The Arab-Israeli Conflict

Volume IV: The Difficult Search for Peace (1975–1988)

PART ONE

EDITED BY

JOHN NORTON MOORE

SPONSORED BY THE

American Society of
International Law

Princeton University Press
Princeton, New Jersey

Copyright © 1991 by Princeton University Press

Published by Princeton University Press, 41 William Street,
Princeton, New Jersey 08540
In the United Kingdom: Princeton University Press, Oxford

Library of Congress Cataloging-in-Publication Data

(Revised for vol. 4)

The Arab-Israeli conflict.

Includes indexes. Bibliography: v. 3, p.
Contents: v. 1. Readings.—v. 2. Readings.—[etc.]—v.
4. The difficult search for peace (1975–1988).
1. Jewish-Arab relations—1917– —Addresses, essays, lectures.
2. Jewish-Arab relations—1917– Sources. I. Moore, John Norton, 1937–
II. American Society of International Law.
DS119.7.A6718   1975   956'.04   72-39792

Vol. 4 Part One ISBN 0-691-05648-X

This book has been composed in Linotron Baskerville

Princeton University Press books are printed on acid-free paper,
and meet the guidelines for permanence and durability of the
Committee on Production Guidelines for Book Longevity of the
Council on Library Resources

Printed in the United States of America by Princeton University Press,
Princeton, New Jersey

10 9 8 7 6 5 4 3 2 1

THE ARAB-ISRAELI CONFLICT

Volume IV: The Difficult Search

for Peace (1975–1988)

PART ONE

Volume Four

THE ARAB-ISRAELI CONFLICT:
THE DIFFICULT SEARCH FOR PEACE (1975–1988)

PART ONE

Introduction by John Norton Moore

Acknowledgments

Maps

PART TWO

Maps

Permissions

Selected Bibliography on the Arab-Israeli Conflict and
International Law: 1975–1988

Introduction

THIS VOLUME of documents, *The Arab-Israeli Conflict: The Difficult Search for Peace (1975–1988)*, is a successor volume to the three-volume compilation of readings and documents on the Arab-Israeli conflict and international law published in 1974 and a one-volume abridged and updated edition published in 1977 under the auspices of the American Society of International Law. The three-volume set is I–III, J. Moore, ed., *The Arab-Israeli Conflict* (Princeton University Press, 1974), and the one-volume abridged edition is J. Moore, ed., *The Arab-Israeli Conflict: Readings and Documents* (Princeton University Press, 1977).

Since the 1974 volumes, the passage of time and major events in the Arab-Israeli conflict such as the 1975 Sinai Agreement between Egypt and Israel, the 1977 Sadat-Begin rapprochement, the Camp David Accords of 1978, the Egyptian-Israeli Peace Treaty of 1979, the 1981 Israeli air strike on Iraq's Osirak reactor, the 1982 Israeli invasion of Lebanon in response to continuing attacks against Israel, the 1982–1983 deployment of the multinational force in Lebanon and its subsequent withdrawal, the continuing conflict in Lebanon, and the intensification of Middle Eastern terrorism and response suggest the need for an updated series. This volume of documents is intended to supplement the three-volume series and one-volume abridgement without significant omission or duplication. It also stands on its own as a documentary history of the Arab-Israeli conflict from the September 1975 Sinai Accords to the Shultz peace initiative of 1988.

Because of the cost of producing a full multivolume set of readings as well as documents, it was felt preferable to produce a documentary volume with an extensive bibliography incorporating a selected range of articles on the Arab-Israeli conflict in an organizational framework that would have been used for the supplemental readings in a multivolume set. As such, it makes available to the reader the editorial judgments on organizational structure and selection of readings that would have been made in a multivolume set. In addition, a list of important recent books and documentary collections on the Middle East has been included in the bibliography.

This volume, like those before it, is sponsored by the American Society of International Law, an association of international legal scholars and practitioners from more than ninety countries. It is not affiliated with any government or ideology other than a commitment to the settlement of international disputes on the basis of law and justice and the free exchange of ideas to that end.

Selection and Arrangement of Documents

The purpose of this documentary compilation is to make more readily available the principal documents relating to the international legal aspects of the Arab-Israeli conflict. It is hoped that such a compilation will prove useful in research and teaching about the conflict and in efforts at settlement. As these documents show, there has been a range of efforts at conflict management in the region spanning more than sixty years. A thorough grounding in the strengths and weaknesses of these past efforts is an indispensable tool for anyone seriously concerned with promoting peaceful settlement.

The documents in this compilation have been selected because of their importance for appraisal of the Arab-Israeli conflict and, in some cases, because of their limited availability. An effort has been made to include all the documents significant for an understanding of the bases on which the different positions rest. Although the compilation is the most complete to date and includes the more important legal documents, it is by no means exhaustive. The historical sweep of the Arab-Israeli conflict has generated a staggering quantity of documents and official statements. United Nations materials alone would fill a number of volumes if all of the Security Council and General Assembly debates, reports of the Secretary-General, and other United Nations proposals, recommendations, and reports were included.

The documents in Volume 4 are arranged in rough chronological sequence. More precisely, they are arranged in five major chronological divisions centering on major events or periods in the Arab-Israeli conflict. These are: "From the Sinai Accords to Camp David: September 1975–September 1978," "Camp David and the Egyptian-Israeli Peace Treaty: August 1978–December 1984," "From Camp David to the War in Lebanon: October 1978–May 1982," "The War in Lebanon: June 1982–August 1982," and "The Search for Peace and the Continuing Conflict in Lebanon: August 1982–December 1988." Within these five major headings the documents are subdivided by principal subjects and within each subject subheadings are presented in chronological sequence.

Most documents are reprinted in their entirety without editorial intervention. When space limitations have forced cuts, the usual scholarly conventions have been followed. On occasion the layout of the documents has been adjusted to provide a consistent presentation throughout the volume. For the reader who would like to refer to the complete document, references are given for each, and occasionally references are also given to related documents or materials.

A Few Words of Caution

A few words of caution may be helpful in using this compilation. First, overreliance on historical documents for analysis of world order disputes may lead to excessive emphasis on historical conditions at the expense of present reality. Although a knowledge of past experience is indispensable for understanding the present, to be most useful, any appraisal must ultimately be focused on present circumstances and conditions. Moreover, history alone does not provide a sufficient basis for normative appraisal. One of the most important principles of the United Nations Charter is that past grievances, no matter how deeply felt, may not be the basis for unilateral coercion to right the perceived wrong. Lawful unilateral coercion is restricted to individual and collective defense. The Charter thus rightly incorporates the present behavioral understanding that perceptions usually differ about the justice or injustice of particular events. The Charter also embodies the judgment that war always has been a destructive mode of change, but that in the present international system it flirts with global catastrophe. Accordingly, the Charter principle that force should not be used as an instrument of national policy except in defense must be considered in any thoughtful appraisal of international disputes.[1]

Second, documents are merely the tip of an iceberg of an ongoing process of social and political interaction. Each document simultaneously represents the outcome of a complex process of interaction and is in turn an influence on subsequent processes. Context, including temporal setting, then, may play an important role in interpretation or understanding. Thus, it would be a mistake simply to add up the General Assembly and Security Council resolutions favoring the Israeli position and those favoring the Arab position as a basis for judgment about comparative fault. Such an effort is of little value without an awareness of the so-called "automatic majority" for the United States position in the General Assembly in the early years of the United Nations and of the radical shift in General Assembly alignment since 1960 toward a Third World "automatic majority." One should also be aware that, beginning about 1953, the Soviet veto has been regularly applied in support of the Arab position in the Security Council.

Last, the inclusion of a large selection of documents and materials may obscure the greater or lesser relative importance of various documents. The importance and legal significance of the documents included in this volume may vary widely. Those that are particularly fundamental in the period September 1975 to July 1986 are the 1975 Sinai Agreement between Egypt and Israel, the Camp David Accords of September 17, 1978, and the Egyptian-Israeli Peace Treaty of 1979. The 1977 Begin-Sadat exchange of addresses in the Knesset and the 1982 peace initiative by President Reagan are of further special interest.

John Norton Moore

---

[1] Because of its general availability, the United Nations Charter has not been included in this compilation. Of particular relevance are articles 1, 2(3), 2(4), 33, and 51.

Acknowledgments

THE PRINCIPAL PURPOSE of this updated collection of documents on the Arab-Israeli conflict is to promote a greater understanding of what continues to be one of the most persistent and explosive challenges to world order of our time. It has been reassuring to see that the original enthusiasm from all quarters for this project has endured. The very enthusiasm of the response, however, makes it impossible to thank all who assisted in the preparation of this volume. Among the special debts that stand out, I should particularly like to thank the institutions that made this project possible by generously giving permission to reprint their documents and the American Society of International Law, under whose auspices this book has been published. A list of contributors and a list of individual permissions appear at the end of the volume.

I am much indebted to Bernard L. Seward, Jr., Tonia L. Horton, Richard Baugh, Christian Smith, and the other research associates on the staff of the Center for Law and National Security for their long and diligent work on this project. I am also indebted to Shabtai Rosenne, Arthur Goodhart Professor in Legal Science at the University of Cambridge, for his review and excellent suggestions. Finally, I wish to thank Sanford Thatcher, former Editor-in-Chief of Princeton University Press, for his continued assistance throughout the project.

The selection of documents in this volume does not imply their endorsement by the American Society of International Law or anyone associated with the project. The final responsibility for any errors and infelicities is my own.

Volume Four

THE ARAB-ISRAELI CONFLICT:

THE DIFFICULT SEARCH FOR PEACE (1975–1988)

PART ONE

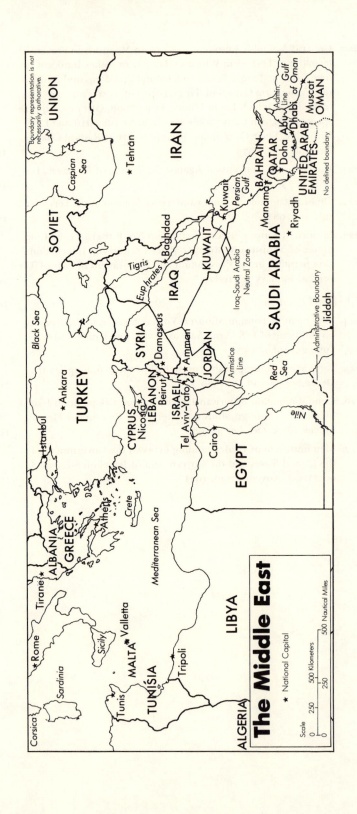

The Middle East

I. From the Sinai Accords to Camp David:

September 1975–September 1978

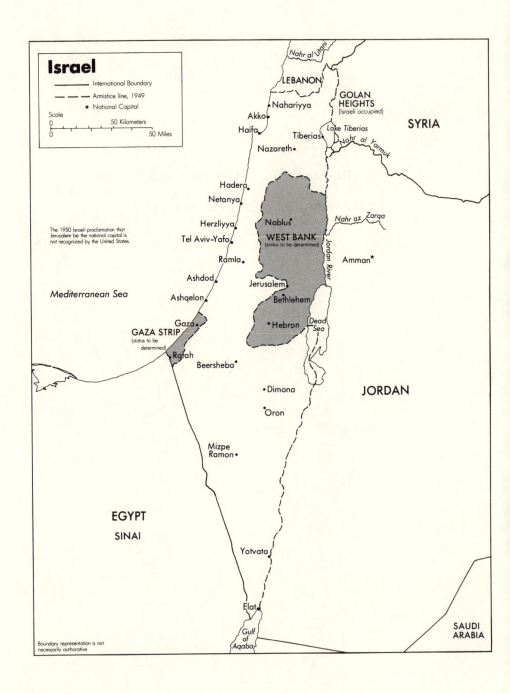

Israel

- International Boundary
- — — Armistice line, 1949
- ★ National Capital

Scale

0 — 50 Kilometers

0 — 50 Miles

The 1950 Israeli proclamation that
Jerusalem be the national capital is
not recognized by the United States.

Mediterranean Sea

EGYPT

SINAI

LEBANON

Nahr al Litani

**GOLAN
HEIGHTS**
(Israeli occupied)

SYRIA

Nahariyya

Akko

Haifa

Lake Tiberias

Tiberias

Nahr al Yarmuk

Nazareth

Hadera

Netanya

Herzliyya

Tel Aviv-Yafo

Nablus

Nahr az Zarqa

WEST BANK
(status to be determined)

Amman ★

Ramla

Jordan River

Ashdod

Ashqelon

Jerusalem

Bethlehem

Gaza

GAZA STRIP
(status to be
determined)

Hebron

*Dead
Sea*

Rafah

Beersheba

JORDAN

Dimona

Oron

Mizpe
Ramon

Yotvata

**SAUDI
ARABIA**

Elat

Gulf
of
Aqaba

Boundary representation is not
necessarily authorative

A. The Sinai Accords

1. Sinai Agreement between Egypt and Israel,

Annex, and U.S. Proposal for Participation in

the Early Warning System, September 1, 1975*

---

* 73 U.S. Dep't State Bull. No. 1892, at 466 (1975).

Agreement Between Egypt and Israel[3]

The Government of the Arab Republic of Egypt and the Government of Israel have agreed that:

ARTICLE I

The conflict between them and in the Middle East shall not be resolved by military force but by peaceful means.

The Agreement concluded by the Parties January 18, 1974, within the framework of the Geneva Peace Conference, constituted a first step towards a just and durable peace according to the provisions of Security Council Resolution 338 of October 22, 1973.

They are determined to reach a final and just peace settlement by means of negotiations called for by Security Council Resolution 338, this Agreement being a significant step toward that end.

ARTICLE II

The Parties hereby undertake not to resort to the threat or use of force or military blockade against each other.

ARTICLE III

The Parties shall continue scrupulously to observe the ceasefire on land, sea, and air and to refrain from all military or para-military actions against each other.

The Parties also confirm that the obligations contained in the Annex and, when concluded, the Protocol shall be an integral part of this Agreement.

ARTICLE IV

A. The military forces of the Parties shall be deployed in accordance with the following principles:

(1) All Israeli forces shall be deployed east of the lines designated as Lines J and M on the attached map.

(2) All Egyptian forces shall be deployed west of the line designated as Line E on the attached map.

(3) The area between the lines designated on the attached map as Lines E and F and the area between the lines designated on the attached map as Lines J and K shall be limited in armament and forces.

(4) The limitations on armament and forces in the areas described by paragraph (3) above shall be agreed as described in the attached Annex.

(5) The zone between the lines designated on the attached map as Lines E and J, will be a buffer zone. In this zone the United Nations Emergency Force will continue to perform its functions as under the Egyptian-Israeli Agreement of January 18, 1974.

(6) In the area south from Line E and west from Line M, as defined on

[3] The agreement and annex were initialed on Sept. 1 at Jerusalem by representatives of Israel and at Alexandria by representatives of Egypt and signed at Geneva on Sept. 4.

the attached map, there will be no military forces, as specified in the attached Annex.

B. The details concerning the new lines, the redeployment of the forces and its timing, the limitation on armaments and forces, aerial reconnaissance, the operation of the early warning and surveillance installations and the use of the roads, the United Nations functions and other arrangements will all be in accordance with the provisions of the Annex and map which are an integral part of this Agreement and of the Protocol which is to result from negotiations pursuant to the Annex and which, when concluded, shall become an integral part of this Agreement.

ARTICLE V

The United Nations Emergency Force is essential and shall continue its functions and its mandate shall be extended annually.

ARTICLE VI

The Parties hereby establish a Joint Commission for the duration of this Agreement. It will function under the aegis of the Chief Coordinator of the United Nations Peacekeeping Missions in the Middle East in order to consider any problem arising from this Agreement and to assist the United Nations Emergency Force in the execution of its mandate. The Joint Commission shall function in accordance with procedures established in the Protocol.

ARTICLE VII

Non-military cargoes destined for or coming from Israel shall be permitted through the Suez Canal.

ARTICLE VIII

This Agreement is regarded by the Parties as a significant step toward a just and lasting peace. It is not a final peace agreement.

The Parties shall continue their efforts to negotiate a final peace agreement within the framework of the Geneva Peace Conference in accordance with Security Council Resolution 338.

ARTICLE IX

This Agreement shall enter into force upon signature of the Protocol and remain in force until superseded by a new agreement.

Done at _____ on the _____ 1975, in four original copies.

For the Government of the Arab   For the Government of Israel
Republic of Egypt

WITNESS

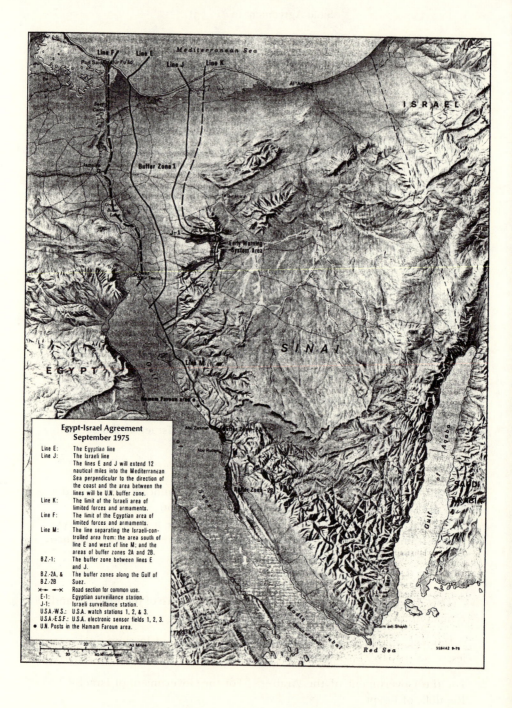

Mediterranean Sea

Line F   Line E
Port Said Abu Fu'ād   Line J   Line K
                                              Al 'Arish
                                                              I S R A E L

Buffer Zone 1

Bir Gifgāfa

J-1
                    Early Warning
                    System Area

                                    S I N A I

Line M

Hamam Faroun area

Abu Zanīma   Buffer Zone 2A
Nu'Rudeis

Buffer Zone 2B   SAUDI
                                                   ARABIA

Sharm ash Shaykh

Red Sea

Egypt-Israel Agreement
September 1975

Line E: The Egyptian line
Line J: The Israeli line
            The lines E and J will extend 12
            nautical miles into the Mediterranean
            Sea perpendicular to the direction of
            the coast and the area between the
            lines will be U.N. buffer zone.
Line K: The limit of the Israeli area of
            limited forces and armaments.
Line F: The limit of the Egyptian area of
            limited forces and armaments.
Line M: The line separating the Israeli-con-
            trolled area from: the area south of
            line E and west of line M; and the
            areas of buffer zones 2A and 2B.
B.Z.-1:   The buffer zone between lines E
            and J.
B.Z.-2A, & The buffer zones along the Gulf of
B.Z.-2B   Suez.
×—• •—×   Road section for common use.
E-1:   Egyptian surveillance station.
J-1:   Israeli surveillance station.
U.S.A.-W.S.: U.S.A. watch stations 1, 2, & 3.
U.S.A.-E.S.F.: U.S.A. electronic sensor fields 1, 2, 3.
•   U.N. Posts in the Hamam Faroun area.

0   20   40 Miles
0   20   40 Kilometers

358442 9-75

Annex to Egypt-Israel Agreement

Within 5 days after the signature of the Egypt-Israel Agreement, representatives of the two Parties shall meet in the Military Working Group of the Middle East Peace Conference at Geneva to begin preparation of a detailed Protocol for the implementation of the Agreement. The Working Group will complete the Protocol within 2 weeks. In order to facilitate preparation of the Protocol and implementation of the Agreement, and to assist in maintaining the scrupulous observance of the ceasefire and other elements of the Agreement, the two Parties have agreed on the following principles, which are an integral part of the Agreement, as guidelines for the Working Group.

1. *Definitions of Lines and Areas*

The deployment lines, areas of limited forces and armaments, Buffer Zones, the area south from Line E and west from Line M, other designated areas, road sections for common use and other features referred to in Article IV of the Agreement shall be as indicated on the attached map (1:100,000-U.S. Edition).

2. *Buffer Zones*

(a) Access to the Buffer Zones will be controlled by the United Nations Emergency Force, according to procedures to be worked out by the Working Group and the United Nations Emergency Force.

(b) Aircraft of either Party will be permitted to fly freely up to the forward line of that Party. Reconnaissance aircraft of either Party may fly up to the middle line of the Buffer Zone between E and J on an agreed schedule.

(c) In the Buffer Zone, between line E and J there will be established under Article IV of the Agreement an Early Warning System entrusted to United States civilian personnel as detailed in a separate proposal, which is a part of this Agreement.

(d) Authorized personnel shall have access to the Buffer Zone for transit to and from the Early Warning System; the manner in which this is carried out shall be worked out by the Working Group and the United Nations Emergency Force.

3. *Area South of Line E and West of Line M*

(a) In this area, the United Nations Emergency Force will assure that there are no military or para-military forces of any kind, military fortifications and military installations; it will establish checkpoints and have the freedom of movement necessary to perform this function.

(b) Egyptian civilians and third country civilian oil field personnel shall have the right to enter, exit from, work, and live in the above indicated area, except for Buffer Zones 2A, 2B and the United Nations Posts. Egyptian civilian police shall be allowed in the area to perform normal civil police functions among the civilian population in such numbers and with such weapons and equipment as shall be provided for in the Protocol.

(c) Entry to and exit from the area, by land, by air or by sea, shall be only through United Nations Emergency Force checkpoints. The United Nations Emergency Force shall also establish checkpoints along the road, the dividing line and at other points, with the precise locations and number to be included in the Protocol.

(d) Access to the airspace and the coastal area shall be limited to unarmed Egyptian civilian vessels and unarmed civilian helicopters and transport planes involved in the civilian activities of the area as agreed by the Working Group.

(e) Israel undertakes to leave intact all currently existing civilian installations and infrastructures.

(f) Procedures for use of the common sections of the coastal road along the Gulf of Suez shall be determined by the Working Group and detailed in the Protocol.

4. *Aerial Surveillance*

There shall be a continuation of aerial reconnaissance missions by the United States over the areas covered by the Agreement (the area between lines F and K), following the same procedures already in practice. The missions will ordinarily be carried out at a frequency of one mission every 7–10 days, with either Party or the United Nations Emergency Force empowered to request an earlier mission. The United States Government will make the mission results available expeditiously to Israel, Egypt and the Chief Coordinator of the United Nations Peacekeeping Missions in the Middle East.

5. *Limitation of Forces and Armaments*

(a) Within the Areas of Limited Forces and Armaments (the areas between lines J and K and lines E and F) the major limitations shall be as follows:

(1) Eight (8) standard infantry battalions

(2) Seventy-five (75) tanks

(3) Seventy-two (72) artillery pieces, including heavy mortars (i.e. with caliber larger than 120 mm), whose range shall not exceed twelve (12) km.

(4) The total number of personnel shall not exceed eight thousand (8,000).

(5) Both Parties agree not to station or locate in the area weapons which can reach the line of the other side.

(6) Both Parties agree that in the areas between lines J and K, and between line A (of the Disengagement Agreement of January 18, 1974) and line E, they will construct no new fortifications or installations for forces of a size greater than that agreed herein.

(b) The major limitations beyond the Areas of Limited Forces and Armament will be:

(1) Neither side will station nor locate any weapon in areas from which they can reach the other line.

(2) The Parties will not place antiaircraft missiles within an area of ten (10) kilometers east of Line K and west of Line F, respectively.

(c) The United Nations Emergency Force will conduct inspections in order to ensure the maintenance of the agreed limitations within these areas.

6. *Process of Implementation*

The detailed implementation and timing of the redeployment of forces, turnover of oil fields, and other arrangements called for by the Agreement, Annex and Protocol shall be determined by the Working Group, which will agree on the stages of this process, including the phased movement of Egyptian troops to line E and Israeli troops to line J. The first phase will be the transfer of the oil fields and installations to Egypt. This process will begin within two weeks from the signature of the Protocol with the introduction of the necessary technicians, and it will be completed no later than eight weeks after it begins. The details of the phasing will be worked out in the Military Working Group.

Implementation of the redeployment shall be completed within 5 months after signature of the Protocol.

For the Government
of the Arab Republic
of Egypt

For the Government of Israel

WITNESS

Proposal

In connection with the Early Warning System referred to in Article IV of the Agreement between Egypt and Israel concluded on this date and as an integral part of that Agreement, (hereafter referred to as the Basic Agreement), the United States proposes the following:

1. The Early Warning System to be established in accordance with Article IV in the area shown on the map attached to the Basic Agreement will be entrusted to the United States. It shall have the following elements:

a. There shall be two surveillance stations to provide strategic early warning, one operated by Egyptian and one operated by Israeli personnel. Their locations are shown on the map attached to the Basic Agreement. Each station shall be manned by not more than 250 technical and administrative personnel. They shall perform the functions of visual and electronic surveillance only within their stations.

b. In support of these stations, to provide tactical early warning and to verify access to them, three watch stations shall be established by the United States in the Mitia and Giddi Passes as will be shown on the map attached to the Basic Agreement. These stations shall be operated by United States civilian personnel. In support of these stations, there shall be established three unmanned electronic sensor fields at both ends of each Pass and in the general vicinity of each station and the roads leading to and from those stations.

2. The United States civilian personnel shall perform the following duties in connection with the operation and maintenance of these stations.

a. At the two surveillance stations described in paragraph 1 a. above, United States civilian personnel will verify the nature of the operations of the stations and all movement into and out of each station and will immediately report any detected divergency from its authorized role of visual and electronic surveillance to the Parties to the Basic Agreement and to the United Nations Emergency Force.

b. At each watch station described in paragraph 1 b. above, the United States civilian personnel will immediately report to the Parties to the Basic Agreement and to the United Nations Emergency Force any movement of armed forces, other than the United Nations Emergency Force, into either Pass and any observed preparations for such movement.

c. The total number of United States civilian personnel assigned to functions under this Proposal shall not exceed 200. Only civilian personnel shall be assigned to functions under this Proposal.

3. No arms shall be maintained at the stations and other facilities covered by this Proposal, except for small arms required for their protection.

4. The United States personnel serving the Early Warning System shall be allowed to move freely within the area of the System.

5. The United States and its personnel shall be entitled to have such support facilities as are reasonably necessary to perform their functions.

6. The United States personnel shall be immune from local criminal, civil, tax and customs jurisdiction and may be accorded any other specific privileges and immunities provided for in the United Nations Emergency Force agreement of February 13, 1957.

7. The United States affirms that it will continue to perform the functions described above for the duration of the Basic Agreement.

8. Notwithstanding any other provision of this Proposal, the United States may withdraw its personnel only if it concludes that their safety is jeopardized or that continuation of their role is no longer necessary. In the latter case the Parties to the Basic Agreement will be informed in advance in order to give them the opportunity to make alternative arrangements. If both Parties to the Basic Agreement request the United States to conclude its role under this Proposal, the United States will consider such requests conclusive.

9. Technical problems including the location of the watch stations will be worked out through consultation with the United States.

Henry A. Kissinger
Secretary of State

2. House of Representatives Joint Resolution 683

Implementing the U.S. Proposal for an Early Warning

System in the Sinai, October 13, 1975*

---

* H.R.J. Res. 683, 89 Stat. 572 (1975), *repealed by*, International Securities Act of 1978, Sec. 12(c)(4), 92 Stat. 737 (1978).

To implement the United States proposal for the early-warning system in Sinai.

Whereas an agreement signed on September 4, 1975, by the Government of the Arab Republic of Egypt and the Government of Israel may, when it enters into force, constitute a significant step toward peace in the Middle East;

Whereas the President of the United States on September 1, 1975, transmitted to the Government of the Arab Republic of Egypt and to the Government of Israel identical proposals for United States participation in an early-warning system, the text of which has been submitted to the Congress, providing for the assignment of no more than two hundred United States civilian personnel to carry out certain specified noncombat functions and setting forth the terms and conditions thereof;

Whereas the proposal would permit the Government of the United States to withdraw such personnel if it concludes that their safety is jeopardized or that continuation of their role is no longer necessary; and

Whereas the implementation of the United States proposal for the early-warning system in Sinai may enhance the prospect of compliance in good faith with the terms of the Egyptian-Israeli agreements and thereby promote the cause of peace: Now, therefore, be it

Resolved by the Senate and House of Representatives of the United States of America in Congress assembled, That the President is authorized to implement the "United States Proposal for the Early Warning System in Sinai": *Provided, however,* That United States civilian personnel assigned to Sinai under such proposal shall be removed immediately in the event of an outbreak of hostilities between Egypt and Israel or if the Congress by concurrent resolution determines that the safety of such personnel is jeopardized or that continuation of their role is no longer necessary. Nothing contained in this resolution shall be construed as granting any authority to the President with respect to the introduction of United States Armed Forces into hostilities or into situations wherein involvement in hostilities is clearly indicated by the circumstances which authority he would not have had in the absence of this joint resolution.

SEC. 2. Any concurrent resolution of the type described in the first section of this resolution which is introduced in either House of Congress shall be privileged in the same manner and to the same extent as a concurrent resolution of the type described in section 5(c) of Public Law 93–148 is privileged under section 7 of such law.

SEC. 3. The United States civilian personnel participating in the early warning system in Sinai shall include only individuals who have volunteered to participate in such system.

SEC. 4. Whenever United States civilian personnel, pursuant to this resolution, participate in any early warning system, the President shall, so long as the participation of such personnel continues, submit written reports to the Congress periodically, but no less frequently than once every six months, on (1) the status, scope, and anticipated duration of their participation, and (2) the feasibility of ending or reducing as soon as possible their participation by substituting nationals of other countries or by making technological changes. The appropriate committees of the Congress shall promptly hold hearings on each report of the President and report to the Congress any findings, conclusions, and recommendations.

SEC. 5. The authority contained in this joint resolution to implement the "United States Proposal for the Early Warning System in Sinai" does not signify approval of the Congress of any other agreement, understanding, or commitment made by the executive branch.

Approved October 13, 1975.

3. Executive Order No. 11896 Establishing the United States Sinai Support Mission, January 13, 1976*

* 12 Weekly Comp. Pres. Doc. 34 (January 19, 1976).

By virtue of the authority vested in me by the Constitution and statutes of the United States of America, including the Joint Resolution of October 13, 1975 (Public Law 94–110, 89 Stat. 572, 22 U.S.C. 2441 note), the Foreign Assistance Act of 1961, as amended (22 U.S.C. 2151 *et seq.*), including but not limited to Sections 531, 621, 633, 901, and 903 thereof (22 U.S.C. 2346, 2381, 2393, 2441, 2443), and section 301 of title 3 of the United States Code, and as President of the United States of America, it is hereby ordered as follows:

SECTION 1. (a) In accordance with the Foreign Assistance Act of 1961, as amended, and notwithstanding the provisions of Part I of Executive Order No. 10973, as amended, there is hereby established the United States Sinai Support Mission, hereinafter referred to as the Mission.

(b) The Mission shall, in accordance with the Foreign Assistance Act of 1961, as amended, the Joint Resolution of October 13, 1975, and the provisions of this order, carry out the duties and responsibilities of the United States Government to implement the "United States Proposal for the Early Warning System in Sinai" in connection with the Basic Agreement between Egypt and Israel, signed on September 4, 1975, and the Annex to the Basic Agreement, subject to broad policy guidance received through the Assistant to the President for national security affairs, and the continuous supervision and general direction of the Secretary of State pursuant to Section 622(c) of the Foreign Assistance Act of 1961, as amended (22 U.S.C. 2382(c)).

(c) It shall be the duty and responsibility of the Mission to ensure that the United States role in the Early Warning System enhances the prospect of compliance in good faith with the terms of the Egyptian-Israeli agreement and thereby promotes the cause of peace.

(d) At the head of the Mission there shall be a Director, who shall be appointed by the President. The Director shall be a Special Representative of the President. There shall also be a Deputy Director, who shall be appointed by the President. The Deputy Director shall perform such duties as the Director may direct, and shall serve as the Director in the case of a vacancy in the office of the Director, or during the absence or disability of the Director.

(e) The Director and Deputy Director shall receive such compensation, as permitted by law, as the President may specify.

SEC. 2. (a) The Director shall exercise immediate supervision and direction over the Mission.

(b) The Director may, to the extent permitted by law, employ such staff as may be necessary.

(c) The Director may, to the extent permitted by law and the provisions of this order, enter into such contracts as may be necessary to carry out the purposes of this order.

(d) The Director may procure the temporary or intermittent services of experts or consultants, in accordance with the provisions of Section 626 of the Foreign Assistance Act of 1961, as amended (22 U.S.C. 2386), and section 3109 of title 5 of the United States Code.

(e) As requested by the Director, the agencies of the Executive branch shall, to the extent permitted by law and to the extent practicable, provide the Mission with such administrative services, information, advice, and facilities as may be necessary for the fulfillment of the Mission's functions under this order.

Sec. 3. (a) In accordance with the provisions of Section 633 of the Foreign Assistance Act of 1961, as amended (22 U.S.C. 2393), it is hereby determined to be in furtherance of the purposes of the Foreign Assistance Act of 1961, as amended, that the functions authorized by that act and required by this order, may be performed, subject to the provisions of subsection (b) of this Section, by the Director without regard to the following specified provisions of law and limitations of authority:

(1) Section 3648 of the Revised Statutes, as amended (31 U.S.C. 529).

(2) Section 3710 of the Revised Statutes (41 U.S.C. 8).

(3) Section 2 of Title III of the Act of March 3, 1933 (47 Stat. 1520, 41 U.S.C. 10a).

(4) Section 3735 of the Revised Statutes (41 U.S.C. 13).

(5) Section 3679 of the Revised Statutes, as amended (31 U.S.C. 665), Section 3732 of the Revised Statutes, as amended (41 U.S.C. 11), and Section 9 of the Act of June 30, 1906 (34 Stat. 764, 31 U.S.C. 627), so as to permit the indemnification of contractors against unusually hazardous risks, as defined in Mission contracts, consistent, to the extent practicable, with regulations prescribed by the Department of Defense pursuant to the provisions of the Act of August 28, 1958, as amended (50 U.S.C. 1431 *et seq.*) and Executive Order No. 10789 of November 14, 1958, as amended.

(6) Section 302(a) of the Federal Property and Administrative Services Act of 1949, as amended (41 U.S.C. 252(a)), so as to permit the Sinai Support Mission to utilize the procurement regulations promulgated by the Department of Defense pursuant to Section 2202 of Title 10 of the United States Code.

(7) Section 304(b) of the Federal Property and Administrative Services Act of 1949, as amended (41 U.S.C. 254(b)), so as to permit the payment of fees in excess of the prescribed fee limitations but nothing herein contained shall be construed to constitute authorization hereunder for the use of the cost-plus-a-percentage-of-cost system of contracting.

(8) Section 305 of the Federal Property and Administrative Services Act of 1949, as amended (41 U.S.C. 255).

(9) Section 901(a) of the Merchant Marine Act, 1936, as amended (46 U.S.C. 1241 (a)).

(b) It is directed that each specific use of the waivers of statutes and limitations of authority authorized by this Section shall be made only when determined in writing by the Director that such use is specifically necessary and in furtherance of the purposes of this Order and in the interests of the United States.

SEC. 4. (a) There is hereby established the Sinai Interagency Board, hereinafter referred to as the Board, which shall be composed of the following:

(1) The Secretary of State or his representative.

(2) The Secretary of Defense or his representative.

(3) The Administrator, Agency for International Development, or his representative.

(4) The Director of the United States Arms Control and Disarmament Agency or his representative.

(5) The Director of Central Intelligence or his representative.

(6) The Director of the United States Sinai Support Mission or his representative.

(b) The Director of the United States Sinai Support Mission or his representative shall be Chairman of the Board.

(c) The President may from time to time designate others to serve on, or participate in the activities of, the Board. The Board may invite representatives of other departments and agencies to participate in its activities.

(d) The Board shall meet at the call of the Chairman to assist, coordinate, and advise concerning the activities of the United States Sinai Support Mission.

SEC. 5. The Secretary of State shall, pursuant to the provisions of Executive Order No. 10973, as amended, including Part V thereof, and this order, provide from funds made available to the President the funds necessary for the activities of the United States Sinai Support Mission.

SEC. 6. All activities now being undertaken by the Secretary of State to implement the "United States Proposal for the Early Warning System in Sinai" shall be continued until such time as the Mission has become operational and the Director requests the transfer of those activities to the Mission. The Secretary of State may exercise any of the authority or responsibility vested in the Director, by this order, in order to continue the performance of activities related to the Early Warning System until transferred to the Director. All such activities undertaken by the Secretary of State shall be deemed to have been taken by the Director.

GERALD R. FORD

The White House,
January 13, 1976.

[Filed with the Office of the Federal Register, 11:40 a.m., January 13, 1976]

B. Conflict in Lebanon

4. Senate Resolution 293 Deploring the Violence in Lebanon, November 4, 1975*

* S. Res. 293, 94th Cong., 1st Sess., 121 Cong. Rec. 34874 (1975).

Whereas Lebanon is a peaceful country which has consistently attempted to maintain a non-combatant position in the current Middle East situation; and

Whereas Lebanon has been a longtime friend and ally of the United States; and

Whereas Lebanon has been a haven for peoples from all over the world; and

Whereas the current disorder constitutes a tragedy in domestic terms and a threat to the peace and stability of the region and the world: Therefore be it

Resolved, That it is the sense of the Senate that the current violence taking place in Lebanon is deplored.

That the United States views with disfavor any unilateral, uninvited intervention of any nation or armed force in the current conflict.

That the shipment of arms and continued encouragement of the conflict by external forces is deplored.

That the United States supports all efforts to resolve the internal conflict and achieve a return to normalcy through peaceful negotiations and the Lebanese political process.

That the United States should provide, through the United Nations, on request of the Government of Lebanon, such immediate, emergency, and appropriate humanitarian aid and assistance as may be necessary to further the cause of peace, humanity and stability in that area.

5. Resolution Adopted by the Arab League Sending an Arab Peace Force into Lebanon to Replace Syrian Troops, Cairo, June 9–10, 1976*

* 6 J. Palestine Stud. 169 (Autumn 1976).

The Council of the League. . .

1. Thanks the Secretary General of the League for having convened the extraordinary meeting.

2. Asks all parties to ceasefire immediately and asks for the stabilization of the ceasefire.

3. Decides to place symbolic Arab security forces under the supervision of the Secretariat of the League, in order to preserve security and stability in Lebanon. These forces will replace the Syrian forces. Their mission is subject to the demands of the President-elect before taking effect.

4. Decides upon the immediate sending of a committee, representing the Council of the League. The committee is to be comprised of the Minister of Foreign Affairs of Bahrain, the Secretary General of the League, and the chiefs of the delegations of Libya and Algeria. This committee must collaborate with all parties in Lebanon to observe the situation and assure the security and the stability in this country.

5. Invites all the parties in Lebanon to a national reconciliation under the aegis of the President-elect, in order to safeguard the unity of the Lebanese people and its territorial integrity.

6. Affirms the Arab pledge to consolidate the Palestinian revolution and to protect it against all dangers.

7. Considers itself in permanent assembly in order to follow the developments of the situation.

6. Senate Resolution 448 on U.S. Policy with

Respect to Lebanon, June 10, 1976*

* S. Res. 448, 94th Cong., 2d Sess., 122 Cong. Rec. 17539, 17540 (1976).

Whereas Lebanon has been a long time friend of the United States; and

Whereas Lebanon is a peaceful country which has consistently attempted to maintain a noncombatant position in the current Middle East situation; and

Whereas the current disorder constitutes a tragedy in domestic terms and a threat to the peace and stability of the region and the world; and

Whereas the current disorder has taken so many lives and caused so much physical and psychological damage to Lebanon:

Now, therefore be it

Resolved, That it is the sense of the Senate that the Government and people of the United States welcome the election of a new President by the Assembly of Lebanon and anticipate an end to the civil strife in Lebanon which has taken so many lives and caused so much physical and psychological damage to a democratic, pluralistic society which has traditionally maintained close, cordial, and cooperative relations with the United States; and be it further

Resolved, That the Congress welcomes the President's requests for appropriate funds to assist in the relief and rehabilitation of victims of the armed strife which has caused so much damage to the essential fabric of life in Lebanon over the past year; and be it further

Resolved, That the Congress urges the President to declare the willingness of the United States to participate in multilateral assistance programs to help in the reconstruction of the bady [sic] damaged national infrastructure of Lebanon for the purpose of speeding a return to normal economic conditions of prosperity there; and be it further

Resolved, That the Congress urges the President immediately to request the Secretary General of the United Nations to renew his appeal for a cease-fire for that purpose and call for such other United Nations action as may be appropriate.

The Secretary of the Senate is directed to transmit a copy of this resolution to the President of the United States and to the Secretary of State.

7. Agreement Signed by Syrian Foreign Minister Abdul Halim Khaddam and PLO Political Department Chairman Farouq Qaddoumi on the Fundamental Points for Ending the Fighting in Lebanon, Damascus, July 29, 1976*

---

* 6 J. Palestine Stud. 189 (Autumn 1976).

Out of a consciousness of national responsibility and an awareness of the dangers implicit in the continuation of the fighting in Lebanon, and in harmony with the Arab League resolutions affirming the necessity of ending the fighting in Lebanon, agreement has been reached on the following:

1. All parties concerned are to announce their acceptance of a complete ceasefire on all Lebanese territories effective from the time to be specified by the committee mentioned in Article 2 of this agreement.

2. Pending the assumption by the President-elect of his constitutional functions, a Higher Lebanese-Syrian-Palestinian committee shall immediately be formed under the chairmanship of the Arab League envoy to undertake the supervision of the ceasefire, the enforcing of security and the establishment of a timetable for the phased withdrawal of all show of arms within a period of ten days, employing for that purpose the Arab peace force units currently available and any other suitable and appropriate forces.

3. Concerning the Lebanese situation: Proceeding from concern for the unity of Lebanon, its land and people, and its independence and integrity, and out of a conviction of the necessity of realizing governmental reforms to assure a genuine and effective participation of all elements in the government, the Syrian and Palestinian sides encourage all sides to conduct a national dialogue under the chairmanship of President Elias Sarkis on the basis of the Document of February 14, 1976 and on the basis of any additional Lebanese issues agreed upon by those quarters. Moreover, the Syrian and Palestinian sides encourage all Lebanese sides to work for the formation of a national union cabinet to work for the restoration and unification of governmental institutions and the implementation of accepted reforms.

4. Lebanese-Palestinian relations: proceeding from the stipulation that it is Lebanon's right that the Palestinian side should not interfere in internal Lebanese affairs, as well as the resistance's right to carry out its struggle from the Lebanese arena in accordance with the agreements contracted between the resistance and the Lebanese authorities, agreement has been reached on the organization of those relations in conformity with the attached Syrian working paper which was approved by all parties and announced on February 14, 1976, and also in accordance with the Cairo Agreement and its appendices. A Lebanese-Palestinian committee will be formed to establish a timetable for the implementation of those principles including the Cairo Agreement and its appendices.

C. U.S. Legislative Response to the Arab Boycott

8. Excerpts from the Tax Reform Act of 1976 Pertaining to International Boycotts and Bribes, October 4, 1976*

* Tax Reform Act of 1976, Pub. L. No. 94–455, 90 Stat. 1520, 1649 (codified as amended in scattered sections of 26 U.S.C.).

PART VI—DENIAL OF CERTAIN TAX BENEFITS FOR COOPERATION WITH
OR PARTICIPATION IN INTERNATIONAL BOYCOTTS AND IN CONNECTION
WITH THE PAYMENT OF CERTAIN BRIBES

SEC. 1061. DENIAL OF FOREIGN TAX CREDIT.

(a) IN GENERAL.—Subpart A of part III of subchapter N (relating to income from sources without the United States) is amended by adding at the end thereof the following new section:

"SEC. 908. REDUCTION OF CREDIT FOR PARTICIPATION IN OR COOPERATION WITH AN INTERNATIONAL BOYCOTT.

(a) IN GENERAL.—If a person, or a member of a controlled group (within the meaning of section 993(a)(3)) which includes such person, participates in or cooperates with an international boycott during the taxable year (within the meaning of section 999(b)), the amount of the credit allowable under section 901 to such person, or under section 902 or 960 to United States shareholders of such person, for foreign taxes paid during the taxable year shall be reduced by an amount equal to the product of—

(1) the amount of credit which, but for this section, would be allowed under section 901 for a taxable year, multiplied by

(2) the international boycott factor (determined under section 999).

(b) APPLICATION WITH SECTIONS 275(a)(4) AND 78.—Section 275(a)(4) and section 78 shall not apply to any amount of taxes denied credit under subsection (a)."

(b) CLERICAL AMENDMENT.—The table of sections for such subpart is amended by adding at the end thereof the following new item:

Sec. 908. Reduction of credit for participation in or cooperation
with an international boycott.

SEC. 1062. DENIAL OF DEFERRAL OF INTERNATIONAL BOYCOTT AMOUNTS.

(a) DENIAL OF DEFERRAL.—Section 952(a) (relating to general definition of subpart F income) is amended—

(1) by striking out "and" at the end of paragraph (1),

(2) by striking out the period at the end of paragraph (2) and inserting in lieu thereof a comma, and the word "and", and

(3) by adding at the end thereof the following new paragraph:

"(3) an amount equal to the product of—

(A) the income of such corporation other than income which—

(i) is attributable to earnings and profits of the foreign corporation included in the gross income of a United States person under section 951 (other than by reason of this paragraph), or

(ii) is described in subsection (b),

multiplied by

(B) the international boycott factor (as determined under section 999)."

SEC. 1063. DENIAL OF DISC BENEFITS.

(a) INTERNATIONAL BOYCOTT ACTIVITY.—Subparagraph (D) of section 995(b)(1) (relating to distributions in qualified years) is amended to read as follows:

"(D) the sum of—

"(i) one-half of the excess of the taxable income of the DISC for the taxable year, before reduction for any distributions during the year, over the sum of the amounts deemed distributed for the taxable year under subparagraphs (A), (B), and (C), and

"(ii) an amount equal to the amount determined under clause (i) multiplied by the international boycott factor determined under section 999, and.

SEC. 1064. DETERMINATIONS AS TO PARTICIPATION IN OR COOPERATION WITH AN INTERNATIONAL BOYCOTT.

(a) IN GENERAL.—Subchapter N of chapter 1 (relating to tax based on income from sources within or without the United States) is amended by adding at the end thereof the following new part:

"PART V—INTERNATIONAL BOYCOTT DETERMINATIONS

Sec. 999. Reports by taxpayers: determinations.

SEC. 999. REPORTS BY TAXPAYERS; DETERMINATIONS.

(a) INTERNATIONAL BOYCOTT REPORTS BY TAXPAYERS.—

(1) REPORT REQUIRED.—If any person, or a member of a controlled group (within the meaning of section 993(a)(3)) which includes that person, has operations in, or related to—

(A) a country (or with the government, a company, or a national of a country) which is on the list maintained by the Secretary under paragraph (3), or

(B) any other country (or with the government, a company, or a national of that country) in which such person or such member had operations during the taxable year if such person (or, if such person is a foreign corporation, any United States shareholder of that corporation) knows or has reason to know that participation in or cooperation with an international boycott is required as a condition of doing business within such country or with such government, company, or national,

that person or shareholder (within the meaning of section 951(b)) shall report such operations to the Secretary at such time and in such manner as the Secretary prescribes, except that in the case of a foreign corporation such report shall be required only of a United States shareholder (within the meaning of such section) of such corporation.

(2) PARTICIPATION AND COOPERATION; REQUEST THEREFOR.—A tax-

payer shall report whether he, a foreign corporation of which he is a United States shareholder, or any member of a controlled group which includes the taxpayer or such foreign corporation has participated in or cooperated with an international boycott at any time during the taxable year, or has been requested to participate in or cooperate with such a boycott, and, if so, the nature of any operation in connection with which there was participation in or cooperation with such boycott (or there was a request to participate or cooperate).

(3) List to be maintained.—The Secretary shall maintain and publish not less frequently than quarterly a current list of countries which require or may require participation in or cooperation with an international boycott (within the meaning of subsection (b)(3)).

(b) Participation in or Cooperation With an International Boycott.—

(1) General rule.—If the person or a member of a controlled group (within the meaning of section 993 (a)(3)) which includes the person participates in or cooperates with an international boycott in the taxable year, all operations of the taxpayer or such group in that country and in any other country which requires participation in or cooperation with the boycott as a condition of doing business within that country, or with the government, a company, or a national of that country, shall be treated as operations in connection with which such participation of cooperation occurred, except to the extent that the person can clearly demonstrate that a particular operation is a clearly separate and identifiable operation in connection with which there was no participation in or cooperation with an international boycott.

(2) Special rule.—

(A) Nonboycott operations.—A clearly separate and identifiable operation of a person, or of a member of the controlled group (within the meaning of section 993(a)(3)) which includes that person, in or related to any country within the group of countries referred to in paragraph (1) shall not be treated as an operation in or related to a group of countries associated in carrying out an international boycott if the person can clearly demonstrate that he, or that such member, did not participate in or cooperate with the international boycott in connection with that operation.

(B) Separate and identifiable operations.—A taxpayer may show that different operations within the same country, or operations in different countries, are clearly separate and identifiable operations.

(3) Definition of boycott participation and cooperation.—For purposes of this section, a person participates in or cooperates with an international boycott if he agrees—

(A) as a condition of doing business directly or indirectly within a country or with the government, a company, or a national of a country—

(i) to refrain from doing business with or in a country which is the object of the boycott or with the government, companies, or nationals of that country;

(ii) to refrain from doing business with any United States person engaged in trade in a country which is the object of the boycott or with the government, companies, or nationals of that country;

(iii) to refrain from doing business with any company whose ownership or management is made up, all or in part, of individuals of a particular nationality, race, or religion, or to remove (or refrain from selecting) corporate directors who are individuals of a particular nationality, race, or religion; or

(iv) to refrain from employing individuals of a particular nationality, race, or religion; or

(B) as a condition of the sale of a product to the government, a company, or a national of a country, to refrain from shipping or insuring that product on a carrier owned, leased, or operated by a person who does not participate in or cooperate with an international boycott (within the meaning of subparagraph (A)).

(4) COMPLIANCE WITH CERTAIN LAWS.—This section shall not apply to any agreement by a person (or such member)—

(A) to meet requirements imposed by a foreign country with respect to an international boycott if United States law or regulations, or an Executive Order, sanctions participation in, or cooperation with, that international boycott,

(B) to comply with a prohibition on the importation of goods produced in whole or in part in any country which is the object of an international boycott, or

(C) to comply with a prohibition imposed by a country on the exportation of products obtained in such country to any country which is the object of an international boycott.

(c) INTERNATIONAL BOYCOTT FACTOR.—

(1) INTERNATIONAL BOYCOTT FACTOR.—For purposes of sections 908(a), 952(a)(3), and 995(b)(3), the international boycott factor is a fraction, determined under regulations prescribed by the Secretary, the numerator of which reflects the world-wide operations of a person (or, in the case of a controlled group (within the meaning of section 993(a)(3)) which includes that person, of the group) which are operations in or related to a group of countries associated in carrying out an international boycott in or with which that person or a member of that controlled group has participated or cooperated in the taxable year, and the denominator of which reflects the world-wide operations of that person or group.

(2) SPECIFICALLY ATTRIBUTABLE TAXES AND INCOME.—If the taxpayer clearly demonstrates that the foreign taxes paid and income earned for the taxable year are attributable to specific operations, then, in lieu of applying the international boycott factor for such taxable year, the

amount of the credit disallowed under section 908(a), the addition to sub-part F income under section 952(a)(3), and the amount of deemed distri-bution under section 995(b)(1)(D)(ii) for the taxable year, if any, shall be the amount specifically attributable to the operations in which there was participation in or cooperation with an international boycott under sec-tion 999(b)(1).

(3) WORLD-WIDE OPERATIONS.—For purposes of this subsection, the term 'world-wide operations' means operations in or related to countries other than the United States.

(d) DETERMINATIONS WITH RESPECT TO PARTICULAR OPERATIONS.—Upon a request made by the taxpayer, the Secretary shall issue a determination with respect to whether a particular operation of a person, or of a member of a controlled group which includes that person, constitutes participation in or cooperation with an international boycott. The Secretary may issue such a determination in advance of such operation in cases which are of such a nature that an advance determination is possible and appropriate under the circumstances. If the request is made before the operation is com-menced, or before the end of a taxable year in which the operation is car-ried out, the Secretary may decline to issue such a determination before close of the taxable year.

(e) PARTICIPATION OR COOPERATION BY RELATED PERSONS.—If a person controls (within the meaning of section 304(c)), a corporation—

(1) participation in or cooperation with an international boycott by such corporation shall be presumed to be such participation or coopera-tion by such person, and

(2) participation in or cooperation with such a boycott by such person shall be presumed to be such participation or cooperation by such cor-poration.

(f) WILLFUL FAILURE TO REPORT.—Any person (within the meaning of section 6671 (b)) required to report under this section who willfully fails to make such report shall, in addition to other penalties provided by law, be fined not more than $25,000, imprisoned for not more than one year, or both.".

(b) CLERICAL AMENDMENT.—The table of parts for such subchapter is amended by adding at the end thereof the following new item:

Part V. International boycott determinations.

SEC. 1065. FOREIGN BRIBES.

(a) DENIAL OF DEFERRAL.—

(1) CONTROLLED FOREIGN CORPORATIONS.—Section 952(a) (relating to general definition of subpart F income) is amended—

(A) by striking out "and" at the end of paragraph (2),

(B) by striking out the period at the end of paragraph (3) and in-serting in lieu of thereof a comma and the word "and", and

(C) by adding at the end thereof the following new paragraph:

"(4) the sum of the amounts of any illegal bribes, kickbacks, or other payments (within the meaning of section 162(c)) paid by or on behalf of the corporation during the taxable year of the corporation directly or indirectly to an official, employee, or agent in fact of a government."

(2) DISC's.—Subparagraph (D) of section 995(b)(1) (relating to distributions in qualified years) is amended—

(A) by striking out "and" at the end of clause (i),

(B) by adding at the end thereof the following new clause:

(iii) any illegal bribe, kickback, or other payment (within the meaning of section 162(c)) paid by or on behalf of the DISC directly or indirectly to an official, employee, or agent in fact of a government, and.

(b) Bribes Not To Reduce Foreign Earnings and Profits.—Section 964(a) (relating to earnings and profits of foreign corporations) is amended by adding at the end thereof the following sentence: "In determining such earnings and profits, or the deficit in such earnings and profits, the amount of any illegal bribe, kickback, or other payment (within the meaning of section 162(c)) shall not be taken into account to decrease such earnings and profits or to increase such deficit."

SEC. 1066. EFFECTIVE DATES.

(a) International Boycotts.—

(1) General rule.—The amendments made by this part (other than by section 1065) apply to participation in or cooperation with an international boycott more than 30 days after the date of enactment of this Act.

(2) Existing contracts.—In the case of operations which constitute participation in or cooperation with an international boycott and which are carried out in accordance with the terms of a binding contract entered into before September 2, 1976, the amendments made by this part (other than by section 1065) apply to such participation or cooperation after December 31, 1977.

(b) Foreign Bribes.—The amendments made by section 1065 apply to payments described in section 162(c) of the Internal Revenue Code of 1954 made more than 30 days after the date of enactment of this Act.

SEC. 1067. REPORTS BY SECRETARY.

(a) Reports to the Congress.—As soon after the close of each calendar year as the data become available, the Secretary shall transmit a report to the Committee on Ways and Means of the House of Representatives and to the Committee on Finance of the Senate setting forth, for that calendar year—

(1) the number of reports filed under section 999(a) of the Internal Revenue Code of 1954 for taxable years ending with or within such taxable year,

(2) the number of such reports on which the taxpayer indicated inter-

national boycott participation or cooperation (within the meaning of section 999(b)(3) of such Code), and

(3) a detailed description of the manner in which the provisions of such Code relating to international boycott activity have been administered during such calendar year.

(b) INITIAL LIST.—The Secretary of the Treasury shall publish an initial list of those countries which may require participation in or cooperation with an international boycott as a condition of doing business within such country, or with the government, a company, or a national of such country (within the meaning of section 999(b) of the Internal Revenue Code of 1954) within 30 days after the enactment of this Act.

9. Secretary of State Vance's Statement Before
the House Committee on International Relations on
Antiboycott Legislation and Nuclear Nonproliferation,
March 1, 1977*

* 76 U.S. Dep't State Bull. No. 1969, at 267 (1977).

This is my first formal appearance before this committee. I hope and expect it will inaugurate a most fruitful relationship under your newly chosen and distinguished chairman [Representative Clement J. Zablocki].

I am pleased today to address the boycott issue and the Administration's position concerning proposed new antiboycott legislation.

We favor renewal of the Export Administration Act of 1969 in order to provide specific legislative authority for the Secretary of Commerce to control exports for reasons of national security, foreign policy, and short supply. A number of agencies will be submitting to your committee reports on title I of the bills to renew the Export Administration Act, and later in the morning, as agreed, I will talk briefly about title III, concerning nuclear exports.

Question of Foreign Boycotts

Let me turn to the question of boycotts.

As the first representative of the new Administration to address this issue before the Congress, let me say that we want to work closely with you on the problems that foreign boycotts present to American commerce and American firms, especially as they involve conduct that is contrary to commonly accepted American principles and standards. The President has often made clear his concern, and I share his deep feelings on this issue. We deplore discrimination on the basis of race, religion, and national origin. We also oppose boycott practices requiring American firms not to deal with friendly countries or other American firms. Let me summarize the principles on which we believe an approach to these problems should be based:

1. *Any foreign-boycott-motivated discrimination against U.S. persons on the basis of religion, race, or national origin should be explicitly outlawed.* Firms should be prohibited from responding to boycott-related requests for information on religion, race, or national origin.

2. *Refusals by American firms to deal with any friendly foreign country, demonstrably related to a foreign boycott, should be prohibited. So, in general, should refusals to deal with other U.S. firms.* We believe that decisions as to what commerce U.S. firms may or may not have with other countries or with other U.S. firms should be made, consonant with American policy, by Americans and only Americans. This principle raises difficult questions about enforcement—turning on judgments about a company's intent when it does not do business with a friendly country or another company. We need to examine, both within the executive branch and in consultation with the Congress, how this principle can most effectively be expressed in legislation. We need to provide our companies with clear and realistic guidance on how to conduct trade in boycott-related situations. We must consider, for example, such difficult problems as whether an American company might be required to ship goods to a foreign country when it knew that these goods would be turned back or confiscated at the port of entry.

3. *The prohibitions affecting U.S. firms should not, in general, apply to transactions of foreign subsidiaries of U.S. firms which involve the commerce of a foreign country and not U.S. exports.* But they should apply in cases in which any U.S. firm seeks to use foreign subsidiaries in a manner intended to circumvent the law.

4. *The new law should preempt provisions of state laws dealing with foreign boycotts.* This should be done in the interests of uniformity and to remove elements of confusion and uncertainty from the conduct of our foreign commerce.

5. To enable an orderly transition to be made to the new legislative requirements, *some kind of grandfather clause or grace period should be provided with regard to transactions under existing commitments.*

6. *The new law should substantially cut back the reporting requirements on U.S. firms.* Many of the reports now required would not be needed in enforcing a new law. The benefits of maintaining such information-gathering regulations would be disproportionate to the burden on individual firms.

7. *All boycott reports submitted to Commerce should be publicly released.* Only proprietary business information should be protected.

We recognize that this issue stems, at this time, primarily from concerns about the Arab boycott of Israel. We believe that, in cooperation with Congress, we can make progress on these issues without seriously impairing opportunities for foreign trade or inhibiting our diplomacy in the Middle East. And we commit ourselves to cooperating with Congress to achieve this result.

We are strongly opposed to foreign boycotts directed against friendly countries. But we understand that states do exercise their sovereign rights to regulate their commerce and to decide, if they wish, to refuse to deal with other nations or the firms of other nations. They have the right to control the source of their imports as well as the destination of their exports.

We view as a different matter, however, efforts by any foreign countries to influence decisions and activities of American firms in connection with any primary boycott of another country. Thus, secondary-boycott practices of other countries can intrude seriously into the business practices of American firms engaged in U.S. commerce and can have the effect of using U.S. commerce to harm third countries with whom we are friends. I believe we will all agree that U.S. firms should not be required, by the decision of a foreign nation, to avoid commercial relations with other friendly countries or with other U.S. firms.

One specific problem arising from foreign boycott practices has been the requirement for use of negative certifications, e.g., certifications that goods do not originate in a given country or are not produced by a firm blacklisted by another country or are not shipped on a blacklisted vessel. The members of this committee should be aware that diplomatic efforts and the efforts of the U.S. business community over many months have brought about some encouraging changes in this area of concern. I am happy to report that during my visit to Saudi Arabia its leaders informed us that Saudi Arabia will accept positive certifications of origin. We are continuing our efforts to bring about further voluntary changes by foreign governments in this and other areas of intrusive boycott practices.

We agree, Mr. Chairman, on the need to prohibit by law in absolute terms any discriminatory actions arising from foreign boycotts, based on race, religion, or national origin. Forthright diplomacy is another way to pursue our efforts, and we have found a forthcoming response. The Government of Saudi Arabia had very recently informed us again that its boycott "has no connection with or basis in matters of race or creed." When specific instances of discriminatory requests have been reported in isolated instances, we have approached foreign governments and received assurances that discrimination was contrary to the policy of the government in question. We appreciate the responsiveness of the boycotting countries to our concern in seeking to remedy and avoid recurrence of any such discrimination, which all of us abhor. We will remain vigilant on this point.

Core Issues of Middle East Settlement

My appearance here follows closely on my return from the Middle East. I believe it would be appropriate to talk for a moment about our Middle East policy as a whole and about our hopes and our efforts for a peace settlement in the area.

President Carter asked me to travel to the Middle East in my first mission abroad as Secretary of State because he believes that the Middle East situation must be given very high and early priority.

My trip had several purposes:

—To demonstrate the importance the President and I attach to the achievement of a just and durable peace in the Middle East and to the maintenance of close ties between the United States and the nations I visited;

—To meet the leaders of those nations and establish the personal relationships that are so important to a diplomacy of confidence and trust; and

—To learn from them their views, so we might define more clearly areas of both agreement and disagreement and establish a base for our own diplomacy in pursuit of peace.

I am satisfied that these purposes were met. We face a long and difficult process, with no assurance of success. But this has been a good beginning, and we are determined to proceed.

I was encouraged to find a number of areas of general agreement among the leaders I met:

—There is a common commitment to working for peace so that they may turn the energies of their governments to bringing the economic and social benefits of peace to their peoples.

–There is a consensus on the desirability of reconvening the Geneva conference sometime during the second half of 1977.

–Each agreed to attend such a conference without preconditions, assuming the resolution of disagreements on procedural questions.

–They would like to see the United States play an active role in facilitating the search for a settlement.

–And each leader accepted an invitation to meet with President Carter during the next three months.

This is a base on which we can build. But there are complex procedural and substantive issues that will require imagination and flexibility from us all.

While there was general agreement on what the core issues of a settlement must be, there are strongly differing views on how these issues should be resolved. These core issues are the nature of peaceful relations between Israel and her neighbors, the boundaries of peace, and the future of the Palestinians. In addition, there are sharp disagreements over whether and how the PLO [Palestine Liberation Organization] should be involved in a Geneva conference.

No one can promise success. But we are committed to a serious effort at helping the nations of the Middle East find a just and lasting solution to the conflicts and tensions that have plagued them and threatened the world for nearly three decades.

Boycott Legislation and Middle East Relations

Given the inherent difficulty of this challenge, and the very high stakes we have in meeting it successfully, we believe we are bound to do what we can to enhance the chances of success by our handling of related issues.

I must also report that I did find concern in Arab capitals about the effects of legislation on commercial relations between the United States and those countries.

They also attach importance to good bilateral relations with the United States. Our shared economic and commercial interests are an important part of these relations.

The magnitude of these interests is reflected in the latest statistics on economic relations between the United States and Middle Eastern countries. Over the past four years, the Middle East market for U.S. exports has doubled in importance (from about 5 percent of total U.S. exports to nearly 10 percent of this total). During this period, our exports to the Arab countries have nearly quadrupled, to a present level of $7 billion a year. Our current exports to Israel and the Arab countries of the Middle East now total some $8.5 billion. U.S. oil imports from Arab countries now account for more than a third of total U.S. imports and more than 15 percent of total U.S. oil consumption. Reflows to the United States of petrodollars in the form of investment from the Arab states are running some $10 billion a year.

I believe that a forthright but carefully considered policy emphasizing that U.S. legislation deals—as is entirely appropriate—with U.S. commerce and the activities of U.S. persons will be understood by Arab leaders.

We have weighed carefully the risks to our important political and economic interests in the Middle East which attend further legislation directed at activities of U.S. firms related to foreign boycotts. We believe that carefully directed legislation combined with diplomatic action can protect our interests. I want to emphasize our intention to maintain close and friendly relations with the countries of the Middle East.

There is much common ground between these principles of the Administration and the objectives of the current proposals for new legislation. This Administration wants to work out with the Congress language for antiboycott legislation on which we can both agree.

I also hope it will be possible, as these hearings proceed, for the various business and other groups to reconcile their views on the provisions of some new legislation. In this respect I have received encouraging reports that the meetings between the Anti-Defamation League and the Business Roundtable have been constructive. A substantial meeting of minds by these representative groups on a set of principles on which legislation might be based will be a great help to us in our deliberations.

The other Cabinet members concerned and I would be happy to make available our experts to work with your committee staff to formulate new legislative language on which we can agree. As issues are developed for decision, I will also be happy personally to consult further with the members of this committee.

Nuclear Exports and Nonproliferation

Mr. Chairman, at this time I will turn to the provisions of the bills to renew the Export Administration Act having to do with nuclear exports.

I believe you know the deep concern of the new Administration about the global spread of nuclear weapons materials and the technology for producing them.

I, in turn, know of the pioneer work of this committee over the past several years in examining the proliferation implications of our nuclear export policies. You were among the earliest in Congress to recognize the urgency of this difficult problem, and your efforts have been pursued in a truly bipartisan fashion. The International Relations Committee has been a focal point for wide-ranging discussions of the key nonproliferation issues, though in the past the legislative jurisdiction of the committee was narrowly defined to the issue of nuclear exports. Now, appropriately, your legislative jurisdiction has been broadened considerably, and the House Committee on International Relations will be the key committee in the House to consider the broad aspects of our nuclear export policies. That bodes well for our shared purpose of formulating a coherent nonproliferation policy.

As you know, the President has directed an urgent and comprehensive review of U.S. nuclear export and nonproliferation policies. We and other concerned agencies have been developing policy options on the entire range of proliferation issues confronting us, including those dealt with in the proposed bill. In the course of these preparations, we have been in direct touch with Members of Congress and intend to be in close consultation with you as we complete our work. Our policy options will be submitted shortly to the President, and I would expect decisions on them this month.

On the basis of those decisions, we will develop legislative recommendations by the end of this month regarding nuclear export and nonproliferation proposals. We believe this approach would have significant advantages. It would clarify U.S. nonproliferation policy and provide a sound basis from which to assure U.S. leadership in this field. Meanwhile, we suggest that the concerned congressional committees not enact legislation in the nonproliferation area before giving full consideration to the executive branch's recommendations.

Certainly legislation will have to be workable not only from our standpoint but also from that of other nations—both recipient and supplier nations. We think that it should encompass not only U.S. nuclear export criteria but incentives and effective disincentives for preventing proliferation. In this regard, the campaign statements of President Carter and the Presidential statement of October 28 by President Ford provide a strong bipartisan basis from which to proceed.

I might add that because of the overriding importance this Administration attaches to this issue, we have centralized responsibility for our nuclear policy within the State Department in the office of the Under Secretary for Security Assistance. This will, I believe, improve the coherent formulation and implementation of our nuclear export policy.

10. Section 2407 of the Export Administration
Amendments Act of 1977 Concerning Foreign Boycotts,
June 22, 1977 (as amended)*

---

* 50 U.S.C. App. Sec. 2407 (1982).

§2407. Foreign boycotts

(a) Prohibitions and exceptions

(1) For the purpose of implementing the policies set forth in subparagraph (A) or (B) of paragraph (5) of section 3 of this Act [section 2402(5)(A) or (B) of this Appendix], the President shall issue regulations prohibiting any United States person, with respect to his activities in the interstate or foreign commerce of the United States, from taking or knowingly agreeing to take any of the following actions with intent to comply with, further, or support any boycott fostered or imposed by a foreign country against a country which is friendly to the United States and which is not itself the object of any form of boycott pursuant to United States law or regulation:

(A) Refusing, or requiring any other person to refuse, to do business with or in the boycotted country, with any business concern organized under the laws of the boycotted country, with any national or resident of the boycotted country, or with any other person, pursuant to an agreement with, a requirement of, or a request from or on behalf of the boycotting country. The mere absence of a business relationship with or in the boycotted country with any business concern organized under the laws of the boycotted country, with any national or resident of the boycotted country, or with any other person, does not indicate the existence of the intent required to establish a violation of regulations issued to carry out this subparagraph.

(B) Refusing, or requiring any other person to refuse, to employ or otherwise discriminating against any United States person on the basis of race, religion, sex, or national origin of that person or of any owner, officer, director, or employee of such person.

(C) Furnishing information with respect to the race, religion, sex, or national origin of any United States person or of any owner, officer, director, or employee of such person.

(D) Furnishing information about whether any person has, has had, or proposes to have any business relationship (including a relationship by way of sale, purchase, legal or commercial representation, shipping or other transport, insurance, investment, or supply) with or in the boycotted country, with any business concern organized under the laws of the boycotted country, with any national or resident of the boycotted country, or with any other person which is known or believed to be restricted from having any business relationship with or in the boycotting country. Nothing in this paragraph shall prohibit the furnishing of normal business information in a commercial context as defined by the Secretary.

(E) Furnishing information about whether any person is a member of, has made contributions to, or is otherwise associated with or involved in the activities of any charitable or fraternal organization which supports the boycotted country.

(F) Paying, honoring, confirming, or otherwise implementing a letter of credit which contains any condition or requirement compliance with which is prohibited by regulations issued pursuant to this paragraph, and no United States person shall, as a result of the application of this paragraph, be obligated to pay or otherwise honor or implement such letter of credit.

(2) Regulations issued pursuant to paragraph (1) shall provide exceptions for—

(A) complying or agreeing to comply with requirements (i) prohibiting the import of goods or services from the boycotted country or goods produced or services provided by any business concern organized under the laws of the boycotted country or by nationals or residents of the boycotted country, or (ii) prohibiting the shipment of goods to the boycotting country on a carrier of the boycotted country, or by a route other than that prescribed by the boycotting country or the recipient of the shipment;

(B) complying or agreeing to comply with import and shipping document requirements with respect to the country of origin, the name of the carrier and route of shipment, the name of the supplier of the shipment or the name of the provider of other services, except that no information knowingly furnished or conveyed in response to such requirements may be stated in negative, black-listing, or similar exclusionary terms, other than with respect to carriers or route of shipment as may be permitted by such regulations in order to comply with precautionary requirements protecting against war risks and confiscation;

(C) complying or agreeing to comply in the normal course of business with the unilateral and specific selection by a boycotting country, or national or resident thereof, of carriers, insurers, suppliers of services to be performed within the boycotting country or specific goods which, in the normal course of business, are identifiable by source when imported into the boycotting country;

(D) complying or agreeing to comply with export requirements of the boycotting country relating to shipments or transshipments of exports to the boycotted country, to any business concern of or organized under the laws of the boycotted country, or to any national or resident of the boycotted country;

(E) compliance by an individual or agreement by an individual to comply with the immigration or passport requirements of any country with respect to such individual or any member of such individual's family or with requests for information regarding requirements of employment of such individual within the boycotting country; and

(F) compliance by a United States person resident in a foreign country or agreement by such person to comply with the laws of that country with respect to his activities exclusively therein, and such regulations may contain exceptions for such resident complying with the laws or regulations of that foreign country governing imports into such country of trademarked, trade named, or similarly specifically identifiable products, or components of products for his own use, including the performance of contractual services within that country, as may be defined by such regulations.

(3) Regulations issued pursuant to paragraphs (2)(C) and (2)(F) shall not provide exceptions from paragraphs (1)(B) and (1)(C).

(4) Nothing in this subsection may be construed to supersede or limit the operation of the antitrust or civil rights laws of the United States.

(5) This section shall apply to any transaction or activity undertaken, by or through a United States person or any other person, with intent to evade the provisions of this section as implemented by the regulations issued pursuant to this subsection, and such regulations shall expressly provide that the exceptions set forth in paragraph (2) shall not permit activities or agreements (expressed or implied by a course of conduct, including a pattern of responses) otherwise prohibited, which are not within the intent of such exceptions.

(b) Foreign policy controls

(1) In addition to the regulations issued pursuant to subsection (a) of this section, regulations issued under section 6 of this Act [section 2405 of this Appendix] shall implement the policies set forth in section 3(5) [section 2402(5) of this Appendix].

(2) Such regulations shall require that any United States person receiving a request for the furnishing of information, the entering into or implementing of agreements, or the taking of any other action referred to in section 3(5) [section 2402(5) of this Appendix] shall report that fact to the Secretary, together with such other information concerning such request as the Secretary may require for such action as the Secretary considers appropriate for carrying out the policies of that section. Such person shall also report to the Secretary whether such person intends to comply and whether such person has complied with such request. Any report filed pursuant to this paragraph shall be made available promptly for public inspection and copying, except that information regarding the quantity, description, and value of any goods or technology to which such report relates may be kept confidential if the Secretary determines that disclosure thereof would place the United States person involved at a competitive disadvantage. The Secretary shall periodically transmit summaries of the information contained in such reports to the Secretary of State for such action as the Secretary of State, in consultation with the Secretary, considers appropriate for carrying out the policies set forth in section 3(5) of this Act [section 2402(5) of this Appendix].

(c) Preemption

The provisions of this section and the regulations issued pursuant thereto shall preempt any law, rule, or regulation of any of the several States or the

District of Columbia, or any of the territories or possessions of the United States, or of any governmental subdivision thereof, which law, rule, or regulation pertains to participation in, compliance with, implementation of, or the furnishing of information regarding restrictive trade practices or boycotts fostered or imposed by foreign countries against other countries.

(Pub. L. 96–72, § 8, Sept. 29, 1979, 93 Stat. 521.)

REFERENCES IN TEXT

The antitrust laws of the United States, referred to in subsec. (a)(4), are classified generally to chapter 1 (§ 1 et seq.) of Title 15, Commerce and Trade.

The civil rights laws of the United States, referred to in subsec. (a)(4), are classified generally to chapter 21 (§ 1981 et seq.) of Title 42, The Public Health and Welfare.

PRIOR PROVISIONS

A prior section 2407, Pub. L. 91–184, § 8, Dec. 30, 1969, 83 Stat. 846; Pub. L. 95–52, title II, § 203(b), June 22, 1977, 91 Stat. 247, relating to exemption from administrative procedure and judicial review provisions, expired on Sept. 30, 1979.

DELEGATION OF FUNCTIONS

The functions conferred upon the President under this section were delegated to the Secretary of Commerce by Ex. Ord. No. 12214, May 2, 1980, 45 F.R. 29783, set out under section 2403 of this Appendix.

D. The Early Carter Efforts within

the Geneva Framework

11. Prime Minister Begin's Press Conference on Relations between Israel and the United States, the PLO, and Alternatives to the Geneva Conference, July 20, 1977*

---

* Embassy of Israel, Washington, D.C.

Ladies and Gentlemen of the press. I feel I must start with a personal statement.

The elections in Israel were a surprise. I apologize to you for the surprise. And secondly, my name does not rhyme with Fagan.

And now into the merits of the main problem.

U.S.-Israel Relations

The discussion with the President went very well indeed. The President was very gracious to me. We held discussions for nearly five hours; three official meetings and one long nocturnal talk in complete privacy. I think I can say that we established a personal rapport, which will, I hope, work not only in the next few months, but for years to come.

Ladies and gentlemen, no confrontation between the United States and Israel. Some people were apprehensive lest such confrontation arises of the talks. I can assure and reassure all the friends of Israel and of America there isn't any confrontation between our two countries. To the contrary, during the last few days, friendship between the United States and Israel has been deepened. And that personal rapport between the President and myself will be helpful in the future.

I am very impressed by the personality of the President of the United States, by his warm heart and by his extraordinary intelligence, by his quick grasp of the crux of the problem, and by his capability to take decisions.

I said during the ceremony at the White House lawn that we see the President of the United States not only as the first citizen of this great country, but also as the leader and defender of the Free World. After our conversations, I was fortified in this belief.

We shall continue to work together for the common interests of the United States and Israel and the Free World.

Peace Proposal

On behalf of the government of Israel, I brought to the President a proposal about the framework for the peace-making process. For nearly two weeks, I had to reply to all the questions about the contents of that decision taken unanimously by the cabinet in Israel. Please, out of respect for the President, he should be the first to hear from me. Believe me, those ten days were days of very heavy pressure. But somehow I withstood it. And indeed, the President was the first man, after the government of Israel took their decision, to hear about our proposals.

The proposals themselves shouldn't be any secret to public opinion. And I will now explain the contents of what we tell—the framework for the peace-making process.

RECONVENING OF THE GENEVA CONFERENCE

The government of Israel will be prepared, beginning October the 10th, 1977 to participate in a new additional session of the Geneva Peace Conference. It should be reconvened by the two chairmen on the basis of Paragraph III of United Nations Security Council Resolution 338, which stipulates—I quote: "The Security Council decides that immediately and concurrently with the cease-fire, negotiations start between the parties concerned under appropriate auspices aimed at the establishing of a just and durable peace in the Middle East."

The government of Israel acknowledges that Resolution 338 includes and makes reference to Security Council Resolution 242 of November the 22nd, 1967. Participation in the reconvened session of the Geneva Peace Conference. Accredited delegations of sovereign states will participate in the reconvened session of the Geneva Peace Conference; namely, representatives of Israel, Egypt, Syria and Jordan. And may I add that if the suggestion is made that Lebanon participates, we will agree.

FREE NEGOTIATIONS—NO PRIOR CONDITIONS

The participating states in the Geneva Peace Conference will present no prior conditions for the taking part in the conference.

I have to dwell and elaborate on the term "no prior conditions," because sometimes it was not only interpreted, but also misinterpreted. To clarify the issue, I will give two examples on both sides. As you know, ladies and gentlemen, the President of Egypt demands that Israel should withdraw totally to the lines of 4th of June, 1967, the lines preceding the Six Day War; that a so-called Palestinian state be formed in Judea, Samaria, the Gaza Strip and they be linked through an extraterritorial corridor. And this demand, if it should come at any time into realization—I believe it won't—would create the following situation.

We would be nine miles from the seashore, ten miles from the seashore, and maximum, twenty miles from the seashore. Around Netanya, almost in the middle of the country, we would be only nine miles from the seashore. And there by an onslaught of a tank column, the country can be cut into two in ten or fifteen minutes.

Soviet artillery now has a range of forth-three [*sic*] kilometers eight hundred meters. So in other words, from every point of what was in the past termed Green Line, the conventional artillery possessed by our neighbors can reach every city and town and township. In fact, every house. In fact, every man, woman and child.

To sum it up, it would be a mortal danger to the state of Israel. It would mean the beginning of the end of our statehood, independence and liberty.

However, the Geneva Conference should mean an open negotiation. Therefore, I state here that President Sadat or his emissary will be entitled to bring his proposal to the conference table at Geneva. However, should President Sadat say in advance, "You, the Israelis, have to accept my demand so that I should come to the conference table; you, the Israelis, should accept my proposal in advance of the Geneva Conference," that is a precondition, and that will not be accepted. That will not be accepted by Israel.

No preconditions by either side.

For the sake of objectivity, I will give an example on our side. We have a national consensus. In other words, all parties, except one, the Communist Party, which is completely subservient to Moscow, agree that Jerusalem should stay undivided and should be the capital city of the state of Israel. Such is and will be our proposal. But should we ask that the Arabs accept in advance that proposal by Israel so that they come to the—the Israelis come to the peace conference at Geneva, that would mean an Israeli precondition. And as it is a precondition or a prior condition, we don't put it out at all.

They are entitled to bring their proposals; we shall be entitled to bring our proposals. And the negotiation will be a free negotiation between the parties concerned, as it is the law and the practice in the relations amongst nations. No prior conditions.

NO PRIOR COMMITMENTS

To the same effect, I will add no prior commitments by either side. Prior commitments will not be asked by either side. Prior commitments will not be given by either side. This is the basis for a free negotiation.

MIXED COMMISSIONS

At the public session of the reconvened Geneva Peace Conference, the representatives of the parties will make public statements. When the session, the public session comes to a conclusion, we suggest that the instrument for negotiations of peace treaties between Israel and the neighboring countries be established. And we call that instrument three or four, if Lebanon is added, mixed commissions; one an Egyptian-Israeli commission; a Syrian-Israeli commission; and a Jordanian-Israeli commission; and there may be a Lebanese-Israeli commission.

The chairmanship of these commissions will rotate between the Israeli emissary and the emissary of the neighboring country. In the framework of these three or four mixed commissions, peace treaties between the parties concerned will be negotiated and concluded.

I have to dwell and elaborate on the term "peace treaties."

PEACE TREATIES

I was glad to hear some two weeks ago the spokesman of the State Department who states that there should be peace treaties between Israel and the neighboring countries. Our concept is that this is, as every authority on international law will prove, and mainly the quotations are from the well-known book of Law of Oppenheim, that the usual, the accepted way to bring about the termination of a state of war itself is through a peace treaty. There are a few exceptions, admittedly. For instance, Germany after the

Second World War did not yet sign a peace treaty, for reasons which in themselves are exceptional. There are two Germanys, with Russia in Eastern Prussia, the Allied Armies on German soil, etcetera. But this is an exception which proves the rule, because both after the First World War and after the Second World War, peace treaties were signed between the parties concerned.

The United States of America and her allies also signed peace treaties with Japan after the Second World War. The Soviet Union signed a peace declaration with Japan in October, 1956 in Moscow, which is declared by the signatories not to be a peace treaty. And the Soviet Union promises in that document that when a peace treaty is signed between the two countries, they will return the Kuril Islands, Shikotan and Habomai to Japanese sovereignty.

But the first article even of that document is that the state of war between the two countries has come to an end, will cease from . . . . . , etcetera.

Now when we say a peace treaty, we actually include all the elements of the essence of peace, which are lately being discussed. The first article of any peace treaty is to the effect "The state of war has been terminated." Then comes the territorial clauses, a chapter of a peace treaty in which you determine, also with the help of a map attached to the peace treaty, the boundary, the permanent boundary between the countries involved. Then comes the chapter about diplomatic clauses, and there you give a solution for diplomatic exchanges. Then comes a chapter about economic clauses, and other chapters sometimes about tourism, sometimes about fisheries, about specific problems concerning, as they put it usually, "The High Contracting Parties."

So when we say a peace treaty, we mean mainly the termination of the state of war, the determination of permanent boundaries, diplomatic relations, the economic clauses, etcetera. And when the three or the four mixed commissions will work out the conditions and the details of those peace treaties and they will conclude them, then another session of the Geneva Peace Conference will be reconvened, and the peace treaties so concluded will be signed by the parties concerned. And then with the famous stipulation about ratification at a proper time, they will come into force. And there will be a commitment by all the parties concerned.

Such is the framework proposed by us for the peace-making process. I believe it can be used. I believe it can bring us nearer to real peace in the Middle East.

PLO—No Partner for Negotiations

And now, ladies and gentlemen, my final remark in the opening statement. Even before you put this question, I will realistically assume that the problem of participation will arise; namely that the Arab countries may ask or insist on the participation, in addition to the state delegations, of the organization called PLO. We cannot accept participation of that organization. They declared in their covenant or charter, in Article XIX of their charter, that the state of Israel is null and void fundamentally. They also declare that only those Jews who were born or lived in Palestine until the beginning of the "Zionist invasion," as they put it—in other words, until the proclamation of the Balfour Declaration—will be regarded Palestinians, and all the others, as the assumption goes, will have to leave the country. And other articles whose contents are quite known.

So we do know what is their design, what they strive for. To put it bluntly and simply, their design is to destroy our country and to destroy our people. Therefore, they cannot be a partner to any negotiations with Israel.

If, therefore, the Arab countries will make it impossible to reconvene a full-fledged additional new session of the Geneva Conference through insisting on the participation of the organization called the PLO, then we must look for alternatives. And we suggest two alternatives:

Alternatives to Geneva

MIXED COMMISSIONS

One alternative is that the good offices of the United States be used to bring about the establishment of the three or four mixed commissions through diplomatic contacts with the respective capitals. That's one possibility, and it is based on the method used in 1949 during the negotiations for the armistice in Rhodes Island. It is a well-tried method which brought about very good results. The armistice agreements—the three armistice agreements, with Syria, Jordan and with Egypt, are documents of great national importance. In one of their articles it is stipulated there that those armistice agreements are an indispensable step towards the establishment of a full peace in Palestine. Twenty-nine years, twenty-eight years elapses then. So we are late. And during the intervening years there were four wars. It is very regrettable.

Yet, let us start now, at least now, with the delay of almost a generation, and let us carry out the mutual pledge given by the parties concerned that we shall establish a real peace.

So, we suggest as one of the alternative possibilities to have such mixed commissions established through diplomatic contacts in the respective capitals. And they may sit either in their respective capitals or on any neutral soil, as the decision will be taken by the parties concerned.

PROXIMITY TALKS

The second alternative possibility is what is termed the proximity talks. In 1972 the United States Government suggested that proximity talks be held in New York. In other words, an Israeli delegation and an Arab delegation, and the United States delegation giving their good offices to bring the parties together. We will be willing to adopt such a method as well.

   Ladies and gentlemen, the Government of Israel adopted this decision to bring to the knowledge of the President, and of public opinion at large, our proposal for the framework of the peacemaking process. Now it depends on the other side whether it will put into realization. We want peace. We yearn and pray for peace. We want real peace based on security, without which peace becomes devoid of the real meaning.

   We should start negotiating seriously peace treaties, and here we give the instruments which are necessary for such negotiations to be conducted and concluded successfully. We hope it will mean progress toward real peace in the Middle East.

   Ladies and gentlemen, thank you for your attention; and now, please fire your questions.

12. Israeli Government Policy Statement Delivered

in the Knesset by the Minister of Foreign Affairs,

Moshe Dayan, on Relations with the U.S., the Arabs,

and the Palestinians, September 1, 1977*

---

* Embassy of Israel, Washington, D.C.

Mr. Speaker, Members of the Knesset, I do not propose this time to deliver a comprehensive review of foreign policy. I wish to review only one issue, the central issue of our diplomatic activity—the peace negotiations. Technically—and I stress technically, and not in essence—the negotiating process is proceeding apace.

This process commenced with the meetings the President of the United States held, at his initiative, with the Arab Heads of State and with both the former and the incumbent Prime Ministers of Israel. Thereafter, the U.S. Secretary of State visited the Arab States and Israel, and now we face the next round—the indirect talks between the Foreign Ministers, to be held in Washington with effect from the second half of September.

The Arab Positions

The Arab positions, as reported to us by the Secretary of State and in accordance with the Arab leader's public pronouncements, are in the main:

(A) On the territorial issue, insistence on our total withdrawal to the lines of June 4th, 1967 and return of the vacated territories to the Arab States. This entails, inter alia, handing over the Gaza Strip to Egyptian authority and East Jerusalem—including Mount Scopus and the Old City's Jewish Quarter—to Jordanian authority.

(B) Establishment of a Palestinian Arab State, or, in other words, granting the right of self-determination to the Palestinian Arabs, whose representative is the PLO: ergo, the PLO representation, with powers similar to those of other states, is to be allowed to participate in the Geneva Conference.

(C) On the issue of peace, only one Arab State announced its readiness in the advent of peace, to establish diplomatic relations with Israel. The other Arab States contend that a peace treaty does not obligate them to establish diplomatic and commercial relations with Israel.

(D) On the refugee resettlement issue, over and above the PLO, the Syrian President too, in his public pronouncements, insists that even after establishment of a Palestinian State in the Gaza Strip and in Judea and Samaria, the right should be reserved for the refugees to return to their homes and land located in Israel; in addition to establishment of a Palestinian State.

The Position of the United States

As for the United States' position, this is known to the Members of the House, its main points being:

(A) Israeli withdrawal to the boundaries of June 4th, 1967, with minor adjustments to be made by mutual agreement.

(B) Giving the Palestinian Arabs the right of self-determination.

(C) Peace that includes diplomatic ties and commercial relations. This American position was determined during the term of office of the previous

Israel Governments, and has not changed since—neither for the better nor for the worse.

Points of Dispute Between the United States and Israel

I will neither dwell at length, nor go into detail on these matters, since they are well known. All the same, I would like to remark on two points of dispute that have cropped up between the U.S. and ourselves at this juncture, even before negotiations have begun with the Arabs on peace treaties.

The first is on the settlement issue. The U.S. position regarding the settlements is that settling Israeli citizens in the administered areas is in contradiction to the Geneva Convention, hence the settlements are not legal, and that this act also creates an obstacle to peace or to peace negotiations. The Israel Government's position on the subject which is a continuation of the line adopted by all Israel Governments since 1967, is that Israel does not and cannot accept the assertion that Jewish settlement in Eretz Israel is illegal. The Government reiterates that such settlement does not, nor shall, constitute, in any sense, an obstacle to negotiations for peace treaties.

The Arabs' position—and this is also the position of the United States and of the rest of the Nations of the World which emulate the United States—does not, on this matter of settlements, distinguish between one region and another, viewing settlement on the Golan Heights as violation of International Law and an obstacle to peace just like (settlement) in Judea and Samaria.

> Let the Honorable Members take note. I should like Mapam in particular to take note: According to "Al Hamishmar" Mapam adopted a resolution stating that "The Cabinet's decision to establish three civilian settlement-points in Judea and Samaria places an obstacle on the road to political negotiations". I want to reiterate that not only the Arabs' stand, but also that of the United States, is that settlements in the administered areas—regardless of whether on the Golan Heights, in Sinai, or in Judea and Samaria—are illegal and constitute an obstacle to peace. The United States makes no distinction in this matter between Judea and Samaria and the Golan Heights.

The Second sphere in which there are differences of opinion between ourselves and the Americans is that of U.S. recognition of the PLO as a partner for dialogue with the U.S. There has of late been a change for the worse in the position of the U.S. on this issue as compared with its stand some time ago. The present position is that if the PLO accepts Resolution 242—albeit with a reservation to the effect that Resolution 242 should refer to the Palestinians as a people entitled to a homeland, and not as refugees—if the PLO accepts the Resolution with that proviso tagged on, the United States would be ready to maintain contact and dialogue with it. Though the U.S. has not told us, I believe it is correct to say that this approach is ultimately aimed at proposing that the PLO—if not as an independent body then at least as a partner (to another delegation)—participate in one of the delegations to the Geneva Conference or in a unified Arab Delegation to Geneva.

I do not think that the current dealing with the subject of the PLO's legitimation or legalization for the purpose of dialogue between it and the U.S. has any purpose other than the linking and inclusion, in one form or another, of the PLO in peace negotiations. The stand of the Government of Israel vis-a-vis the PLO is clear and explicit. We oppose both U.S. dialogue with the PLO and that organization's participation in the peace conference for two reasons: first, the PLO's murderous essence and nature and its rejection of Israel's very existence; second, the Geneva Conference is one conducted between States and its objective is to bring about the signing of peace treaties between States, and not with any organization which is not a State.

The PLO and Jordan

I would like to add a few remarks at this point. The U.S. position vis-a-vis the State, a Homeland, or self-determination—different expressions designed for the Palestinian Arabs—is that the same entity which we shall call, in plain language, "The Palestinian State", should be connected with Jordan. But that position, and that assumption, utterly contradict the other. The second, tendency of the United States, to present the PLO as representing the Palestinian State—a conception by which the PLO might head the Palestinian State.

First of all, as regards Jordan, there might one day be a different regime in Jordan. There might one day be a revolution in Jordan with the PLO then taking over Jordan and the situation being different. But the present Jordanian regime totally rejects any link with the PLO. That regime holds no dialogue with the PLO, places no faith in it, and regards it as a subversive element against the regime. Jordan is not ready to maintain any connection with a Palestinian State, should such a State be established in the West Bank, if it is headed by the PLO. Hence these two views cannot be reconciled: one cannot want to see a connection between Judea and Samaria and the Gaza Strip and Jordan and at the same time want to see the PLO heading that West Bank-Gaza Strip entity, heading those Palestinian Arabs.

These two contingencies are impossible under the present Jordanian regime, and anyone who wants proof need only look at what is happening at this very time when the King of Jordan invited the Mayors of Nablus, Hebron, Jenin, and Ramallah to pay a courtesy visit to Jordan to bring their greetings on the twenty fifth anniversary of the regime in Jordan. The four mayors of Nablus, Hebron, Tulkarm and Ramallah refused to go to Jordan—every one of those mayors is a Jordanian citizen, and representatives of their towns are members of the parliament in Amman. They would not have refused had it not been for the tendency to place the PLO at the head of the Arabs of these areas, and the instructions they received to refuse the invitation—and it was an insult to refuse the King's request—came from the PLO. (The American trend, from the time of the Rabat Conference, of legitimizing and raising up the PLO, to its most recent policy which posits the PLO as representative of the Palestinian Arabs, totally contradicts the line which sees a link between the Jordanian Government and the Palestinian Arabs who are residents of Judea and Samaria and the Gaza Strip).

No Reliance on U.S. Guarantees of a Settlement

In connection with the American stand, I would like to draw the attention of the House to one further matter. In the course of the ongoing public discussion in Israel—in the press and in various political parties—from time to time there has been talk and suggestions concerning American guarantees for our security as part of a peace settlement between ourselves and the Arab States.

Well, neither in any American initiative nor in their replies to our queries have we, in my opinion, found any basis whatsoever upon which to build our security in such a context. In my view we have heard nothing of the sort, nor do I see any basis for our security which could rely on any serious, fundamental American tendency or readiness—operationally and concretely with its own forces—to guarantee Israel's security as part of the settlement. The United States would not refuse and would not hold back from giving guarantees, along with other States (its position is very similar to that of the U.S.S.R.), if requested by all the parties to append its signature to a peace agreement after it has been attained. But it is a very far call from that to regarding this as a concrete-operative element upon which we can rely as one of the security components.

Israel's Position Prior to the Washington Talks

And, finally, I would like to present Israel's position, in general lines, anticipatory to the talks to be held in Washington. Israel's proposals and aims vis-a-vis the issues to be discussed in Washington—on the substantive—not the procedural issues are divided into two sections.

The first is a draft text for a full peace treaty, in all its articles. The second indicates our approach vis-a-vis discussion and negotiation on the various issues. The second section is subdivided into two components: first, a presentation of the questions involved in a peace agreement between ourselves and each of our neighbors, such as, Israel's security, guaranteeing freedom of navigation of the Gulf of Eilat and the Suez Canal, expression given to Israel's national and historic affinity to Judea and Samaria, securing of the Jordan River sources in the North, and other topics of like nature. That is, presentation of the questions which we believe we must contend with when we are to arrive at a peace agreement between ourselves and each of the neighboring Arab States.

The second element in this approach is our stand and our proposals for resolving these questions. A third component is the principle that the negotiations be conducted without prior conditions. This principle says not only that neither side obligates the other to agree in advance to any condition whatsoever, but also that all issues and areas are open to negotiation, and that we shall be totally open and sincere in listening to, discussing, and examining the proposals of the other parties. To illustrate this we believe that the settlement concerning Judea and Samaria and the Gaza Strip should be based on our living together with the Palestinian Arabs in these areas, and not on partition of the territory. But should the Arabs propose partitioning these territories between ourselves and them, we would discuss and examine their proposal and afterward conclude whether we were ready to agree to their proposals or not.

In connection with this example, I should like to tell the Members of the House that we have re-examined the positions of Jordan, of the Palestinian Arabs, and of the United States, and we have found no inclination on the part of any of them for a solution based on the partition of Judea and Samaria and the Gaza Strip between ourselves and them. We have found no hint of this on the part of Jordan, of the Americans, or of any of the Arab States. I should like to propose to the factions and the parties that think otherwise, that if they find any indication at all of such readiness on the part of the Arabs, they raise the matter before the public, and then we shall know what the debate is about—things that exist or things that do not exist.

The Cardinal Objective Is Peace

In conclusion, I want to say that while there is of course no telling if we shall succeed in reaching an agreement with the Arabs, we must nonetheless make a supreme effort to attain that goal. There is no need to enlarge on the overriding need for its attainment. The entire nation accepts that attainment of true peace with our neighbors is the cardinal objective of our policy. However, in this connection I would like to underscore four facts due to which, I believe, the prospects for reaching a settlement in this period are better than those that existed in the past:

(A) The increased influence of the United States on the Arab countries, and their reduced dependence—particularly that of Egypt—on the Soviet Union.

(B) The Arab leaders' readiness in principle to terminate the state of war with Israel. I have never suggested, and I do not now suggest, that Israel relax its alertness and its military and political preparations against the eventuality that the Arab States—headed by Egypt—launch a war against us. We must view that possibility as a real one at all times, and particularly if the peace talks reach a dead end. Nonetheless, we must not ignore the difference between Nasser's policy—a policy of "what was taken by force shall be restored by force" and of "no negotiations with no recognition of and no peace with Israel"—and that of Sadat, who seeks to attain his goals by political means and declares publicly his readiness to accept Israel. I do not think we should treat his words as deception and fraud. I do not think so. We must try to put those declarations to the test of reality while, as noted, at the same time taking into account the possibility that Egypt will—Sadat's statements notwithstanding—launch war on us.

(C) The third fact is our military and civilian control of the administered areas. Not even the Yom Kippur War, with all its difficulties, led to a change in that situation. We can therefore, conduct peace negotiations without requiring any Arab territorial concession whatsoever. We are in a position to give territories without asking for others in exchange for them.

(D) And lastly, the way of life "alongside one another" which has prevailed for ten years now between ourselves and the Arabs in Jerusalem, in Judea and Samaria, in the Gaza Strip and in Sinai: the present way of life is not the ideal one, and it should not be viewed as the final aim in this regard, either—but so long as we do not arrive at a better arrangement we will be able to continue with it, and we—and our neighbors—must be aware of this.

These are the observations I have found proper to bring before you at the opening of this debate. I presume that there will be place for further debate at the next session of the Knesset, following the talks to be held in Washington.

13. Joint U.S.-Soviet Statement on the Middle East,

October 1, 1977*

* 77 U.S. Dep't State Bull. No. 2002, at 639 (1977).

Having exchanged views regarding the unsafe situation which remains in the Middle East, U.S. Secretary of State Cyrus Vance and Member of the Politbureau of the Central Committee of the CPSU, Minister for Foreign Affairs of the U.S.S.R. A.A. Gromyko have the following statement to make on behalf of their countries, which are cochairmen of the Geneva Peace Conference on the Middle East:

1. Both governments are convinced that vital interests of the peoples of this area, as well as the interests of strengthening peace and international security in general, urgently dictate the necessity of achieving, as soon as possible, a just and lasting settlement of the Arab-Israel conflict. This settlement should be comprehensive, incorporating all parties concerned and all questions.

The United States and the Soviet Union believe that, within the framework of a comprehensive settlement of the Middle East problem, all specific questions of the settlement should be resolved, including such key issues as withdrawal of Israeli Armed Forces from territories occupied in the 1967 conflict; the resolution of the Palestinian question, including insuring the legitimate rights of the Palestinian people; termination of the state of war and establishment of normal peaceful relations on the basis of mutual recognition of the principles of sovereignty, territorial integrity, and political independence.

The two governments believe that, in addition to such measures for insuring the security of the borders between Israel and the neighboring Arab states as the establishment of demilitarized zones and the agreed stationing in them of U.N. troops or observers, international guarantees of such borders as well as of the observance of the terms of the settlement can also be established should the contracting parties so desire. The United States and the Soviet Union are ready to participate in these guarantees, subject to their constitutional processes.

2. The United States and the Soviet Union believe that the only right and effective way for achieving a fundamental solution to all aspects of the Middle East problem in its entirety is negotiations within the framework of the Geneva peace conference, specially convened for these purposes, with participation in its work of the representatives of all the parties involved in the conflict including those of the Palestinian people, and legal and contractual formalization of the decisions reached at the conference.

In their capacity as cochairmen of the Geneva conference, the United States and the U.S.S.R. affirm their intention, through joint efforts and in their contacts with the parties concerned, to facilitate in every way the resumption of the work of the conference not later than December 1977. The cochairmen note that there still exist several questions of a procedural and organizational nature which remain to be agreed upon by the participants to the conference.

3. Guided by the goal of achieving a just political settlement in the Middle East and of eliminating the explosive situation in this area of the world, the United States and the U.S.S.R. appeal to all the parties in the conflict to understand the necessity for careful consideration of each other's legitimate rights and interests and to demonstrate mutual readiness to act accordingly.

14. Joint U.S.-Israel Statement on the Geneva Peace Conference on the Middle East, October 5, 1977*

* 13 Weekly Comp. Press Doc. 1482 (October 10, 1977).

The U.S. and Israel agree that Security Council Resolutions 242 and 338 remain the agreed basis for the resumption of the Geneva Peace Conference and that all the understandings and agreements between them on this subject remain in force.

Proposals for removing remaining obstacles to reconvening the Geneva Conference were developed. Foreign Minister Dayan will consult his Government on the results of these discussions. Secretary Vance will discuss these proposals with the other parties to the Geneva Conference.

Acceptance of the Joint U.S.-U.S.S.R. Statement of October 1, 1977, by the parties is not a prerequisite for the reconvening and conduct of the Geneva Conference.

NOTE: The text of the joint statement was released at New York, N.Y.

E. The Sadat-Begin Rapprochement

15. Address by President Sadat to Israel's Knesset,
November 20, 1977*

* 24 Keesing's Contemporary Archives: Record of World Events 29155 (1978).

"In the name of God, Mr Speaker of the *Knesset*, ladies and gentlemen, permit me first to address a special thanks to the Speaker of the *Knesset* [Mr Itzhak Shamir] for giving me this opportunity to address you.

"I begin my speech by saying God's peace and mercy be with you: God willing, peace for us all; peace for us all in the Arab land and in Israel and in every part of the land of this wide world, this world which is made complex by its bloody conflicts and which is made tense by its sharp contradictions and which is threatened every now and then by destructive wars—wars made by man to kill his brother man. In the end, amid the debris and mutilated bodies of men, there is neither victor nor vanquished; the true vanquished one is always man—man who is the best of God's creation, man whom God created, as Gandhi, the saint of peace, has stated, to walk on his feet to build life and worship God.

"Today I come to you with both feet firmly on the ground, in order that we may build a new life and so that we may establish peace. All of us in this land, the land of God, Moslems, Christians and Jews, worship God and no other god. God's decrees and commandments are: love, honesty, chastity and peace.

Decision to Visit Israel

"I can excuse all those who received my decision to attend your assembly, when I made that decision known to the whole world, with astonishment, or rather who were flabbergasted. Some, under the effect of this violent surprise, thought that my decision was nothing more than a verbal manoeuvre, for home consumption and before world opinion; others described it as a political tactic to conceal my intentions to wage a fresh war.

"I do not want to conceal from you that one of my aides at the President's Office contacted me at a late hour, after I returned home from the People's Assembly [see above], to ask me with concern: 'What are you going to do if Israel actually addresses an invitation to you?' I replied quite calmly: 'I shall immediately accept it. I have declared that I am ready to go to the end of the world; I shall go to Israel, because I want to put before the people of Israel the full facts.'

"I can excuse anyone who was flabbergasted by the decision or who had doubts about the sound intentions behind that declaration. No one could imagine that the President of the largest Arab state, which bears the greatest burden and first responsibility over the question of war or peace in the Middle East region, could take a decision to be prepared to go to enemy territory when we are in a state of war, and we and you are still suffering the effects of four severe wars in a period of 30 years. All this at the time when the families of the war of October 1973 are still living out the tragedies of losing husbands and sons and the martyrdom of fathers and brothers.

"However, as I have already declared, I did not discuss this decision with any of my colleagues and brother heads of the Arab states, not even those of the [other] confrontation states [i.e. Syria and Jordan]; some of them who got in touch with me after the announcement opposed the decision, because a state of total doubt still existed in everybody's mind, a state of complete lack of confidence between the Arab states, including the Palestinian people, and Israel.

"Suffice it to say that long months during which peace could have been established have been wasted in useless differences and discussions over procedures concerning the convening of the Geneva conference; all of them reflected this total doubt, this total lack of confidence. But I tell you frankly and with complete sincerity that I took this decision after long thought; and I know quite well that it is a big gamble. But if almighty God has made it my destiny to assume responsibility for the people of Egypt, and to have a share in the responsibility for the destiny of the entire Arab people, then I think that the first duty dictated by this responsibility is that I must exhaust every possibility in order to stop the Arab people of Egypt, and all the Arab peoples, from enduring the sufferings of other horrendous, destructive wars of which only God knows the extent.

"After long thought, I was convinced that my responsibility to God and the people imposes on me the obligation to go to the furthest place in the world and, indeed, to come to Jerusalem to speak to the members of the *Knesset*, the representatives of the people of Israel, about all the facts which I have in my own mind. Afterwards, I shall let you decide by yourselves, and let almighty God do whatever he wishes with us after that.

"There are moments in the life of nations and peoples when those who are known for their wisdom and foresight are required to look beyond the past, with all its complications and remnants, for the sake of a courageous upsurge towards new horizons. These people who, like ourselves, shoulder that responsibility entrusted to us are the first people who must have the courage to take fateful decisions in harmony with the sublimity of the situation.

"We must all rise above all forms of fanaticism and self-deception and obsolete theories of superiority. It is important that we should never forget that virtue is God's alone. If I say that I want to protect all the Arab people from the terrors of new, terrifying wars, I declare before you with all sincerity that I have the same feelings and I carry the same responsibility for every human being in the world and, most certainly, for the Israeli people.

"A life which is taken away in war is the life of a human being, whether it is an Arab or an Israeli life. The wife who becomes a widow is a human being and has the right to live in a happy family environment whether she is an Arab or an Israeli. The innocent children who lose the care and love of their parents are all our children; they are all our children, whether in the land of the Arabs or in Israel; we have a great responsibility to provide them with a prosperous present and a better future. For all these reasons and to protect the life of all our sons and sisters and in order that our communities may produce in safety and security for the development and happiness of man and give him the right to a dignified life, and out of our responsibility to the future generations, in order to achieve a smile on the face of every child born in our land—for all these reasons I have taken my decision to come to you and speak directly to you.

"I have borne, and shall continue to bear, the requirements of a historic responsibility. For this reason some years ago—to be precise on Feb. 4, 1971—I declared that I was ready to sign a peace agreement with Israel [see also page 24504]. This was the first such declaration to come from a responsible Arab since the beginning of the Arab-Israeli conflict.

"With all these motives, which are made necessary by the responsibility of leadership, I declared on Oct. 16, 1973, and before the Egyptian People's Assembly that an international conference should be called to determine a lasting and just peace [see page 26176]. I was not then in a position to beg for peace or seek a ceasefire. With all these motives, which are made imperative by the duty of history and leadership, we signed the first Sinai disengagement agreement and then the second one [respectively in January 1974 and September 1975—see pages 26319-20; 27429 A]. Then we tried to knock on open and closed doors to find a specific road towards a lasting and just peace. We have opened our hearts to all the peoples of the world so that they may understand our motives and aims and so that they may really be convinced that we are advocates of justice and seekers of peace.

"For all these reasons too, I decided to come to you with an open mind and an open heart and a conscientious will so that we may establish a lasting and just peace. Destiny has decreed that my visit to you, my visit of peace, should come on the day of the great Islamic feast, the blessed Id ul-Adha, the feast of sacrifice and redemption when our father Ibrahim [Abraham]— may peace be upon him, the forefather of both the Arabs and the Jews— submitted to God and dedicated himself completely to Him, not through weakness but through colossal spiritual power and through his free choice to sacrifice his son, which arose from his firm, unshakable belief in the sublime ideals which give a deep meaning to life. Perhaps this coincidence has a new meaning for us all; perhaps it forms a concrete hope for the good signs of security and safety and peace.

Five Facts.—No Separate or Partial Peace

"Let us be frank with each other, using straightforward words and clear thoughts which cannot be twisted. Let us be frank with each other today when the whole world, East and West, is following this unique event, this event which could be a turning-point, which could mean a radical change in the history of this part of the world, if not in the whole world. Let us be frank with each other when answering the big question: how can we achieve a just and lasting peace?

"First of all, I have come to you bringing with me a clear and frank answer to this major question, so that the people of Israel can hear it; the whole world can hear it; all those whose sincere calls reach me can hear it; and so that the results hoped for by millions of people may materialize from this historic meeting.

"Before I make my answer known to you, I want to stress that in this clear and frank answer I rely on a number of facts, facts which no one can deny. The first fact is that there can be no happiness for some [people] at the expense of the misery of others. The second fact is that I have not spoken and will not speak in two tongues, nor have I used, nor shall I use, two policies; I deal with everyone with one tongue, one policy and one face. The third fact is that direct confrontation and a straight line are the nearest and most useful methods to achieve the clear aim. The fourth fact is that the call for a just and lasting peace based on the implementation of the UN resolutions has today become the call of all the world, and has become a clear expression of the will of the international community, both at the level of the official capitals—where policy is decided and decisions made—and at the level of world opinion, which influences the policy and decisions.

"The fifth fact—and perhaps it is the most obvious one—is that, in its efforts to achieve a just and lasting peace, the Arab nation is not proceeding from a position of weakness or instability. Quite the contrary: its strength and stability are such that its efforts must stem from a genuine desire for peace, from a realization that for the spirit of civilization to survive, for us, you and the whole world to avoid a real disaster, there is no alternative to the establishment of a lasting and just peace that no storms can shake, no doubts can spoil, and no ill intentions can undermine.

"On the basis of these facts—these facts that I wanted to convey to you as I see them—I would like with complete sincerity to warn you about certain thoughts that might cross your minds. The duty to be sincere means that I must state the following:

"Firstly, I did not come to you with a view to concluding a separate agreement between Egypt and Israel; this is not provided for in Egypt's policy. The problem does not lie just between Egypt and Israel; moreover, no separate peace between Egypt and Israel—or between any confrontation state and Israel—could secure a lasting and just peace in the region as a whole. Even if a peace agreement was achieved between all the confrontation states and Israel, without a just solution to the Palestinian problem it would never ensure the establishment of the durable, lasting peace the entire world is now trying to achieve.

"Secondly, I did not come with a view to securing a partial peace, a peace such that we end the state of war at this stage, and then postpone the whole problem to a second phase. This is not the fundamental solution that will lead us to a lasting peace. Linked to this is the fact that I did not come to you in order that we may agree to a third disengagement of forces either in Sinai alone, or in Sinai, the Golan and the West Bank; this would be merely a postponement of an explosion until a later time. It would also mean that we lacked the courage to face up to peace, that we were too weak to shoulder the burden and responsibilities of a lasting and just peace.

Acceptance of Israel

"I have come to you so that together we can build a lasting and just peace, so that not one more drop of the blood of either side may be shed. For this reason I stated that I was willing to go to the ends of the earth. At this point I shall answer the question: how are we going to achieve permanent and just peace? In my opinion, and I say it from this platform to the whole world, to find an answer is not impossible and neither is it difficult, despite the long years of blood revenge, hatred and rancour, of bringing up generations on terms of complete estrangement and entrenched enmity. The answer is not difficult nor impossible to find, if we follow the path of a straight line with all honesty and faith. You want to live with us in this area of the world, and I say to you with all sincerity that we welcome you among us with security and safety.

"This in itself forms a giant turning-point, a decisive landmark of an historic transformation. We used to reject you, and we had our reasons and grievances. Yes, we used to reject meeting you anywhere. Yes, we used to describe you as 'so-called Israel'. Yes, conferences and international organizations used to bring us together. Our representatives have never and still do not exchange greetings and salaams. Yes, this is what happened, and it still goes on. For any talks, we used to make it conditional that a mediator met each side separately. Yes, this is how the talks on the first disengagement were conducted and this is also how the talks on the second disengagement were held. Our representatives met at the first Geneva conference [of December 1973–January 1974—see 26317 A] without exchanging one direct word. Yes, this is what went on. But I say to you today and I say to the whole world that we accept that we should live with you in a lasting and just peace. We do not want to surround you or to be surrounded ourselves with missiles which are ready to destroy, with the missiles of hatred and bitterness.

"More than once, I have said that Israel has become a living reality. The world recognized it and the two super-powers shouldered the responsibility of its security and the defence of its existence. And when we want peace both in theory and in practice we welcome you to live amongst us in security and peace, in theory and practice. There existed between you and us a huge high wall. You tried to build it over a quarter of a century, but it was demolished in 1973 [i.e. in the October 1973 war—see 26173 A]. In its ferocity the wall continues the war psychologically. Your wall was a threat with a force capable of destroying the Arab nation from end to end. The wall was based on the view that the Arab peoples had turned into a nation with no defences. Indeed some of you said that even after another 50 years the Arabs would never achieve a position of any strength. This wall has always threatened, with a long arm capable of reaching any position over any distance. This wall has threatened us with annihilation and extinction if we tried to exercise our legitimate right of liberating the occupied territory.

"We must admit together that this wall has fallen; it collapsed in 1973. But there is still another wall. This second wall forms a complex psychological barrier between us and you. It is a barrier of doubt, a barrier of hatred, a barrier of fear of deception, a barrier of illusions about behaviour, actions or decisions, a barrier of cautious and mistaken interpretation of every event or statement. This psychological barrier is the one I have mentioned in official statements, which in my opinion constitutes 70 per cent of the problem.

"On my visit to you, I ask you today why do we not extend our hands in sincerity, faith and truth so that we may together destroy this barrier; why do we not make our intentions the same in truth, faith and sincerity so that we may together eliminate all the doubt, the fear of treachery and ill-intentions, and prove the sincerity of our intentions; why do we not join together, with the courage of men and the daring of heroes, of those who risk their lives for the sake of a sublime idea; why do we not join together with this courage and daring to set up a mammoth edifice of peace, an edifice that builds and does not destroy, that emits to our future generations the light of the human spirit for building, development and the good of man. Why should we leave for these generations the consequences of the bloodletting, the killing of souls, the orphaning of children, the making of widows, the destruction of families and the agony of victims?

"Why do we not believe in the wisdom of the creator, as conveyed in the proverbs of the wise Solomon: 'Deceit is in the heart of those who imagine evil, but to the advocates of peace will come joy; better a morsel and peace than a house full of meat with strife.' Why don't we repeat together, why don't we sing together, from the psalms of David: 'Hear the voice of my supplications when I cry unto Thee, when I lift up my hands towards Thy holy oracle. Put me not with the wicked and with the evil-doers, who speak of peace to their neighbours, but have evil in their hearts. Treat them according to their actions, according to the wickedness of their deeds. I ask for peace and seek it.'

Insistence on Complete Israeli Withdrawal

"The truth is—and it is the truth that I am telling you—that there can be no peace in the true sense of the word unless this peace is based on justice and not on the occupation of the territory of others. It is not right that you seek for yourselves what you deny to others. In all frankness and in the spirit which prompted me to come to you today, I say to you: you have finally to abandon the dreams of tomorrow and you have also to abandon the belief that force is the best means of dealing with the Arabs. You have to absorb very well the lessons of confrontation between ourselves and you; expansion will be of no avail to you.

"To put it clearly: our territory is not a subject of bargaining; it is not a topic for wrangling. To us, the national and nationalist soil occupies the same position which the sacred valley of Tuwa occupies—the valley in which God spoke to Moses, may the peace of God be on him. None of us has the right to accept or to forfeit one inch of it, or to accept the principle of bargaining and wrangling about it. The truth is—and it is the truth that I am telling you—that before us today is a favourable opportunity for peace; it is an opportunity the like of which time will not provide again, if we are really serious in the struggle for peace. It is an opportunity which, if we miss it or waste it, the curse of mankind and of history will be on those who plotted against it.

"What is peace to Israel? To live in the region, together with her Arab neighbours, in security and safety—this is a logic to which I say: 'Yes'. For Israel to live within her borders secure from any aggression—this is a logic to which I say: 'Yes'. For Israel to get all kinds of assurances that ensure for her these two facts—this is a demand to which I say: 'Yes'. Furthermore, we declare that we accept all the international assurances which you can imagine and from those whom you approve. We declare that we accept all assurances you want from the two super-powers; or from one of them; or from the big five; or from some of them. I repeat and I declare quite clearly that we accept any guarantees you need because in return we shall take the same guarantees.

"The upshot of the matter then is this: when we put the question 'What is peace to Israel?', the answer would be that it lives within its borders together with its Arab neighbours in security and safety and within the framework of all that it likes in the way of guarantees which the other side obtains. But how can this be achieved? How can we arrive at this result so that it can take us to a permanent and just peace?

"There are facts which must be confronted with all courage and clarity. There is Arab land which Israel has occupied and still occupies by armed force. And we insist that complete withdrawal from this land be undertaken and this includes Arab Jerusalem—Jerusalem to which I have come, as it is considered the city of peace and which has been and will always be the living embodiment of coexistence between believers of the three religions. It is inadmissible for anyone to think of Jerusalem's special position within the context of annexation and expansion. It must be made a free city, open to all the faithful. What is more important is that the city must not be closed to those who have chosen it as a place of residence for several centuries.

"Instead of inflaming the feuds of the wars of the crusades we must revive the spirit of Umar Bin al-Khattab and Saladin, that is, the spirit of tolerance and respect for rights. The Moslem and Christian houses of worship are not mere places for the performance of religious rites and prayers. They are the true testimonies of our uninterrupted existence in this place, politically, morally and ideologically. Here, nobody must miscalculate the importance and veneration we hold for Jerusalem, we Christians and Moslems.

"Let me tell you without hesitation that I have not come to you, under this dome, to beg you to withdraw your forces from the occupied territory. This is because complete withdrawal from the Arab territories occupied after 1967 is a matter that goes without saying, over which we accept no controversy and in respect of which there is no begging to anyone or from anyone. There will be no meaning to talk about a lasting, just peace and there will be no meaning to any step to guarantee our lives together in this part of the world in peace and security while you occupy an Arab land by armed force. There can never be peace established or built with the occupation of others' land. Yes, this is a self-evident truth, which accepts no controversy or dicussion once the intentions are true—once the intentions are true, as is the struggle for the establishment of a lasting, just peace for our generation and for all the generations that will follow us.

The Palestinian Question

"As regards the Palestine question, nobody denies that it is the essence of the entire problem. Nobody throughout the entire world accepts today slogans raised here in Israel which disregard the existence of the people of Palestine and even ask where the people of Palestine are. The problem of the Palestinian people, and the legitimate rights of the Palestinian people are now no longer ignored or rejected by anybody; no thinking mind supposes that they could be ignored or rejected; they are facts that meet with the support and recognition of the international community both in the West and the East and in international documents and official declarations. No one could turn a deaf ear to their loud, resounding sound, or turn a blind eye to their historic reality.

"Even the USA—your first ally, which is the most committed to the protection of the existence and security of Israel and which has been giving Israel and continues to give it moral, material and military aid—I say even the USA has opted for facing up to the reality and to facts, to recognize that the Palestinian people have legitimate rights, and that the Palestine question is the crux and essence of the conflict; and that so long as this question remains suspended without a solution the conflict will increase, grow more intense and reach new magnitudes. In all sincerity, I tell you that peace cannot be achieved without the Palestinians, and that it would be a great mistake, the effect of which no one knows, to turn a blind eye to this question or to set it aside.

"I shall not recall events of the past, since the issue of the Balfour Declaration 60 years ago. You know the facts quite well. And if you have found it legally and morally justified to set up a national homeland on a land that was not totally yours, you are well placed to show understanding to the insistence of the Palestinian people to set up their own state anew, on their homeland. When some hardliners and extremists demand that the Palestinians should abandon this higher aim it means, in reality and in actual fact, that this is a demand that they should abandon their identity and every hope they have for the future. I salute some Israeli voices which demanded that the rights of the Palestinian people should be recognized in order to achieve and guarantee peace [see page 28534 for Israeli political groups favouring recognition of Palestinian rights]. Therefore, I say to you that there is no benefit from not recognizing the Palestinian people and their rights to establish their state and to return home. We, the Arabs, have earlier experienced this, over you and the truth of the existence of Israel. The struggle took us from one war to another and from victims to more victims, until we and you have reached today the brink of a terrifying abyss and a frightening disaster if, today, we do not seize together the chance of a permanent and just peace.

"You must face the reality courageously, as I have faced it. It is no solution to a problem to run away from it or to be above it. There can never be peace through an attempt to impose imaginary situations on which the entire world has turned its back and declared its unanimous appeal that right and justice should be respected. There is no need to enter the vicious circle of Palestinian rights. There is no use in creating obstacles, for either they will delay the march of peace or peace itself will be killed.

"As I have already told you, there can be no happiness for some at the expense of the misery of others; direct confrontation and the straight line are the surest and most useful ways of reaching the clear aim. Dealing directly with the Palestine problem and tackling it in the only language that will bring a just and lasting peace involve establishing a Palestinian state, with all the international reassurances you want. You must have no fear of a young state which needs the assistance of all the states in the world to establish itself.

Ingredients of Peace

"When the bells of peace ring, there will be no hand to beat the drums of war; should such a hand exist, it will not be heard. Imagine with me the peace agreement in Geneva, the good news of which we herald to a world thirsty for peace: [firstly] a peace agreement based on ending the Israeli occupation of the Arab territory occupied in 1967; [secondly] the realization of basic rights of the Palestinian people and this people's right to self-determination, including their right to setting up their own state; thirdly, the right of all the countries of the region to live in peace within their secure and guaranteed borders, through agreed measures for the appropriate security of international borders, in addition to the appropriate international guarantees; fourthly, all the states in the region will undertake to administer relations among themselves in accordance with the principles and aims of the UN Charter, in particular eschewing the use of force and settling differences among them by peaceful means; and fifthly, ending the state of war that exists in the region.

"Peace is not the putting of a signature under written lines. It is a new writing of history. Peace is not a competition in calling for peace so as to defend any greedy designs or to conceal any ambitions. In essence, peace is a mammoth struggle against all greedy designs and ambitions. The experiences of past and contemporary history teach us all that missiles, warships and nuclear weapons perhaps, cannot establish security. On the contrary, they destroy all that was built by security. For the sake of our peoples, for the sake of a civilization made by man, we must protect man in every place from the rule of the force of arms. We must raise high the rule of humanity with the full force of principles and values which hold man high.

"If you will permit me to address an appeal from this platform to the people of Israel, I address a genuine sincere word to every man, woman and child in Israel, and tell them: I bring to you from the people of Egypt, who bless this sacred mission for peace, the mission of peace, the mission of the Egyptian people who are not fanatics and whose sons, Moslems, Christians and Jews, live in a spirit of amity, love and tolerance. This is the Egypt whose people have entrusted me with carrying the sacred mission to you, the mission of security, hope and peace. Every man and woman, every child in Israel, encourage your leaders to struggle for peace. Let all the efforts be directed towards the building of a mammoth edifice of peace instead of the building of fortresses and shelters fortified with missiles of destruction. Give to the whole world the picture of the new man in this part of the world so that he may be an example for the man of the age, the man of peace in every position and in every place. Give your children the good tidings that what has passed is the last of wars and the end of agonies, and that what is coming is the new beginning of the new life, the life of love and good, freedom and peace. Mothers who have lost their sons, widowed wife, son who has lost a brother or a father, all victims of wars, fill the earth and space with the praise of peace. Fill the hearts and breasts with the hopes of peace. Make the song a fact, one that lives and bears fruit. Make hope an article of work and struggle. The will of the peoples is from the will of God.

Conclusion

"Before coming to this place, I turned with every pulse in my heart and every spark in my conscience to almighty God while I performed the Id prayers in the Al Aksa Mosque and when I visited the Church of the Holy Sepulchre. I turned to almighty God praying to Him to grant the power and to strengthen my conviction that this visit should achieve its objectives, objectives I aspire to for the sake of a happy present and a happier future.

"I have chosen to depart from all precedents and traditions known to countries at war and despite the fact that the Arab territory is still under occupation. Indeed, my announcement of my readiness to come to Israel was a big surprise which has upset many feelings, astounded many minds and aroused suspicions about what lies behind it. Despite all that, I took my decision in full, open and honest faith and with the full, true expression of the will and intentions of my people. I chose this hard path, which in the eyes of many is the hardest path.

"I have chosen to come to you with an open heart and an open mind, to give this momentum to all the international efforts made to achieve peace. I have chosen to put forward to you, and in your own house, the real facts, free from any scheme or whim; not to conduct manoeuvres, or to gain a round, but in order that we may, together, win the most grave round and battle in contemporary history—the battle of a just and lasting peace. It is not just my battle, nor is it just the battle of leaderships in Israel; it is truly the battle of all citizens of all our lands, who have the right to live in peace. It is a commitment of the conscience and responsibility in the hearts of millions of people.

"When I put forward this initiative, many wondered about how I envisaged the achievements that could be reached by this visit, and about where I expected it to lead. Just as I have answered those who put questions to me, I declare before you that I did not think of making this initiative from the point of view of what could be achieved during the visit, but I have come here to deliver a message. Have I delivered the message? God be my witness. God, I repeat what Zachariah said: 'I love right and peace'; and I take inspiration from what God had said in the Holy Book: 'Say: we believe in God, and in what God has sent down on us, and in what has been sent down on Ibrahim, Isma'il, Isaac, Jacob and the tribes and what was bestowed on Moses and the Christ and prophets by their God; we do not single out any of them, in whom we believe' [Koran]. God say the truth. Peace be upon you."

16. Response by Prime Minister Begin to President Sadat's

Knesset Speech, November 20, 1977*

* 24 Keesing's Contemporary Archives: Record of World Events 29158 (1978).

"Mr Speaker, Mr President of the state of Israel, Mr President of the Arab Republic of Egypt, ladies and gentlemen, members of the *Knesset*, we send our greetings to the President, to all the people of the Islamic religion in our country, and wherever they may be, on this the occasion of the Feast of the Sacrifice, Id ul-Adha. This feast reminds us of the binding of Isaac. This was the way in which the creator of the world tested the faith of our forefather, Abraham—our common forefather—and Abraham passed this test. However, from the moral aspect and the advancement of humanity it was forbidden to sacrifice human beings. Our two peoples in their ancient traditions know and taught what the Lord—blessed be He—taught while peoples around us still sacrificed human beings to their gods. Thus we contributed, the people of Israel and the Arab people, to the progress of mankind, and thus we are continuing to contribute to human culture to this day.

"I greet and welcome the President of Egypt for coming to our country and on his participating in the *Knesset* session. The flight time between Cairo and Jerusalem is short, but the distance between Cairo and Jerusalem was until last night almost endless. President Sadat crossed this distance courageously. We, the Jews, know how to appreciate such courage, and we know how to appreciate it in our guest, because it is with courage that we are here and this is how we continue to exist, and we shall continue to exist.

Israel's Desire for Peace

"Mr Speaker, this small nation, the remaining refuge of the Jewish people which returned to its historic homeland, has always wanted peace and, since the dawn of our independence, on May 14, 1948 [see page 9275], in the Declaration of Independence, in the founding scroll of our national freedom, David Ben-Gurion said: 'We extend a hand of peace and good-neighbourliness to all the neighbouring countries and their peoples. We call upon them to co-operate, to help each other, with the Hebrew people independent in its own country.' One year earlier, even from the underground, when we were in the midst of the fateful struggle for the liberation of the country and the redemption of the people, we called on our neighbours in these terms: 'In this country we shall live together and we shall advance together and we shall live lives of freedom and happiness. Our Arab neighbours: do not reject the hand stretched out to you in peace.'

"But it is my bounden duty, Mr Speaker, and not only my right, not to pass over the truth, that our hand outstretched for peace was not grasped and, one day after we had renewed our independence—as was our right, our eternal right, which cannot be disputed—we were attacked on three fronts and we stood almost without arms, the few against many, the weak against the strong, while an attempt was made, one day after the Declaration of Independence, to strangle it at birth, to put an end to the last hope of the Jewish people, the yearning renewed after the years of destruction and holocaust.

"No, we do not believe in might and we have never based our attitude to the Arab people on might; quite the contrary, force was used against us. Over all the years of this generation we have never stopped being attacked by might, the might of the strong arm stretched out to exterminate our people, to destroy our independence, to deny our rights. We defended ourselves, it is true. We defended our rights, our existence, our honour, our women and children, against these repeated and recurring attempts to crush us through the force of arms and not only on one front. That, too, is true. With the help of almighty God we overcame the forces of aggression, and we have guaranteed the existence of our nation, not only for this generation, but for the coming generations, too. We do not believe in might; we believe in right—only in right—and therefore our aspiration, from the depth of our hearts, has always been, to this very day, for peace.

"Mr Speaker, Mr President of Egypt, the commanders of all the underground Hebrew fighting organizations are sitting in this democratic house. They had to conduct a campaign of the few against the many, against a huge, a world power. Here are sitting the veteran commanders and captains who had to go forth into battle because it was forced upon them and forward to victory which was unavoidable because they were defending their rights. They belong to different parties. They have different views, but I am sure, Mr President, that I am expressing the views of everyone with no exceptions that we have one aspiration in our hearts—one desire in our souls and all of us are united in all these aspirations and desires—to bring peace, peace for our nation, which has not known peace for even one day since we started returning to Zion, and peace for our neighbours, whom we wish all the best. And we believe that if we make peace, real peace, we shall be able to help our neighbours in all walks of life and a new era will open in the Middle East, an era of blossoming and growth, development and expansion of the economy, its growth as it was in the past.

Peace Programme

"Therefore, permit me, today, to set out the peace programme as we understand it. We want full, real peace, with complete reconciliation between the Jewish and the Arab peoples. I do not wish to dwell on the memories of the past, but there have been wars; there has been blood spilt; wonderful young people have been killed on both sides. We shall live all our life with the memories of our heroes who gave their lives so this day would arrive, this day, too, would come, and we respect the bravery of a rival and we honour all the members of the younger generation among the Arab people who also fell.

"I do not wish to dwell on memories of the past, although they are bitter memories. We shall bury them, we shall worry about the future, about our people, our children, our joint and common future. For it is true indeed that we shall have to live in this area, all of us together shall live here, for generations upon generations; the great Arab people in their various states and countries and the Jewish people in their country, *Eretz Israel*. Therefore we must determine what peace means.

"Let us conduct negotiations, Mr President, as free negotiating partners for a peace treaty and, with the aid of the Lord, we fully believe the day will come when we can sign it with mutual respect, and we shall then know that the era of wars is over, that hands have been extended between friends, that each has shaken the hand of his brother and the future will be shining for all the peoples of this area. The beginning of wisdom in a peace treaty is the abolition of the state of war. I agree, Mr President, that you did not come here, we did not invite you to our country, in order, as has been said in recent days, to divide the Arab peoples. Somebody quoted an ancient Roman saying: Divide and rule. Israel does not want to rule and therefore does not need to divide. We want peace with all our neighbours, with Egypt, with Jordan, with Syria and with Lebanon. We would like to negotiate peace treaties. [At this point Mr Begin was interrupted by Mr Tawfiq Toubi (Communist), who asked why he was not prepared to talk to the PLO; after explaining the identity of the interrupter to President Sadat in English, Mr Begin added that he was glad that the interruption had not come during the Egyptian leader's speech; he then resumed his speech in Hebrew.]

"And there is no need to distinguish between a peace treaty and an abolition of the state of war. Quite the contrary, we are not proposing this nor are we asking for it. The first clause of a peace treaty is cessation of the state of war, for ever. We want to establish normal relations between us, as they exist between all nations, even after wars. We have learned from history, Mr President, that war is avoidable, peace is unavoidable. Many nations have waged war between each other and sometimes they used the tragic term, a perennial enemy. There are no perennial enemies. And after all the wars the inevitable comes—peace. And so we want to establish, in a peace treaty, diplomatic relations, as is the custom among civilized nations.

"Today two flags are flying over Jerusalem—the Egyptian flag and the Israeli flag. And we saw together, Mr President, little children waving both the flags. Let us sign a peace treaty and let us establish this situation for ever, both in Jerusalem and in Cairo; and I hope the day will come when the Egyptian children wave the Israeli flag and the Egyptian flag just as the children of Israel waved both these flags in Jerusalem. And you, Mr President, will have a loyal ambassador in Jerusalem and we shall have an ambassador in Cairo. And even if differences of opinion arise between us, we shall clarify them, like civilized peoples, through our authorized envoys.

"We are proposing economic co-operation for the development of our countries. There are wonderful countries in the Middle East, the Lord created it thus: oases in the desert; but we can make the deserts flourish as well. Let us co-operate in this field; let us develop our countries; let us eliminate poverty, hunger, homelessness. Let us raise our peoples to the level of developed countries; let them call us developing countries no longer.

"With all due respect, I am willing to repeat the words of His Majesty the King of Morocco, who said in public that if peace came about in the Middle East the combination of Arab genius and Jewish genius together could turn this area into a paradise on earth.

"Let us open our countries to free traffic. You come to our country and we shall visit yours. I am ready to announce, Mr Speaker, this very day, that our country is open to the citizens of Egypt, and I make no conditions. I think it is only proper and just that there should be a joint announcement on this matter. But just as there are Egyptian flags in our streets, and there is an honoured delegation from Egypt in our country, in our capital, let the number of visitors increase; our border with you will be open, as will be all [our] other borders.

"As I pointed out, we want this in the south, in the north, in the east; so I am renewing my invitation to the President of Syria to follow in your footsteps, Mr President, and come to us to open negotiations for a peace between Israel and Syria, so that we may sign a peace treaty between us. I am sorry but I must say that there is no justification for the mourning they have declared beyond our northern border. Quite the contrary, such visits, such links, such clarifications can and must be days of joy, days of the raising of spirits of all people. I invite King Hussein to come to us to discuss all the problems which need to be discussed between us. And genuine representatives of the Arabs of *Eretz Israel*, I invite them to come and hold clarification talks with us about our common future, about guaranteeing the freedom of man, social justice, peace, mutual respect. And if they invite us to come to their capitals, we shall accept their invitations. If they invite us to open negotiations in Damascus, in Amman or in Beirut [i.e. in Syria, Jordan or Lebanon], we shall go to those capitals in order to hold negotiations with them there. We do not want to divide; we want real peace with all our neighbours, to be expressed in peace treaties whose contents I have already made clear.

Jewish Right to Eretz Israel

"Mr Speaker, it is my duty today to tell our guest and the peoples watching us and listening to our words about the link between our people and this land. The President [of Egypt] recalled the Balfour Declaration. No, sir, we did not take over any strange land; we returned to our homeland. The link between our people and this land is eternal. It arose in the earliest days of the history of humanity and was never altered. In this country we developed our civilization. We had our prophets here, and their sacred words stand to this day. Here the Kings of Judah and Israel knelt before their God. This is where we became a people, here we established our kingdom. And when we were expelled from our land, when force was used against us, no matter how far we went from our land, we never forgot it for even one day. We prayed for it, we longed for it, we believed in our return to it from the day these words were spoken: 'When the Lord restores the fortunes of

Zion, we shall be like dreamers. Our mouths will be filled with laughter, and our tongues will speak with shouts of joy.' These verses apply to all our exiles and all our sufferings, giving us the consolation that the return to Zion would come.

"This, our right, was recognized. The Balfour Declaration was included in the [1922 League of Nations Palestine] mandate [to Britain] laid down by the nations of the world, including the United States of America, and the preface to this recognized international document says: 'Whereas recognition has thereby been given to the historical connexion of the Jewish people with Palestine and to the grounds for reconstituting their national home in that country'. The historic connexion between the Jewish people and Palestine or, in Hebrew, *Eretz Israel*, was given confirmation—reconfirmation—as the national homeland in that country, that is, in *Eretz Israel*. In 1919 we also won recognition of this right by the spokesman of the Arab people in the agreement of Jan. 3, 1919, which was signed by Prince Faisal and Chaim Weizmann. It reads: 'Mindful of the racial kinship and ancient bonds existing between the Arabs and the Jewish people and realizing that the surest means of working out the consummation of the national aspirations in the closest possible collaboration in the development of the Arab state and of Palestine.' And afterwards come all the clauses about co-operation between the Arab state and *Eretz Israel*. This is our right. The existence—truthful existence.

The Hitler Period

"What happened to us when our homeland was taken from us? I accompanied you this morning, Mr President, to Yad Vashem. With your own eyes you saw the fate of our people when this homeland was taken from it. It cannot be told. Both of us agreed, Mr President, that anyone who has not seen with his own eyes everything there is in Yad Vashem cannot understand what happened to this people when it was without a homeland, when its own homeland was taken from it. And both of us read a document dated Jan. 30, 1939, where the word *'Vernichtung'*—annihilation—appears. If war breaks out, the Jewish race in Europe will be exterminated. Then, too, we were told that we should not pay attention to the racists. The whole world heard. Nobody came to save us. Not during the nine fateful, decisive months after the announcement was made, the like of which had not been seen since the Lord created man and man created the Devil.

"And during those six years, too, when millions of our people, among them one and a half million of the little children of Israel, were burnt . . . , nobody came to save them, not from the East and not from the West. And because of this, we took a solemn oath, this entire generation—the generation of extermination and revival—that we would never again put our people in danger, that we would never again put our women and our children, whom it is our duty to defend—if there is a need for this, even at the cost of our lives—in the hell of the exterminating fire of an enemy. It is our duty for generations to come to remember that certain things said about our people must be taken with complete seriousness. And we must not, heaven forbid, for the sake of the future of our people, accept any advice whatsoever against taking these things seriously.

Negotiations

"President Sadat knows, and he knew from us before he came to Jerusalem, that we have a different position from his with regard to the permanent borders between us and our neighbours. However, I say to the President of Egypt and to all our neighbours: do not say that there will not be negotiations about any particular issue. I propose, with the agreement of the decisive majority of this Parliament, that everything be open to negotiation. Anyone who says, with reference to relations between the Arab people or between the Arab peoples around us and the state of Israel, that there are things which should be omitted from negotiations is taking upon himself a grave responsibility; everything can be negotiated. No side will say the contrary. No side will present prior conditions. We shall conduct the negotiations honourably. If there are differences of opinion between us, this is not unusual. Anyone who has studied the histories of wars and the signing of peace treaties knows that all negotiations over a peace treaty began with differences of opinion between the sides. And in the course of the negotiations they came to an agreement which permitted the signing of peace treaties and agreements. And this is the road that we propose to take.

"We shall conduct the negotiations as equals. There are no vanquished and there are no victors. All the peoples of the area are equal and all of them should treat each other with due respect. In this spirit of openness, of willingness to listen to each other, to hear the facts and the reasoning and the explanations, accepting all the accumulated knowledge of human persuasion, let us conduct the negotiations as I have asked and am proposing, open them and carry them out, carry them on constantly until we reach the longed-for hour of the signing of a peace treaty between us.

"We are not only ready to sit with the representatives of Egypt, and also with the representatives of Jordan and Syria, and Lebanon if it is ready, but we are also ready to sit together at a peace conference in Geneva. We propose that the Geneva conference be renewed, on the basis of the two Security Council Resolutions 242 and 338. If there are problems between us over holding the Geneva conference, we shall be able to clarify them. And if the President of Egypt wants to continue clarifying them in Cairo, I am in favour of it; if in a neutral place, there is no objection. Let us clarify anywhere, even before the Geneva conference meets, the problems which should be clarified before it is held. And our eyes will be open and our ears will listen to all proposals.

Jerusalem

"Permit me to say a word about Jerusalem. Mr President, you prayed to-day in the house of prayer sacred to the Islamic religion and from there you went to the church of the Holy Sepulchre. You realized, as those coming from all over the world realize, that ever since this city was unified [i.e. since the Israeli capture of East Jerusalem in the 1967 war] there has been completely free access, without interference and without any obstacle, for the members of every religion to the places sacred to them. This positive phenomenon did not exist for 19 years. It has existed for about 11 years and we can promise the Moslem world and the Christian world, all the peoples, that there will always be free access to the sacred places of every religion. We shall defend this right to free access, for we believe in it. We believe in equal rights for all men and citizens and respect for every faith.

Conclusion

"Mr Speaker, this is a special day for our legislative chamber, and certainly this day will be remembered for many years in the history of our nation, and perhaps also in the history of the Egyptian nation, maybe in the history of all nations. And this day, with your agreement, ladies and gentlemen, members of the *Knesset*, let us pray that the God of our fathers, our common fathers, will give us the wisdom needed to overcome difficulties and obstacles, calumnies and slander, incitement and attacks. And with the help of God, may we arrive at the longed-for day for which all our people pray—peace. For it is indeed true that the sweet singer of Israel [King David] said: 'Righteousness and peace will kiss each other'; and that the prophet Zachariah said: 'Love, truth and peace'."

17. European Parliament Resolution on the Historic
Meeting between Mr. Anwar El-Sadat, President of
the Arab Republic of Egypt, and
Mr. Menachem Begin, Head of the Government
of the State of Israel, January 9, 1978*

* 21 O.J. Eur. Comm. (No. C 6) 47 (1978).

The European Parliament,

— conscious of its responsibility to promote, both within and outside the Community, the attainment of a just and lasting peace in the Middle East,

1. Welcomes the courageous and historic initiative by Mr Sadat and Mr Begin who, through their meeting in Jerusalem, have for the first time established direct contact between the Governments of two countries that are parties to the conflict in the Middle East;

2. Places great hopes in the dialogue thus begun for the success of the peace efforts in the Middle East and hopes that the Geneva Conference will be resumed at the earliest possible date;

3. Appeals to the representatives of the peoples concerned to join in this dialogue and support the efforts made to open overall negotiations;

4. Is firmly convinced that a just and lasting peace in this part of the world must be based on the principles laid down in the declaration on the Middle East adopted by the European Council on 29 June 1977;

5. Urgently appeals to the Community institutions and the Governments of the Member States to encourage, within the framework of Community activities and of European Political Cooperation, progress towards the establishment of a just and lasting peace in the Middle East;

6. Instructs its President to forward this resolution to the Council and Commission and to the Governments of the Member States.

18. Senate Concurrent Resolution 72 Condemning Acts of Terrorism Resulting from Sadat's Visit to Israel, June 19, 1978*

---

* S. Con. Res. 72, 95th Cong., 2d Sess., 124 Cong. Rec. 18157 (1978).

Whereas a series of unprovoked terrorist attacks have been conducted against citizens of Israel, Egypt, and Jordan since President Sadat's trip to Jerusalem last November;

Whereas the attacks have resulted in the loss of life and the wounding of civilians, including several Jordanian citizens living on the West Bank, the editor of the Egyptian newspaper Al Ahram on February 18, 1978, and men, women, and children who were trapped in a burning bus or deliberately shot during the attack in Israel March 11, 1978;

Whereas the Palestine Liberation Organization has publicly accepted responsibility for the March 11 attack: Now, therefore, be it

Resolved by the Senate (the House of Representatives concurring), That—

(1) such acts of terrorism are strongly condemned and are obstacles to peace in the Middle East and thus are against the national interest of the United States;

(2) the Congress extends its condolences and deep sympathy to those wounded and the families of those killed in the terrorist attacks;

(3) the President should direct the executive branch to intensify its efforts to counter international terrorism including use of diplomatic, economic, and security measures taken unilaterally or in cooperation with other nations to terminate assistance received by (a) organizations, groups, or individuals which commit or attempt to commit acts of terrorism and (b) governments which provide any assistance to organizations, groups, and individuals which conspire to commit or actually commit terrorism;

(4) the President should report to Congress within thirty days after the adoption of this resolution with respect to action the executive branch has taken to implement existing laws regarding terrorism, including section 3(8) of the Export Administration Act of 1969, as amended and section 18 of the International Security Assistance Act of 1977 in regard to countries cited under (6) which provide assistance to the Palestine Liberation Organization and other groups involved in terrorist activities;

(5) the President should report to Congress within thirty days on the nature and extent of the activities of the Palestine Liberation Organization office in New York; and

(6) the President should report to the Senate Foreign Relations Committee and the House of Representatives International Relations Committee within thirty days the names of nations which provide to the Palestine Liberation Organization and its constituent groups financial assistance, training, weapons, sanctuary, bases, escape routes, transportation assistance and documents, and other forms of assistance.

F. Conflict in Lebanon and the Israeli Incursion of 1978

19. Security Council Resolution 425 Establishing the U.N. Interim Force in Lebanon and Requesting Israeli Withdrawal from Lebanon, March 19, 1978*

* S.C. Res. 425, 33 U.N. SCOR (2074th mtg.) at 5, U.N. Doc. S/INF/34 (1978). *See also* subsequent resolution, S.C. Res. 426, 33 U.N. SCOR (2075th mtg.) at 5, U.N. Doc. S/INF/34 (1978).

The Security Council,

Taking note of the letters from the Permanent Representative of Lebanon[19] and from the Permanent Representative of Israel,[20]

Having heard the statements of the Permanent Representatives of Lebanon and Israel,[21]

Gravely concerned at the deterioration of the situation in the Middle East and its consequences to the maintenance of international peace,

Convinced that the present situation impedes the achievement of a just peace in the Middle East,

1. *Calls* for strict respect for the territorial integrity, sovereignty and political independence of Lebanon within its internationally recognized boundaries;

2. *Calls upon* Israel immediately to cease its military action against Lebanese territorial integrity and withdraw forthwith its forces from all Lebanese territory;

3. *Decides*, in the light of the request of the Government of Lebanon, to establish immediately under its authority a United Nations interim force for Southern Lebanon for the purpose of confirming the withdrawal of Israeli forces, restoring international peace and security and assisting the Government of Lebanon in ensuring the return of its effective authority in the area, the force to be composed of personnel drawn from Member States;

4. *Requests* the Secretary-General to report to the Council within twenty-four hours on the implementation of the present resolution.

Adopted at the 2074th meeting by 12 votes to none, with 2 abstentions (Czechoslovakia, Union of Soviet Socialist Republics).[22]

[19] *Ibid.* [*Official Records of the Security Council, Thirty-third Year, Supplement for January, February and March 1978*], documents S/12600 and S/12606.

[20] *Ibid.*, document S/12607.

[21] *Ibid., Thirty-third Year*, 2071st meeting.

[22] One member (China) did not participate in the voting.

20. Report of the Secretary-General on the Implementation of Security Council Resolution 425 (1978), March 19, 1978*

* 33 U.N. SCOR Supp. (Jan.–Mar. 1978) at 61, U.N. Doc. S/12611 (1978).

1. The present report is submitted in pursuance of Security Council resolution 425 (1978) of 19 March 1978 in which the Council, among other things, decided to set up a United Nations force in Lebanon under its authority and requested the Secretary-General to submit a report to it on the implementation of the resolution.

Terms of Reference

2. The terms of reference of the United Nations Interim Force in Lebanon (UNIFIL) are:

(a) The Force will determine compliance with paragraph 2 of Security Council resolution 425 (1978);

(b) The Force will confirm the withdrawal of Israeli forces, restore international peace and security and assist the Government of Lebanon in ensuring the return of its effective authority in the area;

(c) The Force will establish and maintain itself in an area of operation to be defined in the light of subparagraph b above;

(d) The Force will use its best efforts to prevent the recurrence of fighting and to ensure that its area of operation will not be utilized for hostile activities of any kind;

(e) In the fulfilment of this task, the Force will have the co-operation of the Military Observers of the United Nations Truce Supervision Organization (UNTSO), who will continue to function on the Armistice Demarcation Line after the termination of the mandate of UNIFIL.

General Considerations

3. Three essential conditions must be met for the Force to be effective. First, it must have at all times the full confidence and backing of the Security Council. Secondly, it must operate with the full co-operation of all the parties concerned. Thirdly, it must be able to function as an integrated and efficient military unit.

4. Although the general context of UNIFIL is not comparable with that of the United Nations Emergency Force (UNEF) and the United Nations Disengagement Observer Force (UNDOF), the guidelines for those operations, having proved satisfactory, are deemed suitable for practical application to the new Force. These guidelines are, *mutatis mutandis*, as follows:

(a) The Force will be under the command of the United Nations, vested in the Secretary-General, under the authority of the Security Council. The command in the field will be exercised by a Force Commander appointed by the Secretary-General with the consent of the Security Council. The Commander will be responsible to the Secretary-General. The Secretary-General will keep the Security Council fully informed of developments relating to the functioning of the Force. All matters which may affect the nature or the continued effective functioning of the Force will be referred to the Council for its decision.

(b) The Force must enjoy the freedom of movement and communication and other facilities that are necessary for the performance of its tasks. The Force and its personnel should be granted all relevant privileges and immunities provided for by the Convention on the Privileges and Immunities of the United Nations.

(c) The Force will be composed of a number of contingents to be provided by selected countries, upon the request of the Secretary-General. The contingents will be selected in consultation with the Security Council and with the parties concerned, bearing in mind the accepted principle of equitable geographic representation.

(d) The Force will be provided with weapons of a defensive character. It will not use force except in self-defence. Self-defence would include resistance to attempts by forceful means to prevent it from discharging its duties under the mandate of the Security Council. The Force will proceed on the assumption that the parties to the conflict will take all the necessary steps for compliance with the decisions of the Council.

(e) In performing its functions, the Force will act with complete impartiality.

(f) The supporting personnel of the Force will be provided as a rule by the Secretary-General from among existing United Nations staff. Those personnel will, of course, follow the rules and regulations of the United Nations Secretariat.

5. UNIFIL, like any other United Nations peacekeeping operation, cannot and must not take on responsibilities which fall under the Government of the country in which it is operating. These responsibilities must be exercised by the competent Lebanese authorities. It is assumed that the Lebanese Government will take the necessary measures to co-operate with UNIFIL in this regard. It should be recalled that UNIFIL will have to operate in an area which is quite densely inhabited.

6. I envisage the responsibility of UNIFIL as a two-stage operation. In the first stage, the Force will confirm the withdrawal of Israeli forces from Lebanese territory to the international border. Once this is achieved, it will establish and maintain an area of operation as defined. In this connexion, it will supervise the cessation of hostilities, ensure the peaceful character of the area of operation, control movement and take all measures deemed necessary to assure the effective restoration of Lebanese sovereignty.

7. The Force is being established on the assumption that it represents an interim measure until the Government of Lebanon assumes its full responsibilities in Southern Lebanon. The termination of the mandate of UNIFIL by the Security Council will not affect the continued functioning of the Israel-Lebanon Mixed Armistice Commission, as set out in the appropriate Security Council decision [see S/10611 of 19 April 1972].

8. With a view to facilitating the task of UNIFIL, particularly as it con-

cerns procedures for the expeditious withdrawal of Israeli forces and related matters, it may be necessary to work out arrangements with Israel and
Lebanon as a preliminary measure for the implementation of the Security
Council resolution. It is assumed that both parties will give their full co-
operation to UNIFIL in this regard.

Proposed Plan of Action

9. If the Security Council is in agreement with the principles and conditions outlined above, I intend to take the following steps:

(a) I shall instruct Lieutenant-General Ensio Siilasvuo, Chief Co-ordinator
of the United Nations Peace-keeping Missions in the Middle East, to contact
immediately the Governments of Israel and Lebanon and initiate meetings
with their representatives for the purpose of reaching agreement on the
modalities of the withdrawal of Israeli forces and the establishment of a
United Nations area of operation. This should not delay in any way the
establishment of the Force.

(b) Pending the appointment of a Force Commander, I propose to appoint Major-General E. A. Erskine, the Chief of Staff of UNTSO, Interim
Commander. Pending the arrival of the first contingents of the Force, he
will perform his tasks with the assistance of a selected number of UNTSO
military observers. At the same time, urgent measures will be taken to secure and arrange for the early arrival in the area of contingents of the
Force.

(c) In order that the Force may fulfil its responsibilities, it is considered,
as a preliminary estimate, that it must have at least five battalions each of
about 600 all ranks, in addition to the necessary logistics units. This means
a total strength of the order of 4,000.

(d) Bearing in mind the principles set out in paragraph 4 c above, I am
making preliminary inquiries as to the availability of contingents from suitable countries.

(e) In view of the difficulty in obtaining logistics contingents and of the
necessity for economy, it would be my intention to examine the possibility
of building on the existing logistics arrangements. If this should not prove
possible, it will be necessary to seek other suitable arrangements.

(f) It is proposed also that an appropriate number of observers of
UNTSO should be assigned to assist UNIFIL in the fulfilment of its task in
the same way as for UNEF.

(g) It is suggested that the Force would initially be stationed in the area
for a period of six months.

Estimated Cost and Method of Financing

10. At the present time there are many unknown factors. The best possible preliminary estimate based upon current experience and rates with re-

spect to other peace-keeping forces of comparable size is approximately $68 million for a Force of 4,000 all ranks for a period of six months. This figure is made up of initial setting-up costs (excluding the cost of initial airlift) of $29 million and ongoing costs for the six-month period of $39 million.

11. The costs of the Force shall be considered as expenses of the Organization to be borne by the Members in accordance with Article 17, paragraph 2, of the Charter.

21. Resolutions on the Arab Situation, Passed

by the Sixty-Ninth Session of the Council

of the Arab League, Following the Israeli

Invasion of Lebanon, Cairo, April 1, 1978*

---

* 7 J. Palestine Stud. 191 (Summer 1978).

The Council of the Arab League has studied with the greatest concern the situation in the Middle East and the Israeli aggression against Lebanon.

The Council believes that, by persisting in her aggressive and expansionist policy and her refusal to admit the national rights of the Palestinian people, including their right to self-determination in conformity with the Charter of the United Nations, Israel is impeding the achievement of a just peace in the area.

While stressing the vital importance of national solidarity and of current disputes being settled, the Council resolves the following:

1. That an Arab summit conference should meet as soon as possible to mobilize all Arab forces and potentials to confront Israel's aggressive challenges and to face up to our joint national responsibility in conformity with the resolutions of the Algiers and Rabat summit conferences held in 1973 and 1974 respectively.

2. That a high-level committee for Arab solidarity should be formed, with the Secretary-General taking part, to settle Arab disputes, and to ensure a favourable atmosphere for the meeting of the Arab summit. The Council entrusts its President, Mr. al-Rashid al-Tahir, Vice President and Foreign Minister of the Democratic Republic of Sudan, with the task of contacting President Jaafar Numeiri of the Democratic Republic of Sudan to request him to chair the committee and to choose its members.

3. That continued efforts be made to support the PLO, the sole legitimate representative of the Palestinian people, to reinforce its achievements at the international level and to develop its capacities within the framework of collective Arab commitment.

4. To condemn the Israeli aggression against Lebanon and to continue collective action to ensure the early withdrawal of the Israeli forces and to affirm absolute respect for Lebanon's unity, security, territorial integrity, sovereignty and political independence within her internationally recognized frontiers.

5. That the Arab states should promptly provide the humanitarian aid so urgently required by those, both Lebanese and Palestinians, who have suffered as a result of the Israeli invasion of Lebanon, through the Lebanese government and the PLO.

6. That support for the Arab League be given to enable it to perform an effective role in joint Arab action in all fields, as being the national organization qualified to assume the responsibility for this action in the fields of Arab liberation and development.

22. Security Council Resolution 427 Increasing
the U.N. Interim Force in Lebanon from 4,000 to 6,000
Troops and Taking Note of the Partial Israeli
Withdrawal, May 3, 1978*

---

* S.C. Res. 427, 33 U.N. SCOR (2076th mtg.) at 5, U.N. Doc. S/INF/34 (1978).

The Security Council,

Having considered the letter dated 1 May 1978 from the Secretary-General to the President of the Security Council,[26]

Recalling its resolutions 425 (1978) and 426 (1978) of 19 March 1978,

1. *Approves* the increase in the strength of the United Nations Interim Force in Lebanon requested by the Secretary-General from 4,000 to approximately 6,000 troops;

2. *Takes note* of the withdrawal of Israeli forces that has taken place so far;

3. *Calls upon* Israel to complete its withdrawal from all Lebanese territory without any further delay;

4. *Deplores* the attacks on the United Nations Force that have occurred and demands full respect for the United Nations Force from all parties in Lebanon.

Adopted at the 2076th meeting by 12 votes to none, with 2 abstentions (Czechoslovakia, Union of Soviet Socialist Republics).[27]

[26] *Ibid.* [*Official Records of the Security Council, Thirty-third Year, Supplement for April, May and June 1978*], document S/12675.

[27] One member (China) did not participate in the voting.

23. Security Council Resolution 434 Renewing
the U.N. Interim Force in Lebanon Mandate,
September 18, 1978*

* S.C. Res. 434, 33 U.N. SCOR (2085th mtg.) at 6, U.N. Doc. S/INF/34 (1978).

The Security Council.

Recalling its resolutions 425 (1978) and 426 (1978) of 19 March and 427 (1978) of 3 May 1978,

Recalling in particular that, in its resolution 425 (1978), the Council called for strict respect for the territorial integrity, sovereignty and political independence of Lebanon within its internationally recognized boundaries,

Gravely concerned at the serious conditions in Lebanon, which continue to endanger the achievement of a just and lasting solution of the Middle East question,

Having considered the report of the Secretary-General dated 13 September 1978[32] on the implementation of the above-mentioned resolutions,

Commending the outstanding performance of the United Nations Interim Force in Lebanon in seeking to carry out its mandate as established in resolutions 425 (1978) and 426 (1978),

Deeply grieved at the loss of life suffered by the Force,

Conscious of the progress already achieved by the Force towards the establishment of peace and security in Southern Lebanon,

Noting with concern that the Force has encountered obstacles in deploying freely throughout its area of operation and that it has not been possible as yet for the Lebanese Government fully to restore its authority over all its territory in accordance with resolution 425 (1978),

Supporting the efforts of the Secretary-General and taking into account the observations in his report describing the problems encountered by the Force in carrying out its mandate,

Determined to secure urgently the total fulfilment of the mandate and objectives of the Force in accordance with resolutions 425 (1978) and 426 (1978),

Acting in response to the request of the Lebanese Government,

1. *Decides* to renew the mandate of the United Nations Interim Force in Lebanon for a period of four months, that is, until 19 January 1979;

2. *Calls upon* Israel, Lebanon and all others concerned to co-operate fully and urgently with the United Nations in the implementation of Security Council resolutions 425 (1978) and 426 (1978);

3. *Requests* the Secretary-General to report to the Security Council in two months on the implementation of the present resolution in order to allow it to assess the situation and to examine what further measures should be taken, and to report again at the end of the four-month period.

Adopted at the 2085th meeting by 12 votes to none, with 2 abstentions (Czechoslovakia, Union of Soviet Socialist Republics).[33]

---

[32] *Ibid.* [*Official Records of the Security Council, Thirty-third Year, Supplement for July, August and September 1978*], document S/12845.

[33] One member (China) did not participate in the voting.

G. Israeli Security and Palestinian Autonomy

24. Security Council Resolution 378 Renewing

the U.N. Emergency Force Mandate,

October 23, 1975*

* S.C. Res. 378, 30 U.N. SCOR (1851st mtg.) at 6, U.N. Doc. S/INF/31 (1975). *See also* subsequent resolutions, S.C. Res. 396, 31 U.N. SCOR (1964th mtg.) at 3, U.N. Doc. S/INF/32 (1976) and S.C. Res. 416, 32 U.N. SCOR (2035th mtg.) at 13, U.N. Doc. S/INF/33 (1977).

The Security Council,

Recalling its resolutions 338 (1973) of 22 October, 340 (1973) of 25 October and 341 (1973) of 27 October 1973, 346 (1974) of 8 April and 362 (1974) of 23 October 1974, 368 (1975) of 17 April and 371 (1975) of 24 July 1975,

Having considered the report of the Secretary-General on the United Nations Emergency Force,[21]

Having noted the developments in the situation in the Middle East,

Having further noted the Secretary-General's view that any relaxation of the search for a comprehensive settlement covering all aspects of the Middle East problem could be especially dangerous in the months to come and that it is his hope, therefore, that urgent efforts will be undertaken by all concerned to tackle the Middle East problem in all its aspects, with a view both to maintaining quiet in the region and to arriving at the comprehensive settlement called for by the Security Council in its resolution 338 (1973),

1. *Decides:*

(*a*) To call upon all the parties concerned to implement immediately Security Council resolution 338 (1973);

(*b*) To renew the mandate of the United Nations Emergency Force for a period of one year, that is, until 24 October 1976;

(*c*) To request the Secretary-General to submit at the end of this period a report on the developments in the situation and the steps taken to implement resolution 338 (1973);

2. *Express its confidence* that the Force will be maintained with maximum efficiency and economy.

Adopted at the 1851st meeting by 13 votes to none.[22]

[21] *Ibid.* [*Official Records of the Security Council, Thirtieth Year*], *Supplement for October, November and December 1975*, document S/11849.

[22] Two members (China and Iraq) did not participate in the voting.

25. Security Council Resolution 381 Renewing the U.N. Disengagement Observer Force Mandate, November 30, 1975*

* S.C. Res. 381, 30 U.N. SCOR (1856th mtg.) at 7, U.N. Doc. S/INF/31 (1975). *See also* subsequent resolution, S.C. Res. 390, 31 U.N. SCOR (1923rd mtg.) at 2, U.N. Doc. S/INF/32 (1976).

The Security Council,

Having considered the report of the Secretary-General on the United Nations Disengagement Observer Force,[23]

Having noted the discussions of the Secretary-General with all parties concerned on the situation in the Middle East,

Expressing concern over the continued state of tension in the area,

Decides:

(*a*) To reconvene on 12 January 1976, to continue the debate on the Middle East problem including the Palestinian question, taking into account all relevant United Nations resolutions;

(*b*) To renew the mandate of the United Nations Disengagement Observer Force for another period of six months;

(*c*) To request the Secretary-General to keep the Security Council informed on further developments.

Adopted at the 1856th meeting by 13 votes to none.[24]

[23] *Official Records of the Security Council, Thirtieth Year, Supplement for October, November and December 1975*, documents S/11883 and Add.1.

[24] Two members (China and Iraq) did not participate in the voting.

26. General Assembly Resolution 3525 (XXX)
on the Report of the Special Committee to
Investigate Israeli Practices Affecting
the Human Rights of the Population of
the Occupied Territories, December 15, 1975*

* G.A. Res. 3525 (XXX), 30 U.N. GAOR Supp. (No. 34) at 41, U.N. Doc. A/10034 (1975).

A

The General Assembly,

Guided by the purposes and principles of the Charter of the United Nations as well as the principles and provisions of the Universal Declaration of Human Rights,

Bearing in mind the provisions of the Geneva Convention relative to the Protection of Civilian Persons in Time of War, of 12 August 1949,[13] as well as of other relevant conventions and regulations,

Recalling its resolutions on the subject, as well as those adopted by the Security Council, the Commission on Human Rights and other United Nations bodies concerned and by specialized agencies,

Having considered the report of the Special Committee to Investigate Israeli Practices Affecting the Human Rights of the Population of the Occupied Territories,[14] which contains, *inter alia*, public statements made by leaders of the Government of Israel,

1. *Commends* the Special Committee to Investigate Israeli Practices Affecting the Human Rights of the Population of the Occupied Territories for its efforts in performing the tasks assigned to it by the General Assembly;

2. *Deplores* the continued refusal by Israel to allow the Special Committee access to the occupied territories;

3. *Calls again upon* Israel to allow the Special Committee access to the occupied territories;

4. *Deplores* the continued and persistent violation by Israel of the Geneva Convention relative to the Protection of Civilian Persons in Time of War, of 12 August 1949, and other applicable international instruments;

5. *Condemns*, in particular, the following Israeli policies and practices:

(*a*) The annexation of parts of the occupied territories;

(*b*) The establishment of Israeli settlements therein and the transfer of an alien population thereto;

(*c*) The destruction and demolition of Arab houses;

(*d*) The confiscation and expropriation of Arab property in the occupied territories and all other transactions for the acquisition of land involving the Israeli authorities, institutions or nationals on the one hand, and the inhabitants or institutions of the occupied territories on the other;

(*e*) The evacuation, deportation, expulsion, displacement and transfer of Arab inhabitants of the occupied territories, and the denial of their right to return;

(*f*) Mass arrests, administrative detention and ill-treatment of the Arab population;

(*g*) The pillaging of archaeological and cultural property;

[13] United Nations, *Treaty Series*, vol. 75, No. 973, p. 287.
[14] A/10272.

(h) The interference with religious freedoms and practices, as well as family rights and customs;

(i) The illegal exploitation of the natural wealth, resources and population of the occupied territories;

6. *Declares* that those policies and practices of Israel constitute grave violations of the Charter of the United Nations, in particular the principles of sovereignty and territorial integrity, and the principles and provisions of international law concerning occupation, and constitute as well an impediment to the establishment of a just and lasting peace;

7. *Reaffirms* that all measures taken by Israel to change the physical character, demographic composition, institutional structure or status of the occupied territories, or any part thereof, are null and void;

8. *Reaffirms further* that Israel's policy of settling parts of its population and new immigrants in the occupied territories is a flagrant violation of the Geneva Convention relative to the Protection of Civilian Persons in Time of War and of the relevant United Nations resolutions, and urges all States to refrain from any action which Israel will exploit in carrying out its policy of colonizing the occupied territories;

9. *Demands* that Israel desist forthwith from the annexation and colonization of the occupied Arab territories as well as from all the policies and practices referred to in paragraph 5 above;

10. *Reiterates* its call upon all States, international organizations and specialized agencies not to recognize any changes carried out by Israel in the occupied territories and to avoid actions, including actions in the field of aid, which might be used by Israel in its pursuit of the policies and practices referred to in the present resolution;

11. *Requests* the Special Committee, pending the early termination of the Israeli occupation, to continue to investigate Israeli policies and practices in the Arab territories occupied by Israel since 1967, to consult, as appropriate, with the International Committee of the Red Cross in order to ensure the safeguarding of the welfare and human rights of the population of the occupied territories, and to report to the Secretary-General as soon as possible and whenever the need arises thereafter;

12. *Requests* the Secretary-General:

(a) To render all necessary facilities to the Special Committee, including those required for its visits to the occupied territories with a view to investigating Israeli policies and practices referred to in the present resolution;

(b) To make available additional staff as may be necessary to assist the Special Committee in the performance of its tasks;

(c) To ensure the widest circulation of the reports of the Special Committee, and of information regarding its activities and findings, by all means available through the Office of Public Information of the Secretariat;

(d) To report to the General Assembly at its thirty-first session on the tasks entrusted to him;

13. *Decides* to include in the provisional agenda of its thirty-first session

the item entitled "Report of the Special Committee to Investigate Israeli Practices Affecting the Human Rights of the Population of the Occupied Territories".

2441st plenary meeting
15 December 1975

B

The General Assembly,

Recalling its resolutions 3092 A (XXVIII) of 7 December 1973 and 3240 B (XXIX) of 29 November 1974,

Considering that the promotion of respect for the obligations arising from the Charter of the United Nations and other instruments and rules of international law is among the basic purposes and principles of the United Nations,

Bearing in mind the provisions of the Geneva Convention relative to the Protection of Civilian Persons in Time of War, of 12 August 1949,[13]

Noting that Israel and those Arab States whose territories have been occupied by Israel since June 1967 are parties to that Convention,

Taking into account that States parties to that Convention undertake, in accordance with article 1 thereof, not only to respect but also to ensure respect for the Convention in all circumstances,

1. *Reaffirms* that the Geneva Convention relative to the Protection of Civilian Persons in Time of War, of 12 August 1949, is applicable to all the Arab territories occupied by Israel since 1967, including Jerusalem;

2. *Deplores* the failure of Israel to acknowledge the applicability of that Convention to the territories it has occupied since 1967;

3. *Calls once more upon* Israel to acknowledge and to comply with the provisions of that Convention in all the Arab territories it has occupied since 1967, including Jerusalem;

4. *Urges* all States parties to that Convention to exert all efforts in order to ensure respect for and compliance with the provisions thereof in all the Arab territories occupied by Israel since 1967, including Jerusalem.

2441st plenary meeting
15 December 1975

C

The General Assembly,

Recalling its resolution 3240 C (XXIX) of 29 November 1974,

Having considered the report of the Special Committee to Investigate Israeli Practices Affecting the Human Rights of the Population of the Occupied Territories,[14] in particular section V thereof concerning action by the Special Committee to implement the provisions of paragraph 3 of resolution 3240 C (XXIX),

Noting that the Special Committee was not able to submit to the General Assembly at its current session a full report in accordance with the request made in paragraph 3 of resolution 3240 C (XXIX),

1. *Requests* the Special Committee to Investigate Israeli Practices Affecting the Human Rights of the Population of the Occupied Territories to continue its efforts to undertake a survey of the destruction in Quneitra and to assess the nature, extent and value of the damage caused by such destruction;

2. *Requests* the Secretary-General to continue to make available to the Special Committee all the facilities necessary in the performance of its tasks and to report to the General Assembly at its thirty-first session.

2441st plenary meeting
15 December 1975

D

The General Assembly,

Recalling its resolutions 2253 (ES-V) of 4 July 1967, 2254 (ES-V) of 14 July 1967 and 3240 (XXIX) of 29 November 1974 and Security Council resolutions 252 (1968) of 21 May 1968, 267 (1969) of 3 July 1969, 271 (1969) of 15 September 1969 and 298 (1971) of 25 September 1971,

Taking note of the information contained in the report of the Special Committee to Investigate Israeli Practices Affecting the Human Rights of the Population of the Occupied Territories,[14]

Noting with concern the actions of the Israeli authorities in changing the institutional structure and established religious practices in the sanctuary of Al-Ibrahimi Mosque in the city of Al-Khalil,

Considering that these actions constitute grave violations of human rights and religious freedom and of the norms of international law, in particular article 27 of the Geneva Convention relative to the Protection of Civilian Persons in Time of War, of 12 August 1949,[13]

Considering also that these violations of established religious rights are a challenge to the susceptibilities of hundreds of millions of Moslems all over the world,

Considering furthermore that these violations, which have already caused civil and religious disturbances, constitute a new threat to peace and security in the area,

1. *Declares* all measures taken by the Israeli authorities with a view to changing the institutional structure and established religious practices in the sanctuary of Al-Ibrahimi Mosque in the city of Al-Khalil null and void;

2. *Calls upon* Israel to rescind and to desist forthwith from all such measures;

3. *Requests* the Secretary-General to investigate the situation in Al-Ibrahimi Mosque by contacting the Islamic, Arab and other authorities con-

cerned, and to report as soon as possible on the implementation of paragraph 2 above;

4. *Calls upon* Israel to co-operate with the Secretary-General and to facilitate his task.

2441st plenary meeting
15 December 1975

27. General Assembly Resolution 31/15 on

the U.N. Relief and Works Agency for

Palestine Refugees in the Near East,

November 23, 1976*

* G.A. Res. 15, 31 U.N. GAOR Supp. (No. 39) at 48, U.N. Doc. A/31/39 (1976). *See also* subsequent resolutions, G.A. Res. 112, 33 U.N. GAOR Supp. (No. 45) at 67, U.N. Doc. A/33/45 (1978), G.A. Res. 52, 34 U.N. GAOR Supp. (No. 46) at 72, U.N. Doc. A/34/46 (1979) and G.A. Res. 13, 35 U.N. GAOR Supp. (No. 48) at 84, U.N. Doc. A/35/48 (1980).

A

ASSISTANCE TO PALESTINE REFUGEES

The General Assembly,

Recalling its resolution 3419 (XXX) of 8 December 1975 and all previous resolutions referred to therein, including resolution 194 (III) of 11 December 1948,

Taking note of the annual report of the Commissioner-General of the United Nations Relief and Works Agency for Palestine Refugees in the Near East, covering the period from 1 July 1975 to 30 June 1976,[3]

1. *Notes with deep regret* that repatriation or compensation of the refugees as provided for in paragraph 11 of General Assembly resolution 194 (III) has not been effected, that no substantial progress has been made in the programme endorsed by the Assembly in paragraph 2 of resolution 513 (VI) of 26 January 1952 for the reintegration of refugees either by repatriation or resettlement and that, therefore, the situation of the refugees continues to be a matter of serious concern;

2. *Expresses its thanks* to the Commissioner-General and to the staff of the United Nations Relief and Works Agency for Palestine Refugees in the Near East for their continued dedicated and effective efforts under difficult circumstances to provide essential services for the Palestine refugees, and to the specialized agencies and private organizations for their valuable work in assisting the refugees;

3. *Notes with regret* that the United Nations Conciliation Commission for Palestine has been unable to find a means of achieving progress in the implementation of paragraph 11 of General Assembly resolution 194 (III)[4] and requests the Commission to exert continued efforts towards the implementation of that paragraph and to report as appropriate, but no later than 1 October 1977;

4. *Directs attention* to the continuing seriousness of the financial position of the United Nations Relief and Works Agency for Palestine Refugees in the Near East, as outlined in the Commissioner-General's report;

5. *Notes with profound concern* that, despite the commendable and successful efforts of the Commissioner-General to collect additional contributions, this increased level of income to the United Nations Relief and Works Agency for Palestine Refugees in the Near East is still insufficient to cover essential budget requirements in the present year, and that, at presently foreseen levels of giving, deficits will recur each year;

6. *Calls upon* all Governments as a matter of urgency to make the most

---

[3] *Ibid.* [*Official Records of the General Assembly*], *Thirty-first Session, Supplement No. 13* (A/31/13 and Corr.1).

[4] For the report of the United Nations Conciliation Commission for Palestine covering the period from 30 September 1975 to 30 September 1976, see *Official Records of the General Assembly, Thirty-first Session, Annexes,* agenda item 53, document A/31/254, annex.

generous efforts possible to meet the anticipated needs of the United Nations Relief and Works Agency for Palestine Refugees in the Near East, particularly in the light of the budgetary deficit projected in the Commissioner-General's report, and therefore urges non-contributing Governments to contribute regularly and contributing Governments to consider increasing their regular contributions.

76th plenary meeting
23 November 1976

B

ASSISTANCE TO PERSONS DISPLACED AS A RESULT OF THE JUNE 1967 HOSTILITIES

The General Assembly,

Recalling its resolutions 2252 (ES-V) of 4 July 1967, 2341 B (XXII) of 19 December 1967, 2452 C (XXIII) of 19 December 1968, 2535 C (XXIV) of 10 December 1969, 2672 B (XXV) of 8 December 1970, 2792 B (XXVI) of 6 December 1971, 2963 B (XXVII) of 13 December 1972, 3089 A (XXVIII) of 7 December 1973, 3331 C (XXIX) of 17 December 1974 and 3419 A (XXX) Of 8 December 1975,

Taking note of the annual report of the Commissioner-General of the United Nations Relief and Works Agency for Palestine Refugees in the Near East, covering the period from 1 July 1975 to 30 June 1976,[5]

Concerned about the continued human suffering resulting from the June 1967 hostilities in the Middle East,

1. *Reaffirms* its resolutions 2252 (ES-V), 2341 B (XXII), 2452 C (XXIII), 2535 C (XXIV), 2672 B (XXV), 2792 B (XXVI), 2963 B (XXVII), 3089 A (XXVIII), 3331 C (XXIX) and 3419 A (XXX);

2. *Endorses*, bearing in mind the objectives of those resolutions, the efforts of the Commissioner-General of the United Nations Relief and Works Agency for Palestine Refugees in the Near East to continue to provide humanitarian assistance, as far as practicable, on an emergency basis and as a temporary measure, to other persons in the area who are at present displaced and in serious need of continued assistance as a result of the June 1967 hostilities;

3. *Strongly appeals* to all Governments and to organizations and individuals to contribute generously for the above purposes to the United Nations Relief and Works Agency for Palestine Refugees in the Near East and to the other intergovernmental and non-governmental organizations concerned.

76th plenary meeting
23 November 1976

---

[5] *Official Records of the General Assembly, Thirty-first Session, Supplement No. 13* (A/31/13 and Corr.1).

C

WORKING GROUP ON THE FINANCING OF THE UNITED NATIONS RELIEF AND WORKS AGENCY FOR PALESTINE REFUGEES IN THE NEAR EAST

The General Assembly,

Recalling its resolutions 2656 (XXV) of 7 December 1970, 2728 (XXV) of 15 December 1970, 2791 (XXVI) of 6 December 1971, 2964 (XXVII) of 13 December 1972, 3090 (XXVIII) of 7 December 1973, 3330 (XXIX) of 17 December 1974 and 3419 D (XXX) of 8 December 1975,

Having considered the report of the Working Group on the Financing of the United Nations Relief and Works Agency for Palestine Refugees in the Near East,[6]

Taking into account the annual report of the Commissioner-General of the United Nations Relief and Works Agency for Palestine Refugees in the Near East, covering the period from 1 July 1975 to 30 June 1976,[7]

Gravely concerned at the alarming financial situation of the United Nations Relief and Works Agency for Palestine Refugees in the Near East, imminently endangering the essential minimum services being provided to the Palestine refugees,

Emphasizing the urgent need for extraordinary efforts in order to maintain, at least at their present minimum level, the activities of the United Nations Relief and Works Agency for Palestine Refugees in the Near East,

1. *Commends* the Working Group on the Financing of the United Nations Relief and Works Agency for Palestine Refugees in the Near East for its work;

2. *Notes with appreciation* the report of the Working Group;

3. *Requests* the Working Group to continue its efforts, in co-operation with the Secretary-General and the Commissioner-General, for the financing of the United Nations Relief and Works Agency for Palestine Refugees in the Near East for a further period of one year;

4. *Requests* the Secretary-General to provide the necessary services and assistance to the Working Group for the conduct of its work.

76th plenary meeting
23 November 1976

D

POPULATION AND REFUGEES DISPLACED SINCE 1967

The General Assembly,

Recalling Security Council resolution 237 (1967) of 14 June 1967,

Recalling also its resolutions 2252 (ES-V) of 4 July 1967, 2452 A (XXIII) of 19 December 1968, 2535 B (XXIV) of 10 December 1969, 2672 D (XXV)

---

[6] *Ibid., Thirty-first Session, Annexes*, agenda item 53, document A/31/279.
[7] *Ibid., Thirty-first Session, Supplement No. 13* (A/31/13 and Corr.1).

of 8 December 1970, 2792 E (XXVI) of 6 December 1971, 2963 C and D (XXVII) of 13 December 1972, 3089 C (XXVIII) of 7 December 1973, 3331 D (XXIX) of 17 December 1974 and 3419 C (XXX) of 8 December 1975,

Having considered the report of the Commissioner-General of the United Nations Relief and Works Agency for Palestine Refugees in the Near East, covering the period from 1 July 1975 to 30 June 1976,[8] and the report of the Secretary-General of 4 October 1976,[9]

1. *Reaffirms* the right of the displaced inhabitants to return to their homes and camps in the territories occupied by Israel since 1967;

2. *Deplores* the continued refusal of the Israeli authorities to take steps for the return of the displaced inhabitants;

3. *Calls once more upon* Israel:

(*a*) To take immediate steps for the return of the displaced inhabitants;

(*b*) To desist from all measures that obstruct the return of the displaced inhabitants, including measures affecting the physical and demographic structure of the occupied territories;

4. *Requests* the Secretary-General, after consulting with the Commissioner-General of the United Nations Relief and Works Agency for Palestine Refugees in the Near East, to report to the General Assembly by the opening of the thirty-second session on Israel's compliance with paragraph 3 of the present resolution.

76th plenary meeting
23 November 1976

E

PALESTINE REFUGEES IN THE GAZA STRIP

The General Assembly,

Recalling Security Council resolution 237 (1967) of 14 June 1967,

Recalling also its resolutions 2792 C (XXVI) of 6 December 1971, 2963 C (XXVII) of 13 December 1972, 3089 C (XXVIII) of 7 December 1973, 3331 D (XXIX) of 17 December 1974 and 3419 C (XXX) of 8 December 1975,

Having considered the report of the Commissioner-General of the United Nations Relief and Works Agency for Palestine Refugees in the Near East, covering the period from 1 July 1975 to 30 June 1976,[10] and the report of the Secretary-General of 4 October 1976,[11]

1. *Calls once more upon* Israel:

(*a*) To take effective steps immediately for the return of the refugees concerned to the camps from which they were removed in the Gaza Strip and to provide adequate shelters for their accommodation;

[8] *Ibid.*
[9] *Ibid., Thirty-first Session, Annexes*, agenda item 53, document A/31/240.
[10] *Ibid., Thirty-first Session, Supplement No. 13* (A/31/13 and Corr.1).
[11] *Ibid., Thirty-first Session, Annexes*, agenda item 53, document A/31/240.

(*b*) To desist from further removal of refugees and destruction of their shelters;

2. *Requests* the Secretary-General, after consulting with the Commissioner-General of the United Nations Relief and Works Agency for Palestine Refugees in the Near East, to report to the General Assembly by the opening of the thirty-second session on Israel's compliance with paragraph 1 of the present resolution.

76th plenary meeting
23 November 1976

28. General Assembly Resolution 31/20 on the Question of Palestine, November 24, 1976*

* G.A. Res. 20, 31 U.N. GAOR Supp. (No. 39) at 21, U.N. Doc. A/31/39 (1976).

The General Assembly,

Recalling its resolution 3376 (XXX) of 10 November 1975,

Having considered the report of the Committee on the Exercise of the Inalienable Rights of the Palestinian People,[37]

Deeply concerned that no just solution to the problem of Palestine has been achieved and that this problem therefore continues to aggravate the Middle East conflict, of which it is the core, and to endanger international peace and security,

Reaffirming that a just and lasting peace in the Middle East cannot be established without the achievement, *inter alia*, of a just solution of the problem of Palestine on the basis of the attainment of the inalienable rights of the Palestinian people, including the right of return and the right to national independence and sovereignty in Palestine, in accordance with the Charter of the United Nations,

1. *Expresses its appreciation* to the Committee on the Exercise of the Inalienable Rights of the Palestinian People for its efforts in performing the tasks assigned to it by the General Assembly;

2. *Takes note* of the report of the Committee and endorses the recommendations contained therein, as a basis for the solution of the question of Palestine;

3. *Decides* to circulate the report to all the competent bodies of the United Nations and urges them to take necessary action, as appropriate, in accordance with the Committee's programme of implementation;

4. *Urges* the Security Council to consider once again as soon as possible the recommendations contained in the report, taking fully into account the observations made thereon during the debate in the General Assembly at its thirty-first session, in order to take the necessary measures to implement the above-mentioned recommendations of the Committee so as to achieve early progress towards a solution of the problem of Palestine and the establishment of a just and lasting peace in the Middle East;

5. *Authorizes* the Committee to exert all efforts to promote the implementation of its recommendations and to report thereon to the General Assembly at its thirty-second session;

6. *Requests* the Committee to promote the greatest possible dissemination of information on its programme of implementation through non-governmental organizations and other appropriate means;

7. *Requests* the Secretary-General to give the widest possible publicity to the Committee's work and to provide the Committee with all the necessary

---

[37] *Ibid.* [*Official Records of the General Assembly*], *Thirty-first Session, Supplement No. 35* (A/31/35).

facilities for the performance of its tasks, including summary records of its meetings;

8. *Decides* to include the item entitled "Question of Palestine" in the provisional agenda of its thirty-second session.

77th plenary meeting
24 November 1976

29. Security Council Resolution 398 Calling for
the Implementation of Security Council Resolution 338
(1973) and Renewing the U.N. Disengagement Observer
Force Mandate, November 30, 1976*

* S.C. Res. 398, 31 U.N. SCOR (1975th mtg.) at 2, U.N. Doc. S/INF/32
(1976). *See also* subsequent resolutions, S.C. Res. 408, 32 U.N. SCOR
(2010th mtg.) at 11, U.N. Doc. S/INF/33 (1977), S.C. Res. 420, 32 U.N.
SCOR (2051st mtg.) at 12, U.N. Doc. S/INF/33 (1977), and S.C. Res. 429,
33 U.N. SCOR (2079th mtg.) at 6, U.N. Doc. S/INF/34 (1978).

The Security Council,

Having considered the report of the Secretary-General on the United Nations Disengagement Observer Force,[4]

Having noted the efforts made to establish a durable and just peace in the Middle East area and the urgent need to continue and intensify such efforts,

Expressing concern over the prevailing state of tension in the area,

Decides:

(a) To call upon the parties concerned to implement immediately Security Council resolution 338 (1973) of 22 October 1973;

(b) To renew the mandate of the United Nations Disengagement Observer Force for another period of six months, that is, until 31 May 1977;

(c) To request the Secretary-General to submit at the end of this period a report on the developments in the situation and the measures taken to implement resolution 338 (1973).

Adopted at the 1975th meeting by 12 votes to none.[5]

[4] *Official Records of the Security Council, Thirty-first Year, Supplement for October, November and December 1976*, document S/12235.

[5] Three members (Benin, China and Libyan Arab Republic) did not participate in the voting.

30. General Assembly Resolution 31/61 on

the Situation in the Middle East,

December 9, 1976*

* G.A. Res. 61, 31 U.N. GAOR Supp. (No. 39) at 22, U.N. Doc. A/31/39 (1976).

The General Assembly,

Recalling its resolution 3414 (XXX) of 5 December 1975 and noting with concern that no progress has been achieved towards the implementation of that resolution, in particular its paragraph 4,

Recalling the debate held in the Security Council in January 1976[44] on the Middle East problem including the Palestinian question, in implementation of subparagraph (*a*) of Council resolution 381 (1975) of 30 November 1975,

Deeply concerned at the increasing deterioration of the situation in the Middle East due to continued Israeli occupation and Israel's refusal to implement United Nations resolutions,

Reaffirming the necessity of establishing a just and lasting peace in the region based on full respect for the purposes and principles of the Charter of the United Nations as well as for the resolutions concerning the problem of the Middle East and the question of Palestine,

1. *Affirms* that the early resumption of the Peace Conference on the Middle East with the participation of all the parties concerned, including the Palestine Liberation Organization, in accordance with General Assembly resolution 3375 (XXX) of 10 November 1975, is essential for the realization of a just and lasting settlement in the region;

2. *Condemns* Israel's continued occupation of Arab territories in violation of the Charter of the United Nations, the principles of international law and repeated United Nations resolutions;

3. *Reaffirms* that a just and lasting peace in the Middle East cannot be achieved without Israel's withdrawal from all Arab territories occupied since 1967 and the attainment by the Palestinian people of their inalienable rights, which are the basic prerequisites enabling all countries and peoples in the Middle East to live in peace;

4. *Condemns* all measures taken by Israel in the occupied territories to change the demographic and geographic character and institutional structure of these territories;

5. *Requests once again* all States to desist from supplying Israel with military and other forms of aid or any assistance which would enable it to consolidate its occupation or to exploit the natural resources of the occupied territories;

6. *Requests* the Security Council to take effective measures, within an appropriate time-table, for the implementation of all relevant resolutions of the Council and the General Assembly on the Middle East and Palestine;

7. *Requests* the Secretary-General to inform the Co-Chairmen of the Peace Conference on the Middle East of the present resolution and to submit a report on the follow-up of its implementation to the General Assembly at its thirty-second session.

95th plenary meeting
9 December 1976

---

[44] See *Official Records of the Security Council, Thirty-first Year*, 1870th to 1879th meetings.

31. General Assembly Resolution 31/62 on the Peace Conference on the Middle East, December 9, 1976*

---

* G.A. Res. 62, 31 U.N. GAOR Supp. (No. 39) at 23, U.N. Doc. A/31/39 (1976).

The General Assembly,

Having discussed the item entitled "The situation in the Middle East",

Noting the report of the Secretary-General on this item[45] and his initiative of 1 April 1976,[46]

Gravely concerned at the lack of progress towards the achievement of a just and lasting peace in the Middle East,

Convinced that any relaxation in the search for a comprehensive settlement covering all aspects of the Middle East problem to achieve a just peace in the area constitutes a grave threat to the prospects of peace in the Middle East as well as a threat to international peace and security,

1. *Requests* the Secretary-General:

(*a*) To resume contacts with all the parties to the conflict and the Co-Chairmen of the Peace Conference on the Middle East, in accordance with his initiative of 1 April 1976, in preparation for the early convening of the Peace Conference on the Middle East;

(*b*) To submit a report to the Security Council on the results of his contacts and on the situation in the Middle East not later than 1 March 1977;

2. *Calls* for the early convening of the Peace Conference on the Middle East, under the auspices of the United Nations and the co-chairmanship of the Union of Soviet Socialist Republics and the United States of America, not later than the end of March 1977;

3. *Requests* the Security Countil [*sic*] to convene subsequent to the submission by the Secretary-General of the report referred to in paragraph 1 (*b*) above, in order to consider the situation in the area in the light of that report and to promote the process towards the establishment of a just and lasting peace in the area;

4. *Further requests* the Secretary-General to inform the Co-Chairmen of the Peace Conference on the Middle East of the present resolution.

95th plenary meeting
9 December 1976

---

[45] A/31/270-S/12210. For the printed text, see *Official Records of the Security Council, Thirty-first Year, Supplement for October, November and December 1976.*

[46] A/31/270-S/12210, para. 8. For the printed text, see *Official Records of the Security Council, Thirty-first Year, Supplement for October, November and December 1976.*

32. General Assembly Resolution 31/106 on

the Report of the Special Committee to

Investigate Israeli Practices Affecting the Human Rights

of the Population of the Occupied Territories,

December 16, 1976*

* G.A. Res. 106, 31 U.N. GAOR Supp. (No. 39) at 50, U.N. Doc. A/31/39 (1976).

A

The General Assembly,

Guided by the principles of the Charter of the United Nations, in particular the principles of sovereignty and territorial integrity,

Bearing in mind the rules of international law concerning occupation, in
particular the provisions of the Geneva Convention relative to the Protection of Civilian Persons in Time of War, of 12 August 1949,[14]

1. *Strongly deplores* the measures taken by Israel in the Arab territories
occupied since 1967 that alter their demographic composition or geographical nature, and particularly the establishment of settlements;

2. *Declares* that such measures have no legal validity and cannot prejudice
the outcome of the search for the establishment of peace, and considers that
such measures constitute an obstacle to the achievement of a just and lasting
peace in the area;

3. *Declares further* that all legislative and administrative measures taken by
Israel, including the expropriation of land and properties thereon and the
transfer of populations, which purport to change the legal status of Jerusalem are invalid and cannot change that status;

4. *Urgently calls once more upon* Israel to rescind all those measures and to
desist forthwith from taking any further measures which tend to change the
demographic composition, geographical nature or status of the occupied
Arab territories or any part thereof, including Jerusalem.

101st plenary meeting
16 December 1976

B

The General Assembly,

Recalling its resolutions 3092 A (XXVIII) of 7 December 1973, 3240 B
(XXIX) of 29 November 1974 and 3525 B (XXX) of 15 December 1975,

Considering that the promotion of respect for the obligations arising from
the Charter of the United Nations and other instruments and rules of international law is among the basic purposes and principles of the United
Nations,

Bearing in mind the provisions of the Geneva Convention relative to the
Protection of Civilian Persons in Time of War, of 12 August 1949,[15]

Noting that Israel and those Arab States whose territories have been occupied by Israel since June 1967 are parties to that Convention,

Taking into account that States parties to that Convention undertake, in
accordance with article 1 thereof, not only to respect but also to ensure respect for the Convention in all circumstances,

1. *Reaffirms* that the Geneva Convention relative to the Protection of Ci-

[14] United Nations, *Treaty Series*, vol. 75, No. 973, p. 287.
[15] *Ibid.*

vilian Persons in Time of War, of 12 August 1949, is applicable to all the Arab territories occupied by Israel since 1967, including Jerusalem;

2. *Deplores* the failure of Israel to acknowledge the applicability of that Convention to the territories it has occupied since 1967;

3. *Calls again upon* Israel to acknowledge and to comply with the provisions of that Convention in all the Arab territories it has occupied since 1967, including Jerusalem;

4. *Urges once more* all States parties to that Convention to exert all efforts in order to ensure respect for and compliance with the provisions thereof in all the Arab territories occupied by Israel since 1967, including Jerusalem.

101st plenary meeting
16 December 1976

C

The General Assembly,

Guided by the purposes and principles of the Charter of the United Nations as well as the principles and provisions of the Universal Declaration of Human Rights,

Bearing in mind the provisions of the Geneva Convention relative to the Protection of Civilian Persons in Time of War, of 12 August 1949,[16] as well as of other relevant conventions and regulations,

Recalling its resolutions on the subject, as well as those adopted by the Security Council, the Commission on Human Rights and other United Nations bodies concerned and by specialized agencies,

Having considered the report of the Special Committee to Investigate Israeli Practices Affecting the Human Rights of the Population of the Occupied Territories,[17] which contains, *inter alia*, public statements made by leaders of the Government of Israel,

1. *Commends* the Special Committee to Investigate Israeli Practices Affecting the Human Rights of the Population of the Occupied Territories for its efforts in performing the tasks assigned to it by the General Assembly;

2. *Deplores* the continued refusal by Israel to allow the Special Committee access to the occupied territories;

3. *Calls again upon* Israel to allow the Special Committee access to the occupied territories;

4. *Deplores* the continued and persistent violation by Israel of the Geneva Convention relative to the Protection of Civilian Persons in Time of War, of 12 August 1949, and other applicable international instruments;

5. *Condemns*, in particular, the following Israeli policies and practices:

(a) The annexation of parts of the occupied territories;

[16] *Ibid.*
[17] A/31/218.

(b) The establishment of Israeli settlements therein and the transfer of an alien population thereto;

(c) The evacuation, deportation, expulsion, displacement and transfer of Arab inhabitants of the occupied territories, and the denial of their right to return;

(d) The confiscation and expropriation of Arab property in the occupied territories and all other transactions for the acquisition of land involving the Israeli authorities, institutions or nationals on the one hand, and the inhabitants or institutions of the occupied territories on the other;

(e) The destruction and demolition of Arab houses;

(f) Mass arrests, administrative detention and ill-treatment of the Arab population;

(g) The ill-treatment of persons under detention;

(h) The pillaging of archaeological and cultural property;

(i) The interference with religious freedoms and practices, particularly as manifested most recently in Al-Khalil, as well as family rights and customs;

(j) The illegal exploitation of the natural wealth, resources and population of the occupied territories;

6. *Reaffirms* that all measures taken by Israel to change the physical character, demographic composition, institutional structure or status of the occupied territories, or any part thereof, including Jerusalem, are null and void, and that Israel's policy of settling parts of its population and new immigrants in the occupied territories constitutes a flagrant violation of the Geneva Convention relative to the Protection of Civilian Persons in Time of War and of the relevant United Nations resolutions;

7. *Demands* that Israel desist forthwith from the policies and practices referred to in paragraphs 5 and 6 above;

8. *Reiterates* its call upon all States, international organizations and specialized agencies not to recognize any changes carried out by Israel in the occupied territories and to avoid actions, including those in the field of aid, which might be used by Israel in its pursuit of the policies of annexation and colonization or any of the other policies and practices referred to in the present resolution;

9. *Requests* the Special Committee, pending the early termination of the Israeli occupation, to continue to investigate Israeli policies and practices in the Arab territories occupied by Israel since 1967, to consult, as appropriate, with the International Committee of the Red Cross in order to ensure the safeguarding of the welfare and human rights of the population of the occupied territories, and to report to the Secretary-General as soon as possible and whenever the need arises thereafter;

10. *Requests* the Secretary-General:

(a) To render all necessary facilities to the Special Committee, including those required for its visits to the occupied territories, with a view to investigating the Israeli policies and practices referred to in the present resolution;

(*b*) To continue to make available additional staff as may be necessary to assist the Special Committee in the performance of its tasks;

(*c*) To ensure the widest circulation of the reports of the Special Committee, and of information regarding its activities and findings, by all means available through the Office of Public Information of the Secretariat and, where necessary, to reprint those reports of the Special Committee which are no longer available;

(*d*) To report to the General Assembly at its thirty-second session on the tasks entrusted to him in the present paragraph;

11. *Decides* to include in the provisional agenda of its thirty-second session the item entitled "Report of the Special Committee to Investigate Israeli Practices Affecting the Human Rights of the Population of the Occupied Territories".

101st plenary meeting
16 December 1976

D

The General Assembly,

Recalling its resolutions 3240 C (XXIX) of 29 November 1974 and 3525 C (XXX) of 15 December 1975,

Having considered the report of the Special Committee to Investigate Israeli Practices Affecting the Human Rights of the Population of the Occupied Territories,[18] in particular section V thereof, entitled "Quneitra", and annex III thereto, a report entitled "Quneitra: report on nature, extent and value of damage", submitted by a Swiss expert engaged by the Special Committee,

1. *Expresses its appreciation* of the thoroughness and impartiality with which the expert engaged by the Special Committee to Investigate Israeli Practices Affecting the Human Rights of the Population of the Occupied Territories discharged the tasks entrusted to him;

2. *Condemns* the massive, deliberate destruction of Quneitra perpetrated during the Israeli occupation and prior to the withdrawal of Israeli forces from that city in 1974;

3. *Recognizes* that the Syrian Arab Republic is entitled to full and adequate compensation, under international law and in equity, for the massive damage and deliberate destruction perpetrated in Quneitra while it was under Israeli occupation, and to all other legal remedies in accordance with applicable international law and practice;

4. *Takes note* of the statements made by the representative of the Syrian Arab Republic before the Special Political Committee, to the effect that his Government reserves all rights to full compensation in regard to all damages resulting from Israel's deliberate destruction of Quneitra, including

[18] *Ibid.*

those not covered by the expert's above-mentioned report or not falling within the scope of his assignment;

5. *Requests* the Special Committee to complete its survey on all the aspects referred to in paragraph 4 above and to report thereon to the General Assembly at its thirty-second session;

6. *Requests* the Secretary-General to provide the Special Committee with all the facilities required for the completion of the tasks referred to in the previous paragraphs.

101st plenary meeting
16 December 1976

33. General Assembly Resolution 31/110 on
the Living Conditions of the Palestinian People,
December 16, 1976*

* G.A. Res. 110, 31 U.N. GAOR Supp. (No. 39) at 59, U.N. Doc. A/31/39 (1976). *See also* subsequent resolutions, G.A. Res. 171, 32 U.N. GAOR Supp. (No. 45) at 105, U.N. Doc. A/32/45 (1977), G.A. Res. 110, 33 U.N. GAOR Supp. (No. 45) at 91, U.N. Doc. A/33/45 (1978) and G.A. Res. 113, 34 U.N. GAOR Supp. (No. 46) at 105, U.N. Doc. A/34/46 (1979).

The General Assembly,

Recalling the Vancouver Declaration on Human Settlements, 1976,[21] and the recommendations for national action[22] adopted by Habitat: United Nations Conference on Human Settlements, held at Vancouver from 31 May to 11 June 1976,

Recalling also resolution 3 of the Conference[23] on living conditions of the Palestinians in occupied territories, and Economic and Social Council resolution 2026 (LXI) of 4 August 1976,

Recalling further the recommendation adopted at the Regional Preparatory Conference for Asia and the Pacific, held at Teheran from 14 to 19 June 1975,

1. *Requests* the Secretary-General, in collaboration with the relevant United Nations organs and specialized agencies, to prepare and submit to the General Assembly at its thirty-second session a report on the living conditions of the Palestinian people in the occupied territories;

2. *Requests* the Secretary-General, in preparing the above-mentioned report, to consult and co-operate with the Palestine Liberation Organization, the representative of the Palestinian people;

3. *Urges* all States to co-operate with the Secretary-General in this matter.

101st plenary session,
16 December 1976

[21] *Report of Habitat: United Nations Conference on Human Settlements* (United Nations publication, Sales No. E.76.IV.7 and corrigendum), chap. I.

[22] *Ibid.,* chap. II.

[23] *Ibid.,* chap. III.

34. Resolutions of the Thirteenth Palestine National Council, Cairo, March 21–25, 1977*

* 6 J. Palestine Stud. 188 (Spring 1977).

(a) Political Resolutions

On the basis of the Palestinian National Covenant and of the resolutions of the previous National Council; from its concern for the political resolutions and gains achieved by the PLO at the Arab and international levels in the period since the twelfth Council; after discussion and study of the latest developments in the Palestine cause and in reassertion of support for Palestinian national struggle in Arab and international forums, the Palestine National Council stresses the following:

1. The Council stresses that the Palestine cause is the core and basis of the Arab-Zionist conflict, and that Security Council Resolution 242 ignores the Palestinian people and their inalienable rights, and therefore the Council reaffirms its rejection of this resolution and of action taken on the basis of it, at either the Arab or international levels.

2. The Council stresses the PLO's determination to pursue armed struggle, accompanied by various forms of political and mass struggle, to achieve the non-negotiable national rights of the Palestinian Arab people.

3. The Council affirms that all forms of struggle—whether military, political or popular—in the occupied territories, constitute the central link in its programme of struggle. On this basis, the PLO strives to escalate armed struggle in the occupied territories, as well as all other forms of struggle accompanying it, while giving every moral support to our masses in the occupied territory so that they may escalate this struggle and consolidate their steadfastness in their efforts to liquidate the occupation.

4. The Council stresses the PLO's rejection of all types of American capitulationist settlements as well as any liquidationist projects. It also stresses the PLO's determination to confront and foil any settlement achieved at the expense of our people's inalienable national rights. It calls on the Arab nation to shoulder its national responsibilities and concentrate all its potentials for the confrontation of these imperialist-Zionist schemes.

5. The Council stresses the importance and necessity of national unity, both military and political, among all factions of the Palestinian Revolution within the framework of the PLO, for national unity is an essential precondition of victory. Therefore it is essential to consolidate national unity at all levels, on the basis of commitment to these resolutions, and to draw up the required programmes for their implementation.

6. The Council stresses its commitment to the right of the Palestinian Revolution to remain in the territory of Lebanon within the context of the Cairo Agreement, and its annexes, concluded between the PLO and the Lebanese authorities; and stresses its commitment to their implementation in letter and in spirit; and in as much as they provide for the protection of the Revolution's right to bear arms and the security of the camps rejects any unilateral interpretation of this agreement and its annexes, while at the same time fully observing the sovereignty and security of Lebanon.

7. The Council salutes the heroic Lebanese people and affirms the PLO's

concern for the unity of its land and people, for its security, independence and sovereignty, for its Arab character; it stresses its pride in the support provided by this heroic people to the PLO, in its struggle to recover the national rights of our people in their homeland, and their right to return to that homeland, and strongly stresses the necessity of deepening and consolidating the cohesion between all Lebanese nationalist forces and the Palestinian Revolution.

8. The Council stresses the necessity of strengthening the Arab Front for the Support of the Palestinian Revolution and of deepening [the Revolution's] cohesion with all participating Arab nationalist forces in all Arab states. It also stresses the necessity of escalating the joint Arab struggle and of putting forward a formula of support for the Palestinian Revolution in its confrontation of Zionist-imperialist schemes.

9. The Council resolves to intensify Arab struggle and solidarity on the basis of anti-imperialist, anti-Zionist struggle and of action for the liberation of all occupied Arab territories, and in support of the Revolution in recovering the inalienable national rights of the Palestinian Arab people, without peace or recognition of Israel.

10. The Council reaffirms the PLO's right to meet its responsibilities at the Arab level in the struggle to liberate the occupied territory.

11. The Council resolves to pursue the struggle to recover our people's national rights and first and foremost, their right to return, to exercise self-determination and to establish their independent national state on their own land.

12. The Council stresses the necessity of consolidating cooperation and solidarity with the socialist countries, the non-aligned states, the Islamic states, the African states and with all national liberation movements in the world.

13. The Council salutes the attitude and endeavours of all states and forces which have taken a stand against Zionism as a form of racism, and against its aggressive practices.

14. The Council stresses the importance of relations and coordination with Jewish democratic and progressive forces inside and outside the occupied homeland, which are struggling against the ideology and practice of Zionism; and calls on all freedom-, peace-, and justice-loving forces and states in the world to discontinue all forms of aid to and cooperation with the racist Zionist regime, to condemn it and to reject all contacts with it.

15. Taking into consideration what has been achieved at the Arab and international levels since the end of the twelfth session of the Council, and after reviewing the political report submitted by the Executive Committee, the Council resolves the following:-

A. Stresses its commitment to the PLO's right to participate, independently and on a basis of equality, in all international conferences, forums and efforts related to the Palestine question and the Arab-Zionist conflict with the intention of realizing our non-negotiable national rights which have been recognized by the UN General Assembly since 1974, in particular resolution 3236.

B. The Council declares that any settlement or agreement prejudicial to the rights of our Palestinian people concluded without reference to them is absolutely null and void.

(b) Resolutions on Occupied Palestine. [1]

1. The Council, while asserting the unity of destiny and struggle of our people in all of Palestine and outside it, is proud to salute the struggle of our people in occupied Palestine and their continued steadfastness in spite of all Zionist, imperialist, particularly American, as well as Arab reactionary plots and measures, and praise the heroic mass uprising over the past few years which is an expression of our people's firm stand in rejecting Zionist occupation, in holding tenaciously to their land and their national rights in rallying around the PLO and its programme in its capacity as the sole legitimate representative of the Palestinian people, in confronting all plots to create an alternative leadership, and in insisting on foiling all attempts to harm their national rights to national independence and liberation. The Council also salutes the struggle and steadfastness of our militants in Israeli jails who are being subjected to the worst forms of degradation, torture and persecution, which treatment contradicts human rights and international conventions and affirms the fascist nature of the racist Zionist movement.

2. The Council praises the firm cohesion of our Palestinian masses throughout the occupied homeland in their battles for the defence of the land and their struggle against settlement projects; expropriation of land, repressive measures, inhuman mass punishments, deportation, desecration of holy places and the policy of suppression of national culture and all other such measures. The way our people under occupation have stood by their Revolution both politically and materially during the Lebanese crisis is the greatest proof of their unity, the strength of their commitment to the goals of the Revolution and their determination to defend it.

3. In order to intensify and escalate the struggle of our people in occupied Palestine and in consolidation of the unity of their national forces, sectors and institutions, the Council reaffirms the importance of supporting the Palestinian National Front in the occupied homeland and of ensuring the participation of all national groups and forces in it.

4. In order to reinforce the United Nations resolution regarding Zionism as a racist movement, the Council stresses the importance of the support provided by progressive and democratic anti-Zionist forces which defend the national rights of our people inside occupied Palestine.

5. Efforts to ensure that the Arab states agree to the repatriation of their Jewish citizens who have emigrated to occupied Palestine, and support for all Arab activities directed to this end.

[1] Wafa, *March 22, 1977*—Ed.

6. The Council stresses the extreme political, social and moral importance of the question of Palestinian detainees in the prisons of the occupation and calls for:

A. Support for the families of prisoners and detainees by making the Institution for the Families of Prisoners and Martyrs into a Palestinian public institution capable of helping all such families, particularly in occupied Palestine.

B. The adoption of their problems, and support for their struggle inside the prisons; the formation of permanent committees to defend their rights; and the contacting of peace committees, Amnesty International and other committees which defend human rights, in order to gain support for their just cause and to expose the measures taken against them by the enemy.

C. Providing material and moral support to the committee which defends political detainees in occupied Palestine.

7. The Council stresses the importance of supporting the struggle of the Palestinian working class inside the occupied homeland and of helping them through trade unions and economic projects to ensure the improvement of their living conditions and to prevent their emigration in order that they may be able to play their leading role in the struggle against Zionist occupation.

8. The Council affirms the importance of full support for all national institutions in the occupied homeland through:

1. Efforts to establish a Fund to support the steadfastness of our people in the occupied homeland.

2. Efforts to secure the implementation of the Jerusalem Fund project which was recommended by the last Islamic conference in Amman.

3. Greater efforts to secure the release of the deposits in Arab countries of individuals and institutions which belong to our people in the occupied homeland.

4. Encouragement and support of projects to increase steadfastness in occupied Palestine, particularly housing societies, agricultural cooperatives, national industries, and the development of national products.

5. Developing national educational institutions and efforts to establish a Palestinian university, so as to provide our students in occupied Palestine with better chances of scientific education and guarantee their remaining in their homeland. In addition, exerting all possible efforts to secure the admission of our students to Arab and foreign universities, and to ensure their welfare in these countries.

6. Offering the greatest possible medical support to our people inside occupied Palestine, through financial and technical aid, and the provision of supplies to all national institutions, so as to deter the emigration of medical personnel from the occupied homeland and to prevent the deterioration of our people's conditions.

7. Efforts to ensure that Palestinian information media, in particular the radio, devote the greatest possible attention to the needs of our masses in

the occupied areas as regards clear and accurate political orientation, as well as giving due attention to the solving of their day-to-day problems. The Council also affirms the necessity of establishing a special research institution for occupied Palestine affairs, to follow up objectively the affairs of our masses, issue information bulletins on the subject, and form a committee of specialists charged with the task of drawing up a long-term programme in all sectors. The Council also stresses the necessity of establishing an information centre on the affairs of occupied Palestine, which would issue specialized bulletins.

8. The Council affirms the necessity of developing the Department for Occupied Homeland Affairs and furnishing it with the funds and powers necessary for the execution of its functions.

9. The Palestine National Council, in reaffirming the Arab character of all Palestine and particularly Jerusalem, rejects all demographic arguments; and all measures involving annexation, settlement, confiscation or any other form of transference of land title; whether through collateral, forcible acquisition or any other illegitimate methods.

10. The council affirms that the defence of Palestinian territory is a sacred national duty which should be given priority over other matters with which the PLO is concerned. The most extensive backing should be given to the struggle of our people—which was manifested in such a splendid manner on Land Day—against racist Zionism. The council calls on the Executive Committee to:

A. Ensure recognition by Palestinians of Land Day as a national day of solidarity with the struggle of our people in the occupied homeland.

B. Make efforts to ensure that Land Day is recognized by all Arabs as a national day on which the Arab masses express their solidarity with the struggle of our people.

C. Support the struggle of the Committee for the Defence of the Land in the occupied homeland.

11. Take all measures to prevent the Palestinian land falling into the hands of the enmey [sic] and launch a campaign against all Zionist attempts to buy such land.

(c) Resolutions of the Committee of National Unity.[1]

During its thirteenth session, the Palestine National Council approved the following recommendations of the Committee of National Unity:

1. The PLO constitutes the general framework for the unity of all Palestinian national forces, on the basis of commitment to the Palestinian National Charter and the PLO's political programme.

2. This framework shall include all the PLO's controlling bodies, institutions and departments.

3. The national unity of the different sections of the revolution shall be in the form of a front.

[1] Wafa, *March 24, 1977*—Ed.

4. All the controlling bodies, institutions and departments, shall enforce the principle of collective leadership, and observe the need to reinforce democratic relations at all levels of action, and any problems that may arise between organizations shall be solved on the basis of democratic dialogue. In the light of these principles the Committee recommends the following:

(A) That the PLO's controlling bodies, namely, the National Council, the Executive Committee and the Central Council be constituted on the basis of a front.

(B) The Council calls on the Executive Committee to prepare plans to ensure that the Revolution's armed forces are united in a unified army and a unified popular militia.

(C) That all revenue and expenditure be unified within the framework of the Palestinian National Fund and be placed under its control, the Executive Committee amending the financial schedules of the National Fund to ensure that the demands of Palestinian revolutionary action are met.

(D) That the information agencies and media of all sections of the Palestinian Revolution be unified within the framework of a single central agency and unified media, on the basis of the political programme of the PLO.

(E) That the agencies of all the organizations that deal with foreign relations be unified, under the appropriate PLO department, which will be responsible for the foreign relations of the Palestinian Revolution, including its diplomatic representation in Arab, friendly and foreign countries.

(F) That the Executive Committee form a committee to study organizational affairs in occupied Palestine and Jordan, with a view to devising an appropriate formula for unification in the light of the demands of the struggle and of security.

(G) That every section should maintain its ideological and organizational independence, within the framework of the political programme of the PLO.

(H) That members of the Palestine National Council living in every country where there is a PLO office should form a consultative committee to cooperate with the director of the office in coping with problems, the director of the office keeping the committee informed of new developments and the committee meeting monthly.

(I) That the Popular Organization Department of the Executive Committee should, with due regard for the principle of representation on the basis of a front, be responsible for laying down the general outlines of action by Palestinian mass and trade union organizations, on the basis of the principle of proportional representation, which will ensure democratic competition and strengthen the role of the mass organizations in the national struggle of the Palestinian people.

(J) The Council authorizes the Chairman of the Executive Committee to resolve the disputes within the Popular Front-General Command.

(K) The Council has decided to transmit all the recommendations of this committee to the Executive Committee, so that it may choose the measures which it considers appropriate.

(d) Resolutions of the Education Committee.[1]

Inasmuch as the Palestinian people's power to survive and to support and develop their Revolution depends to a great extent on education and educated personnel, education, its level and its goals are matters of the greatest importance to the Palestinian people. And inasmuch as the PLO is the sole legitimate representative of the Palestinian people, it bears the full responsibility for providing education and determining its level, for meeting the requirements of the Palestinian people both inside and outside the occupied homeland and for the education of new generations capable of bearing the burdens and achieving the objectives of Palestinian struggle.

In view of the continued occupation of our territory by the Zionist enemy, of the fact that the Palestinian people are dispersed in various countries, of the repeated attacks on them, the latest of which has been in Lebanon during the last two years, and of the resulting acute educational problems that are in urgent need of solutions, the Palestine National Council, at its last session, decided on the following measures:

1. The Executive Council of the PLO is called on to establish a Higher Council for Culture, Education and Higher Education, which shall be directly responsible to the Chairman of the Executive Committee and shall perform the following tasks:

(a) Drafting the higher policy for culture, education and higher education.

(b) Establishing the general outlines of educational planning and approving the detailed plans submitted by the information offices of the PLO's specialized agencies.

(c) Ensuring coordination between the agencies operating in this field.

(d) Supervising the implementation of these projects.

(e) Mobilizing Palestinian and Arab specialists and making use of their qualifications in educational, scientific and cultural fields.

This Council shall consist of the heads of the organizations operating in the field of Palestinian education and culture, and of highly qualified Palestinians, selected on the basis of their specialized qualifications in the various fields of education, and representing the different Palestinian communities.

2. Developing and supporting the PLO's Department for Educational and Cultural Affairs, so that it may be able to perform its duties in a proper manner, by increasing its budget, supplying it with the necessary qualified personnel and increasing its executive powers.

3. Developing and supporting the Palestinian Planning and Research Centres to enable them to perform their roles of preparing educational and cultural projects and submitting them to the Higher Council.

4. Establishing a Palestinian Arab University in occupied Palestine.

5. Providing annual financial aid to the Arab higher education institutions

[1] Wafa, *March 28, 1977*—Ed.

in the occupied territory with a view to developing them and increasing their capacity.

6. Establishing intermediate technical institutions in occupied Palestine.

7. Studying means of ensuring that Palestinians wishing to complete their higher education outside the occupied territory are able to do so, including the projects for a people's university, a public university and a conventional university, and any other available means.

8. Establishing a central office to arrange for the enrolment of Palestinian students in Arab and foreign universities, priority being given to students from occupied Palestine, the children of martyrs and combatants and students from Arab countries in which they are not treated, as regards university enrolment, on a footing of equality with native-born students.

9. The PLO shall assume responsibility for the problem of providing secondary education for Palestinian pupils in Lebanon, by establishing new schools and increasing the capacity of existing schools for absorbing more Palestinian and Lebanese students.

10. Taking steps, with the assistance of international organizations, to ensure that elementary, secondary and university education is available to Palestinians in the territories occupied before 1948.

11. The PLO shall be responsible, through its specialized agencies, for orienting and supervising the elementary and secondary education provided by UNRWA, and for ensuring that its standards are raised and its scope extended.

12. The Arab host governments are requested to treat Palestinian students on an equal footing with their own students.

13. Supplying the General Union of Palestinian Women with financial support for its kindergarten projects, the PLO assisting it in drawing up its programmes.

14. Supplying material and moral support to the Educational City for the Children of Palestinian Martyrs and Combatants in Syria and the children's Recreational School in Lebanon, and ensuring that they have the necessary qualified and specialist staff.

15. Publishing a series of school textbooks on the Palestine problem suitable for pre-university teaching in all Arab countries. It is recommended that the series be based on the project of the PLO Planning Centre.

16. Supplying all possible financial aid to the Palestinian Student Fund, which shall act in coordination with the central office for the enrolment of Palestinian students.

(e) Resolutions of the Military Committee.[1]

In the course of the meetings of the Palestine National Council in Cairo, the Military Committee proposed the following military recommendations, which were unanimously approved by the Council.

---

[1] Wafa, *March 23, 1977*—Ed.

1. That the combat forces of all sections of the Palestinian Revolution, including the forces of the Palestinian Armed Struggle Command, militia forces, and the PLA, be unified under "the Palestinian Revolution's Army and Armed Forces," which is to be considered the PLO's military institution.

2. That the Palestinian Revolution should consist of:

A. Regular forces consisting of the army and the armed forces of the "Palestinian National Army," to which all Palestinian regular forces should be attached.

B. Semi-regular forces.

C. Militia forces, including youth organizations, and male and female cubs [sic].

3. That the Chairman of the PLO Executive Committee should be the Supreme Commander of the army and the armed forces of the Palestinian Revolution, as well as the Commander-in-Chief of these forces, until such time as a Commander-in-Chief is chosen.

4. That a Supreme Military Council be established, headed by the Supreme Commander and including the military commanders of organizations, the Commander-in-Chief and the commanders of the regular, semiregular and militia forces as members. That council should be responsible for drawing up the regulations and schedules regarding the organization of the army and the armed forces, the appointment of commanders and the constituting of military units, and for drafting the plans, programmes and budget required for the organization, support and development of the army and the armed forces.

5. That the Palestinian National Fund should meet the expenses of this army, in the light of the regulations drawn up by the Supreme Military Council, with the organizations continuing their financial contributions to the Fund for a transitional period until such time as financial unification is achieved.

6. That all Palestinian military men not serving in the army and the armed forces be retained as reserves liable to be called up by the command as and when necessary.

7. That national service be compulsory for all Palestinians in all Arab countries, and be arranged in coordination with the Arab host countries. That they should serve in the Palestinian army and armed forces.

8. That the military agreements between the PLO and Arab countries in which PLA units are stationed be reconsidered with a view to the conclusion of new agreements enabling the political leadership of the Organization to fully control and direct this army.

9. That the necessity of escalating armed struggle inside the occupied territories be asserted and that the Arab confrontation countries be called on to open their fronts to the forces of the Palestinian Revolution for action against the Zionist enemy to safeguard the existence and freedom of movement of these forces in the countries.

10. That the right of the Palestinian Resistance to retain all its arms in Lebanon be asserted, as also its right to defend the Palestinian camps.

11. That the Chairman of the PLO Executive Committee and Commander-in-Chief of the army and the armed forces of the Palestinian Revolution be called on to implement these resolutions as soon as possible in cooperation with the Supreme Military Council.

(f) Resolutions of the Social Affairs and Labour Committee.[1]

The Palestine National Council resolved during its thirteenth session to establish an independent Department for Social Affairs and Labour in the PLO. There follow the recommendations, submitted by the Council's Social Affairs and Labour Committee, which were approved by the Council:

1. *The Palestinian Camps in Lebanon*:

A. That the necessary solutions for the problems of the refugee camps in Lebanon be found and that all the requirements of their inhabitants be met.

B. That the search for persons still missing as a result of the Lebanese war be continued, all available means being employed to find out what has happened to them.

C. That medical services be provided by the establishment of clinics and hospitals, and that the existing ones in the camps be improved. That the Palestinian Red Crescent Society be authorized to do this within the limits of its means and priorities.

D. That drinking water supplies be ensured in the camps, by drilling artesian wells, with all houses being connected to the water and drainage systems.

2. That the families of Palestinian martyrs, prisoners, detainees, disabled and wounded be cared for by:

A. The Association for the Care of the Families of Palestinian Combatants and Martyrs.

B. That the PLO's Executive Committee be called on to support the Association for the Care of the Families of Palestinian Combatants and Martyrs in all fields and by every possible means to enable it to perform its social duties and achieve its humanitarian aims.

C. That a resolution be adopted to the effect that this association is the sole authority responsible for the care of the families of Palestinian martyrs, and for providing them with social services in the PLO and at the Arab and international levels, according to resolution 123 of 1973.

D. The Council recommends continued support for the Association of Wounded Combatants in Jerusalem and the Association of War Veterans in Gaza.

E. That the PLO Executive Committee be called on to continue its efforts to secure the release of all Palestinian detainees in Israeli prisons by exerting

[1] Wafa, *March 25, 1977*—Ed.

all possible pressures; and to work assiduously to ensure the enforcement of the Geneva Convention with regard to all prisoners and detainees in Israeli prisons.

3. A. That more extensive social and financial aid be provided to the families of all Palestinian detainees in occupied Palestine, to support their heroic steadfastness and continued resistance to the Zionist occupation.

B. That appropriate compensation be provided for those whose homes have been destroyed by the Zionist enemy for resisting the occupation.

C. That the PLO's regulations be amended so as to ensure continued social welfare and medical insurance for PLO employees and their families.

4. *Medical Affairs*

That the Palestinian Red Crescent organization be supported on the basis of resolutions of previous National Councils, so that it may continue to provide medical services to the Palestinian people inside and outside the occupied homeland.

5. *Care of Palestinian Children*

That a study be undertaken of all projects related to the care of Palestinian children with a view to making nurseries, kindergartens and family welfare centres available to all, supporting already established projects and those submitted by the General Union of Palestinian Women, and other specialized Palestinian institutions, and providing the necessary funds to support these projects.

6. *Labour and Workers*

A. That every effort be made to establish a social security fund for Palestinian workers, under the supervision of the department and in cooperation with the General Union of Palestinian Workers.

B. That every effort be made to establish a health insurance fund for Palestinian workers under the supervision of the General Union of Palestinian Workers.

C. That a study by [*sic*] undertaken of production and cooperation projects and that funds be allocated for projects of this kind, priority being given to projects submitted by the General Union of Palestinian Workers—Lebanon Branch—for implementation in Lebanon, in view of the serious labour situation resulting from the recent events there.

D. That the activities of the General Union of Palestinian Workers and its branches among migrant workers, particularly in Western Europe, be stepped up.

E. That attention be drawn to the dangers arising from the emigration to certain European countries of Palestinian workers because of the financial inducements offered them there, and that plans be drawn up to cope with this problem and the underlying economic reasons.

F. That special attention paid to the professional rehabilitation of the war-

wounded and disabled, through support for training, cooperative and production institutions, mother and child welfare, health insurance and social
security projects.

G. That social and cultural clubs for Palestinian communities abroad be
developed and supported, and that the establishment of new clubs in the
Palestinian camps and the Arab host countries be encouraged.

35. Prime Minister Begin's Speech to the Knesset Presenting the New Government and Outlines of Its Policy, June 21, 1977*

* Embassy of Israel, Washington, D.C.

The Change of Government

In a democratic decision of which we are proud, the people of Israel on May 17, 1977 resolved upon a change of guard in the administration. A party that had for a long time been the party of leadership and government became the second party in the Knesset, while a political bloc that had served the Nation patiently and loyally according to the rules of democracy—in parliamentary opposition—now became the first party, and was called upon to form a new government.

On Tuesday June 7, 1977, the President—by virtue of his powers, and upon the recommendation of Knesset factions representing a decisive majority of members of the House—entrusted me with forming the Government. I have come today to present the Government—its composition and the distribution of functions therein—to the Knesset and to request, therefore, the confidence of the House of Representatives.

The electorate has placed its trust in us—but we shall not boast of victory. We are aware that the principal tasks lie ahead of us. And since the Government and its policy are new, I request the House and the Nation to grant it moral credit, for at least the first year of its tenure. In one day we will not rectify the situation, nor advance the State in the social, economic and political spheres; but our resolve is to so advance, and we shall make a supreme effort, through hard work, to implement the positive program for whose execution we received the confidence of the people. But that takes time. I hope that moral credit will be given us and that we shall be able—in conditions of national consensus—to improve the lot of our people in all walks of life.

The Desire for Peace

Upon assuming his high office, the President of the United States, Mr. Carter, quoted from the Prophet Micah, as follows:

> It hath been told Thee, O Man, what is good, and what the Lord doth requite of Thee: Only to do justly, and to love mercy, and to walk humbly with Thy God.

These words have served in the past—and will always serve—as a guiding light to us. But Micah the Morashtite also had a vision of 'Acharit Hayamim'—a vision wonderfully resembling, although with certain differences, that of Isaiah the son of Amos. To this day the heart of every person who pursues freedom, peace, and justice is stirred when reading those immortal words:

> And they shall beat their swords into plowshares and their spears into pruning hooks: Nation shall not lift up sword against Nation, neither shall they learn war anymore.

In the light of this vision we too shall proceed out of faith and the knowledge that this is one of the most prodigious contributions of Jewish perception to human civilization, and that the day will come when wars between people shall cease and lethal weapons shall be no more and peace shall reign on the Earth. And this too shall we remember: After raising his universal vision Micah the Morashtite asserts: "For let all the peoples walk each one in the name of its God: But we shall walk in the name of the Lord Our God for ever and ever".

The Right to Exist

By virtue of this age long heritage of our fathers I wish to declare that the Government of Israel will not ask any nation, be it near or far, mighty or small, to recognize our right to exist. The right to exist? It would not enter the mind of any Briton or Frenchman, Belgian or Dutchman, Hungarian or Bulgarian, Russian or American, to request for his people recognition of its right to exist. Their existence per se is their right to exist. The same holds true for Israel. We were granted our right to exist by the God of Our Fathers, at the glimmer of the dawn of human civilization nearly four thousand years ago. For that right which has been sanctified in Jewish blood from generation to generation, we have paid a price unexampled in the annals of the nations. Certainly this fact does not diminish or enfeeble our right. On the contrary. Therefore, I re-emphasize that we do not expect anyone to request on our behalf that our right to exist in the land of our fathers be recognized. It is a different form of recognition which is required between ourselves and our neighbors: recognition of sovereignty and of the mutual need for a life of peace and understanding. It is this mutual recognition that we look forward to: for it we shall make every possible effort.

Our Attachment to the Land of Israel

The Land of Israel, our sole country, the beloved land of our fathers, we have clung to it throughout the generations, never did we sever the link with it. We prayed for it, longed for it, loved it with all our heart and with all our soul. Not for one day did we forget it in our wanderings in exile, and its name was upon the lips of our saintly forefathers when they were dragged by destructive enemies to wanton death. We were exiled from its soul and we returned unto it, with faith and by right and with sacrifice, with glorious pioneering building and in a fight for self-liberation.

No one gave us our freedom as a present. We conquered it, with the vestige of our national strength, in a generation in which a third of our people was destroyed and no one came to their rescue.

Over seventy years ago, Ze'ev Jabotinsky wrote, of this land:

Indeed the true core of our national uniqueness is the pure fruit of the
Land of Israel. Before we came to the Land of Israel we were not a
nation and we had no existence. On the soil of the Land of Israel, from
the fragments of diverse tribes was the Hebrew Nation formed. On the
soil of the Land of Israel did we grow up. Upon it we became citizens,
we fortified the faith of the One God, we inhaled the breath of the land
and in our struggle for independence and rule we were enveloped by
its atmosphere, the grain that flourished on its soil sustained us. It was
in the Land of Israel that the concepts of our prophets developed, and
in the Land of Israel the Song of Songs was first uttered. All that is
Hebrew within us has been bestowed upon us by the Land of Israel.
Everything else that is within us is not Hebrew. The People of Israel
and the Land of Israel are one.

And so it is, as we have asserted in our basic guidelines: the Jewish people
has an historic eternal and inalienable right to the Land of Israel, the Land
of our Forefathers.

Israel and the Nations

We shall endeavour to deepen the friendship between ourselves and the
United States of America. This will be the firm foundation of the Government's policy. America and Israel have in common not only profound feelings for, and faith in the values of morality and democracy. We believe they
are united also by a true and profound partnership of interests. Israel is an
integral part of the free world. But the free—the democratic world has of
late greatly shrunk. It may be likened to an island whose shores are swept
by stormy waves and the tempestuous seas of foul totalitarianism. A famous
19th Century slogan must be altered in our day: Free men of all countries,
unite. We must all stand together to repulse the threat and preserve the
freedom of man.

We shall work for renewal of the friendship between Israel and France.
There existed more than friendship: there was an alliance between our two
countries. I hereby call on the President of France and its government to
resume those relations with Israel—of course, on a basis of reciprocity.
France has many friends in Israel and Israel has excellent friends in France.
From the two ends of the Mediterranean we shall stretch out a hand to one
another and work for the revival of the friendship between the two peoples.

We are interested in normalization of relations between Israel and the
Soviet Union. Three periods have there been in relations between Zionism
and the Land of Israel, and the Soviet Union. Starting with the Bolshevik
Revolution for close on thirty years relations were unbridgeable hostility instigated by Moscow. In the late 'forties came the great turn. Under the influence of the War of Liberation against British rule, Moscow began to view
the aspiration for the Jewish State's renaissance as one of human progress—

and we all recall the speeches by Messrs. Gromyko and Tsarapkin about the urgent need for establishing the Jewish State. And then the 'fifties in which there came a turn for the worse, Moscow lending a hand to our enemies and equipping them with lethal weapons—knowing well that one day these would be directed against the remnants of the Jewish people whose destruction its rulers had seen with their own eyes on the soil of their country and elsewhere.

Upon the outbreak of the Six Day War, the Soviet Union severed diplomatic relations with Israel. Resumption of these normal relations depends, in the nature of things, on Moscow's initiative. Should such initiative be forthcoming, we shall demand that an end be put to persecution of Judaism and Zionism, and to the incitement against them, that all Prisoners-of-Zion be released and that every Jew throughout the Soviet Union so desiring be allowed to emigrate, to return to the Land of Israel—or, in the words of our brethren, the seekers of Zion in the Soviet Union, to the "Jewish people's historic homeland".

Negotiations with the Arab Countries

Our prime concern is prevention of a new war in the Middle East. I call upon King Hussein, President Sadat and President Assad to meet with me—whether in our capitals or on neutral soil, in public or away from the spotlights of publicity—in order to discuss the establishment of true peace between their countries and Israel. Much blood, too much, has been shed in the region—Jewish and Arab. Let us put an end to the blood shedding that is abhorrent to us, and sit down at the negotiating table in sincerity and seriousness. Should this plea encounter refusal, we shall note the Arab intransigence. It will not be new. Five Prime Ministers who preceeded me—David Ben-Gurion, Moshe Sharett and Levi Eshkol of blessed memory, and Mrs. Golda Meir and Yitzhak Rabin, to whom I wish long life—repeatedly called for the holding of such meetings. There was no response—or rather, there was a negative response—from the other side. But we shall not weary of sounding the call—not for propaganda purposes, but for the vital needs of our peoples and our countries.

The Call to Israelis Abroad to Return Home

And now, the appeal to ourselves, to our people. I call on all citizens of Israel who have left the country to return home. In days past, Jew-haters were wont to say that the Jew pursues the following rule: Ubi Bene, Ibi Patria (Wherever I feel good—there my homeland be)—even though it be difficult for me. The government will act to ease matters for the returning families. We shall not address these people by derogatory terms: insults solve no problems. We shall say to them simply—the time has come to return home.

We call on the young generation, in the homeland and in the Diaspora, to arise, go forth and settle. Come from East and West, North and South, to build together the Land of Israel. There is room in it for millions of returnees to Zion. We do not wish to evict, nor shall we evict, any Arab resident from his land. Jews and Arabs, Druze and Circassians, can live together in this land. And they must live together in peace, mutual respect, equal rights, in freedom and with social-economic progress.

The Government's Legislative Program

The Government's legislative program for this brief term and for the Knesset's winter term will include, inter alia:

(a) a universal state health insurance law
(b) a state-juridical arbitration law for the services essential to the public and the country
(c) a minimum wage law
(d) a pension law, in accordance with the prayer which is sacred to the Jewish people: "Cast me not off in the time of old age"
(e) a housing-rights law

Likewise, should the need arise, we shall introduce bills aimed at uprooting violent crimes. We must all make an effort to return to the lofty tradition of the Jewish people in the Diaspora and in the Pre-State Yishuv: the Jewish people were unacquainted with certain types of crime against other men or women or against themselves. We must build a beautiful Land of Israel, but we must also have a beautiful, honest, pure people of Israel, who show respect in human relations and maintain civil law and order, serving as a paragon to their fellow-men.

Not a few citizens have gone astray in economic offenses, whether because of the severity of certain restrictive laws or for other reasons. The Government will consider the possibility of extending a line across the past, of opening a new leaf in this area as well. We are looking towards the future. The State will respect the citizen, and the citizen will respect the State's laws. We shall all educate the young generation in the humane and Jewish values which the soul of the Jewish people has clung to from generation to generation: love of man, love of liberty and justice, love of homeland. We have a wonderful young generation: serene, devoted, loyal, we have seen it tested and it has passed honorably and dedicatedly. It has all our concern and love and we hope that, when the day comes, with God's help, we shall hand over to the young generation a land and a state which our people and all free men everywhere may be proud of.

Streamlining the Government

It is our intention to make innovations in the structure of government, for purposes of saving and streamlining. We shall eliminate ministries and unite ministries. We shall eliminate the Ministry of Police, which is unexampled in any democratic country, and we shall transfer its areas of responsibility to the Ministry of the Interior. We shall unite the Ministry of Tourism with the Ministry of Commerce and Industry, and we shall have one ministry for affairs of commerce, industry, and tourism. We shall establish a new ministry, to be called the Ministry for Social Betterment, whose sphere will include the functions of the Ministry of Social Welfare and the Ministry of Labor, along with the National Insurance Institution. For the time being, we shall retain the Ministry of Health, but should there be a change in the Government's makeup, requiring the Health Ministry's unification with the Ministry for Social Betterment, we shall give this possibility positive consideration. We shall transfer to the sphere of activity and responsibility of the Housing Minister—who will henceforth be called Minister of Construction—functions which are at present within the sphere of the Ministry of Labor and which have to do with construction. We shall unite the Ministry of Transport with the Ministry of Communications, and we shall have one Ministry for Transport and Communications.

We shall establish a new Ministry for Energy and Infrastructure, whose spheres of activity will include, inter alia, subjects having to do with energy, which are at present in the spheres of the Ministry of Finance and the Ministry of Commerce and Industry, and infrastructure matters at present located in other government ministries.

I have cited a number of examples of changes which we intend to make in the structure of the Government and its ministries, and the Government will, at an early date, submit, for Knesset approval, as required by law, its proposals for the designation and reorganization of the structure of the Government and its ministries.

Composition of the Cabinet

And now, I have the honor to present to the Knesset the composition of the cabinet, as follows:

Menachem Begin—Prime Minister
Simha Erlich—Minister of Finance
Aharon Abu Hatzeira—Minister of Religious Affairs
Yosef Burg—Minister of the Interior and Minister of Police
Moshe Dayan—Minister of Foreign Affairs
Yigal Hurvitz—Minister of Commerce and Industry and
                 Minister of Tourism
Zevulun Hammer—Minister of Education and Culture
Ezer Weizman—Minister of Defence
David Levi—Minister of Immigrant Absorption
Yitzhak Moda'i—Minister of Energy and Infrastructure
Gideon Patt—Minister of Construction

Eliezer Shostak–Minister of Health
Ariel Sharon–Minister of Agriculture

As you see, Members of the Knesset, I have not included in the list ministers appointed over the Ministry of Justice, over the Ministry of Social Welfare and the Ministry of Labor (which will be included in the new Ministry for Social Betterment once it is established) and over the Ministry of Transport and the Ministry of Communications (which will be unified in one ministry). The functions of these ministers will be borne, pro tem, by the Prime Minister. We have done this in order to maintain the possibility for the Democratic Movement for Change to join the Government. Owing to the importance of these ministries, and for the sake of the Government's efficiency, we shall not be able to leave open this situation for more than four to five weeks. We should like to hope that until then, negotiations will have been resumed with the representatives of the Democratic Movement for Change and that it will join the Government, its emmissaries taking over these ministries.

Basic Outline of the Government's Policy

I. *Peace, Negotiations, the Land of Israel, and the Jewish People*
   A. Recognition of the shared fate and the common struggle for the survival of the Jewish people in the Land of Israel and in the Diaspora.
   B. The Jewish people has an eternal historic right to the Land of Israel. The inalienable legacy of our Forefathers.
   C. The Government shall plan, create and encourage urban and rural settlements on the soil of the homeland.
   D. The Government shall give the encouragement of aliya primacy in the tasks facing the Nation.
   E. The Government shall make the aspiration for peace its prime concern.
   F. The Government shall invite Israel's neighbors jointly and severally, directly or through a friendly state, to conduct direct negotiations for the signing of peace agreements between them, without prior conditions on the part of anyone, and without any formulated solution from without.
   G. The Government declares its readiness to participate in the Geneva Conference if and when it shall be convened by the United States and the Soviet Union on the basis of Security Council Resolutions 242 and 338.
   H. With the approach of the Geneva Conference and direct negotiations, the Government declares Israel's readiness to conduct the said negotiations in order to achieve a genuine, contractual, and workable peace which will bring about normalization of life in the region.

I.   In the absence of peace agreements the parties shall be bound by the agreements between them which were signed by the previous governments.

J.   The Knesset has legally empowered the Government to extend by decree the State's law, jurisdiction, and administration over the entire area of the Land of Israel as shall be specified in the decree. This legal and parliamentary authority is at the Government's discretion. It shall not be implemented so long as negotiations over peace agreements are being conducted between Israel and its neighbors. It shall involve the selection of a suitable time, the Government's political consideration, a special date in the Knesset and approval by the Knesset.

K.   Equal rights for all citizens and inhabitants regardless of religion, race, sex, ethnic and communal affiliation.

L.   The Government shall ensure individual freedom and civil rights. The encouragement of private initiative and equality of opportunity, and the individual's advancement and wellbeing.

M.   An ongoing campaign for the return to Zion of all who desire it in the Soviet Union and for the rescue of the Jews of Syria and the other Arab States.

II. *Internal Affairs*

A.   The curbing of inflation, stabilization of the currency, and insurance of a decent standard of living for all inhabitants of the State.

B.   Action for the elimination of poverty and for the provision of aid to large families, particularly in housing and education.

C.   A continuous effort aimed at increasing capital investments from abroad and the renewal of economic growth. A special effort will be made for the construction of rental housing.

D.   The Government shall strive to ensure employment and shall foster joy of creativity and labor morality.

E.   The Government shall encourage and stimulate increased productivity and output in a combined effort to bring about a rapid growth in the gross national product and a continuous increase in exports.

F.   The Government shall act to improve labor relations and to reduce disputes in the economy. Action to this end shall include legislation of compulsory arbitration in essential services.

G.   The Government shall act to encourage and expand agriculture and agricultural settlements of every variety and type.

H.   The adoption of means to prevent emigration, to bring about the return of citizens who have left and to increase immigration from East and West alike.

I.   Respect for the Law and the uprooting of crime and violence.

J.   The institution of a long school day and an education based on the values of Judaism and Zionism, love of Israel and love of the homeland.

K. The Government shall guarantee freedom of conscience and religion to every citizen, shall see to the provision of public religious needs by means of the State and shall ensure a religious education for all children whose parents desire it.

L. The status quo in matters of religion shall be maintained.

M. The Government shall respect the international agreement signed by the previous governments.

36. European Council Statement on the Middle East, June 30, 1977*

* 10 Bull. Eur. Comm. (No. 6) 62 (1977).

1. At the present critical stage in the Middle East, the Nine welcome all efforts now being made to bring to an end the tragic conflict there. They emphasize the crucial interest which they see in early and successful negotiations towards a just and lasting peace. They call on all the parties concerned to agree urgently to participate in such negotiations in a constructive and realistic spirit; at this juncture in particular all parties should refrain from statements or policies which could constitute an obstacle to the pursuit of peace.

2. The Nine set out on many occasions in the past, for example, in their statements of 6 November 1973,[1] 28 September 1976[2] and 7 December 1976,[2] their view that a peace settlement should be based on Security Council Resolutions 242 and 338 and on:

(i) The inadmissibility of the acquisition of territory by force;

(ii) The need for Israel to end the territorial occupation which it has maintained since the conflict of 1967;

(iii) Respect for the sovereignty, territorial integrity and independence of every State in the area and their right to live in peace within secure and recognized boundaries;

(iv) Recognition that in the establishment of a just and lasting peace account must be taken of the legitimate rights of the Palestinians.

It remains their firm view that all these aspects must be taken as a whole.

3. The Nine have affirmed their belief that a solution to the conflict in the Middle East will be possible only if the legitimate right of the Palestinian people to give effective expression to its national identity is translated into fact, which would take into account the need for a homeland for the Palestinian people. They consider that the representatives of the parties to the conflict including the Palestinian people, must participate in the negotiations in an appropriate manner to be worked out in consultation between all the parties concerned. In the context of an overall settlement, Israel must be ready to recognize the legitimate rights of the Palestinian people: equally, the Arab side must be ready to recognize the right of Israel to live in peace within secure and recognized boundaries. It is not through the acquisition of territory by force that the security of the States of the region can be assured; but it must be based on commitments to peace exchanged between all the parties concerned with a view to establishing truly peaceful relations.

4. The Nine believe that the peace negotiations must be resumed urgently, with the aim of agreeing and implementing a comprehensive, just and lasting settlement of the conflict. They remain ready to contribute to the extent the parties wish in finding a settlement and in putting it into effect. They are also ready to consider participating in guarantees in the framework of the United Nations.

[1] Bull. EC 10-1973, point 2502.

[2] Statements made on behalf of the Community by the Dutch Presidency in United Nations General Assembly debates.

37. Excerpts from the Speech to the U.N. General

Assembly on the Middle East by the President

of the Council of the European Communities,

September 26, 1977*

*10 Bull. Eur. Comm. (No. 9) 85 (1977).

3.2.2. Anything that affects the stability and prosperity of the countries of Africa and the Middle East is of the greatest interest to the Nine. We have close historical ties with these countries which are deepening in all fields of human activity.

With regard to the situation in the Middle East, over which the Nine continue to be gravely concerned, they remain convinced, as a matter of principle, that any solution must be based on Security Council Resolutions 242 and 338, as they affirmed on 29 July 1977,[2] and on the following fundamental principles:

(i) acquisition of territory by force is unacceptable;

(ii) Israel must end its occupation of territories it has held since the 1967 war;

(iii) the sovereignty, territorial integrity and the independence of each State in the region must be respected, as well as the right of each State in the region to live in peace within secure and recognized borders;

(iv) the establishment of a just and durable peace must give due consideration to the rights of the Palestinians.

The Nine also continue to believe that a solution to the conflict will be possible only if the legitimate right of the Palestinian people to give effective expression to its national identity is translated into fact. This would take into account the need for a homeland for the Palestinian people.

It remains the firm view of the Nine that all these aspects must be taken as a whole.

They consider that the representatives of the parties in the conflict, including the Palestinian people, must participate in the negotiations in an appropriate manner to be worked out in consultation between all the parties concerned. In the context of an overall settlement, Israel must be ready to recognize the legitimate rights of the Palestinian people; equally, the Arab side must be ready to recognize the right of Israel to live in peace within secure and recognized boundaries.

Speaking practically, the Nine are prepared to collaborate, to the extent desired by the interested parties, in the search for a general and definitive solution, and to implement this, notably through participation in the context of the United Nations, in guarantees that the Nine consider of the greatest importance for a general solution of the problems of the Middle East.

One should recall that the Nine have publicly stated their concern over the illegal measures taken recently by the Government of Israel in the occupied territories, and which will be the subject of a new point on the agenda of our Assembly. These measures are contrary to the basic principles which I have just stated. Moreover, they constitute an additional obstacle in the process of negotiation which should lead to a peaceful solution.

Looking forward to peace negotiations, the Nine reaffirm what they have

[2] Bull. EC 6-1977, point 2.2.3.

expressed on many occasions, in that the parties to the conflict should refrain from making any declarations and adopting any measures, administrative, legal, military or other, which would constitute an obstacle to the process of peace.

Moreover, the Nine reaffirm their continuing support for Lebanon's independence and territorial integrity. They deplore that the south of the country should be the scene of bloodshed, endangering the efforts to establish peace in the Middle East, and they call upon all parties concerned to halt the fighting.

38. General Assembly Resolution 32/5 on Recent Illegal Israeli Measures in the Occupied Arab Territories Designed to Change the Legal Status, Geographic Nature and Demographic Composition of Those Territories in Contravention of the Principles of the Charter of the United Nations, of Israel's International Obligations Under the Fourth Geneva Convention of 1949 and of United Nations Resolutions, and Obstruction of Efforts Aimed at Achieving a Just and Lasting Peace in the Middle East, October 28, 1977*

---

* G.A. Res. 5, 32 U.N. GAOR Supp. (No. 45) at 13, U.N. Doc. A/32/45 (1977).

The General Assembly,

Stressing the urgent need to achieve a just and lasting peace in the Middle East,

Expressing grave anxiety and concern over the present serious situation in the occupied Arab territories as a result of the continued Israeli occupation and the measures and actions taken by the Government of Israel, as the occupying Power, and designed to change the legal status, geographical nature and demographic composition of those territories,

Considering that the Geneva Convention relative to the Protection of Civilian Persons in Time of War, of 12 August 1949,[6] is applicable to all the Arab territories occupied since 5 June 1967,

1. *Determines* that all such measures and actions taken by Israel in the Palestinian and other Arab territories occupied since 1967 have no legal validity and constitute a serious obstruction of efforts aimed at achieving a just and lasting peace in the Middle East;

2. *Strongly deplores* the persistence of Israel in carrying out such measures, in particular the establishment of settlements in the occupied Arab territories;

3. *Calls upon* Israel to comply strictly with its international obligations in accordance with the principles of international law and the provisions of the Geneva Convention relative to the Protection of Civilian Persons in Time of War, of 12 August 1949;

4. *Calls once more upon* the Government of Israel, as the occupying Power, to desist forthwith from taking any action which would result in changing the legal status, geographical nature or demographic composition of the Arab territories occupied since 1967, including Jerusalem;

5. *Urges* all States parties to the Geneva Convention relative to the Protection of Civilian Persons in Time of War to ensure respect for and compliance with its provisions in all the Arab territories occupied by Israel since 1967, including Jerusalem;

6. *Requests* the Secretary-General:

(*a*) To undertake urgent contacts with the Government of Israel to ensure the prompt implementation of the present resolution;

(*b*) To submit a report to the General Assembly and the Security Council, not later than 31 December 1977, on the results of his contacts;

7. *Requests* the Security Council to review the situation in the light of the present resolution and of the report of the Secretary-General.

52nd plenary meeting
28 October 1977

---

[6] United Nations, *Treaty Series*, vol. 75, No. 973, p. 287.

39. General Assembly Resolution 32/20 on the Situation in the Middle East, November 25, 1977*

* G.A. Res. 20, 32 U.N. GAOR Supp. (No. 45) at 23, U.N. Doc. A/32/45 (1977).

The General Assembly,

Having discussed the item entitled "The situation in the Middle East",

Recalling its previous resolutions on the subject, in particular resolutions 3414 (XXX) of 5 December 1975 and 31/61 of 9 December 1976,

Taking into account the decisions of the Fifth Conference of Heads of State or Government of Non-Aligned Countries, held at Colombo from 16 to 19 August 1976, concerning the situation in the Middle East and the question of Palestine,[42]

Deeply concerned that the Arab territories occupied since 1967 have continued, for more than ten years, to be under illegal Israeli occupation and that the Palestinian people, after three decades, are still deprived of the exercise of their inalienable national rights,

Reaffirming that the acquisition of territory by force is inadmissible and that all territories thus occupied must be returned,

Reaffirming also the urgent necessity of the establishment of a just and lasting peace in the region, based on full respect for the purposes and principles of the Charter of the United Nations as well as for its resolutions concerning the problem of the Middle East including the question of Palestine,

Taking note with satisfaction of the joint statement on the Middle East issued on 1 October 1977 by the Minister for Foreign Affairs of the Union of Soviet Socialist Republics and the Secretary of State of the United States of America in their capacities as Co-Chairmen of the Peace Conference on the Middle East,

Reaffirming that peace is indivisible and that a just and lasting settlement of the Middle East problem must be based on a comprehensive solution, under the auspices of the United Nations, which takes into account all aspects of the Arab-Israeli conflict, in particular the attainment by the Palestinian people of all their inalienable national rights and the Israeli withdrawal from all the occupied Arab territories,

Convinced that the early convening of the Peace Conference on the Middle East with the participation of all parties concerned, including the Palestine Liberation Organization, in accordance with relevant resolutions of the General Assembly, is essential for the realization of a just and lasting settlement in the region,

1. *Condemns* Israel's continued occupation of Arab territories, in violation of the Charter of the United Nations, the principles of international law and repeated resolutions of the United Nations;

2. *Reaffirms* that a just and lasting peace in the Middle East, in which all countries and peoples in the region can live in peace and security within recognized and secure boundaries, cannot be achieved without Israel's withdrawal from all Arab territories occupied since 5 June 1967 and the attainment by the Palestinian people of their inalienable national rights;

[42] See A/31/197.

3. *Calls anew* for the early convening of the Peace Conference on the Middle East, under the auspices of the United Nations and the co-chairmanship of the Union of Soviet Socialist Republics and the United States of America, with the participation on an equal footing of all parties concerned, including the Palestine Liberation Organization;

4. *Urges* the parties to the conflict and all other interested parties to work towards the achievement of a comprehensive settlement covering all aspects of the problems and worked out with the participation of all parties concerned within the framework of the United Nations;

5. *Requests* the Security Council, in the exercise of its responsibilities under the Charter, to take all necessary measures in order to ensure the implementation of relevant resolutions of the United Nations and to facilitate the achievement of such a comprehensive settlement aiming at the establishment of a just and lasting peace in the region;

6. *Requests* the Secretary-General to follow up the implementation of the present resolution and to inform all concerned, including the Co-Chairmen of the Peace Conference on the Middle East;

7. *Also requests* the Secretary-General to report to the Security Council periodically on the development of the situation and to submit to the General Assembly at its thirty-third session a comprehensive report covering, in all their aspects, the developments in the Middle East.

82nd plenary meeting
25 November 1977

40. General Assembly Resolution 32/40 on

the Question of Palestine,

December 2, 1977*

* G.A. Res. 40, 32 U.N. GAOR Supp. (No. 45) at 24, U.N. Doc. A/32/45 (1977).

A

The General Assembly,

Recalling its resolutions 3236 (XXIX) of 22 November 1974, 3376 (XXX) of 10 November 1975 and 31/20 of 24 November 1976,

Having considered the report of the Committee on the Exercise of the Inalienable Rights of the Palestinian People,[45]

Having heard the statement of the Palestine Liberation Organization, the representative of the Palestinian people,[46]

Deeply concerned that no just solution to the problem of Palestine has been achieved and that this problem therefore continues to aggravate the Middle East conflict, of which it is the core, and to endanger international peace and security,

Reaffirming that a just and lasting peace in the Middle East cannot be established without the achievement, *inter alia*, of a just solution of the problem of Palestine on the basis of the attainment of the inalienable rights of the Palestinian people, including the right of return and the right to national independence and sovereignty in Palestine, in accordance with the Charter of the United Nations,

Taking note of the resolution on the question of Palestine adopted by the Council of Ministers of the Organization of African Unity at its twenty-ninth ordinary session, held at Libreville from 23 June to 3 July 1977,[47]

Taking note of the Declaration on the situation in the Middle East and the question of Palestine adopted by the Ministers for Foreign Affairs of non-aligned countries at their extraordinary meeting in New York on 30 September 1977,[48]

Taking note also of the final communiqué of the extraordinary meeting of the Ministers for Foreign Affairs of the States members of the Islamic Conference, held in New York on 3 October 1977,[49]

1. *Expresses its appreciation* to the Committee on the Exercise of the Inalienable Rights of the Palestinian People for its efforts in performing the tasks assigned to it by the General Assembly;

2. *Takes note* of the report of the Committee and endorses the recommendations contained in paragraphs 43 and 44 of that report;

3. *Notes with satisfaction* that, during the consideration of the report of the Committee by the Security Council at its 2041st meeting, on 27 October 1977, all members of the Council who participated in the discussion reaffirmed that a just and lasting peace in the Middle East could not be estab-

---

[45] *Ibid.* [*Official Records of the General Assembly*], *Thirty-second Session, Supplement No. 35* (A/32/35).

[46] *Ibid., Thirty-second Session, Plenary Meetings,* 84th meeting, paras. 46–79.

[47] A/32/310, annex I, resolution CM/Res.580 (XXIX).

[48] A/32/255-S/12410, annex. For the printed text, see *Official Records of the Security Council, Thirty-second Year, Supplement for October, November and December 1977.*

[49] A/32/261, annex.

lished without the achievement, in particular, of a just solution of the problem of Palestine on the basis of the attainment of the inalienable rights of the Palestinian people;

4. *Urges* the Security Council to take as soon as possible a decision on the recommendations endorsed by the General Assembly in its resolution 31/20 as a basis for the solution of the problem of Palestine;

5. *Decides* to circulate the report to all the competent bodies of the United Nations and urges them to take necessary action, as appropriate, in accordance with the Committee's programme of implementation;

6. *Requests* the Secretary-General to transmit the reports of the Committee to all conferences on the Middle East held under the auspices of the United Nations, including the Geneva Peace Conference on the Middle East;

7. *Authorizes* the Committee to continue to exert all efforts to promote the implementation of its recommendations, to send delegations or representatives to international conferences where such representation would be considered by it to be appropriate, and to report thereon to the General Assembly at its thirty-third session;

8. *Further requests* the Secretary-General to continue to provide the Committee with all the necessary facilities for the performance of its tasks, including summary records of its meetings;

9. *Decides* to include the item entitled "Question of Palestine" in the provisional agenda of its thirty-third session.

91st plenary meeting
2 December 1977

B

The General Assembly,

Having considered the report of the Committee on the Exercise of the Inalienable Rights of the Palestinian People,[50]

Noting, in particular, the observations contained in paragraphs 38 to 42 of that report,

Recognizing the need for the greatest possible dissemination of information on the inalienable rights of the Palestinian people and on the efforts of the United Nations to promote the attainment of those rights,

1. *Requests* the Secretary-General to establish within the Secretariat of the United Nations a Special Unit on Palestinian Rights which would:

(a) Prepare, under the guidance of the Committee on the Exercise of the Inalienable Rights of the Palestinian People, studies and publications relating to:

   (i) The inalienable rights of the Palestinian people;

   (ii) Relevant resolutions of the General Assembly and other organs of the United Nations;

[50] *Official Records of the General Assembly, Thirty-second Session, Supplement No. 35* (A/32/35).

(iii) The activities of the Committee and other United Nations organs, in order to promote the attainment of those rights;

(*b*) Promote maximum publicity for such studies and publications through all appropriate means;

(*c*) Organize in consultation with the Committee, commencing in 1978, the annual observance of 29 November as the International Day of Solidarity with the Palestinian People;

2. *Further requests* the Secretary-General to ensure the full co-operation of the Office of Public Information and other units of the Secretariat in enabling the Special Unit on Palestinian Rights to perform its tasks;

3. *Invites* all Governments and organizations to lend their co-operation to the Committee on the Exercise of the Inalienable Rights of the Palestinian People and the Special Unit on Palestinian Rights in the implementation of the present resolution.

91st plenary meeting
2 December 1977

41. Six-Point Programme Agreed by All Palestinian Factions, Announced by Fateh Central Council Member Salah Khalaf at a Press Conference in Tripoli, December 4, 1977*

* 7 J. Palestine Stud. 188 (Spring 1978).

In the wake of Sadat's treasonous visit to the Zionist entity, all factions of the Palestinian Resistance Movement have decided to make a practical answer to this step. On this basis, they met and issued the following document:

We, all factions of the PLO, announce the following:

First: We call for the formation of a "Steadfastness and Confrontation Front" composed of Libya, Algeria, Iraq, Democratic Yemen, Syria and the PLO, to oppose all capitulationist solutions planned by imperialism, Zionism and their Arab tools.

Second: We fully condemn any Arab party in the Tripoli Summit which rejects the formation of this Front, and we announce this.

Third: We reaffirm our rejection of Security Council resolutions 242 and 338.

Fourth: We reaffirm our rejection of all international conferences based on these two resolutions, including the Geneva Conference.

Fifth: To strive for the realization of the Palestinian people's rights to return and self-determination within the context of an independent Palestinian national state on any part of Palestinian land, without reconciliation, recognition or negotiations, as an interim aim of the Palestinian Revolution.

Sixth: To apply the measures related to the political boycott of the Sadat regime.

In the name of all the factions, we ratify this unificatory document:

— The Palestinian National Liberation Movement, Fateh: Abu Ayyad [Salah Khalaf]
— The Popular Front for the Liberation of Palestine: Dr. George Habbash
— The Democratic Front for the Liberation of Palestine: Nayef Hawatmeh
— The P.F.L.P.—General Command: Ahmad Jabril
— Vanguards of the People's Liberation War, Saiqa: Zuhair Muhsin
— Arab Liberation Front: Abdul-Rahim Ahmad
— Palestinian Liberation Front: Talaat Ya'qoub
— P.L.O.: Hamed Abu-Sitta.

42. General Assembly Resolution 32/90 on the U.N. Relief and Works Agency for Palestine Refugees in the Near East, December 13, 1977*

* G.A. Res. 90, 32 U.N. GAOR Supp. (No. 45) at 66, U.N. Doc. A/32/45 (1977).

A

The General Assembly,

Recalling its resolution 31/15 A of 23 November 1976 and all previous resolutions referred to therein, including resolution 194 (III) of 11 December 1948,

Taking note of the annual report of the Commissioner-General of the United Nations Relief and Works Agency for Palestine Refugees in the Near East, covering the period from 1 July 1976 to 30 June 1977,[10]

1. *Notes with deep regret* that repatriation or compensation of the refugees as provided for in paragraph 11 of General Assembly resolution 194 (III) has not been effected, that no substantial progress has been made in the programme endorsed by the Assembly in paragraph 2 of resolution 513 (VI) of 26 January 1952 for the reintegration of refugees either by repatriation or resettlement and that, therefore, the situation of the refugees continues to be a matter of serious concern;

2. *Expresses its sincere appreciation* to Sir John Rennie, who retired this year as Commissioner-General of the United Nations Relief and Works Agency for Palestine Refugees in the Near East, for his efficient administration of the Agency and for his dedicated service to the welfare of the refugees during the past nine years;

3. *Expresses its thanks* to the Commissioner-General and to the staff of the United Nations Relief and Works Agency for Palestine Refugees in the Near East for their continued dedicated and effective efforts under difficult circumstances to provide essential services for the Palestine refugees, recognizing that the Agency is doing all it can within the limits of available resources, and also expresses its thanks to the specialized agencies and private organizations for their valuable work in assisting the refugees;

4. *Notes with regret* that the United Nations Conciliation Commission for Palestine has been unable to find a means of achieving progress in the implementation of paragraph 11 of General Assembly resolution 194 (III)[11] and requests the Commission to exert continued efforts towards the implementation of that paragraph and to report as appropriate, but no later than 1 October 1978;

5. *Directs attention* to the continuing seriousness of the financial position of the United Nations Relief and Works Agency for Palestine Refugees in the Near East, as outlined in the report of the Commissioner-General;

6. *Notes with profound concern* that, despite the commendable and successful efforts of the Commissioner-General to collect additional contributions,

[10] *Official Records of the General Assembly, Thirty-second Session, Supplement No. 13* (A/32/13 and Corr.1 and 2).

[11] For the report of the United Nations Conciliation Commission for Palestine covering the period from 1 October 1976 to 30 September 1977, see *Official Records of the General Assembly, Thirty-second Session, Annexes*, agenda item 55, document A/32/238, annex.

this increased level of income to the United Nations Relief and Works Agency for Palestine Refugees in the Near East is still insufficient to cover essential budget requirements in the present year, and that, at presently foreseen levels of giving, deficits will recur each year;

7. *Calls upon* all Governments as a matter of urgency to make the most generous efforts possible to meet the anticipated needs of the United Nations Relief and Works Agency for Palestine Refugees in the Near East, particularly in the light of the budgetary deficit projected in the report of the Commissioner-General, and therefore urges non-contributing Governments to contribute regularly and contributing Governments to consider increasing their regular contributions;

8. *Decides* to extend until 30 June 1981, without prejudice to the provisions of paragraph 11 of General Assembly resolution 194 (III), the mandate of the United Nations Relief and Works Agency for Palestine Refugees in the Near East.

101st plenary meeting
13 December 1977

B

ASSISTANCE TO PERSONS DISPLACED AS A RESULT OF THE JUNE 1967 HOSTILITIES

The General Assembly,

Recalling its resolutions 2252 (ES-V) of 4 July 1967, 2341 B (XXII) of 19 December 1967, 2452 C (XXIII) of 19 December 1968, 2535 C (XXIV) of 10 December 1969, 2672 B (XXV) of 8 December 1970, 2792 B (XXVI) of 6 December 1971, 2963 B (XXVII) of 13 December 1972, 3089 A (XXVIII) of 7 December 1973, 3331 C (XXIX) of 17 December 1974, 3419 A (XXX) of 8 December 1975 and 31/15 B of 23 November 1976,

Taking note of the annual report of the Commissioner-General of the United Nations Relief and Works Agency for Palestine Refugees in the Near East, covering the period from 1 July 1976 to 30 June 1977,[12]

Concerned about the continued human suffering resulting from the June 1967 hostilities in the Middle East,

1. *Reaffirms* its resolutions 2252 (ES-V), 2341 B (XXII), 2452 C (XXIII), 2535 C (XXIV), 2672 B (XXV), 2792 B (XXVI), 2963 B (XXVII), 3089 A (XXVIII), 3331 C (XXIX), 3419 A (XXX) and 31/15 B;

2. *Endorses*, bearing in mind the objectives of those resolutions, the efforts of the Commissioner-General of the United Nations Relief and Works Agency for Palestine Refugees in the Near East to continue to provide humanitarian assistance, as far as practicable, on an emergency basis and as a temporary measure, to other persons in the area who are at present dis-

---

[12] *Official Records of the General Assembly, Thirty-second Session, Supplement No. 13* (A/32/13 and Corr.1 and 2).

placed and in serious need of continued assistance as a result of the June 1967 hostilities;

3. *Strongly appeals* to all Governments and to organizations and individuals to contribute generously for the above purposes to the United Nations Relief and Works Agency for Palestine Refugees in the Near East and to the other intergovernmental and non-governmental organizations concerned.

101st plenary meeting
13 December 1977

C

PALESTINE REFUGEES IN THE GAZA STRIP

The General Assembly,

Recalling Security Council resolution 237 (1967) of 14 June 1967,

Recalling also its resolutions 2792 C (XXVI) of 6 December 1971, 2963 C (XXVII) of 13 December 1972, 3089 C (XXVIII) of 7 December 1973, 3331 D (XXIX) of 17 December 1974, 3419 C (XXX) of 8 December 1975 and 31/15 E of 23 November 1976,

Having considered the report of the Commissioner-General of the United Nations Relief and Works Agency for Palestine Refugees in the Near East, covering the period from 1 July 1976 to 30 June 1977,[13] and the reports of the Secretary-General of 6 and 21 October 1977,[14]

1. *Calls once more upon* Israel:

(a) To take effective steps immediately for the return of the refugees concerned to the camps from which they were removed in the Gaza Strip and to provide adequate shelters for their accommodation;

(b) To desist from further removal of refugees and destruction of their shelters;

2. *Requests* the Secretary-General, after consulting with the Commissioner-General of the United Nations Relief and Works Agency for Palestine Refugees in the Near East, to report to the General Assembly by the opening of its thirty-third session on Israel's compliance with paragraph 1 of the present resolution.

101st plenary meeting
13 December 1977

D

WORKING GROUP ON THE FINANCING OF THE UNITED NATIONS RELIEF AND
WORKS AGENCY FOR PALESTINE REFUGEES IN THE NEAR EAST

The General Assembly,

Recalling its resolutions 2656 (XXV) of 7 December 1970, 2728 (XXV) of 15 December 1970, 2791 (XXVI) of 6 December 1971, 2964 (XXVII) of 13

[13] *Ibid.*
[14] *Ibid., Thirty-second Session, Annexes*, agenda item 55, documents A/32/264 and Add.1.

December 1972, 3090 (XXVIII) of 7 December 1973, 3330 (XXIX) of 17 December 1974, 3419 D (XXX) of 8 December 1975 and 31/15 C of 23 November 1976,

Having considered the report of the Working Group on the Financing of the United Nations Relief and Works Agency for Palestine Refugees in the Near East,[15]

Taking into account the annual report of the Commissioner-General of the United Nations Relief and Works Agency for Palestine Refugees in the Near East, covering the period from 1 July 1976 to 30 June 1977,[16]

Gravely concerned at the critical financial situation of the United Nations Relief and Works Agency for Palestine Refugees in the Near East, which has already reduced the essential minimum services being provided to the Palestine refugees and which threatens even greater reductions in the future,

Emphasizing the urgent need for extraordinary efforts in order to maintain, at least at their present minimum level, the activities of the United Nations Relief and Works Agency for Palestine Refugees in the Near East,

1. *Commends* the Working Group on the Financing of the United Nations Relief and Works Agency for Palestine Refugees in the Near East for its efforts to assist in ensuring the Agency's financial security;

2. *Notes with approval* the report of the Working Group;

3. *Requests* the Working Group to continue its efforts, in co-operation with the Secretary-General and the Commissioner-General, for the financing of the United Nations Relief and Works Agency for Palestine Refugees in the Near East for a further period of one year;

4. *Requests* the Secretary-General to provide the necessary services and assistance to the Working Group for the conduct of its work.

101st plenary meeting
13 December 1977

E

POPULATION AND REFUGEES DISPLACED SINCE 1967

The General Assembly,

Recalling Security Council resolution 237 (1967) of 14 June 1967,

Recalling also its resolutions 2252 (ES-V) of 4 July 1967, 2452 A (XXIII) of 19 December 1968, 2535 B (XXIV) of 10 December 1969, 2672 D (XXV) of 8 December 1970, 2792 E (XXVI) of 6 December 1971, 2963 C and D (XXVII) of 13 December 1972, 3089 C (XXVIII) of 7 December 1973, 3331 D (XXIX) of 17 December 1974, 3419 C (XXX) of 8 December 1975 and 31/15 D of 23 November 1976,

Having considered the report of the Commissioner-General of the United Nations Relief and Works Agency for Palestine Refugees in the Near East,

---

[15] *Ibid.*, document A/32/278.
[16] *Ibid., Thirty-second Session, Supplement No. 13* (A/32/13 and Corr.1 and 2).

covering the period from 1 July 1976 to 30 June 1977,[17] and the reports of the Secretary-General of 6 and 21 October 1977,[18]

1. *Reaffirms* the right of the displaced inhabitants to return to their homes and camps in the territories occupied by Israel since 1967;

2. *Deplores* the continued refusal of the Israeli authorities to take steps for the return of the displaced inhabitants;

3. *Calls once more upon* Israel:

(*a*) To take immediate steps for the return of the displaced inhabitants:

(*b*) To desist from all measures that obstruct the return of the displaced inhabitants, including measures affecting the physical and demographic structure of the occupied territories;

4. *Requests* the Secretary-General, after consulting with the Commissioner-General of the United Nations Relief and Works Agency for Palestine Refugees in the Near East, to report to the General Assembly by the opening of its thirty-third session on Israel's compliance with paragraph 3 of the present resolution.

101st plenary meeting
13 December 1977

F

OFFERS BY MEMBER STATES OF GRANTS AND SCHOLARSHIPS FOR HIGHER
EDUCATION, INCLUDING VOCATIONAL TRAINING, FOR THE PALESTINE REFUGEES

The General Assembly,

Recalling its resolution 212 (III) of 19 November 1948 on assistance to Palestine refugees,

Cognizant of the fact that the Palestinian refugees have, for the last three decades, lost their lands and means of livelihood,

Having examined with appreciation the report of the Commissioner-General of the United Nations Relief and Works Agency for Palestine Refugees in the Near East, covering the period from 1 July 1976 to 30 June 1977,[19]

Noting that less than one per thousand of the Palestinian refugee students has the chance to continue higher education, including vocational training,

Noting also that over the past five years the number of scholarships offered by the United Nations Relief and Works Agency for Palestine Refugees in the Near East has dwindled to half of what it was because of the Agency's regular budgetary difficulties,

1. *Expresses its appreciation* to those Member States which have provided scholarships to Palestinian refugees;

2. *Appeals* to all States to make special allocations, scholarships and grants to Palestinian refugees, in addition to their contributions to the regular bud-

---

[17] *Ibid.*
[18] *Ibid., Thirty-second Session, Annexes*, agenda item 55, documents A/32/264 and Add.1.
[19] *Ibid., Thirty-second Session, Supplement No. 13* (A/32/13 and Corr.1 and 2).

get of the United Nations Relief and Works Agency for Palestine Refugees in the Near East;

3. *Invites* relevant United Nations agencies to consider the inclusion, within their respective spheres of competence, of assistance for higher education for Palestinian refugee students;

4. *Requests* the United Nations Relief and Works Agency for Palestine Refugees in the Near East to act as recipient and trustee for such special allocations and scholarships and to award them to qualified Palestinian refugee candidates;

5. *Requests* the Secretary-General to report to the General Assembly at its thirty-third session on the implementation of the present resolution.

101st plenary meeting
13 December 1977

43. General Assembly Resolution 32/91 on the Report of
the Special Committee to Investigate Israeli Practices
Affecting the Human Rights of the Population of the
Occupied Territories, December 13, 1977*

* G.A. Res. 91, 32 U.N. GAOR Supp. (No. 45) at 69, U.N. Doc. A/32/45
(1977).

A

The General Assembly,

Recalling its resolutions 3092 A (XXVIII) of 7 December 1973, 3240 B (XXIX) of 29 November 1974, 3525 B (XXX) of 15 December 1975 and 31/106 B of 16 December 1976,

Considering that the promotion of respect for the obligations arising from the Charter of the United Nations and other instruments and rules of international law is among the basic purposes and principles of the United Nations,

Bearing in mind the provisions of the Geneva Convention relative to the Protection of Civilian Persons in Time of War, of 12 August 1949,[20]

Noting that Israel and those Arab States whose territories have been occupied by Israel since June 1967 are parties to that Convention,

Taking into account that States parties to that Convention undertake, in accordance with article 1 thereof, not only to respect but also to ensure respect for the Convention in all circumstances,

1. *Reaffirms* that the Geneva Convention relative to the Protection of Civilian Persons in Time of War, of 12 August 1949, is applicable to all the Arab territories occupied by Israel since 1967, including Jerusalem;

2. *Strongly deplores* the failure of Israel to acknowledge the applicability of that Convention to the territories it has occupied since 1967;

3. *Calls again upon* Israel to acknowledge and to comply with the provisions of that Convention in all the Arab territories it has occupied since 1967, including Jerusalem;

4. *Urges once more* all States parties to that Convention to exert all efforts in order to ensure respect for and compliance with the provisions thereof in all the Arab territories occupied by Israel since 1967, including Jerusalem.

101st plenary meeting
13 December 1977

B

The General Assembly,

Recalling its resolutions 3240 C (XXIX) of 29 November 1974, 3525 C (XXX) of 15 December 1975 and 31/106 D of 16 December 1976,

Having considered the report of the Special Committee to Investigate Israeli Practices Affecting the Human Rights of the Population of the Occupied Territories,[21] in particular annex II thereof, entitled "Report on damage at Quneitra", a report on the nature, extent and value of damage, submitted by a Swiss expert engaged by the Special Committee,

1. *Expresses its appreciation* of the thoroughness and impartiality with which

---

[20] United Nations, *Treaty Series*, vol. 75, No. 973, p. 287.
[21] A/32/284.

the expert engaged by the Special Committee to Investigate Israeli Practices Affecting the Human Rights of the Population of the Occupied Territories discharged the tasks entrusted to him;

2. *Condemns* the massive, deliberate destruction of Quneitra perpetrated during the Israeli occupation and prior to the withdrawal of Israeli forces from that city in 1974;

3. *Reaffirms* that the Syrian Arab Republic is entitled to full and adequate compensation, under international law and in equity, for the massive damage and deliberate destruction perpetrated in Quneitra while it was under Israeli occupation, and to all other legal remedies in accordance with applicable international law and practice;

4. *Takes note* of the statements made by the representative of the Syrian Arab Republic before the Special Political Committee at the thirty-first[22] and thirty-second[23] sessions of the General Assembly to the effect that his Government reserves all rights to full compensation in regard to all damages resulting from Israel's deliberate destruction of Quneitra, including those not covered by the expert's above-mentioned report or not falling within the scope of his assignment;

5. *Requests* the Special Committee to complete its survey on all the aspects referred to in paragraph 4 of the present resolution and to report thereon to the General Assembly at its thirty-third session;

6. *Requests* the Secretary-General to provide the Special Committee with all the facilities required for the completion of the tasks referred to in the previous paragraphs.

101st plenary meeting
13 December 1977

C

The General Assembly,

Guided by the purposes and principles of the Charter of the United Nations as well as the principles and provisions of the Universal Declaration of Human Rights,

Bearing in mind the provisions of the Geneva Convention relative to the Protection of Civilian Persons in Time of War, of 12 August 1949,[24] as well as of other relevant conventions and regulations,

Recalling its resolutions on the subject, as well as those adopted by the Security Council, the Commission on Human Rights and other United Nations bodies concerned and by the specialized agencies,

Having considered the report of the Special Committee to Investigate Israeli Practices Affecting the Human Rights of the Population of the Occu-

---

[22] *Official Records of the General Assembly, Thirty-second Session, Special Political Committee,* 30th meeting, para. 12.

[23] *Ibid.,* 34th meeting, paras. 7-10.

[24] United Nations, *Treaty Series,* vol. 75, No. 973, p. 287.

pied Territories,[25] which contains, *inter alia*, public statements made by leaders of the Government of Israel,

1. *Commends* the Special Committee to Investigate Israeli Practices Affecting the Human Rights of the Population of the Occupied Territories for its efforts in performing the tasks assigned to it by the General Assembly;

2. *Deplores* the continued refusal by Israel to allow the Special Committee access to the occupied territories;

3. *Calls again upon* Israel to allow the Special Committee access to the occupied territories;

4. *Deplores* the continued and persistent violation by Israel of the Geneva Convention relative to the Protection of Civilian Persons in Time of War, of 12 August 1949, and other applicable international instruments, and condemns in particular those violations which that Convention designates as "grave breaches" thereof;

5. *Condemns* the following Israeli policies and practices:

(a) The annexation of parts of the occupied territories;

(b) The establishment of Israeli settlements therein and the transfer of an alien population thereto;

(c) The evacuation, deportation, expulsion, displacement and transfer of Arab inhabitants of the occupied territories, and the denial of their right to return;

(d) The confiscation and expropriation of Arab property in the occupied territories and all other transactions for the acquisition of land involving the Israeli authorities, institutions or nationals on the one hand, and the inhabitants or institutions of the occupied territories on the other;

(e) The destruction and demolition of Arab houses;

(f) Mass arrests, administrative detention and ill-treatment of the Arab population;

(g) The ill-treatment and torture of persons under detention;

(h) The pillaging of archaeological and cultural property;

(i) The interference with religious freedoms and practices as well as with family rights and customs;

(j) The illegal exploitation of the natural wealth, resources and population of the occupied territories;

6. *Reaffirms* that all measures taken by Israel to change the physical character, demographic composition, institutional structure or status of the occupied territories, or any part thereof, including Jerusalem, are null and void, and that Israel's policy of settling parts of its population and new immigrants in the occupied territories constitutes a flagrant violation of the Geneva Convention relative to the Protection of Civilian Persons in Time of War and of the relevant United Nations resolutions;

7. *Demands* that Israel desist forthwith from the policies and practices referred to in paragraphs 5 and 6 of the present resolution;

[25] A/32/284.

8. *Reiterates* its call upon all States, in particular those States parties to the Geneva Convention relative to the Protection of Civilian Persons in Time of War, in accordance with article 1 of that Convention, and upon international organizations and specialized agencies not to recognize any changes carried out by Israel in the occupied territories and to avoid actions, including those in the field of aid, which might be used by Israel in its pursuit of the policies of annexation and colonization or any of the other policies and practices referred to in the present resolution;

9. *Requests* the Special Committee, pending the early termination of the Israeli occupation, to continue to investigate Israel policies and practices in the Arab territories occupied by Israel since 1967, to consult, as appropriate, with the International Committee of the Red Cross in order to ensure the safeguarding of the welfare and human rights of the population of the occupied territories, and to report to the Secretary-General as soon as possible and whenever the need arises thereafter;

10. *Requests* the Special Committee to continue to investigate the treatment of civilians in detention in the Arab territories occupied by Israel since 1967 and to submit to the Secretary-General a special report on that subject as soon as possible and whenever the need arises thereafter;

11. *Requests* the Secretary-General:

(*a*) To render all necessary facilities to the Special Committee, including those required for its visits to the occupied territories, with a view to investigating the Israeli policies and practices referred to in the present resolution;

(*b*) To continue to make available additional staff as may be necessary to assist the Special Committee in the performance of its tasks;

(*c*) To ensure the widest circulation of the reports of the Special Committee, and of information regarding its activities and findings, by all means available through the Office of Public Information of the Secretariat and, where necessary, to reprint those reports of the Special Committee which are no longer available;

(*d*) To report to the General Assembly at its thirty-third session on the tasks entrusted to him in the present paragraph;

12. *Decides* to include in the provisional agenda of its thirty-third session the item entitled "Report of the Special Committee to Investigate Israeli Practices Affecting the Human Rights of the Population of the Occupied Territories".

101st plenary meeting
13 December 1977

44. State Department Legal Advisor's Letter to the Congress Concerning the Legality of Israeli Settlements in the Occupied Territories, April 21, 1978*

* U.S. Congress, House of Representatives, Committee Print, *Israeli Settlements in the Occupied Territories*, Hearings Before the Subcommittee on International Organizations and on Europe and the Middle East 167–72 (Washington, D.C.: GPO, 1978), *reprinted in* 17 Int'l Legal Materials 777 (1978).

Dear Chairmen Fraser and Hamilton:

Secretary Vance has asked me to reply to your request for a statement of legal considerations underlying the United States view that the establishment of the Israeli civilian settlements in the territories occupied by Israel is inconsistent with international law. Accordingly, I am providing the following in response to that request:

The Territories Involved

The Sinai Peninsula, Gaza, the West Bank and the Golan Heights were ruled by the Ottoman Empire before World War I. Following World War I, Sinai was part of Egypt; the Gaza Strip and the West Bank (as well as the area east of the Jordan) were part of the British Mandate for Palestine; and the Golan Heights were part of the French Mandate for Syria. Syria and Jordan later became independent. The West Bank and Gaza continued under British Mandate until May, 1948.

The Honorable
 Donald M. Fraser, Chairman
  Subcommittee on International
   Organizations,
    Committee on International Relations
     House of Representatives.

The Honorable
 Lee H. Hamilton, Chairman
  Subcommittee on Europe and the
   Middle East,
    Committee on International Relations,
     House of Representatives.

In 1947, the United Nations recommended a plan of partition, never effectuated, that allocated some territory to a Jewish state and other territory (including the West Bank and Gaza) to an Arab state. On May 14, 1948, immediately prior to British termination of the Mandate, a provisional government of Israel proclaimed the establishment of a Jewish state in the areas allocated to it under the partition plan. The Arab League rejected partition and commenced hostilities. When the hostilities ceased, Egypt occupied Gaza, and Jordan occupied the West Bank. These territorial lines of demarcation were incorporated, with minor changes, in the armistice agreements concluded in 1949. The armistice agreements expressly denied political significance to the new lines, but they were de facto boundaries until June, 1967.

During the June, 1967 war, Israeli forces occupied Gaza, the Sinai Peninsula, the West Bank and the Golan Heights. Egypt regained some territory in Sinai during the October, 1973 war and in subsequent disengagement agreements, but Israeli control of the other occupied territories was not af-

fected, except for minor changes on the Golan Heights through a disengagement agreement with Syria.

The Settlements

Some seventy-five Israeli settlements have been established in the above
territories (excluding military camps on the West Bank into which small
groups of civilians have recently moved). Israel established its first settlements in the occupied territories in 1967 as para-military "nahals". A number of "nahals" have become civilian settlements as they have become economically viable.

Israel began establishing civilian settlements in 1968. Civilian settlements
are supported by the government, and also by non-governmental settlement
movements affiliated in most cases with political parties. Most are reportedly
built on public lands outside the boundaries of any municipality, but some
are built on private or municipal lands expropriated for the purpose.

Legal Considerations

1. As noted above, Israeli armed forces entered Gaza, the West Bank,
Sinai and the Golan Heights in June, 1967, in the course of an armed conflict. Those areas had not previously been part of Israel's sovereign territory
nor otherwise under its administration. By reason of such entry of its armed
forces, Israel established control and began to exercise authority over these
territories; and under international law, Israel thus became a belligerent occupant of these territories.

Territory coming under the control of a belligerent occupant does not
thereby become its sovereign territory. International law confers upon the
occupying state authority to undertake interim military administration over
the territory and its inhabitants; that authority is not unlimited. The governing rules are designed to permit pursuit of its military needs by the occupying power, to protect the security of the occupying forces, to provide
for orderly government, to protect the rights and interests of the inhabitants and to reserve questions of territorial change and sovereignty to a later
stage when the war is ended. See L. Oppenheim, 2 International Law 432-
438 (7th ed., H. Lauterpacht ed., 1952); E. Feilchenfeld, The International
Economic Law of Belligerent Occupation 4-5, 11-12, 15-17, 87 (1942);
M. McDougal & F. Feliciano, Law and Minimum World Public Order 734-
46, 751-7 (1961); Regulations annexed to the 1907 Hague Convention on
the Laws and Customs of War on Land, Articles 42-56, 1 Bevans 643; Department of the Army, The Law of Land Warfare, Chapter 6 (1956) (FM-
27-10).

In positive terms, and broadly stated, the Occupant's powers are (1) to
continue orderly government, (2) to exercise control over and utilize
the resources of the country so far as necessary for that purpose and to

meet his own military needs. He may thus, under the latter head, apply its resources to his own military objects, claim services from the inhabitants, use, requisition, seize or destroy their property, within the limits of what is required for the army of occupation and the needs of the local population. But beyond the limits of quality, quantum and duration thus implied, the Occupant's acts will not have legal effect, although they may in fact be unchallengeable until the territory is liberated. He is not entitled to treat the country as his own territory or its inhabitants as his own subjects, . . . and over a wide range of public property, he can confer rights only as against himself, and within his own limited period of *de facto* rule. J. Stone, Legal Controls of International Conflict, 697 (1959).

On the basis of the available information, the civilian settlements in the territories occupied by Israel do not appear to be consistent with these limits on Israel's authority as belligerent occupant in that they do not seem intended to be of limited duration or established to provide orderly government of the territories and, though some may serve incidental security purposes, they do not appear to be required to meet military needs during the occupation.

2. Article 49 of the Fourth Geneva Convention relative to the Protection of Civilian Persons in Time of War, August 12, 1949, 6 UST 3516, provides, in paragraph 6:

The Occupying Power shall not deport or transfer parts of its own civilian population into the territory it occupies.

Paragraph 6 appears to apply by its terms to any transfer by an occupying power of parts of its civilian population, whatever the objective and whether involuntary or voluntary.* It seems clearly to reach such involvements of the occupying power as determining the location of settlements, making land available and financing of settlements, as well as other kinds of assistance and participation in their creation. And the paragraph appears applicable whether or not harm is done by a particular transfer. The language and history of the provision lead to the conclusion that transfers of a belligerent occupant's civilian population into occupied territory are broadly proscribed as beyond the scope of interim military administration.

The view has been advanced that a transfer is prohibited under paragraph 6 only to the extent that it involves the displacement of the local population. Although one respected authority, Lauterpacht, evidently took this view, it is otherwise unsupported in the literature, in the rules of international law or in the language and negotiating history of the Convention, and it clearly seems not correct. Displacement of protected persons is dealt with separately in the Convention and paragraph 6 would be redundant if lim-

---

* Paragraph 1 of Article 49, prohibits "forcible" transfers of protected persons out of occupied territory; paragraph 6 is not so limited.

ited to cases of displacement. Another view of paragraph 6 is that it is directed against mass population transfers such as occurred in World War II for political, racial or colonization ends; but there is no apparent support or reason for limiting its application to such cases.

The Israeli civilian settlements thus appear to constitute a "transfer of parts of its own civilian population into the territory it occupies" within the scope of paragraph 6.

3. Under Article 6 of the Fourth Geneva Convention, paragraph 6 of Article 49 would cease to be applicable to Israel in the territories occupied by it if and when it discontinues the exercise of governmental functions in those territories. The laws of belligerent occupation generally would continue to apply with respect to particular occupied territory until Israel leaves it or the war ends between Israel and its neighbors concerned with the particular territory. The war can end in many ways, including by express agreement or by de facto acceptance of the status quo by the belligerents.

4. It has been suggested that the principles of belligerent occupation, including Article 49, paragraph 6, of the Fourth Geneva Convention, may not apply in the West Bank and Gaza because Jordan and Egypt were not the respective legitimate sovereigns of these territories. However, those principles appear applicable whether or not Jordan and Egypt possessed legitimate sovereign rights in respect of those territories. Protecting the reversionary interest of an ousted sovereign is not their sole or essential purpose; the paramount purposes are protecting the civilian population of an occupied territory and reserving permanent territorial changes, if any, until settlement of the conflict. The Fourth Geneva Convention, to which Israel, Egypt and Jordan are parties, binds signatories with respect to their territories and the territory of other contracting parties, and "in all circumstances" (Article 1), in "all cases" of armed conflict among them (Article 2) and with respect to all persons who "in any manner whatsoever" find themselves under the control of a party of which they are not nationals (Article 4).

Conclusion

While Israel may undertake, in the occupied territories, actions necessary to meet its military needs and to provide for orderly government during the occupation, for the reasons indicated above the establishment of the civilian settlements in those territories is inconsistent with international law.

Very truly yours,
Herbert J. Hansell

H. Natural Resources in the Occupied Territories

45. General Assembly Resolution 3516 (XXX) on Permanent Sovereignty Over National Resources in the Occupied Arab Territories, December 15, 1975*

---

* G.A. Res. 3516 (XXX), 30 U.N. GAOR Supp. (No. 34) at 70, U.N. Doc. A/10034 (1975).

The General Assembly,

Recalling its resolution 3336 (XXIX) of 17 December 1974, entitled "Permanent sovereignty over national resources in the occupied Arab territories", in paragraph 5 of which it requested the Secretary-General, with the assistance of relevant specialized agencies and United Nations organs, including the United Nations Conference on Trade and Development, to prepare a report on the adverse economic effects on the Arab States and peoples resulting from repeated Israeli aggression and continued occupation of their territories,

Recalling the statement, made at the twenty-ninth session of the General Assembly[86] on behalf of the co-sponsors in introducing the revised draft resolution,[87] underlining the need to seek the assistance of relevant United Nations organizations in preparing the report requested of the Secretary-General, as these organizations had the machinery needed to carry out studies and research which would be useful in preparing the report,

Recalling further the statements on administrative and financial implications submitted by the Secretary-General[88] in which he proposed that the report would be prepared on the basis of inquiries from and visits to the States concerned and consultations with the relevant specialized agencies and United Nations organs, including the United Nations Conference on Trade and Development,

Recalling also that, in his two statements, the Secretary-General indicated that a large part of the work involved would be carried out in co-operation with the Economic Commission for Western Asia, and that the Commission would require four economists, appointed for six months each, and General Service secretarial support as well as travel funds for the preparation of the report,

Noting that, in view of the staffing proposals for the Economic Commission for Western Asia, the Advisory Committee on Administrative and Budgetary Questions recommended[89] an additional provision in the amount of $37,000 to cover the cost of two economists only for a period of six months each and that the General Assembly approved this additional appropriation to supplement the staff and resources of the Commission in the work involved in the preparation of the report,

Noting also that the report of the Secretary-General[90] was not prepared in conformity with paragraph 5 of General Assembly resolution 3336 (XXIX), the related statements made on behalf of the co-sponsors and by the Secretary-General, and the administrative and financial implications and provi-

---

[86] See *Official Records of the General Assembly, Twenty-ninth Session, Second Committee,* 1635th meeting.

[87] A/C.2/L.1372/Rev.1.

[88] A/C.2/L.1385, A/C.5/1649.

[89] *Official Records of the General Assembly, Twenty-ninth Session, Annexes,* agenda item 73, document A/9978/Add.1, para. 4.

[90] A/10290 and Add.2.

sions approved by the Assembly, but contained only annexes setting forth information available to Governments and to some of the relevant specialized agencies and United Nations organs which were not involved in the preparation of substantive studies related to the report,

1. *Notes* that the report of the Secretary-General is inadequate as it did not incorporate the necessary substantive and comprehensive studies required in conformity with paragraph 5 of General Assembly resolution 3336 (XXIX) and related documents, including the record of the meeting of the Second Committee,[86] the statements on administrative and financial implications[88] and the recommendation of the Advisory Committee on Administrative and Budgetary Questions;[89]

2. *Requests* the heads of the relevant specialized agencies and United Nations organs, particularly the United Nations Conference on Trade and Development and the Economic Commission for Western Asia, to co-operate actively and adequately with the Secretary-General in the preparation of a final comprehensive report;

3. *Requests* the Secretary-General to submit to the General Assembly at its thirty-first session his final comprehensive report, which should fulfil the above-mentioned requirements.

2441st plenary meeting
15 December 1975

46. State Department Memorandum of Law on Israel's Right to Develop New Oil Fields in Sinai and the Gulf of Suez, October 1, 1976*

* U.S. Department of State Memorandum dated October 1, 1976, *reprinted in* 16 Int'l Legal Materials 733 (1977).

This memorandum addresses the question of Israel's right to develop new oil fields in Sinai and the Gulf of Suez.

The question is addressed in light of the following understanding of the Israeli legal position (which does not, necessarily, constitute the considered legal view of the Israeli government): Oil in the ground is public immovable property subject to Article 55 of the Hague Regulations of 1907. The Occupant has usufructory rights to such property. The law of usufruct, while prohibiting waste of excessive extraction, permits the reasonable operation of old wells and new. In fact, searching for and discovering new oil deposits is an enhancement of the land's value, and thus not prohibited waste. The Occupant may grant commercial concessions to develop and exploit new wells, but the absent sovereign may not do so during the occupation. There is a twelve mile territorial sea in the Gulf of Suez in which, at least out to the median line, where this is less than twelve miles from shore, the Occupant has the same rights of military occupation as on shore.

The memorandum concludes that Israel's oil development plans in Sinai and the Gulf of Suez are contrary to international law, even if the latter area were "occupied territory". An occupant's rights under international law do not include the right to develop a new oil field, to use the oil resources of occupied territory for the general benefit of the home economy or to grant oil concessions. Further, Israel must respect the oil concessions held by Amoco in the Gulf of Suez all of which are valid, whether granted before or after June 1967.

1. *An occupier has those limited military rights regarding property set out in the Hague Regulations.*

An occupier does not acquire the rights of a sovereign in occupied territory, but only those limited military rights allowed to him under the international law of belligerent occupation.[1] Those rights with regard to property in occupied territory are spelled out in the Hague Regulations of 1907, which are still universally accepted as the codification of existing international law on the subject.[2]

---

[1] See, E.H. Feilchenfeld, *The International Economic Law of Occupation* (1942) p. 817: "The textbooks are agreed that an occupant is not a sovereign." Feilchenfeld cites, C.C. Hyde, *International Law, Chiefly as Interpreted and Applied by the United States,* (1922) p. 362; Oppenheim, 5th Edition, p. 345; F. von Liszt, *Das Voelkerrecht systematisch dargestellt,* (1898), p. 228; and P. Fauchille, *Traite de droit international public,* (1921), Tome II, Guerre et Neutralite, p. 215. As Fauchille puts it, [f]or as long as the war lasts, the invader is not juridically substituted for the legal government. He is not the sovereign of the territory. His powers are limited to the necessities of the war" (Fauchille, p. 218, informally translated). See also, Oppenheim's *International Law,* Lauterpacht ed., 7th Edition, Vol. II, pp. 432-434, hereafter cited as Oppenheim.

[2] See, e.g., *Judgment of the International Military Tribunal, Nuernberg,* 1 *Trial of the Major War Criminals* 253-54 (1947); *U.S. v. Von Leeb,* 11 *Trials of War Criminals Before the Nuernberg Military Tribunals Under Control Council Law No. 1,* at 533; Oppenheim (7th), Vol. II, pp. 234-35 and 397-415; Property in occupied territories must be disposed of "according

2. *The occupant's right to state-owned oil in the ground is that of a usufructuary under Article 55 and does not include the right to open new oil fields.*

Oil in the ground is classified as an 'immovable' as are appurtenances to real estate generally.[3] Under Egyptian law, it is public property of the state,[4] although this would not preclude the creation of private rights regarding such oil through a concession granted by the sovereign. Publicists, courts and military manuals dealing with the law of land warfare treat the subject of immovable public property as regulated by Article 55 of the Hague Regulations,[5] which provides:

> The occupying State shall be regarded only as administrator and usufructuary of public buildings, real estate, forests, and agricultural estates belonging to the hostile State, and situated in the occupied country. It must safeguard the capital of these properties, and administer them in accordance with the rules of usufruct.

There is little in the negotiating history of this Article to indicate just what its drafters meant by it, but rules of usufruct in civil law countries and of the common law analogue, life tenancy and waste, as well as international practice regarding public enemy property give the Article definition. The right of a usufructuary is, literally, the right to use the fruits of the property—not the broader right of ownership.[6] The civil law tradition generally recognizes a usufructuary's right to continue, at the previous rate of exploitation, to work mines that had already been opened by the owner at the time the usufruct began.[7] The usufructuary may not open new mines and exploit them, even at a reasonable rate.[8] This position is supported in common law

---

to the strict rules laid down in the Hague Regulations" *U.S. v. Krupp*, 9 *Trials of War Criminals Before the Nuernberg Tribunals* 1341; The taking of property "must be judged by reference exclusively to the Hague Regulations", E. Lauterpacht, *The Hague Regulations and the Seizure of Munitions de Guerre*, 32 Brit. Y.B. Int'l L. 218, 220 (1955).

[3] C.P. Sherman, *Roman Law in the Modern World*, (1937) p. 142; E.R. Cummings, "Oil Resources in Occupied Arab Territories Under the Law of Belligerent Occupation", 9 *The Journal of Int'l Law and Econ.* 533, 557-558.

[4] S. Siksek, *The Legal Framework for Oil Concessions in the Arab World*, 9, 11 (1960).

[5] Oppenheim, p. 397; Department of the Army Field Manual, *The Law of Land Warfare*, FM 27-10, p. 151; Cummings, pp. 558-559.

[6] Department of the Army, *International Law*, (1962) Vol. II, p. 183.

[7] Some civil code jurisdictions have not adopted even this permissive a rule and prohibit exploitation by a usufructuary of already operating mines, unless expressly authorized by the deed creating the usufruct. See, for example, Mexico, Article 1001; Puerto Rico, Article 1516; and Spain, Article 476. Spain, however, provides a limited exception, in Article 477, for operating existing mines on a profit-sharing basis with the owner.

[8] The French Civil Code, Article 598, for example, provides: "He also has the use, in the same manner as the owner, of mines and quarries which are being exploited at the beginning of the usufruct; and, nevertheless, if the exploitation is one which requires a concession, the usufructuary can only enjoy it after having obtained the permission of the King (President of the Republic).

"He has no right to unopened mines and quarries nor to peat-bogs which have not

countries by the prohibition of "waste" under a life tenancy. Under the doctrine, a life tenant ordinarily is not entitled to extract oil, gas or other minerals since that depletes the corpus or inheritance and, thus, constitutes waste.[9] To continue working open mines or pits, however, is recognized as an exception of the prohibition, for, as Blackstone states, "it has now become the mere annual profit of the land."

While the majority rule appears to be that set out above, there are some more permissive exceptions; the German civil code, although somewhat obscure, seems to allow the usufructuary a freer hand than the French does to open new mines, as long as opening them does not change the economic dedication of the property and the exploitation is at a reasonable rate (Art. 1037). Even within the German tradition it is apparent that opening new mines (or wells) in areas where there has never before been mineral exploitation constitutes a change in the economic dedication of the land. Thus, even that most permissive rule would not appear to accord Israel the right to make oil fields of lands and waters that Egypt was not using for that purpose when the occupation began. Further, the German system provides safeguards which allow an owner to require that exploitation by a usufructuary follow either an agreed plan or one established by a court. These safeguards are not available in an occupation situation. Modified by being stripped of these safeguards, the German rule would provide less protection for property than any known civil law system. Such a modified and novel rule cannot be deemed to represent the intended and proper meaning of Article 55.

It should be noted that there are more restrictive regimes than the French which might be advanced with some justification as the proper rule, since they are more consistent with the basic duty of a usufructuary to preserve the property's capital.[10] If any particular minority rule is to be applied it might logically be that of the Egyptian code, which is derived from the French, but differs in not providing for any usufructuary right to the minerals in the land. Its silence on the subject gives a more restrictive result than any of the other rules cited, since it is a reflection of the fact that mineral rights do not belong to the private landowner, but rather to the Egyptian state, and thus are not among the rights which a usufructuary of land can acquire in Egypt.

Equally important, the text of Article 55 and the international practice

---

begun to be exploited nor to treasure which might be discovered during the period of the usufruct." (Informal translation.) A partial survey shows similar express provisions are found in the civil codes of Argentina, Article 2900; Belgium, Article 598; Italy, Article 987; Louisiana, Article 552; and the Netherlands, Article 823. See also, G. Pugliese, "On Roman Usufruct", 40 Tulane L. Rev. 523, 546-47; Sherman, C.P., *Roman Law in the Modern World*, (1937) p. 165.

[9] E. Kuntz, *A Treatise on the Law of Oil and Gas*, p. 168 (1962). Blackstone, *Commentaries on the Laws of England*, Book 2, Ch. 18.

[10] See footnote 7 above.

under it indicate that the international law of usufruct under Article 55 is at most as liberal as the law of usufruct under the French code and the law of waste in the common law system.

First, there is the emphasis of the text itself. The Article says not only that the occupant must abide by the rules of usufruct, but, independently of that obligation, it states that he "must safeguard the capital of these properties". Resources such as oil deposits, which are irreplaceable and have value only as they are consumed, cannot be used without impairing the capital of oil bearing land. While the French and similar codes, as well as the common law, have made an illogical compromise in considering the continued operation of existing wells as a permitted annual fruit or profit, the separate emphasis in Article 55 on the occupant's duty to safeguard the capital of the property precludes any rule which provides even less protection for that capital than the French or common law interpretations.

Second, the continued recognition of a usufructuary right to operate existing mines is one which appears to be limited, at least in international law, by the requirement of exploitation at normal or pre-existing levels.[11] Taking consumables at the rate established previously might be viewed as taking a fruit or annual profit of the land; or from another perspective a prior rate might be viewed as a standard established by the owner himself regarding the conservation of the value, or capital, of the particular piece of land. Under either view, an occupant may not open wells in areas where none existed at the time the occupation began, since the prior or normal rate of exploitation was zero.

Finally, the attempt to exercise such a right as a belligerent occupant appears to be unprecedented in state practice.

Recognizing that the rules regarding public immovable property do not permit the occupant very much leeway with regard to the general public resources of occupied territory, despite the chronic shortages involved in modern economic mobilization, one leading writer states that the occupant's power over such property "is a mere incident of his status as the governing authority *pro tempore*. As such, his power is measured not by his own needs, but by the duty to maintain the integrity of the corpus."[12] Article 55 thus plainly enacts at least a normally restrictive version of usufructory rights, and, at minimum, precludes an occupant from opening and exploiting new oil fields and wells.

    3. Even if new oil fields could be opened, the oil could not be taken for the broad purposes apparently contemplated.

Certainly there would be no basis for arguing that an occupant had greater freedom regarding the use or disposition of oil found in the ground

---

[11] Fauchille, pp. 253–54; Gerhard von Glahn, *The Occupation of Enemy Territory*, (1957), p. 177.

[12] Stone, Julius, *Legal Controls of International Conflict*, (1959), p. 714.

(public immovable property) than of oil he found already lifted (public movable property). Writing before World War II with regard to the right of an occupant to public movable property under Article 53, one leading authority noted that the occupant did not receive unlimited title to seized chattels and put in doubt the right of the occupant to sell seized chattels abroad to enrich the occupant's home treasury. Since the war, the rule has been stated with greater certainty, in light of the post-war legal decisions.[13]

Under the interpretation of the Hague Regulations set out in the resolution of the London International Law Conference in 1943 and the decisions in the trials of German war criminals, property can be taken only for purposes of the occupation itself, whatever rubric of the regulations the taking is under.[14]

---

[13] Writing during World War II, Feilchenfeld stated: "[T]he Hague Regulations speak of 'seizure' [of public chattels] not of 'appropriation'. It would seem therefore, that no unlimited title is acquired. . . . It seems admitted that the occupant may sell, spend, otherwise dispose of seized public chattels during the occupation; but it is at least not beyond doubt that seized food stores, for instance, may be sold abroad in order to enrich the home treasury of the occupant. The French word *saisie* does not necessarily connote unlimited rights." Feilchenfeld, pp. 53-54; A later writer stated that "[s]ome jurists go so far as to justify the sale of [lawfully seized enemy movable public property], but the present writer believes that such a sale would violate the important restriction imposed by Article 53 of the Hague Regulations, that is, that the property in question must be usable for military purposes. If seized enemy property is not to be utilized by an occupant at a given time, his authorities should appoint property custodians who should be placed in control of the property in question" von Glahn, p. 183; "The Occupant may take possession of [the property of the occupied State under Article 53], provided that it may be used for operations of war. This is a power of requisition which the Occupant enjoys in relation to private property under Article 52. It is wider principally because the Occupant is not limited by the restriction that property should be required only for the necessities of the army of occupation. It is narrower for the reason that the Occupant does not acquire title by his act of seizure, but only obtains a right to use the property (if necessary to the point of consumption or destruction)" E. Lauterpacht, p. 221.

[14] A sweeping statement on this point was contained in a resolution adopted by the London International Law Conference of 1943: "The rights of the occupant do not include any right to dispose of property, rights or interests for purposes other than the maintenance of public order and safety in the occupied territory. In particular, the occupant is not, in international law, vested with any power to transfer a title which will be valid outside that territory to any property, rights or interests which he purports to acquire or create or dispose of; this applies whether such property, rights or interests are those of the State or of private persons or bodies." (Entire resolution is set out in von Glahn, pp. 194-96).

The judgment in the trial of the major German war criminals included the following: "Article 49 of the Hague Convention provides that an occupying power may levy a contribution of money from the occupied territory to pay for the needs of the army of occupation, and for the administration of the territory in question. Article 52 of the Hague Convention provides that an occupying power may make requisitions in kind only for the needs of the army of occupation, and that these requisitions shall be in proportion to the resources of the country. These articles, together with Article 48 . . . 53, 55 and 56 . . . make it clear that under the rules of war, the economy of an occupied country can only be required to bear the expenses of the occupation, and these should not be greater than

The law, in this regard, appears to be properly stated by Stone:

"In positive terms and broadly stated, the Occupant's powers are (1) to continue orderly government, (2) to exercise control over and utilize the resources of the country so far as necessary for that purpose and to meet his own military needs. He may thus, under the latter head, apply its resources to his own military objects, claim services from the inhabitants, use, requisition, seize or destroy their property, *within the limits of what is required for the army of occupation and the needs of the local population.* But beyond the limits of quality, quantum and duration thus implied, the Occupant's acts will not have legal effect. . . ."[15] (emphasis supplied)

While there is authority for a broader proposition that "munitions de guerre" may be taken for use in military operations outside occupied territory and in other theaters of war,[16] this narrow exception, if it is valid, would not be relevant to the treatment of public immovable property under Article 55. Further, it appears doubtful at best, that in the present stage of the Israeli-Egyptian conflict, the taking of any significant amounts of property out of occupied territory, even "munitions de guerre", could be justified by the requirements of any relevant military operations.

These limitations are entirely consistent with, if not compelled by, the limited purposes for which force may be used under the U.N. Charter. It is difficult to justify a rule that the use of force in self-defense may, during any resulting occupation, give the occupant rights against the enemy sovereign not related to the original self-defense requirement, or not required as concomitants of the occupation itself and the occupant's duties. A rule holding out the prospect of acquiring unrestricted access to and use of resources and raw materials, would constitute an incentive to territorial occupation by a country needing raw materials, and a disincentive to withdrawal.

It has not been disputed that the purpose of the activity in the Sinai and Gulf of Suez is the acquisition of oil to meet the needs of Israel generally. The activity could not credibly be justified by reference to the needs of the occupied territory or the army of occupation itself. Further, the arrangements presumably would involve commercial trade outside occupied terri-

---

the economy of the country can reasonably be expected to bear." Judgment, I *Trial of the Major War Criminals Before the International Military Tribunal* 239 (1947). See *In re Flick, In re Krupp* and *In re Krauch.* This reasoning was followed by Whyatt, C.J., in the *Singapore Oil Stocks Case,* who noted that the Japanese exploitation of Sumatran oil fields was part of a Japanese plan to "secure the oil resources of the Netherlands Indies, not merely for the purpose of meeting the requirements of an army of occupation but for supplying the naval, military and civilian needs of Japan both at home and abroad, during the course of the war against the Allied Powers." Citing the decisions of the International and United States Military Tribunals, Whyatt concluded that "the seizure and the subsequent exploitation by the Japanese armed forces of the oil resources of the appellants in Sumatra was in violation of the laws and customs of war and, consequently, did not operate to transfer the appellants' title to the belligerent occupant." 51 Am. J. Int'l L. at 808 (1957).

[15] Stone, p. 697.
[16] E. Lauterpacht, p. 222.

tory, which would exceed the purposes for which the occupant is permitted to take enemy property. Such trade would also necessitate the transfer of title, though, under the authorities cited above, the occupant would, arguably, not acquire adequate title for such transfer.

4. An occupant is not entitled to grant a commercial concession to exploit oil fields.

A further difficulty with the contemplated development of oil fields in Sinai and the Gulf of Suez is that it is reportedly being carried out through commercial concessions which Israel claims it has the power, as occupant, to grant. However, this aspect, as well, appears to be without precedent in international practice.[17]

A concession for the exploitation of mineral resources in Egyptian territory is a legislative act, under the Egyptian legal system. Article 43 of the 1907 Hague Regulations requires the occupier "[to respect] unless absolutely prevented, the laws in force in the country". The legislative and regulatory right which an occupier has under international law is founded upon his duty to ensure public order and safety and his right to pursue his own military ends.[18] It may accordingly be argued that the occupier may not enact new legislation in this area, since it would be difficult to argue that the occupier was "absolutely prevented" from respecting the existing laws on mineral exploitation or that a new "law" on such exploitation flowed from his duties or military needs.

This reasoning appears to underlie the statement of one leading authority that "[n]ormally only the legitimate sovereign would seem to have the power to grant concessions." While this writer also argues the desirability of the occupant having such a power, "in the interest of the native population", it is clear that such considerations are non-existent in the Sinai and the Gulf of Suez.[19]

The terms and purposes of the activities under the Israeli concession would be impermissible under international law, involving, as they presumably do, transfer of title which the occupant arguably does not have, the commercial trading in the extracted petroleum and its use for purposes beyond the needs of the occupied territory and army of occupation.

5. The taking of oil in certain areas might violate the private property rights held by a U.S. company.

Israeli authorized oil exploitation in the waters of the Gulf of Suez would violate the concession rights held by Amoco.[19a] Only a small area of the Gulf

[17] von Glahn, p. 209.
[18] see, Stone, p. 698.
[19] von Glahn, p.

[19a] It has been asserted that the oil activities and rights in the Gulf are those of GUPCO (the Gulf of Suez Petroleum Company) and not those of Amoco. However, GUPCO is a non-profit Egyptian corporation which carries out operations under the concession agree-

east of the median line (the area claimed by Israel) is not subject to Amoco concessions.

First, the status of Israel as an occupying power in the Gulf of Suez is open to doubt, not only for the reasons advanced in the 1968 exchange of memoranda, but also because of the fact that the waters of the Gulf, except for a three mile strip out from the low-water line, constitute high seas.[20] The concept of belligerent occupation is exclusively one of the law of land warfare. While the notion of occupation of the territorial sea may be somewhat problematic, it is clear that high seas are not subject to belligerent occupation and that neither party to the Egyptian-Israeli dispute at present enjoys any right to belligerent activity on the high seas.

Second, assuming, *arguendo*, that Israel does have occupation rights in areas of the Gulf of Suez, it would have to respect the Amoco concessions as private property protected under the law of belligerent occupation.[21] Thus, the permission granted to others to carry out activities regarding which Amoco (together with its partners) enjoys an exclusive concessionary right, must be judged illegal as a taking of private property not within the rights of an occupant under the private property provisions of the Hague Regulations.

It has been suggested that Israel's oil development plans in the Gulf of Suez might not conflict with any rights held by Amoco because the Amoco concession in the relevant area was only granted in 1974. This is not persuasive. Even were Israel considered to have belligerent occupant status in the relevant areas of the Gulf, this would not have the result of invalidating Egypt's grant of an oil concession in areas occupied at the time of the grant.[22]

---

ment as the agent of Amoco and EGPC (Egyptian General Petroleum Company). The use of an agent does not affect the status of Amoco as a principal in the operations conducted and rights held under a concession.

[20] This is the considered opinion of the State Department Geographer. Egypt has taken none of the actions which would have been necessary to extend the territorial sea through baselines, or to close the Gulf and make its waters internal. While Egypt claims a twelve mile territorial sea, the United States continues to refuse recognition to any claims beyond three.

[21] Even in a case of state succession, acquired rights of a concessionaire must be respected by a successor state. D.P. O'Connel, "Economic Concessions in the Law of State Succession", 27 Brit. Y.B. Int'l L. 93, 116 (1951). *A fortiori*, they must be respected by a belligerent occupant whose rights fall far short of a successor sovereign's. The United States appears to have considered property rights based on concessions to be protected, and the occupant bound to respect those rights, even prior to the Hague Regulations. See Cummings, n. 148, pp. 570-571, and the numerous authorities cited therein.

[22] In the Lighthouse Case, the Permanent Court of International Justice considered as binding a concession contract for the usufruct of public immovable property granted in 1913 by the absent sovereign, Turkey, while the territory was under Greek belligerent occupation. The ad hoc judge appointed by the Greek Government argued that the occupant has the exclusive right to grant a concession to the usufruct of public immovable property. However, the majority did not acknowledge such a rule. The Court found it could decide without ruling on the point. The concession agreement, while concluded in

Since the granting of an oil concession is a legislative act in Egypt (as the grant of a lighthouse concession was in Turkey at the time of the Balkan Wars when Turkey effectively made such a grant in territory occupied by Greece), the question may be analyzed in terms of the right of the ousted sovereign to legislate in general with respect to the occupied territories. Consistent with the ruling of courts of various countries, including the United States, it is now accepted that the absent sovereign can legislate with respect to property in occupied territory, at least where such action does not conflict with valid rights of the occupier.[23]

This rule would preclude the legislative grant by the absent sovereign of a concession conflicting with the occupant's rights. However, it would not invalidate Egypt's oil concessions in this case, given the absence of any right in the belligerent occupant to open new mines or oil fields. There is no conflict with any valid rights of the occupier in the ousted sovereign's grant of a concession for such purposes, although the concessionaire might be unable to exploit the concession area during the occupation if the concession is in an area which is occupied, e.g., not on the high seas.

Thus, the concessions granted by Egypt to Amoco appear equally valid, whether granted prior to or post June 1967.

Conclusion:

Israel's rights *vis-a-vis* the undeveloped oil fields in occupied Egyptian territory, those of a usufructuary, do not include the right to develop a new oil field.

Any rights Israel might be able to assert with respect to the oil resources of occupied territory would, in any event, be limited by the purposes and underlying principles of the law of war which preclude their use for the general benefit of the Israeli economy, or their sale for commercial or non-military use.

International law does not support the assertion of a right in the occupant to grant an oil development concession.

1913, covered the period 1924-1949, long before which the occupant, Greece, had become the sovereign. *World Court Reports*, Hudson, ed., Vol. III, pp. 368, 383, 388-89, 407-409.

[23] Looking to pre-World War II authority, McNair stated: "It is at any rate arguable that, assuming the new law to fall within the category of that large portion of national law which persists during the occupation and which the enemy occupant cannot lawfully change or annul, it ought to operate in occupied territory in spite of the absence of power to make it effective during the occupation." McNair, *Legal Effects of War* (1948) p. 383. The matter is somewhat differently stated in the leading American case: "In short, the legitimate sovereign should be entitled to legislate over occupied territory insofar as such enactments do not conflict with the legitimate rule of the occupying power." *State of Netherlands v. Federal Reserve Bank of New York et. al.*, 201 F.2d 455 at 462 (U.S.C.A. 2nd Circuit 1953). See this opinion for a thorough statement of the law and for citations to the relevant cases. "The currently accepted principle appears to be that the legitimate sovereign may legislate for an occupied portion of his territory, provided that his laws do not conflict with the powers of the occupant as outlined in conventional international law." von Glahn, p. 35, Apparently, only the post-war decisions of Greek courts are contra.

Amoco's concessions, whether pre or post 1967, are valid and must be respected.

Thus, the oil development plans of Israel in Sinai and the Gulf of Suez, even if the latter area were "occupied territory", are contrary to international law.

Monroe Leigh
Legal Adviser

47. General Assembly Resolution 31/186 on Permanent Sovereignty Over National Resources in the Occupied Arab Territories, December 21, 1976*

* G.A. Res. 186, 31 U.N. GAOR Supp. (No. 39) at 87, U.N. Doc. A/31/39 (1976).

The General Assembly,

Recalling its resolution 3336 (XXIX) of 17 December 1974 entitled "Permanent sovereignty over national resources in the occupied Arab territories",

Recalling further its resolution 3516 (XXX) of 15 December 1975 on the same subject, in which it was noted that the report of the Secretary-General on the adverse economic effects on the Arab States and peoples resulting from repeated Israeli aggression and continued occupation of their territories[127] was inadequate in that it did not incorporate the necessary substantive and comprehensive studies required in conformity with paragraph 5 of resolution 3336 (XXIX), the related statements made at the twenty-ninth session of the General Assembly on behalf of the co-sponsors of the resolution[128] and submitted by the Secretary-General on the administrative and financial implications,[129] as well as the recommendation of the Advisory Committee on Administrative and Budgetary Questions,[130]

Noting that in its resolution 3516 (XXX) the Secretary-General was requested to submit to the General Assembly at its thirty-first session his final comprehensive report, which should fulfill the above-mentioned requirements, taking into account the related statements on the administrative and financial implications submitted by the Secretary-General[131] and approved by the Assembly at its thirtieth session,

Taking into account the note by the Secretary-General of 1 November 1976,[132]

Bearing in mind the pertinent provisions of its resolutions 3201 (S-VI) and 3202 (S-VI) of 1 May 1974, containing the Declaration and the Programme of Action on the Establishment of a New International Economic Order, and 3281 (XXIX) of 12 December 1974, containing the Charter of Economic Rights and Duties of States,

1. *Reaffirms* the right of the Arab States and peoples whose territories are under Israeli occupation to regain full and effective control over their natural and all other resources and economic activities, as well as the rights of those States, territories and peoples to the restitution and full compensation for the exploitation, loss and depletion of, and damage to, their natural and all other resources and economic activities;

2. *Takes note* of the regret expressed in the note by the Secretary-General that the submission of the report as requested by the General Assembly in

[127] A/10290 and Add.2.

[128] See *Official Records of the General Assembly, Twenty-ninth Session, Second Committee,* 1635th meeting.

[129] A/C.2/L.1385, A/C.5/1649.

[130] *Official Records of the General Assembly, Twenty-ninth Session, Annexes,* agenda item 73, document A/9978/Add.1, para. 4.

[131] A/C.2/L.1494, A/C.5/1759.

[132] A/31/284.

resolutions 3336 (XXIX) and 3516 (XXX) and of the related statements will be postponed until the thirty-second session of the Assembly;

3. *Requests* the Secretary-General to take immediately all the measures necessary to secure the submission to the General Assembly at its thirty-second session of his final substantive comprehensive report, which should fulfill all of the above-mentioned requirements;

4. *Requests* the heads of the relevant specialized agencies and United Nations organs, particularly the United Nations Conference on Trade and Development and the Economic Commission for Western Asia, to co-operate actively and adequately with the Secretary-General in the preparation of his final substantive comprehensive report.

106th plenary meeting
21 December 1976

48. Israeli Ministry of Foreign Affairs Memorandum of Law on the Right to Develop New Oil Fields in Sinai and the Gulf of Suez, August 1, 1977*

* Text provided by the Ministry of Foreign Affairs of Israel, *reprinted in* 17 Int'l Legal Materials 432 (1978). The memorandum was originally submitted to the U.S. Department of State on October 27, 1977.

The Department of State, in its Memorandum of Law of October 1, 1976, submitted on 18 January 1977, puts forward the proposition, as we understand it, that although Israel as a belligerent occupant of Sinai has rights of usufructus to State owned oil in existing oil fields;

a) there is no legal right to develop new oil fields;
b) even if new oil fields could be developed the oil could be used only for purposes of the occupation;
c) there is no right of the occupant to grant commercial concessions for the exploration of the oil fields;
d) oil concessions granted by Egypt to U.S. Companies in Sinai must be respected even if such concessions were granted after 1967.

The Government of Israel finds these four points raised in the U.S. Memorandum of Law to be unfounded in law and without precedent in the practice of States including the practice of the U.S. itself.

It is debatable as to how far section III of the 1907 Hague Regulations are relevant and valid to the situation in Sinai, and a leading authority referred to in the U.S. Memorandum states on this point—

Section III of the Hague Regulations applies expressly only to the typical case of belligerent occupation where one belligerent has overrun a part of the territory belonging to an enemy state, *where both armies are still fighting in the field and where no armistice or other agreement has been concluded.* [1] (emphasis added)

However, on the assumption for present purposes that section III of the 1907 Hague Regulations is applicable to Sinai, Israel's understanding of the law is as follows:

A. *The Right to Develop New Oil Fields*
1) The Hague Regulations of 1907 contain no reference to new oil fields and the onus of proof that they contain an implied prohibition on opening such new fields is on a party that opposes such use. The right to usufruct referred to in Article 55 of the Hague Regulations is not stated to be limited to existing mines and there is no mention of any such limitation in the Article.

Both the British [2] and the U.S. Military Manuals [3] quote Article 55 as referring to the working of mines without limiting it to existing mines. The Memorandum of Law presented by the Department of State quotes no international law precedent for such a distinction and we are aware of no precedent in the matter.

2) The term 'usufruct' in Article 55 of the Hague Regulations has been

---

[1] *The International Economic Law of Belligerent Occupation* Feilchenfeld, Washington, 1942 p. 6
[2] Para 610 of the *British Military Manual*
[3] Para 402 of the *USA Field Manual on the Law of Land Warfare*

interpreted by the leading authorities on the subject as requiring the duty to refrain from "wantonly dissipating or destroying the public resources." [4] "It must not constitute abusive exploitation" [5] "Such exploitation must not exceed what is usual or necessary" [6] and the occupant must "act like a bonus paterfamilias and limit its exploitation to the enjoyment of its natural and legal fruits." [7]

None of the leading authorities make any distinction between the right to exploit existing oil fields and the right to exploit new oil fields

3) The restriction proposed in the U.S. Memorandum of Law in addition to being without precedent would in our opinion be contrary to the purposes and objectives of the 1907 Hague Regulations.

Assuming an occupied area whose population and industry is based on local oil fields the proposed restriction could mean that if existing oil wells dry up, the Military Administration would be forbidden to dig new wells and would be bound by law to so assist in the severe economic deprivation of the territory. We find such an interpretation unfounded.

4) Since in practice adjacent oil fields and oil wells often derive their oil from the same underground source, the proposed restriction to existing drillings only would in practice be an arbitrary and illogical distinction.

5) Prospecting for oil, if successful, enhances the value of the land on it being eventually restored to the sovereign State. The converse is also true; if over a long period, such as in the case of the present occupation of Sinai, oil exploitation had been prevented, the development of the territory would have been delayed by that number of years.

6) The U.S. Memorandum of Law attempts to base its proposition on the technical meaning of the phrase usufructus given in a number of Civil Law Countries. It should be pointed out that there is no consensus even among the legal systems of these countries on the matter. The German Civil code states: The usufructuary of a piece of land may erect new structures for the purpose of obtaining stone, gravel, sand, loam, clay, marl, peat and other component parts of the soil, insofar as the economic purpose of the land is not thereby essentially altered. [8]

7) A phrase used in an international agreement is not to be commonly interpreted by the application of National Law systems. The Permanent Court of Justice in 1925 when asked to consider the phrase "établis" in the Lausanne Agreement ruled [9] at p. 18

> The Court will now, in the light of these considerations, proceed firstly to consider the meaning and scope of the word éta-

---

[4] *Law and Minimum World Public Order* McDougal and Feliciano 1961, p. 812

[5] *British Military Manual*, para 610

[6] *Modern Law of Land Warfare* M. Greenspan, p. 288

[7] *International Law Vol. II—The Law of Armed Conflict* G. Schwarzenberger 1968, p. 248

[8] Paragraph 1037 (2) of the German Civil Code

[9] Exchange of Greek and Turkish Populations—P.C.I.J., Series B-10

blis in general, and, secondly, the question whether the situation contemplated by this word should be determined with the aid of the legislation in force in the two countries concerned . . .

p.19   From this point of view, therefore, it becomes necessary to consider whether the Convention contains any express or implicit reference to national legislation for the purpose of determining what persons are to be regarded as "established". No express reference is to be found; it remains to be ascertained whether in regard to the matter before the Court, the Convention makes implicit reference to national legislation . . . .

Nor is there any indication that the authors of the Convention, when they adopted the word which has given rise to the present controversy, had in mind municipal legislation at all. Everything therefore seems to indicate that, in regard to this point, the Convention is self-sufficing and that the Mixed Commission in order to decide what constitutes an established inhabitant must rely on the natural meaning of the words as already explained.

And in 1950 when the South African Government claimed in the International Court of Justice that the word "Mandate" should be interpreted in the light of National Legislation the Court found in its advisory opinion [10]—

The League was not, as alleged by that Government, a "mandator" in the sense in which this term is used in the national law of certain States. It had only assumed an international function of supervision and control. The "Mandate" had only the name in common with the several notions of mandate in national law. The object of the Mandate regulated by international rules far exceeded that of contractual relations regulated by national law. The Mandate was created, in the interest of the inhabitants of the territory, and of humanity in general, as an international institution with an international object—a sacred trust of civilization. It is therefore not possible to draw any conclusion by analogy from the notions of mandate in national law or from any other legal conception of that law.

And even Sir Arnold McNair who in his separate opinion disagreed with the opinion of the Court states on this point [11]

The way in which international law borrows from this source is not by means of importing private law institutions "lock, stock and barrel",

[10] International Status of South West Africa—Reports of the I.C.J., 1950, p. 127
[11] ibid at p. 148

ready-made and fully equipped with a set of rules. It would be difficult to reconcile such a process with the application of "the general principles of Law". In my opinion, the true view of the duty of international tribunals in this matter is to regard any features or terminology which are reminiscent of the rules and institutions of private law as an indication of policy and principles rather than as directly importing these rules and institutions.

8) The phrase "Usufructus" as used in Article 55 has been given a clear meaning by the leading authorities. In such circumstances to attempt to replace this meaning with an interpretation given it by some, but not all Civil legal systems is unfounded.

9) Because of the nature of the relationship between the sovereign state and the occupant there can be no room whatsoever for analogies based on the contractual relationship between a lessor and a lesse [*sic*].

10) The Israel Government accpets [*sic*] the obligation to utilize and exploit the oil fields only as a bonus paterfamilias would. We feel there can be no doubt that such definition includes the obligation and right to continue reasonable considered and orderly new drillings. We cannot consider that the Hague Rules are intended to cause economic paralysis of occupied territory and we do not think that that is a reasonable interpretation.

11) The above position taken has been on the understanding that Article 55 of the Hague Regulations is the applicable article, it should be pointed out however that there is precedent for the proposition that oil in the ground is to be regarded as movable property having military value, and therefore by analogy the first paragraph of Article 53 would apply and the oil thus not be subject to the limitations of usufruct set out in Article 55.

In N. U. Da Bataafsche Petroleum Maatschappij and others v. War Damage Commission [12] the majority of the Singapore Court of the Appeal held that oil in the ground was immovable and not susceptible of direct military use. However, Whitton J., in his dissenting judgment, argued that the concept had to be interpreted according to the changing necessities of warfare. "If it is conceded" he wrote "that a belligerent is entitled to seize petrol which is ready for immediate use, it seems to me it cannot be logically maintained he is not entitled to seize the crude material out of which the finished products are created, since the protection afforded private property by the Regulations is obviously limited by the exclusion of what the signatories to the Convention presumably regarded as the legitimate necessaries of a belligerent Occupant in the execution of his war effort, as the modern phrase has it, and once it is allowed that a certain kind of property is a necessity for the conduct of a war, there scarcely seems reason to maintain that private interest can prevail in respect of the raw material out of which the property is made simply because in such circumstances extraction and processing have first to be carried out."

[12] *International Law Reports* 1956, vol. 23, p. 810

Authoritative legal opinion commenting on this case tends to support the dissenting judgment of Whitton J., quoted above.

McDougal and Feliciano criticise the majority decision and refer to "the enous nature of this ruling's contact with reality" and continue, "the opinion of Whitton J. which in this particular respect at least displays much greater awareness of the exigencies of modern warfare [13]. Furthermore, the British Manual of Military Law, states clearly "for example crude oil could be included in the term 'war material' ". [14]

There is both logic and precedent in claiming that in modern conditions of warfare state-owned oil should come within the meaning of "stores and supplies" which may be used for military operation" and thus may be seized by the occupying army.

B. Restrictions on the Use of the Oil

12) Article 55 of the Hague Regulations specificaly [sic] and categorically allows the Occupant to enjoy the fruits of public property. No restriction is made as to the purposes for which it is to be used. Article 55 must be read in contrast to the other "property articles". Article 48, 49 and 52, which all made specific reference to the fact that income under these articles is subject to the needs of the Army of Occupation. J. Stone who is quoted in the U.S. Memorandum on this point explicitly states that the Occupant may sell lease or contract the products subject only to the restriction against "abusive exploitation". [15]

The 1863 Lieber instructions to the U.S. Army (Article 31) state on this issue "and *sequesters for its own benefit* all the revenues of real property belonging to the hostile government."

13) One leading authority even goes so far as to say that other than the restriction of the right to immovables to usufructus the Hague regulations on the subject of public property provide no protection whatsoever even against complete ruination [16]. There is of course no claim that Israel practice has led to ruination nor are we submitting that it would be permittable.

14) None of the authorities apparently refer directly to any restrictions whatsoever on the use of usufructus and it is our understanding that this omission is based on the reasoning that usufructus implies the right to uti-

[13] *Law and Minimum World Public Order* McDougal and Feliciano 1961, p. 818
[14] Footnote 7 at paragraph 597, Part III, 1958
[15] *Legal Control of International Conflict*, J. Stone 1954, p. 714
[16] *Feilchenfeld*, at p. 14
"The Hague regulations do not succeed in excluding ruination even where occupants stay within their limits" .... "Moreover public property is excluded from this whole type of protection with the exception of the usufructory rule for land and a few similar rules."
It should be noted that the U.S. Memorandum of Law at page 11 quotes Feilchenfeld at p. 53, according to thom [sic] "It would seem therefore that no unlimited title is acquired ... however the complete sentence reads "and that seized chattels left behind in an evacuation belong ipso facto to the occupied state and not to the former occupant". The quote is thus far more limited than might possibly be understood by the reader of the U.S. Memorandum.

lize such produce and is thus different from the rights to other income and property which are indeed subject to the restrictions referred to in the U.S. Memorandum.

15) Alternatively it should be pointed out that the military costs of maintaining the Israel Defense Forces in the occupied areas, there, as a result of Arab aggression, far exceed any income derived from the oil wells in question.

C. The Right to Grant Commercial Concessions

16) The U.S. position on this issue appears to be unclear. Since there is no dispute that existing oil fields can be exploited and assuming that the Israel position on exploiting new oil fields is accepted is it then the U.S. position that the exploitation must be done by an Israel Government agency and must not be leased to a commercial body ? There do not appear to be any grounds for such a distinction.

J. Stone who is quoted in the U.S. Memorandum of Law specificaly [*sic*] states on this issue—

And though it permits the Occupant to *let* or utilize public land and buildings *sell* crops on public land cut and *sell* timber and work mines such contract or lease *must not extend beyond the termination* of the war. [17] (emphasis added).

17) The Permanent Court of International Justice in the *Lighthouse Case between France and Greece* Separate Opinion of Judge Seferiadese stated: [18]

Without going into the general legal aspects of the question, I will examine more particularly the granting of leases or concessions in respect of public property belonging to the State whose territory is occupied.

Naturally, these learned writers do not mention lighthouses; but they have definitely decided the issue in the case of railways. I will give some extracts, substituting the word "lighthouses" for "railways":

(Fauchille, Vol. II p. 257) "The occupying Power may have the operating of the lights for the duration of the occupation. But he may not alienate the lighthouses, for he is not yet the owner, and he will only become the owner if the conquest is definitive."

Consequently, and all the more certainly after the conquest had become definitive, the occupying State—i.e., Greece in this case—could alone have had power to grant concessions.'

Of course, the occupying State, when leasing an object, that is to say, when granting concessions, is bound to respect acquired rights, but only those that were acquired before the occupation. For during the occupation—it is self-evident—the occupying State alone enjoys the usufruct of the public property in the territories which he occupies. All

---

[17] *J. Stone*, at p. 714
[18] P.C.I.J. Series/7/B62, p. 50

learned writers, or at least all that I have read, are agreed upon this general principle.

and at p. 51.

However, if the preparatory discussions of the Hague Conference and the terms of Article 55 of Convention V concerning the laws and customs of war on land are read in conjunction, can it really be contended that, when that Article lays down that the occupying State is the administrator and usufructuary of the public property of the enemy State, that Article, at the same time, DEPRIVES the occupying State of the above rights and declares that they only pertain to the State that possesses the sovereignty? In my opinion, if such an interpretation were correct, Article 55 would have to be considered as laying down rules which flatly contradict one another.

Such a conclusion is inadmissible. When Article 55 of the Hague Convention No. IV admitted the right of the occupying Power to be the administrator and usufructuary of the public property of the occupied State, its object was—it is true—to set a limit to the powers of the occupying State—powers which are often pushed very much further; but the Article certainly did not set out to abolish those rights altogether, for then all administration of occupied territories would become an impossibility. So when it is contended that the Hague Convention does not allow any rights to the occupying Power, and that all rights continue to be vested in the occupied State, that—at any rate in my opinion—is assuredly an erroneous view, both from the standpoint of fact and of international law.

This judgment although given in a separate opinion was not on this point contradicted by the majority decisions of the Court and is quoted with approval by a leading authority [19] and is the only clear international authority on this issue.

18) During the U.S. Occupation of Cuba the specific question of mining concessions arose and the U.S. Attorney General was requested to give his opinion. He wrote: [20]

> Department of Justice
> Washington, D.C.
> September 8, 1900

Sir,

I have the honour to acknowledge the receipt of your communication of August 7, 1900, submitting for my opinion the following questions:

1) Did the Spanish mining laws continue in force in Cuba by virtue of the laws of war and of nations after the American occupation of the island?

[19] *Schwarzenberger*, p. 323

[20] *The Law of Civil Government in Territory Subject to Military Occupation by the Military Forces of the United States* Washington, Government Printing Office, 1902

2) May the military government in Cuba continue the granting of mineral claims in that island upon compliance with the provisions of the mining law as existing prior to the American occupation?

The Attorney General reached the conclusion that the Spanish Laws did not continue in force, however, he added:

> Cuba, therefore, rightly continues to be governed under the laws of the United States. According to the law of belligerent right, the will of the conqueror supplants the former political laws and powers which prevailed in the conquered territory, and the conqueror may make such new laws, rules and regulations as he sees fit.
> (Brown v. U.S., 8 Cranch, 110).
> Under this principle it is lawful for the conqueror, in administering the conquered territory, to make such use of the property previously belonging to the former sovereign as he sees fit. There is, therefore, in the President of the United States, acting by virtues of his constitutional authority as Commander in Chief of the Army and Navy, adequate power to use and make disposition of property in Cuba formerly belonging to the Crown of Spain, or subject to the imperial prorogative, and this includes the right to dispose of mining and other property formerly belonging to the Spanish Crown.
> . . .
> In my judgment, the President, as Commander in Chief, could authorize the military governor of Cuba to make grants of mining rights, if the President desired to do so.
>
> John W. Griggs
> Attorney General

It should be pointed out that the opinion of the U.S. Attorney General is indeed given in very broad language and was written in 1900 that is prior to the 1907 Hague Convention, however, the relevant article of the 1907 Hague Regulations (Article 55) is almost identical with Article 55 of the 1899 Convention which stated:

> Art. 55. The occupying State shall only be regarded as administrator and usufructuary of the public buildings, real property, forests and agricultural works belonging to the hostile State, and situated in the occupied country. It must protect the capital of these properties, and administer it according to the rules of usufruct.

And the principle stated above had already been expressed in the 1863 "Lieber" instructions for the U.S. army.

> Art. 31. A victorious army appropriates all public money, seizes all public movable property until further direction by its government, and sequesters for its own benefit or of that of its government all the revenues of real property belonging to the hostile government or nation.

The title to such real property remains in abeyance during military occupation, and until the conquest is made complete.

Thus the opinion of the U.S. Attorney General was given many years after the principle set out in Art. 55 of the 1907 Hague Regulations had already been incorporated into the laws of war.

19) This principle, that an occupant may well produce and grant concessions, has been incorporated into present day U.S. Army Field Mannual [*sic*] which states:

> He (the occupant) may however *lease* or utilize public lands or buildings, *sell* the crops, cut and *sell* timber and work the mines. The term of a *lease* or contract should not extend beyond the conclusion of the war. (emphasis added) [21]

20) The Memorandum quotes a leading authority as saying that "normally only the legitimate sovereign would seem to have the power to grant concessions" although it would be desirable to have such a power "in the interests of the native population." [22]

The U.S. Memorandum fails to quote the same author's comment later on at the same page where he sums up the issue by stating:

> It would seem reasonable to assume however that an occupant in principle ought to be free to grant concessions for the exploitations of the usufruct of public real or immovable property, with the obvious reservations that no such concession could exceed the duration of the belligerent occupation. [23]

D. Respect for Oil Concessions Granted by Egypt to U.S. Companies

21) Israel accepts in principle the obligation to respect these valid oil leases granted by Egypt to foreign countries prior to the Israel occupation. The Israel government reiterates its willingness to enter into negotiations on this issue with any company claiming that it was granted an oil lease by Egypt prior to June 1967.

22) Israel is of the opinion that its status as an occupant of the Gulf of Suez up to the median line is not open to doubt and we would wish to refer to the Israel Memoranda of Law on this issue in 1963. The further objection raised by the U.S. Memorandum of Law is that the Gulf, other than the three-mile strip from the lower water line, is High Seas. The Memorandum states that "while Egypt claims a twelve-mile limit the United States continues to refuse recognition to any claims beyond three."

Since presumably the U.S. recognizes as valid these Egyptian concessions granted to U.S. Companies in the Gulf of Suez beyond the three-mile limit the same reasoning behind such recognition, apparently on a "continental

---

[21] *U.S. Army Field Manual on the Law of Land Warfare,* para 402
[22] P. 17 of the U.S. Memorandum quoting *The Occupation of Enemy Territory* Van Glahn 1957, p. 209
[23] ibid

shelf basis", would be valid for any occupant of Sinai under the laws of belligerent occupation.

23) The further U.S. proposition that after the commencement of the
occupation Egypt can grant concessions that have effect during the occupation is untenable. Such a proposition is incompatible with the right of an
occupant to grant leases *for the period of the occupation*. Such a proposal would
mean that two states are each entitled to grant a valid concession for the
same area to take effect at the same time.

24) The U.S. proposition would presumably be valid for all cases of public, immovable property and would mean that although not occupying
them, the absent-sovereign could grant leases for use of land, both residential and agricultural, railways, ports, canals etc., to be executed during the
period of occupation.

Such a proposition implies either a high degree of cooperation between
the absent sovereign and the occupant, a situation not usually prevalent, or
alternately, the complete economic standstill of the economy as regards
State property.

25) The U.S. Memorandum does not put forward any authority or precedent for this approach to the laws of belligerent occupation.

26) The authorities and precedents granted in section 13-18 above which
provide that during and for the period of occupation the occupier may
grant concessions is clear authority that the absent sovereign cannot grant
such concessions during the period of occupation for both rights cannot
exist simultaneously.

27) The U.S. Memorandum of Law further analyses the question from
the aspect of legislation.

The Israel position is that the granting of mining concessions and leases
does not necessarily come within the ambit of legislation.

Concessions granted by the Israel military authorities are granted in the
form of contractual arrangements and are not of a legislative nature. Although some concessions granted by Egypt received Egyptian legislative approval, the leases themselves were not of a legislative character.

28) Any Egyptian legislation subsequent to the occupation purporting to
grant concessions is invalid for the period of the occupation.

There is precedent for the position that the disseised sovereign has no
right at all to enact legislation which would take effect within the areas under occupation [24], however, even according to the theories which grant
some rights to the disseised sovereign it is accepted that such legislation cannot be effective in these fields where the Occupant has the right to take
measures.

The wartime legislation of the disseised sovereign is invalid in relation
to the occupied territory in all matters which, while the occupation lasts,
are the legitimate legislative concern of the Occupying Power. [25]

[24] Van Glahn, p. 34
[25] Schwarzenberger, Vol. II, p. 201

As regards what is the legislative concern of the occupant, a U.S. authority writes:

> The application of these regulatory powers extends over practically all fields of life includes the whole field of economics and finance . . . and the whole economic process, including production, distribution, finance and consumption becomes subject to permitted changes. [26]

Conclusion

There is doubt as to the continuing validity of the 1907 Hague Rules in regard to Sinai. However, on the assumption that they are applicable:—

The Hague Rules contain no prohibition as to the opening of new oil fields. The right of usufructus granted to the occupant is interpreted by all leading authorities as prohibiting waste or excessive extraction, no authority refers to it as prohibiting reasonable exploitation of new wells. The interpretation given in some Civil Law countries, but not in all, to the municipal law term of usufructus is not valid for an international law agreement. Alternatively, oil can be regarded as a material liable to seizure under Art. 53 para 1.

The duty of an occupant is inter alia to maintain economic prosperity of occupied territory and this is met by a reasonable development of new oil fields. Such development enhances the value of the land.

The occupier being entitled to work the mines and enjoy the "fruit" of the mines can also grant leases and concessions for there is no logic nor precedent for allowing such reasonable exploitation to be carried out by the occupier but not by a concessionaire on behalf of the occupier.

On the assumption that the occupier can work the mines for the period of the occupation, it is untenable to hold that the absent sovereign can also grant concessions to work the mines to be executed during the period of occupation. The two rights are incompatible.

The occupier is bound to respect valid oil leases granted to foreign companies prior to the occupation, this obligation cannot apply to such lease granted by the absent sovereign after the commencement of the occupation.

[26] Feilchenfeld, p. 86

49. General Assembly Resolution 32/161 on Permanent Sovereignty Over National Resources in the Occupied Arab Territories, December 19, 1977*

* G.A. Res. 161, 32 U.N. GAOR Supp. (No. 45) at 97, U.N. Doc. A/32/45 (1977).

The General Assembly,

Bearing in mind the relevant principles of international law and the provisions of the international conventions and regulations, in particular the Hague Convention IV of 1907[77] and the fourth Geneva Convention of 12 August 1949,[78] concerning the obligations and responsibilities of the occupying Power,

Recalling its previous resolutions on permanent sovereignty over natural resources, particularly their provisions supporting resolutely the efforts of the developing countries and the peoples of the territories under colonial and racial domination and foreign occupation in their struggle to regain effective control over their natural and all other resources, wealth and economic activities,

Bearing in mind the pertinent provisions of its resolutions 3201 (S-VI) and 3202 (S-VI) of 1 May 1974 containing the Declaration and the Programme of Action on the Establishment of a New International Economic Order and 3281 (XXIX) of 12 December 1974 containing the Charter of Economic Rights and Duties of States,

Recalling further its resolutions 3175 (XXVIII) of 17 December 1973, 3336 (XXIX) of 17 December 1974, 3516 (XXX) of 15 December 1975 and 31/ 186 of 21 December 1976 on permanent sovereignty over national resources in the occupied Arab territories,

1. *Takes note* of the report of the Secretary-General[79] on the adverse economic effects on the Arab States and peoples resulting from repeated Israeli aggression and continued occupation of their territories;

2. *Notes* that, owing to the time constraint, incomplete coverage and technical and other limitations, the report did not cover all pertinent losses, such as:

(*a*) The adverse economic effects extending beyond the year 1975;

(*b*) Losses in the Arab territories still under Israeli occupation;

(*c*) Human and military losses;

(*d*) The loss of and damage to items of the national, religious and cultural heritage,

(*e*) Losses in the traditional sectors, including the retail trading, small industries and farming sectors;

(*f*) The full impact on the development process of the Arab States, territories and peoples subjected to Israeli aggression and occupation;

3. *Emphasizes* the right of the Arab States and peoples whose territories are under Israeli occupation to full and effective permanent sovereignty and control over their natural and all other resources, wealth and economic activities;

[77] Carnegie Endowment for International Peace, *The Hague Conventions and Declarations 1899-1907* (New York, Oxford University Press, 1915), p. 100.
[78] United Nations, *Treaty Series*, vol. 75, No. 973, p. 287.
[79] A/32/204.

4. *Reaffirms* that all measures undertaken by Israel to exploit the human, natural and all other resources, wealth and economic activities in the occupied Arab territories are illegal and calls upon Israel immediately to desist forthwith from all such measures;

5. *Further reaffirms* the right of the Arab States and peoples subjected to Israeli aggression and occupation to the restitution of, and full compensation for the exploitation, depletion and loss of and damages to, their natural, human and all other resources, wealth and economic activities, and calls upon Israel to meet their just claims;

6. *Calls upon* all States to support and assist the Arab States and peoples in the exercise of their above-mentioned rights;

7. *Calls upon* all States, international organizations, specialized agencies, investment corporations and all other institutions not to recognize, or cooperate with or assist in any manner in, any measures undertaken by Israel to exploit the resources of the occupied territories or to effect any changes in the demographic composition or geographic character or institutional structure of those territories.

107th plenary meeting
19 December 1977

I. Nuclear Proliferation and Associated Issues

50. General Assembly Resolution 3474 (XXX) on the Establishment of a Nuclear-Weapon-Free Zone in the Region of the Middle East, December 11, 1975*

* G.A. Res. 3474 (XXX), 30 U.N. GAOR Supp. (No. 34) at 24, U.N. Doc. A/10034 (1975).

The General Assembly,

Recalling its resolution 3263 (XXIX) of 9 December 1974, in which it overwhelmingly commended the idea of the establishment of a nuclear-weapon-free zone in the region of the Middle East,

Taking note of the reports of the Secretary-General to the Security Council and the General Assembly,[39] and the replies contained therein, on the question of the establishment of a nuclear-weapon-free zone in the region of the Middle East,

Recognizing, on the basis of the above-mentioned reports, that the establishment of a nuclear-weapon-free zone in the Middle East enjoys wide support in the region,

Mindful of the prevailing political situation in the region and of the potential danger emanating therefrom, which would be further aggravated by the introduction of nuclear weapons in the area,

Conscious, therefore, of the need to keep the countries of the region from becoming involved in a ruinous nuclear arms race,

Taking note of the comprehensive study of the question of nuclear-weapon-free zones in all its aspects,[40] prepared by the *Ad Hoc* Group of Qualified Governmental Experts pursuant to General Assembly resolution 3261 F (XXIX) of 9 December 1974,

Recalling its resolution 2373 (XXII) of 12 June 1968, in which it expressed the hope for the widest possible adherence to the Treaty on the Non-Proliferation of Nuclear Weapons[41] by both nuclear-weapon and non-nuclear weapon States,

1. *Expresses the opinion* that the Member States with which the Secretary-General has consulted through his notes verbales of 19 March 1975 and 13 June 1975 pursuant to General Assembly resolution 3263 (XXIX) should exert efforts towards the realization of the objective of establishing a nuclear-weapon-free zone in the region of the Middle East;

2. *Urges* all parties directly concerned to adhere to the Treaty on the Non-Proliferation of Nuclear Weapons as a means of promoting this objective;

3. *Recommends* that the Member States referred to in paragraph 1 above, pending the establishment of the nuclear-weapon-free zone under an effective system of safeguards, should:

(a) Proclaim solemnly and immediately their intention to refrain, on a reciprocal basis, from producing, acquiring or in any other way possessing nuclear weapons and nuclear explosive devices, and from permitting the

---

[39] *Official Records of the Security Council, Thirtieth Year, Supplement for July, August and September 1975*, documents S/11778 and Add.1-3 and *ibid., Supplement for October, November and December 1975*, document S/11778/Add.4; A/10221 and Add.1 and 2.

[40] *Official Records of the General Assembly, Thirtieth Session, Supplement No. 27A* (A/10027/Add.1), annex I.

[41] Resolution 2373 (XXII), annex.

stationing of nuclear weapons, in their territory under their control, by any third party;

(*b*) Refrain, on a reciprocal basis, from any other action that would facilitate the acquisition, testing or use of such weapons, or would be in any other way detrimental to the objective of the establishment of a nuclear-weapon-free zone in the region under an effective system of safeguards;

4. *Recommends* to the nuclear-weapon States to refrain from any action contrary to the purpose of the present resolution and the objective of establishing, in the region of the Middle East, a nuclear-weapon-free zone under an effective system of safeguards and to extend their co-operation to the States of the region in their efforts to promote this objective;

5. *Decides* to include in the provisional agenda of its thirty-first session the item entitled "Establishment of a nuclear-weapon-free zone in the region of the Middle East".

2437th plenary meeting
11 December 1975

51. Senate Resolution 523 Authorizing a Senate Study of United States Security and Foreign Policy Matters with Emphasis on the Middle East and Nuclear Proliferation, August 26, 1976*

* S. Res. 523, 94th Cong., 2d Sess., 122 Cong. Rec. 27916 (1976).

RESOLUTION

Authorizing a Senate study of United States security and
foreign policy matters.

Resolved, That the President of the Senate is authorized to appoint a special delegation of Members of the Senate upon the recommendation of the majority and minority leaders to visit certain countries in the Middle East, Europe, and other areas as needed to conduct a study on United States security and foreign policy interests in those areas with particular emphasis on worldwide nuclear proliferation and to designate the co-chairman of said delegation.

SEC. 2. (a) The expenses of the delegation, including staff members designated by the co-chairman to assist said delegation, shall not exceed $35,000, and shall be paid from the contingent fund of the Senate upon vouchers approved by the co-chairman of said delegation.

(b) The expenses of the delegation shall include such special expenses as the co-chairman may deem appropriate, including reimbursements to any agency of the Government for (1) expenses incurred on behalf of the delegation, (2) compensation (including overtime) of employees officially detailed to the delegation, and (3) expenses incurred in connection with providing appropriate hospitality.

(c) The Secretary of the Senate is authorized to advance funds to the co-chairman of the delegation in the same manner provided for committees of the Senate under the authority of Public Law 118, Eighty-first Congress, approved June 22, 1949.

52. General Assembly Resolution 31/71 on the Establishment of a Nuclear-Weapon-Free Zone in the Region of the Middle East, December 10, 1976*

* G.A. Res. 71, 31 U.N. GAOR Supp. (No. 39) at 36, U.N. Doc. A/31/39 (1976). *See also* subsequent resolution, G.A. Res. 82, 32 U.N. GAOR Supp. (No. 45) at 48, U.N. Doc. A/32/45 (1977).

The General Assembly,

Recalling its resolution 3263 (XXIX) of 9 December 1974, in which it over-whelmingly commended the idea of the establishment of a nuclear-weapon-free zone in the region of the Middle East,

Recalling also its resolution 3474 (XXX) of 11 December 1975, in which it recognized that the establishment of a nuclear-weapon-free zone in the Middle East enjoys wide support in the region,

Mindful of the prevailing political situation in the region and the potential danger emanating therefrom that would be further aggravated by the intro-duction of nuclear weapons in the area,

Concerned that the lack of any appreciable progress in the direction of the establishment of a nuclear-weapon-free zone, in the present atmosphere in the region, will further complicate the situation,

Convinced that progress towards the establishment of a nuclear-weapon-free zone in the Middle East will greatly enhance the cause of peace both in the region and in the world,

Conscious of the particular nature of the problems involved and the com-plexities inherent in the situation in the Middle East, and the urgency of keeping the region free from involvement in a ruinous nuclear-arms race,

1. *Expresses the need* for further action to generate momentum towards realization of the establishment of a nuclear-weapon-free zone in the Mid-dle East;

2. *Urges* all parties directly concerned to adhere to the Treaty on the Non-Proliferation of Nuclear Weapons[27] as a means of promoting this objective;

3. *Reiterates* its recommendation that the Member States referred to in paragraph 2 above, pending the establishment of the nuclear-weapon-free zone under an effective system of safeguards, should:

(*a*) Proclaim solemnly and immediately their intention to refrain, on a reciprocal basis, from producing, acquiring or in any other way possessing nuclear weapons and nuclear explosive devices and from permitting the sta-tioning of nuclear weapons in their territory or the territory under their control by any third party;

(*b*) Refrain, on a reciprocal basis, from any other action that would facili-tate the acquisition, testing or use of such weapons, or would be in any other way detrimental to the objective of the establishment of a nuclear-weapon-free zone in the region under an effective system of safeguards;

(*c*) Agree to place all their nuclear activities under the International Atomic Energy Agency safeguards;

4. *Reaffirms* the recommendations to the nuclear-weapon States to refrain from any action contrary to the purpose of the present resolution and the objective of establishing, in the region of the Middle East, a nuclear-weapon-free zone under an effective system of safeguards and to extend

---

[27] Resolution 2373 (XXII), annex.

their co-operation to the States of the region in their efforts to promote this objective;

5. *Invites* the Secretary-General to explore the possibilities of making progress towards the establishment of a nuclear-weapon-free zone in the area of the Middle East;

6. *Decides* to include in the provisional agenda of its thirty-second session the item entitled "Establishment of a nuclear-weapon-free zone in the region of the Middle East".

96th plenary meeting
10 December 1976

53. Excerpt from the Senate Delegation Report on American Foreign Policy and Nonproliferation Interests in the Middle East, June 1977*

* S. Doc. No. 47, 95th Cong., 1st Sess. at 41 (1977).

III. Nuclear Energy and Non-Proliferation

Nuclear proliferation as used in this report refers to the spread of nuclear weapons through the world. Five countries are known to have nuclear weapons: the United States, the Soviet Union, France, the United Kingdom, and the People's Republic of China. India's detonation of a nuclear device in 1974 demonstrated that it has the capacity to become the sixth member of the nuclear club. American foreign policy has been directed toward containment of the further spread of nuclear weapons. But there have proven to be no means within acceptable foreign policy options to prevent a modestly industrial nation from acquiring a few nuclear weapons if it decides to make its own plutonium in small, hidden installations. The possession of nuclear power plants of current design does not provide a country with direct access to fissionable materials suitable to make a nuclear explosive. The risk occurs when a country has its own facilities to enrich uranium or to recover plutonium from used nuclear fuels. Even if nuclear exporting countries were to restrict commerce to materials and processes required for electricity generation, the important problem of storing plutonium-bearing used fuel would remain. It is essential that storage be tightly safeguarded in known locations and unavailable for diversion by the producing country.

Congressional interest in the problems of nuclear proliferation led to adoption of Senate Resolution 523. The delegation discussed problems of nuclear energy and non-proliferation with officials of the International Atomic Energy Agency and with national leaders in Israel, Jordan, Egypt, and Iran, and had summary discussions in London with a group of Parliamentarians.

The International Atomic Energy Agency

The United States maintains a mission to the International Atomic Energy Agency (IAEA); both the U.S. mission and the IAEA received the Senate delegation on November 6, 1976. The delegation met with Ambassador Galen Stone, Deputy Director of the United States mission and with members of his staff, and with several management level officials of the IAEA. The Director General of the IAEA, Dr. Sigvard Eklund, was at the United Nations in New York to deliver his annual report at the time.

The IAEA was established in 1957 as an autonomous international organization to promote and provide international regulation for nuclear power. The United States has been and remains the most active participant in the IAEA. American participation is authorized by U.S. ratification of the international statute which created the Agency and by the International Atomic Energy Agency Participation Act of 1957. The United States is a permanent member of the Agency's Board of Governors. Many key personnel are U.S. citizens, some of whom are on leave from ERDA. The United States and the Soviet Union control many of the top posts. Given their shared interest in non-proliferation, the Soviets and the Americans share a common interest in strengthening the effectiveness of the IAEA.

The IAEA is not a specialized agency under United Nations direction or control but cooperates with the United Nations. The IAEA reports annually to the U.N. General Assembly and in some instances to the Security Council and to the Economic and Social Council. It has concluded relationship agreements with five specialized agencies of the United Nations. The stated objective of the Agency is to:

> ... accelerate and enlarge the contribution of atomic energy to peace, health and prosperity throughout the world. It shall ensure, so far as it is able, that assistance provided by it is not used in such a way as to further any military purposes.

The IAEA is responsible for international activities concerned with the peaceful uses of atomic energy including establishing and administering international safeguards. Other Agency functions include providing assistance to member nations in the development and practical application of atomic energy for peaceful purposes, the exchange of scientific information, the training and exchange of scientists and experts, and the development of international standards for health, safety and environmental protection.

At the end of 1976, 109 countries belonged to IAEA. Representatives of all member nations meet once a year in the General Conference to debate general policy and to consider recommendations from the Board of Governors. The Board of Governors is composed of representatives of 34 countries; it has broad authority to direct the functions of the IAEA including authority to establish policies and to recommend budgets and programs. The Agency's programs are implemented by the IAEA Secretariat, which is organized in five major departments and headed by the Director General. The present Director General, Dr. Sigvard Eklund of Sweden, was appointed by the Board of Governors with the approval of the General Conference for a 4-year term expiring in 1977. The Secretariat has about 1,250 employees including about 380 in the professional and higher staff categories. The United States supplies the largest number of IAEA professional personnel, about 20 percent.

Funding for IAEA is mainly through assessed contributions and voluntary and special contributions from member nations. IAEA also receives assistance in kind in fellowships, equipment, supplies, special nuclear materials, the services of experts, the sales of publications and films, and other arrangements by member nations. The annual budget is about 50 million. In 1976 the United States contributed about $9.5 million, or almost 28 percent of assessed contributions to the Agency. The U.S. also contributed about $1.5 million or 27 percent of voluntary contributions, and about $3 million of contributions in kind. The Soviet Union was the second largest contributor: $6 million, or 16 percent of assessed contributions and $860,000 or 16 percent of voluntary contributions.

Since the Agency was founded the United States has taken a leading role in developing an effective IAEA safeguards system and has helped to transfer to the Agency responsibility for applying safeguards on the nuclear materials and facilities which the United States provides bilaterally to other countries. There are two principal objectives of the IAEA safeguards system. One is to assure timely detection of any diversion of significant quantities of sensitive nuclear material (principally plutonium or enriched uranium) which could be used to manufacture nuclear explosive devices. The second is to deter such diversion by establishing the risk of detection and the consequent threat of international exposure.

The IAEA and the Non-Proliferation Treaty

The IAEA has safeguards agreements with individual member nations. In accordance with such agreements the Agency reviews the designs of safeguarded facilities, conducts periodic inspections to verify the absence of diversion, and imposes reporting, recordkeeping, containment, and monitoring requirements for safeguarded materials. With the advent of the Treaty on Non-Proliferation of Nuclear Weapons (NPT), signed in Washington in July 1968, the Agency's safeguards functions have assumed increased importance. The NPT commits the United States, the Soviet Union and all weapons states to reduce nuclear armaments in exchange for commitments by other states not to acquire nuclear weapons or explosives. The non-weapons states party to the treaty (there are almost 100) agree to place all of their nuclear power activities under IAEA safeguards including inspections by IAEA personnel. In return for these commitments, the non-weapons states are assured of U.S. and U.S.S.R. cooperation in developing peaceful uses of nuclear energy, and of access to whatever benefits may be derived from the peaceful uses of nuclear explosives. In addition, a number of IAEA members which have not ratified the NPT have entered into safeguards agreements with the IAEA. These agreements provide for application of agency safeguards to specific nuclear facilities, but not necessarily to all of the nation's peaceful nuclear activities.

All of the non-nuclear weapons states of Western Europe (except Spain and Portugal) and Japan and Canada are parties to the NPT. Except for Albania, all East European states are parties to the NPT as well. Unfortunately, of 22 countries with an industrial base strong enough to have produced nuclear weapons or to produce them in the future, only 11 have ratified the treaty. Among the important countries which have not ratified the treaty are Argentina, Brazil, Egypt, France, India, Israel, Pakistan, the People's Republic of China, South Africa, and Spain. Although not required to do so, the United States and the United Kingdom have offered to permit the IAEA to apply its safeguards to their peaceful nuclear activities when such safeguards are applied generally to non-nuclear weapons states which have signed the NPT.

Discussions with the U.S. Mission to the IAEA

Ambassador Galen Stone described the work of his mission and responded to a series of questions from the delegation. The United States is one of 52 countries maintaining missions to IAEA. About half the American personnel in the U.S. mission are Foreign Service Officers and the remaining are technical specialists from other government agencies. The State Department instructs the U.S. Mission after coordination with such agencies as the Energy Research and Development Agency, the Nuclear Regulatory Commission, and the Arms Control and Disarmament Agency.

Ambassador Stone described policy authority as normally operating on a consensus basis within the 34-member Board of Governors. There have been no votes in the Board in the past 3 years. Political issues have arisen in the General Conference. At the 1976 Conference meeting in Rio de Janeiro, some political matters were raised, such as observer status for the Palestine Liberation Organization, and the role of South Africa as permanent member of the Board of Governors for the Africa region. Ambassador Stone stated that in his judgment the IAEA was not becoming as politicized as several United Nations agencies. The less developed countries belong to the Agency mainly to obtain certain benefits such as technical assistance. The Soviets and Americans share the same interest in promoting effective safeguards. The Ambassador noted that the Soviets usually do not raise political issues themselves but will weigh in if others raise them. He described the Soviets as being generally cooperative with the United States on Agency matters. The main channel for Soviet/American discussions on IAEA matters is in Washington between the Soviet Ambassador and the Director of the U.S. Mission to the IAEA, Ambassador Gerald Tape. Ambassador Stone suggested that another possible reason for the relatively low level of polemics is that Director General Eklund has made serious effort to work fairly and impartially with all members.

Ambassador Stone reviewed IAEA safeguards and told the delegation that to his knowledge the official position of the IAEA was accurate: there had been no diversion of "significant amounts" of nuclear materials. Significant amounts are defined as enough to make one nuclear bomb, or approximately 8 kilograms of plutonium or 25 kilograms of uranium-235. Ambassador Stone said that a major hindrance upon the IAEA's effectiveness in controlling proliferation was the number of important countries which had not accepted the Non-Proliferation Treaty.

The delegation asked Ambassador Stone and Counsellor Allan Labowitz how safeguards could be expanded and strengthened. They replied that gradual progress in the development of a universal safeguards system is being made through the London Nuclear Suppliers Conference. The IAEA was considering proposals to make public more information regarding the Agency's safeguards activities and the results of its inspections.

Discussions with IAEA Officials

The delegation discussed with IAEA officials several issues regarding nuclear power, efforts to prevent diversion of nuclear materials, and means to restrict the possibilities of proliferating nuclear weapons technology. Dr. John Hall, Deputy Director for Administration, chaired a group including Dr. Rudolf Rometsch, Inspector General, and Mr. David Fischer, Assistant Director General and Director of External Relations. Dr. Hall is the highest ranking American at the Agency and was previously Assistant General Manager for international relations at the U.S. Atomic Energy Commission. Dr. Hall described the use of the $45 million annual budget and the organization and work of the 1,300 staff members. The IAEA group emphasized the need to develop and apply IAEA safeguards to all critical nuclear facilities and materials in all countries with nuclear energy programs. Such a universal safeguards system could be realized if all countries subscribed to the NPT. Dr. Rometsch stated that presently about 20 percent of the world's nuclear facilities are being safeguarded. He stated that this share could increase significantly to about 80 percent when the Euratom facilities and the peaceful facilities in the United States and the United Kingdom were placed under IAEA safeguards. An additional problem is that some non-NPT countries have safeguards but not for the entire fuel cycle. Despite progress in applying the IAEA safeguards system, the number of countries outside the system make it impossible to guarantee that a weapons capability would not be developed through diversion of materials from peaceful activities. Dr. Hall stated his conviction that there should be no nuclear traffic to a country which had not signed the Non-Proliferation Treaty or accepted the IAEA complete cycle safeguards.

IAEA officials emphasized that enrichment and reprocessing facilities are especially critical with respect to their proliferation potential. These processes produce nuclear materials suitable for nuclear explosion. The officials recommended that the "front end" or uranium enrichment technology be expanded to obtain greater supplies of slightly enriched uranium, the fuel for present light water reactors. But they favored requiring that any reprocessing operations be conducted in regional centers under multinational as opposed to national control.

Performance of IAEA responsibilities requires cooperation of the host member country. The safeguard system requires the active participation of member countries to maintain reporting and recordkeeping standards. Member countries may request that certain IAEA inspectors not be included in the team assigned to review its facilities. The IAEA tries to make inspection teams as international in composition as possible. The inspection staff has personnel from 37 countries. An inspector must be recommended for employment by the Inspector General and approved by the Director General. One must speak the language of the country whose facilities are inspected, but an inspector is not assigned to his own country. Officials displayed and described the system of cameras, seals, and technology and the six to eight reactor inspections each year to determine whether irradiated fuel has been moved.

Several IAEA officials made the point that although the Agency was capable of strengthening safeguards it could only be as strong as the member countries allowed. One official remarked that it was misleading to claim that the IAEA was too weak. A better statement would be that the United States and other countries have decided that the IAEA should not be stronger. While member countries generally are committed to non-proliferation objectives, there is still a reluctance to surrender power to the Agency other than to permit IAEA safeguards inspections. Although the responsibility to protect nuclear materials against the threat of theft or sabotage rests with the member countries and not the IAEA, the Agency has prepared physical protection guidelines.

At present the Agency has only limited powers to enforce sanctions in the event of materials diversion. If the IAEA were to detect a diversion, the formal procedure to be followed provides for notice by the Director General to the member country concerned, to the IAEA Board of Governors, to all members of the Agency, and then to the United Nations General Assembly and Security Council. The Agency may also suspend the offender's rights and privileges as an Agency member, curtail or suspend assistance to the member, and call for the return of all nuclear materials provided to the supplier country. IAEA officials said that although there have been some discrepancies in material balances there has never been a violation of the IAEA safeguards system. According to the Agency, the discrepancies that have occurred have been much less than that needed for a nuclear explosive device, and a satisfactory explanation for the loss was established in each case.

Two Agency Experts, Mr. Skjoldebrand and Mr. Krymm, briefed the delegation on the worldwide development of nuclear power. There are presently 183 power reactors in 19 member countries. An additional 358 reactors are planned for construction in 32 member countries, including 16 in developing countries. Nuclear plants are now generating about 5 percent of the world's electric energy. In response to a question, Mr. Skjoldebrand stated that there were considerable uranium resources available for development. He said that 80 percent of known reserves were in English speaking countries, and that Latin America and Asia are largely unexplored. Mr. Krymm observed that the techniques for projecting the costs and revenues of power plants had not been adequate, and that general economic comparisons are not useful. While the profitability of most nuclear power plants has worsened, they are still attractive in view of the substantial rise in fossil fuel prices for conventional power stations.

IAEA officials were asked whether they approved the idea of dividing the IAEA into two parts: one to perform developmental functions and the other to exercise regulatory responsibility. The officials opposed such a division. They noted that much of the Agency's effectiveness in safeguards depends upon the active participation and cooperation of member nations. Many members participate in the Agency's safeguards system primarily to obtain developmental assistance and secondarily for exchange of information. Detaching assistance and information would reduce the incentive for many nations to belong to IAEA, thereby weakening the safeguards program.

An interesting point arose in discussing assistance rendered to member countries to upgrade their national nuclear energy agencies. The delegation asked whether the IAEA, as a disinterested party, could advise one of the American states on various questions regarding proposed nuclear power plants. An IAEA official replied that if requested to do so by the United States Government, such advice could be rendered.

Asked how additional funds given to the IAEA could best be used, Dr. Hall suggested that one area for increased attention is the management of spent fuel. When asked what an optimum course of action to stem proliferation might be, Dr. Hall replied that a possibility to consider was to use the IAEA as the sole source of nuclear fuel, to serve as broker to the international community. Dr. Hall noted that the United States had raised this idea 10 years ago but that it had not been pursued. IAEA officials agreed that it would be desirable to strengthen international capabilities to analyze all available energy options for those nations seeking assistance.

United States Cooperation in Nuclear Energy

The United States began cooperation with Israel, Egypt, and Iran in the 1950s through its Atoms for Peace Program and provided assistance to these countries in nuclear technology and research. The U.S. has had research Agreements for Cooperation in atomic energy with Israel since 1955 and with Iran since 1959. While there has been no similar agreement with Egypt, the United States has cooperated with Egypt over the past decade in nuclear fields. Israel, Egypt and Iran all have substantial nuclear energy research programs and one or more nuclear research reactors.

Israel, Egypt and Iran and other developing countries have considered for many years possible ways to link nuclear power plants to development plans. In early 1964 President Johnson announced that discussions had begun with Israeli representatives on cooperation in research to use nuclear reactors for desalinization. In 1968 the United States started a study with Middle Eastern countries to explore the technical and economic feasibility of using nuclear power to provide electricity and water for development of arid areas, especially in Israel and Egypt.

In 1974 The United States announced its intention to enter into Agree-

ments for Cooperation with Egypt and Israel to supply nuclear power reactors and nuclear fuel. Although congressional procedures were already
established to review the proposed sales, Congress enacted in October 1974
an amendment to section 123 of the Atomic Energy Act of 1954 which
strengthened congressional review procedures. By the new procedures,
proposed agreements for nuclear power cooperation must lie before the
Congress for 60 days. If during this period Congress adopts a concurrent
resolution disapproving a proposed agreement, the agreement will not become effective.

Agreements on the texts of proposed power reactor agreements with Israel and with Egypt, identical in substance, were initialed in August 1976,
and submitted by the Administrator of ERDA to the President for approval.
They have not yet been transmitted to the Congress. The agreements have
stringent safeguards governing U.S. supplied reactor operation and fuel
transfers. They would permit export from the United States of two light
water power reactors to both Egypt and Israel with aggregate capacities of
up to 1,870 megawatts electrical (MWe) and low-enriched uranium fuel to
sustain operation of the reactors. The proposed term of the agreements is
40 years. Among the agreements' provisions are the following:

(A) Prohibition against use of U.S. material and equipment and any
plutonium produced through the use of that material or equipment for
any military use including any nuclear explosive device;

(B) U.S. supply of material and equipment would be subject to safeguards of the IAEA, with U.S. safeguards rights suspended but not re-
linquished as long as the U.S. agrees that safeguards requirements are
satisfactorily met by IAEA safeguards;

(C) U.S. access to information on the implementation of the IAEA
safeguards;

(D) Physical security measures set by the United States must be established for application to U.S.-supplied nuclear material and equipment;

(E) U.S approval is required for the location of operations involving
plutonium, including the reprocessing of U.S. fuel or non-U.S. fuel in
an American reactor. Explicit understanding is included that fuel reprocessing, storage, or fabrication of the recovered plutonium will take
place outside the recipient country;

(F) U.S. option to take title to and affect disposition of plutonium
produced in U.S. fuel or in non-U.S. fuel in an American reactor;

(G) Enrichment of uranium fuel to be transferred under the agreements is restricted to less than 20 percent in the isotope U-235;

(H) Should plutonium be requested for recycle as reactor fuel, such
supply would be subject to U.S. approval. If permitted, such plutonium
transfer would be in the form of fabricated elements; and

(I) Certain special guarantees have been required from Israel and
Egypt involving constraints on facilities which might be built by either

country as a result of using U.S. technology ("replicated" facilities): requirements for IAEA safeguards, physical security not less stringent than applicable to direct U.S. assistance, and a prohibition against use for any nuclear explosive device.

It was earlier thought that the proposed agreements would permit transfer of reactors having a total capacity of 1,300 MWe. The 1,970 MWe capacity results from Israel's need for two plants with the larger total MWe capacity. The agreements with both countries are for 1,970 MWe, but Egypt is presently considering reactors of less total capacity.

A provisional enrichment services contract is in effect between the United States and Egypt. Provision of the slightly enriched uranium for the proposed reactors would be provided subject to conclusion of the proposed Agreement for Cooperation. In June 1974, Israel signed a contract with ERDA for fixed commitment uranium enrichment services. The contract provides for supply of slightly enriched uranium for a reactor in the 600-660 MWe range and is conditional upon entry into force of the bilateral cooperation agreement. Since Israel has decided to request purchase of a power reactor of 960MWe, an additional 300-360 MWe equivalent of fuel enrichment services will be needed. Israeli officials have had discussions with American firms with respect to obtaining the additional enrichment services required. The United States has informed Israel that ERDA is not in a position to provide additional commitments for enrichment services. Should Egypt decide to seek additional uranium enrichment services by other United States sources, it would be permitted to do so, subject to the same 1970 total MWe ceiling applied to both Israel and Egypt.

Iran and the United States have been negotiating for about 2 years a proposed nuclear power reactor Agreement for Cooperation. Iran had indicated that it would like to purchase from the United States about eight nuclear plants with up to 8,000 MWe and the low-enriched uranium to fuel them. In June 1974 Iran signed two fixed commitment uranium enriching services contracts with ERDA covering fuel for two reactors in the range of 1,000 to 1,200 MWe, subject to conclusion of an appropriate cooperative agreement with the United States. The agreement under negotiation would comply with the basic United States policy that any American assistance would be used only for peaceful purposes and would prohibit use of U.S. assistance for any nuclear explosive devices. The agreement will include provisions regarding physical security, IAEA safeguards, and other standard guarantees. Because Iran has signed the NPT, Iran's entire peaceful nuclear program including planned power reactors, supporting capabilities, and fuel material from any source used in the reactors is subject to IAEA safeguards.

The principle issue in the American-Iranian negotiations has been reprocessing of U.S. supplied fuel or fuel irradiated in U.S. supplied reactors. The United States has taken the position that if sensitive operations such as reprocessing should be done they should be done under multinational control. Iran has been willing to consider regional reprocessing centers under multinational control. But Iran wants guarantees that such arrangements will not result in economic or political penalties to Iran, especially since Iran has signed the NPT and accepted IAEA safeguards.

Conclusions Regarding Nuclear Energy and Non-Proliferation

THE IAEA

The International Atomic Energy Agency has performed a vital role in promoting the peaceful use of nuclear power and safeguarding against diversion of nuclear materials. The United States and other members have a stake in strengthening this organization and in assuring that it continue to pursue its mandated responsibilities without being weakened by politicization.

For the United States the most important responsibility of the IAEA is the management of safeguards. Although the Agency operates as an information gatherer, all significant enforcement powers are reserved to the member nations. It is vital that the members of IAEA take active interest in the degree of cooperation the IAEA receives from the countries under its safeguards. Instances of a safeguarded country objecting to the presence of an individual inspector, the use of a particular piece of monitoring equipment, or disregarding of an Agency guideline could impede the Agency's ability to detect accurately and in a timely manner any significant diversions of safeguarded materials.

All information on both cooperation received by the IAEA Secretariat and on the results of safeguards inspections should be made available to the Board of Governors and to the member nations. More public awareness of such facts would bolster international confidence in the Agency. It would further focus attention on the Board of Governors and the General Conference to consider measures to ensure full cooperation by all countries participating in the Agency's safeguards program.

The rapid growth in the number of nuclear facilities and the increased importance of confidence in IAEA safeguards demand greater American attention to the competence of the IAEA. It is in the American interest to be certain that the management, personnel, equipment and procedures of the Agency are adequate to fulfill its responsibilities as the number of facilities increases.

Under its existing charter, the IAEA has no power to mandate or impose physical security for nuclear materials and facilities. The Agency is aware of this problem and recently published a physical security guideline. In response to a delegation question Agency officials stated that physical security requirements should be a feature of all future safeguards agreements and in all bilateral agreements. The Agency's authority in physical security matters should be reconsidered, perhaps through a convention on physical security to consider measures to strengthen IAEA safeguard functions. While respecting sovereign rights of its members, possible measures might include increasing the authority of the IAEA to set minimum standards for physical protection, to inspect for compliance, and to report to the Board of Governors and member nations the responses to IAEA recommendations.

THE MIDDLE EAST

The possible sales of nuclear power reactors to Israel, Egypt, and Iran offers the United States an opportunity to cooperate with these countries in their energy and development programs and to advance our non-proliferation objectives. Israel, Egypt, and Iran all present convincing need for additional electric power. Israel has virtually no energy resources of its own and wishes to increase its electricity capacity and reduce its dependence on a vulnerable supply of fossil fuels. Egypt needs power to supplement its energy resources to further industrial and agricultural development of a poor, developing nation. And Iran, although presently rich in petroleum, recognizes that its supply of these fuels is finite and that it will need new energy sources. All three countries have nuclear programs of different sorts. And all three have decided to proceed with developing nuclear power facilities.

It is possible for the United States to help these countries respond to their energy development needs while helping to prevent the spread of nuclear explosives. Each country wants to obtain nuclear power plants from the United States and has expressed willingness to accept proliferation safeguards on those facilities as a precondition to the sales. The United States is but one potential supplier in the international market, and Iran has announced its plans to purchase nuclear power reactors from the Federal Republic of Germany and from France. The United States should be satisfied that any sales it licenses are proper and not compromised by competition. It is also true that remaining an active participant in international nuclear commerce enables the United States to exert leverage for the goals of nonproliferation. The most significant potential for diversion is associated not with power plants themselves, but with fuel facilities, such as uranium enrichment and spent fuel reprocessing plants associated with the use of reactors.

The need to discourage development of national enrichment and reprocessing programs in the Middle East is tied to the supply of low enriched uranium fuel to purchasers of nuclear power plants. The United States and other supplier nations must recognize the importance of secure fuel supplies to purchaser nations. Actions to convince other countries that adequate supplies of fuel will be made available will add legitimacy and credibility to U.S. efforts to restrict national enrichment and reprocessing. One possible avenue worthy of further exploration is that of multinational fuel supplier arrangements.

The controls on the specific items requested for export to Israel and Egypt under the proposed Agreements for Cooperation are adequate. Nonetheless, the delegation supports efforts to strengthen controls, such as those pertaining to the disposition of spent reactor fuel. Israel, Egypt, and Iran all demonstrated needs for additional electrical generating capacity. It appears that each of these countries has decided after serious planning to build nuclear plants. Congress will have a full opportunity to review the proposed agreements with safeguard provisions when they are submitted in accordance with statutory procedures. The safeguards should be as tight as practicable. Any important factors related to American relations with a particular customer or with the region could be presented by the President in his request to the Congress for license approval. The delegation recommends that the President pursue with the leaders of the applicant countries all possible efforts to avoid the proliferation of nuclear weapons in the Middle East.

Notwithstanding the adequacy of assurances against diversion in the proposed agreements for Egypt and Israel, the delegation believes that ratification of the NPT by Israel and Egypt, and the placement by Israel of its Dimona facility under IAEA safeguards, would provide added reassurance. Nonetheless, the delegation believes it would be counterproductive to require such measures as a precondition to the pending sales.[1][2]

Unlike Israel and Egypt, Iran has signed and ratified the NPT and accepted full safeguards on all its nuclear facilities. The principal remaining issue between the United States and Iran regarding reprocessing of U.S. supplied fuel should be surmountable by creative thinking and the will to reach an accommodation. One approach would be to provide a guaranteed supply of enriched uranium fuel through the IAEA. Another possibility would be to establish a regional nuclear reprocessing center under multinational control. In meeting with the delegation, the Shah of Iran indicated his willingness to cooperate in developing workable solutions to the reprocessing problem. The delegation is not prepared to submit recommendations regarding an Agreement for Cooperation with Iran until the complete terms of the agreement are known.

The Treaty on the Non-Proliferation of Nuclear Weapons

The Treaty on the Non-Proliferation of Nuclear Weapons (the "NPT") serves as a restraint on the spread of nuclear explosives in the world. The acceptance of the treaty by all but about a dozen countries underscores the widespread importance attached to curbing nuclear explosives. The treaty serves as an indicator of a nation's intentions regarding the diversion of

---

[1] Senator Culver on this sentence: "In my opinion, this trip did not provide adequate information to reach this particular conclusion."

[2] Senator Glenn comments on this paragraph in his additional views.

nuclear materials from peaceful uses and of its commitment to the goal of non-proliferation. Just as adherence to the pledge to forswear development of nuclear weapons and accept IAEA safeguards indicates intent, so withdrawal from the treaty and termination of IAEA safeguards would signal a change of intent.

Progress towards an effective international safeguards system is hampered by the reluctance of the nonsigners. Some of them have already developed nuclear facilities. Their absence from this dedication to stop proliferation means that even a perfectly functioning set of IAEA safeguards where they exist still leave unexamined a number of important nuclear facilities. That failure of some countries to ratify the NPT may be unrelated to a desire to develop nuclear weapons. Moreover, there are few incentives for some countries to ratify the Treaty. The United States must exercise leadership in cooperation with other members of the IAEA to develop incentives which will encourage full acceptance of the Non-Proliferation Treaty.

Nuclear Suppliers Conference

Consultations with other nuclear exporting countries could be an effective way to devise a common set of safeguards and controls over peaceful nuclear exports. The first supplier meetings included the United States, the Soviet Union, the United Kingdom, France, the Federal Republic of Germany, Canada, and Japan. The group was recently expanded to include the Netherlands, Sweden, Belgium, Italy, the German Democratic Republic, and Poland, all of whom are entering the nuclear market.

The United States has adopted principles based on several meetings in London which it expects will be adopted by the other supplier countries regarding future nuclear exports. It will be important for the IAEA to press for a uniform set of policies among nuclear exporting nations. Non-weapons states must be convinced that their survival and national interests do not require them to have nuclear arms. It would be useful to make public some of the discussions of the London conferences in order to attract world support for greater definition of common exporting principles. The U.S. principles of exporting nuclear materials developed thus far are these:

— Application of international (IAEA) safeguards to all nuclear exports;
— Prohibition of the use of nuclear exports to make nuclear explosives for any purpose—peaceful or otherwise;
— Insistence on adequate physical security of nuclear facilities and materials to prevent theft and sabotage; and
— Requirement that the same conditions of any retransfer of nuclear materials or equipment apply to third countries.

A possible contribution to the control of proliferation would be coordinated suppliers' action against nations which terminate commitments under the Non-Proliferation Treaty or detonate a nuclear explosive. Any nation has the right to end its commitments 90 days after notification to the other parties to the NPT. A country with a large inventory of nuclear materials under IAEA safeguards could terminate its safeguards commitments and be left with the means to make a nuclear weapon. At present there are not substantial, prescribed penalties for such withdrawal, such as a coordinated recall of supplies to a withdrawing nation.

Legislation

Regulatory decisions whether to grant export licenses involve a wide range of controversial economic and political issues attracting considerable public attention. The present statutory criteria of the Atomic Energy Act of 1954 is whether the export will constitute an unreasonable risk to the common defense and security. There will undoubtedly be more applications for export licensing in the future. The examination of licenses by the executive branch and by Congress could be well served by a set of criteria to be applied to each case. Such criteria could also assist potential customers to understand the requirements to be imposed on nuclear exports from the United States. Such criteria and a clear policy commitment that necessary fuel services will be provided as needed on a nondiscriminatory basis will add order and predictability to the business of exporting nuclear materials and systems. To make the role of reliable supplier credible, the United States must have adequate production capacity to meet both domestic demand and that of legitimate international customers. Considerable controversy developed in the 94th Congress as to whether additional enrichment capacity in the United States should be in public or private hands. However that issue is resolved, either by policy or legislation, the American enrichment capacity should be maintained at a level sufficient to support the United States non-proliferation policies. Legislation to establish goals for U.S. non-proliferation policy, to set criteria for nuclear export licensing decisions, and to strengthen existing nuclear export agreements should be developed by the 95th Congress.

New Initiatives

There are a number of means by which a nation or group could obtain the nuclear materials to make a weapon—despite non-proliferation progress and the prospects for advancement through bilateral arrangements, the NPT, the IAEA, and the nuclear suppliers meetings. Ways in which people or governments intending to make a nuclear explosive device could obtain highly enriched uranium or plutonium include theft of these materials or use of a small reactor designed solely to produce plutonium which could be separated in a small recovery plant. New enrichment techniques such as the centrifuge method suggest that it may be possible to produce highly enriched uranium with a relatively small plant. Prevention of proliferation will require the cooperation of both supplier nations and of all nations and people interested in the use of nuclear facilities and technology. The IAEA could serve as a forum for exploring the many complexities of the proliferation problem; other, national fora could serve the same purpose. The importance of the problem and the possible dangers of incomplete control should command the attention of all nations.

54. Excerpt from General Assembly Resolution S-10/2 Calling for the Establishment of a Nuclear-Weapon-Free Zone in the Middle East, June 30, 1978*

---

* G.A. Res. S-10/2, para. 63(d), Final Document of the 10th Special Session of the General Assembly Supp. (No. 4) at 8, U.N. Doc. A/S-10/4 (1978).

(*d*) The serious consideration of the practical and urgent steps, as described in the paragraphs above, required for the implementation of the proposal to establish a nuclear-weapon-free zone in the Middle East, in accordance with the relevant General Assembly resolutions, where all parties directly concerned have expressed their support for the concept and where the danger of nuclear-weapon proliferation exists. The establishment of a nuclear-weapon-free zone in the Middle East would greatly enhance international peace and security. Pending the establishment of such a zone in the region, States of the region should solemnly declare that they will refrain on a reciprocal basis from producing, acquiring or in any other way possessing nuclear weapons and nuclear explosive devices and from permitting the stationing of nuclear weapons on their territory by any third party, and agree to place all their nuclear activities under International Atomic Energy Agency safeguards. Consideration should be given to a Security Council role in advancing the establishment of a nuclear-weapon-free zone in the Middle East; . . . .

J. Terrorism and Response

55. General Assembly Resolution 31/102 on Measures to Prevent International Terrorism Which Endangers or Takes Innocent Human Lives or Jeopardizes Fundamental Freedoms and Study of the Underlying Causes of the Forms of Terrorism and Acts of Violence Which Lie in Misery, Frustration, Grievance and Despair and Which Cause Some People to Sacrifice Human Lives, Including Their Own, in an Attempt to Effect Radical Change, December 15, 1976*

---

* G.A. Res. 102, 31 U.N. GAOR Supp. (No. 39) at 185, U.N. Doc. A/31/ 39 (1976). *See also* subsequent resolution, G.A. Res. 147, 32 U.N. GAOR Supp. (No. 45) at 212, U.N. Doc. A/32/45 (1977).

The General Assembly,

Deeply perturbed over acts of international terrorism which are occurring with increasing frequency and which take a toll of innocent human lives,

Recognizing the importance of international cooperation in devising measures effectively to prevent their occurrence and of studying their underlying causes with a view to finding just and peaceful solutions as quickly as possible,

Recalling the Declaration on Principles of International Law concerning Friendly Relations and Cooperation among States in accordance with the Charter of the United Nations,[22]

Noting that the *Ad Hoc* Committee on International Terrorism, established under General Assembly resolution 3034 (XXVII) of 18 December 1972, has been obliged to suspend its work,

Deeply convinced of the importance to mankind of the continuation of the work of the *Ad Hoc* Committee,

1. *Expresses deep concern* over increasing acts of international terrorism which endanger or take innocent human lives or jeopardize fundamental freedoms;

2. *Urges* States to continue to seek just and peaceful solutions to the underlying causes which give rise to such acts of violence;

3. *Reaffirms* the inalienable right to self-determination and independence of all peoples under colonial and racist regimes and other forms of alien domination, and upholds the legitimacy of their struggle, in particular the struggle of national liberation movements, in accordance with the purposes and principles of the Charter and the relevant resolutions of the organs of the United Nations;

4. *Condemns* the continuation of repressive and terrorist acts by colonial, racist and alien régimes in denying peoples their legitimate right to self-determination and independence and other human rights and fundamental freedoms;

5. *Invites* States to become parties to the existing international conventions which relate to various aspects of the problem of international terrorism;

6. *Invites* States to take all appropriate measures at the national level with a view to the speedy and final elimination of the problem, bearing in mind the provisions of paragraph 3 above;

7. *Invites* the *Ad Hoc* Committee on International Terrorism to continue its work in accordance with the mandate entrusted to it under General Assembly resolution 3034 (XXVII);

8. *Invites* the States which have not yet done so to submit their observations and concrete proposals as soon as possible to the Secretary-General so as to enable the *Ad Hoc* Committee to carry out its mandate more efficiently;

9. *Requests* the Secretary-General to transmit to the *Ad Hoc* Committee an

---

[22] Resolution 2625 (XXV), annex.

analytical study of the observations of States submitted under paragraph 8 above;

10. *Requests* the *Ad Hoc* Committee to consider the observations of States under paragraph 8 above and to submit its report with recommendations for possible co-operation for the speedy elimination of the problem, bearing in mind the provisions of paragraph 3, to the General Assembly at its thirty-second session;

11. *Requests* the Secretary-General to provide the *Ad Hoc* Committee with the necessary facilities and services, including summary records;

12. *Decides* to include the item in the provisional agenda of its thirty-second session.

99th plenary meeting
15 December 1976

56. European Convention on the Suppression of Terrorism, January 27, 1977*

* Provisional edition provided by the Council of Europe, *reprinted in* 15 Int'l Legal Materials 1272 (1976).

The member States of the Council of Europe, signatory hereto,

Considering that the aim of the Council of Europe is to achieve a greater unity between its Members;

Aware of the growing concern caused by the increase in acts of terrorism;

Wishing to take effective measures to ensure that the perpetrators of such acts do not escape prosecution and punishment;

Convinced that extradition is a particularly effective measure for achieving this result,

Have agreed as follows:

ARTICLE 1

For the purposes of extradition between Contracting States, none of the following offences shall be regarded as a political offence or as an offence connected with a political offence or as an offence inspired by political motives:

a. an offence within the scope of the Convention for the Suppression of Unlawful Seizure of Aircraft, signed at The Hague on 16 December 1970;

b. an offence within the scope of the Convention for the Suppression of Unlawful Acts against the Safety of Civil Aviation, signed at Montreal on 23 September 1971;

c. a serious offence involving an attack against the life, physical integrity or liberty of internationally protected persons, including diplomatic agents;

d. an offence involving kidnapping, the taking of a hostage or serious unlawful detention;

e. an offence involving the use of a bomb, grenade, rocket, automatic firearm or letter or parcel bomb if this use endangers persons;

f. an attempt to commit any of the foregoing offences or participation as an accomplice of a person who commits or attempts to commit such an offence.

ARTICLE 2

1. For the purposes of extradition between Contracting States, a Contracting State may decide not to regard as a political offence or as an offence connected with a political offence or as an offence inspired by political motives a serious offence involving an act of violence, other than one covered by Article 1, against the life, physical integrity or liberty of a person.

2. The same shall apply to a serious offence involving an act against property, other than one covered by Article 1, if the act created a collective danger for persons.

3. The same shall apply to an attempt to commit any of the foregoing offences or participation as an accomplice of a person who commits or attempts to commit such an offence.

ARTICLE 3

The provisions of all extradition treaties and arrangements applicable between Contracting States, including the European Convention on Extradition, are modified as between Contracting States to the extent that they are incompatible with this Convention.

ARTICLE 4

For the purposes of this Convention and to the extent that any offence mentioned in Article 1 or 2 is not listed as an extraditable offence in any extradition convention or treaty existing between Contracting States, it shall be deemed to be included as such therein.

ARTICLE 5

Nothing in this Convention shall be interpreted as imposing an obligation to extradite if the requested State has substantial grounds for believing that the request for extradition for an offence mentioned in Article 1 or 2 has been made for the purpose of prosecuting or punishing a person on account of his race, religion, nationality or political opinion, or that that person's position may be prejudiced for any of these reasons.

ARTICLE 6

1. Each Contracting State shall take such measures as may be necessary to establish its jurisdiction over an offence mentioned in Article I in the case where the suspected offender is present in its territory and it does not extradite him after receiving a request for extradition from a Contracting State whose jurisdiction is based on a rule of jurisdiction existing equally in the law of the requested State.

2. This Convention does not exclude any criminal jurisdiction exercised in accordance with national law.

ARTICLE 7

A Contracting State in whose territory a person suspected to have committed an offence mentioned in Article 1 is found and which has received a request for extradition under the conditions mentioned in Article 6, paragraph 1, shall, if it does not extradite that person, submit the case, without exception whatsoever and without undue delay, to its competent authorities for the purpose of prosecution. Those authorities shall take their decision in the same manner as in the case of any offence of a serious nature under the law of that State.

ARTICLE 8

1. Contracting States shall afford one another the widest measure of mutual assistance in criminal matters in connection with proceedings brought in respect of the offences mentioned in Article 1 and 2. The law of the requested State concerning mutual assistance in criminal matters shall apply in all cases. Nevertheless this assistance may not be refused on the sole ground that it concerns a political offence or an offence connected with a political offence or an offence inspired by political motives.

2. Nothing in this Convention shall be interpreted as imposing an obli-

gation to afford mutual assistance if the requested State has substantial grounds for believing that the request for mutual assistance in respect to an offence mentioned in Article 1 or 2 has been made for the purpose of prosecuting or punishing a person on account of his race, religion, nationality or political opinion or that that person's position may be prejudiced for any of these reasons.

3. The provisions of all treaties and arrangements concerning mutual assistance in criminal matters applicable between Contracting States, including the European Convention on Mutual Assistance in Criminal Matters, are modified as between Contracting States to the extent that they are incompatible with this Convention.

ARTICLE 9

1. The European Committee on Crime Problems of the Council of Europe shall be kept informed regarding the application of this Convention.

2. It shall do whatever is needful to facilitate a friendly settlement of any difficulty which may arise out of its execution.

ARTICLE 10

1. Any dispute between Contracting States concerning the interpretation or application of this Convention, which has not been settled in the framework of Article 9, paragraph 2, shall, at the request of any Party to the dispute, be referred to arbitration. Each Party shall nominate an arbitrator and the two arbitrators shall nominate a referee. If any Party has not nominated its arbitrator within the three months following the request for arbitration, he shall be nominated at the request of the other Party by the President of the European Court of Human Rights. If the latter should be a national of one of the Parties to the dispute, this duty shall be carried out by the Vice-President of the Court or, if the Vice-President is a national of one of the Parties to the dispute, by the most senior judge of the Court not being a national of one of the Parties to the dispute. The same procedure shall be observed if the arbitrators cannot agree on the choice of referee.

2. The arbitration tribunal shall lay down its own procedure. Its decisions shall be taken by majority vote. Its award shall be final.

ARTICLE 11

1. This Convention shall be open to signature by the member States of the Council of Europe. It shall be subject to ratification, acceptance or approval. Instruments of ratification, acceptance or approval shall be deposited with the Secretary General of the Council of Europe.

2. The Convention shall enter into force three months after the date of the deposit of the third instrument of ratification, acceptance or approval.

3. In respect of a signatory State ratifying, accepting or approving subsequently, the Convention shall come into force three months after the date of the deposit of its instrument of ratification, acceptance or approval.

ARTICLE 12

1. Any State may, at the time of signature or when depositing its instrument of ratification, acceptance or approval, specify the territory or territories to which this Convention shall apply.

2. Any State may, when depositing its instrument of ratification, acceptance or approval or at any later date, by declaration addressed to the Secretary General of the Council of Europe, extend this Convention to any other territory or territories specified in the declaration and for whose international relations it is responsible or on whose behalf it is authorised to give undertakings.

3. Any declaration made in pursuance of the preceding paragraph may, in respect of any territory mentioned in such declaration, be withdrawn by means of a notification addressed to the Secretary General of the Council of Europe. Such withdrawal shall take effect immediately or at such later date as may be specified in the notification.

ARTICLE 13

1. Any State may, at the time of signature or when depositing its instrument of ratification, acceptance or approval, declare that it reserves the right to refuse extradition in respect of any offence mentioned in Article 1 which it considers to be a political offence, an offence connected with a political offence or an offence inspired by political motives, provided that it undertakes to take into due consideration, when evaluating the character of the offence, any particular serious aspects of the offence, including:

a. that it created a collective danger to the life, physical integrity or liberty of persons; or

b. that it affected persons foreign to the motives behind it; or

c. that cruel or vicious means have been used in the commission of the offence.

2. Any State may wholly or partly withdraw a reservation it has made in accordance with the foregoing paragraph by means of a declaration addressed to the Secretary General of the Council of Europe which shall become effective as from the date of its receipt.

3. A State which has made a reservation in accordance with paragraph 1 of this article may not claim the application of Article 1 by any other State; it may, however, if its reservation is partial or conditional, claim the application of that article in so far as it has itself accepted it.

ARTICLE 14

Any Contracting State may denounce this Convention by means of a written notification addressed to the Secretary General of the Council of Europe. Any such denunciation shall take effect immediately or at such later date as may be specified in the notification.

ARTICLE 15

This Convention ceases to have effect in respect to any Contracting State which withdraws from or ceases to be a Member of the Council of Europe.

ARTICLE 16

The Secretary General of the Council of Europe shall notify the member States of the Council of:

a. any signature;

b. any deposit of an instrument of ratification, acceptance or approval;

c. any date of entry into force of this Convention in accordance with Article 11 thereof;

d. any declaration or notification received in pursuance of the provisions of Article 12;

e. any reservations made in pursuance of the provisions of Article 13, paragraph 1;

f. the withdrawal of any reservation effected in pursuance of the provisions of Article 13, paragraph 2;

g. any notification received in pursuance of Article 14 and the date on which denunciation takes effect;

h. any cessation of the effects of the Convention pursuant to Article 15.

In witness whereof, the undersigned, being duly authorised thereto, have signed this Convention.

Done at Strasbourg, this   day of   in English and in French, both texts being equally authoritative, in a single copy which shall remain deposited in the archives of the Council of Europe. The Secretary General of the Council of Europe shall transmit certified copies to each of the signatory and acceding Parties.

57. Bonn Economic Summit Conference Joint Statement on International Terrorism, July 17, 1978*

* 14 Weekly Comp. Pres. Doc. 1308 (July 24, 1978).

The heads of state and government, concerned about terrorism and the taking of hostages, declare that their governments will intensify their joint efforts to combat international terrorism.

To this end, in cases where a country refuses extradition or prosecution of those who have hijacked an aircraft and/or do not return such aircraft, the heads of state and government are jointly resolved that their governments should take immediate action to cease all flights to that country.

At the same time, their governments will initiate action to halt all incoming flights from that country, or from any country by the airlines of the country concerned. The heads of state and government urge other governments to join them in this commitment.

NOTE: Chancellor Helmut Schmidt read the joint statement during his remarks at the Bonn Stadt Theater at the conclusion of the Bonn Economic Summit Conference.

II. Camp David and
the Egyptian-Israeli Peace Treaty:
August 1978–December 1984

A. The Camp David Accords

58. White House Statement Announcing the Summit Meeting, August 8, 1978*

---

* 78 U.S. Dep't State Bull. No. 2018, at 43 (September 1978).

The President is pleased to announce that President Sadat and Prime Minister Begin have accepted an invitation to come to Camp David on September 5 for a meeting with the President to seek a framework for peace in the Middle East.

All three leaders agree that there is no task more important than this search for peace. Secretary Vance has informed the President that both Prime Minister Begin and President Sadat have welcomed this meeting, and the President is gratified by their response.

Each of the three leaders will be accompanied by a small number of their principal advisers, and no specific time has been set for the duration of the meeting.[1]

[1] Read to news correspondents by White House Press Secretary Jody Powell (text from Weekly Compilation of Presidential Documents of Aug. 14, 1978).

59. President Carter's Remarks on Departure for Camp David, September 4, 1978*

---

* 78 U.S. Dep't State Bull. No. 2019, at 3 (October 1978).

I'm leaving now for Camp David to prepare for a very important meeting between myself, President Sadat of Egypt, and Prime Minister Begin of Israel. During the next few days, very important decisions will be made by us, working with our advisers representing three great nations, searching for peace in the Middle East which can help greatly to insure peace in the future throughout the world; by the Congress while I'm gone, in dealing with many very important issues, including the evolution of an energy policy for our nation.

As we meet at Camp David, no one can insure the degree of success which we might enjoy. The issues are very complicated. The disagreements are deep. Four wars have not led to peace in that troubled region of the world. There is no cause for excessive optimism, but there is also no cause for despair.

The greatest single factor which causes me to be encouraged is my sure knowledge that Prime Minister Begin and President Sadat genuinely want peace. They are determined to make progress, and so am I.

We will need the encouragement and the prayers of everyone in our nation, in all three nations, throughout the world, who want success to come from our deliberations. Compromises will be mandatory. Without them, no progress can be expected. Flexibility will be the essence of our hopes. And my own role will be that of a full partner, not trying to impose the will of the United States on others but searching for common ground on which agreements can be reached and searching for exchanges of compromise that are mutually advantageous to all nations involved.

I know the seriousness with which President Sadat and Prime Minister Begin come to our country, and I have tried to prepare myself as well as I possibly could to bring success to these efforts.

It will have to be a mutual thing, and all of us will enter these discussions without prejudice toward one another, with a spirit of good will and with the realization of the sober responsibilities that fall on us.

Lastly, I would say that we will be almost uniquely isolated from the press and from the outside world. My hope is that this degree of personal interchange, without the necessity for political posturing or defense of a transient stand or belief, will be constructive.

There will be a great deal of effort made to insure and enhance mutual trust in one another and to recognize accurately that we all want the same ultimate goal. There is no doubt in my mind about this.

I want to express, in closing, my thanks to these two great leaders for their willingness to come when the political consequences of failure might be very severe and when the prospects of complete success are very remote. We'll do the best we can, and I fervently ask the support and prayers of all those who share with us a hope that we might bring a new prospect for peace to the Middle East.

60. Exchange of Remarks between Vice-President Mondale and President Sadat at Andrews Air Force Base, September 5, 1978*

* 78 U.S. Dep't State Bull. No. 2019, at 4 (October 1978).

VICE PRESIDENT MONDALE: Mr. President, on behalf of President Carter and the people of the United States, we welcome you again to the United States with a warm heart. The people of our country admire greatly your wisdom, your courage, and your statesmanship. Welcome to the United States.

PRESIDENT SADAT: Mr. Vice President, Mr. Vance, thank you for your thoughtful words and the genuine sentiments you express toward me and the Egyptian people.

As you well know, these feelings are mutual. The Egyptian people value very highly the ever-growing friendship and cooperation with the people and leadership of the United States. We are also gratified by the keen interest you are maintaining in the establishment of a comprehensive, just, and lasting peace in the Middle East.

All along, we have held the view that this nation is the most qualified to be a full partner in the peace process. Your heritage is unique and so is your global responsibility. When you demonstrated your determination to assume such responsibility fully, you reaffirmed the faith of my people in the United States and its dedication to the cause of peace.

We come here at the crucial crossroads. The challenge is tremendous, but we have no choice except to accept the challenge. We cannot afford to fail the hopes of nations all over the world. No one has the right to block the road to peace. This is no time for maneuvers and worn out ideas; it is time for magnanimity and reason.

I pray to God Almighty to guide us in this great endeavor and to enable us to achieve the noble goal which inspired President Carter to call for this conference. That inspiration is and shall remain a brave and gallant act of statesmanship. Together we shall proceed to build a viable structure for peace on the solid foundation of law and legitimacy. Together, we shall realize the hopes of those who believe in the supremacy of right and justice, and together we shall overcome.

61. Exchange of Remarks between Vice-President Mondale and Prime Minister Begin at Andrews Air Force Base, September 5, 1978*

---

* 78 U.S. Dep't State Bull. No. 2019, at 4 (October 1978).

VICE PRESIDENT MONDALE: Mr. Prime Minister, on behalf of Mr. Carter and the American people, we welcome you warmly to the United States. The American people deeply admire your leadership—its genius, its strength, its compassion. Above all, we admire your profound commitment to peace, so appropriate at this historic moment. Mr. Prime Minister, we welcome you with a warm heart.

PRIME MINISTER BEGIN: Mr. Vice President, Mr. Secretary of State, ladies and gentlemen, dear friends: Four times I visited the President of the United States in the interests of peace, since we were elected by our peoples to conduct their affairs, to care for the future, and for the preservation of liberty and democracy in our countries and elsewhere. Twice I met with the President of Egypt in a spirit of understanding, in good will and a common striving for peace in Jerusalem and in Ismailia. However, there is no doubt that this fifth meeting with President Carter, and the third with President Sadat, is the most important, the most momentous of them all.

My friends and colleagues, the Foreign Minister, the Defense Minister, and I and our friends and advisers will make all endeavors possible to reach an agreement so that the peace process can continue and ultimately be crowned with peace treaties. This is the peace mission on behalf of which we come now to you, Mr. Vice President, to the United States and to our dear friend, the President of the United States.

We are grateful to the President for the hospitality he bestowed upon us in his retreat at Camp David and let us all hope that out of that unique political conclave a day will come when the nations of the world will say: *"Habemus pacem"*—"We have peace."

62. Joint Statement Issued by President Carter, President Sadat, and Prime Minister Begin at Camp David, September 6, 1978*

* 78 U.S. Dep't State Bull. No. 2019, at 5 (October 1978).

After four wars, despite vast human efforts, the Holy Land does not yet enjoy the blessings of peace.

Conscious of the grave issues which face us, we place our trust in the God of our fathers, from whom we seek wisdom and guidance.

As we meet here at Camp David we ask people of all faiths to pray with us that peace and justice may result from these deliberations.

63. Senate Resolution 554 Urging All People to Pray for a

Successful Outcome of the Middle East Summit

Conference, September 8, 1978*

---

* S. Res. 554, 95th Cong., 2d Sess., 124 Cong. Rec. 28561 (1978).

Whereas President Jimmy Carter, Prime Minister Menachem Begin, and President Anwar Sadat have requested people of all faiths to pray that peace and justice may result from the deliberations of the Middle East Summit Conference: Now, therefore be it

Resolved, That it is the sense of the Senate to urge people of all faiths to pray that the outcome of the Middle East Summit Conference will be successful, and that the deliberations of the Conference will be based on understanding, humility, and willingness to negotiate for solutions acceptable to all sides in order to further the effort for lasting peace and justice in the Middle East.

64. Exchange of Remarks by President Carter, President Sadat, and Prime Minister Begin at the Signing of the Camp David Agreements, September 17, 1978*

* 78 U.S. Dep't State Bull. No. 2019, at 5 (October 1978).

PRESIDENT CARTER: When we first arrived at Camp David, the first thing upon which we agreed was to ask the people of the world to pray that our negotiations would be successful. Those prayers have been answered far beyond any expectations. We are privileged to witness tonight a significant achievement in the cause of peace, an achievement none thought possible a year ago, or even a month ago, an achievement that reflects the courage and wisdom of these two leaders.

Through 13 long days at Camp David, we have seen them display determination and vision and flexibility which was needed to make this agreement come to pass. All of us owe them our gratitude and respect. They know that they will always have my personal admiration.

There are still great difficulties that remain and many hard issues to be settled. The questions that have brought warfare and bitterness to the Middle East for the last 30 years will not be settled overnight. But we should all recognize the substantial achievements that have been made.

One of the agreements that President Sadat and Prime Minister Begin are signing tonight is entitled, "A Framework for Peace in the Middle East [Agreed at Camp David]." [Applause]

This framework concerns the principles and some specifics in the most substantive way which will govern a comprehensive peace settlement. It deals specifically with the future of the West Bank and Gaza and the need to resolve the Palestinian problem in all its aspects. The framework document proposes a 5-year transitional period in the West Bank and Gaza during which the Israeli military government will be withdrawn and a self-governing authority will be elected with full autonomy.

It also provides for Israeli forces to remain in specified locations during this period to protect Israel's security.

The Palestinians will have the right to participate in the determination of their own future, in negotiations which will resolve the final status of the West Bank and Gaza, and then to produce an Israeli-Jordanian peace treaty.

These negotiations will be based on all the provisions and all the principles of U.N. Security Council Resolution 242. And it provides that Israel may live in peace within secure and recognized borders.

And this great aspiration of Israel has been certified without constraint with the greatest degree of enthusiasm by President Sadat, the leader of one of the greatest nations on Earth. [Applause]

The other document is entitled, "Framework for the Conclusion of a Peace Treaty Between Egypt and Israel."

It provides for the full exercise of Egyptian sovereignty over the Sinai. It calls for the full withdrawal of Israeli forces from the Sinai; and after an interim withdrawal which will be accomplished very quickly, the establishment of normal, peaceful relations between the two countries, including diplomatic relations. [Applause]

Together with accompanying letters, which we will make public tomorrow, these two Camp David agreements provide the basis for progress and peace throughout the Middle East.

There is one issue on which agreement has not been reached. Egypt states that the agreement to remove Israeli settlements from Egyptian territory is a prerequisite to a peace treaty. Israel states that the issue of the Israeli settlements should be resolved during the peace negotiations. That's a substantial difference.

Within the next two weeks, the Knesset will decide on the issue of these settlements.

Tomorrow night, I will go before the Congress to explain these agreements more fully and to talk about their implications for the United States and for the world. For the moment, and in closing, I want to speak more personally about my admiration for all of those who have taken part in this process, and my hope that the promise of this moment will be fulfilled.

During the last 2 weeks, the members of all three delegations have spent endless hours, day and night, talking, negotiating, grappling with problems that have divided their people for 30 years. Whenever there was a danger that human energy would fail or patience would be exhausted or good will would run out—and there were many such moments—these two leaders and the able advisers in all delegations found the resources within them to keep the chances for peace alive.

The long days at Camp David are over. But many months of difficult negotiations still lie ahead.

I hope that the foresight and the wisdom that have made this session a success will guide these leaders and the leaders of all nations as they continue the progress toward peace. [Applause]

PRESIDENT SADAT: Dear President Carter, in this historic moment, I would like to express to you my heartfelt congratulations and appreciation. For long days and nights, you devoted your time and energy to the pursuit of peace. You have been most courageous when you took the gigantic step of convening this meeting. The challenge was great, and the risks were high, but so was your determination.

You made a commitment to be a full partner in the peace process. I'm happy to say that you have honored your commitment.

The signing of the framework for the comprehensive peace settlement has a significance far beyond the event. It signals the emergence of a new peace initiative with the American nation in the heart of the entire process.

In the weeks ahead, important decisions have to be made if we are to proceed on the road to peace. We have to reaffirm the faith of the Palestinian people in the ideal of peace.

The continuation of your active role is indispensable. We need your help and the support of the American people. Let me seize this opportunity to thank each and every American for his genuine interest in the cause of people in the Middle East.

Dear friend, we came to Camp David with all the good will and faith we possessed, and we left Camp David a few minutes ago with a renewed sense of hope and inspiration. We are looking forward to the days ahead with an added determination to pursue the noble goal of peace.

Your able assistants spared no effort to bring out this happy conclusion. We appreciate their spirit and dedication. Our hosts at Camp David and the State of Maryland were most generous and hospitable. To each one of them and to all those who are watching this great event, I say thank you.

Let us join in a prayer to God Almighty to guide our path. Let us pledge to make the spirit of Camp David a new chapter in the history of our nations. [Applause]

PRIME MINISTER BEGIN: Mr. President of the United States, Mr. President of the Arab Republic of Egypt, ladies and gentlemen: The Camp David conference should be renamed. It was the "Jimmy Carter conference." [Laughter, applause]

The President undertook an initiative most imaginative in our time and brought President Sadat and myself and our colleagues and friends and advisers together under one roof. In itself it was a great achievement.

But the President took a great risk for himself and did it with great civil courage. And it was a famous French field commander who said that it is much more difficult to show civil courage than military courage. And the President worked. As far as my historic experience is concerned, I think that he worked harder than our forefathers did in Egypt, building the pyramids. [Laughter, applause]

Yes, indeed, he worked day and night, and so did we—[laughter] day and night. We used to go to bed at Camp David between 3:00 and 4:00 o'clock in the morning, arise, as we are used to since our boyhood, between 5:00 and 6:00, and continue working.

The President showed interest in every section, every paragraph, every sentence, every word, every letter [laughter] of the framework agreements.

We had some difficult moments, as usually, there are some crises in negotiations; as usually, somebody gives a hint that perhaps he would like to pick up and go home. [Laughter] It's all usual. But ultimately, ladies and gentlemen, the President of the United States won the day. And peace now celebrates a great victory for the nations of Egypt and Israel and for all mankind.

Mr. President, we, the Israelis, thank you from the bottom of our hearts for all you have done for the sake of peace, for which we prayed and yearned more than 30 years. The Jewish people suffered much, too much. And, therefore, peace to us is a striving, coming innermost from our heart and soul.

Now when I came here to the Camp David conference, I said perhaps as a result of our work, one day people will, in every corner of the world, be able to say *"Habemus pacem"* in the spirit of these days. Can we say so tonight? Not yet. We still have to go a road until my friend President Sadat and I sign the peace treaties. We promised each other that we shall do so within 3 months.

Mr. President [President Sadat], tonight at this celebration of the great historic event, let us promise each other that we shall do it earlier than within 3 months. [Laughter, applause]

Mr. President, you inscribed your name forever in the history of two ancient civilized peoples, the people of Egypt and the people of Israel. Thank you, Mr. President.

I would like to say a few words about my friend, President Sadat. We met for the first time in our lives last November in Jerusalem. He came to us as a guest, a former enemy, and during our first meeting, we became friends.

In the Jewish teachings, there is a tradition that the greatest achievement of a human being is to turn his enemy into a friend, and this we do in reciprocity. Since then, we had some difficult days. [Laughter] I'm not going now to tell you the saga of those days. Everything belongs to the past. Today, I visited President Sadat in his cabin because in Camp David you don't have houses, you only have cabins. [Laughter] And he then came to visit me. We shook hands. And, thank God, we again could have said to each other, "You are my friend." [Applause]

And, indeed, we shall go on working in understanding and in friendship and with good will. We will still have problems to solve. Camp David proved that any problem can be solved, if there is good will and understanding and some, *some* wisdom.

May I thank my own colleagues and friends, the Foreign Minister, the Defense Minister; Professor Barak who was the Attorney General and now he's going to be His Honor, the Justice of the Supreme Court—the Israeli Brandeis—Dr. Rosenne [legal adviser to the Foreign Minister] and our wonderful Ambassador to the United States, Mr. Simcha Dinitz, and all our friends, because without them, that achievement wouldn't have been possible.

I express my thanks to all the members of the American delegation, headed by the Secretary of State, a man whom we love and respect. And so I express my thanks to all the members of the Egyptian delegation who worked so hard together with us, headed by Deputy Prime Minister Mr. Touhamy, for all they have done to achieve this moment. It is a great moment in the history of our nations and, indeed, of mankind.

I looked for a precedent; I didn't find it. It was a unique conference, perhaps one of the most important since the Vienna conference in the 19th century; perhaps.

And now, ladies and gentlemen, allow me to turn to my own people from the White House in my own native tongue.

[Brief remarks in Hebrew.]

PRESIDENT CARTER: The first document that we will sign is entitled, "A Framework for Peace in the Middle East Agreed at Camp David," and the texts of these two documents will be released tomorrow. The documents will be signed by President Sadat and Prime Minister Begin. And it will be witnessed by me.

We have to exchange three documents, so we'll all sign three times for this one.

[The three leaders signed the first document.]

I might say that the first document is quite comprehensive in nature, encompassing a framework by which Israel can later negotiate peace treaties between herself and Lebanon, Syria, Jordan, as well as the outline of this document that we will now sign.

And as you will later see, in studying the documents, it also provides for the realization of the hopes and dreams of the people who live in the West Bank and Gaza Strip and will assure Israel peace in the generations ahead.

This second document is the one relating to a framework for a peace treaty between Egypt and Israel. And this is the document that calls for the completion of the peace treaty negotiations within 3 months. And I have noticed the challenge extended by these two gentlemen to each other. They will complete within 3 months—I might say that this document encompasses almost all of the issues between the two countries and resolves those issues. A few lines remain to be drawn on maps, and the question of the settlements is to be resolved. Other than that, most of the major issues are resolved already in this document. We will now sign this document as well.

[The three leaders signed the second document.]

65. A Framework for Peace in the Middle East Agreed at Camp David, September 17, 1978*

* 78 U.S. Dep't State Bull. No. 2019, at 7 (October 1978) (note omitted).

Muhammad Anwar al-Sadat, President of the Arab Republic of Egypt, and Menachem Begin, Prime Minister of Israel, met with Jimmy Carter, President of the United States of America, at Camp David from September 5 to September 17, 1978, and have agreed on the following framework for peace in the Middle East. They invite other parties to the Arab-Israeli conflict to adhere to it.

Preamble

The search for peace in the Middle East must be guided by the following:

· The agreed basis for a peaceful settlement of the conflict between Israel and its neighbors is United Nations Security Council Resolution 242, in all its parts.

· After four wars during thirty years, despite intensive human efforts, the Middle East, which is the cradle of civilization and the birthplace of three great religions, does not yet enjoy the blessings of peace. The people of the Middle East yearn for peace so that the vast human and natural resources of the region can be turned to the pursuits of peace and so that this area can become a model for coexistence and cooperation among nations.

· The historic initiative of President Sadat in visiting Jerusalem and the reception accorded to him by the Parliament, government and people of Israel, and the reciprocal visit of Prime Minister Begin to Ismailia, the peace proposals made by both leaders, as well as the warm reception of these missions by the peoples of both countries, have created an unprecedented opportunity for peace which must not be lost if this generation and future generations are to be spared the tragedies of war.

· The provisions of the Charter of the United Nations and the other accepted norms of international law and legitimacy now provide accepted standards for the conduct of relations among all states.

· To achieve a relationship of peace, in the spirit of Article 2 of the United Nations Charter, future negotiations between Israel and any neighbor prepared to negotiate peace and security with it, are necessary for the purpose of carrying out all the provisions and principles of Resolution 242 and 338.

· Peace requires respect for the sovereignty, territorial integrity and political independence of every state in the area and their right to live in peace within secure and recognized boundaries free from threats or acts of force. Progress toward that goal can accelerate movement toward a new era of reconciliation in the Middle East marked by cooperation in promoting economic development, in maintaining stability, and in assuring security.

· Security is enhanced by a relationship of peace and by cooperation between nations which enjoy normal relations. In addition, under the terms of peace treaties, the parties can, on the basis of reciprocity, agree to special security arrangements such as demilitarized zones, limited armaments areas, early warning stations, the presence of international forces, liaison, agreed measures for monitoring, and other arrangements that they agree are useful.

Framework

Taking these factors into account, the parties are determined to reach a just, comprehensive, and durable settlement of the Middle East conflict through the conclusion of peace treaties based on Security Council Resolutions 242 and 338 in all their parts. Their purpose is to achieve peace and good neighborly relations. They recognize that, for peace to endure, it must involve all those who have been most deeply affected by the conflict. They therefore agree that this framework as appropriate is intended by them to constitute a basis for peace not only between Egypt and Israel, but also between Israel and each of its other neighbors which is prepared to negotiate peace with Israel on this basis. With that objective in mind, they have agreed to proceed as follows:

A. WEST BANK AND GAZA

1. Egypt, Israel, Jordan and the representatives of the Palestinian people should participate in negotiations on the resolution of the Palestinian problem in all its aspects. To achieve that objective, negotiations relating to the West Bank and Gaza should proceed in three stages:

(a) Egypt and Israel agree that, in order to ensure a peaceful and orderly transfer of authority, and taking into account the security concerns of all the parties, there should be transitional arrangements for the West Bank and Gaza for a period not exceeding five years. In order to provide full autonomy to the inhabitants, under these arrangements the Israeli military government and its civilian administration will be withdrawn as soon as a self-governing authority has been freely elected by the inhabitants of these areas to replace the existing military government. To negotiate the details of a transitional arrangement, the Government of Jordan will be invited to join the negotiations on the basis of this framework. These new arrangements should give due consideration both to the principle of self-government by the inhabitants of these territories and to the legitimate security concerns of the parties involved.

(b) Egypt, Israel, and Jordan will agree on the modalities for establishing the elected self-governing authority in the West Bank and Gaza. The delegations of Egypt and Jordan may include Palestinians from the West Bank and Gaza or other Palestinians as mutually agreed. The parties will negotiate an agreement which will define the powers and responsibilities of the self-governing authority to be exercised in the West Bank and Gaza. A withdrawal of Israeli armed forces will take place and there will be a redeployment of the remaining Israeli forces into specified security locations. The agreement will also include arrangements for assuring internal and external security and public order. A strong local police force will be established, which may include Jordanian citizens. In addition, Israeli and Jordanian forces will participate in joint patrols and in the manning of control posts to assure the security of the borders.

(c) When the self-governing authority (administrative council) in the West Bank and Gaza is established and inaugurated, the transitional period of five years will begin. As soon as possible, but not later than the third year after the beginning of the transitional period, negotiations will take place to determine the final status of the West Bank and Gaza and its relationship with its neighbors, and to conclude a peace treaty between Israel and Jordan by the end of the transitional period. These negotiations will be conducted among Egypt, Israel, Jordan, and the elected representatives of the inhabitants of the West Bank and Gaza. Two separate but related committees will be convened, one committee, consisting of representatives of the four parties which will negotiate and agree on the final status of the West Bank and Gaza, and its relationship with its neighbors, and the second committee, consisting of representatives of Israel and representatives of Jordan to be joined by the elected representatives of the inhabitants of the West Bank and Gaza, to negotiate the peace treaty between Israel and Jordan, taking into account the agreement reached on the final status of the West Bank and Gaza. The negotiations shall be based on all the provisions and principles of UN Security Council Resolution 242. The negotiations will resolve, among other matters, the location of the boundaries and the nature of the security arrangements. The solution from the negotiations must also recognize the legitimate rights of the Palestinian people and their just requirements. In this way, the Palestinians will participate in the determination of their own future through:

1) The negotiations among Egypt, Israel, Jordan and the representatives of the inhabitants of the West Bank and Gaza to agree on the final status of the West Bank and Gaza and other outstanding issues by the end of the transitional period.

2) Submitting their agreement to a vote by the elected representatives of the inhabitants of the West Bank and Gaza.

3) Providing for the elected representatives of the inhabitants of the West Bank and Gaza to decide how they shall govern themselves consistent with the provisions of their agreement.

4) Participating as stated above in the work of the committee negotiating the peace treaty between Israel and Jordan.

2. All necessary measures will be taken and provisions made to assure the security of Israel and its neighbors during the transitional period and beyond. To assist in providing such security, a strong local police force will be constituted by the self-governing authority. It will be composed of inhabitants of the West Bank and Gaza. The police will maintain continuing liaison

on internal security matters with the designated Israeli, Jordanian, and Egyptian officers.

3. During the transitional period, representatives of Egypt, Israel, Jordan, and the self-governing authority will constitute a continuing committee to decide by agreement on the modalities of admission of persons displaced from the West Bank and Gaza in 1967, together with necessary measures to prevent disruption and disorder. Other matters of common concern may also be dealt with by this committee.

4. Egypt and Israel will work with each other and with other interested parties to establish agreed procedures for a prompt, just and permanent implementation of the resolution of the refugee problem.

B. EGYPT-ISRAEL

1. Egypt and Israel undertake not to resort to the threat or the use of force to settle disputes. Any disputes shall be settled by peaceful means in accordance with the provisions of Article 33 of the Charter of the United Nations.

2. In order to achieve peace between them, the parties agree to negotiate in good faith with a goal of concluding within three months from the signing of this Framework a peace treaty between them, while inviting the other parties to the conflict to proceed simultaneously to negotiate and conclude similar peace treaties with a view to achieving a comprehensive peace in the area. The Framework for the Conclusion of a Peace Treaty Between Egypt and Israel will govern the peace negotiations between them. The parties will agree on the modalities and the timetable for the implementation of their obligations under the treaty.

C. ASSOCIATED PRINCIPLES

1. Egypt and Israel state that the principles and provisions described below should apply to peace treaties between Israel and each of its neighbors—Egypt, Jordan, Syria and Lebanon.

2. Signatories shall establish among themselves relationships normal to states at peace with one another. To this end, they should undertake to abide by all the provisions of the Charter of the United Nations. Steps to be taken in this respect include:

(a) full recognition;

(b) abolishing economic boycotts;

(c) guaranteeing that under their jurisdiction the citizens of the other parties shall enjoy the protection of the due process of law.

3. Signatories should explore possibilities for economic development in the context of final peace treaties, with the objective of contributing to the atmosphere of peace, cooperation and friendship which is their common goal.

4. Claims Commissions may be established for the mutual settlement of all financial claims.

5. The United States shall be invited to participate in the talks on matters related to the modalities of the implementation of the agreements and working out the timetable for the carrying out of the obligations of the parties.

6. The United Nations Security Council shall be requested to endorse the peace treaties and ensure that their provisions shall not be violated. The permanent members of the Security Council shall be requested to underwrite the peace treaties and ensure respect for their provisions. They shall also be requested to conform their policies and actions with the undertakings contained in this Framework.

For the Government of the Arab Republic of Egypt:
A. SADAT

For the Government of Israel:
M. BEGIN

Witnessed by:
JIMMY CARTER, President of the United States of America

66. A Framework for the Conclusion of a Peace Treaty between Egypt and Israel, September 17, 1978*

* 78 U.S. Dep't State Bull. No. 2019, at 9 (October 1978).

In order to achieve peace between them, Israel and Egypt agree to negotiate in good faith with a goal of concluding within three months of the signing of this framework a peace treaty between them.

It is agreed that:

The site of the negotiations will be under a United Nations flag at a location or locations to be mutually agreed.

All of the principles of U.N. Resolution 242 will apply to this resolution of the dispute between Israel and Egypt.

Unless otherwise mutually agreed, terms of the peace treaty will be implemented between two and three years after the peace treaty is signed.

The following matters are agreed between the parties:

(a) the full exercise of Egyptian sovereignty up to the internationally recognized border between Egypt and mandated Palestine;

(b) the withdrawal of Israeli armed forces from the Sinai;

(c) the use of airfields left by the Israelis near El Arish, Rafah, Ras en Naqb, and Sharm el Sheikh for civilian purposes only, including possible commercial use by all nations;

(d) the right of free passage by ships of Israel through the Gulf of Suez and the Suez Canal on the basis of the Constantinople Convention of 1888 applying to all nations; the Strait of Tiran and the Gulf of Aqaba are international waterways to be open to all nations for unimpeded and nonsuspendable freedom of navigation and overflight;

(e) the construction of a highway between the Sinai and Jordan near Elat with guaranteed free and peaceful passage by Egypt and Jordan; and

(f) the stationing of military forces listed below.

Stationing of Forces

A. No more than one division (mechanized or infantry) of Egyptian armed forces will be stationed within an area lying approximately 50 kilometers (km) east of the Gulf of Suez and the Suez Canal.

B. Only United Nations forces and civil police equipped with light weapons to perform normal police functions will be stationed within an area lying west of the international border and the Gulf of Aqaba, varying in width from 20 km to 40 km.

C. In the area within 3 km east of the international border there will be Israeli limited military forces not to exceed four infantry battalions and United Nations observers.

D. Border patrol units, not to exceed three battalions, will supplement the civil police in maintaining order in the area not included above.

The exact demarcation of the above areas will be as decided during the peace negotiations.

Early warning stations may exist to insure compliance with the terms of the agreement.

United Nations forces will be stationed: (a) in part of the area in the Sinai lying within about 20 km of the Mediterranean Sea and adjacent to the international border, and (b) in the Sharm el Sheikh area to ensure freedom of passage through the Strait of Tiran; and these forces will not be removed unless such removal is approved by the Security Council of the United Nations with a unanimous vote of the five permanent members.

After a peace treaty is signed, and after the interim withdrawal is complete, normal relations will be established between Egypt and Israel, including: full recognition, including diplomatic, economic and cultural relations; termination of economic boycotts and barriers to the free movement of goods and people; and mutual protection of citizens by the due process of law.

Interim Withdrawal

Between three months and nine months after the signing of the peace treaty, all Israeli forces will withdraw east of a line extending from a point east of El Arish to Ras Muhammad, the exact location of this line to be determined by mutual agreement.

For the Government of the Arab Republic of Egypt:
A. Sadat

For the Government of Israel:
M. Begin

Witnessed by:
Jimmy Carter, President of the United States of America

67. Accompanying Letters on: Sinai Settlements, Jerusalem, Implementation of Comprehensive Settlement, Definition of Terms, and Airbases, September 17–28, 1978*

* 78 U.S. Dep't State Bull. No. 2019, at 10 (October 1978).

Sinai Settlements[9]

September 17, 1978

Dear Mr. President:

I have the honor to inform you that during two weeks after my return home I will submit a motion before Israel's Parliament (the Knesset) to decide on the following question:

If during the negotiations to conclude a peace treaty between Israel and Egypt all outstanding issues are agreed upon, "are you in favor of the removal of the Israeli settlers from the northern and southern Sinai areas or are you in favor of keeping the aforementioned settlers in those areas?"

The vote, Mr. President, on this issue will be completely free from the usual Parliamentary Party discipline to the effect that although the coalition is being now supported by 70 members out of 120, every member of the Knesset, as I believe, both on the Government and the Opposition benches will be enabled to vote in accordance with his own conscience.

Sincerely yours,

(signed)
MENACHEM BEGIN

The President
Camp David
Thurmont, Maryland

September 22, 1978

Dear Mr. President:

I transmit herewith a copy of a letter to me from Prime Minister Begin setting forth how he proposes to present the issue of the Sinai settlements to the Knesset for the latter's decision.

In this connection, I understand from your letter that Knesset approval to withdraw all Israeli settlers from Sinai according to a timetable within the period specified for the implementation of the peace treaty is a prerequisite to any negotiations on a peace treaty between Egypt and Israel.

Sincerely,

(signed)
JIMMY CARTER

Enclosure:
Letter from Prime Minister Begin

His Excellency
Anwar Al-Sadat
President of the Arab
    Republic of Egypt
Cairo

---

[9] Released by the White House on Sept. 22 (text from Weekly Compilation of Sept. 25).

September 17, 1978

Dear Mr. President:

In connection with the "Framework for a Settlement in Sinai" to be signed tonight, I would like to reaffirm the position of the Arab Republic of Egypt with respect to the settlements:

1. All Israeli settlers must be withdrawn from Sinai according to a time-table within the period specified for the implementation of the peace treaty.

2. Agreement by the Israeli Government and its constitutional institutions to this basic principle is therefore a prerequisite to starting peace negotiations for concluding a peace treaty.

3. If Israel fails to meet this commitment, the "Framework" shall be void and invalid.

Sincerely,

(signed)
MOHAMED ANWAR EL SADAT

His Excellency Jimmy Carter
President of the United States

September 22, 1978

Dear Mr. Prime Minister:

I have received your letter of September 17, 1978, describing how you intend to place the question of the future of Israeli settlements in Sinai before the Knesset for its decision.

Enclosed is a copy of President Sadat's letter to me on this subject.

Sincerely,

(signed)
JIMMY CARTER

Enclosure:
Letter from President Sadat

His Excellency
Menachem Begin
Prime Minister of Israel

Jerusalem[10]

September 17, 1978

Dear Mr. President:

I am writing you to reaffirm the position of the Arab Republic of Egypt with respect to Jerusalem:

1. Arab Jerusalem is an integral part of the West Bank. Legal and histor-ical Arab rights in the City must be respected and restored.

2. Arab Jerusalem should be under Arab sovereignty.

[10] Released by the White House on Sept. 22 (text from Weekly Compilation of Sept. 25).

3. The Palestinian inhabitants of Arab Jerusalem are entitled to exercise their legitimate national rights, being part of the Palestinian People in the West Bank.

4. Relevant Security Council Resolutions, particularly Resolutions 242 and 267, must be applied with regard to Jerusalem. All the measures taken by Israel to alter the status of the City are null and void and should be rescinded.

5. All peoples must have free access to the City and enjoy the free exercise of worship and the right to visit and transit to the holy places without distinction or discrimination.

6. The holy places of each faith may be placed under the administration and control of their representatives.

7. Essential functions in the City should be undivided and a joint municipal council composed of an equal number of Arab and Israeli members can supervise the carrying out of these functions. In this way, the City shall be undivided.

Sincerely,

(signed)
MOHAMED ANWAR EL SADAT

His Excellency Jimmy Carter
President of the United States

---

17 September 1978

Dear Mr. President,

I have the honor to inform you, Mr. President, that on 28 June 1967—Israel's Parliament (the Knesset) promulgated and adopted a law to the effect: "the Government is empowered by a decree to apply the law, the jurisdiction and administration of the State to any part of Eretz Israel (land of Israel—Palestine), as stated in that decree."

On the basis of this law, the Government of Israel decreed in July 1967 that Jerusalem is one city indivisible, the Capital of the State of Israel.

Sincerely,

(signed)
MENACHEM BEGIN

The President
Camp David
Thurmont, Maryland

September 22, 1978

Dear Mr. President:

I have received your letter of September 17, 1978, setting forth the Egyptian position on Jerusalem. I am transmitting a copy of that letter to Prime Minister Begin for his information.

The position of the United States on Jerusalem remains as stated by Ambassador Goldberg in the United Nations General Assembly on July 14, 1967,[11] and subsequently by Ambassador Yost in the United Nations Security Council on July 1, 1969.[12]

Sincerely,

(signed)
JIMMY CARTER

His Excellency
Anwar al-Sadat
President of the Arab
  Republic of Egypt
Cairo

Implementation of Comprehensive Settlement[13]

September 17, 1978

Dear Mr. President:

In connection with the "Framework for Peace in the Middle East", I am writing you this letter to inform you of the position of the Arab Republic of Egypt, with respect to the implementation of the comprehensive settlement.

To ensure the implementation of the provisions related to the West Bank and Gaza and in order to safeguard the legitimate rights of the Palestinian people, Egypt will be prepared to assume the Arab role emanating from those provisions, following consultations with Jordan and the representatives of the Palestinian people.

Sincerely,

(signed)
MOHAMED ANWAR EL SADAT

His Excellency
Jimmy Carter
President of the United States
The White House
Washington, D.C.

Definition of Terms[14]

September 22, 1978

Dear Mr. Prime Minister:

I hereby acknowledge that you have informed me as follows:

A) In each paragraph of the Agreed Framework Document the expressions "Palestinians" or "Palestinian People" are being and will be construed and understood by you as "Palestinian Arabs."

---

[11] For text of Ambassador Goldberg's statement, see BULLETIN of July 31, 1967, p. 148.
[12] For text of Ambassador Yost's statement, see BULLETIN of July 28, 1969, p. 76.
[13] Released by the White House on Sept. 22 (text from Weekly Compilation of Sept. 25).
[14] Released by the White House on Sept. 22 (text from Weekly Compilation of Sept. 25).

B) In each paragraph in which the expression "West Bank" appears, it is being, and will be, understood by the Government of Israel as Judea and Samaria.

Sincerely,

(signed)
JIMMY CARTER

His Excellency
Menachem Begin
Prime Minister of Israel

Airbases[15]

September 28, 1978

Dear Mr. Minister:

The U.S. understands that, in connection with carrying out the agreements reached at Camp David, Israel intends to build two military airbases at appropriate sites in the Negev to replace the airbases at Eitam and Etzion which will be evacuated by Israel in accordance with the peace treaty to be concluded between Egypt and Israel. We also understand the special urgency and priority which Israel attaches to preparing the new bases in light of its conviction that it cannot safely leave the Sinai airbases until the new ones are operational.

I suggest that our two governments consult on the scope and costs of the two new airbases as well as on related forms of assistance which the United States might appropriately provide in light of the special problems which may be presented by carrying out such a project on an urgent basis. The President is prepared to seek the necessary Congressional approvals for such assistance as may be agreed upon by the U.S. side as a result of such consultations.

(signed)
HAROLD BROWN
Secretary of Defense

The Honorable
Ezer Weisman
Minister of Defense
Government of Israel

[15] Released by the Department of Defense on Sept. 29.

68. President Carter's Address Before the Congress on

the Camp David Accords, September 18, 1978*

---

* 78 U.S. Dep't State Bull. No. 2019, at 1 (October 1978).

Vice President Mondale, Speaker O'Neill, distinguished Members of the United States Congress, Justices of the Supreme Court, other leaders of our great nation, ladies and gentlemen: It's been more than 2,000 years since there was peace between Egypt and a free Jewish nation. If our present expectations are realized, this year we shall see such peace again.

The first thing I would like to do is to give tribute to the two men who made this impossible dream now become a real possibility—the two great leaders with whom I have met for the last 2 weeks at Camp David—first, President Anwar Sadat of Egypt and the other, of course, is Prime Minister Menahem [*sic*] Begin of the nation of Israel.

I know that all of you would agree that these are two men of great personal courage, representing nations of peoples who are deeply grateful to them for the achievement which they have realized. And I am personally grateful to them for what they have done.

At Camp David we sought a peace that is not only of vital importance to their own two nations, but to all the people of the Middle East, to all the people of the United States, and, indeed, to all the world as well.

The world prayed for the success of our efforts, and I am glad to announce to you that these prayers have been answered.

I've come to discuss with you tonight what these two leaders have accomplished, and what this means to all of us.

The United States has had no choice but to be deeply concerned about the Middle East and to try to use our influence and our efforts to advance the cause of peace. For the last 30 years, through four wars, the people of this troubled region have paid a terrible price in suffering and division and hatred and bloodshed. No two nations have suffered more than Egypt and Israel. But the dangers and the costs of conflicts in this region for our own nation have been great as well. We have longstanding friendships among the nations there and the peoples of the region, and we have profound moral commitments which are deeply rooted in our values as a people.

The strategic location of these countries and the resources that they possess mean that events in the Middle East directly affect people everywhere. We and our friends could not be indifferent if a hostile power were to establish domination there. In few areas of the world is there a greater risk that a local conflict could spread among other nations adjacent to them and then perhaps erupt into a tragic confrontation between us superpowers ourselves.

Our people have come to understand that unfamiliar names—like Sinai, Aqaba, Sharm el Sheikh, Ras en Naqb, Gaza, the West Bank of Jordan—can have a direct and immediate bearing on our own well-being as a nation and our hope for a peaceful world.

That is why we in the United States cannot afford to be idle bystanders and why we have been full partners in the search for peace and why it is so vital to our nation that these meetings at Camp David have been a success.

Through the long years of conflict, four main issues have divided the parties involved.

· One is the nature of peace—whether peace will simply mean that the guns are silenced, that the bombs no longer fall, that the tanks cease to roll, or whether it will mean that the nations of the Middle East can deal with each other as neighbors and as equals and as friends, with a full range of diplomatic and cultural and economic and human relations between them. That's been the basic question. The Camp David agreement has defined such relationships, I'm glad to announce to you, between Israel and Egypt.

· The second main issue is providing for the security of all parties involved, including, or course, our friends the Israelis, so that none of them need fear attack or military threats from one another. When implemented, the Camp David agreement, I'm glad to announce to you, will provide for such mutual security.

· The third is the question of agreement on secure and recognized boundaries, the end of military occupation, and the granting of self-government or else the return to other nations of territories which have been occupied by Israel since the 1967 conflict. The Camp David agreement, I'm glad to announce to you, provides for the realization of all these goals.

· And, finally, there is the painful human question of the fate of the Palestinians who live or who have lived in these disputed regions. The Camp David agreement guarantees that the Palestinian people may participate in the resolution of the Palestinian problem in all its aspects, a commitment that Israel has made in writing and which is supported and appreciated, I'm sure, by all the world.

Over the last 18 months, there has been, of course, some progress on these issues. Egypt and Israel came close to agreeing about the first issue—the nature of peace. Then they saw that the second and third issues—that is, withdrawal and security—were intimately connected, closely entwined. But fundamental divisions still remained in other areas—about the fate of the Palestinians, the future of the West Bank and Gaza, and the future of the Israeli settlements in occupied Arab territories.

We all remember the hopes for peace that were inspired by President Sadat's initiative—that great and historic visit to Jerusalem last November that thrilled the world and by the warm and genuine personal response of Prime Minister Begin and the Israeli people and by the mutual promise between them, publicly made, that there would be no more war. These hopes were sustained when Prime Minister Begin reciprocated by visiting Ismailia on Christmas Day.

That progress continued but at a slower and slower pace through the early part of the year. And by early summer, the negotiations had come to a standstill once again.

It was this stalemate and the prospect for an even worse future that prompted me to invite both President Sadat and Prime Minister Begin to join me at Camp David.

They accepted, as you know, instantly, without delay, without preconditions, without consultation even between them. It's impossible to overstate the courage of these two men or the foresight they have shown. Only through high ideals, through compromises of words and not principle, and through a willingness to look deep into the human heart and to understand the problems and hopes and dreams of one another can progress in a difficult situation like this ever be made.

That's what these men and their wise and diligent advisers who are here with us tonight have done during the last 13 days.

When this conference began, I said that the prospects for success were remote. Enormous barriers of ancient history and nationalism and suspicion would have to be overcome if we were to meet our objectives.

But President Sadat and Prime Minister Begin have overcome these barriers, exceeded our fondest expectations, and have signed two agreements that hold out the possibility of resolving issues that history had taught us could not be resolved.

The first of these documents is entitled "A Framework for Peace in the Middle East Agreed at Camp David." It deals with a comprehensive settlement, comprehensive settlement between Israel and all her neighbors, as well as the difficult question of the Palestinian people and the future of the West Bank and the Gaza area.

The Israeli military government over these areas will be withdrawn and will be replaced with a self-government of the Palestinians who live there. And Israel has committed that this government will have full autonomy. Prime Minister Begin said to me several times, not partial autonomy, but full autonomy.

Israeli forces will be withdrawn and redeployed into specified locations to protect Israel's security. The Palestinians will further participate in determining their own future through talks in which their own elected representatives, the inhabitants of the West Bank and Gaza, will negotiate with Egypt and Israel and Jordan to determine the final status of the West Bank and Gaza.

Israel has agreed, has committed themselves, that the legitimate rights of the Palestinian people will be recognized. After the signing of this framework last night, and during the negotiations concerning the establishment of the Palestinian self-government, no new Israeli settlements will be established in this area. The future settlements issue will be decided among the negotiating parties.

The final status of the West Bank and Gaza will be decided before the end of the 5-year transitional period during which the Palestinian Arabs will have their own government, as part of a negotiation which will produce a peace treaty between Israel and Jordan, specifying borders, withdrawal, all those very crucial issues.

These negotiations will be based on all the provisions and the principles of Security Council Resolution 242, with which you all are so familiar. The agreement on the final status of these areas will then be submitted to a vote by the representatives of the inhabitants of the West Bank and Gaza, and they will have the right for the first time in their history—the Palestinian people—to decide how they will govern themselves permanently.

We also believe, of course, all of us, that there should be a just settlement of the problems of displaced persons and refugees, which takes into account appropriate U.N. resolutions.

Finally, this document also outlines a variety of security arrangements to reinforce peace between Israel and her neighbors.

This is, indeed, a comprehensive and fair framework for peace in the Middle East, and I'm glad to report this to you.

The second agreement is entitled a "Framework for the Conclusion of a Peace Treaty Between Egypt and Israel." It returns to Egypt its full exercise of sovereignty over the Sinai Peninsula and establishes several security zones, recognizing carefully that sovereignty right for the protection of all parties. It also provides that Egypt will extend full diplomatic recognition to Israel at the time the Israelis complete an interim withdrawal from most of the Sinai, which will take place between 3 months and 9 months after the conclusion of the peace treaty. And the peace treaty is to be fully negotiated and signed no later than 3 months from last night.

I think I should also report that Prime Minister Begin and President Sadat have already challenged each other to conclude the treaty even earlier. This final conclusion of a peace treaty will be completed late in December. And it would be a wonderful Christmas present for the world.

Final and complete withdrawal of all Israeli forces will take place between 2 and 3 years following the conclusion of the peace treaty.

While both parties are in total agreement on all the goals that I have just described to you, there is one issue on which agreement has not yet been reached. Egypt states that agreement to remove the Israeli settlements from Egyptian territory is a prerequisite to a peace treaty. Israel says that the issue of the Israeli settlements should be resolved during the peace negotiations themselves.

Now, within 2 weeks with each member of the Knesset, or the Israeli Parliament acting as individuals, not constrained by party loyalty, the Knesset will decide on the issue of the settlements. Our own government's position, my own personal position, is well-known on this issue and has been consistent. It is my strong hope, my prayer, that the question of Israeli settlements on Egyptian territory will not be the final obstacle to peace.

None of us should underestimate the historic importance of what has already been done. This is the first time that an Arab and an Israeli leader have signed a comprehensive framework for peace. It contains the seeds of a time when the Middle East, with all its vast potential, may be a land of human richness and fulfillment, rather than a land of bitterness and continued conflict. No region in the world has greater natural and human resources than this one. And nowhere have they been more heavily weighed down by intense hatred and frequent war. These agreements hold out the real possibility that this burden might finally be lifted.

But we must also not forget the magnitude of the obstacles that still remain. The summit exceeded our highest expectations—but we know that it left many difficult issues which are still to be resolved. These issues will require careful negotiation in the months to come. The Egyptian and Israeli people must recognize the tangible benefits that peace will bring and support the decisions their leaders have made so that a secure and a peaceful future can be achieved for them. The American public, you and I, must also offer our full support to those who have made decisions that are difficult and those who have very difficult decisions still to make.

What lies ahead for all of us is to recognize the statesmanship that President Sadat and Prime Minister Begin have shown and to invite others in that region to follow their example. I have already last night invited the other leaders of the Arab world to help sustain progress toward a comprehensive peace. We must also join in an effort to bring an end to the conflict and the terrible suffering in Lebanon.

This is a subject that President Sadat discussed with me many times while I was in Camp David with him. And the first time that the three of us met together, this was a subject of heated discussion. On the way to Washington last night in the helicopter, we mutually committed ourselves to join with other nations, with the Lebanese people themselves, all factions, with President Sarkis, with Syria and Saudi Arabia, perhaps the European countries like France, to try to move toward a solution of the problem in Lebanon which is so vital to us and to the poor people in Lebanon who have suffered so much.

We will want to consult on this matter and on these documents and their meaning with all of the leaders, particularly the Arab leaders. And I'm pleased to say to you tonight that just a few minutes ago, King Hussein of Jordan and King Khalid of Saudi Arabia—perhaps other leaders later—but these two have already agreed to receive Secretary Vance, who will be leaving tomorrow to explain to them the terms of the Camp David agreement.

And we hope to secure their support for the realization of the new hopes and dreams of the people of the Middle East.

This is an important mission, and this responsibility I can tell you, based on my last 2 weeks with him, could not possibly rest on the shoulders of a more able and dedicated and competent man than Secretary Cyrus Vance.

Finally, let me say that for many years the Middle East has been a textbook for pessimism, a demonstration that diplomatic ingenuity was no match for intractable human conflicts. Today we are privileged to see the chance for one of the sometimes rare bright moments in human history—a chance that may offer the way to peace. We have a chance for peace because these two brave leaders found within themselves the willingness to work together to seek these lasting prospects for peace, which we all want so badly. And for that, I hope that you will share my prayer of thanks and my hope that the promise of this moment shall be fully realized.

The prayers at Camp David were the same as those of the shepherd King David who prayed in the 85th Psalm: "Wilt thou not revive us again: that thy people may rejoice in thee? . . . I will hear that God the Lord will speak: for he will speak peace unto his people, and to his saints: but let them not return again to folly."

And I would like to say, as a Christian, to these two friends of mine, the words of Jesus: "Blessed are the peacemakers: for they shall be the children of God."

69. Statement by the EEC Foreign Ministers on

the Camp David Meeting, September 19, 1978*

* 11 Bull. Eur. Comm. (No. 9) 53 (1978).

2.2.8. When the Foreign Ministers met in the Council on 19 September the President made the following statement on behalf of the Nine:

'The nine countries of the European Community congratulate President Carter on the great courage with which he initiated the Camp David meeting and brought it to a successful conclusion. They also express their appreciation for the great efforts made by President Sadat and Prime Minister Begin.

The Nine have for years advocated a just, comprehensive and lasting peace-settlement on the basis of Resolutions 242 and 338 of the Security Council of the United Nations. The position of the Nine was clearly set out in the Declaration of the European Council of 29 June 1977. This remains their position. On this basis the Nine welcomed the initiative of President Sadat in November 1977.

The nine Governments hope that the outcome of the Camp David conference will be a further major step on the path to a just, comprehensive and lasting peace, and that all parties concerned will find it possible to join in the process to contribute to that end.

For their part the Nine will lend their strong support to all efforts to achieve such a peace.'

70. House of Representatives Concurrent Resolution 715
Commending the Parties and the Results of the Camp
David Summit, September 28, 1978*

---

* H.R. Con. Res. 715, 92 Stat. 3881 (1978).

Whereas the people of the United States earnestly hope and pray that a just and durable peace in the Middle East can be negotiated by the parties to the Arab-Israeli conflict;

Whereas President Carter has responded to this hope by his courageous and dedicated effort in convening the Camp David Summit;

Whereas President Anwar al-Sadat and Prime Minister Menachem Begin have been willing to negotiate with understanding, humility, and a willingness to compromise in order to try to achieve solutions acceptable to all sides and promote lasting peace and justice in the Middle East; and

Whereas continued good will and cooperation will be needed from the leaders of all states in the Middle East: Now, therefore, be it

Resolved by the House of Representatives (the Senate concurring), That the Congress commends President Carter for his leadership in promoting peace in the Middle East and endorses his efforts to further encourage support and understanding among the leaders of all states in the Middle East of the two agreements reached at the Camp David Summit.

Sec. 2. The Congress commends President Sadat and Prime Minister Begin for the courageous steps they have taken to resolve the differences between their nations and to bring about a comprehensive, just, and durable peace between Israel and its Arab neighbors.

Sec. 3. It is the sense of the Congress that the framework for Middle East peace embodied in the two agreements reached at the Camp David Summit provides the basis for peace treaties among the parties to the Arab-Israeli conflict and provides hope that human dignity, justice, and security for all peoples in the Middle East can be achieved.

Sec. 4. It is further the sense of the Congress that the United States should continue to pursue further direct peace talks among parties in the Middle East in order to build on the momentum created by the Camp David agreements to promote a comprehensive settlement among all parties to the conflict.

Passed September 28, 1978.

71. Resolutions Passed at the Gaza National Conference, Gaza, October 16 and 18, 1978*

* 8 J. Palestine Stud. 199 (Winter 1979).

On October 16 and 18, 1978, the municipalities, rural councils, benevolent societies, trade associations, chambers of commerce and industry and business establishments of the Gaza Strip met to discuss the contents of the Camp David agreements and the documents appended thereto.

In affirming the concern of the Palestinian Arab people of the Gaza Strip that a just peace should prevail in the Middle East, and in desiring that all causes and consequences of wars should disappear so that all peoples of the region can live in a permanent peace which will come about by fulfilling the national aspirations of the Palestinian Arab people, they set forth their views, in a positive, constructive and objective spirit:

1. The Camp David agreement ignores the legitimate rights of the Palestinian Arab people, their right to freedom and self-determination and their right to create an independent national state in their homeland. The agreement also violates the UN Charter, the Declaration of the Rights of Man and the provisions of international law.

2. The Camp David agreement violates the consensus of Arab states arrived at in the various Arab summit meetings, especially the resolutions of the Algiers and Rabat summits.

3. The Camp David agreement violates UN General Assembly resolutions, especially resolution 3236 of November 22, 1974 and resolution 3375 of November 10, 1975.

4. The agreement entrenches Israeli occupation for an unlimited period of time, endows it with legality, disrupts the unity of the Palestinian people at home and abroad, creates a new situation and new facts that essentially and basically conflict with the interests of the Palestinian Arab people and, in addition, does not specify the removal of the settlements in the West Bank and Gaza Strip.

5. The agreement ignored the future of Arab Jerusalem. This deliberate oversight represents a grave danger to its Muslim and Christian shrines and to the rights of its Palestinian Arab population.

6. A just solution to the Palestinian question can only be achieved when the rights of the Palestinian Arab people to their soil and homeland and to the exercise of their natural right to freedom, justice and self-determination are respected and when the Israeli forces have completely and immediately withdrawn from all occupied Arab territories.

7. The participants affirm that the PLO is the sole and legitimate representative of the Palestinian Arab people and that its participation on an equal footing with all other sides is essential for the achievement of a just solution to the Palestinian question. The cause of peace in the Middle East is not served by deliberately ignoring the PLO.

8. Self-government according to the Camp David agreement is without content or meaning since it does not fulfill even the minimum demands and rights of the Palestinian Arab people, nor does it represent the correct manner in which that people can exercise their right to freedom and self-determination. This is because it is obscure, ambiguous and complex and lacks

specific and genuine guarantees which ensure for that people their freedom, their return and self-determination on their soil and in their homeland.

9. Accordingly, the participants condemn the Camp David agreement and call upon all who love justice and peace in the world, upon the Arab and Islamic worlds, upon world public opinion and the United Nations to help the Palestinian Arab people obtain their just rights and put an end to their continuing tragedy. The participants affirm that they fully support a just peace. They assert that the Palestinian Arab people aspire to that just peace. Of all nations in the world, they need and desire this most in order to be rid of their sufferings and of the cruel fate imposed upon them against their will. They affirm that they have always been the victim of continuous wars and have been denied their natural right to freedom and a life of dignity on their own soil and in their homeland.

72. European Parliament Resolution on the Outcome of the Camp David Summit, November 6, 1978*

* 21 O.J. Eur. Comm. (No. C261) 32 (1978).

The European Parliament,

— in the desire to see a just and lasting peace in the Middle East,
— aware of the responsibilities of the countries of Europe in this matter and, in particular, of the Member States of the European Community,
— referring to its resolution of 15 December 1977 on the historic meeting between Mr Anwar el-Sadat, *President of the Arab Republic of Egypt*, and Mr Menachem Begin, *Head of the Government of the State of Israel.*

1. Welcomes the successful outcome of the Camp David Summit;

2. Promises its full support for the negotiations to follow, so that they may lead to a just and lasting peace in the whole region;

3. Calls urgently on the other parties involved in the conflict to join in the negotiations;

4. Invites the Council and Commission to draw up, in consultation with the Arab Republic of Egypt and the State of Israel, practical proposals for multilateral cooperation aimed at speeding up the economic, technical and social development of the region;

5. Calls upon the Foreign Ministers meeting in political cooperation to adopt a constructive attitude to the process of achieving peace and to all measures aimed at helping that process, not only within the Community, but also in the international organizations to which they belong;

6. Instructs its Political Affairs Committee to follow developments in the Middle East and to report to it when it judges necessary;

7. Instructs its President to forward this resolution to the Council and Commission and to the Foreign Ministers meeting in political cooperation.

73. Political and Organizational Programme Approved by the Palestine National Council at Its Fourteenth Session, Damascus, January 15–23, 1979*

* 8 J. Palestine Stud. 165 (Spring 1979).

The US settlement of the Arab-Zionist conflict embodied in the Camp David agreements poses grave threats to the cause of Palestine and of Arab national liberation. This settlement condones the Zionist enemy's continued usurpation of the national soil of Palestine, abrogates the inalienable right of the Palestinian Arab people to their homeland, Palestine, as well as their right to return to it and their right to self-determination and to the exercise of their national independence on their soil. It dissipates other Arab territories and overrides the PLO, the leader of our people's national struggle and their sole legitimate representative and spokesman expressing their will.

In addition, these agreements violate Palestinian, Arab and international legitimacy and pave the way for tighter imperialist and Zionist control over our Arab region and Africa, employing the Egyptian regime, in the context of its alliance with imperialism and Zionism, as a tool for the repression of the Arab and African national liberation movements.

Motivated by our awareness of the gravity of this new conspiracy and its implications and by our national responsibilities in the PLO, which represents our Palestinian Arab people with all their national groups and forces, we are obliged to reject this new conspiratorial scheme, to confront it and to defend our people and their inalienable national rights to their homeland, Palestine, as well as to safeguard our Palestinian revolution.

The courageous position adopted by our Palestinian masses inside and outside the occupied homeland and by the masses of our Arab nation through their rejection of the Camp David agreements and their open determination to confront this new conspiracy against our people and their inalienable national rights and our Arab nation strengthen our resolve to resist this conspiracy and our faith in defeating it.

At the same time, we shoulder a great responsibility which can be carried out only by adopting a united national and popular stand, within the framework of the PLO.

In response to the will of our people and to the challenges that we face, and motivated by our faith in national unity within the PLO as the sole means to achieve victory; basing ourselves upon the Palestine National Charter, the resolutions of the Palestine National Councils and the Tripoli document which established unity among the various organizations of the Palestinian revolution; believing in the right of our people to establish a democratic state on the whole of our national soil and in order to confront this critical and dangerous stage in the struggle of our people, we, the representatives of all organizations of the Revolution and Palestinian national forces, declare the following:

In the Palestinian Sphere

1. [That we] adhere to the inalienable national rights of our people to their homeland, Palestine, and to their right to return and to self-determi-

nation on their soil without foreign interference, and to their right to establish their independent state on their soil unconditionally.

2. [That we shall] defend the PLO and adhere to it as the sole legitimate representative of our people, as leader of their national struggle and as their spokesman in all Arab and international forums; resist all attempts to harm, override or circumvent the PLO, or to create alternatives or partners to it as regards representation of our Palestinian people; adhere to the resolutions of the Arab summits of Algiers and Rabat and to UN resolutions—especially resolutions 3236 and 3237—which affirm our inalienable national rights as well as Arab and international recognition of the PLO as the sole legitimate representative of the Palestinian people.

3. [That we] resolve firmly to continue and escalate the armed struggle and use all other forms of political and mass struggle, especially inside the occupied homeland which is the principal arena of conflict with the Zionist enemy, in order to achieve the inalienable and non-negotiable national rights of the Palestinian Arab people.

4. [That we] affirm that the problem of Palestine is the crux and the basis of the Arab-Zionist conflict, and [we] reject all resolutions, agreements and settlements that do not recognize or that impinge upon the inalienable rights of our people to their homeland, Palestine, including their right to return, to self-determination and to the establishment of their independent national state. This applies in particular to Security Council resolution 242.

5. [That we] reject and resist the self-rule scheme in the occupied homeland, which entrenches Zionist settler colonization of our occupied land and denies the rights of our Palestinian people.

6. [That we] affirm the unity of our Palestinian Arab people inside and outside the occupied homeland, and their sole representation through the PLO; [we shall] resist all attempts and schemes that seek to divide our people or to circumvent the PLO; work to support the struggle of our people in the occupied territories and to fortify their unity and their steadfastness.

7. [That we shall] consolidate the framework of the Palestinian National Front inside Palestine since it is an integral part of the PLO, and [shall] furnish it with all means of political and financial aid so that it can mobilize our masses inside to face the Zionist occupation, its schemes and its projects which are inimical to our people and to their inalienable national rights.

8. [That we] cling to Palestine as the historic homeland of the Palestinian people for which there can be no substitute; resist all schemes for resettlement or for an "alternative homeland," which the imperialist and Zionist enemy is proposing in order to liquidate the Palestinian cause and Palestinian national struggle, and to circumvent our right to return.

In the Arab Sphere

1. [That we] emphasize that the task of confronting the Camp David agreements, their annexes and their consequences, with the fateful dangers

they pose to the cause of Arab struggle, is the responsibility of all the Arab masses and their national and progressive forces, that the Arab Front for Steadfastness and Confrontation, with Syria and the PLO as its central link, is the primary base from which to confront the US-Zionist conspiratorial settlement.

2. [That we must] work to fortify and strengthen the Arab Front for Steadfastness and Confrontation and to expand its scope on the basis of resistance to imperialist and Zionist settlement schemes; adhere to the objective of liberating the occupied Palestinian and Arab territories and to the inalienable national rights of the Palestinian people, and not dissipate or infringe upon these rights; [we must] furnish all possible mass and financial support to the Arab Front for Steadfastness and Confrontation, especially to the PLO and the Syrian Arab region.

3. The PLO calls upon all national and progressive parties, movements and forces in the Arab homeland to support the Arab Front for Steadfastness and Confrontation and to furnish it with all possible mass and financial aid. It further calls upon them to unite and to struggle on the basis of resistance to the imperialist and Zionist schemes for settlement.

4. a) The PLO asserts its firm commitment to the unity, Arab character and independence of Lebanon, its respect for Lebanese sovereignty and its adherence to the Cairo Agreement and its sequels which regulate relations between the PLO and Lebanon's legitimate authority.

b) The PLO highly values the role that has been and is being played by the Lebanese people and their national, progressive and patriotic forces in support of and in defence of the struggle of the Palestinian people. In expressing its pride in the solidarity between our Palestinian people and the people of Lebanon and their national, progressive and patriotic forces in defence of Lebanese territory and of the Palestinian revolution against Zionist aggression, its schemes and its local agents, the PLO emphasizes the importance of continuing and strengthening this solidarity.

5. a) the PLO affirms the special character of the relationship linking the two fraternal peoples, Palestinian and Jordanian, and its concern that the solidarity between these two fraternal peoples should continue.

b) The PLO declares its adherence to the resolutions of the Arab summits of Algiers and Rabat which affirm that the PLO is the sole legitimate representative of the Palestinian people and that our people have a right to establish their national and independent state. The PLO considers that the commitment of the Jordanian regime to these resolutions, its rejection of the Camp David agreements and their aftermath as well as its refusal to be involved in them and its role in enabling the PLO to exercise its responsibility for militant and mass struggle against the Zionist enemy, constitute the basis that governs relations between the PLO and the Jordanian regime.

6. The PLO affirms its right to exercise its responsibility for struggle on the Arab and national levels, and across any Arab territory, in order to liberate the occupied Palestinian territories.

7. The PLO declares that its policies toward and its relations with any Arab regime are determined by the policy of that regime as regards adherence to the resolutions of the summits of Algiers and Rabat and to the rejection of and the opposition to the Camp David agreements with their annexes and their consequences.

8. The PLO calls upon all Arab and national forces and all national and friendly regimes to support and aid the Egyptian people and their national movement to enable them to confront the Sadat conspiracy and to foil the Camp David agreement and its effect upon the Egyptian people, their Arabism and their history of struggle against Zionism and imperialism.

In the International Sphere

1. The role played by the US against our Palestinian people and their national struggle and against the Arab national liberation movement and its objectives of liberation and independence, whether this is manifested in its support of the Zionist entity or through its agents in the Arab region, constitutes a naked aggression against our people and their national cause. The PLO, by acting in solidarity with all groups in the Arab national liberation struggle and their national and progressive forces and regimes, declares its determination to resist the policy, objectives and actions of the US in the region.

2. The PLO affirms the importance of alliance with the socialist countries, and first and foremost with the Soviet Union, since this alliance is a national necessity in the context of confronting American-Zionist conspiracies against the Palestine cause, the Arab national liberation movement and their achievements.

3. The PLO affirms the importance of consolidating its cooperation with the non-aligned, Islamic, African and friendly states which support the PLO and its struggle to achieve the national rights of the Palestinian people to return to their homeland, to self-determination and to establish their independent national state.

4. The PLO, as a national liberation movement, expresses its solidarity with national liberation movements throughout the world, especially with Zimbabwe, Namibia and South Africa, and its determination to consolidate relations of struggle with them since the fight against imperialism, Zionism and racism is a joint cause for all forces of liberation and progress in the world.

5. The PLO declares its firm adherence to the achievements won by Palestinian struggle in the international sphere, such as the wide international recognition accorded to the PLO and to the inalienable right of the Palestinian Arab people to their homeland, Palestine, their right to return, to self-determination and to the establishment of their independent national state on their national soil. These are the achievements embodied in UN resolutions adopted since 1974 and up to the present, especially resolutions 3236

and 3237. It underlines the right of the PLO to participate in all meetings and conferences that discuss the Palestine question on these bases and considers that any discussion or agreement that takes place in its absence about matters related to the Palestine question are totally invalid.

In the Sphere of Organization

1. All the organizations of the Revolution and all Palestinian national forces participate in all institutions of the PLO, and principally in the National Council and the Central Council and the Executive Committee, on a representative basis and in a democratic manner.

2. Palestinian leadership is a collective one. This means that decisions are the responsibility of all, both through participation in the adoption of decision and in its execution. This takes place in a democratic manner where the minority adheres to the view of the majority, in accordance with the political and organizational programme and with the resolutions of the National Councils.

3. [The PLO will work] to ensure that the departments, institutions and organs of the PLO carry out their functions in full, each within its own specific sphere as defined in the basic regulations of the PLO. The Executive Committee will form higher organs, composed on a representative basis, which will undertake to formulate the plans for the various institutions of the PLO and supervise their execution by them, especially in the military, informational and financial spheres.

4. The Executive Committee and the Central Council are composed in accordance with what is agreed upon as stated in the basic regulations of the PLO and the resolutions of the National Council.

5. The next Executive Committee undertakes as soon as it commences its activity to lay down the necessary plans to implement the interim programme and to review the departments and organs of the PLO in a manner that would take merit and quality into account in order to achieve optimal performance from these departments and organs.

B. The Egyptian-Israeli Peace Treaty

74. Treaty of Peace between the Arab Republic of Egypt

and the State of Israel, March 26, 1979*

* 79 U.S. Dep't State Bull. No. 2026, at 3 (May 1979).

The Government of the Arab Republic of Egypt and the Government of the State of Israel;

Convinced of the urgent necessity of the establishment of a just, comprehensive and lasting peace in the Middle East in accordance with Security Council Resolutions 242 and 338;

Reaffirming their adherence to the "Framework for Peace in the Middle East Agreed at Camp David," dated September 17, 1978;

Noting that the aforementioned Framework as appropriate is intended to constitute a basis for peace not only between Egypt and Israel but also between Israel and each of its other Arab neighbors which is prepared to negotiate peace with it on this basis;

Desiring to bring to an end the state of war between them and to establish a peace in which every state in the area can live in security;

Convinced that the conclusion of a Treaty of Peace between Egypt and Israel is an important step in the search for comprehensive peace in the area and for the attainment of the settlement of the Arab-Israeli conflict in all its aspects;

Inviting the other Arab parties to this dispute to join the peace process with Israel guided by and based on the principles of the aforementioned Framework;

Desiring as well to develop friendly relations and cooperation between themselves in accordance with the United Nations Charter and the principles of international law governing international relations in times of peace;

Agree to the following provisions in the free exercise of their sovereignty, in order to implement the "Framework for the Conclusion of a Peace Treaty Between Egypt and Israel":

ARTICLE I

1. The state of war between the Parties will be terminated and peace will be established between them upon the exchange of instruments of ratification of this Treaty.

2. Israel will withdraw all its armed forces and civilians from the Sinai behind the international boundary between Egypt and mandated Palestine, as provided in the annexed protocol (Annex I), and Egypt will resume the exercise of its full sovereignty over the Sinai.

3. Upon completion of the interim withdrawal provided for in Annex I, the Parties will establish normal and friendly relations, in accordance with Article III (3).

ARTICLE II

The permanent boundary between Egypt and Israel is the recognized international boundary between Egypt and the former mandated territory of Palestine, as shown on the map at Annex II, without prejudice to the issue of the status of the Gaza Strip. The parties recognize this boundary as inviolable. Each will respect the territorial integrity of the other, including their territorial waters and airspace.

ARTICLE III

1. The Parties will apply between them the provisions of the Charter of the United Nations and the principles of international law governing relations among states in times of peace. In particular:

a. They recognize and will respect each other's sovereignty, territorial integrity and political independence;

b. They recognize and will respect each other's right to live in peace within their secure and recognized boundaries;

c. They will refrain from the threat or use of force, directly or indirectly, against each other and will settle all disputes between them by peaceful means.

2. Each Party undertakes to ensure that acts or threats of belligerency, hostility, or violence do not originate from and are not committed from within its territory, or by any forces subject to its control or by any other forces stationed on its territory, against the population, citizens or property of the other Party. Each Party also undertakes to refrain from organizing, instigating, inciting, assisting or participating in acts or threats of belligerency, hostility, subversion or violence against the other Party, anywhere, and undertakes to ensure that perpetrators of such acts are brought to justice.

3. The Parties agree that the normal relationship established between them will include full recognition, diplomatic, economic and cultural relations, termination of economic boycotts and discriminatory barriers to the free movement of people and goods, and will guarantee the mutual enjoyment of citizens of the due process of law. The process by which they undertake to achieve such a relationship parallel to the implementation of other provisions of this treaty is set out in the annexed protocol (Annex III).

ARTICLE IV

1. In order to provide maximum security for both Parties on the basis of reciprocity, agreed security arrangements will be established including limited force zones in Egyptian and Israeli territory, and United Nations forces and observers, described in detail as to nature and timing in Annex I, and other security arrangements the Parties may agree upon.

2. The Parties agree to the stationing of United Nations personnel in areas described in Annex I. The Parties agree not to request withdrawal of the United Nations personnel and that these personnel will not be removed unless such removal is approved by the Security Council of the United Nations, with the affirmative vote of the five Permanent Members, unless the Parties otherwise agree.

3. A Joint Commission will be established to facilitate the implementation of the Treaty, as provided for in Annex I.

4. The security arrangements provided for in paragraphs 1 and 2 of this Article may at the request of either party be reviewed and amended by mutual agreement of the Parties.

ARTICLE V

1. Ships of Israel, and cargoes destined for or coming from Israel, shall enjoy the right of free passage through the Suez Canal and its approaches through the Gulf of Suez and the Mediterranean Sea on the basis of the Constantinople Convention of 1888, applying to all nations. Israeli nationals, vessels and cargoes, as well as persons, vessels and cargoes destined for or coming from Israel, shall be accorded nondiscriminatory treatment in all matters connected with usage of the canal.

2. The Parties consider the Strait of Tiran and the Gulf of Aqaba to be international waterways open to all nations for unimpeded and nonsuspendable freedom of navigation and overflight. The Parties will respect each others' right to navigation and overflight for access to either country through the Strait of Tiran and the Gulf of Aqaba.

ARTICLE VI

1. This Treaty does not affect and shall not be interpreted as affecting in any way the rights and obligations of the Parties under the Charter of the United Nations.

2. The Parties undertake to fulfill in good faith their obligations under this Treaty, without regard to action or inaction of any other party and independently of any instrument external to this Treaty.

3. They further undertake to take all the necessary measures for the application in their relations of the provisions of the multilateral conventions to which they are parties, including the submission of appropriate notification to the Secretary General of the United Nations and other depositaries of such conventions.

4. The Parties undertake not to enter into any obligation in conflict with this Treaty.

5. Subject to Article 103 of the United Nations Charter, in the event of a conflict between the obligations of the Parties under the present Treaty and any of their other obligations, the obligations under this Treaty will be binding and implemented.

ARTICLE VII

1. Disputes arising out of the application or interpretation of this Treaty shall be resolved by negotiations.

2. Any such disputes which cannot be settled by negotiations shall be resolved by conciliation or submitted to arbitration.

ARTICLE VIII

The Parties agree to establish a claims commission for the mutual settlement of all financial claims.

ARTICLE IX

1. This Treaty shall enter into force upon exchange of instruments of ratification.

2. This Treaty supersedes the Agreement between Egypt and Israel of September, 1975.

3. All protocols, annexes, and maps attached to this Treaty shall be regarded as an integral part hereof.

4. The Treaty shall be communicated to the Secretary General of the United Nations for registration in accordance with the provisions of Article 102 of the Charter of the United Nations.

DONE at Washington, D.C. this 26th day of March, 1979, in triplicate in the English, Arabic, and Hebrew languages, each text being equally authentic. In case of any divergence of interpretation, the English text shall prevail.

For the Government of the Arab Republic of Egypt:
A. SADAT

For the Government of Israel:
M. BEGIN

Witnessed By:
JIMMY CARTER

Jimmy Carter, President of the United States of America

75. Annex I to the Egyptian-Israeli Peace Treaty— Protocol Concerning Israeli Withdrawal and Security Arrangements, with Maps, March 26, 1979*

---

* 79 U.S. Dep't State Bull. No. 2026, at 5 (May 1979).

ARTICLE I
Concept of Withdrawal

1. Israel will complete withdrawal of all its armed forces and civilians from the Sinai not later than three years from the date of exchange of instruments of ratification of this Treaty.

2. To ensure the mutual security of the Parties, the implementation of phased withdrawal will be accompanied by the military measures and establishment of zones set out in this Annex and in Map 1, hereinafter referred to as "the Zones."

3. The withdrawal from the Sinai will be accomplished in two phases:

a. The interim withdrawal behind the line from east of El Arish to Ras Muhammed as delineated on Map 2 within nine months from the date of exchange of instruments of ratification of this Treaty.

b. The final withdrawal from the Sinai behind the international boundary not later than three years from the date of exchange of instruments of ratification of this Treaty.

4. A Joint Commission will be formed immediately after the exchange of instruments of ratification of this Treaty in order to supervise and coordinate movements and schedules during the withdrawal, and to adjust plans and timetables as necessary within the limits established by paragraph 3, above. Details relating to the Joint Commission are set out in Article IV of the attached Appendix. The Joint Commission will be dissolved upon completion of final Israeli withdrawal from the Sinai.

ARTICLE II
Determination of Final Lines and Zones

1. In order to provide maximum security for both Parties after the final withdrawal, the lines and the Zones delineated on Map 1 are to be established and organized as follows:

a. Zone A

(1) Zone A is bounded on the east by line A (red line) and on the west by the Suez Canal and the east coast of the Gulf of Suez, as shown on Map 1.

(2) An Egyptian armed force of one mechanized infantry division and its military installations, and field fortifications, will be in this Zone.

(3) The main elements of that division will consist of:

(a) Three mechanized infantry brigades.

(b) One armored brigade.

(c) Seven field artillery battalions including up to 126 artillery pieces.

(d) Seven anti-aircraft artillery battalions including individual surface-to-air missiles and up to 126 anti-aircraft guns of 37 mm and above.

(e) Up to 230 tanks.

(f) Up to 480 armored personnel vehicles of all types.

(g) Up to a total of twenty-two thousand personnel.

b. Zone B

(1) Zone B is bounded by line B (green line) on the east and by line A (red line) on the west, as shown on Map 1.

(2) Egyptian border units of four battalions equipped with light weapons and wheeled vehicles will provide security and supplement the civil police in maintaining order in Zone B. The main elements of the four border battalions will consist of up to a total of four thousand personnel.

(3) Land based, short range, low power, coastal warning points of the border patrol units may be established on the coast of this Zone.

(4) There will be in Zone B field fortifications and military installations for the four border battalions.

c. Zone C

(1) Zone C is bounded by line B (green line) on the west and the international boundary and the Gulf of Aqaba on the east, as shown on Map 1.

(2) Only United Nations forces and Egyptian civil police will be stationed in Zone C.

(3) The Egyptian civil police armed with light weapons will perform normal police functions within this Zone.

(4) The United Nations Force will be deployed within Zone C and perform its functions as defined in Article VI of this Annex.

(5) The United Nations Force will be stationed mainly in camps located within the following stationing areas shown on Map 1, and will establish its precise locations after consultations with Egypt:

(a) In that part of the area in the Sinai lying within about 20 Km. of the Mediterranean Sea and adjacent to the international boundary.

(b) In the Sharm el Sheikh area.

d. Zone D

(1) Zone D is bounded by line D (blue line) on the east and the international boundary on the west, as shown on Map 1.

(2) In this Zone there will be an Israeli limited force of four infantry battalions, their military installations, and field fortifications, and United Nations observers.

(3) The Israeli forces in Zone D will not include tanks, artillery and anti-aircraft missiles except individual surface-to-air missiles.

(4) The main elements of the four Israeli infantry battalions will consist of up to 180 armored personnel vehicles of all types and up to a total of four thousand personnel.

2. Access across the international boundary shall only be permitted through entry check points designated by each Party and under its control. Such access shall be in accordance with laws and regulations of each country.

3. Only those field fortifications, military installations, forces, and weapons specifically permitted by this Annex shall be in the Zones.

Aerial Military Regime

1. Flights of combat aircraft and reconnaissance flights of Egypt and Israel shall take place only over Zones A and D, respectively.

2. Only unarmed, non-combat aircraft of Egypt and Israel will be stationed in Zones A and D, respectively.

3. Only Egyptian unarmed transport aircraft will take off and land in Zone B and up to eight such aircraft may be maintained in Zone B. The Egyptian border units may be equipped with unarmed helicopters to perform their functions in Zone B.

4. The Egyptian civil police may be equipped with unarmed police helicopters to perform normal police functions in Zone C.

5. Only civilian airfields may be built in the Zones.

6. Without prejudice to the provisions of this Treaty, only those military aerial activities specifically permitted by this Annex shall be allowed in the Zones and the airspace above their territorial waters.

ARTICLE IV
Naval Regime

1. Egypt and Israel may base and operate naval vessels along the coasts of Zones A and D, respectively.

2. Egyptian coast guard boats, lightly armed, may be stationed and operate in the territorial waters of Zone B to assist the border units in performing their functions in this Zone.

3. Egyptian civil police equipped with light boats, lightly armed, shall perform normal police functions within the territorial waters of Zone C.

4. Nothing in this Annex shall be considered as derogating from the right of innocent passage of the naval vessels of either Party.

5. Only civilian maritime ports and installations may be built in the Zones.

6. Without prejudice to the provisions of this Treaty, only those naval activities specifically permitted by this Annex shall be allowed in the Zones and in their territorial waters.

ARTICLE V
Early Warning Systems

Egypt and Israel may establish and operate early warning systems only in Zones A and D, respectively.

ARTICLE VI
United Nations Operations

1. The Parties will request the United Nations to provide forces and observers to supervise the implementation of this Annex and employ their best efforts to prevent any violation of its terms.

2. With respect to these United Nations forces and observers, as appropriate, the Parties agree to request the following arrangements:

a. Operation of check points, reconnaissance patrols, and observation posts along the international boundary and line B, and within Zone C.

b. Periodic verification of the implementation of the provisions of this Annex will be carried out not less than twice a month unless otherwise agreed by the Parties.

c. Additional verifications within 48 hours after the receipt of a request from either Party.

d. Ensuring the freedom of navigation through the Strait of Titan in accordance with Article V of the Treaty of Peace.

3. The arrangements described in this article for each zone will be implemented in Zones A, B, and C by the United Nations Force and in Zone D by the United Nations Observers.

4. United Nations verification teams shall be accompanied by liaison officers of the respective party.

5. The United Nations Force and Observers will report their findings to both Parties.

6. The United Nations Force and Observers operating in the Zones will enjoy freedom of movement and other facilities necessary for the performance of their tasks.

7. The United Nations Force and Observers are not empowered to authorize the crossing of the international boundary.

8. The Parties shall agree on the nations from which the United Nations Force and Observers will be drawn. They will be drawn from nations other than those which are Permanent Members of the United Nations Security Council.

9. The Parties agree that the United Nations should make those command arrangements that will best assure the effective implementation of its responsibilities.

ARTICLE VII
Liaison System

1. Upon dissolution of the Joint Commission, a liaison system between the Parties will be established. This liaison system is intended to provide an effective method to assess progress in the implementation of obligations under the present Annex and to resolve any problem that may arise in the course of implementation, and refer other unresolved matters to the higher military authorities of the two countries respectively for consideration. It is also intended to prevent situations resulting from errors or misinterpretation on the part of either Party.

2. An Egyptian liaison office will be established in the city of El Arish and an Israeli liaison office will be established in the city of Beer-Sheba. Each office will be headed by an officer of the respective country, and assisted by a number of officers.

3. A direct telephone link between the two offices will be set up and also

direct telephone lines with the United Nations command will be maintained by both offices.

ARTICLE VIII
Respect for War Memorials

Each Party undertakes to preserve in good condition the War Memorials erected in the memory of soldiers of the other Party, namely those erected by Israel in the Sinai and those to be erected by Egypt in Israel, and shall permit access to such monuments.

ARTICLE IX
Interim Arrangements

The withdrawal of Israeli armed forces and civilians behind the interim withdrawal line, and the conduct of the forces of the Parties and the United Nations prior to the final withdrawal, will be governed by the attached Appendix and Maps 2 and 3.

MAP 1 – International Boundary and the Lines of the Zones

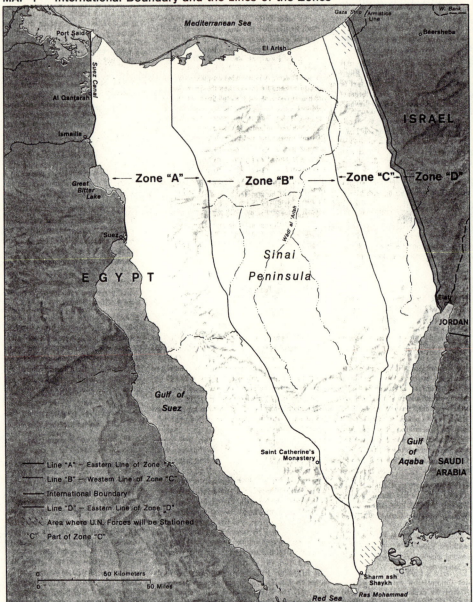

504093 3-79 (544089)

This is a representation of the original map included in the treaty.

MAP 2 – Lines and Zones Effective when Israeli Forces are on the El Arish - Ras Mohammad Line

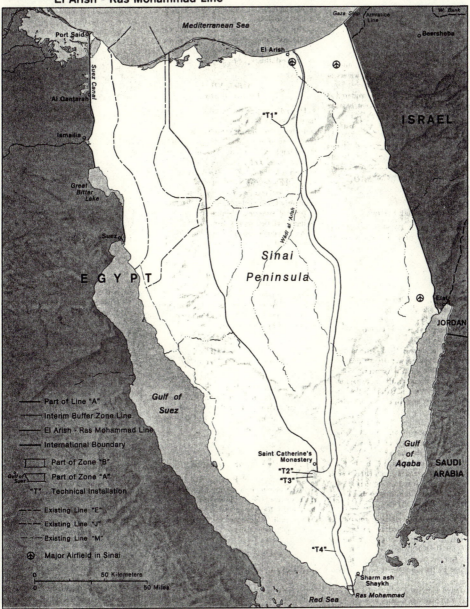

504094 3-79 (544089)

This is a representation of the original map included in the treaty.

MAP 3 – Sub-Phases of Withdrawal to the El Arish-Ras Mohammad Line

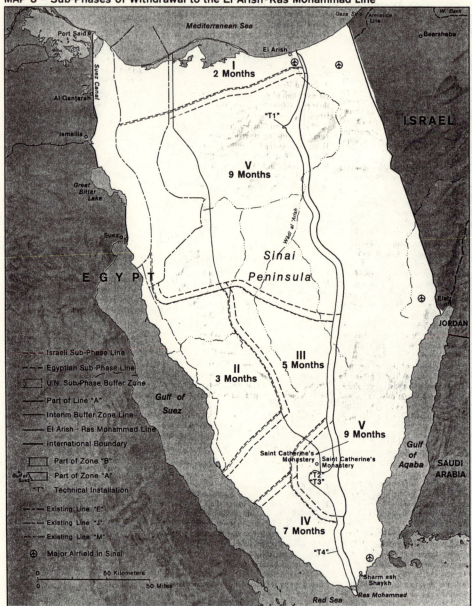

504095 3-79 (544089)

This is a representation of the original map included in the treaty.

76. Appendix to Annex I of the Egyptian-Israeli

Peace Treaty—Organization of Movements in the Sinai,

March 26, 1979*

* 79 U.S. Dep't State Bull. No. 2026, at 7 (May 1979).

ARTICLE I
Principles of Withdrawal

1. The withdrawal of Israeli armed forces and civilians from the Sinai will be accomplished in two phases as described in Article I of Annex I. The description and timing of the withdrawal are included in this Appendix. The Joint Commission will develop and present to the Chief Coordinator of the United Nations forces in the Middle East the details of these phases not later than one month before the initiation of each phase of withdrawal.

2. Both parties agree on the following principles for the sequence of military movements.

a. Not withstanding the provisions of Article IX, paragraph 2, of this Treaty, until Israeli armed forces complete withdrawal from the current J and M Lines established by the Egyptian-Israeli Agreement of September 1975, hereinafter referred to as the 1975 Agreement, up to the interim withdrawal line, all military arrangements existing under that Agreement will remain in effect, except those military arrangements otherwise provided for in this Appendix.

b. As Israeli armed forces withdraw, United Nations forces will immediately enter the evacuated areas to establish interim and temporary buffer zones as shown on Maps 2 and 3, respectively, for the purpose of maintaining a separation of forces. United Nations forces' deployment will precede the movement of any other personnel into these areas.

c. Within a period of seven days after Israeli armed forces have evacuated any area located in Zone A, units of Egyptian armed forces shall deploy in accordance with the provisions of Article II of this Appendix.

d. Within a period of seven days after Israeli armed forces have evacuated any area located in Zones A or B, Egyptian border units shall deploy in accordance with the provisions of Article II of this Appendix, and will function in accordance with the provisions of Article II of Annex I.

e. Egyptian civil police will enter evacuated areas immediately after the United Nations forces to perform normal police functions.

f. Egyptian naval units shall deploy in the Gulf of Suez in accordance with the provisions of Article II of this Appendix.

g. Except those movements mentioned above, deployments of Egyptian armed forces and the activities covered in Annex I will be effected in the evacuated areas when Israeli armed forces have completed their withdrawal behind the interim withdrawal line.

ARTICLE II
Subphases of the Withdrawal to the Interim Withdrawal Line

1. The withdrawal to the interim withdrawal line will be accomplished in subphases as described in this Article and as shown on Map 3. Each subphase will be completed within the indicated number of months from the date of the exchange of instruments of ratification of this Treaty.

a. First subphase: within two months, Israeli armed forces will withdraw from the area of El Arish, including the town of El Arish and its air-field, shown as Area I on Map 3.

b. Second subphase: within three months, Israeli armed forces will withdraw from the area between line M of the 1975 Agreement and line A, shown as Area II on Map 3.

c. Third subphase: within five months, Israeli armed forces will with-draw from the areas east and south of Area II, shown as Area III on Map 3.

d. Fourth subphase: within seven months, Israeli armed forces will withdraw from the area of El Tor-Ras El Kenisa, shown as Area IV on Map 3.

e. Fifth subphase: Within nine months, Israeli armed forces will with-draw from the remaining areas west of the interim withdrawal line, includ-ing the areas of Santa Katrina and the areas east of the Giddi and Mitla passes, shown as Area V on Map 3, thereby completing Israeli withdrawal behind the interim withdrawal line.

2. Egyptian forces will deploy in the areas evacuated by Israeli armed forces as follows:

a. Up to one-third of the Egyptian armed forces in the Sinai in accor-dance with the 1975 Agreement will deploy in the portions of Zone A lying within Area I, until the completion of interim withdrawal. Thereafter, Egyptian armed forces as described in Article II of Annex I will be deployed in Zone A up to the limits of the interim buffer zone.

b. The Egyptian naval activity in accordance with Article IV of Annex I will commence along the coasts of Areas II, III, and IV, upon completion of the second, third, and fourth subphases, respectively.

c. Of the Egyptian border units described in Article II of Annex I, upon completion of the first subphase one battalion will be deployed in Area I. A second battalion will be deployed in Area II upon completion of the second subphase. A third battalion will be deployed in Area III upon completion of the third subphase. The second and third battalions men-tioned above may also be deployed in any of the subsequently evacuated areas of the southern Sinai.

3. United Nations forces in Buffer Zone I of the 1975 Agreement will redeploy to enable the deployment of Egyptian forces described above upon the completion of the first subphase, but will otherwise continue to function in accordance with the provisions of that Agreement in the remainder of that zone until the completion of the interim withdrawal, as indicated in Article I of this Appendix.

4. Israeli convoys may use the roads south and east of the main road junc-tion east of El Arish to evacuate Israeli forces and equipment up to the completion of interim withdrawal. These convoys will proceed in daylight upon four hours notice to the Egyptian liaison group and United Nations forces, will be escorted by United Nations forces, and will be in accordance with schedules coordinated by the Joint Commission. An Egyptian liaison

officer will accompany convoys to assure uninterrupted movement. The Joint Commission may approve other arrangements for convoys.

ARTICLE III
United Nations Forces

1. The Parties shall request that United Nations forces be deployed as necessary to perform the functions described in this Appendix up to the time of completion of final Israeli withdrawal. For that purpose, the Parties agree to the redeployment of the United Nations Emergency Force.

2. United Nations forces will supervise the implementation of this Appendix and will employ their best efforts to prevent any violation of its terms.

3. When United Nations forces deploy in accordance with the provisions of Articles I and II of this appendix, they will perform the functions of verification in limited force zones in accordance with Article VI of Annex I, and will establish check points, reconnaissance patrols, and observation posts in the temporary buffer zones described in Article II above. Other functions of the United Nations forces which concern the interim buffer zone are described in Article V of this Appendix.

ARTICLE IV
Joint Commission and Liaison

1. The Joint Commission referred to in Article IV of this Treaty will function from the date of exchange of instruments of ratification of this Treaty up to the date of completion of final Israeli withdrawal from the Sinai.

2. The Joint Commission will be composed of representatives of each Party headed by senior officers. This Commission shall invite a representative of the United Nations when discussing subjects concerning the United Nations, or when either Party requests United Nations presence. Decisions of the Joint Commission will be reached by agreement of Egypt and Israel.

3. The Joint Commission will supervise the implementation of the arrangements described in Annex I and this Appendix. To this end, and by agreement of both Parties, it will:

a. coordinate military movements described in this Appendix and supervise their implementation;

b. address and seek to resolve any problem arising out of the implementation of Annex I and this appendix, and discuss any violations reported by the United Nations Force and Observers and refer to the Governments of Egypt and Israel any unresolved problems;

c. assist the United Nations Force and Observers in the execution of their mandates, and deal with the timetables of the periodic verifications when referred to it by the Parties as provided for in Annex I and in this Appendix;

d. organize the demarcation of the international boundary and all lines and zones described in Annex I and this Appendix;

e. supervise the handing over of the main installations in the Sinai from Israel to Egypt;

f. agree on necessary arrangements for finding and returning missing bodies of Egyptian and Israeli soldiers;

g. organize the setting up and operation of entry check points along the El Arish—Ras Muhammed line in accordance with the provisions of Article 4 of Annex III;

h. conduct its operations through the use of joint liaison teams consisting of one Israeli representative and one Egyptian representative, provided from a standing Liaison Group, which will conduct activities as directed by the Joint Commission;

i. provide liaison and coordination to the United Nations command implementing provisions of the Treaty, and, through the joint liaison teams, maintain local coordination and cooperation with the United Nations Force stationed in specific areas or United Nations Observers monitoring specific areas for any assistance as needed;

j. discuss any other matters which the Parties by agreement may place before it.

4. Meetings of the Joint Commission shall be held at least once a month. In the event that either Party or the Command of the United Nations Force requests a special meeting, it will be convened within 24 hours.

5. The Joint Commission will meet in the buffer zone until the completion of the interim withdrawal and in El Arish and Beer-Sheba alternately afterwards. The first meeting will be held not later than two weeks after the entry into force of this Treaty.

ARTICLE V

Definition of the Interim Buffer Zone and Its Activities

1. An interim buffer zone, by which the United Nations Force will effect a separation of Egyptian and Israeli elements, will be established west of and adjacent to the interim withdrawal line as shown on Map 2 after implementation of Israeli withdrawal and deployment behind the interim withdrawal line. Egyptian civil police equipped with light weapons will perform normal police functions within this zone.

2. The United Nations Force will operate check points, reconnaissance patrols, and observation posts within the interim buffer zone in order to ensure compliance with the terms of this Article.

3. In accordance with arrangements agreed upon by both Parties and to be coordinated by the Joint Commission, Israeli personnel will operate military technical installations at four specific locations shown on Map 2 and designated as T1 (map central coordinate 57163940), T2 (map central coordinate 59351541), T3 (map central coordinate 59331527), and T4 (map central coordinate 61130979) under the following principles:

a. The technical installations shall be manned by technical and administrative personnel equipped with small arms required for their protection (revolvers, rifles, sub-machine guns, light machine guns, hand grenades, and ammunition), as follows:

T1—up to 150 personnel
T2 and T3—up to 350 personnel
T4—up to 200 personnel.

b. Israeli personnel will not carry weapons outside the sites, except officers who may carry personal weapons.

c. Only a third party agreed to by Egypt and Israel will enter and conduct inspections within the perimeters of technical installations in the buffer zone. The third party will conduct inspections in a random manner at least once a month. The inspections will verify the nature of the operation of the installations and the weapons and personnel therein. The third party will immediately report to the Parties any divergence from an installation's visual and electronic surveillance or communications role.

d. Supply of the installations, visits for technical and administrative purposes, and replacement of personnel and equipment situated in the sites, may occur uninterruptedly from the United Nations check points to the perimeter of the technical installations, after checking and being escorted by only the United Nations forces.

e. Israel will be permitted to introduce into its technical installations items required for the proper functioning of the installations and personnel.

f. As determined by the Joint commission, Israel will be permitted to:

(1) Maintain in its installations firefighting and general maintenance equipment as well as wheeled administrative vehicles and mobile engineering equipment necessary for the maintenance of the sites. All vehicles shall be unarmed.

(2) Within the sites and in the buffer zone, maintain roads, water lines, and communications cables which serve the sites. At each of the three installation locations (T1, T2 and T3, and T4), this maintenance may be performed with up to two unarmed wheeled vehicles and by up to twelve unarmed personnel with only necessary equipment, including heavy engineering equipment if needed. This maintenance may be performed three times a week, except for special problems, and only after giving the United Nations four hours notice. The teams will be escorted by the United Nations.

g. Movement to and from the technical installations will take place only during daylight hours. Access to, and exit from, the technical installations shall be as follows:

(1) T1: through a United Nations check point, and via the road between Abu Aweigila and the intersection of the Abu Aweigila road and the Gebel Libni road (at Km. 161), as shown on Map 2.

(2) T2 and T3: through a United Nations checkpoint and via the

road constructed across the buffer zone to Gebel Katrina, as shown on Map 2.

(3) T2, T3, and T4: via helicopters flying within a corridor at the times, and according to a flight profile, agreed to by the Joint Commission. The helicopters will be checked by the United Nations Force at landing sites outside the perimeter of the installations.

h. Israel will inform the United Nations Force at least one hour in advance of each intended movement to and from the installations.

i. Israel shall be entitled to evacuate sick and wounded and summon medical experts and medical teams at any time after giving immediate notice to the United Nations Force.

4. The details of the above principles and all other matters in this Article requiring coordination by the Parties will be handled by the Joint Commission.

5. These technical installations will be withdrawn when Israeli forces withdraw from the interim withdrawal line, or at a time agreed by the parties.

ARTICLE VI

Disposition of Installations and Military Barriers

Disposition of installations and military barriers will be determined by the Parties in accordance with the following guidelines:

1. Up to three weeks before Israeli withdrawal from any area, the Joint Commission will arrange for Israeli and Egyptian liaison and technical teams to conduct a joint inspection of all appropriate installations to agree upon condition of structures and articles which will be transferred to Egyptian control and to arrange for such transfer. Israel will declare, at that time, its plans for disposition of installations and articles within the installations.

2. Israel undertakes to transfer to Egypt all agreed infrastructure, utilities, and installations intact, inter alia, airfield, roads, pumping stations, and ports. Israel will present to Egypt the information necessary for the maintenance and operations of these facilities. Egyptian technical teams will be permitted to observe and familiarize themselves with the operation of these facilities for a period of up to two weeks prior to transfer.

3. When Israel relinquishes Israeli military water points near El Arish and El Tor, Egyptian technical teams will assume control of those installations and ancillary equipment in accordance with an orderly transfer process arranged beforehand by the Joint Commission. Egypt undertakes to continue to make available at all water supply points the normal quantity of currently available water up to the time Israel withdraws behind the international boundary, unless otherwise agreed in the Joint Commission.

4. Israel will make its best effort to remove or destroy all military barriers, including obstacles and minefields, in the areas and adjacent waters from which it withdraws, according to the following concept:

a. Military barriers will be cleared first from areas near populations, roads, and major installations and utilities.

b. For those obstacles and minefields which cannot be removed or destroyed prior to Israeli withdrawal, Israel will provide detailed maps to Egypt and the United Nations through the Joint Commission not later than 15 days before entry of United Nations forces into the affected areas.

c. Egyptian military engineers will enter those areas after United Nations forces enter to conduct barrier clearance operations in accordance with Egyptian plans to be submitted prior to implementation.

ARTICLE VII
Surveillance Activities

1. Aerial surveillance activities during the withdrawal will be carried out as follows:

a. Both Parties request the United States to continue airborne surveillance flights in accordance with previous agreements until the completion of final Israeli withdrawal.

b. Flight profiles will cover the Limited Forces Zones to monitor the limitations on forces and armaments, and to determine that Israeli armed forces have withdrawn from the areas described in Article II of Annex I, Article II of this appendix, and Maps 2 and 3, and that these forces thereafter remain behind their lines. Special inspection flights may be flown at the request of either Party or of the United Nations.

c. Only the main elements in the military organizations of each Party, as described in Annex I and in this Appendix, will be reported.

2. Both Parties request the United States operated Sinai Field Mission to continue its operations in accordance with previous agreements until completion of the Israeli withdrawal from the area east of the Giddi and Mitla Passes. Thereafter, the Mission will be terminated.

ARTICLE VIII
Exercise of Egyptian Sovereignty

Egypt will resume the exercise of its full sovereignty over evacuated parts of the Sinai upon Israeli withdrawal as provided for in Article I of this Treaty.

77. Annex III to the Egyptian-Israeli Peace Treaty— Protocol Concerning Relations of the Parties, March 26, 1979*

---

* 79 U.S. Dep't State Bull. No. 2026, at 13 (May 1979).

ARTICLE 1
Diplomatic and Consular Relations

The Parties agree to establish diplomatic and consular relations and to exchange ambassadors upon completion of the interim withdrawal.

ARTICLE 2
Economic and Trade Relations

1. The Parties agree to remove all discriminatory barriers to normal economic relations and to terminate economic boycotts of each other upon completion of the interim withdrawal.

2. As soon as possible, and not later than six months after the completion of the interim withdrawal, the Parties will enter negotiations with a view to concluding an agreement on trade and commerce for the purpose of promoting beneficial economic relations.

ARTICLE 3
Cultural Relations

1. The parties agree to establish normal cultural relations following completion of the interim withdrawal.

2. They agree on the desirability of cultural exchanges in all fields, and shall, as soon as possible and not later than six months after completion of the interim withdrawal, enter into negotiations with a view to concluding a cultural agreement for this purpose.

ARTICLE 4
Freedom of Movement

1. Upon completion of the interim withdrawal, each Party will permit the free movement of the nationals and vehicles of the other into and within its territory according to the general rules applicable to nationals and vehicles of other states. Neither Party will impose discriminatory restrictions on the free movement of persons and vehicles from its territory to the territory of the other.

2. Mutual unimpeded access to places of religious and historical significance will be provided on a nondiscriminatory basis.

ARTICLE 5
Cooperation for Development and Good Neighborly Relations

1. The Parties recognize a mutuality of interest in good neighborly relations and agree to consider means to promote such relations.

2. The Parties will cooperate in promoting peace, stability and development in their region. Each agrees to consider proposals the other may wish to make to this end.

3. The Parties shall seek to foster mutual understanding and toler-

ance and will, accordingly, abstain from hostile propaganda against each other.

<h3 style="text-align:center">ARTICLE 6</h3>
<h3 style="text-align:center">Transportation and Telecommunications</h3>

1. The Parties recognize as applicable to each other the rights, privileges and obligations provided for by the aviation agreements to which they are both party, particularly by the Convention on International Civil Aviation, 1944 ("The Chicago Convention") and the International Air Services Transit Agreement, 1944.

2. Upon completion of the interim withdrawal any declaration of national emergency by a party under Article 89 of the Chicago Convention will not be applied to the other party on a discriminatory basis.

3. Egypt agrees that the use of airfields left by Israel near El Arish, Rafah, Ras El Nagb and Sharm el Sheikh shall be for civilian purposes only, including possible commercial use by all nations.

4. As soon as possible and not later than six months after the completion of the interim withdrawal, the Parties shall enter into negotiations for the purpose of concluding a civil aviation agreement.

5. The Parties will reopen and maintain roads and railways between their countries and will consider further road and rail links. The Parties further agree that a highway will be constructed and maintained between Egypt, Israel and Jordan near Eilat with guaranteed free and peaceful passages of persons, vehicles and goods between Egypt and Jordan, without prejudice to their sovereignty over that part of the highway which falls within their respective territory.

6. Upon completion of the interim withdrawal, normal postal, telephone, telex, data facsimile, wireless and cable communications and television relay services by cable, radio and satellite shall be established between the two Parties in accordance with all relevant international conventions and regulations.

7. Upon completion of the interim withdrawal, each Party shall grant normal access to its ports for vessels and cargoes of the other, as well as vessels and cargoes destined for or coming from the other. Such access shall be granted on the same conditions generally applicable to vessels and cargoes of other nations. Article 5 of the Treaty of Peace will be implemented upon the exchange of instruments of ratification of the aforementioned Treaty.

<h3 style="text-align:center">ARTICLE 7</h3>
<h3 style="text-align:center">Enjoyment of Human Rights</h3>

The Parties affirm their commitment to respect and observe human rights and fundamental freedoms for all, and they will promote these rights and freedoms in accordance with the United Nations Charter.

ARTICLE 8
Territorial Seas

Without prejudice to the provisions of Article 5 of the Treaty of Peace each Party recognizes the right of the vessels of the other Party to innocent passage through its territorial sea in accordance with the rules of international law.

78. Agreed Minutes to Articles I, IV, V, and VI and Annexes I and III of the Egyptian-Israeli Peace Treaty, March 26, 1979*

* 79 U.S. Dep't State Bull. No. 2026, at 13 (May 1979).

ARTICLE I

Egypt's resumption of the exercise of full sovereignty over the Sinai provided for in paragraph 2 of Article I shall occur with regard to each area upon Israel's withdrawal from that area.

ARTICLE IV

It is agreed between the parties that the review provided for in Article IV(4) will be undertaken when requested by either party, commencing within three months of such a request, but that any amendment can be made only with the mutual agreement of both parties.

ARTICLE V

The second sentence of paragraph 2 of Article V shall not be construed as limiting the first sentence of that paragraph. The foregoing is not to be construed as contravening the second sentence of paragraph 2 of Article V, which reads as follows:

"The parties will respect each other's right to navigation and overflight for access to either country through the Strait of Tiran and the Gulf of Aqaba."

ARTICLE VI(2)

The provisions of Article VI shall not be construed in contradiction to the provisions of the framework for peace in the Middle East agreed at Camp David. The foregoing is not to be construed as contravening the provisions of Article VI(2) of the treaty, which reads as follows:

"The Parties undertake to fulfill in good faith their obligations under this Treaty, without regard to action or inaction of any other Party and independently of any instrument external to this Treaty."

ARTICLE VI(5)

It is agreed by the Parties that there is no assertion that this Treaty prevails over other Treaties or agreements or that other Treaties or agreements prevail over this Treaty. The foregoing is not to be construed as contravening the provisions of Article VI(5) of the Treaty, which reads as follows:

"Subject to Article 103 of the United Nations Charter, in the event of a conflict between the obligations of the Parties under the present Treaty and any of their other obligations, the obligations under this Treaty will be binding and implemented."

ANNEX I

Article VI, Paragraph 8, of Annex I provides as follows:

"The Parties shall agree on the nations from which the United Nations force and observers will be drawn. They will be drawn from nations other than those which are permanent members of the United Nations Security Council."

The Parties have agreed as follows:

"With respect to the provisions of paragraph 8, Article VI, of Annex I, if no agreement is reached between the Parties, they will accept or support a U.S. proposal concerning the composition of the United Nations force and observers."

ANNEX III

The Treaty of Peace and Annex III thereto provide for establishing normal economic relations between the Parties. In accordance therewith, it is agreed that such relations will include normal commercial sales of oil by Egypt to Israel, and that Israel shall be fully entitled to make bids for Egyptian-origin oil not needed for Egyptian domestic oil consumption, and Egypt and its oil concessionaires will entertain bids made by Israel, on the same basis and terms as apply to other bidders for such oil.

For the Government of the Arab Republic of Egypt:
A. SADAT

For the Government of Israel:
M. BEGIN

Witnessed by:
JIMMY CARTER

Jimmy Carter, President of the United States of America

79. Memoranda of Agreement between the U.S. and Israel, March 26, 1979*

* 79 U.S. Dep't State Bull. No. 2026, at 60 (May 1979).

The oil supply arrangement of September 1, 1975, between the Governments of the United States and Israel, annexed hereto, remains in effect. A memorandum of agreement shall be agreed upon and concluded to provide an oil supply arrangement for a total of 15 years, including the 5 years provided in the September 1, 1975, arrangement.

The memorandum of agreement, including the commencement of this arrangement and pricing provisions, will be mutually agreed upon by the parties within sixty days following the entry into force of the Treaty of Peace between Egypt and Israel.

It is the intention of the parties that prices paid by Israel for oil provided by the United States hereunder shall be comparable to world market prices current at the time of transfer, and that in any event the United States will be reimbursed by Israel for the costs incurred by the United States in providing oil to Israel hereunder.

Experts provided for in the September 1, 1975, arrangement will meet on request to discuss matters arising under this relationship.

The United States administration undertakes to seek promptly additional statutory authorization that may be necessary for full implementation of this arrangement.

[M. DAYAN]
For the Government of Israel

[CYRUS V. VANCE]
For the Government of the United States

ANNEX

Israel will make its own independent arrangements for oil supply to meet its requirements through normal procedures. In the event Israel is unable to secure its needs in this way, the United States Government, upon notification of this fact by the Government of Israel, will act as follows for five years, at the end of which period either side can terminate this arrangement on one year's notice.

(a) If the oil Israel needs to meet all its normal requirements for domestic consumption is unavailable for purchase in circumstances where no quantitative restrictions exist on the ability of the United States to procure oil to meet its normal requirements, the United States Government will promptly make oil available for purchase by Israel to meet all of the aforementioned normal requirements of Israel. If Israel is unable to secure the necessary means to transport such oil to Israel, the United States Government will make every effort to help Israel secure the necessary means of transport.

(b) If the oil Israel needs to meet all of its normal requirements for domestic consumption is unavailable for purchase in circumstances where quantitative restrictions through embargo or otherwise also prevent the United States from procuring oil to meet its normal requirements, the United States Government will promptly make oil available for purchase by

Israel in accordance with the International Energy Agency conservation and allocation formula, as applied by the United States Government, in order to meet Israel's essential requirements. If Israel is unable to secure the necessary means to transport such oil to Israel, the United States Government will make every effort to help Israel secure the necessary means of transport.

Israeli and United States experts will meet annually or more frequently at the request of either party, to review Israel's continuing oil requirement.

Recognizing the significance of the conclusion of the Treaty of Peace between Israel and Egypt and considering the importance of full implementation of the Treaty of Peace to Israel's security interests and the contribution of the conclusion of the Treaty of Peace to the security and development of Israel as well as its significance to peace and stability in the region and to the maintenance of international peace and security: and

Recognizing that the withdrawal from Sinai imposes additional heavy security, military and economic burdens on Israel;

The Governments of the United States of America and of the State of Israel, subject to their constitutional processes and applicable law, confirm as follows:

1. In the light of the role of the United States in achieving the Treaty of Peace and the parties' desire that the United States continue its supportive efforts, the United States will take appropriate measures to promote full observance of the Treaty of Peace.

2. Should it be demonstrated to the satisfaction of the United States that there has been a violation or threat of violation of the Treaty of Peace, the United States will consult with the parties with regard to measures to halt or prevent the violation, ensure observance of the Treaty of Peace, enhance friendly and peaceful relations between the parties and promote peace in the region, and will take such remedial measures as it deems appropriate, which may include diplomatic, economic and military measures as described below.

3. The United States will provide support it deems appropriate for proper actions taken by Israel in response to such demonstrated violations of the Treaty of Peace. In particular, if a violation of the Treaty of Peace is deemed to threaten the security of Israel, including, inter alia, a blockade of Israel's use of international waterways, a violation of the provisions of the Treaty of Peace concerning limitation of forces or an armed attack against Israel, the United States will be prepared to consider, on an urgent basis, such measures as the strengthening of the United States presence in the area, the providing of emergency supplies to Israel, and the exercise of maritime rights in order to put an end to the violation.

4. The United States will support the parties' rights to navigation and

overflight for access to either country through and over the Strait of Tiran and the Gulf of Aqaba pursuant to the Treaty of Peace.

5. The United States will oppose and, if necessary, vote against any action or resolution in the United Nations which in its judgment adversely affects the Treaty of Peace.

6. Subject to Congressional authorization and appropriation, the United States will endeavor to take into account and will endeavor to be responsive to military and economic assistance requirements of Israel.

7. The United States will continue to impose restrictions on weapons supplied by it to any country which prohibit their unauthorized transfer to any third party. The United States will not supply or authorize transfer of such weapons for use in an armed attack against Israel, and will take steps to prevent such unauthorized transfer.

8. Existing agreements and assurances between the United States and Israel are not terminated or altered by the conclusion of the Treaty of Peace, except for those contained in articles 5, 6, 7, 8, 11, 12, 15, and 16 of the Memorandum of Agreement between the Government of the United States and the Government of Israel (United States-Israeli Assurances) of September 1, 1975.

9. This Memorandum of Agreement sets forth the full understanding of the United States and Israel with regard to the subject matters covered between them hereby, and shall be carried out in accordance with its terms.

[CYRUS R. VANCE]
For the Government of the United States of America

[M. DAYAN]
For the Government of Israel

80. Joint Letter Concerning the Egyptian-Israeli Peace Treaty to President Carter from President Sadat and Prime Minister Begin, March 26, 1979*

* 79 U.S. Dep't State Bull. No. 2026, at 14 (May 1979).

March 26, 1979

Dear Mr. President:

This letter confirms that Egypt and Israel have agreed as follows:

The Governments of Egypt and Israel recall that they concluded at Camp David and signed at the White House on September 17, 1978, the annexed documents entitled "A Framework for Peace in the Middle East Agreed at Camp David" and "Framework for the conclusion of a Peace Treaty between Egypt and Israel."

For the purpose of achieving a comprehensive peace settlement in accordance with the above-mentioned Frameworks, Egypt and Israel will proceed with the implementation of those provisions relating to the West Bank and the Gaza Strip. They have agreed to start negotiations within a month after the exchange of the instruments of ratification of the Peace Treaty. In accordance with the "Framework for Peace in the Middle East," the Hashemite Kingdom of Jordan is invited to join the negotiations. The Delegations of Egypt and Jordan may include Palestinians from the West Bank and Gaza Strip or other Palestinians as mutually agreed. The purpose of the negotiation shall be to agree, prior to the elections, on the modalities for establishing the elected self-governing authority (administrative council), define its powers and responsibilities, and agree upon other related issues. In the event Jordan decides not to take part in the negotiations, the negotiations will be held by Egypt and Israel.

The two Governments agree to negotiate continuously and in good faith to conclude these negotiations at the earliest possible date. They also agree that the objective of the negotiations is the establishment of the self-governing authority in the West Bank and Gaza in order to provide full autonomy to the inhabitants.

Egypt and Israel set for themselves the goal of completing the negotiations within one year so that elections will be held as expeditiously as possible after agreement has been reached between the parties. The self-governing authority referred to in the "Framework for Peace in the Middle East" will be established and inaugurated within one month after it has been elected, at which time the transitional period of five years will begin. The Israeli military government and its civilian administration will be withdrawn, to be replaced by the self-governing authority, as specified in the "Framework for Peace in the Middle East." A withdrawal of Israeli armed forces will then take place and there will be a redeployment of the remaining Israeli forces into specified security locations.

This letter also confirms our understasnding that the United States Government will participate fully in all stages of negotiations.

Sincerely yours,

For the Government of Israel:
M. BEGIN
Menachem Begin

For the Government of the Arab Republic of Egypt:

A. SADAT

Mohamed Anwar El-Sadat

The President,
  The White House.

[NOTE: President Carter, upon receipt of the joint letter to him from President Sadat and Prime Minister Begin, added to the American and Israeli copies the notation:

"I have been informed that the expression 'West Bank' is understood by the Government of Israel to mean 'Judea and Samaria'."

This notation is in accordance with similar procedures established at Camp David.]

81. Letters Regarding Exchange of Ambassadors, March 26, 1979*

* 79 U.S. Dep't State Bull. No. 2026, at 14 (May 1979).

March 26, 1979

Dear Mr. President:

In response to your request, I can confirm that, within one month after the completion of Israel's withdrawal to the interim line as provided for in the Treaty of Peace between Egypt and Israel, Egypt will send a resident ambassador to Israel and will receive a resident Israeli ambassador in Egypt.

Sincerely,

A. SADAT
Mohamed Anwar El-Sadat

The President,
   The White House.

March 26, 1979

Dear Mr. Prime Minister:

I have received a letter from President Sadat that, within one month after Israel completes its withdrawal to the interim line in Sinai, as provided for in the Treaty of Peace between Egypt and Israel, Egypt will send a resident ambassador to Israel and will receive in Egypt a resident Israeli ambassador.

I would be grateful if you will confirm that this procedure will be agreeable to the Government of Israel.

Sincerely,

JIMMY CARTER
Jimmy Carter

His Excellency
   Menachem Begin
      Prime Minister of the
         State of Israel.

March 26, 1979

Dear Mr. President:

I am pleased to be able to confirm that the Government of Israel is agreeable to the procedure set out in your letter of March 26, 1979 in which you state:

"I have received a letter from President Sadat that, within one month after Israel completes its withdrawal to the interim line in Sinai, as provided for in the Treaty of Peace between Egypt and Israel, Egypt will send a resident ambassador to Israel and will receive in Egypt a resident Israeli ambassador."

Sincerely,

M. BEGIN
Menachem Begin

The President,
   The White House.

82. Letters Concerning the Egyptian-Israeli Peace Treaty from President Carter to President Sadat and Prime Minister Begin, March 26, 1979*

* 79 U.S. Dep't State Bull. No. 2026, at 15 (May 1979).

March 26, 1979

Dear Mr. President:

I wish to confirm to you that subject to United States Constitutional processes:

In the event of an actual or threatened violation of the Treaty of Peace between Egypt and Israel, the United States will, on request of one or both of the Parties, consult with the Parties with respect thereto and will take such other action as it may deem appropriate and helpful to achieve compliance with the Treaty.

The United States will conduct aerial monitoring as requested by the Parties pursuant to Annex I of the Treaty.

The United States believes the Treaty provision for permanent stationing of United Nations personnel in the designated limited force zone can and should be implemented by the United Nations Security Council. The United States will exert its utmost efforts to obtain the requisite action by the Security Council. If the Security Council fails to establish and maintain the arrangements called for in the Treaty, the President will be prepared to take those steps necessary to ensure the establishment and maintenance of an acceptable alternative multinational force.

Sincerely,

JIMMY CARTER
Jimmy Carter

His Excellency
  Mohamed Anwar El-Sadat,
    President of the Arab
      Republic of Egypt.

March 26, 1979

Dear Mr. Prime Minister:

I wish to confirm to you that subject to United States Constitutional processes:

In the event of an actual or threatened violation of the Treaty of Peace between Israel and Egypt, the United States will, on request of one or both of the Parties, consult with the Parties with respect thereto and will take such other action as it may deem appropriate and helpful to achieve compliance with the Treaty.

The United States will conduct aerial monitoring as requested by the Parties pursuant to Annex I of the Treaty.

The United States believes the Treaty provision for permanent stationing of United Nations personnel in the designated limited force zone can and should be implemented by the United Nations Security Council. The United States will exert its utmost efforts to obtain the requisite action by the Security Council. If the Security Council fails to establish and maintain the arrangements called for in the Treaty, the President will be prepared to take those steps necessary to ensure the establishment and maintenance of an acceptable alternative multinational force.

Sincerely,

JIMMY CARTER
Jimmy Carter

His Excellency
   Menachem Begin,
      Prime Minister of the
         State of Israel.

83. Exchange of Remarks among President Carter, President Sadat, and Prime Minister Begin upon Signing the Peace Treaty between Egypt and Israel, the White House, March 26, 1979*

---

* 79 U.S. Dep't State Bull. No. 2026, at 1 (May 1979).

PRESIDENT CARTER: During the past 30 years, Israel and Egypt have waged war. But for the past 16 months, these same two great nations have waged peace. Today we celebrate a victory—not of a bloody military campaign but of an inspiring peace campaign. Two leaders who will loom large in the history of nations—President Anwar al-Sadat and Prime Minister Menahem Begin—have conducted this campaign with all the courage, tenacity, brilliance, and inspiration of any generals who have ever led men and machines onto the field of battle.

At the end of this campaign, the soil of the two lands is not drenched with young blood. The countrysides of both lands are free from the litter and the carnage of a wasteful war. Mothers in Egypt and Israel are not weeping today for their children fallen in senseless battle. The dedication and determination of these two world statesmen have borne fruit. Peace has come to Israel and to Egypt.

I honor these two leaders and their government officials who have hammered out this peace treaty which we have just signed. But most of all, I honor the people of these two lands whose yearning for peace kept alive the negotiations which today culminate in this glorious event.

We have won at last the first step of peace, a first step on a long and difficult road. We must not minimize the obstacles which still lie ahead. Differences still separate the signatories to this treaty from one another, and also from some of their neighbors who fear what they have just done. To overcome these differences, to dispel these fears, we must rededicate ourselves to the goal of a broader peace with justice for all who have lived in a state of conflict in the Middle East.

We have no illusions—we have hopes, dreams, and prayers, yes, but no illusions.

There now remains the rest of the Arab world, whose support and whose cooperation in the peace process is needed and honestly sought. I am convinced that other Arab people need and want peace. But some of their leaders are not yet willing to honor these needs and desires for peace. We must now demonstrate the advantages of peace and expand its benefits to encompass all those who have suffered so much in the Middle East.

Obviously, time and understanding will be necessary for people, hitherto enemies, to become neighbors in the best sense of the word.

Just because a paper is signed, all the problems will not automatically go away. Future days will require the best from us to give reality to these lofty aspirations.

Let those who would shatter peace, who would callously spill more blood, be aware that we three and all others who may join us will vigorously wage peace.

So let history record that deep and ancient antagonism can be settled without bloodshed and without staggering waste of precious lives, without rapacious destruction of the land.

It has been said, and I quote: "Peace has one thing in common with its enemy, with the fiend it battles, with war; peace is active, not passive; peace is doing, not waiting; peace is aggressive—attacking; peace plans its strategy and encircles the enemy; peace marshals its forces and storms the gates; peace gathers its weapons and pierces the defense; peace, like war, is waged."

It is true that we cannot enforce trust and cooperation between nations, but we can use all our strength to see that nations do not again go to war.

All our religious doctrines give us hope. In the Koran we read: "But if the enemy incline towards peace, do thou also incline towards peace, and trust in God; for He is the One that heareth and knoweth all things."

And the prophet Isaiah said: "Nations shall beat their swords into plowshares and their spears into pruning-hooks: nation shall not lift up sword against nation, neither shall they learn war any more."

So let us now lay aside war. Let us now reward all the children of Abraham who hunger for a comprehensive peace in the Middle East. Let us now enjoy the adventure of becoming fully human, fully neighbors, even brothers and sisters. We pray God, we pray God together, that these dreams will come true. I believe they will.

PRESIDENT SADAT: This is certainly one of the happiest moments in my life. It is an historic turning point of great significance for all peace-loving nations. Those among us who are endowed with vision cannot fail to comprehend the dimensions of our sacred mission. The Egyptian people, with their heritage and unique awareness of history, have realized from the very beginning the meaning and value of this endeavor.

In all the steps I took, I was not performing a personal mission. I was merely expressing the will of a nation. I'm proud of my people and of belonging to them.

Today a new dawn is emerging out of the darkness of the past. A new chapter is being opened in the history of coexistence among nations, one that's worthy of our spiritual values and civilization. Never before had men encountered such a complex dispute, which is highly charged with emotions. Never before did men need that much courage and imagination to confront a single challenge. Never before had any cause generated that much interest in all four corners of the globe.

Men and women of good will have labored day and night to bring about this happy moment. Egyptians and Israelis alike pursued their sacred goal, undeterred by difficulties and complications. Hundreds of dedicated individuals on both sides have given generously of their thought and effort to translate the cherished dream into a living reality.

But the man who performed the miracle was President Carter. Without any exaggeration, what he did constitutes one of the greatest achievements of our time. He devoted his skill, hard work, and, above all, his firm belief in the ultimate triumph of good against evil to insure the success of our mission.

To me he has been the best companion and partner along the road to peace. With his deep sense of justice and genuine commitment to human rights, we were able to surmount the most difficult obstacles.

There came certain moments when hope was eroding and retreating in the face of crisis. However, President Carter remained unshaken in his confidence and determination. He is a man of faith and compassion. Before anything else, the signing of the peace treaty and the exchanged letter is a tribute to the spirit and ability of Jimmy Carter.

Happily, he was armed with the blessing of God and the support of his people. For that we are grateful to each and every American who contributed in his own way to the success of our endeavor.

We are also heartened by the understanding of hundreds of thousands of Israelis who remained unwavering in their commitment to peace. The continuation of this spirit is vital to the coronation of our effort. We realize that difficult times lay ahead. The signing of these documents marks only the beginning of peace. But it is an indispensable start. Other steps remain to be taken without delay or procrastination. Much will depend on the success of these steps.

We are all committed to pursue our efforts until the fruits of the comprehensive settlement we agreed upon are shared by all parties to the conflict.

President Carter once said that the United States is committed without reservation to seeing the peace process through until all parties to the Arab-Israeli conflict are at peace. We value such a pledge from a leader who raised the banners of morality and ethics as a substitute for power politics and opportunism.

The steps we took in the recent past will serve Arab vital interests. The liberation of Arab land and the reinstitution of Arab authority in the West Bank and Gaza would certainly enhance our common strategic interests.

While we take the initiative to protect these interests, we remain faithful to our Arab commitment. To us, this is a matter of destiny. Pursuing peace is the only avenue which is compatible with our culture and creed.

Let there be no more wars or bloodshed between Arabs and Israelis. Let there be no more wars or bloodshed between Arabs and Israelis. Let there be no more suffering or denial of rights. Let there be no more despair or loss of faith. Let no mother lament the loss of her child. Let no young man waste his life on a conflict from which no one benefits. Let us work together until the day comes when they beat their swords into plowshares and their spears into pruning-hooks. And God does call to the abode of peace. He does guide whom he pleases to his way.

[*At this point, President Sadat spoke in Arabic.*]

PRIME MINISTER BEGIN: I have come from the land of Israel, the land of Zion and Jerusalem, and here I am in humility and with pride as a son of the Jewish people, as one of the generation of the Holocaust and redemption.

The ancient Jewish people gave the world a vision of eternal peace, of universal disarmament, of abolishing the teaching and the learning of war.

Two prophets—Yishayahu Ben Amotz and Micah Hamorashti—having foreseen the spiritual unit of man under God, with these words coming forth from Jerusalem, gave the nations of the world the following vision—expressed in identical terms—"And they shall beat their spears into pruninghooks: nation shall not lift up sword against nation, neither shall they learn war any more."

Despite the tragedies and disappointments of the past, we must never foresake that vision, that human dream, that unshakable faith.

Peace is the beauty of life. It is sunshine. It is the smile of a child, the love of a mother, the joy of a father, the togetherness of a family. It is the advancement of man, the victory of a just cause, the triumph of truth. Peace is all of these and more, and more.

These are words I uttered in Oslo, on December 10, 1978, while receiving the second half of the Nobel Peace Prize. The first half went, rightly so, to President Sadat. And I took the liberty to repeat them here on this momentous, historic occasion.

It is a great day in the annals of two ancient nations—Egypt and Israel—whose sons met in battle five times in one generation, fighting and falling.

Let us turn our hearts to our heroes and pay tribute to their eternal memory. It is thanks to them, to our fallen heroes, that we could have reached this day.

However, let us not forget that in ancient times, our two nations met also in alliance. Now we make peace, the cornerstone of cooperation and friendship.

It is a great day in your life, Mr. President of the United States. You have worked so hard, so insistently, so consistently to achieve this goal. And your labors and your devotion bore God-blessed fruit.

Our friend, President Sadat, said that you are the unknown soldier of the peacemaking effort. I agree, but as usual, with an amendment. [Laughter] A soldier in the service of peace, you are. You are, Mr. President, even, *mirabile dictu*, an intransigent fighter for peace. But Jimmy Carter, the President of the United States, is not completely unknown. [Laughter] And so it is his efforts which will be remembered and recorded by generations to come.

It is, of course, a great day in your life, Mr. President of the Arab Republic of Egypt. In the face of adversity and hostility, you have demonstrated the human value that can change history—civil courage.

A great field commander once said: "Civil courage is sometimes more difficult to show than military courage." You showed both, Mr. President. But now it is time for all of us to show civil courage in order to proclaim to our peoples and to others: No more war, no more bloodshed, no more bereavement. Peace unto you—*shalom, salaam* forever.

And it is the third greatest day in my life. The first was May 14, 1948, when our flag was hoisted. Our independence in our ancestors' land was proclaimed after 1,878 years of dispersion, persecution, humiliation, and, ultimately physical destruction.

We fought for our liberation alone, and with God's help, we won the day. That was spring. Such a spring we can never have again.

The second day was when Jerusalem became one city and our brave, perhaps most hardened soldiers, the parachutists, embraced with tears and kissed the ancient stones of the remnants of the wall destined to protect the chosen place of God's glory. Our hearts wept with them in remembrance.

[In Hebrew] "Our feet shall stand within thy gates, O Jerusalem. Jerusalem is builded as a city that is compact together."

This is the third day in my life. I have signed a Treaty of Peace with our great neighbor, with Egypt. The heart is full and overflowing. God gave me the strength to persevere, to survive the horrors of Nazism and of the Stalinite concentration camp and some other dangers, to endure, not to waver in nor flinch from my duty, to accept abuse from foreigners and, what is more painful, from my own people, and even from my close friends. This effort, too, bore some fruit.

Therefore, it is the proper place and the appropriate time to bring back to memory the song and prayer of thanksgiving I learned as a child, in the home of father and mother that doesn't exist anymore because they were among the 6 million people—men, women, and children—who sanctified the Lord's name with the sacred blood which reddened the rivers of Europe from the Rhine to the Danube, from the Bug to the Volga, because—only because—they were born Jews, and because they didn't have a country of their own, and neither a valiant Jewish army to defend them, and because nobody, nobody came to their rescue, although they cried out, "Save us, save us"—*de profundis*, from the depths of the pits and agony. That is the Song of Degrees, written 2 millennia and 500 years ago when our forefathers returned from their first exile to Jerusalem and Zion.

[At this point, Prime Minister Begin spoke in Hebrew.]

I will not translate. Every man, whether Jew or Christian or Moslem, can read it in his own language in the Book of the Books. It is just Psalm 126.

C. Implementation of the Peace Treaty

84. European Community Statement on the Middle East, March 26, 1979*

---

* 12 Bull. Eur. Comm. (No. 3) 86 (1979).

'The nine Member States of the European Community have followed with the greatest attention the negotiations which have resulted in the signature of the agreements between Egypt and Israel. They are fully appreciative of the will for peace which has led President Carter to engage himself personally in these negotiations, as well as of the efforts made by President Sadat and Prime Minister Begin. While a difficult road remains to be trodden before Security Coucil Resolution 242 is implemented in all its aspects and on all fronts, the Nine consider that the Treaty constitutes a correct application of the principles of that Resolution to Egyptian/Israeli relations.

They recall, however, that as they indicated in their declaration of 29 June 1977, the establishment of a just and lasting peace in the Middle East can only take place within the framework of a comprehensive settlement. Such a settlement must be based on Security Council Resolution 242 and 338 and must translate into fact the right of the Palestinian people to a homeland.

In this context they take due note of the will expressed by the signatories to the treaty to consider this not as a separate peace but as a first step in the direction of a comprehensive settlement designed to bring to an end thirty years of hostility and mistrust.

They hope that this will, to which they attach particular importance, can be given practical form soon in a comprehensive agreement in which all the parties concerned, including the representatives of the Palestinian people, would participate and to which the international community could give its endorsement.

The Nine express the hope that all the parties concerned will avoid any statement or action which will impede the search for peace, such as the Israeli policy of settlements in the occupied territories.'

85. Resolutions Passed at the Conference of Arab Foreign,

Economy, and Finance Ministers, Baghdad,

March 26, 1979*

* 8 J. Palestine Stud. 164 (Summer 1979).

Inasmuch as the government of the Arab Republic of Egypt has chosen to ignore the resolutions of the Arab Summit Conferences, and in particular those of the Sixth and Seventh Conferences held at Algiers and Rabat, and has at the same time ignored the resolutions of the Ninth Arab Summit Conference, in particular the call by the Arab kings and heads of state not to sign a peace agreement with the Zionist enemy, and on March 26, 1979 proceeded to sign a peace treaty with Israel, thereby withdrawing from Arab ranks and choosing, in collusion with the United States of America, to side with the Zionist enemy, to act unilaterally as regards the Arab-Zionist conflict, to violate the rights of the Arab nation, to expose the destiny, struggle and goals of the Arab nation to the dangers and challenges that threaten it and to neglect its national duty to liberate the occupied Arab territories, in particular Jerusalem, and to recover the inalienable national rights of the Palestinian Arab people, including the right to return and the right to self-determination and to establish an independent Palestinian state on the soil of their homeland;

In order to maintain Arab solidarity and unity of ranks for the defence of the historic Arab cause;

From an appreciation of the struggle of the Arab people in Egypt and their sacrifices for Arab causes and the Palestinian cause in particular;

In implementation of the resolutions adopted by the Ninth Arab Summit Conference held in Baghdad from November 2-5, 1978;

And at the invitation of the government of the Iraqi Republic, a conference of the Arab League Council at the level of Arab Ministers of Foreign Affairs, Economy and Finance was held in Baghdad from March 27-31, 1979. In the light of the resolutions of the Ninth Arab Summit Conference, the Council studied the latest developments related to the Arab-Zionist conflict, especially in view of the fact that the government of the Arab Republic of Egypt signed a peace treaty with the Zionist enemy on March 26, 1979.

The Arab League Council, meeting at the level of Arab Foreign Ministers, resolved the following:

1. a) To withdraw the ambassadors of the Arab states from Egypt immediately.

b) To recommend that political and diplomatic relations with the Egyptian government be severed, the Arab governments taking the necessary measures to implement this recommendation within a maximum of one month from the adoption of this resolution, in conformity with the constitutional measures in force in each country.

2. To regard the Arab Republic of Egypt as suspended from membership in the Arab League as from the date on which the Egyptian government signed the treaty with the Zionist enemy. This means that it is deprived of all the rights deriving from its membership.

3. a) That the city of Tunis, the capital of the Tunisian Republic, shall be the temporary headquarters of the League of Arab States, its Secretariat-General, specialized ministerial councils and permanent technical commit-

tees, as from the date of the signing of the treaty between the Egyptian government and the Zionist enemy, and that all international and regional organizations and bodies shall be informed of this, and that dealings with the League should be through its Secretariat in the new temporary headquarters.

b) To request the government of the Tunisian Republic to provide all possible assistance to facilitate the establishment of the temporary headquarters of the League and the housing of its officials.

c) To form a committee consisting of representatives of Iraq, Syria, Tunisia, Kuwait, Saudi Arabia and Algeria, in addition to a representative of the Secretariat-General, whose task shall be the implementation of the provisions of the resolution, and to urge the member states to provide such assistance as it requires. The committee shall be entrusted with all such powers of the League Council as may be required for the implementation of this resolution, including the safekeeping of the Arab League's property, funds, documents and records, and of taking the necessary measures against any step that may be taken by the Egyptian government to impede the transfer of the League's headquarters or to impair its rights and property. It shall complete its task of removal to the temporary headquarters within two months from the adoption of this resolution, though this period may be prolonged for a further month at the decision of the committee, which shall submit a report on the completion of its task to the first meeting of the Arab League Council.

d) That the sum of five million dollars shall be placed at the disposal of the committee to meet the expenses of the transfer, this sum being withdrawn from the permanent credits of the various funds. The committee shall be entitled to spend sums in excess of this if necessary, expenditure for this purpose being controlled by the committee or such party as it may authorize, each of the member states contributing to such expenditure in the ratio of its annual contribution to the League's budget.

e) To transfer the personnel of the League Secretariat who are working at the time of the adoption of this resolution from the permanent to the temporary headquarters within the period specified in paragraph 3 (c) of this resolution and the committee mentioned in paragraph 3 above shall be empowered to pay them compensation proportionate to the cost of living in the new headquarters and to facilitate matters for them until such time as permanent arrangements are made.

4. That the specialized Arab organizations set out in Appendix 1[2] shall take the necessary measures to suspend Egypt's membership from them and to transfer such of their headquarters as are situated in Egypt to other Arab countries on a temporary basis, as in the case of the League's Secretariat-General.

[2] For reasons of space, Appendix 1, which enumerates these bodies, has not been included—*Ed.*

The councils and executive committees of these organizations, agencies, institutions and federations shall meet immediately to implement this resolution within a period no longer than that specified in paragraph 3 (c) above.

5. To take action to secure the suspension of the Arab Republic of Egypt's membership in the Non-aligned Movement, the Islamic Conference Organization and the Organization of African Unity, because of her violation of the resolutions of these organizations relative to the Arab-Zionist conflict.

6. To continue to cooperate with the Arab people of Egypt and Egyptian citizens, with the exception of those who cooperate directly or indirectly with the Zionist enemy.

7. That the member states shall inform all foreign countries of their position on the Egypt-Israel treaty and ask them not to support this treaty, which is an infringement on the rights of the Palestinian people and the Arab nation and a threat to world peace and security.

8. To condemn the policy pursued by the United States of America as regards the role it played in the conclusion of the Camp David agreements and the Egypt-Israel treaty.

9. To regard the measures taken in this resolution as temporary ones to be annulled at the decision of the League Council as soon as the circumstances that justified their being taken no longer exist.

10. That the Arab states shall pass the legislation and take the decisions and measures required for the implementation of this resolution.

The Council of the Arab League, meeting at the level of the Arab Foreign, Economy and Finance Ministers, also resolved the following:

A. To halt the granting of any loans, deposits, securities, banking facilities, contributions, or financial or technical aid, or aid in kind by Arab governments or their institutions to the Egyptian government and its institutions, as from the date of the signing of the treaty.

B. To prohibit the granting of economic aid from Arab funds, banks and financial institutions operating within the framework of the Arab League and of joint Arab cooperation to the Egyptian government and its institutions.

C. That Arab governments and institutions shall refrain from acquiring bonds, shares, money orders and government loan stock issued by the Egyptian government and its financial institutions.

D. Following the suspension of the Egyptian government's membership in the Arab League, its membership in the institutions, funds and organizations affiliated thereto shall be suspended, the Egyptian government and its institutions shall no longer benefit from them, and such of them as are based in Egypt shall be transferred to other Arab countries on a temporary basis (Appendix 2).[3]

---

[3] For reasons of space, Appendix 2, which lists the Arab League affiliated bodies with offices in Egypt that are to be transferred abroad, could not be included—*Ed.*

E. In view of the fact that the ill-omened Egypt-Israel treaty and its annexes stipulate that Egypt shall sell oil to Israel, the Arab states shall refrain from providing Egypt with oil and petroleum derivatives.

F. To prohibit commercial exchanges with Egyptian public government and private firms that have dealings with the Zionist enemy.

G. Economic Boycott

1) To enforce the laws, principles and provisions of the Arab boycott against companies, institutions and individuals in the Arab Republic of Egypt that have direct or indirect dealings with the Zionist enemy, the Boycott Office being entrusted with the task of carrying out these tasks.

2) The provisions set out in paragraph (1) shall cover such intellectual, cultural and artistic activities as promote dealings with the Zionist enemy or are linked to his institutions.

3) The Arab states stress the importance of continuing to deal with private national Egyptian institutions whose refusal to deal with the Zionist enemy is confirmed, and to encourage them to operate and be active in the Arab countries in the fields that concern them.

4) The Arab states stress the importance of respecting the feelings of Egyptian citizens who work and live in the Arab countries, protecting their interests and reinforcing their national affiliation to Arabism.

5) So as to strengthen the role of the Arab boycott and to tighten its grip at this stage and to confirm unanimous Arab commitment to its provisions, the Assistant Secretary-General for Economic Affairs is temporarily entrusted with the task of directly supervising the Main Boycott Office in Damascus and is granted the necessary powers to reorganize and reinforce it and to submit proposals for developing the methods, content and scope of the boycott. He shall submit a report thereon to the first meeting of the League Council.

H. The United Nations shall be requested to move the headquarters of its regional offices that serve the Arab area from the Arab Republic of Egypt to any other Arab capital, and the Arab states shall take unified collective action to achieve this goal.

I. The Secretariat-General of the Arab League shall be entrusted with the task of studying the situation of joint Arab projects with a view to taking the measures necessary to protect the interests of the Arab nation in harmony with the goals of these resolutions, and the Secretariat-General shall submit its proposals to the Arab League Council at its first meeting.

J. To confront Zionist schemes by devising an Arab strategy for economic confrontation designed to exploit intrinsic Arab potentials; to stress the importance of achieving Arab economic integration at all levels; to promote joint Arab development and regional development within a pan-Arab context; to initiate further joint Arab projects that will serve the aims of liberation, development and Arab economic integration and to reinforce such as already exist; to improve the methods, organization and content of the economic boycott; also to diversify international relations and strengthen them with the developing countries. The Secretary-General of the Arab League shall as soon as possible submit studies on a strategy for joint Arab economic action to the Arab Economic Council at its next session, in preparation for convening an Arab economic conference.

K. The above-mentioned committee shall supervise the implementation of these resolutions and submit a follow-up report to the League Council at its first meeting.

L. The Arab states shall adopt such resolutions and legislation and take such measures as may be required for the implementation of these resolutions.

M. The measures taken by the Arab Foreign and Economy Ministers shall be regarded as the minimum action required for the confrontation of the dangers involved in the treaty, and it is left to the Arab governments to take such further individual measures as they deem necessary.

N. The Arab Foreign and Economy Ministers call on all countries of the Arab nation to support the economic measures taken against the Zionist enemy and the Egyptian regime.

86. European Parliament Resolution on the Signature of a Peace Treaty between Egypt and Israel and a Community Contribution to a Comprehensive Peace Settlement, May 21, 1979*

* 22 O.J. Eur. Comm. (No. C 127) 59 (1979).

The European Parliament,

- having regard to its resolution on the historic meeting between Mr. Anwar-el-Sadat and Mr. Menachem Begin (¹),
- having regard to its resolution on the outcome of the Camp David Summit (²),
- having regard to the statement on the signature of the Peace Treaty made on 26 March 1979 by the Nine Foreign Ministers meeting in political cooperation,
- having regard to the report of the Political Affairs Committee (Doc. 82/79),

1. Warmly welcomes the signature of a treaty of peace between Egypt and Israel after 30 years of hostilities and shares the desire of its signatories that this event should be considered as the first important step in the direction of a comprehensive peaceful settlement of the Middle East conflict;

2. Congratulates President Carter on his perseverance and dedication, and President Sadat and Prime Minister Begin on their courageous efforts in laying the foundations of a just and lasting peace in this area;

3. Endorses the declaration made by the Foreign Ministers meeting in political cooperation in Paris on 26 March 1979;

4. Urges the Council and Commission and the Governments of the Member States to do all in their power to intensify, within the framework of the Community and of European political cooperation, the existing links between the Community, Egypt and Israel and to offer stronger cooperation to those States of the area which are willing to participate in the process of achieving a comprehensive peace settlement;

5. Requests the Commission to bring forward concrete proposals to increase industrial cooperation between the Community and Israel and the Community and Egypt, as a contribution to the development of the region, and including suggestions for specific projects, in order to increase the industrial capacity of both countries and to diversify their economies;

6. Emphasizes the desire of the European Parliament to seek to make an effective contribution to the Community's efforts to assist in the achievement of a comprehensive settlement;

7. Instructs its President to forward this resolution to the Council and the Commission, to the Foreign Ministers meeting in political cooperation, to the governments of the Member States, the United States of America, Israel and Egypt and to the Knesset and the People's Assembly of Egypt.

¹ OJ No C 6, 9. 1. 1978, p. 47.
² OJ No C 261, 6. 4. 1978, p. 32.

87. Opening Statement by Dr. Josef Burg, Chairman of the Israeli Negotiating Team, at the First Session of the Autonomy Talks, Beersheba, May 25, 1979*

* Embassy of Israel, Washington, D.C.

On September 17, 1978, President Sadat and Prime Minister Menachem Begin signed the Camp David Framework for Peace in the Middle East, witnessed by President Jimmy Carter. This document, and the subsequent joint letter of March 26, 1979, are the mandate that brings us here today.

We are met with the goal of reaching agreement on the establishment of an elected administrative council in order to provide full autonomy for the Arab inhabitants of Samaria, Judea and the Gaza District. Our task is to reach an accord between us, prior to the election of this administrative council, on the modalities of its establishment, define its powers and responsibilities, and agree upon other related issues. Having reached such an agreement we would wish that the envisaged democratic elections speedily take place in Judea, Samaria and the Gaza District.

The tasks ahead of us are great, and no doubt complex. We enter negotiations mindful of the responsibility which history has placed on our shoulders. It is obvious that it is not possible to resolve overnight the bitter conflict which has gone on for so many years. We realize that before us lies a long and difficult road of negotiations. I am confident that we, Egypt and Israel, shall work together to reach understanding and agreement as expeditiously as we can. In this effort we shall benefit, as before, from the valuable assistance of the Government of the United States, whose representatives will participate fully in all stages of the negotiations.

Mr. Secretary, I deem it appropriate at this time and this place to reiterate to you, and through you to the President of the United States, the deepest gratitude for America's important role in advancing the course of our regional peace, as reflected in the first indispensable and historic step, the Treaty of Peace between Egypt and Israel.

We have already proven to each other how the common will for peace provides solutions to problems that otherwise seem elusive, how obstacles to progress fade away in the presence of common purpose, and how a patient ear precludes polemic and misunderstanding. We, Egypt and Israel, both have lived through the convulsions and agonies of our region for so long. Drama and trauma have gone hand in hand, caught in the vicious grip of enmity and warfare and bereavement.

No more. We are now bent on a different course, and already the pure breeze of coexistence plus dialogue and peace is dispersing the ugly pollution of the past.

We meet in Beersheba, the city of our common forefather, Abraham, it is perhaps most appropriate that here in this place we, Egypt and Israel, make our rendezvous with history, ancient and modern, to talk of Eretz Israel. Our founding patriarchs and matriarchs lie buried just to the north, in the town of Hebron. Jerusalem, the eternal capital city of Israel, founded by David the King, crowns the hills of Judea, from where our prophets preached the message of eternal peace in a land which has known so much strife.

Yes, it is to end the strife, to expand the peace, to ensure security and to promote the coexistence of its inhabitants, Jew and Arab, that we are met. Herein lie the justice and the validity of the autonomy, the details of which we shall negotiate in the weeks and months ahead.

At its very heart lies the conviction that the Palestinian Arabs should and must conduct their own daily lives for themselves and by themselves. It was this that motivated the Government of Israel, as early as December 1977, to propose autonomy—fully autonomy—for the Palestinian Arab inhabitants of Judea, Samaria and the Gaza District.

What I must make clear, and what must be understood from the outset, is that autonomy does not and cannot imply sovereignty. It is the peace and welfare of people that we seek—and this above all has to be our common task ahead—then we must by definition reject a priori an independent Palestinian statehood. Israel will not agree, and indeed totally rejects, the proposition, declaration or establishment of a Palestinian state in Judea, Samaria and the Gaza District. By everything we know to be true, it would be the certain prescription for violence and war. Indeed, it would be a mortal danger to Israel and a grave peril to the whole free world. No hostile element or agent or force dare control the heartland of this land to threaten the lives of its city dwellers and villagers and thereby hold a knife to the jugular vein of Israel.

Twenty-two independent Arab states, astride Africa and Asia, from the Persian Gulf to the Atlantic ocean—surely there has never been such an expression in the families of nations of self-determination and sovereignty. Our world has but one Jewish state—as of right in its ancient land—and the people of this land—nay, people of goodwill and decency everywhere—will not and cannot acquiese to any measure that will put that surviving remnant of our unspeakable holocaust in jeopardy. After having walked through the valley of the shadow of death, we shall never again allow life, liberty—indeed, existence itself—to be imperilled.

This is acknowledged and reflected in the Camp David Accord, which addresses itself to Israel's right to security as an essential condition of the peace. It is an integral feature of the autonomy. It is upon this foundation that the autonomy shall be built: Thereby the Arab inhabitants of Judea, Samaria and the Gaza District shall exercise control over their own daily lives and activities through their self-elected administrative council. Israel shall enjoy security. These are the principles and provisions stipulated in the Camp David Agreement.

Distinguished Members of the Delegations:

We meet here in sincere purpose. We meet with you with a sense of responsibility to the past and towards the generations of the future. We meet together for the sake of the peace with all our neighbors, with whom we wish to live always in mutual respect and cooperation.

We have problems to solve—together, challenges to overcome—together. I am confident that we shall find the appropriate solutions. To do so with courage and caution, as befits the historic responsibility we share. There is urgency to our work but there is also much need for the patient draftsmanship of devoted negotiators who are moved by high purpose.

Let us now set about constructing the next step on the ladder of peace. We hope that others might join us in our work. I call upon the Arab inhabitants of Judea, Samaria and the Gaza District to seize this opportunity to embark upon this new beginning and to share with us, Egypt and Israel both, in mapping a future that will guarantee the peace and welfare of this land in which we are destined to live together for all time.

"To everything there is a season, and a time to every purpose under heaven. A time to keep silent and a time to speak, a time to love and a time to hate, a time of war and a time of peace." We pray that the almighty might grant us his guidance in our efforts.

Thank you very much.

88. Excerpts from the Political Report Approved by the Central Committee of the Democratic Front for the Liberation of Palestine at the End of Its Meetings in Mid-July, 1979*

* 9 J. Palestine Stud. 200 (Autumn 1979).

The Struggle Against the Camp David Agreements: The Current Tasks of the Arab Steadfastness Movement

The thwarting of the Egyptian-Israeli treaty and the self-government plan is the most immediate task on the agenda of the forces of the revolution and the Arab liberation movement. This task is the central link in the current struggle against the Camp David agreements. In order to combat these agreements the peoples of our nation, the Arab Steadfastness movement and the Arab national liberation movement as a whole must without fail:

— Ensure the firm implementation of the resolutions of the two Baghdad conferences on the comprehensive economic, oil, political and diplomatic boycott of the Egyptian regime and the neutralization of any attempt to sidestep or water down the implementation of these resolutions.

— Complete the international political isolation of Sadat's regime. Now that the Egyptian regime's membership of the Conference of Islamic States has been suspended, it is the national duty of all to take action to suspend this regime's membership in the Organization of African Unity and the Non-Aligned Movement. It is also their duty to condemn the Camp David agreements and Sadat's treasonable treaty in all international and regional gatherings, and to prevent their being granted international legitimacy either at the UN or through UN supervision of the treaty in Sinai.

— Apply unremitting and systematic mass pressure for a policy of firm confrontation leading to the economic, oil and political boycott of American imperialism, the principal enemy of the peoples of our Arab nation, the main ally of the Zionist enemy, the ringleader of the Camp David agreements and the guarantor of the implementation of the treaty and the normalization of Egyptian-Israeli relations as a *fait accompli*, and of the self-government plan, whose aim is the liquidation of the Palestinian national cause and rights.

— Rebut all claims that new American initiatives are being launched and disclose their suspect objectives so that no one may be deluded into rehabilitating American policy and solutions.

— Give impetus to the Arab Steadfastness Front and ensure that it holds its fourth summit conference. The successful boycotting of imperialism requires a number of steps at the Arab level, the most important of which, in the present circumstances, is the convening of a summit of the Arab Steadfastness Front and efforts to ensure that Iraq joins it, so that it may be in a position to fulfil the conditions of steadfastness, first and foremost of which is taking the initiative in the economic, oil and political boycott of the US in conformity with national necessity and with the resolutions of the third Steadfastness summit.

In this way the other Arab regimes will have to face a new common denominator that constitutes the basic criterion of their hostility to the Camp David agreements, the bilateral capitulationist treaty and the self-government plan, and of the seriousness of their determination to repel the aggressiveness of American imperialism and its capitulationist solutions to Arab causes, and force it to withdraw and reconsider the whole of its policy of alliance with the Zionist enemy in this area.

. . . .

— Establish a progressive Arab front comprising all parties and nationalist, political and trade union movements throughout the Arab homeland, which has become an urgent necessity affirmed by the daily requirements of the current conflict with the Camp David alliance, the bilateral capitulationist treaty, the self-government plan and the war of steadfastness against the Zionist war of attrition on the front lines of confrontation. If the situation prior to the Camp David agreements made it impossible to establish such a front in view of the political differences between many Arab parties and movements as regards the nature of the present stage, the ensuing tasks and the manner of performing them, the current situation has given rise to the political base essential for the establishment of a nationalist and progressive Arab front. This is because the struggle to destroy the Camp David agreements, the Egyptian-Israeli capitulationist treaty and the liquidationist self-government plan constitutes the broad framework for the establishment of such a front. Moreover, all organizations of the resistance and the overwhelming majority of the sectors of the Arab national liberation movement have agreed on an interim national programme based on the slogans of the liberation of the Arab territories occupied in 1967 and the recovery of the national rights of the people of Palestine, headed by the right to return, to self-determination and to an independent state; this programme is the direct opposite of the Camp David agreements, the treaty and the self-government plan, and is an offensive weapon in the hands of all the forces of the liberation movement and the Arab peoples in their confrontation of the surrender projects embodied in the Camp David agreements and their annexes.

. . . .

At the level of the Arab mass movement, it is the duty of the Arab revolutionary forces—parties, popular movements and trade unions—to launch a vigorous campaign against all attempts to rehabilitate the policies and settlements of American colonialism that certain reactionary Arab quarters are advocating. It is also the duty of the Arab revolutionary forces to engage in unremitting struggle against the course of vacillation, hesitancy and unprincipled compromise that is being pursued by the ruling national bourgeoisie and its rightist trends. This course must be combated on the basis of unrelenting hostility to the treaty, the Camp David agreements and American policy in the Middle East, and on the basis of the national interim programme for the steadfastness and Arab struggle movement.

Also at the level of the mass movement, priority in joint national action must be accorded to ensuring that all parties and nationalist and progressive movements come together in a united front in every Arab country, on the basis of genuinely democratic relations between these forces and of their right to freedom of action in all fields on the basis of their ideological, political and organizational independence, with no question of any kind of coercion or restriction on the movement of any force in any field.

— Grant democratic freedoms to the masses and effective struggle against all kinds of repression or coercion to which their parties, organizations and trade union and professional institutions are being subjected.

. . . .

The performance of these tasks will besiege the Sadat-Begin treaties and prevent bilateral and separate surrender agreements spreading to other Arab fronts, and ensure that the Camp David agreements are confined within the limits of the Egyptian front until such time as it is checked and thrown back.

. . . .

The Occupied Territories

. . . .

The central link in national struggle within the occupied areas is resistance to the self-government plan, the employment of all kinds of struggle to frustrate it and the elimination of all groups who try to become party to it in the future.

Although the situation in the Arab environment, especially since the surrender of the Egyptian regime, indicates that we are to be confronted with a relentless long-term battle, the important feature of the situation in the occupied areas is that the deterioration in the Arab situation has not been reflected in the frame of mind of the masses or affected their high level of readiness for struggle. This in itself provides a firm foundation for the fighting of a battle, in which final victory is assured, against the self-government plan, for closing the door on those who advocate it and for resolute insistence on Palestinian national rights, first and foremost of which is the right to establish an independent state.

The defeat of the self-government project and the plans for [Israeli] settlement [in the occupied territories] requires of us, and of all nationalist forces, that we undertake the following:

— [We must take] prompt action to establish the organizations and institutions required by the national front in all areas, towns and camps. The growth of the national front and its organizational structures from base to apex is the essential weapon for the unification of all nationalist forces in the occupied territories and for the mobilization and organization of the widest possible mass base that will take part in the organized and unremitting struggle under the banner of the political programme of the PLO.

It will be the task of the national front to organize all kinds of national struggle so as to induce the workers, the peasants and the national bourgeoisie to rally round the front, as constituting a genuine leadership of their struggle against occupation and settlement and for self-determination and national independence. It will also provide genuine leadership in the defence of the rights and interests of the masses, which will increase their readiness for effort and sacrifice throughout the long struggle, until such time as the occupiers are defeated and the independent state is established.

– Here we must stress the importance of resisting all rightist trends aimed at impeding and fragmenting the activities of the national front, and also the responsibility of radical and progressive forces for closing their ranks and unifying their action toward this end.

– [We must] isolate agents of the occupation and all defeatist reactionary elements who make propaganda on behalf of the self-government project, and stress that it is the duty of the leadership of the PLO outside the occupied areas to sever links with these elements and to combat their capitulationist trend.

– Efforts [must be made] to ensure that the "steadfastness funds" are used to support nationalist institutions, bodies and municipalities, and [there must be] resistance to all trends leading to their being wasted or withheld from nationalist quarters. This is especially important inasmuch as the trend followed by the Jordanian regime in the past will now have increased its influence since the adoption by the Baghdad summit of resolutions making it a partner with the PLO in the distribution of these funds.

– [We must] develop the trade unions by widening their social bases and encouraging the use of democratic methods in their daily life, so that they may play their vanguard role in the national struggle of the working class in support of their demands and develop their aptitudes and capacities in the field of struggle, organization and politics in the nationalist and revolutionary process now in progress in the occupied homeland against occupation, settlement and the self-government plan.

So far the size of the working class has not been reflected in the nationalist and trade union role they have played, or in their struggle for their demands. While this class accounts for 62 percent of the labour force in the West Bank and the Gaza Strip, their nationalist leadership role is still limited.

Similarly the size of the working class is not reflected in the ratio of membership of the unions: the trade union base is not more than 7 percent of the working class.

.   .   .   .

– Armed struggle against the enemy and its military and economic institutions is the principal factor in the escalation and development of all forms of mass and political struggle against the enemy. In this connection we welcome the escalation and development of operations of armed struggle on the part of our front and the forces of the revolution throughout the period that has just passed. If the enemy's confrontation with the operations of the Palestinian revolution within the occupied territories has taken the form of an aggressive war of attrition against the revolution and the camps of our people in Lebanon, it is up to us and all organizations of the revolution to increase armed struggle and to develop its quantity and quality within occupied Palestine.

In Galilee, the Triangle, the Negev and all concentrations of the Palestinian people that have held out in their land since 1948, nationalist struggle is growing under the leadership of the democratic forces within which the Communist Party (Rakah) is playing a vanguard role. The spirit of unity that welds this section of the Palestinian people, their insistence on holding on to their national territory, on political resistance to settlement and the seizure of lands in Galilee and the Negev and on retaining their national identity, are all reinforcing the trend toward the reunification of the ranks of the Palestinian people in these areas with other groupings in the West Bank, Jerusalem and the Gaza Strip and outside the homeland, on the basis of struggle against Zionism and national dissolution and to ensure national rights as regards the return of the refugees to their homeland and the achievement of the full independence of the Palestinian people in their land. This unity is reflected in the battles that are being fought daily against the plundering of lands from Ma'lia to the Negev, and in Nablus and all areas of the occupied homeland. This calls for the strengthening of relations in struggle between all sectors active in the ranks of the Palestinian people in all their concentrations, and also with democratic anti-Zionist Jewish forces. This requires the effective implementation of the resolutions of the Palestinian National Council on the promotion of these links and the development of all kinds of mutual political and practical militant support, with a view to reinforcing the unity of the struggle and the common goals that have brought these forces together.

All sectors and groupings of the Palestinian people have been unanimous in their opposition to the Camp David conspiracy, including those who live in Galilee, the Triangle and the Negev, from a consciousness that they are a part of the Palestinian people as a whole, and from a realization that the establishment of an independent state for the Palestinian people will mark the start of the deliverance of the whole of our people and their full liberation from Zionist persecution.

The present stage in the Palestinian struggle to defeat occupation, settlement and the self-government plan gives greater emphasis than ever before to the fundamental importance of the role of the revolution and the popular movement in the occupied areas. Hence the need to direct the principal efforts in our struggle and that of all organizations of the resistance toward the development of the nationalist movement and armed struggle inside the occupied territories where, to a great extent, will be decided the destiny of the self-government project and the plans of the occupation, and also the destiny and the future of our national cause for many years to come.

89. Written Question to the EEC Foreign Ministers on the U.N. Resolution of 29 November 1979 on the Camp David Agreements, January 15, 1980—Answer, March 31, 1980*

---

* 23 O.J. Eur. Comm. (No. C 110) 50 (1980).

WRITTEN QUESTION No 1484/79
by Mr Schwartzenberg
to the Ministers for Foreign Affairs meeting in political cooperation
(15 January 1980)

Subject: UN resolution of 29 November 1979 on the Camp David Agreements

On 29 November 1979 the General Assembly of the United Nations adopted by 75 votes to 33 with 37 abstentions a resolution condemning the Agreements between Israel, Egypt and the United States of America at Camp David.

How did the Nine vote on that occasion and why?

ANSWER
(31 March 1980)

On 28 November 1979, the Nine either abstained or voted against resolution 34/65 B taken under item 'Palestinian Question' on the agenda. This does not imply that they have fundamentally different interpretations of the Camp David Agreements.

The Nine made known their position on these Agreements in their statements of 19 September 1978 and 26 March 1979 and in the address delivered to the United Nations General Assembly on 25 September 1979 by the Irish Minister for Foreign Affairs speaking on behalf of the Nine.

The Nine fully appreciate the desire for peace behind President Carter's personal commitment, and the efforts of President Sadat and Prime Minister Begin in the negotiation of the Camp David Agreements.

They have noted that the peace treaty is a correct application to Israeli-Egypt relations of the principles of the relevant resolutions of the United Nations Security Council. They have expressly noted the will of the signatories to the Treaty to consider this not as a separate peace but as a first step towards a global solution in which all the interested parties, including the representatives of the Palestinian people, will participate.

90. Autonomy—the Wisdom of Camp David,

Policy Background, May 2, 1980*

---

* Embassy of Israel, Washington, D.C.

This is the first time that the Palestinian Arabs have a chance of securing something, of making some progress in their standing in this country and in the region. For there is little they can gain from the declarations of European statesmen, or from UN resolutions, or from terrorist activities . . . Experience shows that, by their extremist behaviour, they have been unable to achieve anything in practice. The only concrete proposal that gives them a chance, today, to attain a serious position and to play a role in determining that position in the region is the autonomy plan.

> (Israel Foreign Minister, Yitzhak Shamir,
> in an interview broadcast by Israel radio,
> 21 March 1980.)

The current negotiations on granting autonomy to the Palestinian Arab inhabitants of Judea, Samaria and Gaza are the outcome of a negotiated agreement upon which Israel, Egypt—the major state of the Arab world—and the United States came to terms at Camp David. That framework package is the fruit of difficult negotiations which lasted some ten months; it represents a triumph for compromise and illuminates the one secure path through the conflicting concerns and interests which have pitted the Arab world against Israel in five major wars; it rests upon Security Council Resolutions 242 and 338.

As recognized both by the Armistice Accords of 1949—which ended the War of Independence of 1948—and the Interim Accord of 1975—which ended the Yom Kippur War of 1973—peace must, of necessity, be made by the same parties that had participated in the fighting. Thus, in Israel's view, the major priority has always been the establishment of peace with any one of her neighbours so willing. Clearly the corollary of that desire has been that the Arab states should forego their sworn intentions to destroy Israel, and accept her as a sovereign and recognized neighbour. It was on that basis that President Sadat came to Jerusalem in 1977, and that the process which led to the Camp David Accords and the Israel-Egypt peace treaty started.

During his visit to Ismailia in December 1977, the Prime Minister of Israel proposed that, in addition to peace between Israel and Egypt, the problem of the Palestinian Arab inhabitants of Judea, Samaria and Gaza be considered for resolution, and the idea of autonomy was first brought up.

Israel's Proposal

Israel's proposal for a self-governing authority was presented in the absence of any other acceptable formula for the resolution of a problem which had been created by the Arab states.

It was a historic turning point for the Palestinian Arabs, since it offered them a status and advantages which no one had hitherto proposed.

The autonomy agreement was intended as a practical solution to the status of the Palestinian Arabs. This solution would answer the needs of all parties concerned: Israel's need for security and defense in depth on her eastern border; the Egyptian wish to adhere to the Arab cause; and last, but not least, the need of the Palestinian Arabs to govern their own affairs.

The essence of the plan is simple. The Arab inhabitants will be allowed to fully manage all those areas of legitimate internal administration, but matters which could be detrimental to Israel would be excluded. Israel will retain those powers and functions which are essential to her defense and security.

In Mena House, Giza, on January 16, 1980, the Israeli delegation to the autonomy talks presented a carefully prepared, detailed model for the proposed administrative council. The plan offers the inhabitants of Judea-Samaria and Gaza, for the first time in history, full control over all matters affecting their daily lives, as well as a real opportunity to participate in the determination of their future.

The model defines three categories of powers and responsibilities:

1. those to be transferred in full to the administrative council, grouped into ten divisions, and the general power to issue regulations, to determine and administer budgets, to enter into contracts, to sue and be sued and to employ personnel;

2. those to be administered jointly and through cooperation—such as foreign trade, water supply, regional planning, etc.;

3. those reserved powers to remain under Israel's authority—such as defense and security, foreign affairs, stamps and currency, etc.

In contrast, Cairo's own proposals have, in many ways, no basis in the Camp David Accords, and run counter to some of their basic principles. Pending the initial five-year period of autonomy, all options will remain open, and at that time the claims of the parties will be negotiated. These negotiations "shall be based on all the provisions and principles of UN Security Council Resolution 242" and will "determine the final status" of the areas. According to the Camp David Agreements, two separate but related committees will convene, one consisting of Israel, Egypt, Jordan and the elected representatives of the inhabitants of Judea, Samaria and the Gaza district, to agree on the final status of these areas, and the second committee, consisting of the representatives of Israel and Jordan and the inhabitants of the areas, to negotiate the peace treaty between Israel and Jordan.

The Israeli and Egyptian Positions—A Comparison

If adopted, the Egyptian proposals would set in motion an irreversible process which would lead to the establishment of an independent Arab-Palestinian state. Such a process would effectively destroy any option of territorial compromise or functional division of authority and would thus severly [sic] jeopardize whatever prospects exist for achieving peace with Jordan. The Camp David Agreements clearly state that the final disposition of the status of the administered areas, following the five-year transitional period, is to be negotiated separately in talks which are to commence three years after the implementation of autonomy.

Positions Compared

While significant agreement has been reached on the election modalities, substantial differences between the Egyptian and Israeli positions remain in the following realms:

a) The nature of the Autonomy: In conformity with the Camp David accords, Israel's position is that autonomy should extend to the inhabitants of Judea, Samaria and the Gaza district. Egypt, on the other hand believes that the autonomy should extend to lands as well.

b) The nature of the Self-Governing Authority: Israel's position is that there should be an administrative council—as stipulated in the Accords, the term "administrative council" defines but also qualifies the powers of this Authority. Egypt, on the other hand, requests full legislative and executive authority, in addition to the administration of justice. An administrative council, by definition, cannot exercise such powers—these are the prerogatives of an independent state.

c) The powers of the Self-Governing Authority: According to the Camp David agreement these should be negotiated between the parties. Israel therefore believes that these powers should be jointly defined. Egypt, on the other hand, requests that all the powers currently exercised by the Military Government should be handed over to the self-governing authority. This position is unacceptable to Israel. Since there are certain powers—such as security, which for obvious reasons cannot be transferred.

d) The Source of Authority: Every autonomy arrangement (and examples are numerous) has had a power above it; this is particularly true of one which is to provide for a transitional period of 5 years. It is Israel's view that the source of authority should be the Military Government. To adopt any other position would be to preordain the ultimate result after the 5 year period and would vest the self-governing authority with the attributes of an independent state. The Egyptian view is that the self-governing authority should be a self-generating authority, and that no outside source should vest it with authority. To adopt that position would mean, again, an independent state, rather than autonomy.

e) Security: The role of the self-governing authority described in the Camp David accords is "to assist in providing such security, a strong local police will be constituted and . . . will maintain continuing liaison on internal security matters with the designated Israel, Jordanian and Egyptian officers." It follows from this that internal (as well as external) security must be in Israel's hands. Israel believes that in order to counter the twin threat of terrorism and armed invasion, the role of the self-governing authority should be defined as "assistance" by its police force.

Egypt's Position	*Camp David Agreements*	*Israel's Position*
NATURE OF AUTONOMY		
"Authority of the Self-Governing Authority extends to the inhabitants as well as the land in the West Bank and Gaza Strip."	" . . . full autonomy to the inhabitants (of the West Bank and Gaza) . . . "	Autonomy is specifically intended for "the inhabitants" of the areas, not for the territory, as such.
NATURE OF THE SELF-GOVERNING AUTHORITY		
" . . . the powers and responsibilities to be exercised by the self-governing authority include full legislative and executive authority (and) . . . administration of justice."	"When the self-governing authority (administrative council) in the West Bank and Gaza is established and inaugurated, the transitional period of five years will begin.	The term "administrative council" defines and qualifies the power of the self-governing authority. An administrative council cannot exercise executive legislative and judicial functions.
POWERS OF THE SELF-GOVERNING AUTHORITY		
"The transfer of authority (to the self-governing authority) implies the handing over of all powers and responsibilities presently exercised by the Military Government and its civilian administration."	"The parties will negotiate an agreement which will define the powers and responsibilities of the self-governing authority . . . "	The parties must negotiate to "define" which of the Military Government's powers and responsibilities are to be transferred to the self-governing authority and which are to remain in Israel's hands.
PALESTINIAN ARABS		
"The purpose (is) . . . the realization of their (the Palestinian people's) legitimate rights, including their right to self-determination."	" . . . the Palestinians will participate in the determination of their own future . . . "	To exceed Palestinian "participation" in the determination of their future, at this time, would be to prejudge the ultimate disposition of the areas.

Egypt's Position	*Camp David Agreements*	*Israel's Position*
SOURCE OF AUTHORITY "It (the self-governing authority) is a self-generating authority. No outside source vests it with its authority."		Every autonomy arrangement ever implemented has had a power over it. The source of authority here is the Israel Military Government.
JERUSALEM "The annexation of East Jerusalem is null and void and must be rescinded. Jerusalem is an integral part of the West Bank. The seat of the self-governing authority will be East Jerusalem.	Subject not included in the Camp David accords.	Jerusalem, the capital of the State of Israel, is one and indivisible.
SETTLEMENT Israeli settlements in the West Bank and the Gaza Strip are illegal and, in the course of a final settlement, should be withdrawn. During the transition, there should be a ban on the establishment of new settlements or enlarging the existing ones. After the inauguration of the self-governing authority, all settlers in the West Bank and Gaza will come under the authority of the self-governing authority.	(At the request of President Carter, Israel agreed to a three-month freeze on the establishment of new settlements in the areas following the conclusion of the Camp David Agreements.)	Eretz Israel ("Palestine") is the Jewish homeland to which Jews have returned as of right. Just as they are entitled to dwell in Tel Aviv, Haifa and Jerusalem, so do Jews have the right to live in Judea-Samaria and the district of Gaza—as indeed they did for centuries until the Arab invasion of 1948. This right is inseperably linked to the requirements of Israel's vital national security.
SECURITY The self-governing authority will assume	" . . . there will be a redeployment of the	Ultimate responsibility for internal as well

Egypt's Position	Camp David Agreements	Israel's Position
SECURITY (cont.) "responsibility for . . . public order and internal security . . . (and) has full power in . . . internal security . . . Permission (of the self-governing authority) will be required for any movement of military troops into or through the territory . . . Responsibility for security and public order will be decided jointly by the parties, including the Palestinians . . ."	remaining Israeli forces into specified security locations. The agreement will also include arrangements for assuring internal and external security and public order . . . All necessary measures will be taken and provisions made to assure the security of Israel and its neighbours during the transitional period and beyond. To assist in providing such security, a strong local police force will be constituted by the self-governing authority (and) . . . will maintain continuing liaison on internal security matters with the designated Israeli, Jordanian and Egyptian officers."	as external security must remain in Israel's hands, so that it can counter the twin threat of terrorism and armed invasion. The role of the self-governing authority in these matters is clearly defined as "assistance" and "liaison" by its police force, rather than shared (let alone full) responsibility. Also, there is no basis whatsoever for the proposal to require the self-governing authority's permission for the movement of troops to and from, and among, the specified security locations, and it is inconceivable that Israel would allow anyone veto power over such movements.

The Past: Unaccepted Solutions

Israel's autonomy proposal was put forward following a long history of abortive proposals which had been unacceptable to one or more of the parties.

a) An Independant Palestinian State

This solution was put forward following the 1967 war by the recently founded terrorist organizations. Previous to that time, Judea and Samaria had been annexed by Jordan in 1950 (with the exception of Great Britain and Pakistan, the entire international community, including the countries of the Arab League, refused to recognize this annexation); the Gaza district had been ruled by Egypt. The inhabitants of Judea and Samaria continued to hold Jordanian citizenship after 1967, and the proposal was promoted in the main by Arab terrorist organizations based in Beirut. In this context it is worth noting that within the historic area of Palestine, two states already exist, and that one of them, Jordan, is composed of an ethnic majority of Palestinians. This proposal suggested, in effect, the creation of a second Palestinian Arab state, that is, a twenty-third Arab state.

Such a solution cannot be acceptable to Israel under any circumstances. The establishment of another Palestinian Arab state would create a political vacuum which would be filled by the terrorist organizations; it would provide a strategic foothold for the Soviet Union or its Cuban surrogates in this area, and would threaten the long-tern [*sic*] interests of the West and the very existence of Israel. The American view of this crucial issue has repeatedly been stated by President Carter. On August 11, 1979, he said:

> I am against any creation of a separate Palestinian state. I don't think it would be good for the Palestinians. I don't think it would be good for Israel. I don't think it would be good for the Arab neighbors of such a state . . .

The President further stated on February 25, 1980:

> I am opposed to an independent Palestinian state because in my own judgement and in the judgement of many leaders in the Middle East, including Arab leaders, this would be a destabilizing factor and would not be in the US interest.

On August 31, 1979, the President also told a group of newspaper editors:

> I have never met an Arab leader that in private professed a desire for an independent Palestinian state.

b) *Territorial Partition*

Previous governments of Israel have put forward proposals to partition Judea and Samaria. In essence such proposals called for "secure and recognized boundaries," in place of the insecure lines of 1949, and the "withdrawal of the armed forces from territories occupied in the recent conflict" (but not all the territories). Thus, Israel would retain areas essential to her security, whilst the populated heartlands of Judea and Samaria would be returned to the control of Jordan

These proposals were consistently rejected, again as recently as April 24, 1980, by King Hussein of Jordan, who insists on the complete and unconditional evacuation of all the territories by Israel.

One should note, in this context, that the great majority of Israelis reject a return to the vulnerable 1967 borders. No other viable solution has ever been put forward by any other party. The autonomy proposal is therefore the only solution which has been agreed upon by an Arab state. It is a solution which has grown out of a long and difficult process of negotiations, and which represents, in fact, the other part of the Camp David accords, based on these countries' acceptance of Resolution 242. Moreover, it is a solution which is conditional upon the original terms of the same resolution, calling for a peace "in which every state in the area can live in security." It is in this spirit that Israel in the treaty with Egypt has made far-reaching territorial sacrifices, and has opened the way to autonomy in Judea, Samaria and Gaza. Egypt recognized the wisdom of the phased approach to the question of the final status of the areas, and thus the Camp David accords were agreed upon.

Any change in these basic tenets would prejudge the final status of the areas and would thus undermine the only agreed upon solution. It would also destroy all possibility of sound and constructive negotiations in the future.

Israel's security was a basic tenet of both Resolution 242 and Camp David accords. To negate that tenet would mean putting Israel's security in jeopardy, and would endanger the whole area.

The Continuing Committee

The Camp David accords also proposed that during the proposed transitional period, a continuing committee should be established. This committee would deal with the admission of displaced persons from the Six-Day War of 1967, matters of public order, and other matters of public concern. The members of the committee would be Israel, Egypt, Jordan and representatives of the self-governing authority in the autonomous regions.

Since the conclusion of the accords Israel has continued to demonstrate flexibility and a willingness to reach practical working arrangements for the work of this committee. She has agreed to the inclusion of US representatives on the committee and to the inclusion on its agenda of matters not considered susceptible to immediate agreement such as the development of common water resources and other economic matters.

Jerusalem

It should be noted that the autonomy plan does not include Jerusalem, and that any questions concerning the future of the city are not included in the terms of reference of the negotiating committees.

Whilst being a topic of discussion at Camp David, the subject of Jerusalem was not included in the Camp David accords. Clearly it was considered to be outside the boundaries of the proposed autonomous areas and any agreement pertaining to the future regulation of life and resources in those areas would be applicable only to them.

Jerusalem is, and always has been, the capital of the Jewish people. It has maintained, throughout the ages, a Jewish majority. Today, its population, more than 75% of which is Jewish, is reunited in an open, developing and vibrant city whose growth has been in the interest of all and from which all have benefited. The desecration and neglect of the Jordanian occupation of

East Jerusalem have been consigned to history. That small part of Jerusalem which was under Jordanian occupation is now an integral part of the city and the State of Israel and all its inhabitants enjoy and exercise the right of participation in municipal elections. A return to any form of division within the city would be not only artificial and impractical, but would be contrary to all future harmony, co-existence and the spirit of mutual respect and tolerance which has developed since reunification. Israel does not wish to include any part of Jerusalem in the autonomy plan precisely because this would imply a redivision of the city. Such a redivision, in any shape or form, would be totally unacceptable to Israel. American policy relating to Jerusalem was summed up in a message from President Carter to Prime Minister Begin on March 3, 1980:

> . . . As to Jerusalem, we strongly believe that Jerusalem should be undivided with free access to the holy places for all faiths and that its status should be determined in the negotiations for a comprehensive peace settlement.

A Mid-Way Point

Israel can look back with a sense of accomplishment on the achievements of the peace-building process thus far. For Israel this has been the realization of a dream—the dream of peace. It is an achievement which Israel does not wish to jeopardize. That peace process can be brought to fruition only in an unfettered process of negotiations free from outside pressure or interference, and based upon what has been achieved thus far. Israel believes, therefore, that within the parameters determined by the necessities of her security, and the continuous threat of Arab aggression from the east, it is possible to achieve full autonomy as agreed upon at Camp David, and extend the benefits of peace to other elements in the Middle East who genuinely desire them, above all to the Palestinian inhabitants of Judea, Samaria and Gaza. When President Sadat visited Jerusalem in November 1977, a peace treaty between Egypt and Israel was envisaged within a year. As matters turned out, it took 16 months to complete the negotiations; that fact does not render the treaty that was ultimately signed between the two countries less valid—or less of an historic achievement.

Similarly in the case of the autonomy talks, there is no call for a sense of impending doom because the target date of May 26 is approaching and the possibility exists that agreement will not have been reached by that time. With both sides determined—as they have repeatedly stated they are—to bring these negotiations to a successful conclusion as speedily as possible, agreement will surely be reached before of [sic] after May 26.

91. Protocol Establishing the Sinai Multinational Force and Observers, with Annex and Appendix, and Secretary of State Haig's Letter to Egyptian and Israeli Foreign Ministers, August 3, 1981*

* 81 U.S. Dep't State Bull. No. 2054, at 44 (September 1981).

Secretary's Letter to Egyptian and Israeli Foreign Ministers, Aug. 3, 1981

Dear Mr. Minister:

I wish to confirm the understandings concerning the United States' role reached in your negotiations on the establishment and maintenance of the Multinational Force and Observers:

1. The post of the Director-General will be held by U.S. nationals suggested by the United States.

2. Egypt and Israel will accept proposals made by the United States concerning the appointment of the Director-General, the appointment of the Commander, and the financial issues related to paragraphs 24-26 of the Annex to the Protocol, if no agreement is reached on any of these issues between the Parties. The United States will participate in deliberations concerning financial matters. In the event of differences of view between the Parties over the composition of the MFO, the two sides will invite the United States to join them in resolving any issues.

3. Subject to Congressional authorization and appropriations:

A. The United States will contribute an infantry battalion and a logistics support unit from its armed forces and will provide a group of civilian observers to the MFO.

B. The United States will contribute one-third of the annual operating expenses of the MFO. The United States will be reimbursed by the MFO for the costs incurred in the change of station of U.S. Armed Forces provided to the MFO and for the costs incurred in providing civilian observers to the MFO. For the initial period (July 17, 1981-September 30, 1982) during which there will be exceptional costs connected with the establishment of the MFO, the United States agrees to provide three-fifths of the costs, subject to the same understanding concerning reimbursement.

C. The United States will use its best efforts to find acceptable replacements for contingents that withdraw from the MFO.

D. The United States remains prepared to take those steps necessary to ensure the maintenance of an acceptable MFO.

I wish to inform you that I sent today to the Minister of Foreign Affairs of Israel [of Egypt] an identical letter, and I propose that my letters and the replies thereto constitute an agreement among the three States.

Sincerely,

ALEXANDER M. HAIG, JR.

Protocol

In view of the fact that the Egyptian-Israeli Treaty of Peace dated March 26, 1979 (hereinafter, "the Treaty"), provides for the fulfillment of certain functions by the United Nations Forces and Observers and that the President of the Security Council indicated on 18 May 1981, that the Security Council was unable to reach the necessary agreement on the proposal to establish the UN Forces and Observers, Egypt and Israel, acting in full respect for the purposes and principles of the United Nations Charter, have reached the following agreement:

1. A Multinational Force and Observers (hereinafter, "MFO") is hereby established as an alternative to the United Nations Forces and Observers. The two parties may consider the possibility of replacing the arrangements hereby established with alternative arrangements by mutual agreement.

2. The provisions of the Treaty which relate to the establishment and functions and responsibilities of the UN Forces and Observers shall apply mutatis mutandis to the establishment and functions and responsibilities of the MFO or as provided in this Protocol.

3. The provisions of Article IV of the Treaty and the Agreed Minute thereto shall apply to the MFO. In accordance with paragraph 2 of this Protocol, the words "through the procedures indicated in paragraph 4 of Article IV and the Agreed Minute thereto" shall be substituted for "by the Security Council of the United Nations with the affirmative vote of the five permanent members" in paragraph 2 of Article IV of the Treaty.

4. The Parties shall agree on the nations from which the MFO will be drawn.

5. The mission of the MFO shall be to undertake the functions and responsibilities stipulated in the Treaty for the United Nations Forces and Observers. Details relating to the international nature, size, structure and operation of the MFO are set out in the attached Annex.

6. The Parties shall appoint a Director-General who shall be responsible for the direction of the MFO. The Director-General shall, subject to the approval of the Parties, appoint a Commander, who shall be responsible for the daily command of the MFO. Details relating to the Director-General and the Commander are set out in the attached Annex.

7. The expenses of the MFO which are not covered by other sources shall be borne equally by the Parties.

8. Disputes arising from the interpretation and application of this Protocol shall be resolved according to Article VII of the Treaty.

9. This Protocol shall enter into force when each Party has notified the other that all its Constitutional requirements have been fulfilled. The attached Annex shall be regarded as an integral part hereof. This Protocol shall be communicated to the Secretary General of the United Nations for registration in accordance with the provisions of Article 102 of the Charter of the United Nations.

For the Government of the Arab Republic of Egypt:
Ashraf A. Gorbal

For the Government of the State of Israel:
Ephraim Evron

Witnessed by:
Alexander M. Haig, Jr.
For the Government of the United States of America

Annex

DIRECTOR-GENERAL

1. The Parties shall appoint a Director-General of the MFO within one month of the signing of this Protocol. The Director-General shall serve a term of four years, which may be renewed. The Parties may replace the Director-General prior to the expiration of his term.

2. The Director-General shall be responsible for the direction of the MFO in the fulfillment of its functions and in this respect is authorized to act on behalf of the MFO. In accordance with local laws and regulations and the privileges and immunities of the MFO, the Director-General is authorized to engage an adequate staff, to institute legal proceedings, to contract, to acquire and dispose of property, and to take those other actions necessary and proper for the fulfillment of his responsibilities. The MFO shall not own immovable property in the territory of either Party without the agreement of the respective government. The Director-General shall determine the location of his office, subject to the consent of the country in which the office will be located.

3. Subject to the authorization of the Parties, the Director-General shall request those nations agreeable to the Parties to supply contingents to the MFO and to receive the agreement of contributing nations that the contingents will conduct themselves in accordance with the terms of this Protocol. The Director-General shall impress upon contributing nations the importance of continuity of service in units with the MFO so that the Commander may be in a position to plan his operations with knowledge of what units will be available. The Director-General shall obtain the agreement of contributing nations that the national contingents shall not be withdrawn without adequate prior notification to the Director-General.

4. The Director-General shall report to the Parties on developments relating to the functioning of the MFO. He may raise with either or both Parties, as appropriate, any matter concerning the functioning of the MFO. For this purpose, Egypt and Israel shall designate senior responsible officials as agreed points of contact for the Director-General. In the event that either Party or the Director-General requests a meeting, it will be convened in the location determined by the Director-General within 48 hours. Access across the international boundary shall only be permitted through entry checkpoints designated by each Party. Such access will be in accordance with the laws and regulations of each country. Adequate procedures will be established by each Party to facilitate such entries.

MILITARY COMMAND STRUCTURE

5. In accordance with paragraph 6 of the Protocol, the Director-General shall appoint a Commander of the MFO within one month of the appointment of the Director-General. The Commander will be an officer of general rank and shall serve a term of three years which may, with the approval of

the Parties, be renewed or curtailed. He shall not be of the same nationality as the Director-General.

6. Subject to paragraph 2 of this Annex, the Commander shall have full command authority over the MFO, and shall promulgate its Standing Operating Procedures. In making the command arrangements stipulated in paragraph 9 of Article VI of Annex I of the Treaty (hereinafter "Annex I"), the Commander shall establish a chain of command for the MFO linked to the commanders of the national contingents made available by contributing nations. The members of the MFO, although remaining in their national service, are, during the period of their assignment to the MFO, under the Director-General and subject to the authority of the Commander through the chain of command.

7. The Commander shall also have general responsibility for the good order of the MFO. Responsibility for disciplinary action in national contingents provided for the MFO rests with the commanders of the national contingents.

FUNCTIONS AND RESPONSIBILITIES OF THE MFO

8. The mission of the MFO shall be to undertake the functions and responsibilities stipulated in the Treaty for the United Nations Forces and Observers.

9. The MFO shall supervise the implementation of Annex I and employ its best efforts to prevent any violation of its terms.

10. With respect to the MFO, as appropriate, the Parties agree to the following arrangements:

(a) Operation of checkpoints, reconnaissance patrols, and observation posts along the international boundary and Line B, and within Zone C.

(b) Periodic verification of the implementation of the provisions of Annex I will be carried out not less than twice a month unless otherwise agreed by the Parties.

(c) Additional verifications within 48 hours after the receipt of a request from either Party.

(d) Ensuring the freedom of navigation through the Strait of Tiran in accordance with Article V of the Treaty of Peace.

11. When a violation has been confirmed by the MFO, it shall be rectified by the respective Party within 48 hours. The Party shall notify the MFO of the rectification.

12. The operations of the MFO shall not be construed as substituting for the undertakings by the Parties described in paragraph 2 of Article III of the Treaty. MFO personnel will report such acts by individuals as described in that paragraph in the first instance to the police of the respective Party.

13. Pursuant to paragraph 2 of Article II of Annex I, and in accordance with paragraph 7 of Article VI of Annex I, at the checkpoints at the international boundary, normal border crossing functions, such as passport in-

spection and customs control, will be carried out by officials of the respective Party.

14. The MFO operating in the Zones will enjoy freedom of movement necessary for the performance of its tasks.

15. MFO support flights to Egypt or Israel will follow normal rules and procedures for international flights. Egypt and Israel will undertake to facilitate clearances for such flights.

16. Verification flights by MFO aircraft in the Zones will be cleared with the authorities of the respective Party, in accordance with procedures to ensure that the flights can be undertaken in a timely manner.

17. MFO aircraft will not cross the international boundary without prior notification and clearance by each of the Parties.

18. MFO reconnaissance aircraft operating in Zone C will provide notification to the civil air control center and, thereby, to the Egyptian liaison officer therein.

SIZE AND ORGANIZATION

19. The MFO shall consist of a headquarters, three infantry battalions totalling not more than 2,000 troops, a coastal patrol unit and an observer unit, an aviation element and logistics, and signal units.

20. The MFO units will have standard armament and equipment appropriate to their peacekeeping mission as stipulated in this Annex.

21. The MFO headquarters will be organized to fulfill its duties in accordance with the Treaty and this Annex. It shall be manned by staff-trained officers of appropriate rank provided by the troop contributing nations as part of their national contingents. Its organization will be determined by the Commander, who will assign staff positions to each contributor on an equitable basis.

REPORTS

22. The Commander will report findings simultaneously to the Parties as soon as possible, but not later than 24 hours, after a verification or after a violation has been confirmed. The Commander will also provide the Parties simultaneously a monthly report summarizing the findings of the checkpoints, observation posts, and reconnaissance patrols.

23. Reporting formats will be worked out by the Commander with the Parties in the Joint Commission. Reports to the Parties will be transmitted to the liaison offices to be established in accordance with paragraph 31 below.

FINANCING, ADMINISTRATION, AND FACILITIES

24. The budget for each financial year shall be prepared by the Director-General and shall be approved by the Parties. The financial year shall be from October 1 through September 30. Contributions shall be paid in U.S. dollars, unless the Director-General requests contributions in some other form. Contributions shall be committed the first day of the financial year

and made available as the Director-General determines necessary to meet expenditures of the MFO.

25. For the period prior to October 1, 1981, the budget of the MFO shall consist of such sums as the Director-General shall receive. Any contributions during that period will be credited to the share of the budget of the contributing state in Financial Year 1982, and thereafter as necessary, so that the contribution is fully credited.

26. The Director-General shall prepare financial and administrative regulations consistent with this Protocol and submit them no later than December 1, 1981, for the approval of the Parties. These financial regulations shall include a budgetary process which takes into account the budgetary cycles of the contributing states.

27. The Commander shall request the approval of the respective Party for the use of facilities on its territory necessary for the proper functioning of the MFO. In this connection, the respective Party, after giving its approval for the use by the MFO of land or existing buildings and their fixtures, will not be reimbursed by the MFO for such use.

RESPONSIBILITIES OF THE JOINT COMMISSION PRIOR TO ITS DISSOLUTION

28. In accordance with Article IV of the Appendix to Annex I, the Joint Commission will supervise the implementation of the arrangements described in Annex I and its Appendix, as indicated in subparagraphs b, c, h, i, and j of paragraph 3 of Article IV.

29. The Joint Commission will implement the preparations required to enable the Liaison System to undertake its responsibilities in accordance with Article VII of Annex I.

30. The Joint Commission will determine the modalities and procedures for the implementation of Phase Two, as described in paragraph 3(b) of Article I of Annex I, based on the modalities and procedures that were implemented in Phase One.

LIAISON SYSTEM

31. The Liaison System will undertake the responsibilities indicated in paragraph 1 of Article VII of Annex I, and may discuss any other matters which the Parties by agreement may place before it. Meetings will be held at least once a month. In the event that either Party or the Commander requests a special meeting, it will be convened within 24 hours. The first meeting will be held in El-Arish not later than two weeks after the MFO assumes its functions. Meetings will alternate between El-Arish and Beer Sheba, unless the Parties otherwise agree. The Commander shall be invited to any meeting in which subjects concerning the MFO are discussed, or when either Party requests MFO presence. Decisions will be reached by agreement of Egypt and Israel.

32. The Commander and each chief liaison officer will have access to one another in their respective offices. Adequate procedures will be worked out

between the Parties with a view to facilitating the entry for this purpose of the representatives of either Party to the territory of the other.

PRIVILEGES AND IMMUNITIES

33. Each Party will accord to the MFO the privileges and immunities indicated in the attached Appendix.

SCHEDULE

34. The MFO shall assume its functions at 1300 hours on April 25, 1982.

35. The MFO shall be in place by 1300 hours, on March 20, 1982.

Appendix

DEFINITIONS

1. The "Multinational Force and Observers" (hereinafter referred to as "the MFO") is that organization established by the Protocol.

2. For the purposes of this Appendix, the term "Member of the MFO" refers to the Director-General, the Commander and any person, other than a resident of the Receiving State, belonging to the military contingent of a Participating State or otherwise under the authority of the Director-General, and his spouse and minor children, as appropriate.

3. The "Receiving State" means the authorities of Egypt or Israel as appropriate, and the territories under their control. "Government authorities" includes all national and local, civil and military authorities called upon to perform functions relating to the MFO under the provisions of this Appendix, without prejudice to the ultimate responsibility of the Government of the Receiving State.

4. "Resident of the Receiving State" includes (a) a person with citizenship of the Receiving State, (b) a person resident therein, or (c) a person present in the territory of the Receiving State other than a member of the MFO.

5. "Participating State" means a State that contributes personnel to the MFO.

DUTIES OF MEMBERS OF THE MFO IN THE RECEIVING STATE:

6. (a) Members of the MFO shall respect the laws and regulations of the Receiving State and shall refrain from any activity of a political character in the Receiving State and from any action incompatible with the international nature of their duties or inconsistent with the spirit of the present arrangements. The Director-General shall take all appropriate measures to ensure the observance of these obligations.

(b) In the performance of their duties for the MFO, members of the MFO shall receive their instructions only from the Director-General and the chain of command designated by him.

(c) Members of the MFO shall exercise the utmost discretion in regard to all matters relating to their duties and functions. They shall not communicate to any person any information known to them by reason of their position with the MFO which has not been made public, except in the course of their duties or by authorization of the Director-General. These obligations do not cease upon the termination of their assignment with the MFO.

(d) The Director-General will ensure that in the Standing Operating Procedures of the MFO, there will be arrangements to avoid accidental or inadvertent threats to the safety of MFO members.

ENTRY AND EXIT: IDENTIFICATION

7. Individual or collective passports shall be issued by the Participating States for members of the MFO. The Director-General shall notify the Receiving State of the names and scheduled time of arrival of MFO members, and other necessary information. The Receiving State shall issue an individual or collective multiple entry visa as appropriate prior to that travel. No other documents shall be required for a member of the MFO to enter or leave the Receiving State. Members of the MFO shall be exempt from immigration inspection and restrictions on entering or departing from the territory of the Receiving State. They shall also be exempt from any regulations governing the residence of aliens in the Receiving State, including registration, but shall not be considered as acquiring any right to permanent residence or domicile in the Receiving State. The Receiving State shall also provide each member of the Force with a personal identity card prior to or upon his arrival.

8. Members of the MFO will at all times carry their personal identity cards issued by the Receiving State. Members of the MFO may be required to present, but not to surrender, their passport or identity cards upon demand of an appropriate authority of the Receiving State. Except as provided in paragraph 7 of this Appendix, the passport or identity card will be the only document required for a member of the MFO.

9. If a member of the MFO leaves the services of the Participating State to which he belongs and is not repatriated, the Director-General shall immediately inform the authorities of the Receiving State, giving such particulars as may be required. The Director-General shall similarly inform the authorities of the Receiving State of any member of the MFO who has absented himself for more than twenty-one days. If an expulsion order against the ex-member of the MFO has been made, the Director-General shall be responsible for ensuring that the person concerned shall be received within the territory of the Participating State concerned.

JURISDICTION

10. The following arrangements respecting criminal and civil jurisdiction are made having regard to the special functions of the MFO and not for the personal benefit of the members of the MFO. The Director-General shall cooperate at all times with the appropriate authorities of the Receiving State to facilitate the proper administration of justice, secure the observance of laws and regulations, and prevent the occurrence of any abuse in connec-

tion with the privileges, immunities, and facilities mentioned in this Appendix.

11. (a) Military members of the MFO and members of the civilian observer group of the MFO shall be subject to the exclusive jurisdiction of their respective national states in respect of any criminal offenses which may be committed by them in the Receiving State. Any such person who is charged with the commission of a crime will be brought to trial by the respective Participating State, in accordance with its laws.

(b) Subject to paragraph 25, other members of the MFO shall be immune from the criminal jurisdiction of the Receiving State in respect of words spoken or written and all acts performed by them in their official capacity.

(c) The Director-General shall obtain the assurances of each Participating State that it will be prepared to take the necessary measures to assure proper discipline of its personnel and to exercise jurisdiction with respect to any crime or offense which might be committed by its personnel. The Director-General shall comply with requests of the Receiving State for the withdrawal from its territory of any member of the MFO who violates its laws, regulations, customs, or traditions. The Director-General, with the consent of the Participating State, may waive the immunity of a member of the MFO.

(d) Without prejudice to the foregoing, a Participating State may enter into a supplementary arrangement with the Receiving State to limit or waive the immunities of its members of the MFO who are on periods of leave while in the Receiving State.

12. (a) Members of the MFO shall not be subject to the civil jurisdiction of the courts of the Receiving State or to other legal process in any matter relating to their official duties. In a case arising from a matter relating to official duties and which involves a member of the MFO and a resident of the Receiving State, and in other disputes as agreed, the procedure provided in paragraph 38(b) of this Appendix shall apply to the settlement.

(b) If the Director-General certifies that a member of the MFO is unable because of official duties or authorized absence to protect his interests in a civil proceeding in which he is a participant, the court or authority shall at his request suspend the proceeding until the elimination of the disability, but for not more than ninety days. Property of a member of the MFO which is certified by the Director-General to be needed by him for the fulfillment of his official duties shall be free from seizure for the satisfaction of a judgment, decision, or order, together with other property not subject thereto under the law of the Receiving State. The personal liberty of a member of the MFO shall not be restricted by a court or other authority of the Receiving State in a civil proceeding, whether to enforce a judgment, decision, or order, to compel an oath of disclosure, or for any other reason.

(c) In the cases provided for in subparagraph (b) above, the claimant may elect to have his claim dealt with in accordance with the procedure set out in paragraph 38(b) of this Appendix. Where a claim adjudicated or an award made in favor of the claimant by a court of the Receiving State or the Claims Commission under paragraph 38(b) of this Appendix has not been satisfied, the authorities of the Receiving State may without prejudice to the claimant's rights, seek the good offices of the Director-General to obtain satisfaction.

NOTIFICATION: CERTIFICATION

13. If any civil proceeding is instituted against a member of the MFO, before any court of the Receiving State having jurisdiction, notification shall be given to the Director-General. The Director-General shall certify to the court whether or not the proceeding is related to the official duties of such member.

MILITARY POLICE: ARREST: TRANSFER OF CUSTODY AND MUTUAL ASSISTANCE

14. The Director-General shall take all appropriate measures to ensure maintenance of discipline and good order among members of the MFO. To this end military police designated by the Director-General shall police the premises referred to in paragraph 19 of this Appendix, and such areas where the MFO is functioning.

15. The military police of the MFO shall immediately transfer to the civilian police of the Receiving State any individual, who is not a member of the MFO, of whom it takes temporary custody.

16. The police of the Receiving State shall immediately transfer to the MFO any member of the MFO, of whom it takes temporary custody, pending a determination concerning jurisdiction.

17. The Director-General and the authorities of the Receiving State shall assist each other concerning all offenses in respect of which either or both have an interest, including the production of witnesses, and in the collection and production of evidence, including the seizure and, in proper cases, the handing over, of things connected with an offense. The handing over of any such things may be made subject to their return within the time specified by the authority delivering them. Each shall notify the other of the disposition of any case in the outcome of which the other may have an interest or in which there has been a transfer of custody under the provisions of paragraphs 15 and 16 of this Appendix.

18. The government of the Receiving State will ensure the prosecution of persons subject to its criminal jurisdiction who are accused of acts in relation to the MFO or its members which, if committed in relation to the forces of the Receiving State or their members, would have rendered them liable to prosecution. The Director-General will take the measures within his power with respect to crimes or offenses committed against citizens of the Receiving State by members of the MFO.

PREMISES OF THE MFO

19. Without prejudice to the fact that all the premises of the MFO remain the territory of the Receiving State, they shall be inviolable and subject to the exclusive control and authority of the Director-General, who alone may consent to the entry of officials to perform duties on such premises.

MFO FLAG

20. The Receiving States permit the MFO to display a special flag or insignia, of design agreed upon by them, on its headquarters, camps, posts, or other premises, vehicles, boats, and otherwise as decided by the Director-General. Other flags or pennants may be displayed only in exceptional cases and in accordance with conditions prescribed by the Director-General. Sympathetic consideration will be given to observations or requests of the authorities of the Receiving State concerning this last-mentioned matter. If the MFO flag or other flag is flown, the flag of the Receiving State shall be flown alongside it.

UNIFORM: VEHICLE, BOATS AND AIRCRAFT MARKINGS AND REGISTRATION: OPERATING PERMITS

21. Military members of the MFO shall normally wear their national uniform with such identifying MFO insignia as the Director-General may prescribe. The conditions on which the wearing of civilian dress is authorized shall be notified by the Director-General to the authorities of the Receiving State and sympathetic consideration will be given to observations or requests of the authorities of the Receiving State concerning this matter. Members of the MFO shall wear civilian dress while outside the areas where they are functioning. Service vehicles, boats, and aircraft shall not carry the marks or license plates of any Participating State, but shall carry the distinctive MFO identification mark and license which shall be notified by the Director-General to the authorities of the Receiving State. Such vehicles, boats, and aircraft shall not be subject to registration and licensing under the laws and regulations of the Receiving State. Authorities of the Receiving State shall accept as valid, without a test or fee, a permit, or license for the operation of service vehicles, boats, and aircraft issued by the Director-General. MFO drivers shall be given permits by the Receiving State to enable them to drive outside the areas where they are functioning, if these permits are required by the Receiving State.

ARMS

22. Members of the MFO who are off-duty shall not carry arms while outside the areas where they are functioning.

PRIVILEGES AND IMMUNITIES OF THE MFO

23. The MFO shall enjoy the status, privileges, and immunities accorded in Article II of the Convention on the Privileges and Immunities of the United Nations (hereinafter, "the Convention"). The provisions of Article

II of the Convention shall also apply to the property, funds, and assets of Participating States used in the Receiving State in connection with the activities of the MFO. Such Participating States may not acquire immovable property in the Receiving State without agreement of the government of the Receiving State. The government of the Receiving State recognizes that the right of the MFO to import free of duty equipment for the MFO and provisions, supplies, and other goods for the exclusive use of members of the MFO, includes the right of the MFO to establish, maintain, and operate at headquarters, camps, and posts, service institutes providing amenities for the members of the MFO. The amenities that may be provided by service institutes shall be goods of a consumable nature (tobacco and tobacco products, beer, etc.), and other customary articles of small value. To the end that duty-free importation for the MFO may be effected with the least possible delay, having regard to the interests of the government of the Receiving State, a mutually satisfactory procedure, including documentation, shall be arranged between the Director-General and the customs authorities of the Receiving State. The Director-General shall take all necessary measures to prevent any abuse of the exemption and to prevent the sale or resale of such goods to persons other than the members of the MFO. Sympathetic consideration shall be given by the Director-General to observations or requests of the authorities of the Receiving State concerning the operation of service institutes.

PRIVILEGES AND IMMUNITIES AND DELEGATION OF AUTHORITY OF DIRECTOR-GENERAL

24. The Director-General of the MFO may delegate his powers to other members of the MFO.

25. The Director-General, his deputy, the Commander, and his deputy, shall be accorded in respect of themselves, their spouses, and minor children, the privileges and immunities, exemptions, and facilities accorded to diplomatic envoys in accordance with international law.

MEMBERS OF THE MFO: TAXATION, CUSTOMS, AND FISCAL REGULATIONS

26. Members of the MFO shall be exempt from taxation by the Receiving State on the pay and emoluments received from their national governments or from the MFO. They shall also be exempt from all other direct taxes, fees, and charges, except for those levied for services rendered.

27. Members of the MFO shall have the right to import free of duty their personal effects in connection with their first taking up their post in the Receiving State. They shall be subject to the laws and regulations of the Receiving State governing customs and foreign exchange with respect to personal property not required by them by reason of their presence in the Receiving State with the MFO. Special facilities for entry or exit shall be granted by the immigration, customs, and fiscal authorities of the Receiving State to regularly constituted units of the MFO provided that the authorities

concerned have been duly notified sufficiently in advance. Members of the MFO on departure from the area may, notwithstanding the foreign exchange regulations, take with them such funds as the Director-General certifies were received in pay and emoluments from their respective national governments or from the MFO and are a reasonable residue thereof. Special arrangements between the Director-General and the authorities of the Receiving State shall be made for the implementation of the foregoing provisions in the interests of the government of the Receiving State and members of the MFO.

28. The Director-General will cooperate with the customs and fiscal authorities of the Receiving State and will render all assistance within his power in ensuring the observance of the customs and fiscal laws and regulations of the Receiving State by the members of the MFO in accordance with this Appendix or any relevant supplemental arrangements.

COMMUNICATIONS AND POSTAL SERVICES

29. The MFO shall enjoy the facilities in respect to communications provided for in Article III of the Convention. The Director-General shall have authority to install and operate communications systems as are necessary to perform its functions subject to the provisions of Article 35 of the International Telecommunications Convention of April 11, 1973, relating to harmful interference. The frequencies on which any such station may be operated will be duly communicated by the MFO to the appropriate authorities of the Receiving State. Appropriate consultations will be held between the MFO and the authorities of the Receiving State to avoid harmful interference. The right of the Director-General is likewise recognized to enjoy the priorities of government telegrams and telephone calls as provided for the United Nations in Article 39 and Annex 3 of the latter Convention and in Article 5, No. 10 of the telegraph regulations annexed thereto.

30. The MFO shall also enjoy, within the areas where it is functioning, the right of unrestricted communication by radio, telephone, telegraph, or any other means, and of establishing the necessary facilities for maintaining such communications within and between premises of the MFO, including the laying of cables and land lines and the establishment of fixed and mobile radio sending and receiving stations. It is understood that the telegraph and telephone cables and lines herein referred to will be situated within or directly between the premises of the MFO and the areas where it is functioning, and that connection with the system of telegraphs and telephones of the Receiving State will be made in accordance with arrangements with the appropriate authorities of the Receiving State.

31. The government of the Receiving State recognizes the right of the MFO to make arrangements through its own facilities for the processing and transport of private mail addressed to or emanating from members of the MFO. The government of the Receiving State will be informed of the nature of such arrangements. No interference shall take place with, and no

censorship shall be applied to, the mail of the MFO by the government of the Receiving State. In the event that postal arrangements applying to private mail of members of the MFO are extended to operations involving transfer of currency, or transport of packages or parcels from the Receiving State, the conditions under which such operations shall be conducted in the Receiving State will be agreed upon between the government of the Receiving State and the Director-General.

MOTOR VEHICLE INSURANCE

32. The MFO will take necessary arrangements to ensure that all MFO motor vehicles shall be covered by third party liability insurance in accordance with the laws and regulations of the Receiving State.

USE OF ROADS, WATERWAYS, PORT FACILITIES, AIRFIELDS, AND RAILWAYS

33. When the MFO uses roads, bridges, port facilities, and airfields it shall not be subject to payment of dues, tolls, or charges either by way of registration or otherwise, in the areas where it is functioning and the normal points of access, except for charges that are related directly to services rendered. The authorities of the Receiving State, subject to special arrangements, will give the most favorable consideration to requests for the grant to members of the MFO of traveling facilities on its railways and of concessions with regard to fares.

WATER, ELECTRICITY, AND OTHER PUBLIC UTILITIES

34. The MFO shall have the right to the use of water, electricity, and other public utilities at rates not less favorable to the MFO than those to comparable consumers. The authorities of the Receiving State will, upon the request of the Director-General, assist the MFO in obtaining water, electricity, and other utilities required, and in the case of interruption or threatened interruption of service, will give the same priority to the needs of the MFO as to essential government services. The MFO shall have the right where necessary to generate, within the premises of the MFO either on land or water, electricity for the use of the MFO and to transmit and distribute such electricity as required by the MFO.

CURRENCY OF THE RECEIVING STATE

35. The Government of the Receiving State will, if requested by the Director-General, make available to the MFO, against reimbursement in U.S. dollars or other currency mutually acceptable, currency of the Receiving State required for the use of the MFO, including the pay of the members of the national contingents, at the rate of exchange most favorable to the MFO that is officially recognized by the government of the Receiving State.

PROVISIONS, SUPPLIES, AND SERVICES

36. The authorities of the Receiving State will, upon the request of the Director-General, assist the MFO in obtaining equipment, provisions, sup-

plies, and other goods and services required from local sources for its subsistence and operation. Sympathetic consideration will be given by the Director-General in purchases on the local market to requests or observations of the authorities of the Receiving State in order to avoid any adverse effect on the local economy. Members of the MFO may purchase locally goods necessary for their own consumption, and such services as they need, under conditions prevailing in the open market.

If members of the MFO should require medical or dental facilities beyond those available within the MFO, arrangements shall be made with the appropriate authorities of the Receiving State under which such facilities may be made available. The Director-General and the appropriate local authorities will cooperate with respect to sanitary services. The Director-General and the authorities of the Receiving State shall extend to each other the fullest cooperation in matters concerning health, particularly with respect to the control of communicable diseases in accordance with international conventions; such cooperation shall extend to the exchange of relevant information and statistics.

LOCALLY RECRUITED PERSONNEL

37. The MFO may recruit locally such personnel as required. The authorities of the Receiving State will, upon the request of the Director-General, assist the MFO in the recruitment of such personnel. Sympathetic consideration will be given by the Director-General in the recruitment of local personnel to requests or observations of authorities of the Receiving State in order to avoid any adverse effect on the local economy. The terms and conditions of employment for locally recruited personnel shall be prescribed by the Director-General and shall generally, to the extent practicable, be no less favorable than the practice prevailing in the Receiving State.

SETTLEMENT OF DISPUTES OR CLAIMS

38. Disputes or claims of a private law character shall be settled in accordance with the following provisions:

(a) The MFO shall make provisions for the appropriate modes of settlement of disputes or claims arising out of contract or other disputes or claims of a private law character to which the MFO is a party other than those covered in subparagraph (b) and paragraph 39 following. When no such provisions have been made with the contracting party, such claims shall be settled according to subparagraph (b) below.

(b) Any claim made by:

(i) a resident of the Receiving State against the MFO or a member thereof, in respect of any damages alleged to result from an act or omission of such member of the MFO relating to his official duties;

(ii) the Government of the Receiving State against a member of the MFO;

(iii) the MFO or the Government of the Receiving State against one another, that is not covered by paragraph 40 of this Appendix;

shall be settled by a Claims Commission established for that purpose. One member of the Commission shall be appointed by the Director-General, one member by the Government of the Receiving State, and a Chairman jointly by the two. If the Director-General and the Government of the Receiving State fail to agree on the appointment of a chairman, the two members selected by them shall select a chairman from the list of the Permanent Court of Arbitration. An award made by the Claims Commission against the MFO or a member or other employee thereof or against the Government of the Receiving State shall be notified to the Director-General or the authorities of the Receiving State as the case may be, to make satisfaction thereof.

39. Disputes concerning the terms of employment and conditions of service of locally recruited personnel shall be settled by administrative procedure to be established by the Director-General.

40. All disputes between the MFO and the Government of the Receiving State concerning the interpretation or application of this Appendix which are not settled by negotiation or other agreed mode of settlement shall be referred for final settlement to a tribunal of three arbitrators, one to be named by the Director-General, one by the Government of the Receiving State, and an umpire to be chosen jointly who shall preside over the proceedings of this tribunal.

41. If the two parties fail to agree on the appointment of the umpire within one month of the proposal of arbitration by one of the parties, the two members selected by them shall select a chairman from the list of the Permanent Court of Arbitration. Should a vacancy occur for any reason, the vacancy shall be filled within thirty days by the methods laid down in this paragraph for the original appointment. The tribunal shall come into existence upon the appointment of the chairman and at least one of the other members of the tribunal. Two members of the tribunal shall constitute a quorum for the performance of its functions, and for all deliberations and decisions of the tribunal a favorable vote of two members shall be sufficient.

DECEASED MEMBERS: DISPOSITION OF PERSONAL PROPERTY

42. The Director-General shall have the right to take charge of and dispose of the body of a member of the MFO who dies in the territory of the Receiving State and may dispose of his property after the debts of the deceased person incurred in the territory of the Receiving State and owing to residents of the Receiving State have been settled.

SUPPLEMENTAL ARRANGEMENTS

43. Supplemental details for the carrying out of this Appendix shall be made as required between the Director-General and appropriate authorities designated by the Government of the Receiving State.

EFFECTIVE DATE AND DURATION

44. This Appendix shall take effect from the date of the entry into force of the Protocol and shall remain in force for the duration of the Protocol. The provisions of paragraphs 38, 39, 40, and 41 of this Appendix, relating to the settlement of disputes, however, shall remain in force until all claims arising prior to the date of termination of this Appendix and submitted prior to or within three months following the date of termination, have been settled.

92. Senate Joint Resolution 100 Authorizing U.S.
Participation in the Sinai Peacekeeping Force,
October 7, 1981*

* S.J. Res. 100, 97th Cong., 1st Sess., 127 Cong. Rec. 23698 (1981).

Whereas the treaty of peace between Egypt and Israel signed on March 26, 1979, calls for the supervision of security arrangements to be undertaken by United Nations forces and observers; and

Whereas the United Nations has been unable to assume those responsibilities; and

Whereas a protocol initialed on July 17, 1981, by the Government of the Arab Republic of Egypt and the Government of the State of Israel provides for the creation of an alternative multinational force and observers to implement the treaty of peace; and

Whereas the Government of the Arab Republic of Egypt and the Government of the State of Israel have requested that the United States participate in the multinational force and observers: Now, therefore, be it

Resolved by the Senate and House of Representatives of the United States of America in Congress assembled, That the President is authorized to assign, under such terms and conditions as he may determine, personnel of the Armed Forces of the United States to participate in the multinational force and observers to be established in accordance with the protocol between Egypt and Israel initialed July 17, 1981, relating to the implementation of the security arrangements of the treaty of peace. The President is also authorized to provide, under such terms and conditions as he may determine, United States civilian personnel to participate as observers in the multinational force and observers. The status of United States Government personnel assigned to the multinational force and observers shall be as provided in section 629 of the Foreign Assistance Act of 1961, as amended.

Sec. 2. The President is authorized to agree with Egypt and Israel that the United States will contribute a share of the costs of such multinational force and observers in accordance with the protocol, subject to the authorization and appropriation of necessary funds.

In accordance with the agreement among the United States, Egypt, and Israel, effected by an exchange of letters signed August 3, 1981, such United States share shall not exceed 60 per centum of the budget for the expenses connected with the establishment and initial operation of the multinational force and observers during the period ending September 30, 1982, and shall not exceed 33 1/3 per centum of the budget for the annual operating expenses of the multinational forces and observers for each financial year beginning after that date.

Sec. 3. There are authorized to be appropriated to the President to carry out chapter 6 of part II of the Foreign Assistance Act of 1961, in addition to amounts otherwise available to carry out that chapter, $125,000,000 for the fiscal year 1982 for contributions as authorized by section 2 of this resolution. Amounts appropriated under this section are authorized to remain available until expended.

Sec. 4. (a) Any agency of the United States Government is authorized to provide administrative and technical support and services to the multinational force and observers without reimbursement and upon such terms and conditions as the President may direct when such provision of support or services would not result in significant incremental costs to the United States.

(b) The President is authorized to provide military training to the armed forces of other countries participating in the multinational force upon such terms and conditions as the President may direct.

SEC. 5. Nothing in this resolution shall affect the responsibilities of the President or the Congress under the War Powers Resolution (Public Law 93-148) nor does this resolution authorize the use of United States Armed Forces or civilian personnel in circumstances or for purposes beyond those specified in the protocol with the Governments of Egypt and Israel signed on August 3, 1981.

SEC. 6. It is the sense of the Congress that the President should give careful consideration to assigning responsibility for the coordination of United States support of the Multinational Force and Observers to the Director of the United States Arms Control and Disarmament Agency consistent with his statutory responsibilities.

93. Statement by the EEC Foreign Ministers on
Participation by Community Members in the Sinai
Multinational Force, November 23, 1981*

---

* 14 Bull. Eur. Comm. (No. 11) 59 (1981).

'The Ten consider that the decision of France, Italy, The Netherlands and the United Kingdom to participate in the multinational force in Sinai meets the wish frequently expressed by the members of the Community to facilitate any progress in the direction of a comprehensive peace settlement in the Middle East on the basis of the mutual acceptance of the right to existence and security of all States in the area and the need for the Palestinian people to exercise fully its right to self-determination'.

94. U.S.-Israel Statement on Multinational Force and Observers Participation, December 3, 1981*

* 82 U.S. Dep't State Bull. No. 2058, at 46 (January 1982).

The United States and Israel note the decision of the United Kingdom, France, Italy, and the Netherlands to contribute to the multinational force and observers (MFO) to be established in accordance with the Treaty of Peace Between Egypt and Israel.[2]

The United States and Israel reviewed the participation of these four countries in light of the following clarifications which they have provided to the United States on November 26, 1981:

· That they recognize that the function of the MFO is as defined in the relevant Egyptian-Israeli agreements and includes that of insuring freedom of navigation through the Strait of Tiran in accordance with Article V of the Treaty of Peace; and

· That they have attached no political conditions, linked to Venice or otherwise, to their participation.

The United States and Israel understand that the participation of the four and any other participating state is based upon the following.

· The basis for participation in the MFO is the Treaty of Peace Between Egypt and Israel originated in the Camp David accords and the protocol signed between Egypt and Israel and witnessed by the United States on August 3, 1981, based upon the letter from President Carter to President Sadat and Prime Minister Begin of March 26, 1979.

· All of the functions and responsibilities of the MFO and of its constituent elements, including any contingents that may be formed through European participation, are defined in the Treaty of Peace and protocol, and there can be no derogation or reservation from any of them. As provided in the protocol, all participants in the MFO undertake to conduct themselves in accordance with the terms of the protocol under the direction of the Director General appointed by Egypt and Israel. The MFO shall employ its best efforts to prevent any violation of the terms of the Treaty of Peace. The functions of the MFO will specifically include the following in accordance with the Treaty of Peace and the protocol:

(a) Operation of checkpoints, reconnaissance patrols, and observation posts along the international boundary and Line B, and within Zone C;

(b) Periodic verification of the implementation of the provisions of Annex I will be carried out not less than twice a month unless otherwise agreed by the parties;

(c) Additional verifications within 48 hours after the receipt of a request from either party; and

(d) Insuring the freedom of navigation through the Strait of Tiran in accordance with Article V of the Treaty of Peace.

The United States understands and appreciates the concerns expressed by the Government of Israel regarding the statements made by the four European contributors in explaining their decision to participate in the MFO to their own legislatures and publics. The United States recognizes

---

[2] For text of the treaty, see BULLETIN of May 1979.

that some positions set forth in the statements are at variance with its own positions with respect to the future of the peace process, as well as with positions held by Israel as a party to the Treaty of Peace. The United States and Israel recognize that the positions held on any other aspects of the problem in the area by any state which agrees to participate in the MFO do not affect the obligation of that state to comply fully with the terms of the protocol which was negotiated in accordance with the letter from President Carter to President Sadat and Prime Minister Begin of March 26, 1979, and which is designed to help implement the Treaty of Peace, which was concluded pursuant to the Camp David accords.

The Treaty of Peace, in accordance with which the MFO is established, represents the first step in a process agreed on at Camp David whose ultimate goal is a just, comprehensive, and durable settlement of the Middle East conflict through the conclusion of peace treaties based on Security Council Resolutions 242 and 338. The United States and Israel reiterate their commitment to the Camp David accords as the only viable and ongoing negotiating process. They renew their determination to make early meaningful progress in the autonomy talks.

95. Multinational Force and Observers Participation
Resolution, December 29, 1981*

---

* 22 U.S.C. Secs. 3421–27 (1982).

§ 3421. Congressional declaration of policy

The Congress considers the establishment of the Multinational Force and Observers to be an essential stage in the development of a comprehensive settlement in the Middle East. The Congress enacts this subchapter with the hope and expectation that establishment of the Multinational Force and Observers will assist Egypt and Israel in fulfilling the Camp David accords and bringing about the establishment of a self-governing authority in order to provide full autonomy in the West Bank and Gaza.

(Pub. L. 97-132, § 2, Dec. 29, 1981, 95 Stat. 1693.)

SHORT TITLE

For short title of Pub. L. 97-132, which enacted this subchapter, as the Multinational Force and Observers Participation Resolution, see section 1 of Pub. L. 97-132, set out as a Short Title note under section 3401 of this title.

§ 3422. Participation of United States personnel in the Multinational Force and Observers

(a) Participation by United States Armed Forces; maximum limit on the number of members

(1) Subject to the limitations contained in this subchapter, the President is authorized to assign, under such terms and conditions as he may determine, members of the United States Armed Forces to participate in the Multinational Force and Observers.

(2) The Congress declares that the participation of the military personnel of other countries in the Multinational Force and Observers is essential to maintain the international character of the peacekeeping function in the Sinai. Accordingly—

(A) before the President assigns or details members of the United States Armed Forces to the Multinational Force and Observers, he shall notify the Congress of the names of the other countries that have agreed to provide military personnel for the Multinational Force and Observers, the number of military personnel to be provided by each country, and the functions to be performed by such personnel; and

(B) if a country withdraws from the Multinational Force and Observers with the result that the military personnel of less than four foreign countries remain, every possible effort must be made by the United States to find promptly a country to replace that country.

(3) Members of the United States Armed Forces, and United States civilian personnel, who are assigned, detailed, or otherwise provided to the Multinational Force and Observers may perform only those functions or responsibilities which are specified for United Nations Forces and Observers in the Treaty of Peace and in accordance with the Protocol.

(4) The number of members of the United States Armed Forces who are assigned or detailed by the United States Government to the Multinational Force and Observers may not exceed one thousand two hundred at any one time.

(b) Participation by civilian personnel

Subject to the limitations contained in this subchapter, the President is authorized to provide, under such terms and conditions as he may determine, United States civilian personnel to participate as observers in the Multinational Force and Observers.

(c) Status of United States personnel

The status of United States Government personnel assigned to the Multinational Force and Observers under subsection (a)(1) or (b) of this section shall be as provided in section 2389 of this title.
(Pub. L. 97-132, § 3, Dec. 29, 1981, 95 Stat. 1693.)

SECTION REFERRED TO IN OTHER SECTIONS

This section is referred to in section 3424 of this title.

§ 3423. United States contributions to costs

(a) United States share of the costs

In accordance with the agreement set forth in the exchanges of letters between the United States and Egypt and between the United States and Israel which were signed on August 3, 1981, the United States share of the costs of the Multinational Force and Observers—

(1) shall not exceed 60 per centum of the budget for the expenses connected with the establishment and initial operation of the Multinational Force and Observers during the period ending September 30, 1982; and

(2) shall not exceed 33 1/3 per centum of the budget for the annual operating expenses of the Multinational Force and Observers for each financial year beginning after that date.

(b) Authorization of appropriations

(1) There are authorized to be appropriated to the President to carry out chapter 6 of part II of the Foreign Assistance Act of 1961 [22 U.S.C. 2348 et seq.], in addition to amounts otherwise available to carry out that chapter, $125,000,000 for the fiscal year 1982 for use in paying the United States contribution to the budget of the Multinational Force and Observers. Amounts appropriated under this subsection are authorized to remain available until expended.

(2) Expenditures made pursuant to section 138 of the joint resolution entitled "Joint resolution making continuing appropriations for the fiscal year 1982, and for other purposes", approved October 1, 1981 (Public Law 97-51), or pursuant to any subsequent corresponding provision applicable to the fiscal year 1982, shall be charged to the appropriation authorized by this subsection.

(c) Reimbursements to the United States

Unless required by law, reimbursements to the United States by the Multinational Force and Observers shall be on the basis of identifiable costs actually incurred as a result of requirements imposed by the Multinational Force and Observers, and shall not include administrative surcharges. (Pub. L. 97-132, § 4, Dec. 29, 1981, 95 Stat. 1694.)

REFERENCES IN TEXT

The Foreign Assistance Act of 1961, referred to in subsec. (b)(1), is Pub. L. 87-195, Sept. 4, 1961, 75 Stat. 424, as amended. Chapter 6 of part II of the Foreign Assistance Act of 1961 is classified to part VI (§ 2348 et seq.) of subchapter II of chapter 32 of this title. For complete classification of this Act to the Code, see Short Title note set out under section 2151 of this title and Tables.

Section 138 of the joint resolution entitled "Joint resolution making continuing appropriations for the fiscal year 1982, and for other purposes", approved October 1, 1981 (Public Law 97-51), referred to in subsec. (b)(2), is section 138 of Pub. L. 97-51, Oct. 1, 1981, 95 Stat. 967, which is not classified to the Code.

§ 3424. Nonreimbursed costs

(a) Administrative and technical support and services

Any agency of the United States Government is authorized to provide administrative and technical support and services to the Multinational Force and Observers, without reimbursement and upon such terms and conditions as the President may direct, when the provision of such support or services would not result in significant incremental costs to the United States.

(b) Costs to be kept at minimum level

The provision by the United States to the Multinational Force and Observers under the authority of this subchapter or any other law of any property, support, or services, including the provision of military and civilian personnel under section 3422 of this title, on other than a reimbursable basis shall be kept to a minimum.

(c) Military training of armed forces of other countries

The President may provide military training to members of the armed forces of other countries participating in the Multinational Force and Observers. (Pub. L. 97-132, § 5, Dec. 29, 1981, 95 Stat. 1695.)

SECTION REFERRED TO IN OTHER SECTIONS

This section is referred to in section 3425 of this title.

§ 3425. Reports to Congress

(a) Initial report

Not later than April 30, 1982, the President shall transmit to the Speaker of the House of Representatives, and to the chairman of the Committee on Foreign Relations of the Senate, a detailed written report with respect to the period ending two weeks prior to that date which contains the information specified in subsection (b) of this section.

(b) Annual report; content

Not later than January 15 of each year (beginning in 1983), the President shall transmit to the Speaker of the House of Representatives, and to the chairman of the Committee on Foreign Relations of the Senate, a written report which describes—

(1) the activities performed by the Multinational Force and Observers during the preceding year;

(2) the composition of the Multinational Force and Observers, including a description of the responsibilities and deployment of the military personnel of each participating country;

(3) All costs incurred by the United States Government (including both normal and incremental costs), set forth by category, which are associated with the United States relationship with the Multinational Force and Observers and which were incurred during the preceding fiscal year (whether or not the United States was reimbursed for those costs), specifically including but not limited to—

(A) the costs associated with the United States units and personnel participating in the Multinational Force and Observers (including salaries, allowances, retirement and other benefits, transportation, housing, and operating and maintenance costs), and

(B) the identifiable costs relating to property, support, and services provided by the United States to the Multinational Force and Observers;

(4) the costs which the United States Government would have incurred in maintaining in the United States those United States units and personnel participating in the Multinational Force and Observers;

(5) amounts received by the United States Government from the Multinational Force and Observers as reimbursement;

(6) the types of property, support, or services provided to the Multinational Force and Observers by the United States Government, including identification of the types of property, support, or services provided on a nonreimbursable basis; and

(7) the results of any discussions with Egypt and Israel regarding the future of the Multinational Force and Observers and its possible reduction or elimination.

(c) Description, detail, and accuracy of reports

(1) The reports required by this section shall be as detailed as possible.

(2) The information pursuant to subsection (b)(3) of this section shall, in the case of costs which are not identifiable, be set forth with reasonable accuracy.

(3) The information with respect to any administrative and technical support and services provided on a nonreimbursed basis under section 3424(a) of this title shall include a description of the types of support and services

which have been provided and an estimate of both the total costs of such
support and services and the incremental costs incurred by the United
States with respect to such support and services.

(Pub. L. 97-132, § 6, Dec. 29, 1981, 95 Stat. 1695.)

EX. ORD. NO. 12361. DELEGATION OF FUNCTIONS FOR

MULTINATIONAL FORCE AND OBSERVERS REPORTS

Ex. Ord. No. 12361, Apr. 27, 1982, 47 F.R. 18313, provided:

By the authority vested in me as President of the United States of America by the Multinational Force and Observers Participation Resolution (Public Law 97-132, 95 Stat. 1693) [this subchapter] and Section 301 of Title 3
of the United States Code, it is hereby ordered as follows:

SECTION 1. *Delegation of Functions.* The reporting function conferred upon
the President by Section 6 of the Multinational Force and Observers Participation Resolution (22 U.S.C. 3425) is delegated to the Secretary of State.

SEC. 2. *Interagency Coordination.* In the exercise of the function conferred
on the Secretary of State by Section 1 of this Order, the Secretary of State
shall consult with the Director of the Office of Management and Budget,
the Secretary of Defense, the Director of the United States Arms Control
and Disarmament Agency, the Assistant to the President for National Security Affairs, and the heads of other Executive agencies as appropriate.

RONALD REAGAN.

§ 3426. Statements of Congressional intent

(a) Disclaimer of Congressional approval of other agreements, understand-
ings, or commitments

Nothing in this subchapter is intended to signify approval by the Congress of any agreement, understanding, or commitment made by the executive branch other than the agreement to participate in the Multinational
Force and Observers as set forth in the exchanges of letters between the
United States and Egypt and between the United States and Israel which
were signed on August 3, 1981.

(b) Limitations on United States participation

The limitations contained in this subchapter with respect to United States
participation in the Multinational Force and Observers apply to the exercise
of the authorities provided by this subchapter or provided by any other provision of law. No funds appropriated by the Congress may be obligated or
expended for any activity which is contrary to the limitations contained in
this subchapter.

(c) War Powers Resolution

Nothing in this subchapter shall affect the responsibilities of the President
or the Congress under the War Powers Resolution (Public Law 93-148) [50
U.S.C. 1541 et seq.].

(Pub. L. 97-132, § 7, Dec. 29, 1981, 95 Stat. 1696.)

REFERENCES IN TEXT

The War Powers Resolution, referred to in subsec. (c), is Pub. L. 93-148, Nov. 7, 1973, 87 Stat, 555, which is classified generally to chapter 33 (§ 1541 et seq.) of Title 50, War and National Defense. For complete classification of this Resolution to the Code, see Short Title note set out under section 1541 of Title 50 and Tables.

§ 3427. Definitions

As used in this subchapter—

(1) the term "Multinational Force and Observers" means the Multinational Force and Observers established in accordance with the Protocol between Egypt and Israel signed on August 3, 1981, relating to the implementation of the security arrangements of the Treaty of Peace; and

(2) the term "Treaty of Peace" means the Treaty of Peace between the Arab Republic of Egypt and the State of Israel signed on March 26, 1979, including the Annexes thereto.

(Pub. L. 97-132, § 8, Dec. 29, 1981, 95 Stat. 1697.)

96. Ambassador Malone's Statement on the Effect of
the Proposed Law of the Sea Convention on Navigational
and Overflight Freedom for the Strait of Tiran and
the Gulf of Aqaba, January 29, 1982*

---

* 128 Cong. Rec. 7865 (1982).

The U.S. fully supports the continuing applicability and force of freedom of navigation and overflight for the Strait of Tiran and the Gulf of Aqaba as set out in the peace treaty between Egypt and Israel. In the U.S. view, the treaty of peace is fully compatible with the LOS convention and will continue to prevail. The conclusion of the LOS convention will not affect these provisions in any way.

97. President Reagan's Letter to the Congress Explaining U.S. Participation in the Multinational Force and Observers in the Sinai, March 19, 1982*

* 82 U.S. Dep't State Bull. No. 2063, at 68 (June 1982).

On December 29, 1981 I signed into law Public Law 97-132, a Joint Resolution authorizing the participation of the United States in the Multinational Force and Observers (MFO) which will assist in the implementation of the 1979 Treaty of Peace between Egypt and Israel. The U.S. military personnel and equipment which the United States will contribute to the MFO are now in the process of deployment to the Sinai. In accordance with my desire that the Congress be fully informed on this matter, and consistent with Section 4(a)(2) of the War Powers Resolution, I am hereby providing a report on the deployment and mission of these members of the U.S. Armed Forces.

As you know, the 1979 Treaty of Peace between Egypt and Israel terminated the existing state of war between those countries, provided for the complete withdrawal from the Sinai of Israeli armed forces and civilians within three years after the date of the Treaty's entry into force (that is, by April 25, 1982), and provided for the establishment of normal friendly relations. To assist in assuring compliance with the terms of Annex I to the Treaty, so as to enhance the mutual confidence of the parties in the security of the Sinai border area, the Treaty calls for the establishment of a peacekeeping force and observers to be deployed prior to the final Israeli withdrawal. Although the Treaty called on the parties to request the United Nations to provide the peacekeeping force and observers, it was also recognized during the negotiations that it might not be possible to reach agreement in the United Nations for this purpose. For this reason, President Carter assured Israel and Egypt in separate letters that "if the Security Council fails to establish and maintain the arrangements called for in the Treaty, the President will be prepared to take those steps necessary to ensure the establishment and maintenance of an acceptable alternative multinational force."

In fact, it proved impossible to secure U.N. action. As a result, Egypt and Israel, with the participation of the United States, entered into negotiations for the creation of an alternative multinational force and observers. These negotiations resulted in the signing on August 3, 1981 by Egypt and Israel of a Protocol for that purpose. The Protocol established the MFO and provided in effect that the MFO would have the same functions and responsibilities as those provided in the 1979 Treaty for the planned U.N. force. Included are: the operation of checkpoints, reconnaissance patrols, and observation posts; verification of the implementation of Annex I of the Peace Treaty; and ensuring freedom of navigation through the Strait of Tiran in accordance with Article V of the Peace Treaty. By means of an exchange of letters with Egypt and Israel dated August 3, 1981, the United States agreed, subject to Congressional authorization and appropriations, to contribute an infantry battalion, a logistics support unit and civilian observers to the MFO, as well as a specified portion of the annual costs of the MFO. The U.S. military personnel to be contributed comprise less than half of the anticipated total MFO military complement of approximately 2,500 personnel.

In Public Law 97-132, the Multinational Force and Observers Participation Resolution, Congress affirmed that it considered the establishment of the MFO to be an essential stage in the development of a comprehensive settlement in the Middle East. The President was authorized to assign, under such terms and conditions as he might determine, members of the United States Armed Forces to participate in the MFO, provided that these personnel perform only the functions and responsibilities specified in the 1979 Treaty and the 1981 Protocol, and that their number not exceed 1,200 at any one time.

In accordance with the 1981 Egypt-Israel Protocol, the MFO must be in place by 1300 hours on March 20, 1982, and will assume its functions at 1300 hours on April 25, 1982. Accordingly, the movement of U.S. personnel and equipment for deployment to the Sinai is currently under way. On February 26 five unarmed UH-1H helicopters (which will provide air transportation in the Sinai for MFO personnel), together with their crews and support personnel, arrived at Tel Aviv; on March 2 approximately 88 logistics personnel arrived at Tel Aviv; on March 17, the first infantry troops of the First Battalion, 505th Infantry, 82nd Airborne Division arrived in the Southern Sinai; and by March 18 a total of 808 infantry troops, together with their equipment will have arrived. These troops will be equipped with standard light infantry weapons, including M-16 automatic rifles, M-60 machine guns, M203 grenade launchers and Dragon anti-tank missiles.

The duration of this involvement of U.S. forces in the Sinai will depend, of course, on the strengthening of mutual confidence between Egypt and Israel. The U.S. contribution to the MFO is not limited to any specific period; however, each country which contributes military forces to the MFO retains a right of withdrawal upon adequate prior notification to the MFO Director-General. U.S. participation in future years will, of course, be subject to the congressional authorization and appropriations process.

I want to emphasize that there is no intention or expectation that these members of the U.S. Armed Forces will become involved in hostilities. Egypt and Israel are at peace, and we expect them to remain at peace. No hostilities are occurring in the area and we have no expectation of hostilities. MFO forces will carry combat equipment appropriate for their peacekeeping missions, to meet the expectations of the parties as reflected in the 1981 Protocol and related documents, and as a prudent precaution for the safety of MFO personnel.

The deployment of U.S. forces to the Sinai for this purpose is being undertaken pursuant to Public Law 97-132 of December 29, 1981, and pursuant to the President's constitutional authority with respect to the conduct of foreign relations and as Commander-in-Chief of U.S. Armed Forces.

Sincerely,

RONALD REAGAN

98. Senate Resolution 374 Commending Egypt and Israel for Completion of the Current Phase of the Egyptian-Israeli Peace Treaty Withdrawal from the Sinai, April 26, 1982*

* S. Res. 374, 97th Cong., 2d Sess., 128 Cong. Rec. 7665 (1982).

Whereas, on Sunday, the 25th of April, 1982, in accordance with the Treaty of Peace between the Arab Republic of Egypt and the State of Israel, Israel completed final withdrawal from the Sinai Peninsula; and

Whereas, this step represents the willingness of the Government and the people of Israel to make difficult and painful decisions and also to take risks for peace; and

Whereas, this step symbolizes the continuing and enduring commitment of Israel and Egypt to the process of achieving a comprehensive peace in the region envisioned in the Camp David Accords;

Therefore be it resolved, That the Senate of the United States:

Commends the Government and the people of Israel for this historic and courageous step in the name of peace; and

Expressed confidence that Israel and Egypt will continue the process of normalization and realize fully the fruits of peaceful coexistence.

99. Statement by the EEC Foreign Ministers on the Withdrawal from the Sinai, April 27, 1982*

* 15 Bull. Eur. Comm. (No. 4) 48 (1982).

2.2.68. 'The Ten welcome the complete withdrawal of Israel from Sinai, which took place on 25 April.

They consider this an important step forward—not only for the development of peaceful relations between Israel and Egypt but also for efforts to achieve a peaceful settlement in the Middle East in accordance with Security Council Resolution 242.

The Ten hope that this event, which is the fruit of negotiations, may be followed by further negotiations leading to a comprehensive, just and lasting peace on the basis of the two principles on which they have repeatedly insisted, namely the right to existence and security for all the countries in the region and justice for all peoples, which implies the recognition of the legitimate rights of the Palestinian people, including their right to self-determination.

The Ten stress their concern regarding the situation in Lebanon, as expressed in their statement of 25 April.'

100. Israeli Ambassador's Statement on the Strait of Tiran at the 190th Meeting of the Third U.N. Conference on the Law of the Sea, December 8, 1982*

* Official Records of the Third United Nations Conference on the Law of the Sea, Volume XVII, at 84 (1984).

18. Mr. ROSENNE (Israel): After the adoption of the Convention and related resolutions on 30 April last, my delegation issued a statement to the
press supplementary to my explanations of vote at the 182nd meeting. We
explained *inter alia* that Israel's interests on the sea are complex and include
the maintenance of freedom of navigation and overflight through all kinds
of geographical formations, security interests, fisheries on a small scale, the
preservation of the marine environment and related ecological issues. We
should also like to take advantage of the new arrangements for the diffusion
of marine technology and scientific research and shall be happy to make
available to others our own expertise, centred above all in our oceano-
graphic institutes and institutes of higher learning.

19. On the question of straits used for international navigation, we feel
that Part III contains regressive elements caused by distortions introduced
in the interests of political opportunism. My delegation maintains the view
that the fundamental rule of law controlling this aspect is that a single legal
régime applies to passage through and overflight of all such straits, except
where a different régime is prescribed by treaty. The distortions in the Convention remain a source of great difficulty for us, except to the extent that
particular stipulations and understandings for a passage régime for specific
straits, giving broader rights to their users, are protected, as is the case for
some of the straits in my country's region, or of interest to my country.

20. In that respect may I recall what I said in greater detail at the 163rd
meeting of the Conference, on 31 March last. More particularly in relation
to the Strait of Tiran and the Gulf of Aqaba, I wish to quote the statement
of the representative of the United States delegation on 29 January last, as
follows:

> The United States fully supports the continuing applicability and
> force of freedom of navigation and overflight for the Strait of Tiran
> and the Gulf of Aquaba as set out in the Peace Treaty between Egypt
> and Israel. In the United States view, the Treaty of Peace is fully com-
> patible with the Law of the Sea Convention and will continue to prevail.
> The conclusion of the Law of the Sea Convention will not affect those
> provisions in any way.

That quotation can be found in the *Congressional Record*, Volume 128, No.
47, 97th Congress, second session, 27 April 1982, in the Senate part of the
volume at page 4089.

21. One of our main difficulties is that we are not yet satisfied that some
of the major concepts embodied in the new Convention are fully applicable
in the form in which they are presented in the semi-enclosed and narrow
seas on which our two coasts lie—the Mediterranean Sea and the Red Sea.
Conceptually speaking, the main thrust of the Convention is towards the
world's great oceans. It would seem to require adjustments both conceptual
and textual before it can be fully applied in other oceanic formations. We
have expressed these ideas often in the informal meetings of the Confer-

ence, but I want to take this opportunity to place this idea in a succinct form on the record and to stress again the necessity for particular arrangements to meet this type of situation, applicable to all the States concerned.

22. In our later written observations we summarized some other of our major difficulties with regard to the Convention. We have not yet completed our detailed examination of its text, and we shall not, therefore, be signing it on 10 December 1982, the anniversary of the adoption of the Universal Declaration of Human Rights, as a previous speaker has reminded us. We will need to examine very closely some of the statements that have been made here in the course of this concluding session and to establish accurately their implications for the interpretation and application of certain relevant provisions of the Convention, themselves the product of delicate negotiations.

23. When the Final Act of the Conference was adopted on 24 September last, I stated that, having regard for our well-known objections to a certain group purporting to be a national liberation movement being granted any rights whatsoever under the Convention or resolution IV, we were not parties to the consensus by which the Final Act was adopted. At the same time, I stated that we would re-examine it in the light of all the proceedings of the Conference.

24. I am glad to state that we are now able to sign the Final Act. At the same time, I have to make the following statement:

> This signature of this Final Act in no way implies recognition in any manner whatsoever of the group calling itself the Palestine Liberation Organization or of any rights whatsoever conferred upon it within the framework of any of the documents attached to this Final Act, and is subject to the statements of the delegation of Israel at the 163rd, 182nd, 184th and 190th meetings of the Conference and document A/CONF.62/WS/33.[1]

That statement will be appended to my signature of the Final Act.

25. It is now my pleasant duty to thank the two Governments that have acted as hosts of this Conference whenever it has met outside United Nations Headquarters—the Government of Venezuela, for our first substantive session in 1974, and the Government of Jamaica, for this concluding session. Like many others we regret that the Government of Venezuela has difficulties with the Convention, but the name of its illustrious Ambassador Andrés Aguilar, who was the Chairman of the Second Committee through most of its crucial stages, will always be associated with the Convention. In this context I cannot pass in silence over the name of the Ambassador of El Salvador, Mr Galindo Pohl, who in 1975 was instrumental in producing the first informal single negotiating text laying the basis for the settlement of the general law of the sea, which is our main interest. I wish

---

[1] See *Official Records of the Third United Nations Conference on the Law of the Sea*, vol. XVI.

also to express my delegation's great appreciation of the devoted work and valuable contributions of the other leaders of the Conference: the Chairmen of the First and Third Committees, our friends Paul Bamela Engo of Cameroon and Mr. Alexandr Yankov of Bulgaria; the Chairman of the Drafting Committee, Mr. Beesley of Canada; the Committee Rapporteurs, the Chairmen of all the other negotiating, working and language groups; and Mr. Kenneth Rattray of Jamaica, our General Rapporteur.

26. This historic Conference, one of the most difficult ever held, would not have reached this point without the devoted work of its secretariat, headed first by Mr. Constantin Stavropoulos and later by Mr. Bernardo Zuleta as Special Representative of the Secretary-General, so ably backed by Mr. David Hall. If I mention these three gentlemen, I do not wish to be taken as being forgetful of the other members of the secretariat, whatever their ranks and positions, with whom we have had such long and pleasant working relationships and through which I hope bonds of personal friendship transcending political differences have been formed. But I should like to mention particularly the documents officers in New York and in Geneva, always so helpful, especially during the work of the Drafting Committee and its language groups.

27. Finally, I come to the presidency. The late Hamilton Shirley Amerasinghe of Sri Lanka, Chairman of the Committee on the Peaceful Uses of the Sea-Bed and the Ocean Floor beyond the Limits of National Jurisdiction and then of this Conference until his lamented death at the end of 1980, brought inestimable services to the international community. My delegation is glad to see that a memorial fellowship is being established in recognition of his unique contribution to the work of the Conference. His sudden death and your election to the presidency of this Conference, Sir, confronted you with a bundle of seemingly intractable problems which made great demands on all your well-known skills and personal attributes. If my delegation could not accept certain aspects and had to appeal some of your rulings, I am sure you realize that deep political factors lay behind those positions and that our actions do not detract in the slightest from the admiration and esteem in which we hold you for the conduct of the presidency since you took office.

28. Once again my delegation would like to express its thanks to the Government of Jamaica and to the authorities of Montego Bay, who have done so much to make our stay here a pleasant and memorable occasion of a historic event.

101. Egypt's Declaration Concerning Passage through the Strait of Tiran and the Gulf of Aqaba under the U.N. Convention on the Law of the Sea, December 10, 1982*

* Multilateral Treaties Deposited With the Secretary-General: Status at 31 December 1985, at 707, U.N. Doc. ST/LEG/SER.E/4 (1986).

Declaration Concerning Passage through the Strait of Tiran and the Gulf of Aqaba

The provisions of the 1979 Peace Treaty between Egypt and Israel concerning passage through the Strait of Tiran and the Gulf of Aqaba come within the framework of the general régime of waters forming straits referred to in part III of the Convention, wherein it is stipulated that the general régime shall not affect the legal status of waters forming straits and shall include certain obligations with regard to security and the maintenance of order in the State bordering the strait.

102. Israel's Declaration Concerning Passage through the Strait of Tiran and the Gulf of Aqaba under the U.N. Convention on the Law of the Sea, December 11, 1984*

* Multilateral Treaties Deposited With the Secretary-General: Status at 31 December 1985, at 718, U.N. Doc. ST/LEG/SER.E/4 (1986).

The concerns of the Government of Israel, with regard to the law of the sea, relate principally to ensuring maximum freedom of navigation and overflight everywhere and particularly through straits used for international navigation.

In this regard, the Government of Israel states that the regime of navigation and overflight, confirmed by the 1979 Treaty of Peace between Israel and Egypt, in which the Strait of Tiran and the Gulf of Aqaba are considered by the Parties to be international waterways open to all nations for unimpeded and non-suspendable freedom of navigation and overflight, is applicable to the said areas. Moreover, being fully compatible with the United Nations Convention on the Law of the Sea, the regime of the Peace Treaty will continue to prevail and to be applicable to the said areas.

It is the understanding of the Government of Israel that the declaration of the Arab Republic of Egypt in this regard, upon its ratification of the Convention [. . .], is consonant with the above declaration [made by Egypt].

III. From Camp David to the War in Lebanon:

October 1978–May 1982

A. Conflict in Lebanon

103. Security Council Resolution 436 Calling for

a Cease-Fire in Lebanon, October 6, 1978*

---

* S.C. Res. 436, 33 U.N. SCOR (2089th mtg.) at 7, U.N. Doc. S/INF/34 (1978).

The Security Council,

Noting with grave concern the deteriorating situation in Beirut and its surroundings,

Deeply grieved at the consequent loss of life, human suffering and physical destruction,

Noting the appeal made on 4 October 1978 by the President of the Security Council and the Secretary-General,

1. *Calls upon* all those involved in hostilities in Lebanon to put an end to acts of violence and observe scrupulously an immediate and effective cease-fire and cessation of hostilities so that internal peace and national reconciliation may be restored based on the preservation of Lebanese unity, territorial integrity, independence and national sovereignty;

2. *Calls upon* all involved to allow units of the International Committee of the Red Cross into the area of conflict to evacuate the wounded and provide humanitarian assistance;

3. *Supports* the Secretary-General in his efforts and requests him to continue these efforts to bring about a durable cease-fire and to keep the Security Council informed on the implementation of the cease-fire.

Adopted unanimously at the 2089th meeting

104. European Parliament Resolution on the Situation in Lebanon, November 6, 1978*

* 21 O.J. Eur. Comm. (No. C 261) 38 (1978).

The European Parliament,

— deeply disturbed by current events in Lebanon where repeated acts of brutality are threatening the life of the country and the very survival of vital sectors of the Lebanese community,

1. Appeals urgently to the Commission, the Council and the Foreign Ministers meeting in political cooperation, earnestly requesting them to:
— take all possible measures as a matter of extreme urgency to help to maintain the cease-fire and further a return to peace based on respect for the country's unity and the preservation and security of all the communities living in Lebanon,
— grant immediate humanitarian aid to Lebanon, together with the economic and technical resources essential for it to rebuild democratically a sovereign State within its own frontiers;

2. Instructs its Political Affairs Committee to follow developments in Lebanon closely and to report to it regularly;

3. Instructs its President to forward this resolution to the Council, the Commission and the Foreign Ministers meeting in political cooperation.

105. General Assembly Resolution 33/146 on Assistance

for the Reconstruction and Development of Lebanon,

December 20, 1978*

* G.A. Res. 146, 33 U.N. GAOR Supp. (No. 45) at 111, U.N. Doc. A/33/45 (1978). *See also* subsequent resolutions, G.A. Res. 135, 34 U.N. GAOR Supp. (No. 46) at 125, U.N. Doc. A/34/46 (1979), G.A. Res. 85, 35 U.N. GAOR Supp. (No. 48) at 143, U.N. Doc. A/35/48 (1980), G.A. Res. 205, 36 U.N. GAOR Supp. (No. 51) at 137, U.N. Doc. A/36/51 (1981), G.A. Res. 163, 37 U.N. GAOR Supp. (No. 51) at 133, U.N. Doc. A/37/51 (1982), G.A. Res. 220, 38 U.N. GAOR Supp. (No. 47) at 171, U.N. Doc. A/38/47 (1983) and G.A. 197, 39 U.N. GAOR Supp. (No. 51) at 150, U.N. Doc. A/39/51 (1984).

The General Assembly,

Deeply concerned about the tragic loss of life and the immense damage to the economic structure and to property, and about the disruption of society in Lebanon resulting from the hostilities during the past four years,

Aware of the magnitude of the unmet needs for the relief of the Lebanese people and the reconstruction and development of Lebanon,

Bearing in mind the concern expressed by Member States about the grave situation in Lebanon and their interest in its return to normal conditions of life and its reconstruction and development,

Affirming the urgent need for international action to assist the Government of Lebanon in its efforts for relief, reconstruction and development,

Noting the appeals of the Secretary-General for relief and other forms of assistance to Lebanon and the creation of a special fund for this purpose,

Noting also resolution 65 (V) of 6 October 1978[118] of the Economic Commission for Western Asia in which the Commission considered that the needs of Lebanon exceeded the means within the capacity of the Commission,

1. *Endorses* the appeal of the Secretary-General for international assistance to Lebanon;

2. *Urges* all Governments to contribute to the reconstruction of Lebanon, either through existing bilateral and multilateral channels or, in addition, through a special fund to be established by the Secretary-General for this purpose;

3. *Requests* the Secretary-General to establish at Beirut a joint co-ordinating committee of the specialized agencies and other organizations within the United Nations system to co-ordinate their assistance and advice to the Government of Lebanon in all matters relating to reconstruction and development;

4. *Decides* that the Committee on Assistance for the Reconstruction and Development of Lebanon, headed by a co-ordinator appointed by the Secretary-General, shall also assist the Government of Lebanon in the assessment, formulation and phasing of aid and ensure its implementation within the framework of the needs of Lebanon;

5. *Requests* the Secretary-General to provide all possible assistance to the Committee in discharging its duties and to establish, in the manner he deems appropriate, a mode of consultation with representatives of the countries providing assistance;

6. *Further requests* the Secretary-General to report to the Economic and Social Council at its first regular session of 1979 and to the General Assembly at its thirty-fourth session on the progress achieved in the implementation of the present resolution.

90th plenary meeting
20 December 1978

[118] See *Official Records of the Economic and Social Council, 1979, Supplement No. 14* (E/1979/49), chap. III.

106. Security Council Resolution 444 Renewing the U.N.

Interim Force in Lebanon Mandate and Deploring Israel's

Lack of Cooperation with the Force, January 19, 1979*

* S.C. Res. 444, 34 U.N. SCOR (2113th mtg.) at 2, U.N. Doc. S/INF/35 (1979).

The Security Council,

Recalling its resolutions 425 (1978) and 426 (1978) of 19 March, 427 (1978) of 3 May and 434 (1978) of 18 September 1978,

Recalling also the statement made by the President of the Security Council on 8 December 1978 (S/12958),[7]

Having studied the report of the Secretary-General on the United Nations Interim Force in Lebanon of 12 January 1979, contained in document S/13026 and Corr.1,[6]

Expressing concern at the grave situation in Southern Lebanon resulting from obstacles placed in the way of the full implementation of resolutions 425 (1978) and 426 (1978),

Reiterating its conviction that the continuation of the situation constitutes a challenge to its authority and a defiance of its resolutions,

Noting with regret that the Force has reached the end of its second mandate without being enabled to complete all the tasks assigned to it,

Stressing that free and unhampered movement for the Force is essential for the fulfilment of its mandate within its entire area of operation,

Reaffirming the necessity for the strict respect for the sovereignty, territorial integrity and political independence of Lebanon within its internationally recognized boundaries,

Re-emphasizing the temporary nature of the Force as set out in its terms of reference,

Acting in response to the request of the Government of Lebanon taking into account the report of the Secretary-General,

1. *Deplores* the lack of co-operation, particularly on the part of Israel, with the efforts of the United Nations Interim Force in Lebanon fully to implement its mandate, including assistance lent by Israel to irregular armed groups in Southern Lebanon;

2. *Notes with great appreciation* the efforts being made by the Secretary-General, the commanders and soldiers of the Force and the staff of the United Nations, as well as by Governments which have lent their assistance and co-operation;

3. *Expresses its satisfaction* with the declared policy of the Government of Lebanon and the steps already taken for the deployment of the Lebanese army in the south and encourages it to increase its efforts, in coordination with the Force, to re-establish its authority in that area;

4. *Decides* to renew the mandate of the Force for a period of five months, that is, until 19 June 1979;

5. *Calls upon* the Secretary-General and the Force to continue to take all effective measures deemed necessary in accordance with the approved guidelines and terms of reference of the Force as adopted by the Security

[6] *Ibid. [Official Records of the Security Council, Thirty-fourth Year], Supplement for January, February and March 1979.*

[7] *Ibid., Thirty-third Year, 2106th meeting, para. 7.*

Council[8] and invites the Government of Lebanon to draw up, in consultation with the Secretary-General, a phased programme of activities to be carried out over the next three months to promote the restoration of its authority;

6. *Urges* all Members States which are in a position to do so to bring their influence to bear on those concerned, so that the Force can discharge its responsibilities fully and unhampered;

7. *Reaffirms* its determination, in the event of continuing obstruction of the mandate of the Force, to examine practical ways and means in accordance with relevant provisions of the Charter of the United Nations to secure the full implementation of resolution 425 (1978);

8. *Decides* to remain seized of the question and to meet again within three months to assess the situation.

Adopted at the 2113th meeting by 12 votes to none, with 2 abstentions (Czechoslovakia, Union of Soviet Socialist Republics).[9]

[8] *Ibid., Supplement for January, February and March 1978*, document S/12611.
[9] One member (China) did not participate in the voting.

107. Security Council Resolution 450 Renewing the U.N. Interim Force in Lebanon Mandate and Calling for Israel to Stop Its Actions in Lebanon, June 14, 1979*

---

* S.C. Res. 450, 34 U.N. SCOR (2149th mtg.) at 7, U.N. Doc. S/INF/35 (1979).

The Security Council,

Recalling its resolutions 425 (1978) and 426 (1978) of 19 March, 427 (1978) of 3 May and 434 (1978) of 18 September 1978, and the statement made by the President of the Security Council on 8 December 1978 (S/ 12958),[7]

Recalling also, and particularly, its resolution 444 (1979) of 19 January 1979 and the statements made by the President of the Security Council on 26 April (S/13272)[20] and on 15 May 1979,[21]

Having studied the report of the Secretary-General on the United Nations Interim Force in Lebanon,[22]

Acting in response to the request of the Government of Lebanon and noting with concern the questions raised in its letters addressed to the Security Council on 7 May,[23] 30 May[24] and 11 June 1979,[25]

Reaffirming its call for the strict respect for the territorial integrity, unity, sovereignty and political independence of Lebanon within its internationally recognized boundaries,

Expressing its anxiety about the continued existence of obstacles to the full deployment of the Force and the threats to its very security, its freedom of movement and the safety of its headquarters, which prevented the completion of the phased programme of activities,

Convinced that the present situation has serious consequences for peace and security in the Middle East and impedes the achievement of a just, comprehensive and durable peace in the area,

1. *Strongly deplores* acts of violence against Lebanon that have led to the displacement of civilians, including Palestinians, and brought about destruction and loss of innocent lives;

2. *Calls upon* Israel to cease forthwith its acts against the territorial integrity, unity, sovereignty and political independence of Lebanon, in particular its incursions into Lebanon and the assistance it continues to lend to irresponsible armed groups;

3. *Calls also upon* all parties concerned to refrain from activities inconsistent with the objectives of the United Nations Interim Force in Lebanon and to cooperate for the fulfilment of these objectives;

4. *Reiterates* that the objectives of the Force as set out in resolutions 425 (1978), 426 (1978) and 444 (1979) must be attained;

5. *Highly commends* the performance of the Force and reiterates its terms of reference as set out in the report of the Secretary-General of 19 March

---

[7] *Ibid.* [*Official Records of the Security Council*], *Thirty-third Year,* 2106th meeting, para. 7.

[20] *Ibid., Thirty-fourth Year,* 2141st meeting, para. 2.

[21] *Ibid.,* 2144th meeting, para. 2.

[22] *Ibid., Supplement for April, May and June 1979,* document S/13384.

[23] *Ibid.,* document S/13301.

[24] *Ibid.,* document S/13361.

[25] *Ibid.,* document S/13387.

1978[8] and approved by resolution 426 (1978), in particular that the Force must be enabled to function as an effective military unit, that it must enjoy freedom of movement and communication and other facilities necessary for the performance of its tasks and that it must continue to be able to discharge its duties according to the above-mentioned terms of reference, including the right of self-defence;

6. *Reaffirms* the validity of the General Armistice Agreement[26] between Israel and Lebanon in accordance with its relevant decisions and resolutions and calls upon the parties to take the necessary steps to reactivate the Mixed Armistice Commission and to ensure full respect for the safety and freedom of action of the United Nations Truce Supervision Organization;

7. *Urges* all Member States which are in a position to do so to bring their influence to bear on those concerned, so that the Force can discharge its responsibilities fully and unhampered;

8. *Decides* to renew the mandate of the Force for a period of six months, that is, until 19 December 1979.

9. *Reaffirms* its determination, in the event of continuing obstruction of the mandate of the Force, to examine practical ways and means in accordance with relevant provisions of the Charter of the United Nations to secure the full implementation of resolution 425 (1978);

10. *Decides* to remain seized of the question.

Adopted at the 2149th meeting by 12 votes to none, with 2 abstentions (Czechoslovakia, Union of Soviet Socialist Republics).[27]

[8] *Ibid., Supplement for January, February and March 1978*, document S/12611.
[26] *Ibid., Fourth Year, Special Supplement No. 4.*
[27] One member (China) did not participate in the voting.

108. Statement by the EEC Foreign Ministers on Lebanon, September 11, 1979*

* 12 Bull. Eur. Comm. (No. 9) 68 (1979).

'On repeated occasions in the past few years, in particular in their statement of 18 June,[1] the Nine have expressed deep concern over the continuous deterioration of the situation in Lebanon. Aware as they are of the courageous efforts being made by the Government of President Sarkis to promote the security of its people and restore its authority over the whole of its territory, they have constantly reiterated their support for Lebanon's independence, sovereignty and territorial integrity. They have therefore given their backing to the operations of Unifil[2]—which includes contingents from certain Community Member States. The Nine calls on all parties to do their utmost to assist Unifil in its task and to respect the Security Council's decisions.

In the light of recent developments which caused the Lebanese Government to request a meeting of the Security Council, the Nine wish to confirm their full and unqualified solidarity with a fellow country whose people are exposed to such intense physical and material suffering, thus seriously endangering its precarious balance.

Taking note of the improvement in the situation since the last Security Council debate, the Nine hope that a decisive end will be put to all acts of violence in Lebanon, including the harassment of Unifil.

The Nine formally address an urgent appeal to every single country and party concerned to refrain from any action that might jeopardize Lebanese territorial integrity or the authority of the Lebanese Government. They also call on all Lebanese, regardless of their religion or political sympathies, to give full support to the efforts of their Government to achieve a true political dialogue, which is a prerequisite for the restoration of internal peace and security.

The Nine are willing to back, for instance the United Nations, any action or move that might help to restore peace and stability in Lebanon, which is still a key factor in maintaining balance in the region.[3]

[1] Bull. EC 6-1979, point 2.2.59.
[2] United Nations intervention force in Lebanon.
[3] Non-official translation.

109. Security Council Resolution 459 Renewing the U.N.

Interim Force in Lebanon Mandate and Approving the

General Armistice Agreement, December 19, 1979*

---

* S.C. Res. 459, 34 U.N. SCOR (218oth mtg.) at 11, U.N. Doc. S/INF/35 (1979).

The Security Council,

Recalling its resolutions 425 (1978) and 426 (1978) of 19 March, 427 (1978) of 3 May and 434 (1978) of 18 September 1978, 444 (1979) of 19 January and 450 (1979) of 14 June 1979, as well as the statements made by the President of the Security Council on 8 December 1978 (S/12958),[7] on 26 April (S/13272)[20] and on 15 May 1979,[21]

Recalling its debate on 29 and 30 August 1979[44] and the statements of the Secretary-General concerning the cease-fire,

Having studied the report of the Secretary-General on the United Nations Interim Force in Lebanon,[45]

Acting in response to the request of the Government of Lebanon and noting with concern the continued violations of the cease-fire, the attacks on the Force and the difficulties in implementing Security Council resolutions,

Expressing its anxiety about the continued existence of obstacles to the full deployment of the Force and the threats to its very security, its freedom of movement and the safety of its headquarters,

Convinced that the present situation has serious consequences for peace and security in the Middle East and impedes the achievement of a just, comprehensive and durable peace in the area,

Reaffirming its call for the strict respect for the territorial integrity, unity, sovereignty and political independence of Lebanon within its internationally recognized boundaries, and welcoming the efforts of the Government of Lebanon to reassert its sovereignty and restore its civilian and military authority in Southern Lebanon,

1. *Reaffirms* the objectives of resolutions 425 (1978) and 450 (1979);

2. *Expresses its support* for the efforts of the Secretary-General to consolidate the cease-fire and calls upon all parties concerned to refrain from activities inconsistent with the objectives of the United Nations Interim Force in Lebanon and to co-operate for the fulfilment of these objectives;

3. *Calls upon* the Secretary-General and the Force to continue to take all effective measures deemed necessary in accordance with the approved guidelines and terms of reference of the Force as adopted in resolution 426 (1978);

4. *Takes note* of the determination of the Government of Lebanon to draw up a programme of action, in consultation with the Secretary-General, to promote the restoration of its authority in pursuance of resolution 425 (1978);

5. *Takes note also* of the efforts of the Government of Lebanon to obtain international recognition for the protection of the archaeological and cul-

---

[7] *Ibid. [Official Records of the Security Council], Thirty-third Year,* 2106th meeting, para. 7.

[20] *Ibid., Thirty-fourth Year,* 2141st meeting, para. 2.

[21] *Ibid.,* 2144th meeting, para. 2.

[44] *Official Records of the Security Council, Thirty-fourth Year,* 2164th and 2165th meetings.

[45] *Ibid., Supplement for October, November and December 1979,* document S/13691.

tural sites and monuments in the city of Tyre in accordance with international law and the Convention of The Hague of 1954,[46] under which such cities, sites and monuments are considered to be a heritage of interest to all mankind;

6. *Reaffirms* the validity of the General Armistice Agreement[26] between Israel and Lebanon in accordance with its relevant decisions and resolutions and calls upon the parties, with the assistance of the Secretary-General, to take the necessary steps to reactivate the Mixed Armistice Commission and to ensure full respect for the safety and freedom of action of the United Nations Truce Supervision Organization;

7. *Highly commends* the performance of the Force and its Commander, and reiterates its terms of reference as set out in the report of the Secretary-General of 19 March 1978[8] and approved by resolution 426 (1978), in particular that the Force must be enabled to function as an efficient military unit, that it must enjoy freedom of movement and communication and other facilities necessary for the performance of its tasks and that it must continue to be able to discharge its duties according to the above-mentioned terms of reference, including the right of self-defence;

8. *Urges* all Member States which are in a position to do so to continue to bring their influence to bear on those concerned, so that the Force can discharge its responsibilities fully and unhampered;

9. *Decides* to renew the mandate of the Force for a period of six months, that is, until 19 June 1980;

10. *Reaffirms* its determination, in the event of continuing obstruction of the mandate of the Force, to examine practical ways and means in accordance with relevant provisions of the Charter of the United Nations to secure the full implementation of resolution 425 (1978);

11. *Decides* to remain seized of the question.

Adopted at the 2180th meeting by 12 votes to none, with 2 abstentions (Czechoslovakia, Union of Soviet Socialist Republics).[47]

[8] *Ibid.* [*Thirty-third Year*], *Supplement for January, February and March 1978*, document S/12611.

[26] *Ibid.*, [*Official Records of the Security Council*], *Fourth Year, Special Supplement No. 4.*

[46] Convention for the Protection of Cultural Property in the Event of Armed Conflict (United Nations, *Treaty Series*, vol. 249, p. 240).

[47] One member (China) did not participate in the voting.

110. Statement by the EEC Foreign Ministers on UNIFIL's Position in Southern Lebanon, April 22, 1980*

* 13 Bull. Eur. Comm. (No. 4) 79 (1980).

Statement on UNIFIL's Position in Southern Lebanon

'1. The Foreign Ministers of the nine Member States of the European Community meeting in Luxembourg on 22 April considered recent developments in relation to the United Nations peace-keeping force in southern Lebanon (UNIFIL).

2. They expressed their profound revulsion at the recent killing of soldiers of the force and especially at the brutal and cold-blooded murder on 18 April by the irregular forces of Major Haddad of two unarmed soldiers of the Irish contingent.

3. The Ministers recalled their statement on 11 September 1979 reaffirming their support for the independence, sovereignty and territorial integrity of Lebanon and calling on all parties to give full assistance to the UNIFIL operation and to respect the decisions of the Security Council.[6]

They expressed very serious concern that armed attacks continue to be made on the UNIFIL troops, installations and equipment and that obstacles continue to be placed in the way of the force in its efforts to carry out effectively, and throughout the whole of its area of operation, the peace-keeping mandate it received from the Security Council.

4. The Nine believe it is vital that steps be taken to ensure that UNIFIL is permitted to carry out fully the tasks assigned to it and they support the efforts of the troop-contributing countries to ensure that this will now be done. They note that it is the intention of the Security Council, as stated on behalf of its member states by the President of the Council on 18 April "to take such determined action as the situation calls for to enable UNIFIL to take immediate and total control of the entire area of operation up to the internationally recognized boundaries".

5. The Foreign Ministers of the Nine call strongly on all concerned to give their fullest support to the measures decided on by the Security Council so that UNIFIL may be in a position to carry out in full the important peace-keeping mission with which it has been entrusted on behalf of the international community.'

[6] Bull. EC 9-1979, point 2.2.55.

111. Security Council Resolution 467 Reaffirming the
U.N. Interim Force in Lebanon Mandate and Deploring
Israeli Intervention in Lebanon, April 24, 1980*

---

* S.C. Res. 467, 35 U.N. SCOR (2218th mtg.) at 7, U.N. Doc. S/INF/36 (1980).

The Security Council,

Acting in response to the request of the Government of Lebanon,[29]

Having studied the special report of the Secretary-General on the United Nations Interim Force in Lebanon of 11 April 1980[30] and the subsequent statements, reports and addenda,

Having expressed itself through the statement of the President of the Security Council of 18 April 1980,[27]

Recalling its resolutions 425 (1978), 426 (1978), 427 (1978), 434 (1978), 444 (1979), 450 (1979) and 459 (1979),

Recalling the terms of reference and general guidelines of the Force, as stated in the report of the Secretary-General of 19 March 1978[31] confirmed by resolution 426 (1978), and particularly:

(*a*) That the Force "must be able to function as an integrated and efficient military unit",

(*b*) That the Force "must enjoy the freedom of movement and communication and other facilities that are necessary for the performance of its tasks",

(*c*) That the Force "will not use force except in self-defence",

(*d*) That "self-defence would include resistance to attempts by forceful means to prevent it from discharging its duties under the mandate of the Security Council",

1. *Reaffirms* its determination to implement the above-mentioned resolutions, particularly resolutions 425 (1978), 426 (1978) and 459 (1979), in the totality of the area of operation assigned to the United Nations Interim Force in Lebanon, up to the internationally recognized boundaries;

2. *Condemns* all actions contrary to the provisions of the above-mentioned resolutions and, in particular, strongly deplores:

(*a*) Any violation of Lebanese sovereignty and territorial integrity;

(*b*) The military intervention of Israel in Lebanon;

(*c*) All acts of violence in violation of the General Armistice Agreement between Israel and Lebanon;[32]

(*d*) Provision of military assistance to the so-called *de facto* forces;

(*e*) All acts of interference with the United Nations Truce Supervision Organization;

(*f*) All acts of hostility against the Force and in or through its area of operation as inconsistent with Security Council resolutions;

(*g*) All obstructions of the ability of the Force to confirm the complete withdrawal of Israeli forces from Lebanon, to supervise the cessation of hos-

[27] Document S/13900, incorporated in the record of the 2217th meeting.

[29] *Official Records of the Security Council, Thirty-fifth Year, Supplement for April, May and June 1980*, document S/13885.

[30] *Ibid.*, document S/13888.

[31] *Ibid., Thirty-third Year, Supplement for January, February and March 1978*, document S/12611.

[32] *Ibid., Fourth Year, Special Supplement No. 4.*

tilities, to ensure the peaceful character of the area of operation, to control movement and to take measures deemed necessary to ensure the effective restoration of the sovereignty of Lebanon;

(*h*) Acts that have led to loss of life and physical injuries among the personnel of the Force and of the United Nations Truce Supervision Organization, their harassment and abuse, the disruption of communication, as well as the destruction of property and material;

3. *Condemns* the deliberate shelling of the headquarters of the Force and more particularly the field hospital, which enjoys special protection under international law;

4. *Commends* the efforts undertaken by the Secretary-General and by the interested Governments to bring about the cessation of hostilities and to enable the Force to carry out its mandate effectively without interference;

5. *Commends* the Force for its great restraint in carrying out its duties in very adverse circumstances;

6. *Calls attention* to the provisions in the mandate that would allow the Force to use its right to self-defence;

7. *Calls attention* to the terms of reference of the Force which provide that it will use its best efforts to prevent the recurrence of fighting and to ensure that its area of operation will not be utilized for hostile activities of any kind;

8. *Requests* the Secretary-General to convene a meeting, at an appropriate level, of the Israel-Lebanon Mixed Armistice Commission to agree on precise recommendations and further to reactivate the General Armistice Agreement conducive to the restoration of the sovereignty of Lebanon over all its territory up to the internationally recognized boundaries;

9. *Calls upon* all parties concerned and all those capable of lending any assistance to co-operate with the Secretary-General in enabling the Force to fulfil its mandate;

10. *Recognizes* the urgent need to explore all ways and means of securing the full implementation of resolution 425 (1978), including enhancing the capacity of the Force to fulfil its mandate in all its parts;

11. *Requests* the Secretary-General to report as soon as possible on the progress of these initiatives and the cessation of hostilities.

Adopted at the 2218th meeting by 12 votes to none, with 3 abstentions (German Democratic Republic, Union of Soviet Socialist Republics, United States of America).

112. Security Council Resolution 474 Renewing the U.N.

Interim Force in Lebanon Mandate and Condemning the

Continued Violence, June 17, 1980*

---

* S.C. Res. 474, 35 U.N. SCOR (2232nd mtg.) at 11, U.N. Doc. S/INF/36 (1980).

The Security Council,

Recalling its resolutions 425 (1978), 426 (1978), 427 (1978), 434 (1978), 444 (1979), 450 (1979), 459 (1979) and 467 (1980), as well as the statement by the President of the Security Council of 18 April 1980,

Having studied the report of the Secretary-General on the United Nations Interim Force in Lebanon of 12 June 1980,[42]

Acting in response to the request of the Government of Lebanon and noting with concern the questions raised in its letters addressed to the Security Council on 8 May,[43] 17 May[44] and 27 May 1980,[45]

Convinced that the present situation has serious consequences for peace and security in the Middle East,

Reaffirming its call for the strict respect for the territorial integrity, unity, sovereignty and political independence of Lebanon within its internationally recognized boundaries,

Commending the performance of the Force, yet expressing its concern about the continued existence of obstacles to the full deployment of the Force and its freedom of movement, the threats to its security and the safety of its headquarters,

1. *Decides* to renew the mandate of the United Nations Interim Force in Lebanon for a period of six months, that is, until 19 December 1980, and reiterates its commitment to the full implementation of the mandate of the Force throughout its entire area of operation up to the internationally recognized boundaries, according to the terms of reference and guidelines as stated and confirmed in the appropriate Security Council resolutions;

2. *Takes note* of the report of the Secretary-General on the United Nations Interim Force in Lebanon and fully endorses the conclusions and recommendations expressed therein;

3. *Strongly condemns* all actions contrary to the provisions of the mandate and, in particular, continued acts of violence that prevent the fulfilment of this mandate by the Force;

4. *Takes note* of the steps already taken by the Secretary-General to convene a meeting of the Israel-Lebanon Mixed Armistice Commission and urges the parties concerned to extend to him their full co-operation in accordance with the relevant Security Council decisions and resolutions, including resolution 467 (1980);

5. *Takes note* of the efforts deployed by Member States, and more particularly the troop-contributing countries, in support of the Force and urges all those which are in a position to do so to continue to use their influence

---

[42] *Ibid.* [*Official Records of the Security Council, Thirty-fifth Year, Supplement for April, May and June 1980*], document S/13994.

[43] *Ibid.*, document S/13931.

[44] *Ibid.*, document S/13946.

[45] *Ibid.*, document S/13962.

with those concerned so that the Force can discharge its responsibilities fully and unhampered;

6. *Reaffirms* its determination, in the event of continuing obstruction of the mandate of the Force, to examine practical ways and means to secure the full implementation of resolution 425 (1978);

7. *Decides* to remain seized of the question.

Adopted at the 2232nd meeting by 12 votes to none, with 2 abstentions (German Democratic Republic, Union of Soviet Socialist Republics).[46]

[46] One member (China) did not participate in the voting.

113. Security Council Resolution 483 Renewing the U.N.

Interim Force in Lebanon Mandate and Reactivating the

Israel-Lebanon Mixed Armistice Commission,

December 17, 1980*

---

* S.C. Res. 483, 35 U.N. SCOR (2258th mtg.) at 15, U.N. Doc. S/INF/36 (1980).

The Security Council,

Recalling its resolutions 425 (1978), 426 (1978), 427 (1978), 434 (1978), 444 (1979), 450 (1979), 459 (1979), 467 (1980) and 474 (1980),

Having studied the report of the Secretary-General on the United Nations Interim Force in Lebanon of 12 December 1980,[54]

Noting the letter dated 15 December 1980 from the Permanent Representative of Lebanon to the Secretary-General,[55]

Convinced that the present situation has serious consequences for peace and security in the Middle East,

Reaffirming its call for the strict respect for the territorial integrity, unity, sovereignty and political independence of Lebanon within its internationally recognized boundaries,

1. *Takes note* of the report of the Secretary-General on the United Nations Interim Force in Lebanon;

2. *Decides* to renew the mandate of the Force for a period of six months, that is, until 19 June 1981, and reiterates its commitment to the full implementation of the mandate of the Force throughout its entire area of operation up to the internationally recognized boundaries, according to the terms of reference and guidelines as stated and confirmed in the appropriate Security Council resolutions;

3. *Commends* the performance of the Force and reiterates its terms of reference as set out in the report of the Secretary-General of 19 March 1978[31] and approved by resolution 426 (1978), in particular that the Force must be enabled to function as an efficient military unit, that it must enjoy freedom of movement and communication and other facilities necessary for the performance of its tasks and that it must continue to be able to discharge its duties according to the above-mentioned terms of reference, including the right of self-defence;

4. *Expresses its support* for the Lebanese Government in its efforts to strengthen its authority, both at the civilian and at the military level, in the zone of operation of the Force;

5. *Commends* the Secretary-General for his efforts to reactivate the Israel-Lebanon Mixed Armistice Commission, takes note of the preparatory meeting that was held on Monday, 1 December 1980, and calls on all parties to continue such efforts as are necessary for the total and unconditional implementation of the General Armistice Agreement;[32]

6. *Requests* the Secretary-General to take the necessary measures to intensify discussions among all the parties concerned, so that the Force may com-

[31] *Ibid.*, [*Official Records of the Security Council*], *Thirty-third Year, Supplement for January, February and March 1978*, document S/12611.

[32] *Ibid., Fourth Year, Special Supplement No. 4.*

[54] *Official Records of the Security Council, Thirty-fifth Year, Supplement for October, November and December 1980*, document S/14295.

[55] *Ibid.*, document S/14296.

plete its mandate, and to report periodically on the results of his efforts to the Security Council;

7. *Reaffirms* its determination, in the event of continuing obstruction of the mandate of the Force, to examine practical ways and means to secure the full implementation of resolution 425 (1978).

Adopted at the 2258th meeting by 12 votes to none, with 2 abstentions (German Democratic Republic, Union of Soviet Socialist Republics).[56]

[56] One member (China) did not participate in the voting.

114. European Parliament Resolution on the Crisis

in Lebanon, April 10, 1981*

* 24 O.J. Eur. Comm. (No. C 101) 113 (1981).

The European Parliament,

— concerned at the renewed outbreak of hostilities in the Lebanon, which is causing many casualties among the civilian population, especially in the Christian town of Zahle, thereby exacerbating the dangers of war in that area,
— having regard to United Nations Resolution No 436 of 6 October 1978 calling for a ceasefire and proposing a return to peace and national reconciliation on the basis of the preservation of unity, territorial integrity and sovereignty in the Lebanon.
— having regard to the terms of the communiqué adopted by the European Council at Maastricht,

1. Calls on all the parties concerned to allow the representatives of the International Committee of the Red Cross to enter the areas of conflict in order to evacuate the injured and provide humanitarian assistance;

2. Calls for an immediate ceasefire and ending of the Syrian bombardment;

3. Calls for the withdrawal of all outside forces apart from Unifil and the re-establishment of the legitimate Lebanese Government's authority throughout the territory by its own national, military and police forces;

4. Instructs its President to forward this resolution to the Foreign Ministers meeting in political cooperation, the Secretary-General of the UN, the Governments of the Lebanon, Syria and Israel, and the Secretary-General of the Arab League.

115. House of Representatives Resolution 159 Supporting
Diplomatic Efforts to Resolve the Israel-Syria Missile Crisis
and Congratulating Special Envoy Philip Habib
for His Work, June 16, 1981*

* H.R. Res. 159, 97th Cong., 1st Sess., 127 Cong. Rec. 12544 (1981).

Whereas the ongoing crisis in Lebanon has far-reaching implications for international peace and security and has caused great human suffering and disruption of the economy in that country;

Whereas a diplomatic solution to the present situation in Lebanon which promotes a strong, independent, democratic Lebanon with close ties to the West is a major objective of United States foreign policy;

Whereas Special Envoy Philip C. Habib has demonstrated outstanding diplomatic skills in his effort to reach a peaceful solution which would significantly enhance the prospects of Lebanon once again becoming a peaceful, viable democracy; and

Whereas Philip C. Habib left private life to serve his country in a patriotic and selfless manner in Lebanon and has performed long and distinguished service in the Department of State: Now, therefore, be it

Resolved, That the House of Representatives strongly supports diplomatic efforts to resolve the current crisis in Lebanon and encourages the President to pursue a comprehensive and coordinated policy in Lebanon, including the development of an effective cease-fire, resolution of the issue of Syrian missiles, and promotion of the independence, sovereignty, unity, and territorial integrity of Lebanon.

SEC. 2. The House of Representatives congratulates Special Envoy Philip C. Habib on his tireless efforts to resolve current international problems concerning Lebanon and extends best wishes for success to Philip C. Halbib in the continuation of his mission to Lebanon and in his personal and public endeavors in the future.

116. Security Council Resolution 488 Renewing the U.N. Interim Force in Lebanon Mandate and Reaffirming the Call for Respect of Lebanon's Territorial Integrity, June 19, 1981*

* S.C. Res. 488, 36 U.N. SCOR (2289th mtg.) at 3, U.N. Doc. S/INF/37 (1981).

The Security Council,

Recalling its resolutions 425 (1978), 426 (1978), 427 (1978), 434 (1978), 444 (1979), 450 (1979), 459 (1979), 467 (1980), 474 (1980) and 483 (1980),

Recalling the statement made by the President of the Security Council at the 2266th meeting, on 19 March 1981,

Noting with concern the violations of the relevant Security Council resolutions which had prompted the Government of Lebanon repeatedly to ask the Council for action, and particularly its complaint of 3 March 1981,[19]

Recalling the terms of reference and general guidelines of the United Nations Interim Force in Lebanon, as stated in the report of the Secretary-General of 19 March 1978[20] confirmed by resolution 426 (1978), and particularly:

(*a*) That the Force "must be able to function as an integrated and efficient military unit",

(*b*) That the Force "must enjoy the freedom of movement and communication and other facilities that are necessary for the performance of its tasks",

(*c*) That the Force "will not use force except in self-defence",

(*d*) That "self-defence would include resistance to attempts by forceful means to prevent it from discharging its duties under the mandate of the Security Council",

Having studied the report of the Secretary-General on the United Nations Interim Force in Lebanon of 16 June 1981,[21] and taking note of the conclusions and recommendations expressed therein,

Convinced that the deterioration of the present situation has serious consequences for international security in the Middle East and impedes the achievement of a just, comprehensive and durable peace in the area,

1. *Reaffirms* its repeated call upon all concerned for the strict respect for the political independence, unity, sovereignty and territorial integrity of Lebanon and reiterates the Council's determination to implement resolution 425 (1978) and the ensuing resolutions in the totality of the area of operation assigned to the United Nations Interim Force in Lebanon up to the internationally recognized boundaries;

2. *Condemns* all actions contrary to the provisions of the above-mentioned resolutions that have prevented the full implementation of the mandate of the Force, causing death, injury and destruction to the civilian population as well as among the peace-keeping force;

3. *Supports* the efforts of the Government of Lebanon in the civilian and military fields of rehabilitation and reconstruction in southern Lebanon,

[19] *Official Records of the Security Council, Thirty-sixth Year, Supplement for January, February and March 1981*, document S/14391.

[20] *Ibid., Thirty-third Year, Supplement for January, February and March 1978*, document S/12611.

[21] *Ibid., Thirty-sixth Year, Supplement for April, May and June 1981*, document S/14537.

and supports, in particular, the deployment of substantial contingents of the Lebanese army in the area of operation of the Force;

4. *Decides* to renew the mandate of the Force for another period of six months, that is, until 19 December 1981;

5. *Requests* the Secretary-General to assist the Government of Lebanon in establishing a joint phased programme of activities to be carried out during the present mandate of the Force, aimed at the total implementation of resolution 425 (1978), and to report periodically to the Security Council;

6. *Commends* the efforts of the Secretary-General and the performance of the Force, as well as the support of the troop-contributing Governments and of all Member States who have assisted the Secretary-General, his staff and the Force in discharging their responsibilities under the mandate;

7. *Decides* to remain seized of the question and reaffirms its determination, in the event of continuing obstruction of the mandate of the Force, to examine practical ways and means to secure its unconditional fulfilment.

Adopted at the 2289th meeting by 12 votes to none, with 2 abstentions (German Democratic Republic, Union of Soviet Socialist Republics).[22]

[22] One member (China) did not participate in the voting.

117. Senate Resolution 144 Supporting Diplomatic Efforts to Resolve the Israel-Syria Missile Crisis in Lebanon, June 25, 1981*

* S. Res. 144, 97th Cong., 1st Sess., 127 Cong. Rec. 13796, 13798 (1981).

Resolution to offer strong support for diplomatic efforts to resolve the current crisis in Lebanon, including the issue of the Syrian missiles, and to protect the right of all Lebanese communities to live in freedom and security

Whereas the current situation in Lebanon has caused great human suffering and disruption of the economy of that country;

Whereas the present crisis including violence and PLO terrorism, threatens to further undermine the sovereignty of Lebanon and stability in the Middle East;

Whereas the strengthening of the Lebanese Government authority throughout the country would significantly enhance the prospects of Lebanon once again becoming a peaceful, viable democracy;

Whereas the continuing conflict in Lebanon threatens the survival of the ancient city of Tyre, one of the historical treasures of our world;

Whereas a strong, independent, democratic Lebanon—with its traditional ties to the West—would help promote stability in the region and serve the national interest of the United States;

Whereas the Senate commends and supports the will of the Lebanese people to live in freedom, security and peace; and

Whereas the Senate hopes for the success of diplomatic efforts currently being carried out by special envoy Philip C. Habib.

Resolved, That the Senate of the United States of America strongly supports diplomatic efforts to resolve the current crisis in Lebanon, and that the Government of the United States should continue to pursue a comprehensive and coordinated policy in Lebanon guided by the following principles:

1. Establishment of an immediate and effective cease-fire throughout Lebanon.

2. Resolution of the issue of the Syrian missiles deployed in Lebanon.

3. Freedom, security and opportunity for Christian and all other Lebanese communities, including the Moslem, Druze, and Jewish communities in Lebanon.

4. Reaffirmation of the historic United States-Lebanon relationship and strengthening the longstanding commitment of the United States to the independence, sovereignty, and territorial integrity of Lebanon, without partition, free from terrorism and violence, and free to determine its future without Soviet or other outside interference.

5. Generous international support for relief, rehabilitation, and humanitarian assistance for Lebanon, particularly for those Lebanese citizens who have suffered from the terrorism and violence of recent events.

6. Respect for and strengthening of the authority of a Lebanese Government, based on open national elections free from external interference which will be able to preserve security through its national army and its security forces without outside military presence.

118. Security Council Resolution 490 Calling for a Cessation of All Armed Attacks and Reaffirming Its Commitment to Territorial Integrity in Lebanon, July 21, 1981*

* S.C. Res. 490, 36 U.N. SCOR (2293rd mtg.) at 5, U.N. Doc. S/INF/37 (1981).

The Security Council,

Reaffirming the urgent appeal made by the President and the members of the Security Council on 17 July 1981,[27] which reads as follows:

The President of the Security Council and the members of the Council, after hearing the report of the Secretary-General,[26] express their deep concern at the extent of the loss of life and the scale of the destruction caused by the deplorable events that have been taking place for several days in Lebanon.

They launch an urgent appeal for an immediate end to all armed attacks and for the greatest restraint so that peace and quiet may be established in Lebanon and a just and lasting peace in the Middle East as a whole.

Taking note of the report of the Secretary-General in this respect,

1. *Calls* for an immediate cessation of all armed attacks;

2. *Reaffirms* its commitment to the sovereignty, territorial integrity and independence of Lebanon within its internationally recognized boundaries;

3. *Requests* the Secretary-General to report back to the Security Council on the implementation of the present resolution as soon as possible and not later than forty-eight hours from its adoption.

Adopted unanimously at the 2293rd meeting.

[26] *Official Records of the Security Council, Thirty-sixth Year,* 2292nd meeting.
[27] Document S/14599, incorporated in the record of the 2292nd meeting.

119. Written Question to the European Council on the Conflict between Israel and Lebanon, August 24, 1981— Answer, December 31, 1981*

---

* 25 O.J. Eur. Comm. (No. C 30) 3 (1982).

WRITTEN QUESTION NO 817/81
by Mr Schmid and Mrs Wieczorek-Zeul
to the Council of the European Communities
(24 August 1981)

Subject: Conflict between Israel and Lebanon

On 16 to 18 July 1981 Israeli fighter planes attacked not only units of the Palestinian Liberation Organization but also refugee camps and residential districts of Beirut. In our view this action is not merely a matter between Israel and Lebanon. It also concerns the Community, which maintains relations with both countries through cooperation agreements. It is currently under consideration in what form and for what amounts new financial protocols should be concluded with the Mediterranean countries of the Middle East. What steps will the Council take within the context of the preparatory discussions and ensuing negotiations to persuade Israel to cease such attacks on the civilian population?

ANSWER
(31 December 1981)

As regards the renewal of the Financial Protocols with those Mediterranean countries whose Protocol expires at the end of October 1981 (Maghreb, Mashreq, Israel), the negotiating directives approved by the Council at its meetings in July and September 1981 were the result of an overall assessment based in the main on consideration of the amounts which the Community is able to contribute and the needs and level of economic development of the countries in question in the context of the balanced overall approach on which the Community's Mediterranean policy rests.

As regards the political aspects arising out of the Middle East problem, the Community and the Ten are attempting in other contexts to make a contribution towards an overall peace settlement.

120. Security Council Resolution 498 Calling for a Cease-Fire in Lebanon, Israeli Withdrawal, and Renewing the U.N. Interim Force in Lebanon Mandate, December 18, 1981*

---

* S.C. Res. 498, 36 U.N. SCOR (2320th mtg.) at 6, U.N. Doc. S/INF/37 (1981).

The Security Council,

Recalling its resolutions 425 (1978), 426 (1978), 427 (1978), 434 (1978), 444 (1979), 450 (1979), 459 (1979), 467 (1980), 474 (1980), 483 (1980), 488 (1981) and 490 (1981),

Having studied the report of the Secretary-General on the United Nations Interim Force in Lebanon of 11 December 1981,[35] and taking note of the conclusions and recommendations expressed therein,

Taking note of the letter of the Permanent Representative of Lebanon to the Secretary-General dated 14 December 1981,[36]

Convinced that the deterioration of the present situation has serious consequences for peace and security in the Middle East,

1. *Reaffirms* its resolution 425 (1978), in which it

(a) *Calls* for strict respect for the territorial integrity, sovereignty and political independence of Lebanon within its internationally recognized boundaries;

(b) *Calls upon* Israel immediately to cease its military action against Lebanese territorial integrity and withdraw forthwith its forces from all Lebanese territory;

(c) *Decides*, in the light of the request of the Government of Lebanon, to establish immediately under its authority a United Nations interim force for southern Lebanon for the purpose of confirming the withdrawal of Israeli forces, restoring international peace and security and assisting the Government of Lebanon in ensuring the return of its effective authority in the area, the force to be composed of personnel drawn from Member States;

2. *Reaffirms* its past resolutions and particularly its repeated calls upon all concerned for the strict respect of the political independence, unity, sovereignty and territorial integrity of Lebanon;

3. *Reiterates* its determination to implement resolution 425 (1978) in the totality of the area of operation assigned to the United Nations Interim Force in Lebanon up to the internationally recognized boundaries so that the Force may fulfil its deployment and so that the United Nations Truce Supervision Organization may resume its normal functions, unhindered, under the provisions of the General Armistice Agreement of 1949;[37]

4. *Calls upon* all concerned to work towards the consolidation of the ceasefire called for by the Security Council in resolution 490 (1981) and reiterates its condemnation of all actions contrary to the provisions of the relevant resolutions;

5. *Calls attention* to the terms of reference and general guidelines of the

---

[35] *Official Records of the Security Council, Thirty-sixth Year, Supplement for October, November and December 1981*, document S/14789.

[36] *Ibid.*, document S/14792.

[37] *Ibid., Fourth Year, Special Supplement No. 4.*

Force, as stated in the report of the Secretary-General of 19 March 1978[20] confirmed by resolution 426 (1978), and particularly:

(a) That the Force "must be able to function as an integrated and efficient military unit";

(b) That the Force "must enjoy the freedom of movement and communication and other facilities that are necessary for the performance of its tasks";

(c) That the Force "will not use force except in self-defence";

(d) That "self-defence would include resistance to attempts by forceful means to prevent it from discharging its duties under the mandate of the Security Council";

6. *Supports* the efforts of the Government of Lebanon in the civilian and military fields of rehabilitation and reconstruction in southern Lebanon, and supports, in particular, the restoration of the authority of the Government of Lebanon in that region and deployment of substantial contingents of the Lebanese army in the area of operation of the Force;

7. *Requests* the Secretary-General to continue his discussions with the Government of Lebanon, with a view to establishing a joint phased programme of activities to be carried out during the present mandate of the Force, aimed at the total implementation of resolution 425 (1978), and to report periodically to the Security Council;

8. *Decides* to renew the mandate of the Force for six months, that is, until 19 June 1982;

9. *Commends* the efforts of the Secretary-Genreal and the performance of the Force, as well as the support of the troop-contributing Governments, and of all Member States who have assisted the Secretary-General, his staff and the Force in discharging their responsibilities under the mandate;

10. *Decides* to remain seized of the question and to review, within two months, the situation as a whole in the light of the letter of the Permanent Representative of Lebanon to the Secretary-General dated 14 December 1981.

Adopted at the 2320th meeting by 13 votes to none, with 2 abstentions (German Democratic Republic, Union of Soviet Socialist Republics).

---

[20] *Ibid. [Official Records of the Security Council], Thirty-third Year, Supplement for January, February and March 1978*, document S/12611.

121. Security Council Resolution 501 Reaffirming the
U.N. Interim Force in Lebanon and Increasing Its Size to
7,000 Troops, February 25, 1982*

---

* S.C. Res. 501, 37 U.N. SCOR (2332nd mtg.) at 2, U.N. Doc. S/INF/38 (1982).

The Security Council,

Recalling its resolutions 425 (1978), 426 (1978), 427 (1978), 434 (1978), 444 (1979), 450 (1979), 459 (1979), 467 (1980), 474 (1980), 483 (1980), 488 (1981), 490 (1981) and 498 (1981),

Acting in accordance with its resolution 498 (1981), and in particular with paragraph 10 of that resolution in which it decided to review the situation as a whole,

Having studied the special report of the Secretary-General on the United Nations Interim Force in Lebanon,[6]

Taking note of the letter of the Permanent Representative of Lebanon to the President of the Security Council,[7]

Having reivewed the situation as a whole in the light of the report of the Secretary-General and of the letter of the Permanent Representative of Lebanon,

Noting from the report of the Secretary-General that it is the strong recommendation of the Commander of the United Nations Interim Force in Lebanon, and also the wish of the Government of Lebanon, that the ceiling for troops of the Force should be increased, and that the Secretary-General fully supports the recommendation for an increase by one thousand of the troop strength of the Force,

1. *Reaffirms* its resolution 425 (1978) which reads:

"*The Security Council,*

Taking note of the letters from the Permanent Representative of Lebanon[8] and from the Permanent Representative of Israel,[9]

Having heard the statements of the Permanent Representatives of Lebanon and Israel,[10]

Gravely concerned at the deterioration of the situation in the Middle East and its consequences to the maintenance of international peace,

Convinced that the present situation impedes the achievement of a just peace in the Middle East,

1. *Calls* for strict respect for the territorial integrity, sovereignty and political independence of Lebanon within its internationally recognized boundaries;

2. *Calls upon* Israel immediately to cease its military action against Lebanese territorial integrity and withdraw forthwith its forces from all Lebanese territory;

3. *Decides*, in the light of the request of the Government of Lebanon, to

---

[6] *Official Records of the Security Council, Thirty-seventh Year, Supplement for January, February and March 1982*, document S/14869.

[7] *Ibid.*, document S/14875.

[8] *Ibid., Thirty-third Year, Supplement for January, February and March 1978*, documents S/12600 and S/12606.

[9] *Ibid.*, document S/12607.

[10] *Ibid., Thirty-third Year*, 2071st meeting.

establish immediately under its authority a United Nations interim force for southern Lebanon for the purpose of confirming the withdrawal of Israeli forces, restoring international peace and security and assisting the Government of Lebanon in ensuring the return of its effective authority in the area, the force to be composed of personnel drawn from Member States;

4. *Requests* the Secretary-General to report to the Council within twenty-four hours on the implementation of the present resolution."

2. *Decides* to approve the immediate increase in the strength of the United Nations Interim Force in Lebanon recommended by the Secretary-General in paragraph 6 of his report,[6] from six thousand to approximately seven thousand troops, to reinforce present operations as well as to make further deployment possible on the lines of resolution 425 (1978);

3. *Re-emphasizes* the terms of reference and general guidelines of the Force as stated in the report of the Secretary-General of 19 March 1978[11] confirmed by resolution 426 (1978), and particularly:

(*a*) That the Force "must be able to function as an integrated and efficient military unit";

(*b*) That the Force "must enjoy the freedom of movement and communication and other facilities that are necessary to the performance of its tasks";

(*c*) That the Force "will not use force except in self-defence";

(*d*) That "self-defence would include resistance to attempts by forceful means to prevent it from discharging its duties under the mandate of the Security Council";

4. *Calls upon* the Secretary-General to renew his efforts to reactivate the General Armistice Agreement between Lebanon and Israel of 23 March 1949[12] and, in particular, to convene an early meeting of the Mixed Armistice Commission;

5. *Requests* the Secretary-General to continue his discussions with the Government of Lebanon and the parties concerned with a view to submitting a report by 10 June 1982 on the necessary requirements for achieving further progress in a phased programme of activities with the Government of Lebanon;

6. *Decides* to remain seized of the question and invites the Secretary-General to report to the Security Council on the situation as a whole within two months.

Adopted at the 2332nd meeting by 13 votes to none, with 2 abstentions (Poland, Union of Soviet Socialist Republics).

[11]*Ibid., Thirty-third Year, Supplement for January, February and March 1978*, document S/12611.

[12] *Ibid., Fourth Year, Special Supplement No. 4.*

122. European Community Statement on the Israeli Bombing of Lebanon, April 25, 1982*

* 15 Bull. Eur. Comm. (No. 4) 48 (1982).

'The Ten strongly condemn all acts of violence, notably the bombing by the Israeli air force of various parts of Lebanon on 21 April 1982, which has caused further casualties among the civilian population.

This escalation is a further serious attack on the sovereignty and territorial integrity of Lebanon.

The Ten urgently call upon Israel and the other parties not to resort to force of arms and appeal to them not to return violence for violence, but to leave the way open for a peaceful settlement.'

B. Israeli Security and Palestinian Autonomy

123. Security Council Resolution 438 Renewing the U.N.

Emergency Force Mandate, October 23, 1978*

---

* S.C. Res. 438, 33 U.N. SCOR (2091st mtg.) at 7, U.N. Doc. S/INF/34 (1978).

The Security Council,

Recalling its resolutions 338 (1973) of 22 October, 340 (1973) of 25 October and 341 (1973) of 27 October 1973, 346 (1974) of 8 April and 362 (1974) of 23 October 1974, 368 (1975) of 17 April, 371 (1975) of 24 July and 378 (1975) of 23 October 1975, 396 (1976) of 22 October 1976 and 416 (1977) of 21 October 1977,

Having considered the report of the Secretary-General on the United Nations Emergency Force,[35]

Recalling the Secretary-General's view that the situation in the Middle East as a whole continues to be unstable and potentially dangerous and is likely to remain so unless and until a comprehensive settlement covering all aspects of the Middle East problem can be reached, and his hope that urgent efforts will be pursued by all concerned to tackle the problem in all its aspects, with a view both to maintaining quiet in the region and to arriving at a just and durable peace settlement, as called for by the Security Council in its resolution 338 (1973),

1. *Decides* to renew the mandate of the United Nations Emergency Force for a period of nine months, that is, until 24 July 1979;

2. *Requests* the Secretary-General to submit at the end of this period a report on the developments in the situation and on the steps taken to implement Security Council resolution 338 (1973);

3. *Expresses its confidence* that the Force will be maintained with maximum efficiency and economy.

Adopted at the 2091st meeting by 12 votes to none, with 2 abstentions (Czechoslovakia, Union of Soviet Socialist Republics).[36]

[35] *Ibid.* [*Official Records of the Security Council, Thirty-third Year, Supplement for October, November and December 1978*], document S/12897.

[36] One member (China) did not participate in the voting.

124. Security Council Resolution 441 Calling for the

Implementation of Security Council Resolution 338 (1973)

and Renewing the U.N. Disengagement Observer Force

Mandate, November 30, 1978*

---

* S.C. Res. 441, 33 U.N. SCOR (2101st mtg.) at 8, U.N. Doc. S/INF/34 (1978). *See also* subsequent resolutions, S.C. Res. 449, 34 U.N. SCOR (2154th mtg.) at 6, U.N. Doc. S/INF/35 (1979), S.C. Res. 456, 34 U.N. SCOR (2174th mtg.) at 11, U.N. Doc. S/INF/35 (1979), S.C. Res. 470, 35 U.N. SCOR (2224th mtg.) at 10, U.N. Doc. S/INF/36 (1980), S.C. Res. 481, 35 U.N. SCOR (2256th mtg.) at 15, U.N. Doc. S/INF/36 (1980), S.C. Res. 485, 36 U.N. SCOR (2278th mtg.) at 3, U.N. Doc. S/INF/37 (1981), S.C. Res. 493, 36 U.N. SCOR (2311th mtg.) at 5, U.N. Doc. S/INF/37 (1981), and S.C. Res. 506, 37 U.N. SCOR (2369th mtg.) at 5, U.N. Doc. S/INF/38 (1982).

The Security Council,

Having considered the report of the Secretary-General on the United Nations Disengagement Observer Force,[38]

Decides:

(*a*) To call upon the parties concerned to implement immediately Security Council resolution 338 (1973) of 22 October 1973;

(*b*) To renew the mandate of the United Nations Disengagement Observer Force for another period of six months, that is, until 31 May 1979;

(*c*) To request the Secretary-General to submit at the end of this period a report on the developments in the situation and the measures taken to implement resolution 338 (1973).

Adopted at the 2101st meeting by 14 votes to none.[39]

[38] *Ibid.* [*Official Records of the Security Council, Thirty-third Year, Supplement for October, November and December 1978*], document S/12934.

[39] One member (China) did not participate in the voting.

125. General Assembly Resolution 33/28 on the Question of Palestine, December 7, 1978*

* G.A. Res. 28, 33 U.N. GAOR Supp. (No. 45) at 16, U.N. Doc. A/33/45 (1978).

A

The General Assembly,

Recalling and reaffirming its resolutions 3236 (XXIX) of 22 November 1974, 3375 (XXX) and 3376 (XXX) of 10 November 1975, 31/20 of 24 November 1976 and 32/40 A and B of 2 December 1977,

Having considered the report of the Committee on the Exercise of the Inalienable Rights of the Palestinian People,[19]

Having heard the statement of the Palestine Liberation Organization, the representative of the Palestinian people,[20]

1. *Expresses its grave concern* that no just solution to the problem of Palestine has been achieved and that this problem therefore continues to aggravate the Middle East conflict, of which it is the core, and to endanger international peace and security;

2. *Reaffirms* that a just and lasting peace in the Middle East cannot be established without the achievement, *inter alia*, of a just solution of the problem of Palestine on the basis of the attainment of the inalienable rights of the Palestinian people, including the right of return and the right to national independence and sovereignty in Palestine, in accordance with the Charter of the United Nations;

3. *Calls once more* for the invitation of the Palestine Liberation Organization, the representative of the Palestinian people, to participate, on the basis of General Assembly resolution 3236 (XXIX), in all efforts, deliberations and conferences on the Middle East which are held under the auspices of the United Nations, on an equal footing with other parties;

4. *Declares* that the validity of agreements purporting to solve the problem of Palestine requires that they be within the framework of the United Nations and its Charter and its resolutions on the basis of the full attainment and exercise of the inalienable rights of the Palestinian people, including the right of return and the right to national independence and sovereignty in Palestine, and with the participation of the Palestine Liberation Organization;

5. *Endorses* the recommendations of the Committee on the Exercise of the Inalienable Rights of the Palestinian People as contained in paragraphs 55 to 58 of its report;[18]

6. *Expresses its regret and concern* that the recommendations of the Committee on the Exercise of the Inalienable Rights of the Palestinian People endorsed by the General Assembly in its resolutions 31/20 and 32/40 A have not been implemented;

7. *Notes with regret* that the Security Council has not taken the action it was

[18] *Official Records of the General Assembly, Thirty-third Session, Plenary Meetings,* 10th meeting, paras. 2-63.

[19] *Ibid., Thirty-third Session, Supplement No. 35* (A/33/35 and Corr.1).

[20] *Ibid., Thirty-third Session, Plenary Meetings,* 59th meeting, paras. 73-112.

urged to take by the General Assembly in paragraph 4 of its resolution 32/ 40 A;

8. *Once again urges* the Security Council to consider and take as soon as possible a decision on the recommendations endorsed by the General Assembly in its resolutions 31/20 and 32/40 A and in the present resolution;

9. *Authorizes and requests* the Committee on the Exercise of the Inalienable Rights of the Palestinian People, in the event that the Security Council fails to consider or to take a decision on those recommendations by 1 June 1979, to consider that situation and to make the suggestions it deems appropriate;

10. *Decides* to include the item entitled "Question of Palestine" in the provisional agenda of its thirty-fourth session.

73rd plenary meeting
7 December 1978

B

The General Assembly,

Recalling its resolutions 3376 (XXX) of 10 November 1975, 31/20 of 24 November 1976 and 32/40 A and B of 2 December 1977,

Having considered the report of the Committee on the Exercise of the Inalienable Rights of the Palestinian People,[21]

1. *Expresses its appreciation* to the Committee on the Exercise of the Inalienable Rights of the Palestinian People for its efforts in performing the tasks assigned to it by the General Assembly;

2. *Requests* the Committee on the Exercise of the Inalienable Rights of the Palestinian People to keep the situation relating to the question of Palestine under review and to report and make suggestions to the General Assembly or to the Security Council, as may be appropriate;

3. *Authorizes* the Committee on the Exercise of the Inalienable Rights of the Palestinian People to continue to exert all efforts to promote the implementation of its recommendations, to send delegations or representatives to international conferences where such representation would be considered by it to be appropriate, and to report thereon to the General Assembly at its thirty-fourth session and thereafter;

4. *Requests* the United Nations Conciliation Commission for Palestine, established under General Assembly resolution 194 (III) of 11 December 1948, to co-operate fully with the Committee on the Exercise of the Inalienable Rights of the Palestinian People and to make available to the Committee, at its request, the relevant information and documentation which the Commission has at its disposal;

5. *Decides* to circulate the report of the Committee on the Exercise of the Inalienable Rights of the Palestinian People to all the competent bodies of the United Nations and urges them to take necessary action, as appropriate, in accordance with the Committee's programme of implementation;

---

[21] *Ibid., Thirty-third Session, Supplement No. 35* (A/33/35 and Corr.1/Rev.1).

6. *Requests* the Secretary-General to continue to provide the Committee on the Exercise of the Inalienable Rights of the Palestinian People with all the necessary facilities for the performance of its tasks, including summary records of its meetings.

73rd plenary meeting
7 December 1978

C

The General Assembly,

Recalling its resolution 32/40 B of 2 December 1977,

Having considered the report of the Committee on the Exercise of the Inalienable Rights of the Palestinian People,[22]

Noting, in particular, the information contained in paragraphs 47 to 54 of that report,

1. *Takes note* of the establishment, within the Secretariat of the United Nations, of a Special Unit on Palestinian Rights in accordance with paragraph 1 of General Assembly resolution 32/40 B;

2. *Requests* the Secretary-General to ensure that the Special Unit on Palestinian Rights continues to discharge the tasks assigned to it in paragraph 1 of resolution 32/40 B in consultation with the Committee on the Exercise of the Inalienable Rights of the Palestinian People and under its guidance;

3. *Further requests* the Secretary-General to consider, in consultation with the Committee on the Exercise of the Inalienable Rights of the Palestinian People, the strengthening and the possible reorganization and renaming of the Special Unit on Palestinian Rights;

4. *Also requests* the Secretary-General to ensure the full co-operation of the Department of Public Information and other units of the Secretariat in enabling the Special Unit on Palestinian Rights to perform its tasks;

5. *Invites* all Governments and organizations to lend their co-operation to the Committee on the Exercise of the Inalienable Rights of the Palestinian People and the Special Unit on Palestinian Rights in the performance of their tasks.

73rd plenary meeting
7 December 1978

[22] *Ibid.*

126. General Assembly Resolution 33/29 on the Situation in the Middle East, December 7, 1978*

* G.A. Res. 29, 33 U.N. GAOR Supp. (No. 45) at 18, U.N. Doc. A/33/45 (1978).

The General Assembly,

Having discussed the item entitled "The situation in the Middle East",

Recalling its previous resolutions on the subject, in particular resolutions 3414 (XXX) of 5 December 1975, 31/61 of 9 December 1976, 32/20 of 25 November 1977 and 33/28 of 7 December 1978,

Taking into account the decisions of the Conference of Ministers for Foreign Affairs of Non-Aligned Countries, held at Belgrade from 25 to 30 July 1978, concerning the situation in the Middle East and the question of Palestine,[23]

Deeply concerned that the Arab territories occupied since 1967 have continued, for more than eleven years, to be under illegal Israeli occupation and that the Palestinian people, after three decades, is still deprived of the exercise of its inalienable national rights,

Reaffirming that the acquisition of territory by force is inadmissible and that all territories thus occupied must be returned,

Reaffirming also the urgent necessity of the establishment of a just and lasting peace in the region, based on full respect for the principles of the Charter of the United Nations as well as for its resolutions concerning the problem of the Middle East including the question of Palestine,

Convinced that the early convening of the Peace Conference on the Middle East with the participation of all parties concerned, including the Palestine Liberation Organization, in accordance with relevant resolutions of the General Assembly, is essential for the realization of a just and lasting settlement in the region,

1. *Condemns* Israel's continued occupation of Palestinian and other Arab territories, in violation of the Charter of the United Nations, the principles of international law and repeated resolutions of the United Nations;

2. *Declares* that peace is indivisible and that a just and lasting settlement of the Middle East problem must be based on a comprehensive solution, under the auspices of the United Nations, which takes into account all aspects of the Arab-Israeli conflict, in particular the attainment by the Palestinian people of all its inalienable national rights and the Israeli withdrawal from all the occupied Palestinian and other Arab territories;

3. *Reaffirms* that until Israel withdraws from all occupied Palestinian and other Arab territories, and until the Palestinian people attains and exercises its inalienable national rights, a comprehensive, just and lasting peace in the Middle East, in which all countries and peoples in the region live in peace and security within recognized and secure boundaries, will not be achieved;

4. *Calls anew* for the early convening of the Peace Conference on the Middle East, under the auspices of the United Nations and the co-chairmanship of the Union of Soviet Socialist Republics and the United States of America, with the participation on an equal footing of all parties concerned, including

[23] See A/33/206.

the Palestine Liberation Organization in accordance with General Assembly resolution 3375 (XXX) of 10 November 1975;

5. *Urges* the parties to the conflict and all other interested parties to work towards the achievement of a comprehensive settlement covering all aspects of the problems and worked out with the participation of all parties concerned within the framework of the United Nations;

6. *Requests* the Security Council, in the exercise of its responsibilities under the Charter, to take all necessary measures in order to ensure the implementation of relevant resolutions of the United Nations, including General Assembly resolution 33/28 and the present resolution, and to facilitate the achievement of such a comprehensive settlement aiming at the establishment of a just and lasting peace in the region;

7. *Requests* the Secretary-General to follow up the implementation of the present resolution and to inform all concerned, including the Co-Chairmen of the Peace Conference on the Middle East;

8. *Also requests* the Secretary-General to report to the Security Council periodically on the development of the situation and to submit to the General Assembly at its thirty-fourth session a comprehensive report covering, in all their aspects, the developments in the Middle East.

73rd plenary meeting
7 December 1978

127. Final Communiqué of the Fourth Session of the

General Committee of the Euro-Arab Dialogue, Damascus,

December 9–11, 1978*

* 11 Bull. Eur. Comm. (No. 12) 19 (1978).

I

'1. The General Committee of the Euro-Arab Dialogue held its Fourth Session from 9 to 11 December 1978 in Damascus. The meeting was opened by H.E. Sayed Abdul Halim Khaddam, Minister of Foreign Affairs and Vice Prime-Minister of Syria who delivered a speech.

2. The two parties expressed their profound gratitude for the warm welcome given by the Syrian Government and for its efforts which have ensured the perfect organization of the meeting.

3. The two sides pursued the exchange of views on all the aspects of Euro-Arab cooperation—political, economic, social and cultural—which had taken place during past meetings of the General Committee at Luxemburg in May 1976, at Tunis in February 1977 and at Brussels, in October 1977.

4. They reviewed the situation in the Middle East and its developments since the last meeting of the General Committee held in Brussels from 26 to 28 October 1977. Both sides agreed that the continued Arab-Israeli conflict constitutes a threat to the security and peace in the Middle East and to international peace and security. In this context both sides reaffirmed their conviction that the security of Europe is linked to the security of the Mediterranean region and the Arab region.

5. Both sides recalled their views that the Palestinian question is central to the conflict in the area and that a peaceful, comprehensive and just settlement of the conflict including obviously a solution to the Palestinian problem was not only a matter of vital importance to the Arabs but also of great concern to the Nine in view of the close relations existing between Europe and the Middle East.

6. The European side recalled that the Nine set out on many occasions in the past, for example, in their statements of 6 November 1973, 28 September 1976 and 7 December 1976, their view that a peace settlement should be based on Security Council Resolutions 242 and 338 and on:

- the inadmissibility of the acquisition of territory by force;
- the need for Israel to end the territorial occupation which it has maintained since the conflict in 1967;
- respect for the sovereignty, territorial integrity and independence of every State in the area and their right to live in peace within secure and recognized boundaries;
- recognition that in the establishment of a just and lasting peace account must be taken of the legitimate rights of the Palestinians.

It remains their firm view that all these aspects must be taken as a whole. Such a settlement must also take into account the need for a homeland for the Palestinian people.

In this context, the European side emphasized that the representatives of the parties to the conflict, including the Palestinian people, must participate in the negotiations in an appropriate manner to be worked out in consultation between all the parties concerned.

7. The Arab side reaffirmed that the continued occupation of territories by Israel constitutes a threat to peace and security in the Middle East and to international peace and security. It set forth the Arab position as regards the solution to the Palestine question. It emphasized that such a solution must enable the people of Palestine to establish their independent State on their territory and exercise the right to return to their homeland. The Arab side noted the necessity of not putting any constraints on the rights of the representatives of the Palestinian people to speak in their name. With respect to cooperation between the two sides in order to achieve a comprehensive settlement, the Arab side felt that it was time for the European Community to recognize the Palestine Liberation Organization as the legitimate representative of the Palestinian people, which was already recognized by all the Arab States, most of the other nations of the world, and indeed by the United Nations.

8. The Arab side expressed the hope to receive a positive response to this demand in the forthcoming meeting of the General Committee.

9. The European side took careful note of the elements put forward by the Arab side at the General Committee and undertook to bring them to the attention of their Governments.

10. The Arab side referred to and condemned measures and actions taken by Israel in the occupied territories since 1967, such as the establishment of settlements in addition to changing their legal status and demographic structure including Jerusalem, as well as the coercive and repressive acts perpetrated by Israel against the Arab inhabitants in the occupied territories in flagrant violation of the universal declaration of human rights. The two sides recalled the General Assembly Resolution under agenda item No 126 of October 27, 1977. This resolution, *inter alia:*

> —determines that measures and actions taken by Israel in the Palestinian and other Arab territories occupied since 1967 have no legal validity and constitute a serious obstruction of efforts aimed at achieving a just and lasting peace in the Middle East;
>
> · strongly deplores the persistence of Israel in carrying out such measures, in particular the establishment of settlements in the occupied Arab territories;
>
> · calls upon Israel to comply strictly with its international obligations in accordance with the principles of international law and the provisions of the Geneva Convention relative to the protection of Civilian Persons in Time of War, of 12 August 1949;
>
> · calls once more upon the Government of Israel as the occupying Power to desist forthwith from taking any action which would result in changing the legal status, geographical nature or demographic composition of the Arab territories occupied since 1967, including Jerusalem.

11. The two sides stressed the need to restore peace in Lebanon and expressed the hope that every Lebanese would grant his steadfast support to President Sarkis, the symbol of legitimacy in Lebanon and its safeguard.

The two sides considered that national unity amongst the Lebanese was a pressing need in order to secure the independence of Lebanon, its sovereignty and territorial integrity, to which the two sides pledged support.

The Arab side stressed its refusal to settle Palestinians in Lebanon, an idea rejected by the Lebanese and Palestinians and by all the Arabs. The European side confirmed that such an idea had never been advanced by the Nine.

The two sides expressed their hope that Euro-Arab Dialogue might offer a framework for future projects in Lebanon.

12. The Arab side favoured a meeting as soon as feasible of Arab Foreign Ministers with the Foreign Ministers of the Nine.

13. Both sides expressed the intention to ensure that the forthcoming General Committee should be convened within the due period in a European capital.

II

A. The General Committee reviewed the work carried out by the various Working Committees and specialized groups since its last meeting in Brussels. It expressed its thanks to the Co-chairmen of these Committees and groups for the reports they presented and which enabled the General Committee to assess the progress that has been made in a number of fields of cooperation. The General Committee adopted these Joint Reports.

The General Committee recalled the Joint Memorandum issued in Cairo on 14 June 1975, establishing the special relationship between the two groups as a product of a joint political will that emerged at the highest level. It recalled furthermore the wish stated in the abovementioned Joint Memorandum to rediscover, to renew and to invigorate the existing links between these two neighbouring regions, the intention to establish the bases for future cooperation in a wide area of activities, to the benefit of both sides.

The General Committee recalled the fact that a growing economy in both the European and the Arab region is in the common interest of both sides and essential to a successful, dynamic and lasting cooperation which must be based on the equality of the partners, on their mutual interest, thus completing already existing cooperation links.

The General Committee recognized the mutual advantages in the increased cooperation of each side in the economy of the other. It also stressed the important role that the private sector has in the context of the Dialogue. It invited the competent Working Committees to study ways and means for a closer integration of this sector into the Euro-Arab Dialogue.

The General Committee urged the Working Committees to speed up all the work necessary to the implementation of studies and other activities decided upon. This should be done in conformity with the Code of Financial Procedures, and respecting the deadlines set out therein.

The General Committee was of the opinion that all Working Committees should in their future work, give particular emphasis to the field of vocational training, this being of the utmost importance to the development of the Arab countries.

The General Committee furthermore invited the Working Committees to concentrate their efforts on projects of a regional character or of global interest for the Arab countries.

B. The General Committee examined and approved the studies and activities listed in annex I which were proposed by the Working Committees. The Finance Group has examined the financial aspects of these studies and activities and expressed a favourable opinion. The General Committee fixed the contributions of both sides to finance these studies and activities. The execution of these studies and activities will be realized under the provisions of the Financial Code of Procedure.

The Arab side re-iterated its position expressed during the third meeting of the General Committee in Brussels that the European side should participate in the financing of studies agreed upon by not less than one third of the total costs thereof, while the European participation in the cost of seminars and other activities should be not less than 50%.

Regarding the project for the Arab Polytechnic Institute the two co-presidencies of the Dialogue are empowered to finalize this decision within the ceiling approved for the financing of the project in the light of additional information which will become available from the conclusions of the definition study.

As suggested by the Finance Group, the General Committee recommended that all Working Committees and specialized groups should in future include a contingency reserve of 15% of the total amount in their estimates of costs for studies and other activities. This reserve is considered necessary to take account of fluctuation in exchange rates, inflation and other factors which may affect costs.

C. Further, the General Committee devoted particular attention to the following subjects on which it took relevant decisions as follows:

1. Transfer of Technology

Based on the stand recently taken by the European side, as well as the stand taken by the Arab side, the General Committee approved the establishment of a Euro-Arab Centre for the Transfer of Technology. The General Committee also approved the undertaking of a study by four experts (two experts from each side, terms of reference to be defined by the *ad hoc* Group) on the setting up of the Euro-Arab Centre for the Transfer of Technology in the light of studies carried out within the framework of the Euro-Arab Dialogue and of other studies conducted in this field.

The Committee empowered the Co-chairmen of the *ad hoc* Group, the General Secretariat of the League of Arab States and the Commission of the European Communities, to take the necessary measures in order to undertake the above mentioned study (after each side completes its own procedures). This study will be referred to the *ad hoc* Group on the Transfer of Technology, which will prepare a report thereon for submission to the General Committee at its forthcoming meeting.[1]

2. *Industrialization*

The General Committee expressed its satisfaction with the work accomplished by the Working Committee on Industrialization and its five specialized groups.

The General Committee expressed its hope that the studies approved in the fields of oil-refining and petro-chemical industries would enable the specialized group to continue its work.

The General Committee acknowledged that the specialized group on standardization had already approched [*sic*] a phase of practical implementation. The adopted studies on training and information in the field of standardization and the resulting improvement in standardization facilities in interested Arab countries is a substantial step in the direction of completing the agreed programme of work set up at the beginning of the cooperation in this field.

The General Committee encouraged the specialized group on General Conditions of Contracts to finalize its work on applicable law and arbitration as well as on technical service contracts and to submit the jointly agreed General Conditions of Contracts and/or comments thereon. Thereafter it will take up the "Standard Contract for Mechanical and Electronical Engineering Construction".

3. *Basic Infrastructure*

The General Committee recorded with satisfaction the progress made in the preparation of the four studies concerning port developments on the Syrian and Iraqi coasts, vocational training for port personnel and the harmonization of statistics.

It expressed the wish that the invitations to tender drawn up by the specialized groups should be issued soon.

Noting the in-depth exchanges of views between the European and Arab experts occasioned by the preparation of the symposium on new towns, the General Committee urged the Working Committee on Basic Infrastructure to bring about that meeting in the course of 1979, stressing that this project should not neglect the necessary cultural considerations.

The General Committee also invited the Working Committee to give attention to studies and operations of joint interest for the Arab countries in

---

[1] The Co-chairmen agreed to hold the plenary meeting of the *ad hoc* Group not later than the end of January 1979, preferably in the last week of January 1979. The venue will be fixed through the normal procedures.

the other basic infrastructure fields defined at the Rome meeting in June 1975, and stressed the importance of transport to link the Arab world and Europe more closely.

4. Agriculture and Rural Development

The General Committee expressed its satisfaction with the work accomplished by the specialized group on the Applied Research Programme on Water Resources Development and Use in Rural Areas. It instructed the Working Committee on Agriculture and Rural Development to give the necessary consideration to the report elaborated by the specialized group and to decide on measures for further action. Because of the considerable importance of this programme, the General Committee expressed the hope that more progress will be achieved in this field before the next session of the General Committee.

The General Committee welcomed the initiative taken by the Working Committee to set up two sub-groups of experts for agricultural mechanization and agro-industries. It instructed the Working Committee to examine as soon as possible the proposals made by these two sub-groups and to decide how their work can be furthered.

In accordance with the policy pursued by the Arab Ministers of Agriculture, the General Committee invited the Working Committee to identify new areas of cooperation which are likely to contribute towards increasing self-sufficiency in food production and security in the Arab region, and to promote economic integration in the field of agriculture.

5. Financial Cooperation

The General Committee welcomed the encouraging progress made by the Financial Cooperation working Committee on a multilateral investment promotion and protection convention, and adopted the principles reached by the said Working Committee as a basis for the contents of a convention. The General Committee instructed the sub-group for the protection of investment to meet at experts level in order to carry forward the drafting of treaty language and encouraged the two Co-chairmen to press forward these negotiations to a satisfactory conclusion as soon as possible.

6. Commercial Cooperation

Having taken note of the joint report of the Co-chairmen of the Working Committee on Commercial Co-operation, the General Committee expressed the wish that the Arab and European Delegations should intensify their efforts to transfer into reality in the trade field the special relationship adopted as one of the basic objectives of the Dialogue.

Recalling the previous discussions within the Working Committee, the

General Committee considered that it is appropriate and urgent to examine, from every aspect, the establishment of special institutional links between the two parties in the field of trade cooperation, particularly in the form of a convention.

The objective is to strengthen and diversify trade between the two parties taking into account their respective development levels.

The General Committee reaffirmed, moreover, the importance it attaches to the establishment of a Euro-Arab Centre for Commercial Cooperation within the framework of the Dialogue.

7. Scientific and Technological Cooperation

The General Committee confirmed the importance that it attaches to scientific and technological cooperation, the development of which will promote fruitful and enduring contacts between scientists and instructors in both regions.

It considered that the three projects adopted following proposals by the competent working committee (Arab polytechnic institute, Arab institute for water desalination and resources, survey of marine science in the Arab countries) meet this objective, particularly in respect of their regional character.

The General Committee looks forward to similar involvement and endeavours by the Working Committee on Scientific and Technological cooperation in areas of scientific activity which open promising opportunities for cooperation.

8. Labour and Social Affairs

The General Committee examined the draft Joint Declaration on the principles governing the living and working conditions of foreign workers and their families who are nationals of the States participating in the Dialogue and are resident in the territory of these States, as presented by the Working Committee on Cultural, Social and Labour questions.

The General Committee adopted the draft Declaration and stressed:

(a) that it is important to promote the positive impact of the Declaration on the living and working conditions of these workers;

(b) that it is also important, as stated in the final paragraph of the Declaration, to seek in the future, in the bilateral and multilateral contexts, appropriate solutions to those problems which, in the view of the States concerned, still remained to be solved.

The Arab side repeated the preoccupations which it put forward at the third meeting of the General Committee in Brussels concerning the security and stability of employment of the Arab workers in Europe in the present employment situation.

The General Committee requested the Working Committee to continue the discussion with a view to achieving as rapidly as possible results satisfactory to both sides concerning the organization of a colloquium on the problems of vocational training for Arab migrant workers.

It recommended that the Working Committee implement as soon as possible the Euro-Arab project concerning the creation and operation of the Arab Centre for Vocational Training.

The General Committee requested the Working Committee to continue its examination of a number of topics in the social sector, notably the following:
– labour statistics,
– the training of the handicapped,
– social security.

9. Cultural Cooperation

The General Committee noted with satisfaction the results achieved in the cultural field as described in the Joint Report presented in Damascus by the two Co-chairmen and instructed the Working Committee to intensify its efforts in the following areas:

(a) to make the Hamburg Symposium on the relations between the two civilizations (Hamburg, 17 to 21 September 1979) an event of great significance in the Euro-Arab Dialogue and to involve both sides in publicizing this initiative, which will include a large programme of cultural events proposed by the Specialized Group amongst interested circles in the two regions;

(b) to study the need for organizing in the future similar cultural events in other countries of the two regions in order to highlight different aspects of their cultural links;

(c) to carry out the pilot project of the Catalogue of cultural and scientific institutions;

(d) to publish as quickly as possible the proceedings of the Euro-Arab Seminar in Venice (March 1977) aimed at promoting the diffusion in Europe of the knowledge of Arabic language and civilization;

(e) to consider the special importance of cooperation in the youth field and to implement the Euro-Arab Seminar on the role of sports and physical education in youth welfare, planned for 1979;

(f) to set up a specialized group of experts to examine the history text books used in the two regions;

(g) to continue discussions on cooperation in the field of information, on the basis of the working papers and the offers of scholarships already exchanged, with a view to achieving concrete results;

(h) to go ahead with the preparation of the meeting of Rectors/Vice-Chancellors of Universities of the two regions, of a seminar for librarians and a seminar on the problems of teaching European languages for academic and higher education purposes.'

128. General Assembly Resolution 33/113 on the Report of the Special Committee to Investigate Israeli Practices Affecting the Human Rights of the Population of the Occupied Territories, December 18, 1978*

* G.A. Res. 113, 33 U.N. GAOR Supp. (No. 45) at 70, U.N. Doc. A/33/45 (1978). *See also* subsequent resolution, G.A. Res. 90, 34 U.N. GAOR Supp. (No. 46) at 80, U.N. Doc. A/34/46 (1979).

A

The General Assembly,

Recalling its resolutions 3092 A (XXVIII) of 7 December 1973, 3240 B (XXIX) of 29 November 1974, 3525 B (XXX) of 15 December 1975, 31/106 B of 16 December 1976 and 32/91 A of 13 December 1977,

Considering that the promotion of respect for the obligations arising from the Charter of the United Nations and other instruments and rules of international law is among the basic purposes and principles of the United Nations,

Bearing in mind the provisions of the Geneva Convention relative to the Protection of Civilian Persons in Time of War, of 12 August 1949,[19]

Noting that Israel and those Arab States whose territories have been occupied by Israel since June 1967 are parties to that Convention,

Taking into account that States parties to that Convention undertake, in accordance with article 1 thereof, not only to respect but also to ensure respect for the Convention in all circumstances,

1. *Reaffirms* that the Geneva Convention relative to the Protection of Civilian Persons in Time of War, of 12 August 1949, is applicable to all the Arab territories occupied by Israel since 1967, including Jerusalem;

2. *Strongly deplores* the failure of Israel to acknowledge the applicability of that Convention to the territories it has occupied since 1967;

3. *Calls again upon* Israel to acknowledge and to comply with the provisions of that Convention in all the Arab territories it has occupied since 1967, including Jerusalem;

4. *Urges once more* all States parties to that Convention to exert all efforts in order to ensure respect for and compliance with the provisions thereof in all the Arab territories occupied by Israel since 1967, including Jerusalem.

87th plenary meeting
18 December 1978

B

The General Assembly,

Recalling its resolution 32/5 of 28 October 1977,

Expressing grave anxiety and concern over the present serious situation in the occupied Arab territories as a result of the continued Israeli occupation and the measures and actions taken by the Government of Israel, as the occupying Power, and designed to change the legal status, geographical nature and demographic composition of those territories,

Considering that the Geneva Convention relative to the Protection of Civil-

---

[19] United Nations, *Treaty Series*, vol. 75, No. 973, p. 287.

ian Persons in Time of War, of 12 August 1949,[20] is applicable to all the Arab territories occupied since 5 June 1967,

1. *Determines* that all such measures and actions taken by Israel in the Palestinian and other Arab territories occupied since 1967 have no legal validity and constitute a serious obstruction of efforts aimed at achieving a just and lasting peace in the Middle East;

2. *Strongly deplores* the persistence of Israel in carrying out such measures, in particular the establishment of settlements in the Palestinian and other occupied Arab territories;

3. *Calls upon* Israel to comply strictly with its international obligations in accordance with the principles of international law and the provisions of the Geneva Convention relative to the Protection of Civilian Persons in Time of War, of 12 August 1949;

4. *Calls once more upon* the Government of Israel, as the occupying Power, to desist forthwith from taking any action which would result in changing the legal status, geographical nature or demographic composition of the Arab territories occupied since 1967, including Jerusalem;

5. *Urges* all States parties to the Geneva Convention relative to the Protection of Civilian Persons in Time of War to respect and to exert all efforts in order to ensure respect for and compliance with its provisions in all the Arab territories occupied by Israel since 1967, including Jerusalem.

87th plenary meeting
18 December 1978

C

The General Assembly,

Guided by the purposes and principles of the Charter of the United Nations as well as the principles and provisions of the Universal Declaration of Human Rights,

Bearing in mind the provisions of the Geneva Convention relative to the Protection of Civilian Persons in Time of War, of 12 August 1949,[21] as well as of other relevant conventions and regulations,

Recalling all its resolutions on the subject, in particular resolutions 32/91 B and C of 13 December 1977, as well as those adopted by the Security Council, the Commission on Human Rights and other United Nations organs concerned and by the specialized agencies,

Having considered the report of the Special Committee to Investigate Israeli Practices Affecting the Human Rights of the Population of the Occupied Territories,[22] which contains, *inter alia*, public statements made by leaders of the Government of Israel,

1. *Commends* the Special Committee to Investigate Israeli Practices Affect-

[20] *Ibid.*
[21] *Ibid.*
[22] A/33/356.

ing the Human Rights of the Population of the Occupied Territories for its efforts in performing the tasks assigned to it by the General Assembly and for it thoroughness and impartiality;

2. *Deplores* the continued refusal by Israel to allow the Special Committee access to the occupied territories;

3. *Calls again upon* Israel to allow the Special Committee access to the occupied territories;

4. *Deplores* the continued and persistent violation by Israel of the Geneva Convention relative to the Protection of Civilian Persons in Time of War, of 12 August 1949, and other applicable international instruments, and condemns in particular those violations which that Convention designates as "grave breaches" thereof;

5. *Condemns* the following Israeli policies and practices:

(*a*) Annexation of parts of the occupied territories;

(*b*) Establishment of new Israeli settlements and expansion of the existing settlements on private and public Arab lands, and transfer of an alien population thereto;

(*c*) Evacuation, deportation, expulsion, displacement and transfer of Arab inhabitants of the occupied territories and denial of their right to return;

(*d*) Confiscation and expropriation of private and public Arab property in the occupied territories and all other transactions for the acquisition of land involving the Israeli authorities, institutions or nationals on the one hand, and the inhabitants or institutions of the occupied territories on the other;

(*e*) Destruction and demolition of Arab houses;

(*f*) Mass arrests, administrative detention and ill-treatment of the Arab population;

(*g*) Ill-treatment and torture of persons under detention;

(*h*) Pillaging of archaeological and cultural property;

(*i*) Interference with religious freedoms and practices as well as family rights and customs;

(*j*) Illegal exploitation of the natural wealth, resources and population of the occupied territories;

6. *Reaffirms* that all measures taken by Israel to change the physical character, demographic composition, institutional structure or status of the occupied territories, or any part thereof, including Jerusalem, are null and void, and that Israel's policy of settling parts of its population and new immigrants in the occupied territories constitutes a flagrant violation of the Geneva Convention relative to the Protection of Civilian Persons in Time of War and of the relevant United Nations resolutions;

7. *Demands* that Israel desist forthwith from the policies and practices referred to in paragraphs 5 and 6 of the present resolution;

8. *Reiterates* its call upon all States, in particular those States parties to the Geneva Convention relative to the Protection of Civilian Persons in Time of War, in accordance with article 1 of that Convention, and upon international organizations and the specialized agencies not to recognize any

changes carried out by Israel in the occupied territories and to avoid actions, including those in the field of aid, which might be used by Israel in its pursuit of the policies of annexation and colonization or any of the other policies and practices referred to in the present resolution;

9. *Requests* the Special Committee, pending the early termination of the Israeli occupation, to continue to investigate Israeli policies and practices in the Arab territories occupied by Israel since 1967, to consult, as appropriate, with the International Committee of the Red Cross in order to ensure the safeguarding of the welfare and human rights of the population of the occupied territories and to report to the Secretary-General as soon as possible and whenever the need arises thereafter;

10. *Requests* the Special Committee to continue to investigate the treatment of civilians in detention in the Arab territories occupied by Israel since 1967;

11. *Requests* the Secretary-General:

(*a*) To render all necessary facilities to the Special Committee, including those required for its visits to the occupied territories, with a view to investigating Israeli policies and practices referred to in the present resolution;

(*b*) To continue to make available additional staff as may be necessary to assist the Special Committee in the performance of its tasks;

(*c*) To ensure the widest circulation of the reports of the Special Committee, and of information regarding its activities and findings, by all means available through the Department of Public Information of the Secretariat and, where necessary, to reprint those reports of the Special Committee which are no longer available;

(*d*) To report to the General Assembly at its thirty-fourth session on the tasks entrusted to him in the present paragraph;

12. *Decides* to include in the provisional agenda of its thirty-fourth session the item entitled "Report of the Special Committee to Investigate Israeli Practices Affecting the Human Rights of the Population of the Occupied Territories".

87th plenary meeting
18 December 1978

129. General Assembly Resolution 33/147 on Assistance to the Palestinian People, December 20, 1978*

* G.A. Res. 147, 33 U.N. GAOR Supp. (No. 45) at 112, U.N. Doc. A/33/45 (1978). *See also* subsequent resolution, G.A. Res. 133, 34 U.N. GAOR Supp. (No. 46) at 124, U.N. Doc. A/34/46 (1979).

The General Assembly,

Recalling its resolutions 3236 (XXIX) and 3237 (XXIX) of 22 November 1974,

Recalling also Economic and Social Council resolutions 1978 (LIX) of 31 July 1975, 2026 (LXI) of 4 August 1976 and 2100 (LXIII) of 3 August 1977,

Taking into consideration the reports of the Secretary-General on assistance to the Palestinian people,[119]

Taking note of the report of the Governing Council of the United Nations Development Programme on its twenty-fifth session[120] and of the response of the Administrator of the Programme,[121]

1. *Endorses* the resolutions of the Economic and Social Council concerning assistance to the Palestinian people;

2. *Calls upon* the United Nations Development Programme, in consultation with the specialized agencies and other organizations within the United Nations system, to intensify its efforts, in co-ordination with the Economic Commission for Western Asia, to implement the relevant resolutions of the Economic and Social Council in order to improve the social and economic conditions of the Palestinian people by identifying their social and economic needs and by establishing concrete projects to that end, without prejudice to the sovereignty of the respective Arab host countries, and to provide adequate funds for that purpose.

90th plenary meeting
20 December 1978

[119] E/6005 and Add.1, E/1978/55 and Add.1-3.
[120] *Official Records of the Economic and Social Council, 1978, Supplement No. 13* (E/1978/53/Rev.1).
[121] *Ibid.,* para. 55.

130. Security Council Resolution 446 Calling upon Israel to Cease Changing the Legal Status and the Geographic and Demographic Nature of the Occupied Arab Territories and Establishing a Commission to Examine the Situation, March 22, 1979*

* S.C. Res. 446, 34 U.N. SCOR (2134th mtg.) at 4, U.N. Doc. S/INF/35 (1979).

The Security Council,

Having heard the statement of the Permanent Representative of Jordan and other statements made before the Council,

Stressing the urgent need to achieve a comprehensive, just and lasting peace in the Middle East,

Affirming once more that the Geneva Convention relative to the Protection of Civilian Persons in Time of War, of 12 August 1949,[10] is applicable to the Arab territories occupied by Israel since 1967, including Jerusalem,

1. *Determines* that the policy and practices of Israel in establishing settlements in the Palestinian and other Arab territories occupied since 1967 have no legal validity and constitute a serious obstruction to achieving a comprehensive, just and lasting peace in the Middle East;

2. *Strongly deplores* the failure of Israel to abide by Security Council resolutions 237 (1967) of 14 June 1967, 252 (1968) of 21 May 1968 and 298 (1971) of 25 September 1971, by the consensus statement made by the President of the Council on 11 November 1976[11] and by General Assembly resolutions 2253 (ES-V) and 2254 (ES-V) of 4 and 14 July 1967, 32/5 of 28 October 1977 and 33/113 of 18 December 1978;

3. *Calls once more upon* Israel, as the occupying Power, to abide scrupulously by the Geneva Convention relative to the Protection of Civilian Persons in Time of War, of 12 August 1949, to rescind its previous measures and to desist from taking any action which would result in changing the legal status and geographical nature and materially affecting the demographic composition of the Arab territories occupied since 1967, including Jerusalem, and, in particular, not to transfer parts of its own civilian population into the occupied Arab territories;

4. *Establishes* a commission consisting of three members of the Security Council, to be appointed by the President of the Council after consultation with the members of the Council, to examine the situation relating to settlements in the Arab territories occupied since 1967, including Jerusalem;

5. *Requests* the Commission to submit its report to the Security Council by 1 July 1979;

6. *Requests* the Secretary-General to provide the Commission with the necessary facilities to enable it to carry out its mission;

7. *Decides* to keep the situation in the occupied territories under constant and close scrutiny and to reconvene in July 1979 to review the situation in the light of the findings of the Commission.

Adopted at the 2134th meeting by 12 votes to none, with 3 abstentions (Norway, United Kingdom of Great Britain and Northern Ireland, United States of America).

[10] United Nations, *Treaty Series*, vol. 75, p. 287.
[11] *Official Records of the Security Council, Thirty-first Year*, 1969th meeting.

131. Resolutions on the Palestine Question, Passed at the Conference of the Foreign Ministers of Islamic Countries, Held in Fez, Morocco, May 8–12, 1979*

* 8 J. Palestine Stud. 183 (Summer 1979).

1. The Conference resolves:

a) To reaffirm full and effective support for the Palestinian people in their legitimate struggle, under the leadership of the PLO, their sole legitimate representative inside and outside the occupied homeland, to recover their inalienable national rights in Palestine, including:

— Their right to their homeland, Palestine.

— Their right to return to their homeland and to recover their property, as guaranteed by the UN resolutions.

— Their right to self-determination without any outside interference, in conformity with the principles of the UN and the Declaration of Human rights.

— Their right to the free exercise of their sovereignty over their land.

— Their right to establish their independent national state under the leadership of the PLO, their sole legitimate representative.

b) To struggle in all fields and on the widest international scale to promote recognition of the inalienable national rights of the Palestinian people and the PLO, to draw up a strategy aimed at the liberation of Palestine and at ensuring the exercise by the Palestinian people of their inalienable national rights.

c) To coordinate the activities of the Islamic Conference Organization with those of the PLO with a view to drawing up a strategy aimed at the liberation of Palestine and at ensuring the exercise by the Palestinian people of their inalienable national rights.

2. Affirms the right of the Palestinian people to continue their struggle in all forms, military and political, and by all means, to recover their inalienable national rights and to establish their independent state in Palestine.

3. Calls on all the Islamic states to support with all means the Palestinian people in their legitimate struggle against the racist Zionist occupation of Palestine, for the recovery of their inalienable national rights, this being a fundamental condition for the establishment of a just peace in the Middle East.

4. Calls on all the Islamic states to abide by all the resolutions adopted by the Islamic states' summits and Foreign Ministers' conferences on the Palestine problem and to take action to implement them as soon as possible, particularly the resolutions related to the severing of all forms of political, economic, cultural, technical, touristic and communications relations, and all other relations, with colonialist Zionist Israel.

5. Reaffirms the need to take the necessary measures to ensure that the capitals of the Islamic states accept representatives of the PLO as being the sole legitimate representative of the Palestinian people, to grant such representatives all the rights, privileges and immunities allowed to the diplomatic missions of sovereign states, and calls on the Islamic states that have not yet taken these measures to do so as soon as possible.

6. Affirms that the Palestine problem is the essence of the conflict in the Middle East and that any disregard of this fact is a disservice to peace in the

area. It reaffirms that the attempts and efforts of the USA to promote its interests and influence in the area and to liquidate the problem of occupied Palestine by encouraging bilateral and partial solutions and ignoring the essence of the problem cannot lead to a just solution. The Conference therefore condemns these attempts and efforts and requires that they be resisted. It also condemns all policies, moves and concessions that prejudice or infringe the resolutions of the UN General Assembly and of the conferences of the Islamic states.

7. The Conference condemns the Camp David agreements signed in September 1978 and the Washington Treaty signed on March 26, 1979 by the Israeli government and the Egyptian regime, which it regards as flagrant infringements of the Charter of the Islamic Conference Organization and a violation of international legality and the resolutions of the UN on the Palestine problem and the Palestinian and Arab occupied territories. It rejects all their consequences and results and regards them as null and void and not binding on Arabs and Muslims, and in particular the Palestinian people. It also regards these agreements as a bilateral solution that disregards the essence of the problem, which is the cause of Palestine, and an attempt to liquidate the inalienable national rights of the Palestinian people, in particular their right to return, to self-determination and to establish their independent state on the soil of their homeland. The Conference therefore calls for resistance to these agreements by all ways and means and condemns the role of the US in signing them and endeavouring to impose them on the Palestinian people.

8. Stresses the right of the PLO, the sole legitimate representative of the Palestinian people, to make every effort to reject and thwart all kinds of settlements, proposals and solutions aimed at liquidating the cause of Palestine and impairing the inalienable national rights of the Palestinian people in Palestine and in particular the self-government plan outlined in the Camp David and Washington agreements.

9. Affirms the right of the PLO to independent and equal representation at all international conferences, gatherings and activities concerned with the Palestine problem and the Arab-Zionist conflict, on the basis of the achievement of the inalienable national rights of the Palestinian people as endorsed by the UN General Assembly, and in particular its resolution 3236. The Conference also affirms the right of the PLO to reject and declare null and void any consequences of these activities that does not provide for the PLO's participation in the manner and on the basis mentioned above.

10. Condemns Israel for her continuing refusal to implement the UN resolutions on the Palestine problem, in particular resolution 3236 on the inalienable national rights of the Palestinian people. It also condemns Israel for her refusal to cooperate with the committee set up by the UN General Assembly by its resolution 3376, to ensure that the Palestinian people should exercise their inalienable national rights.

11. Condemns Israel's racist, expansionist and terrorist policies and

moves, and her plans and measures as regards building settlements, judaizing the Palestinian and Arab occupied territories and changing their political, demographic, geographical, cultural and economic character, including the Judaization of Jerusalem, Hebron, Nazareth, the district of Galilee, the Negev, the Golan and Sinai. It resolves that all these measures are null and void and illegal, and that in no way is it possible to recognize them or any of their consequences.

12. Condemns Israel's repeated violations of the human rights of Palestinians and Arabs in the territories occupied in 1948 and 1967 and her refusal to implement the 1949 Geneva Conventions, in particular the Fourth Convention on the Protection of Civilians in Time of War. It also condemns Israeli policies and moves involving the expropriation of lands, the continuing eviction of Palestinians and the destruction of the cultural, historic and religious heritage of Palestinian towns and the Palestinian people, regarding these as crimes committed in defiance of the whole of humanity.

13. The Conference condemns all the states that provide Israel with military, economic, political or manpower support and calls on them to put an immediate end to any kind of material or moral support to Israel.

14. Calls on the Security Council to review the report and resolutions of the committee concerned with the exercise by the Palestinian people of their inalienable national rights in conformity with UN General Assembly resolution 3236 and the annexed resolutions on the Palestine question. It also calls on the Security Council to adopt a resolution embodying the principles and contents of these resolutions, in particular those on the inalienable national rights of the Palestinian people, inasmuch as these resolutions have become an expression of the international will, the obstruction of which involves the infringement of the principles of the UN Charter, the endangering of international peace and security, and the perpetuation of the injustice that has been done to the struggling Palestinian people and the denying of their exercise of their inalienable national rights.

15. Once more calls on all the Islamic states to take all necessary measures to increase pressure on Israel at UN and international gatherings, by imposing the severest sanctions against her, including the possibility of depriving her of membership of the UN, if necessary.

16. Calls on all the Islamic states to take action to implement paragraph 8, which commissions their Foreign Ministers to ensure full cooperation with the PLO during discussion of the Palestine question at the thirty-fourth session of the UN General Assembly.

17. The Conference resolves that at the thirty-fourth session of the UN General Assembly, the Islamic states should adopt a draft resolution stating that the budget of UNRWA should be part of the UN budget and condemning the measures taken by the Agency's administration as regards reducing education and health allotments and services for the refugees, as being contrary to the resolutions of the UN General Assembly.

18. Calls on the Islamic states to request the thirty-fourth session of the

UN General Assembly to hold an extraordinary emergency session devoted to the study of the Palestine question, with a view to taking measures leading to the implementation of the UN resolutions on withdrawal from the occupied Palestinian Arab territories and the achievement of the inalienable national rights of the Palestinian people.

19. Requests the Secretary-General to follow up the implementation of this resolution and to submit a report on what has been done in this respect to the next conference.

132. Statement by the EEC Foreign Ministers on the Middle East, June 18, 1979*

---

* 12 Bull. Eur. Comm. (No. 6) 93 (1979).

2.2.59. The Nine examined the situation in the Middle East. As they indicated in their previous statements of 29 June 1977[2] and 26 March this year[3] the establishment of a just and lasting peace can only take place within the framework of a comprehensive settlement based on Security Council Resolutions 242 and 338 and on:

(i) the inadmissibility of the acquisition of territory by force;

(ii) the need for Israel to end the territorial occupation which it has maintained since the conflict of 1967;

(iii) respect for the sovereignty, territorial integrity and independence of every State in the area and the right to live in peace within secure and recognized boundaries;

(iv) recognition that in the establishment of a just and lasting peace account must be taken of the legitimate rights of the Palestinians, including their right to a homeland.

The Nine deplore any action or statement which could constitute an obstacle to the pursuit of peace. In particular they consider that certain policies and statements of the Israeli Government are likely to impede the pursuit of a comprehensive settlement. This is notably the case with regard to the following:

(i) Israel's claim to eventual sovereignty over the occupied territories, which is incompatible with Resolution 242 establishing the principle of the inadmissibility of the acquisition of territory by force;

(ii) the Israeli Government's policy of establishing settlements in the occupied territories in violation of international law.

With regard to the Lebanon, they support the independence, sovereignty and territorial integrity of that country and deplore any acts that jeopardize the population's safety or impede the reestablishment of the Lebanese Government's authority over all its territory, notably the southern part of the country. They are deeply concerned over the difficulties that Unifil—which includes contingents from certain countries of the Nine—is experiencing in carrying out its task, and call on all parties to comply with the Security Council's decisions.

These are the views which the Nine feel impelled to express at the present juncture. They reserve the right to make further statements in due course on all the matters dealt with above.

[2] Bull. EC 6-1977, point 2.2.3.
[3] Bull. EC 3-1979, point 2.2.74.

133. First Report of the Security Council Commission
Established Under Resolution 446 (1979) and Annexes III,
IV, and V, July 12, 1979*

* 34 U.N. SCOR Supp. (July–Sept. 1979) at 16, U.N. Doc. S/13450 (1979).

CONTENTS

LETTER OF TRANSMITTAL

12 July 1979

In our capacity as members of the Security Council Commission established under resolution 446 (1979), we have the honour to submit herewith
the report prepared by the Commission pursuant to paragraph 5 of the
resolution mentioned above.

This report was adopted unanimously on 12 July 1979.

(*Signed*) Leonardo MATHIAS, *Portugal*,
(*Chairman*)
Julio DE ZAVALA, *Bolivia*,
Kasuka Simwinji MUTUKWA, *Zambia*

I. INTRODUCTION

A. ESTABLISHMENT OF THE COMMISSION

1. The Commission was established by Security Council resolution 446
(1979) with the following mandate: "to examine the situation relating to

settlements in the Arab territories occupied since 1967, including Jerusalem".

2. By a letter dated 23 February 1979 [*S/13115*] to the President of the Security Council, the Permanent Representative of Jordan to the United Nations requested the convening of a meeting of the Council to consider the "most ominous and accelerating erosion of the status of Jerusalem and the rest of the occupied Arab territories in consequence of the Israeli occupation authorities' systematic, relentless and deliberate policy and practice of settlements and colonization of those territories which constitute a grave threat to world peace and security".

3. In response to that request, the Security Council considered the item entitled "The situation in the occupied Arab territories" at its 2123rd to 2128th, 2131st and 2134th meetings held between 9 and 22 March 1979.

4. The relevant documentation before the Council included, *inter alia:*

(*a*) A letter dated 7 March 1979 [*S/13149*] from Jordan transmitting a map and a list of Israeli settlements in the occupied West Bank, along with a letter from the Chairman of the Islamic Commission in Jerusalem to the Prime Minister of Jordan, stating that the Israeli authorities were transforming the Mosque of Hebron into a Jewish synagogue;

(*b*) A letter dated 2 March 1979 [*S/13132*] from the Acting Chairman of the Committee on the Exercise of the Inalienable Rights of the Palestinian People to which were annexed a list of press reports, maps and other documents relating to the situation in the occupied territories.

5. Statements made before the Security Council, including those made by Jordan and Israel, may be found in documents S/PV.2123-2128, 2131 and 2134.

6. At its 2134th meeting the Security Council adopted resolution 446 (1979) which reads as follows:

"*The Security Council,*

Having heard the statement of the Permanent Representative of Jordan and other statements made before the Council,

Stressing the urgent need to achieve a comprehensive, just and lasting peace in the Middle East,

Affirming once more that the Geneva Convention relative to the Protection of Civilian Persons in Time of War of 12 August 1949 is applicable to the Arab territories occupied by Israel since 1967, including Jerusalem,

1. *Determines* that the policy and practices of Israel in establishing settlements in the Palestinian and other Arab territories occupied since 1967 have no legal validity and constitute a serious obstruction to achieving a comprehensive, just and lasting peace in the Middle East;

2. *Strongly deplores* the failure of Israel to abide by Security Council resolutions 237 (1967) of 14 June 1967, 252 (1968) of 21 May 1968 and 298 (1971) of 25 September 1971, by the consensus statement made by the President of the Council on 11 November 1976 and by General Assembly reso-

lutions 2253 (ES-V) and 2254 (ES-V) of 4 and 14 July 1967, 32/5 of 28 October 1977 and 33/113 of 18 December 1978;

3. *Calls once more upon* Israel, as the occupying Power, to abide scrupulously by the Geneva Convention relative to the Protection of Civilian Persons in Time of War, of 12 August 1949, to rescind its previous measures and to desist from taking any action which would result in changing the legal status and geographical nature and materially affecting the demographic composition of the Arab territories occupied since 1967, including Jerusalem, and, in particular, not to transfer parts of its own civilian population into the occupied Arab territories;

4. *Establishes* a commission consisting of three members of the Security Council, to be appointed by the President of the Council after consultation with the members of the Council, to examine the situation relating to settlements in the Arab territories occupied since 1967, including Jerusalem;

5. *Requests* the Commission to submit its report to the Security Council by 1 July 1979;

6. *Requests* the Secretary-General to provide the Commission with the necessary facilities to enable it to carry out its mission;

7. *Decides* to keep the situation in the occupied territories under constant and close scrutiny and to reconvene in July 1979 to review the situation in the light of the findings of the Commission."

B. COMPOSITION, MANDATE AND ORGANIZATION OF THE WORK OF THE COMMISSION

7. In a note dated 3 April 1979 [*S/13218*], the President of the Security Council stated that following his consultations with the members of the Council, an agreement had been reached, according to which the Commission established under paragraph 4 of resolution 446 (1979) would be composed of Bolivia, Portugal and Zambia.

8. At its first meeting held in New York on 10 April 1979, the Commission decided that its chairmanship would be assumed by Portugal.

9. In organizing its programme of work so as to fulfil its mandate, the Commission considered the modalities it should follow "to examine the situation relating to settlements in the Arab territories occupied since 1967, including Jerusalem".

10. The Commission decided, as a first step, to establish direct contacts with the parties involved in the matter with a view to seeking their co-operation in the fulfilment of its mandate and to enter into consultations with relevant United Nations bodies which might be in a position to supply useful information.

C. REQUESTS TO THE PARTIES FOR CO-OPERATION

11. On 13 April 1979, letters were sent to the Permanent Representatives of Egypt, Jordan, Lebanon and the Syrian Arab Republic requesting that the Commission be provided as soon as possible with all available informa-

tion pertinent to its mandate and informing them that the Commission was contemplating to visit the area during the month of May.

12. Also on 13 April, a similar letter was sent to the Permanent Representative of Israel pointing out in addition that his Government's co-operation in facilitating the proposed visit of the Commission to the territories in question would be greatly appreciated.

13. Requests for information were also addressed to the Chairman of the Special Committee to Investigate Israeli Practices Affecting the Human Rights of the Population in the Occupied Territories and the Chairman of the Committee on the Exercise of the Inalienable Rights of the Palestinian People.

14. On 30 April the Commission sent a letter to the Permanent Observer of the Palestine Liberation Organization (PLO), drawing his attention to its mandate and requesting any relevant information.

15. In their replies dated 17, 17 and 25 April respectively, the representatives of Lebanon, Jordan and Egypt assured the Commission of their Governments' full co-operation in the implementation of its mandate. The reply from Jordan included a personal message of support from His Royal Highness, Crown Prince Hassan.

16. Assurances of co-operation and assistance were also received from the Committee on the Exercise of the Inalienable Rights of the Palestinian People and from the Special Committee to Investigate Israeli Practices Affecting the Human Rights of the Population in the Occupied Territories.

17. At the 3rd meeting, on 26 April, the Chairman informed the Commission of the results of his efforts to establish contact with the Permanent Mission of Israel, in order to exchange views on the way in which the Commission intended to fulfil its mandate and on the degree of co-operation it might receive from the Government of Israel. In response, the representative of Israel had stated to the Chairman that the Israeli Government had nothing to hide concerning its actions in the territories under its control; that the situation there had been freely examined by numerous impartial observers who had always confirmed the statements made by the Israeli Government, and that his Mission was not prepared to have any contact with the Commission.

18. After examining the serious consequences which might result from the Israeli attitude concerning its work, the Commission decided that its Chairman should report the matter to the President of the Security Council and draw his attention to the fact that in such circumstances, the Commission would endeavour to implement its mandate in spite of Israel's refusal to allow the Commission to proceed with its planned visit.

19. At the same 3rd meeting, the Chairman also reported on his discussions with the Permanent Observer of the PLO, who had stressed PLO's full co-operation with the Commission.

20. At its 4th meeting on 30 April, the Commission met with members of the office of the Crown Prince of Jordan and with the Permanent Represen-

tative of Jordan, who reiterated their Government's support and provided the Commission with documents and maps relating to the question of settlements. The Commission met also with the Chairman of the Committee on the Exercise of the Inalienable Rights of the Palestinian People, who supplied it with studies prepared by the Committee on the question of the occupied territories.[3]

21. At the 6th meeting on 8 May, the Chairman informed members that in response to his *démarche* concerning Israel's attitude, the President of the Security Council had decided to remind the Permanent Representative in writing that the Commission had not received any answer to its request for co-operation and to ask him of Israel's intentions in that regard.

22. By letters dated 9 May to the Permanent Representatives of Egypt, Jordan, Lebanon and the Syrian Arab Republic, the Commission indicated its plans for a visit to the area and the type of information it was seeking. By another letter of 11 May, the Commission confirmed to the Permanent Observer of the PLO that it would welcome the opportunity to meet Chairman Yasser Arafat during its visit.

23. On the day of its departure for the area concerned, the Commission received a copy of the reply sent by the representative of Israel to the President of the Security Council. In that letter dated 17 May, the Israeli representative informed the President that, in consideration of the circumstances in which resolution 446 (1979) had been adopted, the Government of Israel had rejected that resolution in its entirety and accordingly could not extend any form of co-operation to a Commission set up under it.

24. When preparing its report at Headquarters, the Commission realized that, in view of the heavy schedule of the Security Council and also the extensive volume of testimony and other documentary information received by the Commission during its visit to the area, it would be difficult for the Commission to report to the Council by 1 July 1979, as called for in paragraph 5 of resolution 446 (1979). Accordingly, the Chairman of the Commission requested the President of the Council that the time-limit for the report be postponed until 15 July. Following informal consultations with the other members of the Council, the President informed the Chairman of the Commission that no member of the Council had any objection to the Commission's request [S/13426].

25. The present report is based on elements of information which were gathered from various sources both at Headquarters and during the visit to the area. Section I of the present report relates to the establishment of the Commission and its work at Headquarters and section II to the Commission's visit to the area, including its exchanges of views with Government authorities and with representatives of organizations. Section III is devoted

---

[3] A summary of the statements made by the representatives of Jordan and by the Chairman of the Committee on the Exercise of the Inalienable Rights of the Palestinian People is reproduced in annex I.

to conclusions and recommendations. The annexes deal with the following subjects: annex I, summary of statements made at the 4th meeting of the Commission; annex II, summaries of testimony; annex III, list of settlements; annex IV, Map of settlements; annex V, documentation retained in the custody of the Secretariat.

26. The present report was unanimously adopted at the 19th meeting on 12 July.

II. VISIT TO THE AREA

A. ORGANIZATION OF THE VISIT

27. During its visit to the area, the Commission was composed of the following members: Ambassador Leonardo Mathias (Portugal), Chairman; Ambassador Julio de Zavala (Bolivia); Mr. Kasuka Simwinji Mutukwa (Zambia). They were accompanied by two advisers: Mr. Edgar Pinto (Bolivia); Mr. Luis Crucho Almeida (Portugal).

28. A team of staff members from the Secretariat was assigned by the Secretary-General to assist the Commission in its work.

29. The Commission decided that during the visit, it would hold consultations with the Government authorities concerned and also receive, at hearings or individual interviews, oral or written statements or testimony by other authorities, organizations or private individuals.

30. It was also decided that while, as a general rule, the Commission considered it preferable for the hearings, interviews and working meetings to be held *in camera*, it could decide to hold public meetings should circumstances so require. The Commission could also proceed to specific areas within the countries concerned in order to examine the situation on the spot, whenever feasible, to hear statements, to receive testimony and to obtain all possible information relevant to its mandate.

31. It was further agreed that at the beginning of each series of hearings the Chairman would outline the mandate of the Commission and draw attention to the fact that the Commission expected the witnesses to confine their statements as much as possible within the limits of that mandate. Furthermore, the Commission decided to accept requests by witnesses who expressed the wish to remain anonymous for reasons of safety.

32. Finally, a decision was taken that the Commission would keep a record of its inquiry and would consider information particularly relevant to its mandate in preparing its report. It would also decide which documentation it would annex to its report, bearing in mind that other elements of information obtained would be kept in the custody of the Secretariat.

33. The Commission organized its visit to the area as follows: the Hashemite Kingdom of Jordan, 20-26 May; the Syrian Arab Republic, 26-29 May; Lebanon, 29-30 May; the Arab Republic of Egypt, 30 May-1 June.

34. In accordance with the decisions referred to above, the Commission met in each country with the Government authorities. It also heard a number of witnesses and visited various locations. In Jordan on 23 May, the

Commission went to the Jordan River valley, and on 24 May to a refugee camp. In Syria on 28 May, the Commission went to the location of the town of Quneitra.

35. In the course of its visit, the Commission met with representatives of the Palestine Liberation Organization.

36. The Commission received testimony from 42 witnesses: 22 at Amman (including a written statement), 13 at Damascus and 7 at Cairo, and met spokesmen from local associations. It received also some written documentation, photographs and maps.

37. The Commission returned to Headquarters on 4 June.

38. The Commission wishes to state that in the course of its visit to the area, it received valuable assistance from the Governments and all those concerned in carrying out its mandate. It benefited in particular from fruitful exchanges of views and received informative replies to the points requiring clarification raised by its members. The Commission therefore wishes to express its gratitude to the aforementioned for the co-operation extended to it.

B. VISIT TO THE HASHEMITE KINGDOM OF JORDAN

Meetings with Government Officials

39. The Commission arrived in Jordan on 20 May.

40. The following day, the Commission had a working meeting at Amman at the Ministry of Foreign Affairs where it was received by Mr. Hassan Ibrahim, Minister of State for Foreign Affairs; Mr. Adnan Abu Odeh, Minister of Information and head of the Executive Bureau for Occupied Territories Affairs; Mr. Weal Almasri, Director of the Political Affairs Division of the Ministry of Foreign Affairs; Mr. Faleh Attawel, Director, Department of International Organizations; Mr. Akthem Qusus, Director, United Nations Department; Mr. Shawkat Mahmoud, Director, Bureau of Occupied Territories Affairs; and Mr. George Shamma, of the Permanent Mission of Jordan to the United Nations.

41. The Minister of State for Foreign Affairs welcomed the members of the Commission, wished them success in their "significant and delicate" mission and expressed the hope that the Commission's efforts would help to bring about effective international action towards a comprehensive, just and lasting peace in the Middle East. Israel's settlement policy, which was repeatedly condemned by the General Assembly, the Security Council and even Israel's own friends, was a challenge to the United Nations and a violation of international law.

42. The Minister of State expressed the view that the task of the Commission was rendered particularly difficult by the refusal of Israel to allow it to visit the occupied territories. For its part, his Government was determined to do everything possible to assist the Commission in carrying out its mandate.

43. In reply to the statement by the Minister of State for Foreign Affairs,

the Chairman of the Commission expressed the members' appreciation for the warm welcome afforded them. As an emanation of the Security Council, the Commission shared his apprehensions concerning the situation in the area and would faithfully report its findings to the Council.

44. The Minister of Information then briefed the Commission on the situation concerning the settlements in the occupied West Bank, which so far had reached a total of 78 settlements, covering an area of approximately 370,000 dunums.[4] That was only a part of the 1.5 million dunums of which Israel had taken possession, and which in turn was 27 per cent of the total area of the occupied West Bank.

45. Speaking of the meaning of the settlements for Israel, Mr. Odeh quoted several Israeli sources, including a recent statement attributed to the Minister of the Interior, and others to officials of world Jewish organizations which indicated that Israel's policy of settlements was a step towards the realization of the primary Zionist goal, i.e., the creation of a purely Jewish State in the Middle East. That goal required that space be readily provided for new immigrants until the local Arab population could be outnumbered. The settlements, he said, had always been a "value" in the creed of zionism.

46. As to the methods used by the Israeli authorities to acquire the land, they included acquisitions by virtue of the "restricted area" by-law, which authorized the restriction of land for "security" reasons; the application of the "State domain" policy to the *miri* lands, which are private lands outside city limits with a different legal status; the application of the "absentee owner" policy, under which any Arab who was absent from the West Bank at the time of the Israeli invasion had his property seized; false transactions with Arab inhabitants; a policy of "green zones" which permits land to be frozen and thereby prevents its use by the legal owners; and expropriation for public use, the expropriated property being sold later to private Jewish settlers. Approximately 329,000 dunums have been seized so far under that policy.

47. Turning to the question of policy-making with regard to the settlements, the Minister of Information indicated that for the fiscal year 1979/80, the Israeli Government had allocated a sum of $US 200 million for the settlements. Those settlements were under the control of the Government or non-governmental organizations.

48. Concerning governmental settlements, a ministerial committee chaired by the Israeli Minister of Agriculture was in charge of determining the sites for new settlements, finding the financial support and building the infrastructure.

49. Non-governmental settlements were built under the supervision of various organizations, including the paramilitary Nahal movement for agricultural and military settlements built close to the cease-fire lines, the Gush

4 1 dunum = 1,000 square metres; 1,000 dunums = 1 square kilometre.

Emunim, the Settlements Department of the Jewish Appeal Fund, the Moshav and other organizations.

50. Mr. Odeh then spoke of Israel's policy on the allotment of water resources in the occupied West Bank. The West Bank depended mostly on ground water. The policy of Israel in that regard was to consider the area as one geological basin. Accordingly, it had adopted certain restrictive policies against the Arab farmers, such as the interdiction of drilling artesian wells without a special permit. By contrast Israeli authorities had drilled 24 wells for the exclusive use of Jewish settlers, mostly in the Jordan Valley, thus reducing considerably the amount of water available to Arab farmers. Furthermore, Arab farmers were forced to install meters on their own wells to restrict the amount of water they could use.

51. Regarding the work of the Commission, Mr. Odeh said that Israel had resorted to all kinds of intimidation to prevent potential witnesses from coming to Amman from the occupied territories. Nevertheless, a few people from various walks of life had succeeded in coming from the West Bank in spite of threats of reprisals.

52. Finally, Mr. Odeh gave further information in particular regarding Israel's intimidation policies involving school children.

53. On 21 May the Commission also paid a visit to the Prime Minister, Mr. Mudar Badran, who expressed Jordan's eagerness to make the mission of the United Nations body a success, Mr. Badran emphasized that Jordan had strong ties binding it with the Palestinians, whose problem was the core of the Middle East conflict. He described Israel's settlement policy as a challenge to the United Nations and a violation of international law. The Prime Minister also emphasized that his Government was adhering to the Security Council resolutions which are relevant to the mandate of the Commission. Finally he stressed that the time had come for a solution to the conflict, a solution which would be just and comprehensive.

54. On 22 May the Commission was granted an audience by His Majesty King Hussein of Jordan. King Hussein emphasized in particular the far-reaching consequences of Israel's settlement policy which, he said, was aimed at the eviction of the Arab inhabitants from their lands. This was also part of Israel's attempts to alter the character of the occupied Arab territories in complete disregard of United Nations principles and decisions.

55. King Hussein also explained Jordan's position vis-à-vis the Middle East question, stressing that a just and comprehensive peace could not be achieved without the restoration of Arab Jerusalem to Arab sovereignty, the withdrawal of Israeli forces from all occupied territories in implementation of United Nations resolutions and the safeguarding of Palestinian rights, including the right to self-determination in Palestine.

56. The Chairman expressed the gratitude of the Commission for the words of welcome stated by His Majesty and assured him of the Commission's determined will to implement its mandate with total objectivity.

57. On 24 May, His Highness Crown Prince Hassan received the Com-

mission. On that occasion an extensive exchange of views took place, essentially on Jerusalem and its surroundings. In that connexion Prince Hassan recalled that Jerusalem in addition to being a prestigious centre of the world, was spiritually one of the most sacred places of the Moslem faith. Turning to the question of Israeli settlements he pointed out that, through the establishment of three successive belts of settlements, Israel was creating protective pockets between Jerusalem and the Jordan River. As a result of this, it was "compartmenting" the Arab population. That this action was intentional appeared from the fact that the same policy of fragmentation of the Arab population was also being pursued on the Lebanese border in an effort to balkanize the area.

58. The Crown Price said that since 1967, it had been the official policy of Israel that Jerusalem should stay Jewish, united under Jewish rule. In implementation of that policy many Arab houses had been destroyed and their inhabitants expelled, while settlements had been established all along the eastern side of the Holy City. This settlement policy had had the result of isolating the Arabs living inside the walls and confining them in a ghetto surrounded by hostile groups of settlers. This was no doubt a powerful means of pressure to make them leave.

59. Other means of pressure were being used, some brutal, others financial, such as a 20-year levy raised from Arabs and used to erect new buildings for the Jews. Israel was also modifying the city limits in order to take full advantage of the composition of the population.

60. Prince Hassan reminded the Commission that the position of Jordan concerning Jerusalem and the West Bank had been repeatedly stated. The question was how to proceed towards the return to "Arab Jerusalem", an expression which defined a situation of mutual respect with freedom of worship for every faith.

61. The case of Jerusalem was a very special one which, once solved, could lead to a comprehensive solution. It should be deplored therefore that the question of Jerusalem at its present stage had not been the subject of any complete and impartial study. That should be remedied.

62. The Crown Prince pointed out that an international organ should be requested to make a survey of the various aspects of the situation of Jerusalem—political, religious, social, demographic, economic and any others.

63. He also indicated that the question of Arab properties confiscated by Israel in that area should be examined in detail. In that connexion, the excellent work done by the Conciliation Commission for Palestine with regard to Arab properties confiscated in territories occupied by Israel before 1967 should be kept in mind, as well as in fact the extensive mandate of that commission which was still in force.

64. In conclusion, Prince Hassan emphasized that the road towards a solution might be long and difficult but that, in order to avoid further despair which would inevitably lead to further violence, the present situation should not be allowed to remain frozen.

65. The Chairman thanks Crown Prince Hassan for his most informative briefing and assured him that the contents of his statement would be reflected in the Commission's report.

Visit to the Jordan River Valley and to a Refugee Camp

66. On 23 May, the Commission went to the Jordan Valley area. It stopped over at the King Hussein Bridge and, passing through the villages at Shouna and Karamah, it reached the village of Deir Alla, which overlooks the Jordan River Valley.

67. In the course of a briefing given by a spokesman for the Jordan River Valley Authority, the attention of the Commission was drawn to the intensive exploitation by the Israelis of the water resources in the valley. It was stated in particular that the drawing of water from the Lake of Tiberias and from the Jordan River to irrigate Israeli settlements along the valley and southward to the Negev Desert had not only diminished considerably the flow of the river but noticeably increased its salinity. At the same time, the intensive pumping of underground water through deep artesian wells dug by Israeli settlers was depleting the water resources of the valley, which is a single geological entity.

68. It should be noted that when the Commission departed from Deir Alla at night the Jordanian authorities pointed out, on the West Bank, lines of lights which they said were successive belts of Israeli settlements.

69. On 24 May, the Commission visited Schneller refugee camp, where its members were received by Mr. Abdel Rahim Jarrar, Under-Secretary of the Ministry of Reconstruction; Mr. Mohammad Al-Azzeh, Camp Services Officer; and an official of the United Nations Relief and Works Agency for Palestine Refugees in the Near East (UNRWA). In his welcoming statement, Mr. Jarrar said that the camp housed 30,000 refugees, some of whom had been displaced three times. Even 31 years after displacement, the refugees and the displaced persons were still steadfast in their resolution to return to their homeland. Mr. Jarrar noted that Israel, on the other hand, was continuing its settlement policy and the judaization of the occupied territories in defiance of the United Nations resolutions on the matter. He cited Jerusalem as the best illustration of that policy.

70. The Chairman of the Commission explained the mandate entrusted to the Commission by the Security Council. He emphasized that the mandate of the Commission was to examine the problems, i.e., to determine what they were, in order to get a better understanding and to report back to the Council. The Commission had come to the area, the Chairman observed, because of the conviction of its members that the United Nations could contribute to a just solution of the problem. The Commission believed in the rights of the refugees and displaced persons to return to their homeland in conformity with the Universal Declaration of Human Rights and the relevant resolutions of the United Nations.

71. Mr. Al-Azzeh, the camp services officer, welcomed the Commission

and stated that in view of Israel's oppressive policies in the occupied territories, he was not surprised that Israel had refused the Commission entry.

72. Mr. Abu Jameel, speaking on behalf of the refugees in the camp, wondered how long it would still take for the world to be aware of the cause of the Palestinian people who had been expelled from their homeland. He wondered also why so many resolutions and decisions of the United Nations on this question had not been implemented and why Israel was still able to persist in its policy of defying the United Nations. He emphasized that Palestinians would never accept Jerusalem as an exclusively Jewish city; nor could they accept any form of trusteeship, self-rule or partition. They could not accept any alternative to Palestine. Mr. Abu Jameel further emphasized that Palestinians did not mandate anyone except the Palestine Liberation Organization to speak on their behalf. He wished the Commission success in its endeavours and expressed the hope that that would be the last time that the United Nations would have to send a fact-finding mission to the area.

73. In response to questions put to the Commission by one of the elders of the camp who inquired why the United Nations was not able to compel Israel to recognize the rights of the Palestinian people, the Chairman stated that while he and his colleagues in the Commission understood the despair of the refugees, they were also aware that the question of Palestine was a complex problem, the just and peaceful resolution of which would take time. He recalled in that context the actions conducted at the United Nations by the Arab States. Some progress had already been achieved and the United Nations was continuing its efforts to find a just solution.

74. Mr. Abboud, an officer of UNRWA, said that the despair of the refugees was compounded by the financial crisis in UNRWA. Brigadier Mohammed Sarreef, Executive Secretary of the Supreme Ministerial Committee for Displaced Persons, gave an overview of the situation concerning the movement of refugees and displaced persons from the West Bank to the East Bank. He indicated that the Schneller Camp and five others had been set up by the Jordanian Government in 1968 to accommodate the refugees and the displaced persons who had been forced to leave the Jordan Valley area. The Jordan Government is spending $36 million a year for the subsistence of the refugees, housing, salaries and water supply, as indicated in the last report of the UNRWA Commissioner-General.

Hearings

75. During its stay in Jordan, in addition to meetings with government officials, the Commission held five meetings devoted to the hearing of witnesses. A total of 21 witnesses took the floor. An additional witness presented a written statement which was incorporated in the Commission's records. A number of witnesses asked to remain anonymous, a request which was granted in accordance with a decision previously taken by the Commission.

76. In the course of the hearings, most of the witnesses responded fa-

vourably to the Chairman's appeal to confine their statements to the situation in the settlements in the Arab territories occupied since 1967, including Jerusalem. A number of them, however, expanded their remarks to include grievances of a personal or collective nature which the Commission considered as falling within the purview of human rights violations, rather than within the scope of its mandate (e.g., witnesses Nos. 3 and 10). It should be noted in that connexion that a similar situation occurred at subsequent hearings at Damascus and at Cairo.

77. Most of the witnesses were Palestinians. Some of them—such as Sheik Abdul Hamid El-Sayeh, head of the Islamic Court of Appeal, who was deported from the West Bank in September 1967, Mr. Ruhi El-Khatib, Mayor of Jerusalem, expelled in 1968, Mr. Nadim S. Zaru, Mayor of Ramallah, expelled in 1969 and Mr. Shawkat Mahmoud Hamdi, current Director of the Executive Office of the occupied territories in the Jordanian Government—informed the Commission of their experience while serving in the occupied territories. A church leader, Archdeacon Elya Khoury, referred to his experience in the Anglican Diocese of Jerusalem until his expulsion in 1969. Other witnesses such as Mr. Ibrahim Bakr, a practising lawyer who indicated that he had been expelled in December 1967 from the West Bank, drew particular attention to certain legal aspects of the situation. Most of the other witnesses presented views based on their individual or family experience.

78. Keeping in mind the scope of the mandate established by the Security Council, the Commission would like to draw particular attention to a number of points which were reported by witnesses during its stay in Jordan.

Settlements in the Occupied Territories

79. According to an Arab publication referred to by a witness (No. 15), between 1967 and 1977 the Israelis established in the West Bank, including Jerusalem, 123 settlements, of which 33 were not publicly announced because they were Nahal military settlements.

80. According to another witness (No. 20), it should be noted that while in the past those settlements were established mostly close to the line of the pre-1967 border, the new trend would be to divide the West Bank into large squares, subsequently criss-crossed with roads. As perceived by the inhabitants, the aim of that policy was to divide the whole occupied territory into a number of squares and to build settlements on the corners of each of them in order to isolate the main Arab agglomerations.

81. According to other witnesses, the policy referred to above applied whether the land was publicly or privately owned. In that connexion, a witness (No. 4) challenged what he called an Israeli claim that only public land was being used for those settlements. He pointed out that under the Geneva Convention and the relevant United Nations resolutions, the establishment of a settlement in occupied territories was illegal whether it was set up on public or private land. He then gave an informative briefing on the various categories of private lands under Jordanian law.

82. The witness stated also that out of an estimated 125,630 dunums of cultivable land which were taken by the Israelis for the exclusive use of civilian settlements (thus excluding areas kept for military purposes), 9.4 per cent were public lands and 90.6 per cent private.

83. The pattern and process of land seizure seems to have varied with time. Some witnesses (among them, Nos. 6 and 8) stated that in the wake of the 1967 war, people were expelled from their villages and sometimes their houses were destroyed in front of them. One witness (No. 13) in particular said that, after being expelled from their village to the town of Ramallah, located at a distance of 34 kilometres away, the inhabitants were finally authorized to return. But after walking back approximately 32 kilometres, they were stopped close to their village and saw it being blown up.

84. Since then, according to another witness (No. 4), the land seizure process generally goes as follows: first, the Israeli forces set up boundary markers or barbed wire fences to define the area. Secondly, the leaders of the village are informed that for security reasons the inhabitants are no longer allowed to enter the closed-in area. Thirdly, crops are destroyed and fruit-bearing trees are defoliated and uprooted. That process was confirmed by another witness (No. 14).

85. Concerning the legal aspects of the matter, a witness (No. 21) mentioned the following instruments under which, he said, most of the confiscations of Arab lands were conducted:

(a) The absentee property law, adopted by the Knesset on 14 March 1950, which replaced the emergency decrees concerning absentee property issued on 19 December 1948;

(b) The law of acquisition of land for the public interest, issued in 1943 under the British Mandate and still in use;

(c) Defence and emergency decrees of 1945, also issued under the British Mandate. Under those decrees, the Military Governor can order the deportation of people and the expropriation of property;

(d) Emergency regulations on the exploitation of barren lands, published on 15 October 1948, under which the Minister of Agriculture is empowered to seize barren lands if he is "convinced" that its owner does not intend to utilize it for agricultural purposes;

(e) A law relating to the expropriation of real estate during the 1949 emergency period, under which an *ad hoc* authority may seize any real estate which it believes to be necessary for the national security.

86. With regard to the implementation of the absentee property law mentioned above, it was stated (No. 11) that according to the law, all lands whose owners were not present on 5 June 1967 were considered absentee lands, even when the owner had returned thereafter. All such lands, the witness said, had been put under the authority of the Israeli Custodian of Absentee Property, who collects the rent from the absentee houses.[5]

---

[5] This question was raised on other occasions, in particular at Cairo by the Chairman of the International Law Association (see para. 176).

87. In that connexion some witnesses (Nos. 5 and 17) referred to some cases which had come before an Israeli court. In a recent case, Israeli settlers near Hebron had taken a large piece of land to build 500 housing units. At the request of the Arab owners, the Israeli court had decided that the decision was illegal, but nevertheless, the settlers had kept the land.

88. Another case in which the Israeli judicial system was involved was reported in the village of Anata near Jerusalem. Following the villagers' refusal to lease 4,650 dunums of land, the military authorities had closed off the zone with barbed wire. The case had been submitted to the Israeli High Court of Justice which, on 15 January 1979, had agreed to a reduced demand from the army resulting in the expropriation of 1,740 dunums of fertile land. According to the witness (No. 19), the villagers had not been informed of that decision until 18 March 1979, that is after the 30 days' limit to appeal the decision.

89. As to the use of the land seized, witnesses (Nos. 1, 2, and 4) enumerated a number of settlements which they said had been established on the former location of Arab villages.

90. It was also stated (Nos. 1 and 17) that the military authorities or the settlers themselves resorted to various means of pressure to compel the landowners to leave the area, such as repeated imprisonment linked to an offer to release the person concerned if he agreed to depart from the area, obstacles to children's schooling, confiscation and destruction (under the "absentee law") of houses belonging to Palestinians living abroad, an action sometimes matched with the imprisonment of the tenant who had protested against it (No. 1). Several witnesses referred also in that regard to the control of water as a most powerful means of pressure to compel the inhabitants to leave their property.

91. In that connexion, the water resource policy pursued by the Israelis was frequently mentioned. A witness (No. 4) indicated that to date the Israelis had drilled some 20 deep boreholes from 300 to 600 metres deep in the Jordan Valley and were pumping an estimated 15 to 17 million cubic metres per year exclusively to irrigate the lands seized for their settlements. A number of those wells had been drilled in close proximity to local Arab springs, contrary to Jordanian laws regulating the drilling of new wells. The impact of those practices had been felt all over the West Bank. In Jericho, the saline content of the water pumped from pre-1967 Arab wells (not as deep as the new wells) had noticeably risen while in many areas the flow of water had drastically diminished, such as in the Wadi Fara basin, the Bardala Basin and the region of Al-Anja, where the spring which used to give 11 million cubic metres per year was now down to a trickle, thus threatening the end of any cultivation for the village.

92. In addition, it had become common practice for the Israeli authorities to limit the amount of water which could be pumped from pre-1967 wells by installing water meters (Nos. 1 and 9). To emphasize the importance of water resources, another witness (No. 7) referred to military actions con-

ducted by the Israelis before 1967 across the border against the village of Qalqilia, at which time, he said, 11 artesian wells had been destroyed. Since 1967 when the village was occupied, the Israeli authorities had installed meters on all the wells, thus imposing strict limitations on the use of water. As a result, it was impossible for the Arab inhabitants to carry on any farming but at the same time two Israeli settlements were established in the area. Those settlements, each of them with approximately 150 houses, were now equipped with an artesian well with a motor engine and set of pipelines.

93. The question of whether compensation was given to the deprived landowners was discussed on several occasions. One witness said that the amount offered was merely a tenth of the real value of the property (No. 9); he also added that, furthermore, that was not the point, since the owners did not want to sell it. That latter view was also expressed by another witness (No. 15). Another witness (No. 22) mentioned two relevant cases. In the first one, the owner had refused any compensation which might be construed as an agreement, but the land had nevertheless been used for a military camp and then gradually transformed into a settlement for civilians. In the second, which referred to an area of 400 dunums, no compensation had been paid to the individual owners.

Jerusalem

94. The situation in Jerusalem was described more extensively by four witnesses (Nos. 15, 16, 18 and 21). One of them (No. 21) recalled that the Knesset had adopted on 28 June 1967 a decision of "annexation" on the basis of which the following measures were taken:

(*a*) Abrogation of the Arab Municipal Council of Jerusalem;

(*b*) Elimination of certain municipal services and amalgamation of others with their Israeli counterparts;

(*c*) Application of all Israeli laws to Arab citizens;

(*d*) Closure of the Education Department and transfer of all Arab public schools to the authority of Israel's Ministry of Education, this leading to the use of Israeli curricula including the reading in primary schools of a book entitled *I am an Israeli*;

(*e*) Issuance of Israeli identification cards to all inhabitants;

(*f*) Non-recognition of Jerusalem Islamic Courts;

(*g*) Obligation for professional individuals to register their names with Israeli professional associations;

(*h*) Closure of Arab banks and exclusive use of Israeli currency;

(*i*) Physical transfer to Arab Jerusalem of a number of Israeli ministries and departments.

95. As to the methods used by Israel to judaize the Arab sector, the same witness (No. 21) said that, immediately after the 1967 war, Israel resorted to the demolition, in four different quarters of Jerusalem, of 1,215 houses, 427 shops, 5 mosques, 3 monasteries and 4 schools, i.e., a total of 1,654 buildings. As a result, the witness said, 7,400 inhabitants were forced to

leave (another witness, No. 15, referred to "more than 5,000" people). Then a "Jewish Quarter" was established, which as of today contains 320 housing units built on 116 dunums and inhabited by a Jewish settler population of 1,300 persons. Finally, 94,564 dunums of Arab lands situated within the limits of the municipality of Arab Jerusalem were confiscated.

96. Another witness (No. 15) stated that the aim of those expropriations in Jerusalem was to surround with Jewish settlers three specific areas still mainly occupied by Arabs. Such a policy, he said, was a threat to the very presence and existence of Arabs in the city.

97. A number of witnesses (such as No. 18) referred to the archaeological excavations which, he said, although repeatedly condemned by UNESCO, were still continuing, thus inflicting serious damages to Islamic shrines.

98. As to the number of settlements in Jerusalem, a witness (No. 21) indicated that nine of them had been built within the boundaries of Arab Jerusalem and 10 more within the framework of so-called greater Jerusalem. The same witness concluded his statement, saying that through the policy of settlements Israel's aim was to seize the land and gradually expel its inhabitants. That view was also expressed in various terms by a number of other witnesses.

99. The Commission departed from Amman by road on 26 May.

C. VISIT TO THE SYRIAN ARAB REPUBLIC
Meetings with Government Officials

100. The Commission arrived at Damascus on 26 May and was received the following day at the Ministry of Foreign Affairs by Mr. Abdul Halim Khaddam, Deputy Prime Minister and Minister of Foreign Affairs. He was accompanied by Mr. Kaitham Keylani, Director of the International Organizations Division and other officials from the Foreign Ministry.

101. The Deputy Prime Minister welcomed the Commission and assured it of the full co-operation of his Government in the implementation of its mandate. All that Syria expected from the Commission's efforts, he said, was that the truth be established, because truth was more powerful than military force. In that connexion he described Israel's policy of settlements as nothing but the continuation of the aggressive and expansionist practices which had characterized the Zionist movement since its very beginning and which remained the real obstacle to peace. Mr. Khaddam blamed Israel for the current situation and the United States which, he said, bore a share of the responsibility for facilitating Israel's policy of settlement. He also deplored that the United Nations could not take a stronger stand in that regard.

102. Referring to the policies pursued by Egypt and the United States. Mr. Khaddam emphasized that they did not serve the cause of peace in the area. The so-called autonomy envisaged for the Palestinians of the occupied territories in the peace treaty between Israel and the Egyptian régime would apply only to the inhabitants but the land and its resources would remain indefinitely under the authority of Israel. For the Syrian Government, it was

clear therefore that such an agreement which did not tackle the real problem could not serve the cause of peace in the area. Mr. Keylani noted in that regard as a further proof of it that the number of Israeli air raids over Lebanon had increased 10 times since the signing of the treaty.

103. In his reply, the Chairman expressed the Commission's appreciation for the welcome extended to it and assured the Deputy Prime Minister that the contents of his statement would be reflected in the Commission's report. He recalled the precise terms of the Commission's mandate and, in that context, stressed the position of all three Governments represented on the Commission as to the question of settlements. Their vote in favour of resolution 446 (1979) was a clear indication of that position.

104. On the same day, 27 May, the Commission held an open meeting with a Syrian delegation composed of Mr. Haitham Keylani, Major-General Adnan Tayara, head of the Syrian delegation at the Mixed Armistice Commission, Mr. Taker Houssami, Mr. Bechara Kharou and Mrs. Razan Mahfouz, all from the Ministry of Foreign Affairs.

105. Mr. Keylani stated that, in the view of the Syrian Government, resolution 446 (1979) was a further evidence of the concern with which the international community viewed the explosive situation in the Middle East and that situation was the result of Israel's occupation of Arab territories and its refusal to recognize the national inalienable rights of the Palestinian people. As he pointed out, his Government considered that, in a matter which was related to the maintenance of peace and security, it was imperative for the Security Council not only to express concern but to take the relevant measures provided for in Chapter VII of the United Nations Charter.

106. Mr. Keylani observed also that Israel's practices in the occupied territories—in particular the Golan Heights, where towns and villages had been replaced by Israeli settlements—were consistent with the aims of zionism which involve annexation of occupied territories and the enslavement of the local population.

107. In his reply, the Chairman noted that the purpose of the Commission in coming to Syria was to fulfil to the greatest possible extent the mandate entrusted to it by the Security Council. It had been the intention of the Commission to visit all the parties concerned in the area. However, the possibility for the Commission to go to the occupied Arab territories had to be ruled out because of the attitude of the Government of Israel in that respect. In order to accomplish its task, the Commission resorted to other means of obtaining information. It was in that spirit that the Commission had come to Syria. The information to be provided by the Syrian Government, as well as by the witnesses, would make it possible for the Commission to provide the Council with additional information so that the Council, in its persistent efforts to solve the problems of the Middle East, might in the future adopt appropriate measures.

108. A closed meeting was held at which Mr. Keylani presented the position of the Syrian Government with regard to Israeli policy and practices in

the occupied Arab territories, in particular the Golan Heights. Following a historical review of the occupation of Palestine by Zionist elements, Mr. Keylani pointed out that immediately after its invasion of the Golan Heights in 1967, Israel started implementing its plan to control the whole area and to expel its inhabitants.

109. The Golan Heights before the occupation had been one of the most prosperous areas in Syria, inhabited by 142,000 people, living in 163 towns and villages. After the occupation, Israel completely destroyed all those towns and villages with the exception of five, namely Majdal-Shams, Akaata, Massaada, Al-Ghajar and Ein-Kena, and with the stones from the ruins, Israel built in their place 29 settlements for military and other purposes. The destruction of the town of Quneitra which the Commission was going to visit was an example of what had happened in the 1,770 square kilometres still occupied by Israel.

110. Mr. Keylani pointed out that, of a total of 142,000 Syrian inhabitants in the Golan Heights, only 8,000 had remained while 134,000 had been expelled and compelled to take refuge in other parts of Syria, where there were also approximately 250,000 Palestinian refugees. The Golan Heights was ruled by a military governor with unlimited authority, including the right to appoint local councils and village mayors and to dismiss them at will. By comparison, in the West Bank, those officials were still elected by the population. In an attempt to annex the occupied area to Israel, the occupation authorities were constantly trying to sever all links between the Syrians remaining in the Golan area and their kin elsewhere in Syria. In fact, the freedom of movement of the remaining inhabitants was restricted even within the five villages. To visit another village, the inhabitants had to obtain from the military governor a special authorization, which had to be applied for a month in advance and was valid only for a few hours subjecting the holder to imprisonment and heavy fines in case of violations. Among the measures taken by the occupation authorities which affected more specially the conditions of life in the occupied territories were the imposition of all Israeli laws, the expropriation of large areas of agricultural land for so-called reasons of security, and the refusal to respond to humanitarian appeals by the International Red Cross, among others, for the reunification of families.

111. Commenting on the education policies of the occupation authorities in the Golan Heights, Mr. Keylani said that all Arabic curricula had been replaced with Israeli curricula and the teaching of Hebrew imposed in primary schools. Of the many primary and secondary schools which existed before, only seven primary schools and one secondary school had been allowed to continue functioning. Syrian graduates of the secondary school were not permitted to pursue their higher education in Syrian universities because the aim of the Israeli authorities was to channel these youths into the labour force needed in Israeli factories. Only after repeated efforts and intervention by the International Red Cross were a few students allowed to register in the Syrian universities. Other measures taken by the occupation

authorities in the field of education in the Golan Heights included the intimidation and dismissal of qualified Arab teachers; and educational courses which were compulsory for the 8,000 Syrian inhabitants and aimed at indoctrinating them to serve the aims and purposes of zionism and the Israeli policies. Further information, said Mr. Keylani, on the educational system imposed by the Israeli in the Golan Heights could be found in the reports published by UNESCO, in particular, in documents 104 EX/52 of 31 May and 20C/113 of 28 September 1978.

112. Turning to the question of the geographical changes that had taken place in the Golan Heights as a result of the occupation, Mr. Keylani stated that the whole area had been turned into a military fortress with 29 settlements, a synagogue, a military museum, as well as new roads which are used essentially for military purposes. He recalled by comparison the agricultural prosperity of that area before Israel's occupation.

113. On the question of military rule in the Golan Heights, Mr. Keylani noted that Israel had established a military court at Tiberias to administer Israeli laws over the Golan Heights. Ninety-five per cent of the judgements, he said, delivered by the court related to so-called security matters for which the sentence was life imprisonment or hard labour for life with no possibility of appeal.

114. As to the settlements, Mr. Keylani stated that the 1979 budget of Israel showed the allocations set aside for expanding 11 of the existing 29 settlements. In that connexion, according to a statement by the Israeli chief of Administration of Settlements, Israel intended to establish, in 1979, 20 new settlements, 5 of which would be in the Golan Heights and it would take over all the necessary land in order to settle 58,000 families thereon over a period of five years.

115. To be able to pursue that policy Israel had succeeded in expelling most of the inhabitants of the Golan Heights through various means, including restriction of movement, threats, intimidation, burning of crops, depriving them of their means of livelihood and imposing on them heavy taxation beyond their means. Mr. Keylani also pointed out that those settlements were all military fortresses and that the settlers, who were from Al-Jadna, a military-agricultural organization that worked in liaison with the Israeli army, were of military age. That, he said, was an additional means of pressure on an unarmed population.

116. With regard to the nature of the Israeli settlements, he expressed the conviction of his Government that those settlements were meant to be permanent, as confirmed by statements made by various Israeli officials and by the slogan which Israel had applied to the Golan Heights since 1967, namely "Security before peace". Although the Golan Heights area was included in the security and defence plans of Israel, Mr. Keylani said, security was only a pretext to annex the region since all the relevant United Nations documents indicated that before 1967 the Syrian Army artillery fired only on Israeli military bulldozers entering the no-man's land between Israel and Syria and not on any Israeli settlements.

117. Referring to the differences in the policy of Israel regarding the various Arab territories under occupation, Mr. Keylani observed that Israeli practices varied according to Israel's goals and to the size of the population in each territory. In the Golan Heights, Israel had achieved the following objectives: evacuation of the area by almost all its inhabitants; thwarting of any armed resistance by the remaining inhabitants; reduction to a minimum of the number of violations of human rights, given the small number of inhabitants remaining in the area; exploitation of expropriated fertile lands for Israel's benefit; and establishment of a military zone to defend Israel against Syria. In connexion with the evacuation of inhabitants, he recalled that in 1967 the Syrian inhabitants wanted to stay in the Golan Heights but that they had been forcibly driven out. For example, in the town of Quneitra, Israel had compelled the inhabitants to leave the area at night through minefields, thereby causing heavy casualties.

118. In the course of the exchange of views that ensued, Mr. Keylani said that between 1967 and 1973, Israeli authorities had attempted to impose Israeli citizenship on the Syrian inhabitants. Having met with categorical resistance in that regard, they had continued to deny them the attributes of Syrian citizenship and, furthermore, since 1973, they had imposed Israeli citizenship on the Syrian children born under occupation, in the belief that with time the opposition would disappear.

119. On the question of religion, Mr. Keylani noted that the deliberate destruction of the mosque, particularly in Quneitra, was meant to humiliate the inhabitants and leave them with no choice but to conduct their prayers at home.

120. As to Jerusalem, it was, he said, a sacred Arab Moslem city with the same status as that of any other part of the occupied territories. That occupied city must be liberated and returned to the Palestinian people. Syria would not accept that a single inch of Arab territory, including Jerusalem, remained under Israeli occupation and, in that regard, it supported the resolutions of the General Assembly and the Security Council on the matter.

Visit to Quneitra

121. On 28 May, the Commission visited the location of the town of Quneitra in the Golan Heights.

122. Major-General Adnan Tayara who led the visit recalled that Quneitra and the surrounding area had been taken over by Israel in June 1967 and were returned to Syria in 1974.

123. During the visit through the ruins of the city, the Commission was acquainted with the situation that was reported in 1977 to the General Assembly by the Special Committee to Investigate Israeli Practices Affecting the Human Rights of the Population of the Occupied Territories in its "Report on damage at Quneitra".[6] It was on the basis of that report that the General Assembly, on 13 December 1977, adopted resolution 32/91 by

---

[6] A/32/284, annex II.

which it condemned the "massive, deliberate destruction of Quneitra perpetrated during the Israeli occupation".

124. During that visit, the Syrian authorities pointed out to the Commission several Israeli settlements beyond the area of separation which, they said, were established on land belonging to the city of Quneitra where agricultural work was in progress.

Hearings

125. In addition to the working meeting with the Syrian delegation, the Commission held a number of hearings. Among the witnesses who appeared before the Commission there were three members of the Palestine Liberation Organization, whose statements are reported in part F below.

126. Thirteen other witnesses testified. Among them, a professor of geography (No. 23) briefed the Commission on the economic situation of the Golan Heights before 1967. He pointed out that the region was one of the most prosperous of Syria. The number of inhabitants was about 150,000, with a density of 90 per square kilometre. The arable area amounted to 107,000 hectares. The witness gave figures concerning the various kinds of soil cultivation, fruit-bearing trees and livestock to bear out his assertion that the region, despite its small size, used to produce 10 per cent of the total output of the country.

127. The other witnesses were former inhabitants of the Golan Heights, most of them from Quneitra. Seven of them (Nos. 29, 30, 31, 32, 33, 34 and 35) were municipal officials at the time the Israeli forces entered the region. They concurred in saying that all sorts of pressure including threats of death had been used by the Israelis to make the inhabitants leave the area. Villages had been destroyed, sometimes in the presence of the inhabitants (Nos. 31 and 32) and people had been taken in motor vehicles and dropped at the separation line (Nos. 31, 32 and 33) to compel them to leave.

128. A witness (No. 24) who said that he had seen Israeli bulldozers destroy Arab agglomerations, reported also that he had seen a number of Israeli settlements built on the former location of Arab villages, of which he gave the names.

129. Another witness (No. 29) said that even now, Arab students from the occupied area in the Golan Heights were prevented from pursuing their higher education in Syrian universities. He added that those who, through the mediation of the Red Cross, had been allowed to do so had been prevented from returning to their homes.

D. VISIT TO LEBANON

130. From Damascus, the Commission flew to Beirut on 25 May.

131. The same morning the Commission was received by Mr. Fouad Boutros, Minister for Foreign Affairs. Three members of the Foreign Ministry were also present.

132. The Foreign Minister welcomed the Commission and expressed the hope that its report would assist the Security Council in its efforts to pro-

mote the law of equity and justice, the right of peoples to self-determination and the compliance of Member States with their obligations under the Charter and international law.

133. Although not directly involved in the tasks of the Commission, Lebanon welcomed any effort that could facilitate the return of the Palestinians to their homeland. For its part, Lebanon had felt it its duty to receive on its soil many Palestinian refugees and it was satisfied to have been in a position to assist them in their plight. However, the present disruption which Lebanon was experiencing was linked to that very hospitality. This was therefore one more reason for the Lebanese Government to assure the Commission of its wishes of success in the implementation of the mandate assigned to it by the Security Council.

134. Regarding the situation in Southern Lebanon, Mr. Boutros said that the continuous intensive bombardment by Israel was causing a human tragedy of disastrous dimensions at that time. About 100,000 persons had been forced to flee to the north from the Tyre area. In the present circumstances, Lebanon welcomed the presence of the United Nations Interim Force in Lebanon; it only wished that the mandate of the Force were such that it could better tackle the situation.

135. Summing up the position of his Government, the Foreign Minister emphasized that Lebanon had no problem of frontiers with Israel or of directly occupied territories. However, it could not be indifferent to the question of Israeli settlements established in occupied Arab territories—given the very large number of Palestinians who had taken refuge in Lebanon— or to that of the over-all solution of the Middle East conflict, to which it was a party.

136. The Lebanese Government entirely supported the position of the Arab States concerned. It considered that the establishment of settlements, which in itself was contrary to the norms of international law, aggravated the situation prevailing in the region, gave rise to new causes of discord and new human problems and constituted an obstacle to the return of the Palestinians to their homeland.

137. It also considered that the return of the Palestinians to their homeland, apart from being a necessity for a country like Lebanon, which could not absorb the large number of refugees living in its territory, was the first of the legitimate rights of the Palestinian people, respect for which was called for in Security Council resolutions 242 (1967) and 338 (1973) and in the Soviet-United States communiqué of 1 October 1977.

138. For those reasons Lebanon, which had already on several occasions officially proclaimed, through its Head of State and its accredited representatives in international forums, its refusal to accept the settlement of Palestinians in its territory, reaffirmed its position and its point of view concerning the need to overcome all obstacles, including settlements, that were likely to impede the exercise of the right of the Palestinians to return to their homes.

139. The Chairman said that the Commission had taken due note of the position of Lebanon stated by the Foreign Minister, which would be reflected in its report. He added that although, as stated by the Foreign Minister, the mandate of the Commission did not in a precise way directly apply to Lebanon, it had a bearing on it because Lebanon was a neighbouring country to the occupied territories and gave refuge to an ever-increasing number of Palestinian refugees. The Chairman thanked, therefore, the Foreign Minister for the interest shown by the Lebanese Government in the Commission's efforts.

140. On the same day, the members of the Commission were also received by the Prime Minister of Lebanon, Mr. Salim Al Hoss.

141. Mr. Al Hoss welcomed the Commission and said that Lebanon was concerned by its mandate inasmuch as it dealt with the general situation in the Middle East. Noting with regret that all efforts aimed at settling the Middle East problem, and most particularly the Palestinian question which was at its core, had been unsuccessful, the Prime Minister pointed out that Israel's policy with respect to settlements was still complicating the problem. Such a settlement policy was significant not only in its immediate effects on the occupied territories, but even more so in its future implications in that it made it clear that Israel's intention was to settle in those territories on a permanent basis.

142. At the present time, Lebanon was the country most directly affected by the situation in the Middle East. The acute human problem created by Israel's actions in Southern Lebanon was no less tragic than its policy of settlements in the occupied territories. The Israelis no longer even looked for pretexts, as was the case in the past and, contrary to their allegations, Lebanese civilians were their daily targets.

143. Expressing again his wishes for the success of the Commission, which he saw as a renewed effort toward peace, the Prime Minister assured the members of the full support of his Government and offered any assistance which the Commission might need in the performance of its tasks.

144. The Chairman expressed appreciation for the welcome received by the Commission and assured the Prime Minister of the desire of the Commission to implement as fully as possible the mandate assigned to it by the Security Council.

145. During its stay at Beirut, the Commission also met Mr. Yasser Arafat, Chairman of the Palestine Liberation Organization. That meeting is reported upon in part F below.

E. VISIT TO THE ARAB REPUBLIC OF EGYPT

Meetings with Government Officials

146. The Commission arrived at Cairo on 30 May. In the evening of the same day, the Commission was received by Mr. Boutros Ghali, Minister of State for Foreign Affairs, who was accompanied by Mr. Ahmed Khalil, Under-Secretary for Foreign Affairs, Mr. Ezz Eldin Sharaf, Director, Palestine

Department, Mr. Ahmed Maher, Chef de Cabinet of the Foreign Minister, Mr. Ala Eldin Khariat, Chef de Cabinet of the Minister of State, Mr. Amre Moussa, Director, International Organizations Department, Mr. Abdel Moneim Ghoneim, Cabinet of the Minister of Foreign Affairs, Mr. Said El Masri, Cabinet of the Minister of State, Mr. Mohamed El Dinang, and Ms. Leila Emara, both from the Foreign Ministry.

147. The Minister of State for Foreign Affairs said that Egypt welcomed the Commission most warmly, not only because of Cairo's interest in the United Nations and its role in the achievement of peace but also because of the Commission's mandate, which matched Egypt's concern regarding the settlement policy of Israel.

148. Mr. Boutros Ghali stated that the Egyptian Government had informed the United States and Israel that it condemned the settlement policy and insisted that those settlements should be removed. This had been achieved in the case of the settlements established in the Sinai, and for its part, Egypt would endeavour to have them removed from all the Arab territories, including Arab Jerusalem.

149. Mr. Ghali emphasized that Egypt's aim in the peace process was not the conclusion of a bilateral peace treaty with Israel but a comprehensive peace treaty in the area and the attainment of the settlement of the Arab-Israel conflict in all its aspects. In that connexion, he noted that the Camp David framework agreement set out the principles and procedures for a series of negotiations leading to peace between Israel and each of its Arab neighbours. In the Egypt-Israel peace treaty, Israel had accepted resolution 242 (1967) and thereby the principle of the dissolution of its settlements. That principle had to be applied also in other peace treaties to be concluded between Israel and its other Arab neighbours.

150. In the course of the exchange of views which ensued, Mr. Ghali stated that Arab Jerusalem was an integral part of the West Bank and that Israel must withdraw therefrom. He said that the attainment of a comprehensive peace in the area involved two types of negotiation: negotiation regarding withdrawal of Israel from the Sinai and negotiations concerning the future of the West Bank, including Arab Jerusalem, and of the Gaza Strip. Until a Palestinian authority could be created, what was required was a moratorium on Israeli declarations that there would be more settlements.

151. In conclusion, the Minister of State for Foreign Affairs summed up Egypt's position regarding the problem of settlements as follows: (a) the establishment of the settlements constituted a fundamental obstacle to peace and Egypt condemned that policy; (b) the Geneva Convention signed in 1949 stipulated that it was inadmissible to change the character of the occupied territories and any contrary measures were illegal; (c) Egypt had confirmed that position during the first Camp David discussions and had sent an official letter in that respect to President Carter of the United States on 17 September 1978 requesting his support to obtain the removal of all the settlements; and (d) Egypt had demanded and would continue to demand

during the coming negotiations on autonomy that the settlements be stopped and removed from the West Bank and Gaza Strip.

152. The Chairman expressed the appreciation of the Commission's members for the welcome they had received and reiterated the position of the Commission concerning its mandate and the problems which derived from the fact that the Commission could not go to the occupied territories. The Commission, he added, was grateful to the Minister of State for Foreign Affairs for the data thus provided to it and for stating the position of his Government with regard to the Israeli settlements.

153. On 31 May, the members of the Commission were received by the Prime Minister and Minister of Foreign Affairs, Mr. Mostafa Khalil. Also present at the meeting were Mr. Ahmed Tewfik Khalil, Under-Secretary, Ministry of Foreign Affairs, and Ms. Leila Emara, Ministry of Foreign Affairs.

154. The Prime Minister declared that Egypt regarded the establishment of the settlements as an illegal act incompatible with the resolutions of the United Nations and in no way conducive to the cause of peace and stability in the region. Israel had no right to establish those settlements, and their creation in the West Bank and Gaza Strip constituted a serious problem and impeded the efforts currently being made to bring about a just and comprehensive peace in the Middle East.

155. Referring to the Israeli settlements in the Sinai on land previously reclaimed from the Egyptian Government, which he said were to be removed after the second phase of Israeli withdrawal from the Sinai, the Prime Minister observed that those settlements could serve no military purpose as the area would be demilitarized. If those settlements were to serve a civilian purpose, the Prime Minister drew attention to the difficulties the settlers would face once Egypt resumed the exercise of its full sovereignty over the Sinai since, under Egyptian law, foreigners could not own agricultural lands. Noting that the number of settlers in the Sinai was somewhere around 4,300 to 4,500 people, he pointed out that in comparison to Egypt's population of some 40 million, that number of settlers was insignificant. The real question was the meaning and intention behind those settlements, the question of the right of the settlers to retain their identity and the question of establishing a precedent.

156. Mr. Mostafa Khalil recalled that international law and United Nations resolutions forbade the retention of territories acquired by conquest and also proscribed the exploitation of the resources of such territories during the period of occupation. He pointed out that the framework laid down in the Camp David agreements was based on resolutions 242 (1967) and 338 (1973); this clearly meant that Egypt rejected the pretext of retaining territory in order to obtain security since security could be guaranteed in accordance with agreed arrangements, as was happening in the Sinai, without recourse to the establishment of settlements.

157. The Prime Minister expressed his concern that the settlements

would constitute a future obstacle to the negotiations on self-determination which he said the Palestinians were to conduct three years after the establishment of autonomy in the West Bank and the Gaza Strip.

158. Regarding the present status of Jerusalem, the Prime Minister told the Commission that Arab Jerusalem was part of the West Bank and that the area containing the holy places should be open to all faiths. He affirmed that the Palestinians alone, and no other party, should decided their future and he expressed his conviction that, for the Palestinians, the negotiations on autonomy would represent the beginning of the road towards self-determination.

159. The Chairman thanked the Prime Minister for the opportunity afforded the Commission to acquaint itself with the position of the Egyptian Government on the question of settlements and assured him that the substance of his statement would be reported to the Security Council.

Hearings

160. On 31 May the Commission held a meeting at Cairo during which it heard seven witnesses.

161. In their statements, the first two witnesses introduced themselves as Mr. Yehia Aboubakr, Information Director, League of Arab States (No. 36) and Mr. Ibrahim Shukrallah, Director of the Political Department, League of Arab States (No. 37). Both emphasized that the destruction of Arab villages and the establishment of Jewish settlemetns were interrelated. According to the figures available to their organizations, some 500 Arab villages had already been destroyed for that purpose. They gave specific cases as examples of that policy particularly in the Gaza Strip. They emphasized that that policy, which was a flagrant aggression against human rights, constituted a major obstacle to the establishment of peace. The situation was specially grave because of the clear intention of Israel to establish new settlements.

162. That intention had been stated in particular by the Israeli Minister for Agriculture—also Chairman of the Ministerial Committee for Settlements—who had spoken about several plans such as the increase from 25 to 50 in the number of Israeli settlements in the Jordan Valley; to establish a belt of settlements between the occupied Gaza Strip and the liberated Egyptian Sinai and to encircle Jerusalem with Jewish settlements in order to increase the population of the city to 1 million inhabitants.

163. In addition to the establishment of new settlements, the witnesses noted that the policy to strengthen and enlarge the existing settlements had been advocated repeatedly by Israeli officials. Thus the Israeli Minister of Defence, Mr. Weizman, had recently announced a plan for the creation between Jerusalem and Ramallah of a large settlement town to be called Gabaon.

164. That official attitude was still reinforced by the actions of private groups such as the Gush Emunim group, which acquired lands for further settlements. That group, they said, worked hand-in-glove with the Govern-

ment, and the financing of its operations was partly provided by official Government circles. As to the method used for that purpose, the group would send some of its members during the night to the location concerned. They would build primitive housing in which they would establish residence and gradually would increase their number to the moment when a fait accompli had been established.

165. By implementing that policy, Israel had forced the Palestinians into dispersion, so forefeiting their right to return. Some of those who had remained had been thrown into jail under various pretexts. As to the peasantry, they had been turned into a mobile army of unskilled or semi-skilled labourers that could easily be persuaded to emigrate.

166. But while the Israelis numbered a little over 3 million, Arabs were still the majority in the north, the West Bank and the Gaza Strip. Therefore, to fail to redress such a grave injustice would just keep the cause of contention alive.

167. The chairman stated that the Commission had taken due note of the statements made by the two witnesses as it had taken note of statements made during its visits to other Arab countries when other witnesses were presented to it. The fact that the witnesses had stated that they belonged to the Arab League would not imply, however, on the part of the Commission any involvement in the dispute related to the location of the League headquarters.

168. The four other witnesses (Nos. 38, 39, 40 and 41) referred essentially to the situation in Gaza. One of them (No. 38) described the area as being 45 kilometres long and 8 kilometres wide; half of it, he said, was built up with houses, another quarter bore citrus plantations and the remaining quarter was inhabited by some 500,000 Arabs.

169. Another witness (No. 41) stated that five Israeli settlements had been established on some 12,000 dunums of land. Roads had also been built on Arab land and the owners, said another witness (No. 38), rejected any offer of compensation.

170. Some witnesses referred to different sorts of pressure exerted against the inhabitants to compel them to leave. A witness (No. 41) said that, for example, an Israeli would knock at a door at night, saying that he was an Arab commando and asking refuge. He would stay one hour or two and later on the inhabitant would be arrested and expelled. Another possibility was for the Israeli authorities to grant an authorization to visit relatives outside the Gaza Strip but not let the inhabitant return. A reference was made also to the control of water through meters fixed on wells to limit the supply; the water would be completely shut off if the consumption exceeded the fixed limit (No. 38), thus compelling the inhabitant to leave.

171. The same witness recalled that when Israeli troops entered the Gaza Strip in 1967, they encircled the villages, put the men aged 15 to 30 on trucks and took them to Egypt, thereby expelling some 12,000 young men who were never allowed to return.

172. Another witness (No. 39) stated that the purpose of the settlements

in addition to changing the demographic nature of the area was to terrorize the inhabitants. Those settlements were heavily armed while the local inhabitants had no weapons. Friction and clashes among the two groups left many victims among the Palestinians.

173. As to the procedure followed by the Israeli authorities to establish or extend their settlements, a witness (No. 41), who said that he had left Gaza one month before, stated that when the Eretz settlement had decided to build a road leading to the seashore, the Israelis confiscated his land with its vineyards and also took over several buildings which the United Nations had built for the refugees. In one of those buildings which, the witness said, still belonged to UNRWA, the inhabitants were given 24 hours to leave before it was destroyed.

174. Mr. Ali Khalil, representative of the United Nations Association (No. 42) made an appeal to the Commission to help the Security Council deal with the question of settlements which he emphasized was an obstacle on the road to peace.

Private Meeting

175. During its stay at Cairo, the commission had an opportunity to exchange views with Mr. Hafez Ghanim, Chairman of the International Law Association, and other members of the Association.

176. Among other points, Mr. Ghanim and his colleagues drew particular attention to the illegality of the establishment of settlements in occupied territories with regard to international law. They also questioned the validity of the status and functions of the Office of the Custodian of Absentee Property, which was established in Israel by law in 1950. Mr. Ghanim emphasized that that official was given a free hand over such properties, which could then be disposed of at his whim.

177. The Chairman expressed appreciation to Mr. Ghanim and to the other members of the Association for their informative briefing.

F. STATEMENTS BY THE CHAIRMAN OF THE PALESTINE LIBERATION ORGANIZATION AND OTHER OFFICIALS OF THAT ORGANIZATION

178. In the course of its visit, the members of the Commission had several exchanges of views with representatives of the PLO. At Damascus, on 27 May, the Commission heard a statement by Mr. Najib Al Ahmad, Special Representative, Political Department and, the following day, statements were also made by Mr. Habib Kahwaji, and Mr. Abdul Muhsen Abou Meizar, both members of the Executive Committee. Moreover, at Beirut, on 30 May, the Commission had a private meeting with Mr. Yasser Arafat, Chairman of the Palestine Liberation Organization.

179. In his statement, Chairman Arafat said that the Israeli Defence Minister had recently confirmed his previous declaration that the Israelis wanted to destroy the Palestinians and that the shelling in Southern Lebanon would not stop as long as that goal had not been reached. This ex-

plained the daily killing of children and destruction of schools by fragmentation bombs, although their use was forbidden by international law.[7]

180. As a result of those developments, the number of refugees in Lebanon had increased to some 600,000 of which 150,000 were Palestinians and 450,000 Lebanese. The PLO had to fight not with a view to attacking but just to defend its people. Inside Palestine, the Palestinians who were still there were treated like slaves. They were under the control of the occupation forces for every way of life including the amount of water they were allowed to use in their villages, because water was allocated by priority to Israeli settlements. Meanwhile, the Palestinians who were compelled to leave their country were now used as experimental targets for all new types of those weapons provided to Israel by the United States.

181. Chairman Arafat pointed out the distress of the Palestinian refugees who had been uprooted from their own land and stripped from their national identity. He referred to their daily problems concerning, for instance, the obtaining of a passport or how their children could go to school. Many new-born children, he said, were not even reported because their parents lacked the necessary papers. It was sad indeed that in such circumstances the international community did not take the sort of strong action which could remedy the situation.

182. As to the Camp David agreement, Mr. Arafat said that while it specified that the Israelis should not attack the Jordanians or the Syrians, it did not mention the Palestinians. That omission implied an invitation to Israel to attack the Palestinians; clearly the Israelis were responding to it.

183. More trouble would come up, he said. But in the long run, PLO would succeed just like the many other leaders who, after acting as liberation fighters were now representing their own countries at the United Nations.

184. In the present context the development of Israeli settlements was the centre of the matter, he said. Most of the refugees had to leave their country because Israelis wanted their lands. And now the trend was increasing and the establishment of new settlements demonstrated Israel's policy of colonizing the occupied territories and banning for ever the return of the Palestinian refugees, in violation of United Nations resolutions. For that reason, PLO was hoping very sincerely that the Commission would be successful in its tasks which, it was to be hoped, would bring peace despite Israel's refusal to co-operate with it.

185. The Chairman of the Commission thanked Mr. Arafat for his informative briefing and assured him that the Commission would do its utmost to fulfil faithfully its mandate.

186. When at another meeting at Damascus, Mr. Najib Al Ahmad, special representative of the PLO addressed the Commission, he pointed out that for the establishment of the settlements on Arab lands in the West Bank, the Israeli Government had allocated half a billion Israeli pounds for the

[7] Part of a fragmentation shell was shown to the Commission.

year 1979. Moreover, it had been decided, he said, to build 20 Israeli settlements in the West Bank in 1980 and 45 within the next five years to accommodate 58,000 Jewish families.

187. Mr. Al Ahmad then gave an account of the practices used by authorities to compel Arab inhabitants to leave their lands. Thus the Arabs were prevented from digging any artesian wells without a special authorization, which was difficult to obtain. The owners of the wells were compelled to install water meters and could irrigate their land only with the amount of water allocated to them and only during specified hours. That practice led to a decrease in agricultural production, which compelled the owners to abandon their lands. He referred also to acts of destruction or damage to Arab water pumps perpetrated by the Israeli settlers to prevent the Arabs from irrigating their land and further noted that Arabs in the West Bank and the Gaza Strip needed a special authorization to plant trees or replace those previously planted.

188. Mr. Al Ahmad challenged the Israeli Government claim that it established the settlements only on public lands. He referred to his own experience in 1948 when Israel occupied 90 per cent of the land of his native village, Romana, and in 1967 when it occupied the rest. Mr. Al Ahmad was then put in jail, for security reasons, and after spending 13 months in prison he was expelled with his family.

189. In that connexion, the witness gave some information on the treatment of prisoners in the occupied territories. He also noted that more than 2,000 Arabs had been forcefully deported without even the use of indirect ways of pressure. A large number of these deported people, he said, were professionals such as physicians, engineers, teachers and lawyers.

190. Mr. Al Ahmad also drew attention to the fact that 2,875 Arab houses had been blown up for so-called security reasons.

191. Mr. Habib Kahwaji, member of the Executive Committee of the PLO who indicated that he had been expelled from the West Bank, said that, under the pretext of maintaining security, the Israeli authorities had embarked upon a programme of gradual judaization of the occupied territories. This was pursued through the creation of a wall of settlements between those territories and neighbouring Arab States; the fragmentation of the territorial unity of the West Bank and the Gaza Strip into small areas isolated from each other by Jewish settlements; and the isolation of major Arab cities in the area from their natural Arab surroundings.

192. Over the past 12 years, in order to acquire the lands needed for its settlements in the West Bank and the Gaza Strip, Israel had seized an area equivalent to more than one quarter of the total area of both territories.

193. The various ways resorted to by the Israeli occupation authorities to seize Arab lands included the following:

(a) Acquisition of public lands allocated for public facilities or for the expansion of municipal zones;

(b) Expropriation of privately owned lands by invoking the Emergency Law introduced by the British Mandate Government; that law as revised by

Israel, authorized military governors to declare certain areas as zones closed for military purposes;

(c) The use of the Absentees' Property Law of 1950;

(d) The compulsory purchase of Arab lands, which consisted of seizing privately owned land, then having the owners appear before the military administration official to sign the sale contracts, prepared in advance;

(e) The purchase of land through firms set up abroad either by the Jewish National Fund (JNF) or the Israeli Real Estate Department, such as the Rimanota firms, an American enterprise owned by the JNF;

(f) The seizure of lands under the pretext that they used to be owned by the JNF before 1948.

194. Through these various methods of seizure and confiscation, over 60 per cent of the arable lands of the Jordan Valley, namely, 95,000 dunums, had been seized. In the Hebron area, in addition to public lands, the occupation authorities had expropriated 1,000 dunums in 1968 to set up the settlement of Kiryat Arba, another 1,000 dunums of the Samou' village lands, 230 dunums belonging to the Bani Naeem village in 1975 and about 160 dunums at Hebron itself in 1979.

195. Several thousand dunums had also been seized in the Gosh Etzion area on the Bethlehem-Hebron road, where five settlements were set up. The latest confiscation in that area had happened in the Sheikh Abdulla hill, to the east of Kfar Etzion and south of Bethlehem, where several hundred dunums were seized to be used for a new Jewish town called Efrat. Last year, an area of 60,000 dunums in the Beit Sahor area, to the south of Jerusalem, was closed and fenced.

196. When Israel made its decision to annex Arab Jerusalem in 1967, the outskirts of the city, including an area of 70,000 dunums were also annexed. In the autumn of 1971, Israel closed other lands covering about 70,000 dunums. Those lands ranged from Beit Sahor in the south, through Al-Khan Al-Ahmar on the Jerusalem-Jericho road in the east, to the village of Anata in the north. Inside the city of Jerusalem itself 18,000 dunums were seized. In 1976, a 1,000-dunum area in the Abu Dais village and 750 dunums in the village of Aizariah were expropriated, and 1,000 dunums in the Beit Or village and 800 dunums in the Jila mountain near Beit Jala were closed. Several thousand additional dunums had already been closed in the village of Salwan. Last year the Israeli authorities closed and fenced some 4,000 dunums of the lands of the Anata village to the north of Jerusalem.

197. The same happened in the Ramallah area where, since 1970, the occupation authorities had closed 2,400 dunums in the Al-Beera vicinity, to which were added 1,500 dunums at Jabal El-Taweel, near Al-Beera. In July 1978, lands totalling 7,000 dunums were closed in the same area, half of them belonging to Al-Beera and the other half to the villages of Yabrood and Dora El-Qar'a. Meanwhile, some 600 dunums had been expropriated in the village close to the Ofira settlement to the east of Ramallah and other areas, in the village of Qaryoot and Tar Mas'iya, were expropriated and annexed to the settlement of Shila. Almost at the same time, about 200 du-

nums in the Nabi Salih village, to the northwest of Ramallah, were seized for the purpose of setting up a new settlement there. The same also happened in the Nablus area. In the same year about 1,000 dunums in the village of Tobas were seized.

198. As to the Jewish settlement plans for the future, the witness stated that the Minister of Agriculture and head of the Ministerial Committee for Settlements, Mr. Ariel Sharon, had stressed the necessity of transforming Jerusalem into a city with 1 million Jewish inhabitants within 20 years, surrounded by other smaller Jewish towns.

199. Last year, he said the head of the Settlement Department of the Jewish Agency, Mr. Paanan Weitz, submitted to Israeli Prime Minister Begin, a comprehensive plan for the establishment of 102 settlements by 1983, half of which were to be established in the occupied territories. Mr. Weitz expected that plan to absorb 10,000 Jewish families. Mr. Metitiah Drobless, the Co-Chairman of the Jewish Agency's Settlement Department, explained that, according to the plan, 46 new settlements would be established within five years in the West Bank alone.

200. The witness went on to say that last February, the Israeli Government approved a plan set by the Planning Office in the Jewish Agency's Settlement Department for supplying water from the Lake of Tiberias to a Jewish settlement site in the Jordan Valley and developing a main road to connect the northern part of occupied Palestine with Jerusalem across the eastern slopes of the Nablus Mountains. That plan aimed at the implantation of a wide range of Jewish settlements on the eastern slopes of the Nablus Mountains and the establishment of 33 settlements to absorb 20,000 settlers within four years. The cost of such a plan was estimated by the Israelis at £I 5 billion.

201. For 1979, the Israeli circles were considering the establishment of 10 new settlements in the West Bank and one south of the Gaza Strip. An Israeli official source had announced on 5 December 1978, that by the end of the settlement freezing period, two new settlements would be established in the Jordan Valley and another in the Latrun area—that is on the boundary between Jaffa and Jerusalem—at the first stage. At the second stage, it was intended to establish three further settlements in the Jordan Valley. The Israeli Government had approved a budget of £I 711 million for the improvement and expansion of the present settlements in occupied territories. Later on, the Israeli Government had approved an extra budget of £I 1 billion for further care of the settlements in the occupied territories.

202. Mr. Abdul Muhsen Abou Meizar, member of the PLO Executive Committee, said that, as a Jerusalem attorney, he had been a member of the municipality of that city and a member of its town planning committee. Until his deportation he also had been a member of the High Islamic Council.

203. The witness described some of Israel's practices in the occupied Arab territories, which were in clear violation of the 1949 Geneva Conventions,[8]

---

[8] United Nations, *Treaty Series*, vol. 75, Nos. 970-973.

in particular of articles 2, 4, 27, 47 and 49 of the fourth Convention. As to the settlement policy, it was in flagrant contravention of article 4. Similarly, the annexation of Jerusalem in 1967 was in contradiction to article 47.

204. Contrary to Israel's allegation that the Jewish settlements constituted a private activity of the part of Israeli citizens, it was clear, from the many official statements on the matter, that it was in fact the policy of the Government. Its aim was the judaization of Palestine through the annexation of lands, the expulsion of the Palestinian inhabitants, and the containment and isolation of the remaining Palestinian agglomerations.

III. Conclusions and Recommendations

A. Conclusions

205. When it set out to accomplish the task entrusted to it by the Security Council, i.e., "to examine the situation relating to settlements in the Arab territories occupied since 1967, including Jerusalem", the Commission sought as a matter of priority to secure the co-operation of all the parties concerned in order to carry out its mandate objectively and comprehensively.

206. The Commission felt in that connexion that a visit to the area would be most useful to its work.

207. The Commission, although aware of the views already expressed by the Israeli Government in the matter, made persistent efforts at various levels to secure the co-operation of that Government. As related in section I of the present report, the Commission was much disappointed by Israel's negative response to its approach. It noted in that regard that Israel's attitude deprived the Commission not only of the possibility of examining *in situ* the situation relating to settlements in the occupied territories but also of any opportunity to receive from the Government of Israel the explanations and comments which would have been useful to the Commission in its efforts to assess the situation.

208. The Commission feels compelled to state that it considers such a lack of co-operation on the part of a Member State as an act of disregard for a decision of the Security Council.

209. Having spared no effort to obtain information from a variety of sources, the Commission believes that the present report contains a fairly accurate assessment of the prevailing situation it was entrusted to examine.

210. In its endeavour to fulfil its mandate, the Commission felt that it could assist the Security Council *inter alia* by: (*a*) bringing up to date the basic information already at the disposal of the Council; (*b*) determining the consequences of the settlement policy on the local Arab population; and (*c*) assessing the impact of that policy and its consequences with regard to "the urgent need to achieve a comprehensive, just and lasting peace in the Middle East" stressed by the Council in the preamble of resolution 446 (1979), under which the Commission was created.

211. In drawing its conclusions the Commission did not attribute the same value to every piece of information it had obtained, but evaluated its signif-

icance freely and critically, in accordance with: its relevance to the accomplishment of the mandate of the Commission and its accuracy as determined by its coherence and by the documentary evidence rendered by the witnesses as a supplement to their statements.

Recent Information on the Settlements

212. According to the figures obtained, there are altogether in the occupied territories 133 settlements, including 17 in and around Jerusalem, 62 in the West Bank, 29 in the Golan Heights and 25 in the Gaza Strip and the Sinai.

213. The population of those settlements varies in number, probably depending on the policy purposes predetermined for each settlement. In the area of Jerusalem and the West Bank where the establishment of settlements has been the most intensive, the number of settlers has reached approximately 90,000, while in the Sinai their number would be under 5,000.

214. The land seized by the Israeli authorities as a whole, either specifically for the establishment of those settlements or for other stated reasons, covers 27 per cent of the occupied West Bank and the quasi-totality of the Golan Heights.

215. On the basis of the information received, the Commission is convinced that a number of settlements were established on privately owned land and not only on public land.

216. Many of those settlements are of a military nature, either officially placed under the control of the Israeli army or *de facto* with a settler population of military age. Moreover, those settlers are said to have at their disposal military weapons in the midst of an unarmed Arab population.

217. According to several witnesses, the location of the settlements is determined in accordance with agricultural designs, and also with what Israel considers to be "security" purposes. That may explain, for instance, the existence of three successive belts of settlements reported to have been established between Jerusalem and the Jordan river and which would be aimed at "compartmenting" the local population.

218. Supported by the strong influence of various private groupings, the settlement policy is an official government programme which is implemented by a number of organizations and committees representing both the Government and the private sector inside and outside Israel.

219. In addition to private contributions coming mostly from outside Israel, the financing of the settlement policy is essentially a governmental matter. In that connexion, the Commission was told that the Israeli Government has set aside the equivalent of $US 200 million for expanding and establishing settlements during the fiscal year 1979/80.

220. The Commission found evidence that the Israeli Government is engaged in a wilful, systematic and large-scale process of establishing settlements in the occupied territories for which it should bear full responsibility.

Consequences of the Settlement Policy on the Local Population

221. The Commission is of the view that a correlation exists between the establishment of Israeli settlements and the displacement of the Arab population. Thus it was reported that since 1967, when that policy started, the Arab population has been reduced by 32 per cent in Jerusalem and the West Bank. As to the Golan Heights, the Syrian authorities stated that 134,000 inhabitants had been expelled leaving only 8,000, i.e., 6 per cent of the local population in the occupied Golan Heights.

222. The Commission is convinced that in the implementation of its policy of settlements, Israel has resorted to methods—often coercive and sometimes more subtle—which included the control of water resources, the seizure of private properties, the destruction of houses and the banishment of persons, and has shown disregard for basic human rights, including in particular the right of the refugees to return to their homeland.

223. For the Arab inhabitants still living in those territories, particularly in Jerusalem and the West Bank, they are subjected to continuous pressure to emigrate in order to make room for new settlers who, by contrast, are encouraged to come to the area. The Commission was told also that in the Golan Heights Israeli authorities imposed Israeli citizenship on all new-born children in an effort to assimilate the remaining population.

224. The settlement policy has brought drastic and adverse changes to the economic and social pattern of the daily life of the remaining Arab population. As a mere example of that evolution, the Commission was informed that a number of Arab landowners were now compelled to earn their living and that of their family by working on their own land as the hired employees of the Israeli settlers.

225. The Commission considers that the pattern of that settlement policy, as a consequence, is causing profound and irreversible changes of a geographical and demographic nature in those territories, including Jerusalem.

226. The Commission has no doubt that those changes are of such a profound nature that they constitute a violation of the Geneva Convention relative to the Protection of Civilian Persons in Time of War, of 12 August 1949, and of the relevant decisions adopted by the United Nations in the matter, more specifically: Security Council resolutions 237 (1967), 252 (1968) and 298 (1971); the consensus statement by the President of the Council on 11 November 1976 [*1969th meeting*]; as well as General Assembly resolutions 2253 (ES-V) and 2254 (ES-V), 32/5 and 33/113.

Impact of the Settlement Policy and Its Consequences on the Search for Peace

227. While fully aware of the extreme complexities inherent in the Middle East problem and at the same time recognizing the limitations in the scope of its mandate, the Commission none the less had the opportunity to note a genuine desire for peace in the capitals it visited as well as among the leaders of the Palestine Liberation Organization whom it met.

228. Unfortunately, the Commission has also perceived a deep sense of

despair and helplessness, primarily among the Palestinian refugees. That stems from the realization that Israel's policy with regard to the occupied Arab territories and more particularly its policy of continuing to establish more settlements is unabated and undaunted either by United Nations decisions or any other external factor. The Commission would like to state clearly in that regard that in the course of its various meetings it felt that this settlement policy was widely regarded as a most negative factor in the achievement of peace in the area both by the refugees themselves and all those who support their cause, including the neighbouring Governments for which that policy generates at the national level economic and social problems of grave consequences.

229. Consequently, after examining the situation relating to settlements in the Arab territories occupied since 1967, including Jerusalem, the Commission wishes to reaffirm the determination made in resolution 446 (1979), according to which "the policy and practices of Israel in establishing settlements in the Palestinian and other Arab territories occupied since 1967 have no legal validity and constitute a serious obstruction to achieving a comprehensive, just and lasting peace in the Middle East".

B. RECOMMENDATIONS

230. On the basis of the conclusions reached, the Commission would like, therefore, to recommend that the Security Council, bearing in mind the inalienable right of the Palestinians to return to their homeland, launch a pressing appeal to the Government and people of Israel, drawing again their attention to the disastrous consequences which the settlement policy is bound to have on any attempt to reach a peaceful solution in the Middle East.

231. In the view of the Commission, as a first step, Israel should be called upon to cease on an urgent basis the establishment, construction and planning of settlements in the occupied territories. The question of the existing settlements would then have to be resolved.

232. The Security Council might further wish to consider measures to safeguard the impartial protection of property arbitrarily seized.

233. As to Jerusalem, the Security Council should also call upon the Government of Israel to implement faithfully the resolutions it has adopted on that question as from 1967. Moreover, recalling that Jerusalem is a most sacred place for the three great monotheistic faiths throughout the world, i.e., Christian, Jewish and Moslem, the Council might wish to consider steps to protect and preserve the unique spiritual and religious dimension of the Holy Places in that city, taking into account the views of high-ranking representatives of the three religions.

234. In view of the magnitude of the problem of settlement and its implications for peace in the region, the Security Council should keep the situation under constant survey.

. . . .

ANNEX III

List of settlements

ISRAELI SETTLEMENTS IN THE WEST BANK

A. AREA OF JERUSALEM AND ENVIRONS

Name	Date founded	Location	Type	Economic base	Land used (in dunums)	Original landowners
1. Atrot	1970	Jerusalem: north edge, near airport	Industrial zone	61 factories	10 000	Arab residents of Beit Hanina village
2. Neve Ya'acov	1973	Jerusalem: north of town	Residential suburb	2 500 housing units	10 000	Arab residents of Beit Hanina village
3. Ramot	1973	Jerusalem: north-west, near Nabi Samwil	Residential suburb	750 housing units (8 000 units planned)	30 000	Arab residents of Beit Iksa village; 100 Arab homes demolished
4. Ramat Eshkol ...	1968	Jerusalem: north side	Residential area	1 700 housing units	600	Arab land (expropriated)
5. French Hill	1969	Jerusalem: north side, along Jerusalem-Ramallah road	Residential area	2 100 housing units	15 000	Arab land; land from Catholic convent
6. Nahalat Defna ...		Jerusalem: north side	Residential area	250 housing units	270	Arab families and waqf properties
7. Gilo Sharafat (Gilo)	1973	Jerusalem: south side, near Beit Jala	Residential suburb	1 200 housing units out of 10 000 planned	4 000	Palestinian residents of Jerusalem, Beit Jala, Beit Safafa and Sharafat
8. East Talpiot	1973	Jerusalem: east side, south of Jabal Al-Mukabber where United Nations headquarters was situated	Residential suburb	1 000 housing units (3 000 planned)	20 000	Arab residents of Jerusalem, Sur Bahir, Sheikh Sa'ad and United Nations enclave expropriated

ISRAELI SETTLEMENTS IN THE WEST BANK (*cont.*)

Name	Date founded	Location	Type	Economic base	Land used (in dunums)	Original landowners
9. Jewish Quarter (Old City of Jerusalem)	1967	Jerusalem: "Old City" between western wall of Al Aqsa Mosque and Latin Convent	Residential area	320 housing units and shops		160 Arab houses demolished, 600 homes expropriated, 6 500 Arab residents evacuated
10. Hebrew University	1969	Jerusalem: north side	University campus	Offices, classrooms, dormitories and hospital		Expansion of pre-1948 university for which land was expropriated
11. Sanhedria extension	1973	Jerusalem: north side	Residential area	250 housing units		Former demilitarized zone, entirely expropriated
B. AREA OF RAMALLAH AND EL-BEIREH						
12. Shiloh	1976	East of Nablus-Ramallah road	Gush Emunim		15 000	From villages of Turmus Ayya, Qaryut, Abu-Elfalah and El-Maghireh
					80 to 90	Dunums closed off, almond trees cut down
13. Kochav Hashahar	1975	North-east of Taiyyibe village	Nahal, then kibbutz	Agriculture	4 000	Land from Deir Jarir and Kufur Malik; water from Ain Samia, Ramallah's sole water source

No.	Name	Year	Location	Organization	Activity	Area	Remarks
14.	Ofra (Ba'al Hat/or)	1975	East of Ramallah on Jericho road	Gush Emunim	Workshops and agriculture	350	100 dunums from Ain Yabrud village, 250 dunums from Silwad village
15.	Mevo Horon	1969	Latrun salient	Moshav	Agriculture, 2 wells	16 000	Land from Yalu, Imwas and Beit Nuba villages, destroyed by Israel after 1967 war
16.	Beit Horon	1977	Mid-way on Ramallah-Latrun road, near Tira	Gush Emunim		150	Initial takeover of Arab land
17.	Mevo Horon Dalet (Matityahu)	1977	Latrun area, 3 km from armistice line		Agriculture	350	DMZ (Midya Arab village prior to 1948)
18.	Kfar Ruth	1977	Latrun area; 1 km south-east of Shayelet settlement		Agriculture		DMZ (site of Midya village), thousands of dunums of irrigated lands
19.	Givat Hamivtar ..	1975	On north side of Jerusalem		350 housing units		Land area entirely expropriated
20.	Canada Park	1976	Latrun salient: on Latrun-Ramallah road	Jewish National Fund Park		4 200	Land of destroyed villages of Yalu, Imwas and Beit Nuba (including 1 500 dunums of orchards)
21.	Ramonim	1977	North-east of Taybeh and Rammun villages, north of Ramallah-Jericho road	Nahal		300	Residents of Taybeh village (expropriated lands)
22.	Beit El	1977	North of Ramallah-Nablus road	Gush Emunim		35	Arab land. Settlement to expand on 250 dunums of expropriated land

ISRAELI SETTLEMENTS IN THE WEST BANK (*cont.*)

	Name	Date founded	Location	Type	Economic base	Land used (in dunums)	Original landowners
23.	Giv'on	1977	North-west of Jerusalem; near El-Jib village	Gush Emunim			Previously Jordanian military base, 5 000 dunums needed to be expropriated from El-Jib village
24.	Shayelet (Mevo Horiim)	1977	Latrun area	Moshav	Agriculture		DMZ land (site of Arab village of Midya)
25.	Neve Zuf (Nabi Saleh)	1977	North-west of Ramallah; near Beir Nidham	Gush Emunim		400	Closed off, including 100 dunums of wheat fields and almond trees of Nabi Saleh villagers

C. JORDAN VALLEY AND OTHER AREAS

	Name	Date founded	Location	Type	Economic base	Land used (in dunums)	Original landowners
26.	Mehola	1968	Jordan valley: north end of West Bank	Nahal until Nov. 1969, then moshav	Field crops, metal factory, 1 well, 1 reservoir	3 000	Residents of Bardala and Ain el-Beida villages. Water supply of villages depleted by wells of Mehola
27.	Argaman	1968	Near end of Damya-Nablus road	Nahal until May 1971, then moshav	Agriculture, 5 absentees' wells, 1 reservoir	5 000	Arab agricultural land, including 1 000 dunums from Marj al-Naja
28.	New Massuah	1976	Jordan valley: south of Nablus-Damya road			800	Residents of Arab villages of Al-Ajajra and Jiftlik
29.	Massuah	1970	Jordan valley: just south of settlement No. 28	Nahal until May 1974, then kibbutz	Vegetables, fishpond, water from Hamra, 1 well, 2 reservoirs	3 000	Residents of Al-Ajajra and Jiftlik villages, "expropriated land"

No.	Date	Location	Type	Crops	Number	Remarks
30. Phatza'el B	1977	South of settlement No. 29	Rural settlement		1 500	Arab land
31. Phatza'el	1970	End of south-west road from Aqraba	Moshav	Vegetables, 3 wells, "600 cubic metres per hour", 1 reservoir Hothouse vegetables	3 000	Residents of Fazayil village
32. Tomer	1976	Jordan valley: south of settlement No. 31			Unknown as construction still going on	
33. Gilgal	1970	Jordan valley: south of settlement No. 32	Nahal until May 1973, then moshav	Vegetables, citrus, field crops	3 300	Arab land; "plan to pump water from Jordan river"
34. Netiv Hagdud ...	1976-1977	South of Gilgal settlement (No. 33)	Nahal to become moshav		Unknown as construction still going on	
35. Mivsom (Na'aran)	1977 began construction	Jordan valley: near Arab village of Awja	Nahal to become moshav			Land expropriated from residents of Awja village
36. Yitav	1970	West of Awja village	Nahal until Oct. 1976, then kibbutz	Vegetables, field crops	2 000	Arab land from Awja village "including that of absentee owners", water from Ain Al-Awja and two wells nearby
37. Almog	1977	Jordan valley: north-west of Dead Sea	Nahal			Water supply drawn by 12-inch pipeline from well near Aqbat Jaber, Jeri-

ISRAELI SETTLEMENTS IN THE WEST BANK (*cont.*)

Name	Date founded	Location	Type	Economic base	Land used (in dunums)	Original landowners
38. Kalia	1968	Jordan valley: north-west of Dead Sea	Nahal until 1975, then kibbutz	Vegetables, dairy, vineyards, fish-ponds		Previously Jordan army camp; water supply from Wadi Keit west of Jericho
39. Mitzpe Shalem ..	1970	Dead Sea: west shore	Nahal, then kibbutz	Date palms, vegetables	over 50	
D. ISRAELI SETTLEMENTS ON THE HILLS OVERLOOKING JORDAN VALLEY						
40. Malki Shua	1976	North edge of West Bank: south of Mt. Gibboa; access road from Beit Shean	Nahal			
41. Roï	1974	"Limit of settlements" road (LS): north end	Nahal; moshav by 1978	Agriculture	2 500	Tubas village residents, land cultivated with wheat
42. Bega'ot	1972	LS road, north end: south of Roï (No. 41)	Moshav	Poultry, vegetables, citrus	5 000	Tamun village, land closed off
43. Hamra	1971	LS road: on east of West Nablus-Damya road, in lush valley. Farm land	Moshav	Vegetables, flowers, citrus, poultry; 1 well, 2 reservoirs, 12-inch water pipeline to Massuah (No. 29) in Jordan valley	450	Land from Bab al-Nagab village, valley land near Damya Bridge; 450 dunums of "absentee owner groves"
44. Mekhora	1973	LS road: south of Hamra (No. 43)	Nahal until July 1976, then moshav	Vegetables, fruit	4 000	From Bab al-Nagab, Beit Dajan and Beit Furik villages; water supply includes 1 well, 3 reservoirs

No.	Name	Date	Location	Economy	Type	Area (dunums)	Remarks
45.	Gitit	Aug. 1972	LS road: near east-west Aqraba valley road	Vegetables, field crops	Nahal until Dec. 1975, now kibbutz	5 000	Land from Aqraba closed off, sprayed with defoliants early 1972
46.	Ma'ale Ephraim	1972	LS road: on east-west Aqraba valley road		Regional centre	200	Arab land
47.	Nevo Shiloh (Givat Aduma)	Nov. 1976	South of Ma'ale Ephraim settlement (No. 46)			1 300	Residents of Turmus Ayya, Abu-Fallah and al-Mughayyir villages
48.	Mishor Adomin (Ma'ale Adomin)	Nov. 1974	Dominates Jericho-Jerusalem road	Industry	Industrial estate and army base; Gush Emunim settlers	(81 000)	70 000 dunums closed off Oct. 1972 by Israeli army; additional 700 dunums expropriated from villages of Abu dis, Umaryya and Issawyya, 10 000 dunums from Silwad, 300 dunums from Silwad and Anota Land expropriated from above-mentioned villages
49.	Mizpeh Jericho ..	Early 1978	East of Mishor Adomin settlement (No. 48) overlooking Jericho				
50.	Reihan (Nei'ami Bet)	1977	North-west of Jenin, 3 km beyond armistice line	Agriculture	Nahal, 1978 kibbutz		Arab land

ISRAELI SETTLEMENTS IN THE WEST BANK (cont.)

Name	Date founded	Location	Type	Economic base	Land used (in dunums)	Original landowners
51. Dotan (Sanur) ...	Oct. 1977	Along Nablus-Jenin road in Sanur valley	Gush Emunim			Land of pre-1967 Jordanian police station near Sanur village
52. Natal Ma'ale	Jan. 1978	East of Nablus-Jenin road	Gush Emunim		550	Land confiscated from Silat Al-Dhaha village including 25 olive trees
53. Shomron	Oct. 1977	On Nablus-Jenin road			1 680	Kufr Sur village
54. Sal'it (Tsur Nathan Bet) ...	Aug. 1977	South-east of Tulkarm	Nahal		1 000	Kufr Sur village, half of land privately owned (cultivated), half common land for grazing
55. Elon Moreh (Qaddum)	Dec. 1975	Near Nablus-Qalqilya road	Gush Emunim		300	Arabs of Kufr Qaddum village
56. Qarney-Shomron	Oct. 1977	South side of Nablus-Qalqilya road, near Jinsafut village	Gush Emunim		150	Taken from villages of Jinsafut, Hajj and Kufr Laqif
57. El Qana (Mes'ha Pe'erim)	April 1977	South-east of Qalqilya	Gush Emunim nahal		10 300	Site of former Jordanian police station from Mes'ha village

No.	Name	Date	Location	Type	Economic activity	Population	Notes
58.	Tafuah (Bareget)	Jan. 1978	Along Nablus-Ramallah road 13 km south of Nablus			150	Arab villagers of Yasuf
59.	Haris	Feb. 1978	2 km west of Nablus-Ramallah road, near Salfit junction	Nahal; 2 km access road built		800	300 dunums expropriated for military camp; 500 dunums of pasturage closed off from villages of Kufr Haris, Harda and Salfit
60.	Har Gilo	1976	In Beit Jala village area	Residential suburb		400	Grapevines and fruit trees expropriated from Beit Jala residents, June 1976
61.	Efrat	1978	On road south of Bethlehem			7 000	Expropriated land, most of which cultivated
62.	Tekoah	June 1975	South-east of Bethlehem near Hebron	Nahal		3 000	Land expropriated from Rafidya village
63.	Elazar	Oct. 1975	South of Bethlehem	Religious moshav	Chemical laboratory, electronics	350	Vineyards expropriated from Hadar village, 1973
64.	Rosh Tzurim	July 1969	North of Hebron (Etzion bloc)	Kibbutz	Poultry	3 000	Including site of pre-1948 settlement plus expropriated land from Nahalin village
65.	Alon Shvot	July 1969 settlers, 1972	North of Hebron (Etzion bloc)	Regional centre for religious Jews	Yeshiva students plus families commute to Jerusalem	1 200	Land expropriated in 1969 from Arabs

ISRAELI SETTLEMENTS IN THE WEST BANK (*cont.*)

	Name	Date founded	Location	Type	Economic base	Land used (in dunums)	Original landowners
66.	Kfar Etzion	Sept. 1967 first settlement on the West Bank	North of Hebron (Etzion bloc)	Kibbutz	Some agriculture, a factory		Site (1943-1948) of Jewish settlement and cultivated land (vineyards)
67.	Migdal Oz	1977	West of Hebron (Etzion bloc)	Kibbutz	Agriculture	1 000 to 2 000	Residents of Beit Umar village, closed first as military area; 600 plum and almond trees uprooted in Dec. 1977
68.	Kiryat Arba	1970	Adjoins town of Hebron	Urban settlement	Factories, services, some commute to Jerusalem, 401 housing units	4 250	Individuals from Hebron and Halhoul (1 500 dunums expropriated)
69.	Yattir	July 1977	South of Hebron, near armistice line	Gush Emunim moshav		17 000 planned to be fenced	Pasture land
70.	Zohar						
71.	Sailat Dhahr	1978	On Nablus-Jenin road			550	Expropriated from Arab residents of Sailat Dhahr
72.	Anatot	Late 1978	North of Jerusalem			3 000	Expropriated from residents of Anata village

73.	Ya'afu Horom ...	1978	Near Arab village of Yatta; west of Hebron
74.	Tretseh	Approved 1978	
75.	Jericho		Jericho area
76.	Zif	1978	South of Hebron	Under construction
77.	Neweimeh	1979	Near Jericho
78.	New Kfar Etzion	1979	On road between Bethlehem and Hebron
79.	Huwara	1979	Few miles east of Nablus	600 settlers already live there

Source: List of settlements, map, information supplied by the Government of Jordan [*S/13149 of 7 March 1979*].

ISRAELI SETTLEMENTS IN THE GOLAN HEIGHTS
(June 1967–February 1979)

Name	Date founded	Location	Type	Economic base	Land used (in dunums)	Original landowners
1. Neve Ativ	1971	South slope of Mount Hermon	Moshav	Ski-station/400 dunums apple trees at Benia's spring	Total land of village	Syrian village, dab'at azzayat
2. Snir	1967	Edge of ex-DMZ; pasture on Golan	Nahal up to 1968, then kibbutz	Agriculture		Syrian village lands
3. Har Odem	1976	Mount Oden, between Mas'ada and Bugatha villages	Moshav	Industrial base established	200	Syrian nature reserve 200 dunums from Bugatha
4. El Rom	1971	North, near Bugatha	Kibbutz	Agriculture (apples)	Total land of Ain-kharja, some land of Bugatha	Syrian village of Ain-kharja and some land from Bugatha
5. Merom Golan	July 1967	North, west of Quneitra	Kibbutz	Cattle, 6 000 dunums field crops	6 000	Agricultural land west of Quneitra
6. Ein Zivan	1968	North, west of Quneitra	Kibbutz	Agriculture, 340 dunums orchards in Quneitra valley	340 dunums of orchards	Agricultural land west of Quneitra; near former Syrian village, Ain Ziwane
7. Katzrin	1973	Centre-west; near Yaacov Bridge across Jordan River	Industrial centre, field-school	Industries (200 housing units under construction)		Near Syrian village, Qasrine
8. Keshet	1974	Originally at Quneitra then at Khusniya	Religious moshav; Gush Emunim settlers	Plans for field-school, botanical garden, woodworking, agriculture		Syrian town, Khusniya

No.	Name	Year	Location	Type	Industries		Remarks
9.	Ani'am	1976	South of Katzrin (No. 7)	Industrial moshav	Industries		Syrian village land, Qasrine
10.	Yonatan (Yonati)	1975	Tel Faraz, south of Keshet (No. 8)	Bnei Akiva religious youth movement	Agriculture		
11.	Sha'al	1976	Centre	Moshav	Agriculture, industries planned		Syrian village
12.	Gamla	1976	Overlooks Lake Tiberias	Moshav	Agriculture		Syrian village land
13.	Ramot	1969	Overlooks Lake Tiberias	Moshav	Agriculture		Syrian village land
14.	Merkaz Hisfin (Khisfin)	1973	South Golan	Rural centre			Syrian town, Khisfin
15.	Ramat Magshimim	1968	South-east, 1.8 km from buffer zone	Moshav	Agriculture, cattle		Former Syrian army base
16.	Avni Eitan	1976	South Golan	Moshav	Agriculture		
17.	Nov (Nab)	1972	South Golan	Moshav	Agriculture, reservoir nearby		
18.	Geshur	1969	South; moved west due to 1974 disengagement	Nahal	Field crops		
19.	Eli-Al (El-Al)	1968	South Golan	Nahal until May 1973, then moshav	Agriculture		
20.	Givat Yo'av	1968	South Golan; adjoins No. 21	Histadrut moshav	Field crops, poultry, cattle		
21.	Merkaz Bnei Yehuda	1972	South Golan; joint entrance with No. 20	Rural centre			
22.	Ne'ot Golan	1968	South, overlooks Lake Tiberias	Moshav	Agriculture	100 dunums field crops	Near Syrian town Fiq

ISRAELI SETTLEMENTS IN THE GOLAN HEIGHTS (*cont.*)

	Name	Date founded	Location	Type	Economic base	Land used (in dunums)	Original landowners
23.	Afik	1967	South Golan	Nahal until 1972, then kibbutz	Agriculture		
24.	Kfar Haruv	1973	South, overlooks Lake Tiberias	Kibbutz	Agriculture		Near Syrian village Kafr Hared
25.	Mevo Hamma ...	1968	South, overlooks Lake Tiberias	Kibbutz	Agriculture, tourism at Hamma Springs, pasture	25 000	Syrian village at Hamma Springs
26.	Urtal	1978	Centre-west	Kibbutz	Industries planned		Syrian village land
27.	Ramath Shalom						
28.	Har Shifon						
29.	Dalhmiya						

Source: List by the Syrian Government; information on settlements—Ann Lesch.

ISRAELI SETTLEMENTS IN THE GAZA STRIP

Name	Date founded	Location	Type	Economic base	Land used (in dunums)	Original landowners
1. Netzarim	1972	4 km south of Gaza City, between north-south highway and coast	Nahal became moshav	Agriculture	700	Land exppropriated from Abu Madyan Arab tribe, early 1971
2. Kfar Darom	1970	South of Mughazi refugee camp, east side of north-south highway	Nahal until 1978, then kibbutz	Glasshouse vegetables	200	
3. Netzer Hazani ...	1973	North of Khan Yunis	Nahal until 1977, then moshav	Glasshouse vegetables	300	State land
4. Katif A	1973	West of Netzer Hazani settlement (No. 3), between Deir El Balah and Khan Yunis	Moshav	Glasshouse vegetables	400	
5. Katif B	1978	Close to Katif A settlement		Glasshouse vegetables	150	
6. Morag	1972	On coast between Khan Yunis and Rafah	Nahal, then kibbutz	Agriculture	12 000	Land exppropriated from Umm Kalb village, early 1971
7. Eretz Azooi	1969	North-east of Gaza City		Industries	800	

Source: List of settlements and map showing the location—Najib Al Ahmad, Special Representative, Political Department, Palestine Liberation Organization; information on settlements—Ann Lesch, former representative in the Middle East of the American Friends Service Committee, part of a hearing before the Sub-Committee of the Committee on International Relations, United States House of Representatives, 19 October 1977.

ISRAELI SETTLEMENTS IN THE SINAI

	Name	Date founded	Location	Type	Economic base	Original landowners
1.	Yamit	1973; first settlers, Sept. 1975	Rafah area: on coast 7 km south of Rafah town	Urban settlement	Beach resort	Bedouin lands, most evicted in 1971-1973
2.	Talmei Yosef	1977	Rafah area, near Yamit (No. 1)	Moshav	Tomatoes grown in glass hothouses (2 dunums per family)	Bedouin lands, including almond groves
3.	Pri'el	1977 started	Rafah area: near Yamit (No. 1)	Moshav	(Under construction)	Bedouin lands
4.	Merkaz Avshalom	1973	Rafah area; junction of Gaza Strip-Sinai highway	Rural centre	Gas station, shops, services	Adjoins area where bedouins resettled
5.	Netiv Ha'asara	1973	Rafah area: 7 km south of Rafah	Moshav	Tomatoes, flowers; 40 dunums and 20 000 cu m water yearly per family; hire bedouin labourers	Bedouin lands, including school and cement houses (demolished)
6.	Ogda	1975	Rafah area: 1 km south of settlement No. 5	Moshav	Glasshouse tomatoes; 8 dunums and 9 500 cu m water yearly per family	Bedouin lands
7.	Sufa (Succot)	1974	Rafah area: between Yamit settlement and main highway	Nahal until Jan. 1977, then kibbutz	Field crops, mangoes, glasshouse vegetables	Bedouin lands; almond and peach groves uprooted in 1974-1975
8.	Holit	1977 started	Rafah area: on highway east of Sufa	Nahal	Glasshouse tomatoes, 100 dunums mangoes	Bedouin lands

No.	Name	Year	Location	Type	Activity	Notes
9.	Sadot	1971	Rafah area; just west of No. 5	Moshav	Tomatoes, citrus	Bedouin lands
10.	Nir Avraham	1977 started	Rafah area: 1 km south of Sadot (No. 9)	Moshav	Glasshouse tomatoes	Bedouin lands
11.	Dikla	1969	Rafah area: 11 km south of Rafah town	Nahal until March 1971, then moshav	Tomatoes, packing shed; 10 000 cu m water yearly per family	Site of former Egyptian desert development company
12.	Haruvit	1975	Sinai coast: 18 km south-west of Dikla (No. 11)	Nahal	Tomatoes, vegetables, fishing	
13.	Sinai	1967	Sinai coast: east El Arish city	Nahal	Cultivated 1 000 dunums olives, citrus	Partly expropriated from El Arish
14.	Yam	1967	Sinai coast: lake Bardawil, 70 km south-west of El Arish	Nahal until May 1973, then kibbutz	Fishing	Egyptian fishing site
15.	Kadesh Barnea	Planned in 1977	Sinai: oasis near the 1967 border	Nahal	Archaeological site	Bedouin oasis
16.	Neviot	1971	Gulf of Aqaba: coast road, 60 km south of Eilat	Moshav	Resort area	Nuweibeh oasis
17.	Di-Zahav	1971	Gulf of Aqaba: coast road; 60 km south of Neviot settlement (No. 16)	Moshav	Resort area	Dhahab village, at mouth of Wadi Nasib
18.	Ophira	1967	Gulf of Aqaba: Sharm al-Sheikh	Urban settlement	Military base, port; 190 families (completing 5 000 unit housing project), mostly military	

Source: List of settlements and map supplied by the Egyptian Government (in Arabic).

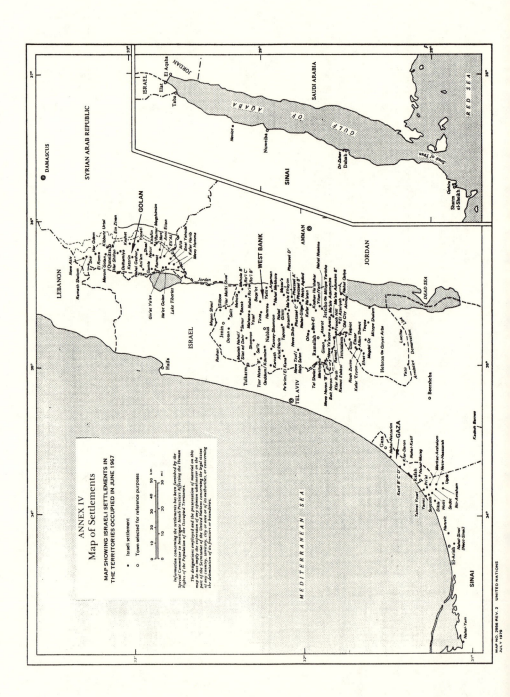

ANNEX IV

Map of Settlements

MAP SHOWING ISRAELI SETTLEMENTS IN
THE TERRITORIES OCCUPIED IN JUNE 1967

• Israeli settlement
○ Town selected for reference purposes

| 0 | 10 | 20 | 30 | 40 | 50 km |
| 0 | | 10 | 20 | | 30 mi |

Information concerning the settlements has been furnished by the Special Committee to Investigate Israeli Practices Affecting the Human Rights of the Population of the Occupied Territories.

The designations employed and the presentation of material on this map do not imply the expression of any opinion whatsoever on the part of the Secretariat of the United Nations concerning the legal status of any country, territory, city or area or of its authorities, or concerning the delimitation of its frontiers or boundaries.

ANNEX V
Documentation retained in the custody of the Secretariat

A. DOCUMENTS RECEIVED BY THE COMMISSION DURING ITS VISIT TO THE AREA

AMMAN, JORDAN

Government of Jordan

–Report on Israeli Settlements in the Occupied West Bank, including Arab Jerusalem since 1967
–Israeli documents relating to Confiscation of Land and Homes in the West Bank, May 1969 (annex to report submitted by the Government of Jordan to Security Council Commission)
–*Economic Development of Jordan in the Regional Context.* Government of Jordan, Amman, January 1978

Witness No. 5 (Anonymous)

–Paper on "The Arabism of Jerusalem", 10 pages
–Copy of memorandum dated 7 April 1978 from P. W. Lapp to R. Chase regarding the "Treatment of Cultural Property and Antiquities Sites in Occupied Jordan", 4 pages
–List of West Bank Settlements dated 9 April 1979 which was compiled by two persons who have travelled extensively in the area (anonymous)
–Clipping from *The Jerusalem Post* showing dead vines on Ja'abari Hill, Hebron; some 550 vines on the hill were cut down systematically in an apparent protest against a government decision not to allow Kiryat Arba settlers to build on the hill
–Copy of telegram sent to President Carter regarding Hebron and Beit Sahour
–Map showing Hebron Municipality borders and confiscated area for Kiryat Arba settlement

Witness No. 15 (Ruhi El-Khatib)

Annex 1. Notice published in *Israel Official Journal* No. 1425 of 11 January 1968 relating to confiscation and expropriation of Arab lands

Annex 2. Order issued by the Israeli Finance Minister and published in the *Israel Official Journal* No. 1443 of 14 April 1968 relating to confiscation and expropriation of land amounting to 116 dunums, with 700 buildings on it

Annex 3. Order issued by the Finance Minister and published in *Official Journal* No. 1443 of 14 April 1968, relating to expropriation of Arab lands outside the walls of Jerusalem

Annex 4. Order relating to expropriation of an area of 11,680 dunums

Annex 5. Map indicating all the sites of expropriated land (above-mentioned 11,680 dunums)

Annex 6. Map showing location of excavations in various places under Arab quarters which had been expropriated, especially in areas near the west and south walls of the Mosque of the Dome of the Rock at Jerusalem

Annexes 7 and 8. Photos showing an Israeli bulldozer striking the last of the remaining real estate neighbouring the south and west sides of the Al Aqsa Mosque

Annex 9. Photo showing a Moslem girls' school which had been demolished

Annex 10. Photocopy of notice sent to all Arab inhabitants asking them to evacuate the area

Annex 11. Clipping from a newspaper, *Al Quds*, reporting the case of an Arab inhabitant who was expelled on 8 August 1973

Annex 12. List of families expelled, names received up to 30 June 1976

Annexes 13 and 14. Copy of map and list of names of Israeli settlements which appeared in *Arab Week*, a Lebanese Arabic magazine

Annex 15. Clipping from *The Jerusalem Post* entitled "On building a fortress Jerusalem", a report full of photographs, documentation and maps concerning the settlements established by the Israelis

Annex 16. Abdul-Hadi, Mahdi. *Israeli Settlements in Occupied Jerusalem and West Bank (1967-1977)*. Jerusalem, 1978

Annex 17. El-Khatib, Ruhi. *The Judaization of Jerusalem*. Amman, Jordan, Al-Tawfiq Press

–Cattan, Henry. *Palestine, the Arabs and Israel*. London: Longmans, Green and Co., Ltd., 1969.

–El-Khatib, Ruhi. *Memorandum regarding the continuation of Israeli acts of aggression towards changing the status of Jerusalem and the surrounding towns and villages*. Amman, Jordan, 1977.

–List of deportees compiled by El-Khatib

–Report No. 35, "Deportations from the West Bank and the Gaza Strip, 1967-1976", compiled by Ann M. Lesch

Witness No. 17 (anonymous)

–Map showing the boundaries of Hebron and the boundaries of the limitation of the area taken away from the Mount of Hebron by a military order

–Photos showing bulldozers demolishing houses and opening new roads

Witness No. 19 (anonymous)

–Land survey of Anata during Hashemite Kingdom rule

–Map of lands in Anata village which had been divided into three zones in accordance with order received from Military Governor of Ramallah on 20 January 1975

–Plan, list of names of landowners at Anata whose lands had been expropriated

–Copy of telegram sent to President Sadat by Anata village Mukhtar requesting him to intervene in order to stop expropriation of villagers' lands

–Copy of a letter addressed to the Military Governor of the West Bank concerning land expropriated from Anata

–Military order confiscating some lands, together with a map showing the area involved

–Israeli map of Anata showing industrial zone planned by Israel

–Order forbidding inhabitants to enter closed zones

–Legal documents from the Israeli High Court pertaining to expropriation of villagers' lands

Witness No. 21 (Shawkat M. Hamdi)

–Copy of his testimony before the Security Council Commission

–Report on the "Policy of Settlements and Its Implications for Arab Jerusalem"

–A study on some Israeli violations of human rights in occupied Arab territories

–A study on the major violations and contraventions on the part of the Israeli authorities

–Map 1, showing the ruins and sacred places of Islam

–Map 2, relating to excavation operations

–Map 3, settlements in the West Bank and at Jerusalem

–Map 4, the "Greater Jerusalem" project

DAMASCUS, SYRIA

Haitham Keylani, Ministry of Foreign Affairs

Map showing location of 29 settlements and location of the Arab Syrian towns and villages which have been destroyed and replaced by new settlements

Najib Al Ahmad, Special Representative, Political Department, PLO

–His written statement to the Security Council Commission

–List of Israeli settlements on the West Bank from 1967-1979

–Map showing Israeli settlements on the West Bank since 1967

–Map of the British Archaeological School at Jerusalem (Burgoyne, M. H., *Some Mameluke Doorways in the Old City of Jerusalem*. Reprinted from "Levant III, 1971")

–Plan for building fortress Jerusalem

–Photos of Al Aqsa Dome taken during the fire and when fire was being put out

–Photo of synagogue built under the Al Aqsa Mosque taken during its installation

–Data on excavations

–List of prisoners who obtained winter clothing during 1978 from the Union of Charitable Organizations at Jerusalem

–Names of prisoners who obtained winter clothing from the Red Cross

–List of Arab inhabitants whose lands have been confiscated in the villages of Majdel and Beni Fadal in the region of Nablus

–List of houses blown up, with description and location of each house

–List of people deported from each village

–Translation of a notice of expropriation as published in Hebrew in *Official Gazette* No. 1656 of 30 August 1970
–Letter of complaint from the Moslem community at Jerusalem concerning the rights of the Palestinian people
–Letter of complaint from Islamic waqf at Jerusalem addressed to the Military Governor of the West Bank concerning acts of desecration committed in Al Aqsa Mosque
–Sample of forgery used to expropriate Arab land
–Report on the Ibrahimi Mosque at Hebron

Witness No. 23 (Abdul Salam)

Le Golan avant l'agression: une étude illustrée

Habib Kahwaji, Member of the Executive Committee, PLO

–Copy of his statement to the Security Council Commission
–Paper on "Racial Discrimination against the Arabs in the Occupied West Bank and Gaza Strip since 1967" (prepared by Kahwaji)
–List of Israeli Settlements in the Occupied West Bank and Gaza Strip (prepared by Kahwaji)
–Paper on "Education in the Occupied West Bank and Gaza Strip since 1967" (prepared by Kahwaji)
–Paper on "Jewish Settlement Plans for the Future" (prepared by Kahwaji)
–Translation by Saif Eddin Zubi, Arab member of the Knesset, of an article on "The König Memorandum" which was published in the Israeli newspapers *Davar* of 25 July and *El Hamishmar* of 7 September 1976

Abdul Abou Meizar, Member of the Executive Committee, PLO

–Report on Political Deportations Carried Out by the Israeli Authorities against Palestinian Citizens
–A booklet which details some activities conducted by the PLO concerning the "Day of the Land" in occupied Palestine
–Deportees from the West Bank

CAIRO, EGYPT

Mr. Boutros Ghali, Minister of State for Foreign Affairs

–Map of Israeli Settlements in the Occupied Arab Territories
–Report on Israeli Settlements in the Occupied Arab Territories, including Jerusalem since 1967 up to the present

Witness No. 36 (Yehia Aboubakr)

–Written statement by the witness

Witness No. 37 (Ibrahim Shukrallah)

–Paper on "Israeli Settlements in the Occupied Arab Territories"
–"Israeli Settlements in the Occupied Territories", compiled by Ann M. Lesch, *Journal of Palestine Studies*.

B. List of documents delivered to the Security Council Commission in New York on 30 April 1979 by the Permanent Mission of the Hashemite Kingdom of Jordan to the United Nations

1. *The Significance of Some West Bank Resources to Israel*, Economics Department, Royal Scientific Society

2. *Information on the Resources of the Occupied West Bank*, Economics Department, Royal Scientific Society

3. Eight maps

4. *The Jerusalem File (1967–1972)*, Council for the Advancement of Arab-British Understanding

5. *The Desecration of Christian Cemeteries and Church Property in Israel*, Beirut, Lebanon, The Institute for Palestine Studies, 1968

6. Background Memorandum on Jerusalem: The Islamic World and Jerusalem

7. Israeli Plans for Jerusalem—The Merip Report

8. David Hirst, "Rush to Annexation: Israel in Jerusalem", *International Journal of Middle East Studies*, vol. 5, No. 2 (April 1974)

9. Ann Mosley Lesch, "Israeli Settlements in the Occupied Territories, 1967–1977", *Journal of Palestine Studies*

10. A Survey of Israeli Settlements—The Merip Report

11. Israeli Settlements—The Merip Reports

12. Paul Quiring, "Israeli Settlements and Palestinian Rights," *Palestine Digest*, No. 9

13. Thesis on "The Legal Status of Jerusalem", The Royal Committee for Jerusalem Affairs

C. Documents received from United Nations bodies

(a) *Committee on the Exercise of the Inalienable Rights of the Palestinian People*

S/12377	Letter dated 28 July 1977 from the Chairman of the Committee to the President of the Security Council
A/33/154	Letter dated 21 June 1978 from the Chairman of the Committee to the Secretary-General
S/13132	Letter dated 2 March 1979 from the Acting Chairman of the Committee to the President of the Security Council
ST/SG/SER.F/1	*The Origins and Evolution of the Palestine Problem* (Part I: 1917–1947, and Part II: 1947–1977)
ST/SG/SER.F/2	*The Right of Return of the Palestinian People*
ST/SG/SER.F/3	*The Right of Self-Determination of the Palestinian People*
A/31/35, A/32/35, A/33/35 and Corr.1 and Corr.1/Rev. 1	Reports and recommendations of the Committee to the General Assembly at its thirty-first, thirty-second and thirty-third sessions

(b) *Special Committee to Investigate Israeli Practices Affecting the Human Rights
of the Population of the Occupied Territories*

A/8089
A/8389 and Corr.1 and 2 and
   Add.1 and Add.1/Corr.1
   and 2
A/8828
A/9148 and Add.1
A/9817
A/10272
A/31/218
A/32/284
A/33/356

Reports submitted by the Special
Committee since its establishment

A/AC.145/R.158 (December 1978), A/AC.145/R.163 (January 1979), A/
   AC.145/R.165 (February 1979)
Map showing Israeli settlements as of April 1979

(c) *Secretariat*

S/AC.21/PV.9–17 Verbatim records of the Security Council Commission
during its mission to the Middle East

134. Security Council Resolution 452 Deploring Israeli Settlements Policy in the Occupied Arab Territories, July 20, 1979*

* S.C. Res. 452, 34 U.N. SCOR (2159th mtg.) at 8, U.N. Doc. S/INF/35 (1979).

The Security Council

Taking note of the report and recommendations of the Security Council Commission established under resolution 446 (1979) of 22 March 1979 to examine the situation relating to settlements in the Arab territories occupied since 1967, including Jerusalem, contained in document S/13450 and Corr.1 and Add.1,[29]

Strongly deploring the lack of co-operation of Israel with the Commission,

Considering that the policy of Israel in establishing settlements in the occupied Arab territories has no legal validity and constitutes a violation of the Geneva Convention relative to the Protection of Civilian Persons in Time of War, of 12 August 1949,[10]

Deeply concerned by the practices of the Israeli authorities in implementing that settlements policy in the occupied Arab territories, including Jerusalem, and its consequences for the local Arab and Palestinian population,

Emphasizing the need for confronting the issue of the existing settlements and the need to consider measures to safeguard the impartial protection of property seized,

Bearing in mind the specific status of Jerusalem and reconfirming pertinent Security Council resolutions concerning Jersualem, and in particular the need to protect and preserve the unique spiritual and religious dimension of the Holy Places in that city,

Drawing attention to the grave consequences which the settlements policy is bound to have on any attempt to reach a peaceful solution in the Middle East,

1. *Commends* the work done by the Security Council Commission established under resolution 446 (1979) in preparing the report on the establishment of Israeli settlements in the Arab territories occupied since 1967, including Jerusalem;

2. *Accepts* the recommendations contained in the report of the Commission;

3. *Calls upon* the Government and people of Israel to cease, on an urgent basis, the establishment, construction and planning of settlements in the Arab territories occupied since 1967, including Jerusalem;

4. *Requests* the Commission, in view of the magnitude of the problem of settlements, to keep under close survey the implementation of the present resolution and to report back to the Security Council before 1 November 1979.

Adopted at the 2159th meeting by 14 votes to none, with 1 abstention (United States of America).

[10] United Nations, Treaty Series, vol. 75, p. 287.

[29] *Ibid. [Official Records of the Security Council, Thirty-fourth Year]*, Supplement for July, August and September 1979.

135. Written Question to the EEC Foreign Ministers
Concerning the Status of the PLO at Meetings of the
International Monetary Fund and the World Bank,
August 7, 1979—Answer, October 23, 1979*

---

* 22 O.J. Eur. Comm. (No. C 288) 9 (1979).

WRITTEN QUESTION NO 360/79

by Mrs Lizin

to the Foreign Ministers of the nine Member States of the European
Community meeting in political cooperation

(7 August 1979)

Subject: Status of the Palestine Liberation Organization at meetings of the
International Monetary Fund and the World Bank

Have the Member States adopted a joint position on the reply to be given
to the PLO's request to attend meetings of the IMF and the World Bank in
an observer capacity?

If so, what is that position?

ANSWER

(23 October 1979)

The PLO made an approach to the IMF and the World Bank earlier this
year to be granted observer status at the annual meeting of the Boards of
the Bank and the International Monetary Fund to be held in Belgrade in
September.

The Nine have taken the view that they could not support this application
as observer status is confined to international organizations or similar bodies
having specialized responsibilities in fields related to the work of the IMF
and the World Bank.

136. Excerpt from Resolutions on the Situation in the
Middle East of the Sixth Conference of Heads of State of
Non-Aligned Countries, Which Met in Havana,
September 3–9, 1979*

* 30 Rev. of Int'l Aff. (Belgrade) No. 707, at 69 (September 20, 1979), *reprinted in* 9 J. Palestine Stud. 165 (Winter 1980).

1. [The conference] *reaffirms* that there can be no solution to the Middle East and Palestinian problems without the integral and simultaneous application of the following basic principles, in consideration of the fact that:

(a) The Palestinian question is the crux of the Middle East problem and the essential cause of the Arab-Israeli conflict,

(b) The Palestinian problem and the Middle East question constitute an indivisible whole in the efforts to find a solution which could in no way be partial or concern only certain parties to the conflict to the exclusion of the others, or be limited to certain aspects of the conflict. Similarly, no partial peace can be instituted, since peace has to be just, must embrace all the parties concerned and eliminate the causes of the conflict,

(c) The establishment of a just peace in the region can be achieved only on the basis of Israel's complete and unconditional withdrawal from all the occupied Palestinian and Arab territories and the recovery by the Palestinian people of all their inalienable national rights, including the right to return to their homeland, to self-determination and to the establishment of an independent state in Palestine,

(d) The Arab city of al-Quds [Jerusalem] forms part of the occupied Palestinian territory It must be fully and unconditionally evacuated by Israel and restored to Arab sovereignty,

(e) The PLO is the sole legitimate representative of the Palestinian people. It alone has the right to represent that people and to participate as a full and sovereign member in all international conferences, activities and forums dealing with the Palestinian problem and the Arab-Zionist conflict with a view to the recovery by the Palestinian people of their inalienable national rights. There can be no general, just and acceptable solution to the problem unless the PLO participates as a sovereign party, on a footing of full equality with the other interested parties, in drawing it up,

(f) All measures and actions by Israel in the Palestinian and Arab territories since their occupation, such as construction work, modification, changes designed to alter the political, cultural, religious, natural, geographical, social, and demographic characteristics thereof, are illegal and invalid,

(g) The establishment of all existing or future settlements in the Palestinian and Arab territories occupied by Israel is unlawful, null and void, and constitutes an obstacle to peace. Accordingly, such settlements must be removed immediately, in conformity with the relevant resolutions of the United Nations and in particular with Security Council resolution 452 (1979),

2. The conference *affirms* that no solution which is not based on these basic principles can lead to a just peace but will give added force to the explosive factors in the region, open the way for the United States policy of eliminating the Palestinian cause, assisting Israel to achieve its political, expansionist, colonialist and racist aims, and encouraging bilateral and partial solutions, disregarding the crux of the problem,

3. *Condemns* the Camp David agreements, signed on 17 September 1978

and the Egypt-Israel Treaty of 26 March 1979, *rejects* their implications and effects, *considers* that those agreements are in no way binding on the Arab states and peoples, including the Palestinian people, and *calls upon* all non-aligned countries to refrain from recognizing or acknowledging them,

4. *Condemns* all the policies, practices and concessions which are in violation of resolutions of the United Nations and of the conferences of the non-aligned countries concerning the Middle East problem and the Palestinian cause,

5. *Affirms* that any violation of the resolutions of the conferences of the non-aligned countries on the Middle East problem and the Palestinian cause leads to a weakening of the struggle for the liberation of the occupied Arab territories and the realization of the inalienable national rights of the Palestinian people and jeopardizes the struggle of the Non-Aligned Movement against colonialism, occupation, racism and Zionism and *considers* that any such violations run counter to the non-aligned countries' determination to put an end to the Israeli occupation of Palestinian and Arab territories and assist the Palestinian people in realizing their inalienable national rights,

6. *Invites* the states and peoples of the world to take a firm stand in the face of Israel's intransigence, persistence in pursuing a policy of aggression and expansion, and steady refusal to implement the United Nations resolutions concerning the Palestinian cause and the Middle East, and

7. *Stresses the fact* that the persistently hostile attitude maintained by the United States of America as regards the inalienable national rights of the Palestinian people and to the question of total withdrawal from all the occupied Palestinian and Arab territories is inconsistent with the resolutions of the United Nations General Assembly concerning the Palestinian cause and is an obstacle to the establishment of a just peace in the region, and *condemns* the policy which the United States is attempting to impose in the region to the detriment of the liberation of all the occupied Palestinian and Arab territories and the realization of the inalienable national rights of the Palestinian people,

8. The conference *invites* all the states and peoples of the world to refrain from providing Israel with any military, human, material or moral support which would encourage it to continue its occupation of Palestinian and Arab territories, and *proclaims* that if those states persist in supporting Israel, the non-aligned countries would be forced to take steps in their regard,

9. *Denounces* the attitude of the states which provide aid and arms to Israel, believing that the true purpose of supplying Israel with enormous quantities of arms which spread death and destruction is to strengthen Israel as a base for colonialism and racism in the Third World in general, and in Africa and Asia in particular,

10. *Condemns* the collusion between Israel and South Africa and their identical aggressive and racist policy, and also condemns their cooperation in all areas in view of the threat which it entails to the security and independence of the African and Arab countries.

137. Address to the 34th General Assembly of the U.N. by Israeli Foreign Minister Moshe Dayan on the PLO, Lebanon, Jerusalem, Syria, Egypt, the U.N. Role in the Peace Process, and the Soviet Union, September 27, 1979*

* 34 U.N. GAOR (11th plen. mtg.) at 232, U.N. Doc. A/34/PV.1–32 (1979).

161. Mr. DAYAN (Israel): Mr. President, please accept my congratulations on your election to the high office of President of the thirty-fourth session of the General Assembly. We are confident that you will guide the work of the Assembly efficiently and fairly.

162. I would also like to express our appreciation to the President of the last session of the General Assembly, Ambassador Liévano of Colombia.

163. It is my pleasure to congratulate Saint Lucia on its independence and admission to the United Nations.

164. As we reflect on the development of the United Nations throughout the past year, we find the spectacle far from encouraging. The fundamental obstacle to the Organization's work is the selectivity which has been forced upon it by an automatic majority of the membership, which is far from impartial and prefers expediency to principles. The United Nations specialized agencies have suffered badly from this. Organs like UNESCO, WHO, and ILO and others have been severely affected by heavy politicization which has influenced their functioning. Instead of dedicating themselves solely to their specific fields in the service of mankind, they have been reduced to forums of political one-sidedness.

165. There must be a return to the United Nations Charter. Consultation and agreement should be restored to their primary place. In particular, the specialized agencies must abandon the dangerous path of politicization along which they have been dragged, so that they may devote themselves to the economic, social, humanitarian, scientific and technological tasks which they were set up to perform and which they perform so well when permitted to do so.

166. There has been little improvement in the situation of the Jews in the Soviet Union during the past year. Even though the number of exit visas for Soviet Jews has increased recently, the gap between the number of Jews applying for exit visas and those granted them is growing, while an even larger number of Soviet Jews have been denied the fundamental right to emigrate—a right guaranteed in the Universal Declaration of Human Rights and in the Helsinki Declaration. Those Jews who do insist on their rights are subjected to continued harassment by the authorities, to dismissal from their places of employment and, in some cases, to arrest and imprisonment. We have taken note of the fact that seven Jewish prisoners were released a few months ago. However, we are particularly concerned by the harsh prison sentences imposed on other Jews whose only crime is their desire to rejoin their families in Israel—Iosif Begun, Boris Kalendarov, Iosif Mendelevich, Ida Nudel, Anatoly Shcharansky, Simon Shnirman, Vladimir Slepak, Aleksandr Vilic and Amner Zavurov. The Soviet Union should release these and other prisoners of conscience and permit everyone who seeks to emigrate to Israel and join his people and his family to do so.

167. We cannot be silent in the face of the rising incitement against the State of Israel and the Jewish people, its religion, culture and national movement, as manifested day by day in the official Soviet media. In this

regard, it must be noted that the Soviet authorities still do not permit Jews to practise their religion and culture. We appeal to the Soviet Union to allow Jewish religion and culture to be practised and expressed freely, and to put an end to anti-Jewish propaganda.

168. We also deeply regret that the Government of Syria continues to violate the Universal Declaration of Human Rights and other international conventions by refusing to permit its Jewish citizens to leave and to be reunited with their relatives living in other lands. We appeal to the Syrian Government to change this policy.

169. The past year witnessed a historic break-through in the Middle East. In March, Israel and Egypt signed the first ever Israel-Arab peace treaty.[9] President El-Sadat of Egypt and Prime Minister Begin of Israel concluded that Treaty after intense negotiations, which lasted a year and a half and which demanded great leadership and courage. Israel wishes to express its appreciation and gratitude to the United States of America and to its President, Mr. Jimmy Carter, personally for the vital role which they played in bringing about this historic achievement, which has created a new reality in our region.

170. Let me recall here that Israel has throughout the first 30 years of its independence constantly extended its hand to its neighbours in the search for peace. This found expression on the very first day of the establishment of our State, in the Israel Declaration of Independence of 14 May 1948. Let me add specifically that as early as in the summer of 1967, very shortly after the six-day war, Israel had taken the initiative and offered to sign a treaty of peace with Egypt, declaring its readiness to withdraw from the Sinai and return it to Egyptian sovereignty in the context of a peace treaty. This Israeli proposal was rejected, and the answer given by Egypt at the time was: "No negotiation, no recognition and no peace with Israel: what was taken by force will be taken back by force." This year, however, has seen the beginning of a new era in the Middle East. After a generation of continued warfare, the realization of a dream begins.

171. The Treaty of Peace, which, as stated in its preamble, is "an important step in the search for comprehensive peace in the area," has provided for a role in its implementation to be fulfilled by the United Nations. United Nations forces and observers were called upon to carry out functions in order to see that the peace treaty was fully implemented. Ironically and paradoxically, that initiative taken by some States Members of the United Nations in the cause of peace was rejected by the United Nations. The Security Council was exposed to the threat of a Soviet veto, and the mandate of UNEF was not renewed, so that the Security Council in effect disassociated itself from the first positive and major step in the great effort to relieve the Middle East from the dangers of war.

172. Although our assumption and hope that the United Nations would

---

[9] Treaty of Peace between the Arab Republic of Egypt and the State of Israel, signed at Washington on 26 March 1979.

assist in the implementation of the Treaty of Peace have been disappointed, we will proceed along the path of peace. The attitude of the United Nations will not damage the peace process; but it will, no doubt, lower the prestige and even the moral stature of the United Nations, one of whose basic principles and purposes is, as stated by the Charter, to "maintain international peace and security . . . and to bring about by peaceful means . . . settlement of international disputes . . . ".

173. As a result of the Treaty of Peace, the process of normalization in the relations between Egypt and Israel has already begun. We are confident that in the months ahead we shall make further progress in cementing new bonds of co-operation.

174. The frequent visits and meetings of the leaders of both countries are also an expression of the common desire to promote understanding and closer personal relationships. The most recent—and most impressive—visit of President El-Sadat to Israel three weeks ago and the reception given him in the city of Haifa, where Jews and Arab coexist in harmony and co-operation, indicated the deep feelings of all the population of Israel towards the era of peace and, we hope, left warm memories in the minds and hearts of our Egyptian guests.

175. Over the past year the situation in Lebanon has become grave. The intervention of Syria has, in fact, plunged the northern part of that formerly prosperous country into a state of anarchy, and the Lebanese Government has become incapable of ruling and exercising its authority over all of its territory. The southern part of Lebanon has been, to a great extent, in the hands of the terrorist groups of the PLO, whose murderous activities have been a source of danger and harassment not only to Israel, but also to the Christian and Moslem Lebanese in that area.

176. UNIFIL was established by Security Council resolution 425 (1978) of 19 March 1978.

177. Israel, having been compelled to act militarily against the PLO in southern Lebanon in a clear act of self-defence, agreed to withdraw its forces, provided that the new United Nations force would undertake to restore peace and security in the area and to assist the Government of Lebanon in ensuring the return of its effective authority in the country.

178. Unfortunately, the aim of restoring Lebanon's integrity has not been achieved, and the Lebanese Government is still incapable of exercising its sovereignty. PLO terrorist groups are still functioning all over Lebanon and, in quite a large number of cases, inside the area of United Nations units. In this region, which was free from any terrorist presence at the time of the Israeli withdrawal, there are now about 700 PLO terrorists, who are acting murderously through the lines of the United Nations Force against the people of Israel. The Force was supposed to act against this. The Secretary-General, in his initial report of 19 March 1978,[10] spoke of the right

[10] See *Official Records of the Security Council, Thirty-third Year, Supplement for January, February and March 1978*, document S/12611.

of self-defence of the Force, including resistance by forceful means to attempts to prevent it from discharging its duties.

179. In his report of 13 September 1978, the Secretary-General stated, among the guidelines and terms of reference of UNIFIL, that "uniformed or armed personnel and military equipment are not allowed to enter the UNIFIL area of operation".[11] However, there are too many cases in which the Force has in fact reconciled itself to the presence and activities of the terrorists in its own area. UNIFIL has not carried out its mandate and duties in this respect, despite the fact that its units have themselves suffered from terrorist activities and at least eight UNIFIL soldiers have been killed in these incidents. The presence and activities of the PLO terrorist groups in the region are in violation of the UNIFIL mandate, and it should be understood that Israel cannot be expected to sit back while terror is being unleashed against its population, no matter where in Lebanon these actions originate.

180. Once again it must be emphasized that terrorism could be virtually eliminated if certain countries ceased to provide arms, training and refuge to its practitioners. No cause can justify terrorism. The issue is, therefore, a fundamental one for the international community, and the struggle against terrorism should continue until terrorism has been brought to an end.

181. The PLO, by its very nature and actions, is a terrorist organization. Its true character is reflected in its so-called "Covenant", which calls for the purging of the Zionist presence from Palestine. The same document denies the existence of the Jewish people and its unbroken historical ties with the land of Israel. It alleges that the establishment of the State of Israel is null and void and rejects outright any plans to settle the Middle East conflict by peaceful means.

182. The PLO has not hesitated to try to translate its vicious doctrine into criminal deeds. It has conducted an unceasing campaign of terror aimed at the mass murder of innocent civilians in Israel. From June 1967 to date, over 640 people have been murdered and 3,300 others have been wounded in Israel by the PLO. It has also terrorized and intimidated Arabs prepared to negotiate peace with Israel, killing more than 350 Arabs and injuring almost 2,000 others.

183. Given the PLO's character and aims, it was, in fact, recognized by the parties at Camp David that the PLO could not be a partner to the peace process. No country can or should be expected to negotiate with a party which denies its very existence, aims at its destruction, and uses terror against its civilian population. On the other hand, careful provision was made in the Camp David agreements to include Palestinian Arab residents of Judea, Samaria and the Gaza District in the peace process.

184. The Framework for Peace in the Middle East, Agreed at Camp David by the President of Egypt and the Prime Minister of Israel, and wit-

---

[11] *Ibid., Supplement for July, August and September 1978*, document S/12845, para. 27 (*a*).

nessed by the President of the United States of America, refers positively and constructively to Palestinian Arab rights, as well as to the rights and security interests of the other parties. It is based on Security Council resolutions 242 (1967) and 338 (1973), which are the only agreed basis for peace negotiations in the Middle East. Any tampering with them can only gravely jeopardize the current peace process.

185. This Framework agreements sees the solution of the question of the Palestinian Arab residents of Judaea, Samaria and the Gaza District in terms of granting them full autonomy, for a transitional period of five years, before reaching an agreement on the final status of the area. For that reason, it was agreed to negotiate on a principle of self-government—exercised through an administrative council—for the Arab inhabitants of the areas in question.

186. Moreover, in the preamble in this Framework, the signatories invited other parties to the Arab-Israel conflict to adhere to it as well. In the letter sent by the President of Egypt and the Prime Minister of Israel to President Carter on 26 March 1979—the date of the signing of the peace treaty—they invited the Hashemite Kingdom of Jordan to join the negotiations.

187. This Framework provides for negotiations on the transitional period of five years, and also for the subsequent negotiations on a peace treaty between Israel and Jordan, in which the location of the boundaries dividing the two countries will be agreed. The option of creating a third State between Israel and Jordan is, therefore, not considered in the Camp David agreements.

188. Thus, the objective of the negotiations being held now, based on the Camp David Framework, is the provision of full autonomy for the inhabitants of Judaea, Samaria and Gaza. The Israeli military government and its civilian administration will be withdrawn as soon as a self-governing authority has been freely elected by the inhabitants. This Framework also specifies measures that will be taken to assure the security of Israel and its neighbours.

189. The only way to keep the process of peace going on is for us to adhere strictly to the Camp David agreements in their letter and spirit, and I should like to assure this Assembly that this is the policy of Israel.

190. Before concluding, let me say a few words about Jerusalem, the eternal capital of Israel and of the Jewish people.

191. Jerusalem has known many foreign rulers during the course of its long history, but none of them regarded it as their capital. Only the Jewish people has always maintained it as the sole centre of its national and spiritual life. For thousands of years, Jews have prayed daily for their return to Jerusalem and, for the past century and a half, Jerusalem has had a continuous and uninterrupted Jewish majority.

192. Jerusalem cannot be divided again by barbed wire and there can be no return to the repeated shooting at our civilians and the barbaric desecration of the Jewish quarter of the City, the Holy Places and cemeteries, as

happened before 1967, when the eastern part of Jerusalem was under the occupation of Jordan. It is relevant to recall that, in grave violation of the 1949 Israel-Jordan General Armistice Agreement,[12] Jordan prevented Jews from having access to their Holy Places and cultural institutions and tried to eliminate systematically every trace of Jerusalem's Jewish past. By contrast, as a result of Israel's policy of free access to all Holy Places, millions of Moslem and Christian tourists and pilgrims—in addition to Jewish visitors—have come to Jerusalem since 1967, and have prayed and worshipped freely at its mosques and churches.

193. Jerusalem is now a city of coexistence between Jews and Arabs. At the same time, the Government of Israel is and has always been conscious of the fact that Jerusalem is of deep concern also to other faiths, and that its religious and cultural sites are precious to Christians and Moslems, as well as to Jews. There should be completely free access to all the holy shrines by believers of all religions, without any exception, completely protected and guaranteed by the law of the country, and those holy shrines should be administered by the respective representatives of the religions concerned, without any interference.

194. The choice before United Nations is clear. This Organization, whose Charter enjoins it to support the cause of international peace and security, must not submit to the designs of those who reject peace. Let the United Nations give peace its full support. Let the Governments of Jordan, Syria and Lebanon and the representatives of the Palestinian Arabs residing in Judaea, Samaria and Gaza join the negotiations in order to achieve the noble goal of a real and durable and comprehensive peace in our area.

[12] *Ibid., Fourth Year, Special Supplement No. 1.*

138. House of Representatives Concurrent Resolution 91

on Syrian Jewish Community-Emigration Rights,

October 10, 1979*

* H.R. Con. Res. 91, 93 Stat. 1425 (1979).

Whereas the United Nations Universal Declaration on Human Rights states unequivocally the right of every individual to emigrate and live in the land of his choice; and

Whereas the Government of Syria is a signatory of the declaration; and

Whereas the Syrian Government has placed restrictions on the right of Syrian Jews to emigrate from that country; and

Whereas the Syrian Jewish community, which numbers nearly five thousand persons, has expressed its desire, through numerous official and unofficial means, to rejoin families and relatives in other lands; and

Whereas numerous private organizations in the United States and other countries have expressed their willingness to facilitate such emigration and to assist in the absorption process; and

Whereas Syria is the only Arab state that has not permitted its Jewish community to exercise the right of emigration: Now, therefore, be it

Resolved by the House of Representatives (the Senate concurring), That the Congress calls upon the Government of Syria, on humanitarian grounds, to permit those members of the Syrian Jewish community desirous of emigrating to do so.

Agreed to October 10, 1979.

139. Israeli Supreme Court Judgment with Regard to

the Elon Moreh Settlement in the Occupied West Bank,

HCJ 390/79, October 22, 1979*

* Unofficial English translation provided by the Ministry of Foreign Affairs of Israel, *reprinted in* 19 Int'l Legal Materials 148 (1980).

In the Supreme Court Sitting as a High Court of Justice

HCJ 390/79

Before: The Acting President, Justice M. Landau
                 Justice A. Vitkon
                 Justice Sh. Asher
                 Justice M. Ben-Porat
                 Justice D. Bekhor

Petitioners: 1. Izat Muhamed Mustafa Dweikat
                 2. Muhamed Abd-Al-Latif Amer Dweikat
                 3. Wafik Sleiman Darwish Dweikat
                 4. Mustafa Abd-El-Latif Amer Dweikat
                 5. Abd-El-Laouf Yusuf Sleiman Al-Asmad
                 6. Jamil Yusuf Sleiman Al-Asmad
                 7. Yusuf Sleiman Yusuf Dweikat
                 8. Salim Sleiman Yusuf Dweikat
                 9. Mahmud Salman Muhamed Ruwajbi
                 10. Salim Hamad Muhamed Ruwajbi
                 11. Ali Shihadeh Hamdan Ruwajbi
                 12. Beir Shihadeh Hamdan Ruwajbi
                 13. Abd-El-Rahim Abd El-Rahman Dweikat
                 14. Muhamed Mahmud Muhamed Dweikat
                 15. Hamda Hamad Muhamed El-Rajba
                 16. Abdullah Muhamed Mahmud El-Rewajba
                 17. Jamil Shihadeh Hamdan El-Rewajba

VERSUS

Respondents: 1. The Government of Israel
                 2. The Minister of Defence
                 3. The Military Commander of the Judaea & Samaria Re-
                    gion
                 4. The Military Commander of the Nablus Subdistrict
                 5. Felix Menachem
                 6. Shvut Avraham

Opposition to order Nisi

Dates of Hearing: 6.9.79, 13.9.79, 14.9.79, 19.9.79, 3.10.79

For Petitioners Nos. 1–16:   Advocate Elias Khoury
For Petitioner No. 17:   Advocates A. Zichroni, A. Feldman
For Respondents Nos. 1–4:   Advocate G. Bach, the State Attorney
For Respondents Nos. 5–6:   Advocates Rahamim Cohen, M. Rimon

JUDGMENT

The Acting President, Justice Landau

In this petition we are asked to judge the question of the legality of the establishment of a civilian settlement at Elon Moreh, adjacent to the town of Nablus, on land which is privately owned by Arab residents. This court dealt with a similar issue in HC 606/78, 610/78 1979 33 *Pskei Din* (2) 113 (hereinafter: the Beit-El case), in which judgment was handed down on 13.3.79. We ruled there that the establishment of two civilian settlements on private land at Beit-El near Ramallah, and at Bekaot B near Tubas, did not infringe upon either Israeli municipal law or customary international law, which constitutes part of the municipal law, because those two settlements were established for military purposes, as we defined that term.

With respect to Beit-El, it was stated, in reference to the justiciability of this issue, that the settlements question "is in dispute between the Government of Israel and other governments and is likely to be on the agenda in fateful international negotiations in which the Government of Israel is engaged in these very days." Since then, the acuteness of the dispute has not faded in the international arena; and it has, moreover, intensified also among the Israeli public domestically. This time it has been reflected also in the very decision to establish a civilian settlement at Elon Moreh, which was adopted by majority vote in the Israeli Cabinet. It is therefore a pressing problem which today excites the public. In H.C. 58/68 (the "Who is a Jew" question) 1969 23 *Piskei Din* (2) 477, at the foot of p. 521, I spoke of "the woeful consequences of the court, as it were, deserting its proper place, above the contentious issues which divide the public, and of judges descending into the arena . . . " and, on p. 530, I explained, as one of the judges in the minority, that it was the duty of the court to refrain from giving judgment in the controversy at issue there, since the court had no proper source for its decision. I added that even in a case like this, "there may be instances when the judge will consider himself forced to give a personal answer to a question which is based on one's philosophy, or outlook on the world, even when the question is a subject of dispute." This time we possess authoritative sources for our judgment and we have no need—indeed, we must not, whilst sitting in judgment—involve our personal views as citizens of the State. But there is still considerable apprehension that the court will be regarded as having left its fitting place and descended into the arena of the public debate, and that its decision will be received by part of the public with cheers, and by the other part with total and emotional rejection. In this sense I regard myself here as one whose duty to rule according to the law in every matter brought before the court is forced upon me, knowing well from the outset that the public at large will not pay attention to the legal reasoning but to the final conclusion only, and the court as an institution is liable to have its fitting status undermined, above the disputes splitting the public. But what can be done, this being our task and this being our duty as justices.

On 7.6.79, in the morning, Israeli citizens, with the help of the Israel Defence Forces (IDF), launched a settlement operation on a hill lying about two kms. east of the Jerusalem-Nablus road, and about the same distance south-east of the junction of that road with the road descending from Nablus to the Jordan Valley. The operation was carried out with the aid of helicopters and heavy equipment which commenced the construction of a road from the main Jerusalem-Nablus road to the hill. The hill is all rocky and uncultivated land (with the exception of a small plot on the north-west part of the site, which was only recently ploughed and seeded and which, in the opinion of an expert for the respondents, in a place where there is no prospect of receiving any economic gain from the produce). But the building of the road, which is 1.7 kilometres long, necessitated the causing of damage to existing sorghum crops, in an area that is 60 metres long by 8 metres wide, and to about six olive seedlings which were approxing four years old.

The land of the hill lies within the boundary of the lands of the village of Rujeib, which is situated close to the hill to the northwest. The seventeen petitioners, who are from the village, have plots of land there, registered in their names in the Nablus Land Registry, after having gone through the land settlement process. The total area of their plots is about 125 dunams. The petitioners have no rights of ownership over the land on which the road was constructed.

On 5 June, 1979, two days before the launching of the settlement operation, Brig-Gen. Benjamin Ben-Eliezer, Commander of the Judaea and Samaria Region, signed "Land Requisition Order No. 16/79". At the beginning of the Order, it is stated that "In accordance with my authority as regional commander, and being of opinion that it is required for military needs, I hereby order as follows . . . " In the main part of the Order, the Commander declared that an area of 700 dunams, marked on the accompanying map, was being "requisitioned for military needs". The petitioners' plots are included in that area. Paragraph 3 of the Order states that any owner or legal occupant of land within the area may present to a staff officer a claim for payment for use of the land and for compensation for any real damage caused by the requisition. According to paragraph 5, "Notice of the contents of the Order will be given to any owner or occupier of land situated in the area." A similar order relating to the road to the hill (No. 17/79) was only signed on 10 June, 1979, 3 days after the initiation of settlement activity. With respect to the conveying of the required notice to the landowners, among whom are the petitioners, it emerges that it was only on the actual day of settlement, at 8 a.m., close on the commencement of work in the field, that a notice of the (requisition) order was made to the mukhtars of the village of Rujeib, who were summoned to the office of the Nablus

Military Governor. The mukhtars were handed written notices—in order to pass them on to the landowners—only on 10.6.79.

In the reply to this petition provided by the Chief of the General Staff, Lt. Gen. Raphael Eitan, the Chief of Staff (hereinafter: C-o-S) states that the landowners should have been given advance notice concerning the intention to execute the seizure, as is usually done in similar instances, and that he has issued directives that henceforth notice be conveyed to the landowners concerned at an appropriate time prior to the requisition of the land. It is not clear why those responsible deviated this time from the custom which had prevailed in the past in similar instances. The impression is created that the settling of the site was organized like a military operation, taking advantage of the element of surprise and in order to ward off the "danger" of this court's intervention in the wake of landowners' applications even before work in the field could begin.

The petitioners applied to this court on 14.6.79, and on 20.6.79 an order nisi was issued against the respondents, the Government of Israel, the Minister of Defence, the Military Commander of Judaea and Samaria and the Military Commander of the Nablus Subdistrict, ordering them, *inter alia*, to show cause, why the requisition orders issued should not be declared null and void, and why the site should not be cleared of the instruments and the structures erected on it and why the establishment there of a civilian settlement be prevented. In addition, an interim order was issued to desist from any further digging or construction work in the area under discussion, or the settlement on it of any additional civilians beyond those who had settled there up to the time the interim order was issued. This interim order remains in force to this day, with certain changes introduced into it at the request of the settlers in the course of the hearing of the petition.

In his affidavit in reply, the C-o-S explains that he arrived at the view that the establishment of the civilian settlement in that place was required for security reasons, and that his position concerning the security importance of the area and of the establishment of the settlement on it was brought to the knowledge of the Ministerial Defence Committee, which in its sessions of 8.5.79 and 10.5.79 decided to approve the seizure of the area with a requisition order for the establishment of the settlement; and in the wake of these decisions, as approved by the Cabinet plenum in its session of 3.6.79, the Commander of the Judaea & Samaria (J & S) Region issued the said requisition order. Lt. Gen. Eitan goes on to dwell on the important contribution of civilian settlements to the defence of the Jewish Yishuv in the country—even before the establishment of the State and in the War of Independence—and he notes the security purposes fulfilled by such settlements, in regional defence and with respect to the IDF's organization in times of quiet and in times of emergency.

The C-o-S laid great stress on his strongly held belief in the importance of regional defence, and his words imply a strong criticism of the views of others who brought the concept of regional defence to its low point, in his opinion, in 1973, when military thinking rested on the laurels of the Six-Day War. But, "after the 1973 war, regional defence was restored to its rightful place which was stolen from it by arrogance and a mistaken attitude to its basic contribution." Today, armed regional defence settlements are fortified and trained properly for the aim of defending the area in which the settlement exists and their location within an area is determined through consideration of their contribution in controlling a wide space and assisting the IDF in its various tasks. The C-o-S explained the special importance of a civilian settlement in particular as opposed to a military base, in that the (military) force on a base, in a time of war, leaves the base on mobile and offensive missions, while the civilian settlement stays on the spot and, being properly armed and equipped, controls the surrounding area for such assignments as observation and protecting nearby lines of transport, so as to prevent enemy control over them. This is particularly so in a time of general mobilization of the reserves on the outbreak of war, and in this case on the outbreak of war on the eastern front. At such a time, the forces are moving to their places of deployment, and control of lines of transport to ensure quick and uninterrupted traffic is of increased importance. Nablus and its surrounding areas are a junction for which there is no alternative, and this is the reason for the special importance of controlling the roads that are near to the city. Elon Moreh overlooks a number of these roads, such as the Ramallah-Nablus, the Nablus-Jordan Valley road via Jiftlik, and another road to the Jordan valley via Akraba and Majdal which passes near the place, from the south.

There is no doubt, and not even the petitioners' lawyers, Mr. Elias Khoury for petitioners 1–16 and Messrs. A. Zichroni and A. Feldman for petitioner 17, dispute it, that Lt. Gen. Eitan holds these views—in a matter which comes within the professional competence of an Army man of such great experience as his—with utter sincerity and with deep inner conviction. But he does not hide the fact that there are those who dispute his conclusion concerning the crucial importance of the establishment of a civilian settlement at the site chosen for Elon Moreh. In Par. 23 (d) of his affidavit he states:

> I am aware of the view of Respondent No. 2, who does not dispute the strategic importance of the region under discussion, but believes that the security needs can be realized by a means other than by the establishment of a settlement at the said site.

Respondent No. 2 is the Minister of Defence. An extraordinary situation has thus been created in which the respondents are divided among themselves over the subject matter of the petition, and the C-o-S should be regarded as declaring his views in the name of the Army authorities and also in the name of the Israeli Cabinet, which decided on the matter by majority vote, in an appeal against the decision of the Ministerial (Defence) Committee made by the Deputy Prime Minister (who is also, like the Minister of

Defence, a salient authority in military matters, having been the IDF's second Chief of Staff). The Petitioners were also permitted to submit additional opinions, one by Lt. Gen. (Res.) Haim Bar-Lev, and the second by Maj. Gen. (Res.) Matityahu Peled. Lt. Gen. (Res.) Bar-Lev expresses his professional assessment that Elon Moreh makes no contribution to Israel's security, neither in the war against hostile terrorist activity during times of tranquillity, nor in the event of a war on the eastern front, because a civilian settlement, situated on a hill some two kms. from the Nablus-Jerusalem road, cannot facilitate the safeguarding of this traffic axis, the more so since close to this road itself is located a large Army camp, which dominates the traffic axes southward and eastward. In fact, says Lt. Gen. (Res.) Bar-Lev, because of hostile terrorist activity in time of war, IDF troops will be tied down to guard the civilian settlement instead of engaging in the war against the enemy's army. The answer to these objections which emerges from Lt. Gen. Eitan's affidavit is that the major importance of a civilian settlement at the site under discussion does not lie in the war against hostile terrorist activity—nor was this the consideration of the C-o-S in requisitioning the site—rather its main importance is likely to be manifested precisely in time of war, because then the base which Lt. Gen. Bar-Lev speaks of will be emptied of its inhabitants; nor does a civilian settlement which is today integrated into the regional defence system resemble a civilian settlement of past years, where the nature of its armament, its equipment and the level of its training are concerned.

The opinion of Maj.-Gen. (Res.) M. Peled is detailed and its conclusion is that "the claim regarding the security value of the Elon Moreh settlement was not put forward in good faith and was made with only one end in sight: to give a justification for the seizure of land which cannot be justified in any other way." However I did not find in the opinion any consideration of C-o-S Eitan's central point, namely that a settlement on that site serves as a stronghold protecting freedom of traffic on the nearby roads at the time of deployment of reserve forces on the eastern front in time of war.

Insofar as concerns Lt.-Gen. Bar-Lev's opinion, and the views of other military experts who think like him, it is not my intention to involve myself in a dispute between experts, and I will only reiterate here what we said in H.C. 258/79 (not yet published): "In a dispute of this sort on military-professional questions, in which the course has no fixed view of its own, we shall presume that the professional views expressed in the affidavit on behalf of the respondents, speaking in the name of those who are responsible for the preservation of security in the administered territories and within the Green Line, are the correct views. Very convincing evidence is needed to contradict this presumption."

In the same case it was also stated that: "In matters of professional military judgment, the Government will certainly be guided first and foremost by the suggestion presented to it by the Chief of Staff."

It is true that in the above case we spoke of "the affidavit on behalf of the respondents" while here the respondents are divided amongst themselves in their opinions. But we heard from Mr. Bach, the learned State Attorney, who argued on behalf of the first four respondents, that the Minister of Defence, despite his contrary opinion, accepted the decision of the majority in the Cabinet, and, fulfilling the statutory duty imposed upon him as the government minister responsible for the Army, under section 2(b) of the "Basic Law: The Army," passed on the decision of the government to the Chief of Staff, for implementation.

At the centre of the hearing of this petition must stand an analysis of the facts, to the extent that these have been revealed from the evidence before us, according to law, and especially in the light of our judgment in the Beit-El issue. But before I come to this, I must first complete the description of the facts themselves, because we received additional factual material in the written reply of the C-o-S to a questionnaire we drew up, after hearing the essence of the advocates' oral arguments, so he could reply to it instead of undergoing an oral cross-examination, as was requested by the petitioners' advocates. The answers to the questionnaire, as well as additional documents which the learned State Attorney was permitted to submit in order to supplement the answers to the questionnaire, threw additional light on the facts of the case, and broadened and deepened our understanding and appraisal of the facts, beyond what was contained in Lt. Gen. Eitan's affidavit and in the first affidavit of Mr. Aryeh Naor, the Government Secretary, which noted the decisions of the Ministerial Defence Committee and of the Cabinet, following an appeal from that Committee. The following is the picture as it was ultimately revealed:

1. On 7.1.79, in the wake of an illegal demonstration ("an unapproved demonstration," as the Government Secretary puts it in his affidavit) of persons from "Gush Emunim" on a road in the Nablus area, a discussion was held by the Ministerial Defence Committee in which the following resolution was adopted:

A)   The Government views the "Elon Moreh" settlement nucleus as a candidate for settlement in the near future.

B)   The Government will decide on the date and place of the settlement in accordance with the appropriate considerations.

C)   When determining the area of settlement for Elon Moreh the Government will, as much as possible, take into consideration the wishes of this nucleus.

D)   The "Elon Moreh" persons must now return to the camp which they left.

2. In the wake of this resolution by the Ministerial Defence Committee, an advance visit was made by representatives of the Ministerial *Settlement Committee* (emphasis in the original—Trans.) aimed at finding a suitable area for the settlement of the "Elon Moreh" nucleus, and five alternative places

were suggested in the area, which were passed on to the IDF for examination. Those in charge of this subject in the Judaea & Samaria Region HQ and in the General Staff examined all the proposed sites, and decided, on the basis of considerations of the IDF, that two of the proposed places should be given a thorough examination. One of these two places was a site recommended by the Minister of Agriculture, who is chairman of the Ministerial Settlement Committee and a member of the Ministerial Defence Committee, and the second site is the one finally selected by the IDF and which is the subject of the petition (the Chief of Staff's replies to the questionnaire, Par. 2(d)).

The Judaea & Samaria Regional HQ looked into the possibility of finding some area in the region which was not privately owned, but no such place was found (ibid., Par. 2(e)).

3. On 11.4.79 (apparently following the abovementioned advance survey and as a result of it) the C-o-S gave his approval to the General Staff elements in charge of the subject to requisition the area for military purposes (ibid., Par. 2(b)).

4. In anticipation of the discussion which was to be held by the Ministerial Defence Committee, the C-o-S was asked to give his opinion, and on 3.5.79 his chef de bureau once again informed the above-mentioned personnel in the General Staff that in his view there was a military need to requisition the area (ibid., loc. cit.).

5. The opinion of the C-o-S was also brought to the knowledge of the Ministerial Defence Committee when it discussed the establishment of the settlement in its session of 8.5.79 (ibid., loc. cit., and also the Government Secretary's first affidavit, Par. 4). In that same session the Ministerial Defence Committee decided to support the order of requisition for military purposes (Government Secretary's first affidavit, Par. 3(a)).

6. On 30.5.79 the Ministerial Defence Committee reaffirmed its decision of 8.5.79 (ibid., Par. 3(b)).

7. The Deputy Prime Minister appealed the decision of the Ministerial Defence Committee before the Cabinet plenum, and on 3.6.79 the Cabinet rejected his appeal and by a majority vote approved the decisions of the Ministerial committees.

8. On 5.6.79 Brig. Gen. Ben-Eliezer (the Military Commander of the Judaea & Samarian Region—Trans.) signed the requisition order, and on 7.6.79 the settlers moved on to the site with the Army's help, as related above.

At this point I shall discuss two arguments put forward by Mr. Zichroni, on behalf of petitioner No. 17, in order to dispose of them before entering into the substance of this petition. He argued that there was a constitutional defect in the process of the decision-taking on the establishment of the settlement, since according to the "Basic Law: The Army," the Minister of Defence is the C-o-S's superior, so that his view on military matters is to be preferred over that of the C-o-S and is also to be preferred over the opinion of the Ministerial Defence Committee and over that of the Cabinet itself, which operate according to the "Basic Law: The Government." Hence, the Cabinet (or the Ministerial Defence Committee) was not authorized to take a decision contrary to the opinion of the Minister of Defence. This argument is insubstantial. While it is true that the Minister of Defence is responsible for the Army on behalf of the Government, according to Par. 2(b) of the "Basic Law: The Government," the Army is under the authority of the Cabinet as a body, according to Par. 2(b) of that same Basic Law, and the C-o-S is also subordinate to the Cabinet, according to Par. 3(b), although he is directly subordinate to the Minister of Defence, as stated in that same paragraph. Hence, as long as the Cabinet has not made its view known on a subject, the C-o-S must execute the orders of the Minister of Defence. But once the matter has been brought before the Cabinet, it is the Cabinet's decision which is binding on the C-o-S; the Minister of Defence is just one member of the Cabinet and as long as he remains a member of the Cabinet he, along with his Ministerial colleagues, bears joint responsibility for its decisions, including for decisions taken by majority vote against his own differing view.

Now the way is open for a discussion of the main question: can the establishment of a civilian settlement at the site under discussion be justified legally, if for that purpose privately owned land was requisitioned? In the Beit-El case we gave an affirmative answer to a similar question, both according to internal municipal, Israeli law and according to customary international law, because we were convinced that the requirements of the Army obligated the establishment of the two civilian settlements discussed in that case at the places where they were established. It is self-evident—and Mr. Bach also informed us that this was clearly explained in the Cabinet's discussions—that in that judgment this court did not give legal authorization in advance for *every* (emphasis in the original—Trans.) seizure of private land for civilian settlement in Judaea & Samaria; rather, each case must be examined to determine whether military purposes, as this term must be interpreted, in fact justify the seizure of the private land.

In this hearing we have—unlike in the Beit-El case—the argument on behalf of two settlers at the "Elon Moreh" site, who are members of the secretariat of the settlers' nucleus, and who were permitted to affiliate themselves to this petition as respondents ... In their affidavit and their pleadings these additional respondents painted a broad picture, far beyond what was argued on behalf of the original respondents. Their affidavit, which was submitted by one of them, Mr. Menachem Reuven Felix, explained that the members of the nucleus settled at Elon Moreh because of the Divine commandment to inherit the land which was given to our forefathers and that "the two elements, therefore, of our sovereignty and our settlement, are intertwined": and that "it is the settlement activity of the People of Israel in the Land of Israel which is the concrete, the most effective and the truest security action. But the settlement itself does not stem from security reasons or physical needs but from the force of destiny and from the force of the Jewish people's return to its land." He goes on to declare:

> Elon Moreh is the very heart of the Land of Israel in the profound sense of the word—also, it is true, from the geographical and the strategic points of view, but first and foremost it is the place where this land was first promised to our first forefather, and it is the place where the first property transaction was made by the father of the nation after whom this land is named—The Land of Israel.

> This being the case, the security reason, with all due deference and about whose genuineness there is no doubt, makes no difference to us.

And after citing Numbers 33:53—"And you shall take possession of the land and settle in it, for I have given the land to you to possess it"—he goes on to say:

> Whether or not the Elon Moreh settlers will be integrated into the regional defence system according to the IDF's plan, settlement in the Land of Israel, which is the mission of the Jewish people and of the State of Israel, is *ipso facto* the security, the wellbeing and the welfare of the nation and the State.

With respect to the petitioners' arguments which are based on international law, including the various international conventions, he adopts an explanation which he got from his lawyer, that they have no relevance whatsoever, since the conflict is an internal conflict between the Jewish people which is returning to its land and the Arab residents of the land of Israel, and that what is involved is neither "occupied territory" nor "administered territory" but the very heart of the Land of Israel, our right to which is in no doubt; and secondly, because factually as well as historically, what is under discussion is Judaea & Samaria, which were part of the British Mandate and which were conquered by force of arms by our neighbour to the east—an occupation and an annexation which were never recognized by anyone (except for England and Pakistan). This is the gist of the affidavit.

Even one who does not hold the views of the respondent and his colleagues will respect their deep religious belief and the devotion spurring them. But we, sitting in judgment in a State based on law in which the *Halakha* is employed only to the degree that this is permitted by the secular law—must employ the law of the State. As to the respondent's view concerning ownership of land in the Land of Israel, I assume that he does not wish to say that according to the *Halakha* anyone who is not a Jew may be deprived of private property at any time. For the Bible states explicitly: "The stranger that sojourneth with you shall be unto you as the home-born among you, and though shalt love him as thyself; for ye were strangers in the land of Egypt" (Leviticus 19:34). In the collection from the literature placed before us by the advocates for the respondents, I found that the Chief Rabbi Y.Z. Hertz, of blessed memory, mentioned this verse when the British Government asked for his opinion on the draft of the Balfour Declaration. In his reply he stated that the mention of the civil and religious rights of the non-Jewish communities in the draft declaration were simply the translation of that same basic principle from the Torah. (Palestine Papers 1917–1922, Seeds of Conflict (John Murray) p. 13). This was the authentic voice of the Zionism which insists on the Jewish people's right of return to its land, as recognized also by the nations of the world—for example, in the preamble to the Palestine Mandate—but has never sought to deprive the residents of the country, members of other peoples, of their civil rights.

This petition contains a decisive reply to the argument whose aim is to interpret the historical right promised to the Jewish people in the Book of Books as abrogating property rights according to the laws of private property. For the framework of the hearing of this petition is delimited first and foremost by the requisition order issued by the Commander of the region, and all agree that the direct source for this order lies in the powers that international law accords to the Military Commander in the area occupied by his forces in a war. The framework of the hearing is also delimited by the legal principles followed by the Israeli Military Commander in the region of Judaea & Samaria also based upon the laws of war in international law. These principles are found in Proclamation No. 1, issued by the Military Commander on 7.6.67, according to which the IDF entered the region on that day and assumed control and the maintenance of security and order in the region; as well as in Proclamation No. 2, of that day, Par. 2 of which states that

> the law which existed in the region on 7.6.67 will remain in force insofar as it contains no contradiction of this proclamation or of any proclamation or order which will be issued by me, and with the changes stemming from the establishment of rule by the IDF in the region.

Par. 4 of that proclamation should also be noted, in which the Commander of the Judaea & Samaria Region declared:

> Movable and immovable property . . . which belonged to or was registered in the name of the Hashemite Jordan State or Government, or any unit thereof or any branch thereof or any part of all these such as are located in the region, shall be transferred to my exclusive holding and shall be under my administration.

These proclamations constitute the legal basis for the Military Government in Judaea & Samaria, which exists there to this day, without having been replaced by another form of rule . . .

Mr. Rahamim Cohen, representing the other respondents (members of the Gush Emunim group), referred us to section 1 of the Area of Jurisdiction and Powers Ordinance, 5708–1948, which states that "Any Law applying to the whole of the State of Israel shall be deemed to apply to the whole of the area including both the area of the State of Israel and any part of Palestine which the Minister of Defence has defined by proclamation as being held by the Israel Defence Forces." The Minister of Defence did not in fact issue any proclamation defining Judaea and Samaria as being occupied by IDF, for the purposes of this section. But, Mr. R. Cohen says, the main point is that the Provisional Council of State, in its capacity as the sovereign legislator of the State of Israel, empowered the Minister of Defence to issue orders in relation to every part of the land of Israel (Palestine). The very fact of this authorization is evidence that the Provisional Council of State, as the legislative authority, saw the State of Israel as having sovereignty over all of the Land of Israel.

The argument is a forceful one, but must be rejected. The fact is that the Minister of Defence did not use his authority under section 1 of that Ordinance to make any order in respect of the Judaea and Samaria region (and the Government of Israel also refrained from applying Israeli law to the same region, as was done in relation to East Jerusalem, by an order on the basis of section 11B of the Law and Administration Ordinance, 5708–1948). When we come to consider the legal bases of Israeli rule in Judaea and Samaria, our interest is in the legal norms which exist, in practice and not just those which exist potentially, and the basic norm upon which Israeli rule in Judaea and Samaria was based was, and is until today, the norm of a military administration, and not the application of Israeli law, which brings with it Israeli sovereignty.

At this point one should note, as in earlier petitions which came before this court, an important argument which Israel puts forward in the international arena. The argument is based on that fact that at the time of the entry of IDF to Judaea and Samaria, this area was not occupied by any sovereign whose occupation had won general international recognition. Mr. Rahamim Cohen repeated this argument with great force. In the Beit-El issue, I said (at page 127) that: "We are not required to consider this problem in this petition and this demurrer joins therefore the group of demurrers of which I spoke in H.C. 302/72, and which remain as open questions in this court."

I believe that the petition before us can only be cleared up by examining the presumptions which are at the base of the requisition order. These presumptions also mark the framework of this hearing for the other respondents.

We must therefore examine the legal validity of the requisition order under discussion according to the international law from which the Military Commander, who issued (the order), derives his authority. In addition, we must also examine whether the order was duly issued in accordance with municipal Israeli law. As in the Rafiah salient case (H.C. 302/72 1973 27

Pskei Din (2) 169, 176) we assume in this case as well that this authority to examine exists personally with respect to the office holders of the military administration who belong to the executive authority of the State, in the role of "people fulfilling public functions according to law", and subject to the supervision of this court, according to section 7(b)(2) of the Courts Law, 5717–1957. From the substantive viewpoint, we must examine according to municipal Israeli law if the requisition order was legally issued in accordance with the powers given to the Government and to the military authorities in "Basic Law: The Government" and "Basic Law: The Army."

In the Beit-El affair we conducted these two examinations, the one according to Israeli municipal law and the other according to international law. Each was considered separately. This time I have already considered the above-mentioned Basic Laws with the argument relating to the decision-making process concerning the requisitioning of land, taken at the governmental level. I can now consider the two tests together insofar as it does not contradict municipal statutory law (see Beit-El case, at p. 129).

Counsel on all sides concentrated their arguments on a comparison of the matter before us with the facts in the Beit-El case, and with what was decided there, with one side seeking to discover the similarity of the two cases, while the other stresses the differences between them. Mr. Bach added to this and repeated the plea of lack of jurisdiction which was already pleaded in the Beit-El case and was rejected there in unambigiuous terms. My distinguished colleague, Vitkon, J. said (at the top of p.124) "I am not in the least impressed by this contention. But supposing—a supposition which does not apply in this case—that a person's property rights have been unlawfully impaired or denied, it is difficult to believe that the court will turn him away because his rights may come up for discussion in political negotiations. This contention has not added weight to the pleading of the respondents."

I, for my part added, at page 128–9, that one must indeed regard the special aspect of the affair which would have required interpreting Article 49(6) of the Geneva Convention as non-justiciable, but that in general this court has jurisdiction to hear petitioners' claims, since private property rights are involved. Mr. Bach says that his argument was not correctly understood, for he intended to say that the question of jurisdiction is but a function of the issue at hand, and the issue is on the one hand subject to acute political dispute, and on the other hand what is being considered is not cultivated land but rocky land, some distance from the village of Rujeib itself. Mr. Bach cited again the article of Professor Jaffe in 74 Harvard Law Review, 1265, 1302–1304.

The argument was well understood at the time and a return to it does not add validity. Article 49 (6) of the Geneva Convention was at the time not considered at all in the hearing, since it belongs to the area of consensual international law which is not in the nature of a law that binds an Israeli court. However I joined my distinguished colleagues in their opinion that jurisdiction over the issue was based on the Hague Rules, which bind the military administration in Judaea and Samaria, being part of customary international law. I will act in a similar fashion this time and will refrain from considering the issue before us on the basis of Article 49(6) of the Geneva Convention. But when the subject matter is private property rights the matter cannot be exempted by a claim of the "relativity" of the right. According to our system of law the right of private property is an important legal value protected by both the civil and criminal law, and it makes no difference, as regards the right of an owner of property to protection of his possession according to law, whether the land is cultivated or rocky land.

The principle of protection of private property also applies in the laws of war, finding their expression in this matter in Article 46 of the Hague Rules. A military administration seeking to affect private property rights must show legal authority, and cannot exempt itself from judicial supervision of its acts by claiming lack of jurisdiction.

For his part, Mr. Zichroni tried to distinguish our decision in the Beit-El case, in that there the court justified the establishment of civilian settlements for military reasons that were connected with the fight against hostile terrorist activity in times of tranquillity while the C-o-S primarily stressed in his affidavit the military necessity in establishing the civilian settlement in the location at issue in the event of a real war on the eastern front. But there is no basis for this distinction. Also in the Beit-El affair the discussion centred [*sic*] on the needs of regional defence designed to fit in with the general defence system of the state at times of war, see the citation of the statement of Maj.-Gen. Orly (p. 125) and see my note at the top of page 131 that "the powers vested in the army in a time of active warfare and in a time of tranquillity cannot be neatly separated. Even if quiet at present prevails in the area near Beit-El, prevention is better than cure." My distinguished colleague Ben Porath, J. said this with greater emphasis in her judgment (p. 132/3).

In the Mattityahu case (H.C. 258/79, not yet published), we again said that one should not simply regard the state of affairs with a static view ignoring what might happen sometime in the future, whether as a result of hostile activity from outside or from within the administered territories and proper military planning must take into account not just existing dangers but also dangers that are likely to be created as a result of dynamic developments in the field.

The question therefore remains: Did the respondents show sufficient legal authority for seizing the petitioners' lands? The requisition order was issued by the Military Commander, which states at the outset, that the order is being issued "by virtue of my authority as Commander of the region, and because I believe that this is required for military purposes." It should be mentioned here that in this order the Commander of the region chose, from the start a more indeterminate formulation than in the order issued in the Beit-El matter, where the requisition order stated that the requisition order for the seizure of the area on which the Beit-El camp stands, and its fringes, was applied only after eight years by the establishment of a civilian settlement, which was necessary "for essential and urgent military purposes." In that instance we justified the establishment of a civilian settlement on the basis of Article 52 of the Hague Regulations, which permits the seizure or possession of land "for the needs of the army of occupation." I also cited there remarks by Oppenheim, who holds that the temporary use of private land is permissible if it is necessary "for all kinds of purposes demanded by the necessities of war," and I cited also the British Manual of Military Law, by which the temporary use of privately owned land or buildings is justified for "military movements, quartering *and the construction of defence positions.*" We also rejected Mr. Khoury's contention that the term "for the needs of an army of occupation" should be taken as including only the immediate needs of the army itself, and we noted that "the main function assigned to the army in occupied territory is 'to safeguard public order and security,' as provided in Article 43 of the Hague Regulations. What is required for the achievement of this purpose is *ipso facto* required for the needs of the army of occupation, within the meaning of Article 52." Similarly, we may say this time that what the army needs in order to fulfil its task of defending the occupied area against hostile acts liable to originate from outside, is also necessary for the army's requirements in the meaning of Article 52.

Up to this point I am in concurrence with Mr. Bach that the seizure of private land for the establishment of a civilian settlement could have been justified in this instance also by the terms of Article 52 of the Hague Regulations—and no other support for this did we find in international law. But what does this entail? When it is proved, according to the facts of the case, that it was the Army's needs which in practice led to the decision to establish a civilian settlement at the site under discussion. I wish to reiterate that there can be no doubt that in Lt. Gen. Eitan's profesional [*sic*] opinion the establishment of the civilian settlement at that site is consistent with the needs of regional defence, which is of special importance in safeguarding the axes of movement during the deployment of the reserve forces in time of war. But I have come to the view that this professional view of the C-o-S would in itself not have led to the taking of the decision on the establishment of the Elon Moreh settlement, had there not been another reason, which was the driving force for the taking of said decision in the Ministerial Defence Committee and in the Cabinet plenum—namely, the powerful desire of the members of Gush Emunim to settle in the heart of Eretz-Israel, as close as possible to the town of Nablus. With respect to the discussions in the Ministerial Committee and in the Cabinet, we were not able to follow them by perusing the minutes of those discussions. But even without this we have enough indications from the evidence before us that both the Ministerial Committee and the Cabinet majority were decisively influenced by reasons lying in a Zionist point of view of the settlement of the whole Land of Israel. This point of view emerges clearly from the statement made by

Mr. Bach in the name of the Prime Minister in the court session of 14.9.79, in reply to the remarks made by the additional respondents, in Par. 6 of that affidavit, to which I had drawn attention in the court session of the previous day. I recorded Mr. Bach's remarks verbatim, as follows, in view of the importance and standing of the person in whose name Mr. Bach was speaking:

> I spoke with the Prime Minister and he authorized me to announce, after the subject came up in yesterday's session, that on many occasions, both in Israel and abroad, the Prime Minister stresses the Jewish people's right to settle in Judaea & Samaria—but these things are not necessarily connected with a discussion held in the Ministerial Defence Committee with regard to the concern for national security and State security, when what is up for discussion and decision is a specific question of the requisition of this or the other site for security needs. In the Prime Minister's views, these are not contradictory matters, though they are, nonetheless, different. As to what was said about the Prime Minister's intervention, this took the form of bringing the matter for discussion before the Ministerial Defence Committee . . . He took part in the committee's discussion and expressed his clear and unequivocal opinion in favour of the issuing of a requisition order for the establishment of that settlement. This, as noted, taking into consideration, *inter alia*, the Chief of staff's opinion.

The view concerning the right of the Jewish people, as mentioned at the outset of the above remarks, is based on the fundamentals of the Zionist doctrine. But the question which is before this court in this petition is whether this view justifies the taking of private property in an area subject to rule by military government—and, as I have tried to make clear, the answer to this depends on the correct interpretation of Article 52 of the Hague Regulations. I am of the opinion that the military needs cited in that article cannot include, according to any reasonable interpretation, national-security needs in their broad sense, as I have just mentioned them. I shall cite Oppenheim:

> According to Article 52 of the Hague Regulations, requisitions may be made from municipalities as well as from the inhabitants, but so far only as they are really necessary for the army of occupation. They must not be made in order to supply the belligerent's general needs.

Military needs in the meaning of Article 52 can, therefore, include the needs that the C-o-S spoke of in his affidavit of response, that is, the needs of regional defence and of defending axes of movement so that reserve forces can deploy uninterruptedly in time of war. In the discussions of the Ministerial Defence Committee the decision was taken "taking into consideration, *inter alia*, the Chief of Staff's opinion" (Justice Landau's emphasis), in the words of Mr. Bach. In the Ministerial committee's decision of 7.1.79, as cited above, Gush Emunim was promised that the Cabinet would decide on the date and place of the settlement "in accordance with the appropriate considerations," and that when determining the area of settlement the Cabinet would take into consideration, as far as possible, the wishes of the "Elon Moreh" settlement nucleus. I shall not err if I assume that what Mr. Bach stated in the name of the Prime Minister reflects the spirit of the discussions in the Ministerial Committee. I do not doubt that the Chief of Staff's opinion was taken into consideration among the rest of the committee's considerations. But in my view this is not sufficient in order to place the decision within the bounds of Article 52. The following are my reasons for this view:

(a) When it is military needs that are involved, I would have expected that the Army authorities would initiate the establishment of the settlement precisely at that site, and that it would be the C-o-S who would, in line with this initiative, bring the Army's request before the political level so that it could approve the settlement's establishment, should it find that there are no political reasons preventing this. The Chief of Staff's affidavit implies that this was in fact the decision-taking process. Were this the case, I would say that the very order of the events attests to the professional military consideration's being the dominant one also in the discussions of the political level. But from the more complete picture formed after the C-o-S replied to the questionnaire presented to him and from the additional documents submitted by Mr. Bach, it emerges that the process was the very opposite: The initiative came from the political level, and the political level asked the C-o-S to give his professional opinion, and then the C-o-S expressed a positive opinion, in accordance with the conception he has always held. This is entirely clear in the replies of the C-o-S to the questionnaire, in Par. 2:

(a) To the best of my knowledge the body that initiated the establishment of the settlement in the Nablus area was the Ministerial Defence Committee.
(b) I did not approach the political level with a suggestion to establish a settlement of Elon Moreh . . .
(c) There was no plan which had been approved by an authorized military element for the establishment of a civilian settlement at the site under discussion . . .

It also emerges from one of the additional documents that on 20.9.73 the then-O/C Central Command, Maj. Gen. Rehavam Ze'evi, submitted to the then-Chief of Staff a detailed proposal for settlement in the Administered Areas. Concerning the establishment of agricultural settlements in Samaria it was stated there that "this is difficult due to a shortage of available land." This shows that the prevailing view at that time was still that no privately owned land should be taken for the establishment of settlements. And this, in fact, was what Maj. Gen. Orly contended in July 1978, in HCJ 321/78 (the Nebbe Sallah case):

7. In locating the area intended for settlement near the village of Nebbe Sallah, those who operated on behalf of the respondents were guided by the principle that was laid down by Government policy not to seize for settlement purposes land which is privately owned.

In the petition before us we find something of a change from this position, because the Government Secretary's first affidavit states, on this subject:

> In answer to the petitioners' contentions . . . concerning Government policy on requisitioning land:
> (a) I hereby make it clear that the Israel Government's aim of not seizing private land, as far as this is possible and is compatible with security needs, remains in force.
> (b) When the Government believes that the security need obligates it, it approves the seizure of private land but directs IDF personnel to remove from the area to be seized, insofar as possible, cultivated land.

As to Maj. Gen. Ze'evi's plan, it should be remarked that his proposals did not gain the approval of any authorized military or civilian body. This plan contained a suggestion to establish a Jewish city near Nablus—not at the site now chosen for the establishment of the Elon Moreh settlement, but not far from it.

In Par. 4 of his replies to the questionnaire, the C-o-S answers the question "Did you approve the establishment of a civilian settlement at the site under discussion because you thought from the start that it was required there for regional defence purposes, or because you found, *post factum*, that if a civilian settlement were to be established at this site it would integrate into the regional defence system?" as follows:

> I approved the seizure of the land which is the subject of the petition for the purpose of establishing the settlement because this is compatible with the military needs in this area as I saw them from the outset, and it is consistent with my security view concerning the State of Israel's defence and security needs, as explained in Pars. 9–20 of the main affidavit.

But when the view of the security needs did not *ab initio* lead to an initiative to establish the settlement at that site—rather the approval came only *post factum* in response to an initiative of the political level—I do not believe that this passive approach attests to there having been from the outset a military necessity to take private land in order to establish the civilian settlement, within the bounds of Article 52 of the Hague Regulations. This time it was not demonstrated therefore, that in the establishment of the civilian settlement the act of settlement was preceded by the military authorities' thought and *military planning* (emphasis in the original—Trans.), as we noted in the Beit-El case.

(d) Further with regard to the question of military necessity: I cited above the text of the Ministerial Defence Committee's decision in its session of 7.1.79, as quoted in the Government Secretary's second affidavit. As will be recalled, the discussion at that meeting was held in the wake of the Gush Emunim members' demonstration on a road near Nablus. The resolution stated that "When determining the area of settlement for Elon Moreh the Government will, as much as possible, take into consideration the wishes of the (settlement) nucleus," and, as though in exchange for this assurance, the Elon Moreh members were called on to return to the camp they had left, that is, to desist from the unlawful demonstration. I regard this as clear proof that it was the pressure of the Gush Emunim members that impelled the Ministerial Committee to take up, in that session, the subject of a civilian settlement in the Nablus area. The matter was subsequently passed on to the Ministerial Settlement Committee so that it could send its representatives for an advance survey in order to select the feasible sites for the establishment of a settlement for the "Elon Moreh" nucleus near Nablus. They selected five sites, and of the five the IDF opted for the site under discussion. It emerges from this that the IDF had no hand in determining those five sites, but was confronted with the choice of selecting one of the five sites determined by the political level. This process is not consistent with the language of Article 52, which in my view necessitates the demarcation in advance of a certain area because precisely that land is needed for military needs; and, as noted, it is natural that the initiative for this should originate with the military level, which is expert in the Army's needs and which plans them in advance with military forethought.

On this matter, Mr. Bach contended that the Army must take into account whether there are candidates for civilian settlement who are ready to go to the place where their settlement is required for military needs. To this I agree, but again this entails the condition that military planning which was approved by a military element precede the search for candidates for settlement at site X. Here the reverse occurred: first came the wish of the members of the "Elon Moreh" nucleus to settle as close as possible to the town of Nablus, and only afterwards, and as a result of the pressure they brought to bear, did the approval of the political level come, and finally also the approval of the military level. The political consideration was, therefore, the dominant factor in the Ministerial Defence Committee's decision to establish the settlement at that site, though I assume that the Committee as well as the Cabinet majority were convinced that its establishment *also* (emphasis in the original—Trans.) fulfills military needs; and I accept the declaration of the C-o-S that he, for his part did not take into account political considerations, including the pressure of the Gush Emunim members, when he came to submit his professional opinion to the military level. But a secondary reason, such as the military reason in the decisions of the political level which initiated the settlement's establishment does not fulfil the precise strictures laid down by the Hague Regulations for preferring the military need to the individual's right of property. In other words: would the decision of the political level to establish the settlement at that site have been taken had it not been for the pressure of Gush Emunim and the political-ideological reasons which were before the political level? I have been convinced that had it not been for these reasons, the decision would not have been taken in the circumstances which prevailed at the time.

I would like to add a few words on the problem of the dominant as opposed to the ascribed purpose in the decision taken by the ruling authority. In H.C. 392/72 1973 27 *Pskei Din* (2) 764 at p. 773, Cahan, J. referred to the discussion on the "plurality of purposes" that appears in the third edition of De Smith's Judicial Review of Administrative Action, at p. 287 et seg., and he selected the following from the five tests proposed there, namely whether the defective exercise of discretion on the invalid purpose had a substantial influence on the decision of the authority. For my part I am prepared to adopt the test which is the more lenient on the authority proposed by De Smith at page 289, viz.

> What was the dominant purpose for which the power was exercized? If the authority is seeking to achieve two or more purposes when one is permitted, expressly or impliedly, the legality of the act is judged according to the dominant purpose.

(And the author, in footnote 74, cites examples of English cases in which this principle was applied.) From what I have explained above at length it is clear what must be the result of the application of this test in the circumstances of the case before us, when the initiative for the establishment of the settlement did not come from the military level. The words of the said author, at p. 291 appear to me also to touch the matter in issue:

> . . . it is sometimes said that the law is concerned with purposes, but not with motives. This view is untenable insofar as motive and purpose share a common area of meaning. Both are capable of meaning a conscious desire to attain a specific end, or the end that is desired. In these senses an improper motive or purpose may, if it affects the quality of the act, have the effect of rendering invalid what is done.

(e) I have still not dwelt on an additional reason which must bring about a revocation of the decision to seize the petitioners' land—a reason which stands on its own, without even taking into consideration the other reasons which I have so far detailed: Already in the matter of Beit-El a considerable question, namely, how is it possible to establish a permanent settlement on land which has been seized only for temporary use? There, we accepted Mr. Bach's answer

> that the civilian settlement can only exist in that place so long as the IDF hold the area by virtue of the requisition order. This occupation can itself come to an end some day as a result of international negotia-

tions, leading to a new arrangement which will take effect under international law and will determine the fate of this settlement as of other settlements existing in the occupied territories.

There, the settlers themselves did not speak out, because they were not affiliated to the hearing. This time, this excuse cannot be accepted as a difficulty. For, as the affidavit submitted on behalf of the settlers states, in Par. 6:

> Basing the seizure on security grounds in their narrow technical sense and not on their basic and comprehensive sense, as explained above, means just one thing: the temporary nature of the settlement and its being transitory. This appalling conclusion we reject out of hand. Nor is it consistent with the Government's decision concerning our settlement in that place. In all the contacts and the many assurances we received from Cabinet Ministers, and above all from the Prime Minister himself—and the requisition order under discussion was issued by the intervention of the Prime Minister himself—they all regard the Elon Moreh settlement as a permanent Jewish settlement, no less than Deganya or Netanya.

This passage, it should be noted, contains two sections: its first part refers to the opinion of the settlers and its second part to comments they heard from Ministers. We were not asked to permit the submission of a counter-affidavit on behalf of the Government or any of its Ministers, to contradict the remarks attributed to them in the second part of this passage—so that these things must be accepted as the absolute truth. But if this is so, the decision to establish a permanent settlement intended from the outset to remain in its place forever—even beyond the duration of the military government which was established in Judaea & Samaria—encounters a legal obstacle which is unsurmountable, because the military government cannot create in its area facts for its military needs which are designed *ab initio* to exist even after the end of the military rule in that area, when the fate of the area after the termination of military rule is still not known. This contains a *prima facie* contradiction which shows also, according to the evidence before us in this petition, that the decisive consideration which led the political level to decide on the establishment of the settlement under discussion was not the military consideration. In these circumstances the legal form of requisitioning the possession only and not expropriating rights of ownership, cannot change the face of things, namely the taking of possession, which is the main content of property, forever.

In view of all the above, I hold that the order nisi should be made absolute, with respect to the petitioners' lands which were seized according to Order No. 16/79.

Signed) M. Landau
Deputy President

[The separate opinions of Justices Vitkon and Bekhor have not been reproduced.]

It was decided to make the order nisi absolute, and to declare requisition order 16/79 null and void with respect to the lands owned by the Petitioners, the particulars of whose registration appear in Para. 2 of the Petition, and to require Respondents 1–4 to evacuate the civilian settlers from Petitioners' lands and every structure raised upon them, as well as any object which was brought upon them. There is no place to issue any order whatsoever with respect to the land seized in accordance with Order No. 17/79, since none of the Petitioners have ownership rights over the lands located in the site of the road.

We give Respondents 1–4 a period of 30 days to carry out the Absolute Order.

Respondents 1–4 will reimburse Petitioners 1–6 for the costs of this Petition, a total sum of IL 5,000—and are to pay an identical sum to Respondent No. 17. There is no order concerning costs with regard to Respondents Nos. 5 and 6.

Given today, 1 Heshvan 5740 (22.10.79)

(signed)
The Permanent Deputy President, Justice M. Landau
Justice A. Vitkon
Justice Sh. Asher
Justice M. Ben-Porat
Justice D. Bekhor

140. Excerpts from the Resolutions of the World
Conference on Palestine, Lisbon, November 2–6, 1979*

* 9 J. Palestine Stud. 174 (Winter 1980).

This world conference held its meetings in Lisbon, Portugal, from November 2–6, 1979, and it was attended by about 750 delegates representing 325 popular groups, organizations and parties from more than one hundred countries.

The conference declared that it condemns all imperialist and Zionist schemes, and in particular the Camp David agreements and the Israeli-Egyptian treaty, declaring that these agreements are invalid because they infringe the inalienable national rights of the Arab people and seek to perpetuate Israel's continued occupation of Palestinian and Arab territories.

The conference reaffirms its support for the struggle of the Arab people, and in particular the Palestinian Arab people, under the leadership of the PLO, which has achieved important political gains in national and international circles. The conference places on record its appreciation of the heroic struggle of the Palestinian Arab people in the occupied territories against Israeli occupation and so-called self-rule, that denies their right to sovereignty and independence. The conference calls for the following:

1. Israel's total, immediate and unconditional withdrawal from all the occupied Arab and Palestinian territories, including Jerusalem.

2. The restoration to the Palestinian Arab people of their legitimate and inalienable rights, including their right to return to their homeland and their right to self-determination and to establish their independent national state, as affirmed by UN General Assembly resolutions, particularly resolution 3236.

3. The reaffirmation of the right of the Palestinian Arab people to engage in all kinds of struggle, including armed struggle, to recover their inalienable national rights, as stipulated by the resolutions of the UN General Assembly and by international law, which are applicable to all national liberation movements.

4. Full support for the resolutions of the UN and other organizations condemning Israel for:

a) Usurping Arab territories and natural resources in the occupied territory and establishing settlements there.

b) The arbitrary imprisonment of fighters for freedom, their torture in Israeli prisons and the imposition of collective penalties and arrests.

c) Changing the political, demographic and cultural character of the occupied territories, including Jerusalem.

5. Full support for the UN General Assembly resolution 3379 which declares that Zionism is a form of racism and racial discrimination, as also full support for the dissemination of information on this matter.

6. Recognition by governments of the PLO.

The conference declares its solidarity with and appreciation of the struggle of the nationalist and progressive forces in Lebanon in defence of Lebanon's unity, territorial integrity, independence and democratic structure. It also declares its support for the presence of the Palestinian resistance in Lebanon, so that it may fulfil its responsibilities in the struggle.

The conference condemns the continuing Israeli attacks on Lebanon, especially in the South. It also condemns the proposals of the fascist isolationists, insofar as they aim at legalizing the occupation of part of South Lebanon. The conference calls for the immediate and radical enforcement of Security Council resolutions 425, 426, 444 and 450, and for the enforcement of the resolutions of Beiteddine and the Baghdad summit conference in this regard, especially those provisions related to Israel and the obstacles that prevent the Arab Deterrent Forces from performing their role of assisting the legitimate authorities to restore sovereignty over their territories.

The conference declares its full solidarity with the Syrian Arab Republic in its steadfast confrontation of Zionism and imperialism, and with the struggle of the Arab Front for Steadfastness and Confrontation: Algeria, Syria, Libya, the Democratic Republic of Yemen and the PLO. It also declares its solidarity with the Arab people in their opposition to the Camp David agreements.

. . . .

The conference condemns the obstructive policy of the US embodied in its use of the veto at the UN, in particular as regards the resolutions on the recognition of the inalienable rights of the Palestinian people. And finally the conference calls on all nationalist organizations and peaceloving forces to provide tangible material aid to the PLO to enable it to achieve its goals and to confront conspiracies and aggression.

141. General Assembly Resolution 34/29 on the Situation in the Occupied Territories, November 16, 1979*

---

* G.A. Res. 29, 34 U.N. GAOR Supp. (No. 46) at 72, U.N. Doc. A/34/46 (1979).

The General Assembly,

Noting with concern the decision of the Israeli authorities to deport the Mayor of Nablus outside the occupied Palestinian territory,

Gravely concerned at the resignation of the mayors of cities and towns in the occupied Palestinian territoriy as a result of the deportation decision,

Expressing grave anxiety and concern about the present serious situation in the occupied Palestinian territory as a result of the deportation decision,

1. *Calls upon* the Israeli authorities to rescind the deportation order;

2. *Requests* the Secretary-General to report to the General Assembly as soon as possible on the implementation of the present resolution.

71st plenary meeting
16 November 1979

142. General Assembly Resolution 34/65 on the Question of Palestine, November 29, 1979*

* G.A. Res. 65, 34 U.N. GAOR Supp. (No. 46) at 19, U.N. Doc. A/34/46 (1979).

A

The General Assembly,

Recalling and reaffirming its resolutions 3236 (XXIX) of 22 November 1974, 3375 (XXX) and 3376 (XXX) of 10 November 1975, 31/20 of 24 November 1976, 32/40 A and B of 2 December 1977 and 33/28 A to C of 7 December 1978,

Having considered the report of the Committee on the Exercise of the Inalienable Rights of the Palestinian People,[28]

Having heard the statement of the Palestinian Liberation Organization, the representative of the Palestinian people,[29]

1. *Expresses its grave concern* that no just solution to the problem of Palestine has been achieved and that this problem therefore continues to aggravate the Middle East conflict, of which it is the core, and to endanger international peace and security;

2. *Reaffirms* that a just and lasting peace in the Middle East cannot be established without the achievement, *inter alia*, of a just solution of the problem of Palestine on the basis of the attainment of the inalienable rights of the Palestinian people, including the right of return and the right to national independence and sovereignty in Palestine, in accordance with the Charter of the United Nations;

3. *Calls once more* for the invitation of the Palestine Liberation Organization, the representative of the Palestinian people, to participate, on the basis of General Assembly resolution 3237 (XXIX), in all efforts, deliberations and conferences on the Middle East which are held under the auspices of the United Nations, on an equal footing with other parties;

4. *Endorses* the recommendations of the Committee on the Exercise of the Inalienable Rights of the Palestinian People contained in paragraphs 52 to 55 of its report;

5. *Expresses its regret and concern* that the recommendations of the Committee on the Exercise of the Inalienable Rights of the Palestinian People endorsed by the General Assembly in its resolutions 31/20, 32/40 A and 33/28 A have not been implemented;

6. *Notes with regret* that the Security Council has not taken the action it was urged to take by the General Assembly in paragraph 4 of its resolution 32/40 A;

7. *Once again urges* the Security Council to consider and take as soon as possible a decision on the recommendations endorsed by the General Assembly in its resolution 31/20, 32/40 A and 33/28 A and in the present resolution;

[28] *Official Records of the General Assembly, Thirty-fourth Session, Supplement No. 35* (A/34/35 and Corr. 1).

[29] *Ibid., Thirty-fourth Session, Plenary Meetings,* 77th meeting, paras. 70-118.

8. *Authorizes and requests* the Committee on the Exercise of the Inalienable Rights of the Palestinian People, in the event of the Security Council failing to consider or to take a decision on those recommendations by 31 March 1980, to consider that situation and to make the suggestions it deems appropriate;

9. *Decides* to include in the provisional agenda of its thirty-fifth session the item entitled "Question of Palestine".

83rd plenary meeting
29 November 1979

B

The General Assembly,

Recalling and reaffirming the declaration, contained in paragraph 4 of its resolution 33/28 A of 7 December 1978, that the validity of agreements purporting to solve the problem of Palestine requires that they be within the framework of the United Nations and its Charter and its resolutions on the basis of the full attainment and exercise of the inalienable rights of the Palestinian people, including the right of return and the right to national independence and sovereignty in Palestine, and with the participation of the Palestine Liberation Organization,

Taking note of paragraphs 33 to 35 of the report of the Committee on the Exercise of the Inalienable Rights of the Palestinian People,[30]

1. *Notes with concern* that the Camp David accords have been concluded outside the framework of the United Nations and without the participation of the Palestine Liberation Organization, the representative of the Palestinian people;

2. *Rejects* those provisions of the accords which ignore, infringe, violate or deny the inalienable rights of the Palestinian people, including the right of return, the right of self-determination and the right to national independence and sovereignty in Palestine, in accordance with the Charter of the United Nations, and which envisage and condone continued Israeli occupation of the Palestinian territories occupied by Israel since 1967;

3. *Strongly condemns* all partial agreements and separate treaties which constitute a flagrant violation of the rights of the Palestinian people, the principles of the Charter and the resolutions adopted in the various international forums on the Palestinian issue;

4. *Declares* that the Camp David accords and other agreements have no validity in so far as they purport to determine the future of the Palestinian people and of the Palestinian territories occupied by Israel since 1967.

83rd plenary meeting
29 November 1979

[30] *Ibid., Thirty-fourth Session, Supplement No. 35* (A/34/35 and Corr.1).

C

The General Assembly,

Recalling its resolutions 3376 (XXX) of 10 November 1975, 31/20 of 24 November 1976, 32/40 A and B of 2 December 1977 and 33/28 A to C of 7 December 1978,

Having considered the report of the Committee on the Exercise of the Inalienable Rights of the Palestinian People,[31]

1. *Expresses its appreciation* to the Committee on the Exercise of the Inalienable Rights of the Palestinian People for its efforts in performing the tasks assigned to it by the General Assembly;

2. *Requests* the Committee on the Exercise of the Inalienable Rights of the Palestinian People to keep the situation relating to the question of Palestine under review and to report and make suggestions to the General Assembly or the Security Council, as appropriate;

3. *Authorizes* the Committee on the Exercise of the Inalienable Rights of the Palestinian People to continue to exert all efforts to promote the implementation of its recommendations, to send delegations or representatives to international conferences where such representation would be considered by it to be appropriate, and to report thereon to the General Assembly at its thirty-fifth session and thereafter;

4. *Requests* the United Nations Conciliation Commission for Palestine, established under General Assembly resolution 94 (III) of 11 December 1948, as well as other United Nations bodies associated with the question of Palestine, to co-operate fully with the Committee on the Exercise of the Inalienable Rights of the Palestinian People and to make available to the Committee, at its request, the relevant information and documentation which they have at their disposal;

5. *Decides* to circulate the report of the Committee on the Exercise of the Inalienable Rights of the Palestinian People to all the competent bodies of the United Nations and urges them to take necessary action, as appropriate, in accordance with the Committee's programme of implementation;

6. *Requests* the Secretary-General to continue to provide the Committee on the Exercise of the Inalienable Rights of the Palestinian People with all the necessary facilities for the performance of its tasks.

100th plenary meeting
12 December 1979

D

The General Assembly,

Having considered the report of the Committee on the Exercise of the Inalienable Rights of the Palestinian People,[32]

[31] *Ibid.*
[32] *Ibid.*

Noting, in particular, the information contained in paragraphs 45 to 51 of that report,

Recalling its resolutions 32/40 B of 2 December 1977 and 33/28 C of 7 December 1978,

1. *Requests* the Secretary-General, in the light of the consultations held in accordance with paragraph 3 of General Assembly resolution 33/28 C, to redesignate the Special Unit on Palestinian Rights as the Division for Palestinian Rights and to provide it with the resources necessary to discharge the increased responsibilities assigned to it by the Assembly;

2. *Also requests* the Secretary-General to ensure that the Division for Palestinian Rights, in consultation with the Committee on the Exercise of the Inalienable Rights of the Palestinian People and under its guidance:

(a) Shall continue to discharge the tasks detailed in paragraph 1 of General Assembly resolution 32/40 B;

(b) Shall undertake an expanded programme of work, including, *inter alia*, the following:

(i) Establishment of closer co-operation within the United Nations framework and with non-governmental organizations;

(ii) Organization of four seminars during the biennium 1980-1981, sponsoring of annual internship programmes and arrangements for lecture tours;

(iii) Monitoring of political and other relevant developments affecting the inalienable rights of Palestinian people;

(iv) Assistance in the preparation of visual material, such as posters;

(v) Expansion of the scope of the bulletin issued by the Division for Palestinian Rights to include all items relevant to the question of Palestinian rights;

3. *Further requests* the Secretary-General to ensure the full co-operation of the Department of Public Information and other units of the Secretariat in enabling the Division for Palestinian Rights to perform its tasks;

4. *Invites* all Governments and organizations to lend their co-operation to the Committee on the Exercise of the Inalienable Rights of the Palestinian People and the Division for Palestinian Rights in the performance of their tasks;

5. *Requests* the Secretary-General to direct the United Nations Postal Administration to issue a series of United Nations commemorative postage stamps to publicize as widely as possible the grave situation and the inalienable rights of the Palestinian people;

6. *Requests* Member States to observe annually on 29 November the International Day of Solidarity with the Palestinian People and to issue special postage stamps for the occasion;

7. *Requests* the Secretary-General to direct the Department of Public Information to set up, in consultation with the Committee on the Exercise of the Inalienable Rights of the Palestinian People, a photographic display in

the public areas of United Nations Headquarters with a view of keeping visitors informed of the grave situation and the inalienable rights of the Palestinian people.

100th plenary meeting
12 December 1979

143. Second Report of the Security Council Commission
Established Under Resolution 446 (1979) and Annex,
December 4, 1979*

* 34 U.N. SCOR (Oct.–Dec. 1979) at 106, U.N. Doc. S/13679 (1979).

CONTENTS

LETTER OF TRANSMITTAL

4 December 1979

In our capacity as members of the Security Council Commission established under resolution 446 (1979), we have the honour to transmit herewith the second report of the Commission, prepared pursuant to paragraph 4 of resolution 452 (1979).

This report was unanimously adopted on 4 December 1979.

We avail ourselves of this opportunity to express the hope that the Commission has fulfilled its mandate to the satisfaction of the Council and our deep appreciation for the confidence shown by the Council in designating our respective delegations to be members of the Commission.

(*Signed*) Leonardo MATHIAS, Portugal
(Chairman)
(*Signed*) Julio DE ZAVALA, Bolivia
(*Signed*) Kasuka Simwinji MUTUKWA Zambia

INTRODUCTION

1. This is the second report presented by the Commission established on 22 March 1979 by Security Council resolution 446 (1979).

2. The original mandate of the Commission was "to examine the situation relating to settlements in the Arab territories occupied since 1967, including Jerusalem".

3. On 3 April, the President of the Security Council announced that the Commission would be composed of Bolivia, Portugal and Zambia.

4. At its 1st meeting, held in New York on 10 April, the Commission decided that its chairmanship would be assumed by Portugal.

5. On 12 July, the Commission submitted its first report [*S/13450 and*

Add. 1] in accordance with paragraph 5 of resolution 446 (1979). The report was considered by the Security Council at its 2156th to 2159th meetings from 18 to 20 July.

6. At the 2159th meeting, the Security Council adopted resolution 452 (1979) which reads as follows:

"*The Security Council,*

Taking note of the report and recommendations of the Security Council Commission, established under resolution 446 (1979) to examine the situation relating to settlements in the Arab territories occupied since 1967, including Jerusalem, contained in document S/13450 and Add.1,

Strongly deploring the lack of co-operation of Israel with the Commission,

Considering that the policy of Israel in establishing settlements in the occupied Arab territories has no legal validity and constitutes a violation of the Geneva Convention relative to the Protection of Civilian Persons in Time of War, of 12 August 1949,

Deeply concerned by the practices of the Israeli authorities in implementing that settlements policy in the occupied Arab territories, including Jerusalem, and its consequences for the local Arab and Palestinian population,

Emphasizing the need for confronting the issue of the existing settlements and the need to consider measures to safeguard the impartial protection of property seized,

Bearing in mind the specific status of Jerusalem, and reconfirming pertinent Security Council resolutions concerning Jerusalem, and in particular the need to protect and preserve the unique spiritual and religious dimension of the Holy Places in that city,

Drawing attention to the grave consequences which the settlements policy is bound to have on any attempt to reach a peaceful solution in the Middle East,

1. *Commends* the work done by the Security Council Commission established under resolution 446 (1979) in preparing the report on the establishment of Israeli settlements in the Arab territories occupied since 1967, including Jerusalem;

2. *Accepts* the recommendations contained in the report of the Commission;

3. *Calls upon* the Government and people of Israel to cease, on an urgent basis, the establishment, construction and planning of settlements in the Arab territories occupied since 1967, including Jerusalem;

4. *Requests* the Commission, in view of the magnitude of the problem of settlements, to keep under close survey the implementation of the present resolution and to report back to the Security Council before 1 November 1979."

7. In organizing its programme of work, the Commission, at its 20th meeting, on 5 September, considered the modalities that it should follow in order to carry out its new mandate, namely, to keep under close survey the implementation of resolution 452 (1979).

8. The Commission decided once more to establish direct contact with the parties involved in the matter, with a view to seeking their co-operation in the fulfilment of its mandate, and also to continue its consultations with relevant United Nations bodies which might be in a position to supply useful current information.

9. Bearing in mind that the Security Council, in resolution 452 (1979), had accepted the recommendations contained in the Commission's first report, particularly with regard to Jerusalem, the Commission also decided to establish contact with a number of high-ranking representatives of the three monotheistic faiths.

10. When preparing its report to the Security Council, the Commission realized that it would be difficult for it to report to the Security Council by 1 November 1979, as called for in paragraph 4 of resolution 452 (1979). Accordingly, the Chairman of the Commission, in a letter to the President of the Council, requested that the time-limit for submission of the report be postponed until 10 December.

11. Following informal consultations with members of the Council, the President informed the Chairman [S/13586] that no member of the Council had any objection to the Commission's request.

12. The Commission held five meetings, from 5 September to 4 December, at Headquarters in New York.

13. The present report was unanimously adopted at the 24th meeting, on 4 December.

I. Activities of the Commission

A. Requests to the Parties for Co-operation

14. In accordance with its previous decisions and in order to carry out its mandate objectively and comprehensively, the Commission requested its Chairman to establish informal contacts with the Israeli delegation in order to ascertain its reaction to the Commission's new mandate.

15. At the 21st meeting on 17 September, the Chairman informed the Commission of the results of his contacts. The Deputy Permanent Representative of Israel had informed him that there had been no change in his Government's policy with regard to the Commission and that the Commission could not count on any co-operation from the Israeli Government in the fulfilment of its mandate. The Chairman had expressed to the Deputy Permanent Representative his regret and disappointment at the position taken by the Israeli Government. In spite of that attitude, however, the Commission intended to fulfil to the best of its ability the mandate entrusted to it by the Security Council and would therefore formally send a letter to the Permanent Representative of Israel requesting his Government's co-operation and expressing the hope that Israel would reconsider its attitude towards the Commission.

16. On 18 September, letters were sent to the Permanent Representatives of Egypt, Jordan, Lebanon and the Syrian Arab Republic requesting that

the Commission be provided as soon as possible with any newly available information pertinent to its mandate.

17. Also on 18 September, the Commission sent a similar letter to the Permanent Observer of the Palestine Liberation Organization (PLO).

18. Requests for information were also addressed to the Chairman of the Special Committee to Investigate Israeli Practices Affecting the Human Rights of the Population in the Occupied Territories and the Chairman of the Committee on the Exercise of the Inalienable Rights of the Palestinian People.

19. On 28 September, the Commission sent a letter to the Permanent Representative of Israel, expressing the hope that his Government would reconsider its position regarding the Commission and co-operate with it by providing it with any available information pertinent to its mandate.

20. In his reply dated 19 September, the Permanent Representative of Egypt again assured the Commission of his Government's intention to co-operate fully in the implementation of its mandate. He also informed the Chairman that Mr. Boutros Boutros Ghali, Minister of State for Foreign Affairs of Egypt and head of that country's delegation to the thirty-fourth session of the General Assembly, would be in New York from 30 September to 7 October and would be happy to meet with the members of the Commission for an exchange of ideas on the mandate of the Commission.

21. In his reply dated 21 September, the Acting Chairman of the Committee on the Exercise of the Inalienable Rights of the Palestinian People transmitted copies of a statement issued by the Committee on 19 September and of letters it addressed on the same day to the President of the Security Council and the Secretary-General [S/13544] regarding the decision by the Government of Israel to abrogate the restrictions hitherto placed on the purchase or acquisition by Israeli citizens and organizations of land in the occupied territories of the West Bank and Gaza. By a subsequent communication dated 18 October, the Chairman of the Committee also transmitted a press communiqué issued by the Committee concerning the decision by the Israeli Cabinet to expand seven existing settlements, as well as a document entitled "Master plan for the development of settlement in Judaea and Samaria", attributed to the World Zionist Organization [see S/13582].

22. On 9 October, the Commission received from the Permanent Observer of the PLO a set of documents, including the "World Zionist Organization's master plan for the development of settlement in Judaea and Samaria"; "Estimated land areas of West Bank settlements" and "Human rights and Israeli settlements".

23. In his reply dated 16 October to the Commission's communication of 28 September, the Deputy Permanent Representative of Israel informed the Commission that the position of his Government remained as set out in the letter of 17 May from the Permanent Representative of Israel to the President of the Security Council, namely, that "in consideration of the circumstances in which resolution 446 (1979) had been adopted, the Government

of Israel had rejected that resolution in its entirety and accordingly could not extend any form of co-operation to a Commission set up under it". The Deputy Permanent Representative further stated that "Israel's reservations were more than justified by the report presented by the Commission of 12 July 1979".

24. In its reply dated 18 October, the Special Committee to Investigate Israeli Practices Affecting the Human Rights of the Population in the Occupied Territories again assured the Commission of its full co-operation in providing precise information relevant to its mandate.

25. In a letter dated 3 December, the representative of Lebanon, referring to the Commission's letter of 18 September, informed the Commission that his Government had nothing further to add to the information it had already given or to what its representative had stated on this matter over the years at the United Nations.

26. As indicated in paragraph 9 above, the Commission, bearing in mind the unique religious and spiritual dimensions of Jerusalem, and guided by its deep concern that Israel's policy of settlement could lead to irreversible situations with regard to the status of the Holy City, has sought to receive the views of representatives of the three great monotheistic religions in that regard. Replies received in time to be included are reproduced in the annex to the present report.

B. MEETINGS WITH OFFICIALS

Meeting with the Minister of State for Foreign Affairs of Egypt

27. On 5 October, the members of the Commission had a meeting at United Nations Headquarters with Mr. Boutros Boutros Ghali, Minister of State for Foreign Affairs of Egypt, with whom they had an exchange of views pertaining to the mandate of the Commission.

28. The Minister of State briefed them on the steps taken by the Egyptian Government since the Commission's visit to Cairo the preceding June with regard to the question of settlements in the occupied Arab territories. He mentioned, in particular, the creation, within his Department, of a special Committee to monitor the latest developments with regard to the settlements, the publication of official communiqués protesting Israel's policy in that regard and the organization of a seminar on the settlements with the participation of specialists from several countries. The purpose of the seminar was to awaken Egyptian, Arab and world opinion to the problem and to emphasize that peace with Israel did not mean agreeing with its policy of settlements.

29. The Minister of State also stated that, taking advantage of the new possibilities offered by the Israeli-Egyptian treaty, he had, on several occasions, directly conveyed to the Israeli public Egypt's conviction that Israel's policy of settlements was an obstacle to the peace process.

30. In answer to questions raised by the representative of Bolivia regard-

ing the position of Egypt on Jerusalem and the creation of new settlements, the Minister of State further stated:

(a) That both during its ongoing negotiations with Israel and in public statements, Egypt had reiterated its position on Jerusalem, namely, that East Jerusalem was part of the West Bank and must be returned to the Arabs. Once that was achieved, it was up to the Palestinians and Israelis to devise modes of co-operation;

(b) That to his knowledge there had been only declarations of intent on the part of the Israelis, but no actual building of new settlements.

Meeting with the Head of the Political Department of the PLO

31. On 5 October, the members of the Commission held a meeting with Mr. Farouk Qaddoumi, head of the Political Department of the PLO, during which they exchanged views pertaining to the Commission's mandate.

32. Mr. Qaddoumi stated that, far from improving, the situation in the occupied territories had, in fact, worsened. It was becoming clear that Israel, through the establishment of new settlements and the enactment of new laws, was forcing people to leave the area and thus paving the way for the annexation of the West Bank. Detailed information on the matter would be shortly sent to the Commission by the PLO observer's office.

33. In response to questions from the representative of Zambia, Mr. Qaddoumi maintained that there was, indeed, evidence that people were still leaving the West Bank, that, contrary to statements by Israeli officials, there was no religious freedom at Jerusalem for Christians and Moslems, and that access to the Holy Places was still restricted.

Meeting with the Permanent Representative of Jordan

34. On 19 October, the members of the Commission had an informal meeting with Mr. Hazem Nuseibeh, Permanent Representative of the Hashemite Kingdom of Jordan, with whom they proceeded to an exchange of views pertaining to the mandate of the Commission.

35. Mr. Nuseibeh expressed the profound concern of his Government at the relentless ongoing process of colonization of the West Bank and at the serious economic and social effects resulting to the Arab population from the seizure by the Israeli occupying authorities of the vital water sources in the territory.

36. While recognizing that the work done by the Commission had helped to "crystallize the picture", he regretted that earlier decisions by the Security Council had had no effect in remedying a situation which was becoming extremely serious.

37. Mr. Nuseibeh again assured the Commission of his Government's co-operation and assistance. His Government hoped to present very shortly an integrated report on the question of settlements. In the meantime he was able to present to the Commission a series of documents, including in particular:

(*a*) A study, in Arabic, concerning the seizure of water resources;

(*b*) A copy, translated from Hebrew, of the World Zionist Organization's "master plan" for the development of settlement in the West Bank of Jordan for the period 1979-1983;

(*c*) Information on the recent decision to allow Israeli nationals to purchase lands and property in the West Bank;

(*d*) Information regarding the expropriation of additional Arab lands;

(*e*) A memorandum prepared by the inhabitants of Jerusalem concerning Israel's plan designed to seize the Al Aqsa Mosque and the Dome of the Rock.

C. REVIEW OF RECENT DEVELOPMENTS REGARDING
THE SETTLEMENTS

38. In preparing this second report, the Commission, in accordance with its mandate, has deemed it necessary to call the attention of the Security Council particularly to those actions undertaken by Israel since the adoption of resolution 452 (1979), which, *inter alia*, called upon the Israeli Government and people to cease, on an urgent basis, the establishment, construction and planning of settlements in the Arab territories occupied since 1967, including Jerusalem.

39. Once more, in its careful endeavour to review the situation most objectively, the Commission decided, as a first step, to approach the interested parties, with a view to receiving any factual information pertinent to its mandate. Regrettably, however, the Commission once again was confronted by Israel's negative response to its approach and by that Government's reaffirmed decision not to co-operate with the Commission.

40. While deploring this persistently negative attitude, which deprives it of the opportunity of receiving explanations and comments from the Government of Israel, the Commission is satisfied that its present report contains an accurate assessment of the current situation, as most of the information upon which it is based was derived from Israeli sources or was widely covered by the media.

41. On the basis of the information available to it, the Commission is able to report the following recent developments:

(*a*) It has come to light that in the last few months, additional private Arab land totalling over 40,000 dunums (1 dunum = 1,000 square metres) has been confiscated by Israeli occupation authorities for the purpose of expanding settlements in the West Bank, mostly in the Nablus, Bethlehem, Beit Shahour and Jerusalem areas.

(*b*) On 16 September, the Israeli Cabinet unanimously adopted a decision allowing Israeli citizens to purchase land in the occupied West Bank and Gaza, thus rescinding a previous decision which had hitherto prohibited Israeli citizens and organizations from purchasing land beyond the armistice lines of the six-day war.

(*c*) On 14 October, the Israeli Cabinet adopted a decision to expand seven existing settlements in the occupied West Bank, using 1,125 acres of land allegedly not privately owned by Arab inhabitants. The Commission issued a statement on 17 October, expressing its disappointment and concern at this new action by the Israeli Government.

(d) On 28 October, the Israeli Cabinet decided that the Elon Moreh (Qaddum) settlement, which Israel's High Court of Justice had ruled illegal, would be moved to a new site on the occupied West Bank. The settlement is built on 220 dunums of land seized from Rujib, near Nablus.

(e) According to information received from various sources, Israel is in the process of implementing a plan prepared by the World Zionist Organization which calls for the building of 46 new settlements in the years 1979-1983. The Commission is calling attention to this project inasmuch as some of the settlements appearing in the plan are already under construction.

(f) The attention of the Commission was drawn again to the increasingly serious problem facing Arab farmers in the occupied territories as a result of Israel's intensive exploitation of the area's traditional water sources for use in Israel proper and by Israeli settlements established in the occupied territories.

42. According to a study on water resources in the West Bank made available to the Commission, Israel pumps away some 500 million cubic metres of the West Bank's total annual supply of 620 million cubic metres by means of artesian wells drilled within its 1948 borders. The traditional water sources, such as wells and springs, are also being depleted through the use of modern drilling equipment to drain off water for the Israeli settlements in the occupied areas. As the water level continues to drop because of excessive Israeli consumption, the Israeli authorities have resorted to restrictive measures on the use of water by the Arab inhabitants, such as the prohibition of drilling new wells on the western side of the West Bank.

43. As a result of the use of powerful modern drilling and pumping equipment by the Israelis and the restrictions imposed upon the Arab inhabitants, the traditional ground-water sources of Arab villages are drying up, resulting in considerable losses.

44. One case in point is the village of Auja (2,000 inhabitants) situated 12 kilometres north of Jericho in the arid part of the Jordan Valley. Last August, the inhabitants of that village protested to the Israeli authorities that their economy was being ruined because Israeli wells and the water network supplying the nearby settlements of Yita'r, Na'aran and Gilgal had drastically depleted the village's water resources, resulting in the loss of banana and citrus planted land.

II. Conclusions and recommendations

A. conclusions

45. In the period since it submitted its first report to the Security Council, the Commission has detected no evidence of any basic positive change in Israel's policy with regard to the construction and planning of settlements

in the Arab territories under occupation, particularly in the West Bank of Jordan. On the contrary, the Commission is of the view that that policy has largely contributed to a deterioration of the situation in the occupied territories and that it is incompatible with the pursuit of peace in the area.

46. In complete disregard of United Nations resolutions and Security Council decisions, Israel is still pursuing its systematic and relentless process of colonization of the occupied territories. This is evidenced by the stated policy of constructing additional settlements in the most viable parts of the West Bank and by the expansion of others already in existence, as well as the long-term planning of still more settlements.

47. The methods used by the occupation authorities to seize the lands needed for the construction or expansion of settlements are those already referred to by the Commission in its first report, as evidenced by the appeals made recently to Israel's High Court of Justice by groups of dispossessed inhabitants.

48. From all indications available, the Commission continues to believe that the Israeli Government has to bear responsibility for the settlement programme, which is being implemented as an official policy.

49. In the case of the Elon Moreh settlement, where a ruling by the Israeli High Court of Justice would seemingly provide some measure of protection against arbitrary seizure of Arab land, the Commission, while taking note of the Court's decision, cannot but deplore the efforts of the Israeli Government to side-step that decision. The Commission is inclined to believe that that episode, unfortunately, does not represent any significant departure from official Israeli policy regarding the settlements or from the ideological claims put forward as justification for that policy.

50. The Commission views with particular concern the decision taken recently by the Israel Cabinet to allow Israeli citizens and organizations to purchase land in the occupied West Bank and Gaza. Even though the measure contains restrictions on the purchase of privately owned lands, it is the considered opinion of the Commission that such a decision, applied as it is to a population under military occupation, could lead to intolerable pressures to obtain lands owned for generations by Arab families.

51. In the light of its findings, the Commission wishes to reiterate most emphatically its view that Israel's policy of settlement, relentlessly pursued in spite of all Security Council decisions and appeals, is incompatible with the pursuit of peace in the area and that it is bound to lead to a further deterioration of the situation in the occupied territories.

B. RECOMMENDATIONS

52. On the basis of its conclusions, the Commission deems it necessary to reiterate its earlier recommendation that the Security Council, bearing in mind the inalienable right of the Palestinians to return to their homeland, again draw the attention of the Government and people of Israel to the

disastrous consequences which the settlement policy is bound to have on any attempt to reach a peaceful solution in the Middle East.

53. It is the view of the Commission that Israel should be made aware of the serious deterioration of the situation in the occupied territories resulting from its policy of settlement and called upon, as a matter of urgency, to cease the establishment, construction, expansion and planning of settlements in those territories.

54. The Commission therefore recommends that the Security Council adopt effective measures to prevail on Israel to cease the establishment of settlements in occupied territories and to dismantle the existing settlements accordingly.

55. In view of the vital importance of water resources for the prosperity of the occupied Arab territories, and of the reported serious depletion of those resources as a result of intensive exploitation by the Israeli authorities, mainly for the benefit of the Israeli settlements, the Security Council might wish to consider measures aiming at investigating the matter further, with a view to ensuring the protection of those important natural resources of the territories under occupation.

56. With regard to Jerusalem, bearing in mind what was already stated in its first report, the Commission again strongly recommends that the Security Council urge the Government of Israel to implement fully the Council resolutions adopted on that question as from 1967 and further desist from taking any measures which would change the status of Jerusalem, including the pluralistic and religious dimensions of that Holy City.

57. In view of the magnitude of the problem of settlements and its direct effect on the over-all deterioration of the situation in the occupied territories and, therefore, its implications for peace in the region, as well as for international peace and security, the Security Council should keep the situation under constant review.

ANNEX
Communications Received by the Commission in Connexion with Paragraph 26 of the Report

A. LETTER DATED 16 NOVEMBER 1979 FROM THE COMMISSION OF THE CHURCHES OF INTERNATIONAL AFFAIRS OF THE WORLD COUNCIL OF CHURCHES ADDRESSED TO THE CHAIRMAN OF THE COMMISSION

With reference to your letter of 14 November 1979, I have the honour to send you the following relevant resolutions on Jerusalem and the Holy Places which state the current official positions of the World Council of Churches:

Statement on Jerusalem, adopted by the Central Committee of the WCC, meeting in Berlin (West), August 1974

Statement on Jerusalem, adopted by the Fifth Assembly of the WCC, meeting in Nairobi, December 1975.

I am also forwarding today a copy of your letter to the Director of this Commission, Mr. Leopoldo F. Niilus, with the request that he send you additional materials arising out of recent discussions on the matters included in the mandate of your Commission.

(*Signed*) Dwain C. Epps
Executive Secretary

ENCLOSURE I

Statement by the Central Committee of the World Council of Churches, Meeting in Berlin (West), August 1974

The Central Committee affirms that, in order to reach a satisfactory position regarding Jerusalem, the following facts should be taken into account:

1. Jerusalem is a holy city for three monotheistic religions: Judaism, Christianity and Islam. The tendency to minimize Jerusalem's importance for any of these three religions should be avoided.

2. Its importance for Christianity is reflected in the following statement of the Executive Committee of the WCC at Bad Saarow (February 1974): "Christian Holy Places in Jerusalem and the neighbouring areas belong to the greatest extent to member churches of the WCC, specifically the Eastern Orthodox and Oriental Orthodox Churches, and are also of concern to other Christians."

But the question of Jerusalem is not only a matter of protection of the Holy Places; it is organically linked with living faiths and communities of people in the Holy City.

Any proposed solution as to the future of the Holy Places in Jerusalem should take into account the legitimate rights of the churches most directly concerned.

3. Any solution on Jerusalem should take into account the rights and needs of the indigenous peoples of the Holy City.

4. We are of the opinion that matters related to jurisdiction over Jerusalem will only find their lasting solution within the context of the settlement of the conflict in its totality.

The Central Committee recommends that the above should be worked out with member churches, initially those churches most directly concerned, and in consultation with the Roman Catholic Church. These issues should also become subjects for dialogue with Jewish and Muslim participants.

ENCLOSURE II

Statement by the Fifth Assembly of the World Council of Churches, Meeting in Nairobi, December 1975

1. For many millions of Christians throughout the world, as well as for the adherents of the two great sister monotheistic religions, namely, Judaism and Islam, Jerusalem continues to be a focus of deepest religious inspiration and attachment. It is therefore their responsibility to co-operate in the creation of conditions that will ensure that Jerusalem is a city open to

the adherents of all three religions, where they can meet and live together. The tendency to minimize Jerusalem's importance for any of these three religions should be avoided.

2. The special legislation regulating the relationship of the Christian communities and the authorities, guaranteed by international treaties (Paris 1856 and Berlin 1878) and the League of Nations and known as the *Status Quo* of the Holy Places must be fully safeguarded and confirmed in any agreement concerning Jerusalem. Christian Holy Places in Jerusalem and neighbouring areas belong to the greatest extent to member churches of the WCC. On the basis of the *Status Quo* none of the church authorities of a given denomination could represent unilaterally and on behalf of all Christians the Christian point of view, each church authority of a given denomination representing only its own point of view.

3. Many member churches of the WCC are deeply concerned about the Christian Holy Places. However, the question of Jerusalem is not only a matter of protection of the Holy Places; it is organically linked with living faiths and communities of people in the Holy City. Therefore the Assembly deems it essential that the Holy Shrines should not become mere monuments of visitation but should serve as living places of worship integrated and responsive to Christian communities who continue to maintain their life and roots within the Holy City and for those who out of religious attachments want to visit them.

4. While recognizing the complexity and emotional implications of the issues surrounding the future status of Jerusalem, the Assembly believes that such status has to be determined within the general context of the settlement of the Middle East conflict in its totality.

5. However, the Assembly thinks that, apart from any politics, the whole settlement of the interreligious problem of the Holy Places should take place under an international aegis and guarantee which ought to be respected by the parties concerned, as well as the ruling authorities.

6. The Assembly recommends that the above should be worked out with the most directly concerned member churches, as well as with the Roman Catholic Church. These issues should also become subjects for dialogue with Jewish and Muslim counterparts.

7. The Assembly expresses its profound hope and fervent prayers for the peace and welfare of the Holy City and all its inhabitants.

B. Statement received from the observer of the Holy See on 3 December 1979

1. It is commonly felt that the failure to find a solution to the question of Jerusalem, or an inadequate solution, or even a resigned postponement of the problem could bring into question the settlement of the whole Middle East crisis. The Holy See also considers it important that in this matter there should not be created irreversible situations which would prejudice the desired solution.

2. In his speech of 21 December 1973, His Holiness Pope Paul VI expressed the confident hope that the Holy See would fittingly be able to make its voice heard when the problem of Jerusalem became the subject of concrete discussions in the context of the peace negotiations for the Middle East.

On his part, His Holiness Pope John Paul II, in his address to the General Assembly on 2 October 1979, stated: "I also hope for a special statute that, under international guarantees—as my predecessor Paul VI indicated—would respect the particular nature of Jerusalem, a heritage sacred to the veneration of millions of believers of the three great monotheistic religions, Judaism, Christianity and Islam."[a]

It hardly seems necessary to emphasize that the Holy See's interest in this question has a spiritual, historical and juridical basis, that its nature is not political but religious and that its aims are conciliation and peace. The intention of the Holy See is to preserve and guarantee to the Holy City its identity as a religious centre, unique and outstanding in the history of the world, in such a way that it may become a stable place of encounter and concord for the three great monotheistic religions (Judaism, Christianity and Islam).

Needless to say, on this subject, the Holy See endeavours to keep in contact not only with the religious authorities of the various Christian Churches but also with the principal leaders of Islam and Judaism.

3. The ideal and historical reality of the Holy City is manifested in the fact that Jerusalem has been and continues to be the most important centre of all three great monotheistic religions, inasmuch as the City is the seat of three religious communities that live together there and is the site of shrines and memorials venerated by the followers of these religions, who, numbering almost 1.5 billion throughout the world, regard Jerusalem as a common sacred patrimony.

This composite presence in Jerusalem of various groups means that an equitable, stable and peaceful solution of the problem of Jerusalem implies, above all, the recognition of an historical and religious pluralism, to be put into practice by according all of the three religions, in their particular expression as communities, full enjoyment of their respective rights, excluding positions of predominance and, indeed, favouring the prospect of a useful human and religious dialogue.

4. The Holy See's view is that such considerations are of primary and determining importance with regard to the problem of political sovereignty itself. That is to say: whatever solution be found to the question of sovereignty over Jerusalem (not excluding the hypothesis of the "internationalization" of the city), the satisfying and safeguarding of the above-mentioned requirements must be ensured, and, at the same time, the international

---

[a] *Official Records of the General Assembly, Thirty-fourth Session, Plenary Meetings*, 17th meeting, para. 24.

community ought to be the guarantor of interests that involve numerous and diverse peoples.

This does not mean, however, that any solution of the political problem of the sovereignty of Jerusalem can be considered irrelevant to the global settlement of the question. Rather, the Holy See, especially because of the particular character of Jerusalem, acknowledges the need for a solution that will be based on the principles of justice and attained by peaceful means.

5. This perspective gives rise to the need for a "special statute, under international guarantees" for Jerusalem, which the Holy See is earnestly hoping for.

The content of this "statute" would include, among other things, two orders of guarantees:

(a) Parity, for three religious communities, of freedom of worship and of access to the Holy Places; of protection of rights of ownership and of other rights acquired by the individual communities; of the preservation and safeguarding of the historical and urban aspects proper to the city.

(b) Equal enjoyment of the rights of the three religious communities, with guarantees for the promotion of their spiritual, cultural, civil and social life, including adequate opportunities for economic process, education and employment.

It will be necessary, furthermore, to define the territory and list the Holy Places, as well as provide for the guarantees and for the supervision which the international community will have to give to the "statute" and for the juridical form of this commitment and of the accord of the interested parties.

6. In many localities of the Holy Land apart from Jerusalem there are important shrines and Holy Places of one or another religious confession. Suitable guarantees, analogous to those for the city of Jerusalem, and in some way linked to an international juridical protection, should be provided for these places also.

144. General Assembly Resolution 34/70 on the Situation in the Middle East, December 6, 1979*

* G.A. Res. 70, 34 U.N. GAOR Supp. (No. 46) at 21, U.N. Doc. A/34/46 (1979).

The General Assembly,

Having discussed the item entitled "The situation in the Middle East",

Recalling its previous resolutions on the subject, in particular resolutions 3414 (XXX) of 5 December 1975, 31/61 of 9 December 1976, 32/20 of 25 November 1977 and 33/28 and 33/29 of 7 December 1978,

Recalling also its resolution 34/65 of 29 November 1979,

Taking into account the support extended to the just cause of the Palestinian people and the other Arab countries in their struggle against Israeli aggression and for a genuine, comprehensive, just and lasting peace in the Middle East and the full exercise of the inalienable national rights of the Palestinian people, both by the Sixth Conference of Heads of State or Government of Non-Aligned Countries, held at Havana from 3 to 9 September 1979,[33] and by the Assembly by Heads of State and Government of the Organization of African Unity at its sixteenth ordinary session, held at Monrovia from 17 to 20 July 1979,[34]

Deeply concerned that the Arab territories occupied since 1967 have continued, for more than twelve years, to be under illegal Israeli occupation and that the Palestinian people, after three decades, is still deprived of the exercise of its inalienable national rights,

Reaffirming that the acquisition of territory by force is inadmissible under the Charter of the United Nations and that all territories thus occupied must be returned,

Reaffirming also the urgent necessity of the establishment of a just, comprehensive and lasting peace in the region, based on full respect for the principles of the Charter of the United Nations as well as for its resolutions concerning the situation in the Middle East and the question of Palestine,

Convinced that the early convening of the Peace Conference on the Middle East with the participation of all parties concerned, including the Palestine Liberation Organization, in accordance with relevant resolutions of the General Assembly, particularly resolution 3375 (XXX) of 10 November 1975, is essential for the realization of a just and lasting settlement in the region,

1. *Condemns* Israel's continued occupation of Palestinian and other Arab territories, in violation of the Charter of the United Nations, the principles of international law and relevant resolutions of the United Nations;

2. *Declares once more* that peace is indivisible and that a just and lasting settlement of the Middle East question must be based on a comprehensive solution, under the auspices of the United Nations, which takes into account all aspects of the Arab-Israeli conflict, in particular the attainment by the Palestinian people of all its inalienable rights and the Israeli withdrawal from all the occupied Arab and Palestinian territories, including Jerusalem;

3 *Condemns* all partial agreements and separate treaties which violate the

[33] See A/34/542.
[34] See A/34/552.

recognized rights of the Palestinian people and contradict the principles of just and comprehensive solutions to the Middle East problem to ensure the establishment of a just peace in the area;

4. *Reaffirms* that until Israel, in accordance with relevant resolutions of the United Nations, withdraws from all the occupied Palestinian and other Arab territories, and until the Palestinian people attains and exercises its inalienable national rights, as affirmed by the General Assembly in resolution 3236 (XXIX) of 22 November 1974, a comprehensive, just and lasting peace in the Middle East, in which all countries and peoples in the region live in peace and security within recognized and secure boundaries, will not be achieved;

5. *Calls anew* for the early convening of the Peace Conference on the Middle East, under the auspices of the United Nations and the co-chairmanship of the Union of Soviet Socialist Republics and the United States of America, with the participation on an equal footing of all parties concerned, including the Palestine Liberation Organization in accordance with General Assembly resolution 3375 (XXX);

6. *Urges* the parties to the conflict and all other interested parties to work towards the achievement of a comprehensive settlement covering all aspects of the problem and worked out with the participation of all parties concerned within the framework of the United Nations;

7. *Requests* the Security Council, in the exercise of its responsibilities under the Charter, to take all necessary measures to ensure the implementation of relevant resolutions of both the Security Council and the General Assembly, including Assembly resolution 34/65 A and the present resolution, and to facilitate the achievement of such a comprehensive settlement aiming at the establishment of a just and lasting peace in the region;

8. *Requests* the Secretary-General to follow the implementation of the present resolution, to transmit the records of the thirty-fourth session of the General Assembly relating to the question of Palestine and the situation in the Middle East to the Security Council and to inform all concerned, including the Co-Chairmen of the Peace Conference on the Middle East;

9. *Also requests* the Secretary-General to report to the Security Council periodically on the development of the situation and to submit to the General Assembly at its thirty-fifth session a report covering, in all their aspects, the developments in the Middle East.

92nd plenary meeting
6 December 1979

145. European Parliament Resolution on the Attack on
the Israeli Ambassador to Portugal, December 10, 1979*

* 22 O.J. Eur. Comm. (No. C 309) 62 (1979).

The European Parliament,

1. Expresses its horror and disgust at the criminal attack on 13 November 1979 on the Israeli Ambassador in Lisbon, and at the resulting loss of life and injuries;

2. Reiterates its firm opposition to the use of murder and violence for political ends;

3. Hopes fervently that it will be possible to continue the building of peace in the Middle East on the basis of justice for the Arab and Israeli peoples and of security for all the states in the area;

4. Instructs its President to forward this resolution to the Council and Commission and to the Head of the Israeli Mission accredited to the European Communities.

146. General Assembly Resolution 34/103 on the Inadmissibility of the Policy of Hegemonism in International Relations, December 14, 1979*

* G.A. Res. 103, 34 U.N. GAOR Supp. (No. 46) at 68, U.N. Doc. A/34/46 (1979).

The General Assembly,

Recognizing the primary responsibility of the United Nations to promote and strengthen international peace and security on the basis of strict respect for the principles of the Charter of the United Nations, especially the principle of sovereignty, sovereign equality and national independence of States,

Recalling the duty of States to refrain in their international relations from military, political, economic or any other form of coercion aimed against the sovereignty, political independence or territorial integrity of any State,

Noting that hegemonism is a manifestation of the policy of a State, or a group of States, to control, dominate and subjugate, politically, economically, ideologically or militarily, other States, peoples or regions of the world,

Considering that imperialism, colonialism, neo-colonialism, racism including zionism and *apartheid* are all forces which seek to perpetuate unequal relations and privileges acquired by force and are, therefore, different manifestations of the policy and practice of hegemonism,

Concerned that hegemonism, global as well as regional, pursued in the context of the policy of division of the world into blocs or by individual States, manifests itself in the use or threat of use of force, foreign domination and intervention,

Concerned also that hegemonism seeks to limit the freedom of States to determine their political systems and pursue economic, social and cultural development without intimidation, hindrance or pressure,

Convinced that hegemonism, global and regional, in all its different forms, leads to a serious threat to international peace and security,

Considering that it is the common desire of all peoples to oppose hegemonism and to preserve the sovereignty and national independence of all States,

Bearing in mind the importance and urgency of creating a new and equitable system of international relations based on the equal participation of all States in the solution of international problems and the maintenance of international peace and security, one which ensures equal security for all States, and progress and prosperity for all peoples, through the establishment of the new international economic order,

1. *Condemns* hegemonism in all its manifestations, including that conducted at the global, regional or sub-regional level, pursued in the context of the policy of division of the world into blocs or by individual States;

2. *Declares* that no State or group of States shall, under any circumstance or for any reason whatsoever, pursue hegemony in international relations or seek a position of dominance, either globally or in any region of the world;

3. *Rejects* all forms of domination, subjugation, interference or intervention and all forms of pressure, whether political, ideological, economic, military or cultural, in international relations;

4. *Resolutely condemns* policies of pressure and use or threat of use of force, direct or indirect aggression, occupation and the growing practice of interference and intervention, overt or covert, in the internal affairs of States;

5. *Resolutely condemns* imperialism, colonialism, neo-colonialism, *apartheid*, racism including zionism and all other forms of foreign aggression, occupation, domination and interference, as well as the creation of spheres of influence and the division of the world into antagonistic political and military blocs;

6. *Calls upon* all States, in the conduct of international relations, to observe strictly the principles of the Charter of the United Nations and those regarding respect for the sovereignty, sovereign equality, national independence, unity and territorial integrity of States, non-interference in their internal affairs, non-aggression, peaceful settlement of disputes and co-operation, as well as the right of peoples under colonial and alien domination to self-determination;

7. *Calls* for the withdrawal of all occupation forces back to their own territories, so as to enable the peoples of all States to determine and administer their own affairs;

8. *Further calls* for strict respect for the right of all States to determine their political and socio-economic systems and pursue their national economic, social and other policies without intimidation, hindrance or interference from outside;

9. *Resolves* to continue the endeavour to establish a new and equitable system of international relations based on the equal participation of all States in the solution of international problems and the maintenance of international peace and security;

10. *Further resolves* to continue the endeavour for the establishment of the new international economic order, so as to ensure the economic emancipation and freedom of all nations, in particular the developing countries.

103rd plenary meeting
14 December 1979

147. Israel's Autonomy Model, January 24, 1980*

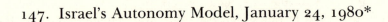

---

* Embassy of Israel, Washington, D.C.

"The purpose of the negotiation shall be to agree, prior to the elections, on the modalities for establishing the elected self-governing authority (administrative council), define its powers and responsibilities, and agree upon other related issues." (Joint letter from President Sadat and Prime Minister Begin to President Carter, March 26, 1979).

"The parties will negotiate an agreement which will define the powers and responsibilities of the self-governing authority to be exercised in the West Bank and Gaza" (The Camp David Accords—The Framework for Peace in the Middle East).

1. In the course of the discussions of the sub-committee which took place recently in Egypt, Israel presented a model of the constituent bodies of the autonomy. This model contains Israel's ideas on the powers and responsibilities of the administrative council. The model, which outlines in great detail the areas of authority to be exercised by the administrative council, represents an important step forward in the negotiations, since the ideas contained in the model are most likely to shift the discussions onto practical lines which is the best way toward reaching an agreement.

2. In devising the model, Israel remained faithful to the letter and spirit of the Camp David Accords, which call for negotiations between the parties on an agreement that will define the powers and responsibilities of the self-governing authority.

3. This is the first time that Israel has presented a concrete model of the proposed administrative council, detailing its organizational structure, as well as the functions and powers covering all the areas of day-to-day life necessary for the implementation of autonomy.

4. The Israeli proposal for the administrative council is for the interim period of five years stipulated in the Camp David Accords.

5. No concrete proposal for the self-governing authority has been made by Egypt. Instead, Egypt has issued statements and made demands which depart from the language and spirit of the Camp David Accords, exceed the terms of reference of the interim autonomy framework, and in effect are liable to pose a serious danger to the security of Israel.

6. Israel recognizes the fact that one of the elements of a settlement of the Arab-Israel conflict is a solution to the question of the Palestinian Arabs, and therefore it was Israel's Prime Minister who suggested granting administrative autonomy to the residents of Judea, Samaria, and the Gaza District. This suggestion became one of the cornerstones of the Camp David Accords. However, Israel is convinced that it is only one of the elements of an overall settlement, and that another fundamental tenet of the Accords is Israel's security—with secure and recognized borders—and above all, recognition by the Arab states bordering Israel of Israel's right to exist as a sovereign Jewish State in the region.

7. When considering the merits of the Israeli proposal it is well to remem-

ber that the Israeli proposal and the Camp David Accords offer the Palestinian Arabs greater opportunities than anything they have ever experienced in their history. When Judea, Samaria, and the Gaza District were under Jordanian and Egyptian occupation between 1948 and 1967, let alone earlier Turkish or British rule, the residents were not allowed to govern themselves to any degree approaching the Israeli proposal.

8. Israel and Egypt agreed at Camp David that the final status of the areas be determined at the end of the five-year interim period by negotiations among Israel, Egypt, Jordan and the elected representatives of the inhabitants of Judea, Samaria, and Gaza.

9. Regrettably, in the course of the discussions between the Israel and Egyptian subcommittees, the Egyptian delegation rejected outright Israel's autonomy model, formulating instead ideas based on geographic definitions and conceptions of legislative authority clearly designed to lead to the creation of another Palestinian Arab state. The creation of such a state not only contradicts the Camp David Accords, and the discussions that led to their conclusion; but the principle of such a state is also opposed by Israel, which sees it as a mortal danger to its security, and by the United States, as stated by President Carter on August 10, 1979: "I am against any creation of a seperate Palestinian state. I don't think it would be good for the Palestinians. I don't think it would be good for Israel. I don't think it would be good for the Arab neighbors of such a state."

10. In order to help clarify the issue we enclose the text of Israel's proposals as well as a graphic outline of the suggested machinery for the autonomous administration.

CHAIRMAN OF THE ADMINISTRATIVE COUNCIL

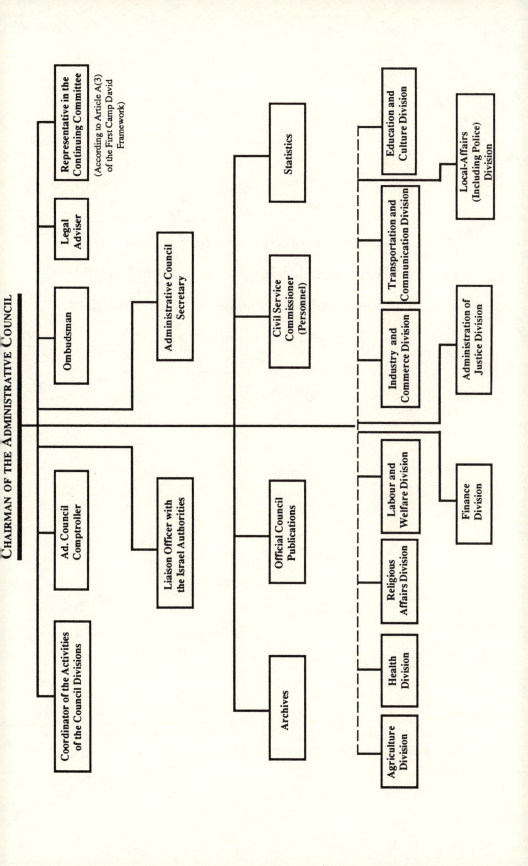

- Coordinator of the Activities of the Council Divisions
- Ad. Council Comptroller
- Ombudsman
- Legal Adviser
- Representative in the Continuing Committee
  (According to Article A(3) of the First Camp David Framework)

- Liaison Officer with the Israel Authorities
- Administrative Council Secretary

- Archives
- Official Council Publications
- Civil Service Commissioner (Personnel)
- Statistics

- Agriculture Division
- Health Division
- Religious Affairs Division
- Labour and Welfare Division
- Industry and Commerce Division
- Transportation and Communication Division
- Education and Culture Division

- Finance Division
- Administration of Justice Division
- Local-Affairs (Including Police) Division

148. Israel's Proposed Model for a Self-Governing
Authority (Administrative Council) to Be Elected by
the Palestinian Arab Inhabitants of Judea, Samaria, and
the Gaza District, January 24, 1980*

---

* Embassy of Israel, Washington, D.C.

The Israeli team expressed its thoughts through this draft model on the organizational concept of the administrative council and its administrative tools.

Israel sees three different categories of powers and responsibilities.

The first is that described in the model, and includes all the powers and responsibilities to be given to the administrative council. In our opinion, this model covers all those elements needed to ensure full autonomy for the Palestinian Arab inhabitants of Judea, Samaria and the Gaza District.

The second category includes powers and responsibilities which will be administered jointly and through cooperation, the so-called "shared powers" between Israel and the administrative council.

The third category includes those powers and responsibilities which will remain in Israel's authority, the so-called "residual" powers.

It should be clear that this is a draft, a proposed model, of the Israeli party to the negotiation.

1. The administrative council will be composed of 11 members, a chairman and 10 members, each of whom will be head of a division.

2. –A– The administrative council will have the following general powers:

    1. To issue regulations.
    2. To determine the budget and mode of financing of the administrative council.
    3. To enter into contracts.
    4. To sue and be sued in the local courts.
    5. To employ personnel.

–B– The administrative council will be entitled to delegate all or part of its powers to heads of divisions functioning within its frame.

3. Following divisions will function within the frame of the council: agriculture, health, religions, labor and welfare, commerce and industry, finance, transport and communications, education and culture, administration of justice and local affairs (including police).

4. Agriculture division will deal with all branches of agriculture and fisheries and with nature reserves and parks.

5. Health division will supervise the hospitals, clinics and other health and sanitary services.

6. Religious division will deal with matters of religious services to all religious communities.

7. Labor and welfare division will be responsible for the welfare, labor and employment services including the operation of labor exchanges, and will be responsible for the rehabilitation of refugees.

8. Industry and commerce division will be responsible for all branches of commerce, industry and workshops.

9. Finance division will deal with the budget of the administrative council

and its distribution among the various divisions, and will be responsible for matters of direct taxation.

10. Transport and communications division will coordinate matters of transport, road traffic, meteorology, shipping and ports, and will be responsible for post and communications services.

11. Education and culture division will operate the local system of educational institutions from kindergarten to institutions of higher education and will supervise culture, art and sports activities.

12. The administration of justice division will supervise the administrative system of the local courts, and also deal with matters of the prosecution framework and with all matters of registration and association under the law (such as—companies, partnerships, patents, trademarks, etc.)

13. The local affairs division will deal with matters of housing and construction inclusive of building licenses, matters of local authorities, tourism and will be responsible for the operation of the local police force, including prisons for criminal offenders sentenced by the local courts.

14. Each division of the administrative council will be managed by its own director-general who will have under his jurisdiction special assistants and section directors. The following sections will function in each of the divisions.

–A– The administration section will deal with organizational and management of the division, employee affairs, budgets, finances and internal audit of the division and its sections. The section will also be responsible for training and professional up-grading for employees of the division.

–B– The legal department of each division will provide legal advice to the head of the division, the director-general, his assistants and the sections.

The chairman of the administrative council will be responsible for coordinating the operation of the various divisions of the council. In addition, there will be in his office a number of non-elected functionaries appointed by the chairman of the council, as follows:

–A– The statistics section.

–B– The civil service commissioner.

–C– The official publications section.

–D– The archives.

The following will function alongside the chairman's office: the legal advisor, ombudsman and comptroller of the administrative council.

–A– The legal advisor will provide legal advice to the council and its divisions in all matters arising from its ongoing functions, and guidance on future affairs. Within its responsibility will also be the regulatory system under the powers of the council: preparation, drafting and coordination of regulations. The legal departments will also be responsible for the function of the legal departments within each division.

–B– The ombudsman will deal with all requests submitted to the chairman of the council or directly to him, and which relate to matters where regular channels cannot provide satisfactory answers.

–C– The comptroller will audit the activities of the various divisions.

The coordinator of divisional activities, alongside the secretary, will coordinate activities between the divisions whenever this is necessary in order to implement council decisions.

149. Excerpt from Resolutions on the Palestine Question
and Jerusalem by the Islamic Conference of Foreign
Ministers Meeting in Its First Extraordinary Session, in
Islamabad, January 27–29, 1980*

---

* 9 J. Palestine Stud. 197 (Spring 1980).

1. [The conference] *condemns* the Egyptian government's policy of establishing relations with the Zionist racist entity and condemns the collusion and cooperation between Egypt, Israel and the USA in all fields, inasmuch as this constitutes a flagrant aggression against the rights of the Palestinian people and a threat to the security and independence of the Arab and Muslim countries.

2. *Calls upon* all Muslim countries to consider joining in boycotting the Egyptian regime politically, economically and culturally and observing the boycott rules of the Arab League and coordinating their efforts with the Arab countries in that respect.

3. *Calls upon* all Islamic states to reaffirm their solidarity with the Palestine Liberation Organization, the sole legitimate representative of the Palestinian people, in its struggle against the Zionist entity and to secure the inalienable national rights of the Palestinian people, including their right to establish an independent state in their usurped homeland.

4. *Condemns* the aggressions perpetrated by Israel against South Lebanon and invites members of the conference to exert their efforts with a view to helping the Lebanese government put an end to these aggressions.

5. *Invites* Islamic countries to reaffirm concretely their solidarity with the Arab states for the liberation of al-Quds [Jerusalem] and all the other occupied territories.

150. Hebron, Information Background,
February 15, 1980*

* Embassy of Israel, Washington, D.C.

HEBRON

The Government affirms that, in accordance with its basic Policy guide-lines, as approved by the Knesset, there is no reason why Jews should not live in Hebron or at any other location in the Land of Israel. The sites and timing of habitation will be determined by the Government. The Government will act with a view to strengthening Kiryat Arba.

Israel Cabinet Decision, Feb. 11, 1980

1. The Jewish Community of Hebron is a vivid example of the continuity of Jewish habitation in the Land of Israel. Apart from short periods follow-ing the expulsions of the Romans and the Crusaders, Jews lived continu-ously in the city for many centuries, until the massacre of the community in 1929 at the hands of an Arab mob.

2. Since the days of the patriarchs, Hebron has been a city of refuge and understanding among the different faiths who shared its holy sites. Only in the twentieth century did rising Arab intolerance put an end to this tradi-tion.

3. In 1948 any possibility of further habitation was temporarily brought to an end with the conquest of Judea and its subsequent annexation in 1950 to the Hashemite Kingdom of Jordan. The entire region of Judea and Sa-maria then became "Judenrein" and any Jewish presence was forbidden. Jewish property was taken over by local Arabs, and some was placed under the guardianship of the Jordanian custodian of absentee property.

4. The right of Jews to return to their property in Hebron, and indeed in the entire region of Judea and Samaria, is based on the following consider-ations:

A. This area was an integral portion of the one-time British Mandate over Palestine in which Jews had full rights of settlement, and, until 1947 owned considerable tracts of property. The entire area of Pal-estine was designated as a national home for the Jewish people and the illegal annexation of Judea and Samaria by the Hashemite King-dom of Jordan cannot negate that right.

B. International law does not prevent persons wishing to return to their property to do so, nor does it prevent the settlement of government land or property which does not involve the displacement of existing population. On the contrary, it encourages the continuation of normal day to day life. There can be no doubt that the right of Jews to play a part in the future everyday life of Hebron is a just reflection of the city's past as a center of religious tolerance and harmony.

5. Following the Six Day War of 1967 and an enforced absence of nine-teen years Jews returned to Hebron. At first they were permitted by the military government to resettle only the ancient site of Kiryat Arba, close by Hebron. Jewish property within Hebron itself was not immediately claimed and remained empty. This property included five houses abandoned in

1929 and until 1967 administered by the Jordanian custodian of absentee property. In 1967 the Israeli military government acceded to control of the property.

6. The current desire to return to Hebron relates to three of these homes, all of which are uninhabited and may be put to use without any disruption of the Arab population. One of the houses had been leased to UNWRA by the Jordanians and, although this organization did not make full use of the property, its status, under local law remains that of a protected tenant. In conformity with international law Israel will respect this status.

7. The current negotiations among the governments of Israel, Egypt and the United States on the issue of autonomy and the establishment of a self-governing authority for the Palestinian Arabs of Judea and Samaria are part of an ongoing process aimed at the settlement of all issues arising from the wars which the Arab states have waged against Israel. Their success cannot be ensured by a unilateral imposition on one of the parties of the forfeiture of all its rights prior to agreement and without any sign of concessions by the other parties to the negotiations. The future of Hebron must be sought in the lessons of its past—a city whose origins go back to the common founder of all three monotheistic faiths, Abraham, "The Friend" a city whose different peoples and faiths have lived together throughout the centuries in harmony and mutual tolerance.

Israel believes that any kind of future arrangement in Judea and Samaria can and must equally involve Jews and Arabs living together side by side in peaceful coexistence.

151. Security Council Resolution 465 Deploring Israeli Policy on Settlements in the Occupied Arab Territories, Jerusalem, and the Holy Places, March 1, 1980*

* S.C. Res. 465, 35 U.N. SCOR (2203rd mtg.) at 5, U.N. Doc. S/INF/36 (1980).

The Security Council,

Taking note of the reports of the Security Council Commission established under resolution 446 (1979) to examine the situation relating to settlements in the Arab territories occupied since 1967, including Jerusalem, contained in documents S/13450 and Corr.1 and Add.1[18] and S/13679,[19]

Taking note also of letters from the Permanent Representative of Jordan[20] and the Permanent Representative of Morocco, Chairman of the Islamic Group,[21]

Strongly deploring the refusal by Israel to co-operate with the Commission and regretting its formal rejection of resolutions 446 (1979) and 452 (1979),

Affirming once more that the Geneva Convention relative to the Protection of Civilian Persons in Time of War, of 12 August 1949,[22] is applicable to the Arab territories occupied by Israel since 1967, including Jerusalem,

Deploring the decision of the Government of Israel officially to support Israeli settlements in the Palestinian and other Arab territories occupied since 1967,

Deeply concerned by the practices of the Israeli authorities in implementing that settlements policy in the occupied Arab territories, including Jerusalem, and its consequences for the local Arab and Palestinian population,

Taking into account the need to consider measures for the impartial protection of private and public land and property, and water resources,

Bearing in mind the specific status of Jerusalem and, in particular, the need to protect and preserve the unique spiritual and religious dimension of the Holy Places in the city,

Drawing attention to the grave consequences which the settlements policy is bound to have on any attempt to reach a comprehensive, just and lasting peace in the Middle East,

Recalling pertinent Security Council resolutions, specifically resolutions 237 (1967), 252 (1968), 267 (1969), 271 (1969) and 298 (1971), as well as the consensus statement made by the President of the Council on 11 November 1976,[23]

Having invited Mr. Fahd Qawasma, Mayor of Al-Khalil (Hebron), in the occupied territory, to supply it with information pursuant to rule 39 of the provisional rules of procedure,

1. *Commends* the work done by the Security Council Commission established under resolution 446 (1979) in preparing the report contained in document S/13679;

[18] See *Official Records of the Security Council, Thirty-fourth Year, Supplement for July, August and September 1979.*

[19] *Ibid., Supplement for October, November and December 1979.*

[20] *Ibid., Thirty-fifth Year, Supplement for January, February and March 1980,* document S/13801.

[21] *Ibid.,* document S/13802.

[22] United Nations, *Treaty Series,* vol. 75, p. 287.

[23] *Official Records of the Security Council, Thirty-first Year,* 1969th meeting.

2. *Accepts* the conclusions and recommendations contained in the report of the Commission;

3. *Calls upon* all parties, particularly the Government of Israel, to co-operate with the Commission;

4. *Strongly deplores* the decision of Israel to prohibit the free travel of Mayor Fahd Qawasma in order to appear before the Security Council and requests Israel to permit his free travel to United Nations Headquarters for that purpose;

5. *Determines* that all measures taken by Israel to change the physical character, demographic composition, institutional structure or status of the Palestinian and other Arab territories occupied since 1967, including Jerusalem, or any part thereof have no legal validity and that Israel's policy and practices of settling parts of its population and new immigrants in those territories constitute a flagrant violation of the Geneva Convention relative to the Protection of Civilian Persons in Time of War and also constitute a serious obstruction to achieving a comprehensive, just and lasting peace in the Middle East;

6. *Strongly deplores* the continuation and persistence of Israel in pursuing those policies and practices and calls upon the Government and people of Israel to rescind those measures, to dismantle the existing settlements and in particular to cease, on an urgent basis, the establishment, construction and planning of settlements in the Arab territories occupied since 1967, including Jerusalem;

7. *Calls upon* all States not to provide Israel with any assistance to be used specifically in connexion with settlements in the occupied territories;

8. *Requests* the Commission to continue to examine the situation relating to settlements in the Arab territories occupied since 1967, including Jerusalem, to investigate the reported serious depletion of natural resources, particularly the water resources, with a view to ensuring the protection of those important natural resources of the territories under occupation, and to keep under close scrutiny the implementation of the present resolution;

9. *Requests* the Commission to report to the Security Council before 1 September 1980 and decides to convene at the earliest possible date thereafter in order to consider the report and the full implementation of the present resolution.

Adopted unanimously at the 2203rd meeting.

152. U.S. Statements with Regard to Security Council Resolution 465, March 1–3, 1980*

* 80 U.S. Dep't State Bull. No. 2037, at 64 (April 1980).

Ambassador McHenry, Mar. 1, 1980[2]

As always, the Middle East is subject to many trends and influences, some of them contradictory in nature. In the view of the United States, one of the positive trends in the area is the current series of negotiations for a comprehensive settlement which resulted from the historic breakthrough at Camp David a year and a half ago. A Peace Treaty has been signed, and large areas of occupied Arab territory have been evacuated by Israel. The parties have taken concrete steps in the cause of peace, even in the face of issues which touch their most vital national interests and on which there are, particularly in Israel, sharp but honest differences of view.

As significant as these developments are, we recognize that there can be no comprehensive peace in the Middle East until the Palestinian problem in all of its aspects is resolved. The ongoing negotiations on the West Bank and Gaza are admittedly difficult and even if successful will constitute only a first step. But progress is being made, and for the first time in 30 years, the core issues are being addressed seriously and with determination.

Everyone recognizes that the problem of Israeli settlements is one of the issues that must be dealt with. The position of the United States on the question of settlements is clear and is consistent. In particular, the United States has had the occasion to state its views both publicly and privately concerning the situation in Hebron.

We regard settlements in the occupied territories as illegal under international law, and we consider them to be an obstacle to the successful outcome to the current negotiations which are aimed at a comprehensive, just, and lasting peace in the Middle East.

We have supported the resolution before us. We have done so despite our reservations with regard to certain of the provisions of the resolution, which we consider to be recommendatory in character. We believe that the report of the settlements commission is generally fair-minded and objective, but we have a question concerning the commission's recommendation in paragraph 54 of its report as to the best means to deal with the settlements in the occupied territories. I should also add that we do not read the reference in operative paragraph 5 of the resolution to changes in the institutional structure of the occupied territories as in any way prejudicing the outcome of the autonomy negotiations.

The basic framework for all our efforts, including the Camp David accords, is Resolution 242 which calls for negotiations to resolve the many and difficult aspects of the Arab-Israeli conflict. Such negotiations are currently underway.

One of the issues which the negotiators will have to address is the matter of existing settlements. There are a number of factors of a practical character that make impractical the call in operative paragraph 6 of the resolution for the dismantling of existing settlements. Some projects are not so

[2] USUN press release 16 of Mar. 1, 1980.

easily dismantled; moreover, whatever the future status of the occupied territories, there will be a need for housing, and there will be a need for related infrastructure for the inhabitants.

My delegation is pleased that the Council has spoken unanimously on this important issue. At the same time, we believe we must all recognize that the solution to the problem lies ultimately in a negotiating process. For our part, we are committed to the negotiations in which we are currently engaged as a full partner, and we are determined that they shall bring a comprehensive peace closer to reality. In the final analysis, all of us here will be judged by the contribution which we make to this objective.

Department Statement, Mar. 3, 1980[3]

There were some questions raised over the weekend about our vote in the Security Council on Saturday. I want, therefore, to make the following points. There is no change in our basic policy on settlements or on Jerusalem. Our policy has been consistently stated over a number of months and remains unchanged. Our support for Israeli security and well-being also remains firm and unwavering.

This is a fundamental element in American foreign policy. We remain totally committed to the success of the negotiations under the Camp David frameworks. We believe they will provide the proper context for dealing with issues such as the Israeli settlements in occupied territory.

As we said yesterday and as Ambassador McHenry made clear in the Security Council, the United States is opposed to the inclusion of the phrase "dismantling of existing settlements" in the Security Council resolution which was passed on Saturday.

The issue of existing settlements in occupied territory will be dealt with in the negotiations now underway. We do not consider the call in this forum—i.e., in the Security Council—in that resolution for dismantling them to be either proper or practical.

As we have said, we believe all the outstanding issues should be dealt with through negotiation, and we are fully committed to the success of the current negotiations.

Finally, to repeat again what we have said before, we have made clear our opposition to any effort to change or amend U.N. Resolution 242 in any way.

President's Statement, Mar. 3, 1980[4]

I want to make it clear that the vote of the United States in the Security Council of the United Nations does not represent a change in our position

[3] Read to news correspondents by acting Department spokesman Tom Reston.
[4] Text from Weekly Compilation of Presidential Documents of Mar. 10, 1980.

regarding the Israeli settlements in the occupied areas nor regarding the status of Jerusalem.

While our opposition to the establishment of the Israeli settlements is longstanding and well-known, we made strenuous efforts to eliminate the language with reference to the dismantling of settlements in the resolution. This call for dismantling was neither proper nor practical. We believe that the future disposition of existing settlements must be determined during the current autonomy negotiations.

As to Jerusalem, we strongly believe that Jerusalem should be undivided with free access to the holy places for all faiths and that its status should be determined in the negotiations for a comprehensive peace settlement.

The U.S. vote in the United Nations was approved with the understanding that all references to Jerusalem would be deleted. The failure to communicate this clearly resulted in a vote in favor of the resolution rather than abstention.

I want to reiterate in the most unequivocal of terms that in the autonomy negotiations and in other fora, the United States will neither support nor accept any position that might jeopardize Israel's vital security interests. Our commitment to Israel's security and well-being remains unqualified and unshakable.

153. The Jewish Quarter of Hebron, Israel Cabinet Decision, March 24, 1980*

* Embassy of Israel, Washington, D.C.

1. The Israel Government decision pertains to the establishment of two cultural and educational institutions in the old Jewish quarter of Hebron. Such institutions existed and flourished there, up until 1929, when, as a result of the massacre of some 60 Jews, Jewish life in Hebron came to an end.

   The Institutions are:
   - A Rabbinical Academy (Yeshiva) on the site of Abraham's synagogue.
   - A field school to be built on the premises of the "Hadassah" clinic by adding one floor to the existing structure.

2. Jewish life existed in Hebron throughout the ages, and it is inconceivable that the right to live or to study there by denied today. Of all places in Judea and Samaria, Hebron is undoubtedly one place where Jewish roots go very deep. It contains the Machpelah Cave, the burial place of the Hebrew patriarchs, one of the holiest shrines in Judaism.

3. The houses used for these institutions are Jewish property and they are presently unoccupied. The present plans will in no way infringe upon the rights of the local residents of the neighborhood, and no one will have to move from his house.

4. The Israeli Government was unanimous on the substance of the decision and the principle involved. Disagreement reflected only considerations of timing.

154. Jewish Settlement in the Land of Israel, April 1980*

---

* Embassy of Israel, Washington, D.C.

Jewish Settlement in the Land of Israel

The Land of Israel—known also as the Holy Land or Palestine—is where the Jewish people founded and developed its national and religious culture, during a period extending over thousands of years. It is the land in which Jews have continued to reside in varying numbers, down through the ages, and that has been the constant focus of the prayers, hopes and yearnings for national redemption of Jews everywhere.

In 1917, after the British conquered the land from the Turks, the British government announced, in what came to be known as the Balfour Declaration, that it favoured the establishment in Palestine of a Jewish National Home.

The mandate over Palestine granted Britain by the League of Nations in 1922 explicitly recognized *"the historical connection of the Jewish people with Palestine"* and *"the grounds for reconstituting their national home in that country."* In that same year, however, Britain arbitrarily partitioned Palestine, designating nearly 80 percent of the land (the section east of the Jordan River, or Transjordan) as a future Arab kingdom.

In 1947 the UN General Assembly resolved to partition Palestine for a second time, calling for the division of western Palestine into what were to become a Jewish state (Israel) and an Arab state. The Arab state, however, was stillborn, because the army of Transjordan (today's Jordan), in flagrant violation of the UN partition resolution and of the UN Charter, invaded Israel in May 1948 together with the other neighbouring Arab states, with the avowed aim of wiping out the newborn Jewish state. Egypt occupied the Gaza district, remaining there as an occupying power until 1967. Jordan occupied Judea-Samaria (the "West Bank") and later annexed these regions, an act that was never recognized internationally. Britain and Pakistan were the only countries in the world to recognize that annexation; even the countries of the Arab League refused to do so. The war of 1948 ended with the signing, early in 1949, of armistice agreements between Israel and each of the four neighbouring Arab states—Egypt, Jordan, Lebanon and Syria.

In the Six-Day War of June 1967, Israel successfully repulsed a coordinated Arab attack across the 1949 armistice line. As a result, Judea-Samaria and the Gaza district came under Israeli administration.

With this background in mind, we may turn our attention to three key questions:

1. *What is the legal status of the areas that came under Israeli administration in 1967?*
2. *Do Israelis have the right to establish and maintain settlements in these areas?*
3. *Are such settlements an obstacle to peace?*

UNALLOCATED TERRITORIES

Judea-Samaria and the Gaza district being an integral part of the historic Jewish homeland, as well as of the League of Nations Palestine mandate

(1922-1948) which recognized that historic connection, Israel reserves the full right to claim sovereignty over these areas—although, to date, it has not exercised this right and has refrained from annexing them.

In its proposals of December 1977 for the establishment of self-rule (autonomy) for the Arab inhabitants of Judea-Samaria and the Gaza district, Israel spelled out its position on the sovereignty question as follows:

> Israel stands by its right and its claim of sovereignty to Judea, Samaria and the Gaza district. In the knowledge that other claims exist, it proposes, for the sake of the agreement and the peace, that the question of sovereignty in these areas be left open.

This proposal later became part of the understanding that lies at the root of the Camp David agreements, which stipulate:

> As soon as possible, but not later than the third year after the beginning of the (five-year) transitional period, negotiations will take place to determine the final status of the West Bank and Gaza and its relationship with its neighbors, and to conclude a peace treaty between Israel and Jordan by the end of the transitional period.

US Secretary of State Cyrus Vance, at a press conference in Washington, DC, on 28 July 1977, gave expression to the undetermined nature of the status of Judea-Samaria when he said:

> There is, I think, an open question as to who has legal right to the West Bank.

Writing in the 26 November 1978 issue of The Washington Star, William O'Brien, Professor of Government at Georgetown University in Washington, DC, describes Judea-Samaria as having the status, today, of "unallocated territory:"

> The West Bank was not and is not clearly the sovereign territory of Jordan, from whom Israel took it in a war of self-defense in 1967. The West Bank is an integral part of the Palestine mandate within which a Jewish national home was to be created. In this sense the territory must be considered today to be unallocated territory.

Professor Stephen M. Schwebel, former legal adviser to the US State Department, goes one step further. Discussing the subject in the May 1970 issue of The American Journal of International Law, he concludes that Israel's title to Judea-Samaria and Gaza is actually better than that of Jordan and Egypt:

> Where the prior holder of territory had seized that territory unlawfully, the state which subsequently takes that territory in the lawful exercise of self-defense has, against that prior holder, better title.

> . . . as between Israel, acting defensively in 1948 and 1967, on the one hand, and her Arab neighbors, acting aggressively in 1948 and 1967, on the other,

Israel has better title in the territory of what was Palestine, including the whole of Jerusalem, than do Jordan and Egypt (the UAR, indeed, has, unlike Jordan, not asserted sovereign title).

(In support of this view, Schwebel cites various instruments of international law, such as the UN Charter and the Vienna Convention on the Law of Treaties, and the well-known authority on international law, E. Lauterpacht.)

THE RIGHT TO SETTLE

The charge has been made that the Jewish settlements in Judea-Samaria are illegal. An examination of the relevant juridical sources, however, will reveal this charge to be entirely unfounded.

The instrument of international law cited in support of the charge is the Fourth Geneva Red Cross Convention of 1949 on the Protection of Civilians in Time of War—Article 49 of which forbids an occupying power to transfer parts of its civilian population to the occupied territory in question.

To begin with, the applicability of the Fourth Geneva Convention to Judea-Samaria and Gaza is highly questionable, since the prior legitimate sovereign in these areas was not Jordan, or any other Arab power, but the British mandate. In fact, the mandate explicitly charged Britain with the duty to encourage *"close settlement by Jews on the land."* Dr. Eugene V. Rostow, Professor of Law and Public Affairs at Yale University and former Under-Secretary of State (1966-1969), in a letter to Mr. I.L. Kenen of Near East Research dated 20 September 1977, pointed out that:

> *Under the mandate, Jewish settlement was contemplated and permitted in the entire area of the mandate. . . That is, the area now known as the West Bank was available to all Palestinians—Muslim, Christian, Druze and Jewish alike. . . The armistice agreements of 1949 do not alter these dispositions. . . They expressly provide that the armistice demarcation lines are not political boundaries, but may be altered by agreement when the parties move from armistice to peace.*

In other words, since Jordan never was the legitimate sovereign in Judea-Samaria, or Egypt in the Gaza district, the provisions of the Fourth Geneva Convention designed to protect the rights of the legitimate sovereign with regard to the transfer of civilians to the occupied territory do not apply with respect to these areas.

Strictly speaking, therefore, Israel is not subject to these provisions and need not consider itself to be restricted by them. Nevertheless, the humanitarian provisions of the convention are scrupulously adhered to by Israel—witness, for example, the judgment of Israel's High Court, discussed below.

As for Article 49, inhabitants of the settlements are not "deported" or "transferred." Their settlement activity is voluntary, generally based on a deep feeling of attachment to the land.

LAND ACQUISITION

Nor can the charge be upheld that land for the settlements has been seized by the Israeli authorities without due process of law. The fact is that all the land acquired for this purpose has been acquired in full conformity with the law, and without the displacement of any of the local population.

Most of the land settled has been in the categories of state domain, ownerless property or property owned by absentee landlords. When owners can be located, they are given the choice of cash compensation or alternative land. Any owner who is dissatisfied with the compensation or procedures of acquisition has the right of appeal to the Supreme Court of Israel, sitting as the High Court of Justice. In a number of instances this right has been duly exercised and the Court, for its part, has issued writs against the government or the military authorities when it has found the grievances to be legitimate.

One example of such a decision was the recent judgment of the High Court ordering the government to evacuate a newly established settlement at Eilon Moreh. (In previous instances, such as Hilu, Tubas and Beit El, the Court had ruled in favour of the government. Moreover, the very right of appeal to the Supreme Court of an "occupying power" is not mentioned at all in the Geneva or Hague Conventions, and far exceeds the legal safeguards outlined in those documents.

In the *Washington Star* on 26 November 1978, Professor O'Brien summed up the issue in these words:

> *The fact is that, while not strictly bound by the traditional international law of belligerent occupation, Israel has maintained an occupation on the West Bank that is fully consonant with the principles of international law and natural justice. The settlements on the West Bank are not "illegal." The manner in which the lands for the settlements have been acquired is violative neither of international law nor of human rights.*

SECURITY CONCERNS

A glance at the map shows clearly that, along Israel's coastal plain, where three-quarters of its population resides, the distance between the pre-1967 armistice lines and the Mediterranean Sea ranges between 9 and 20 miles. Until 1967 all of Israel's major towns and cities, its international airports and the bulk of its industry were within range of medium Arab artillery; Jerusalem, the capital, was within small-arms range of Arab forces.

Moreover, the entire coastal plain is dominated by the stark mountains of Judea-Samaria. Under the conditions of modern aerial and armoured warfare, this topographical inferiority, coupled with the narrowness of the coastal plain, renders Israel's population centres virtually indefensible without security control over Judea-Samaria.

Regardless of the ultimate political settlement in the region, the presence of Jewish villages in Judea-Samaria will serve as an effective form of early warning against attack as well as an important deterrent to terrorist activity directed against Israel.

Thus, rather than being an obstacle to peace, the Israeli settlements are in fact a vital deterrent to war.

AN 'OBSTACLE TO PEACE'?

One of the most common misconceptions about the Jewish settlements in the areas administered by Israel is that they constitute "an obstacle to peace." Nothing could be further from reality.

In the Jordanian invasion of 1948, all the Jewish villages in Judea-Samaria were wiped out, and, for 19 years—from 1948 to 1967—not a single Jew was permitted in these areas. Yet the Arab states persisted, throughout this period, in their refusal to make peace and, indeed, threatened repeatedly to destroy Israel, trying unsuccessfully on several occasions to carry out their threat. The *absence* of settlements, during this period, brought peace no nearer.

From 1967 onwards Israel established settlements in some of these areas—yet that in no way hindered progress towards Israel-Arab agreements, when conditions became ripe for them. In fact, the disengagement agreements with Egypt and Syria in 1974, and the Israel-Egypt interim agreement of 1975, were concluded with no reference to these settlements.

Some say the settlements are harmful "because they create political facts."

Facts can be created not only by action, but also by inaction. Israel knows, from experience, that the absence of Jews from places to which they feel an historical and emotional attachment is liable to lead to the loss of access to those places. For Jews to refrain from settling in locations where they have every right to live, while awaiting the outcome of negotiations, would be a clear signal to the hostile elements that still abound in the Arab world to thwart the peace talks, or prevent their successful consummation in order to paralyze the settlement effort indefinitely. Israel could never agree thus to grant its enemies veto power over the realization of its elementary rights.

William Safire, writing in *The New York Times* on 24 May 1979, put it this way:

> *Sovereignty—who owns the land—is the key. Jordan claims it, the PLO claims it, and Israel, through its continued settlement policy, asserts its own claims. The moment Israel gives up its right to settle, it gives up that claim to sovereignty. If Israel were to admit it is not at least part owner, an independent Palestianian state would be born which—in this decade, at least—would be an intolerable threat to Israel's security.*

ARAB-JEWISH COEXISTENCE

Objections have been raised to the establishment of Jewish settlements in Arab-populated areas. Yet, why should Jews be denied the right to live among Arabs? After all, over half a million Arabs live in Israel, among three million Jews, and no one has ever thought to deny them the right to do so! At a time when old hatreds and hostilities are beginning to thaw, let us not re-introduce the Iron Curtain that once sealed off Jew from Arab.

Israel, for its part, certainly will not consent to a situation in which Jews would be prohibited from living in parts of the Land of Israel.

Israel and Egypt find themselves today at the beginning of a peace process that, it is hoped, will eventually embrace all the countries of the region. It is unthinkable that a true and lasting regional peace can strike root in the area, unless Arab-Jewish coexistence and cooperation are encouraged and given full scope for development. The continued hostility and belligerency of the Arab states over the years, as a matter of ideology and of policy, has been a serious impediment to the development of such coexistence and co-operation. Yet progress has been made: the growth of the Arab community in Israel and its advancement in education, social welfare and economic prosperity; the intermingling of Arab and Jewish Jerusalemites since the reunification of Israel's capital in 1967; the "Open Bridges" policy, transforming Judea-Samaria and the Gaza district, since 1967, into areas of free trade and tourism; the "Good Fence" policy on the Israel-Lebanon border; and, of course, the Egypt-Israel peace treaty.

In this sense, Israel's settlement policy is a natural extension of the Open Bridges and Good Fence policies. Just as in the 1920's and 30's, when Arab-Jewish cooperation in Palestine led to substantial economic growth for both communities—despite the violence and terrorism instigated by extremist Arab leaders—so, too, has current Arab-Jewish economic cooperation overshadowed attempts to disrupt it by the PLO, for its own destructive ends; and both sides have benefited as a result.

A carefully planned, judiciously executed settlement policy performs a highly important twin function: (1) it represents a significant contribution toward protecting Israel from terror and invasion; (2) in the long run, it provides a meaningful framework for helping Jews and Arabs to learn to overcome their hatreds and hostilities, to become accustomed to each other, to build up a relationship of trust and cooperation.

As Jews and Arabs in the Middle East grope for peace, as ways are sought to cast aside the suspicion, the rancour and the strife that have plagued this region for so many years and that continue to prevail in so many places— Israel's settlements have a distinctly positive role to play: in the short run, they are a vital deterrent to war; in the long run, they can become a solid bridge to peace.

IIC/211/April 1980

155. The Jewish Settlements in Judea-Samaria:
A Deterrent to War, April 1980*

---

* Embassy of Israel, Washington, D.C.

The Jewish Settlements in Judea-Samaria: A Deterrent to War

Far from being an obstacle to peace, as has so often been contended in some quarters, the Jewish settlements in Judea-Samaria are actually a vital deterrent to war.

A glance at a map of the area reveals two simple facts:

1. Along the coastal plain, where three-quarters of Israel's population lives, *the distance between the Mediterranean Sea and the pre-1967 armistice lines ranges between 9 and 20 miles.* Until 1967, then, this portion of the land—including all of Israel's major cities, its international airports and much of its industry—was within range of medium Arab artillery. Jerusalem, the capital, was within small-arms range of Arab forces, since the armistice line ran through the very heart of the city, effectively severing it in two.

2. *Judea-Samaria, altogether 30 to 35 miles wide, is hardly more than 2,000 square miles in area*—the size of an average American county—yet its importance for Israel's security is paramount, since its stark mountains dominate all of the coastal plain. Under the conditions of modern aerial and armoured warfare, this topographical inferiority, coupled with the narrowness of the coastal plain, renders Israel's major industrial and population centres virtually indefensible without security control over Judea-Samaria.

STRATEGIC FACTORS

Nature abhors a vacuum. So does *realpolitik*. To forgo a meaningful Jewish civilian as well as military presence in Judea-Samaria (assuming such a surrender to be morally justified and historically-ideologically conceivable) would, within a very short time, cause this area to revert to what it was until 1967: a springboard for attacks on Israel. The question, therefore, of who is in control of the central mountain range running north-south through Judea-Samaria is, for Israel, a matter of life or death.

The steep, largely inaccessible eastern slopes of this range serve as an excellent defensive wall jutting up between the Jordan Valley and Israel's densely populated coastal plain to the west. An attacking armoured force crossing the Jordan River would have to climb that wall, its access to the top of the ridge limited to five existing roads. Such an attacking force, moving slowly, unable to spread out and take advantage of its numbers, could be held back by a small defending force atop the mountains long enough for Israel to mobilize its reserves and send them up to reinforce the defending units, using the gentle western slopes of this mountain range and its many approach roads.

Should the Judea-Samaria region, however, fall into enemy hands, the advantages would be reversed—in favour of the attacker. An armoured force deployed along the ridge of the Judea-Samaria mountain range could swoop down into Israel's coastal plain, the moderate slopes in this sector and the almost infinite array of routes allowing for both speed and manoeuvrability. Effective defence of the country, once an assault of this nature had been launched, would be a virtual impossibility.

Such a situation, which did exist between 1949 and 1967, compelled Israel to pre-empt, in sheer self-defence, whenever an attack appeared imminent. Is Israel to be forced, once again, into the adoption of such a policy?

It has been asserted that the sophistication of modern warfare negates the value of defensible borders and strategic depth. Actually, precisely the opposite is true: the rapid development of conventional weaponry in recent years has boosted the significance of territorial barriers and strategic depth. Bombs and missiles can inflict heavy damage on an opponent's people and cities; but they will not be decisive in war, so long as the other side is resolved to fight back. The German blitz failed to knock England out of World War II; nor did the concentrated Allied air bombardments bring Germany to its knees. This happened only when Allied ground troops defeated the German *Wehrmacht* on the ground and the last bunker in Berlin fell. More recently, again, it was ground action, rather than massive American air raids, that decided the outcome of the war in Vietnam.

Nor is the answer to be found in third-party (UN or Big Power) guarantees—simply because, in today's world, such guarantees have proved worthless. No country has ever been saved from aggression by international guarantees. Ultimately, Israel's success in defending itself against future aggression must depend on the nation's own determination—and its physical capacity—to do so.

THE ROLE OF THE SETTLEMENTS

The conclusion is inescapable. Given Israel's geopolitical situation, the inveterate hostility of most of the nearby Arab countries and the constraints inherent in the global situation, Israel's minimal defence strategy must be based on a continued military and civilian presence in areas whose topography and proximity to its vital centres have a crucial bearing on the nation's security. That means strategically placed army units—as provided for in the Camp David agreements. Such units, equipped with electronic surveillance devices and backed up by strategically placed civilian settlements, can serve as an effective early-warning system in the event of a planned Arab attack and as a deterrent to, and curb against, terrorist activity directed at Israel.

In fact, the restrictions Israel took upon itself, under Camp David, with regard to the deployment of its military forces in Judea-Samaria, render the presence of Jewish settlements at strategic points in these areas imperative for the support of the military units thus deployed. Settlements have therefore been established mainly along a line just west of the Jordan River, along the mountain ridge running north-south through the region and in the vicinity of two east-west road-links.

Recent developments on Israel's eastern front have vindicated these security concerns and confirmed the importance of the settlements in that regard. Apart from Jordan's continued hostile attitude towards Israel and

the Israeli-Egyptian peace process, we have been witnessing an unprecedented military build-up by Syria and Iraq, actively aided and abetted by
such major powers as the Soviet Union and France.

Nothing would better suit the strategic objectives of the Arab "rejection-
ists" on Israel's eastern flank than to have Judea-Samaria cleared of any
Israeli presence that might stand in the way of their bellicose designs.

Israel's Supreme Court, sitting as the High Court of Justice, has firmly
upheld the country's right to establish settlements for security reasons. In a
number of cases, such as Hilu, Tubas and Beit-El, appeals against government expropriation of land for such settlements were rejected. In the more
recent case of Eilon Moreh, the Court ordered a newly established settlement evacuated, on the grounds that the primary considerations for its establishment were held not to have been security ones.

Israel has many deep-rooted reasons for fostering and developing a moderate, controlled settlement policy in Judea-Samaria. But, even if this were
not the case, the strategic and military imperatives outlined here are in
themselves reason enough for the Government of Israel to continue to adhere to this policy—as a minimum programme for maintaining a reasonable
defence posture in the face of the dangers that threaten this country.

IIC/211/April 1980

156. Security Council Resolution 468 Deploring Israeli

Expulsion of Mayors from Hebron and Halhoul,

May 8, 1980*

* S.C. Res. 468, 35 U.N. SCOR (2221st mtg.) at 9, U.N. Doc. S/INF/36 (1980).

The Security Council,

Recalling the Geneva Convention of 1949,[35]

Deeply concerned at the expulsion by the Israeli military occupation authorities of the Mayors of Hebron and Halhoul and of the Sharia Judge of Hebron,

1. *Calls upon* the Government of Israel, as the occupying Power, to rescind
these illegal measures and to facilitate the immediate return of the expelled
Palestinian leaders so that they can resume the functions for which they
were elected and appointed;

2. *Requests* the Secretary-General to report upon the implementation of
the present resolution.

Adopted at the 2221st meeting by 14 votes to none, with 1 abstention (United States of America).

[35] Geneva Convention relative to the Protection of Civilian Persons in Time of War, of
12 August 1949 (United Nations, *Treaty Series*, vol. 75, p. 287).

157. Israel's Statement Before the Security Council Regarding Resolution 468, May 8, 1980*

---

* 35 U.N. SCOR (2221st mtg.) at 16, U.N. Doc. S/P.V.2221 (1980).

(*Mr. Blum, Israel*)

Last Friday, six Jews were callously murdered in Hebron. Sixteen others were wounded, two of them critically. While Israel is still mourning its dead, this Council is already engaged in yet another one-sided exercise against Israel.

Let me acquaint the Council with the facts.

Last Friday night, a group of Jewish worshippers, mostly students at religious seminaries, were returning from their Sabbath eve devotions at the Tomb of the Hebrew Patriarchs—the Cave of Machpelah—in Hebron, on foot, in accordance with Jewish religious law regarding the Sabbath. While they were walking down a narrow alley, PLO terrorists attacked them from the roofs of two buildings, first by hailing them with bullets from the rear and then by hurling hand grenades and explosives at them from several directions.

As I have just said, six persons were killed in that brutal and cowardly attack and 16 others were wounded, among them women and children; two of the wounded remain in critical condition.

Within hours, the gang of terrorists called *Fatah*, which is headed by Yasser Arafat and is the largest constituent group within the criminal PLO, took responsibility for this outrage in a statement broadcast on the terrorists' radio in Lebanon. On 3 May 1980 Arafat himself applauded that atrocity on arrival in Kuwait for a visit and he again justified it in unqualified terms in Beirut yesterday, as reported in today's *New York Times*.

It will be recalled that in 1929 the existence of the millennia-old Jewish community of Hebron was virtually brought to a close, as a result of a brutal pogrom staged by the forerunners of the terrorist PLO. At that time the community consisted mainly of pious scholars and students. More than 60 of them were brutally murdered and scores of others were wounded and tortured, their homes pillaged and their places of worship desecrated. That pogrom was instigated by the notorious Mufti of Jerusalem, Haj Amin al-Husseini, who during World War II collaborated with the Nazis in the extermination of the Jews of Europe and was wanted thereafter as a war criminal to answer at Nuremberg for his crimes.

By perpetrating this latest outrage in Hebron, the terrorist PLO has proved once again that its criminals are the faithful disciples of their infamous mentor.

Once again the aim was mass murder for its own sake. The target was a peaceful group of worshippers returning from prayer, and the timing was the Sabbath eve.

Beyond indiscriminate murder, the object of this unconscionable atrocity was to inflame religious sentiments among local Arabs, and to foment incitement in an attempt to interfere with the ongoing peace process in the Middle East and in particular with the negotiations on full autonomy for the Palestinian Arabs in Judea, Samaria and the Gaza District.

The fact is that the outrage which took place in Hebron last Friday night is known to the whole world. People everywhere were shocked when they heard about it on their radios and saw the gruesome aftermath on their television screens. But for some reason, that atrocity has escaped the attention of this Council.

I say "escaped the attention" advisedly, because that is the most charitable construction that can be put on the Council's meeting this afternoon and on the resolution which has just been adopted.

But such an assumption is hardly credible, since I brought the facts to the Council's attention in my letter of 4 May 1980 to the Secretary-General, which was also circulated as an official document of the Security Council under the symbol S/13923.

We are thus left with an even more uncomfortable alternative—namely, that while this Council, like the rest of the world, is aware of the wanton murder perpetrated in Hebron last Friday, it has purposely chosen to ignore it.

Such "oversights" have long characterized the Council's debates on matters regarding the Arab-Israel conflict. This familiar pattern has been highlighted in the last three months when the opponents of peace in the Middle East, both in the region and beyond, have kept the Council in almost constant session on selected aspects of the conflict, invariably abstracted from their proper and full context.

Indeed, anyone reviewing the agenda of the Council in recent months would be obliged to conclude that there are no international crises in the world, other than the Arab-Israel conflict. The Soviet Union has withdrawn from Afghanistan; its troops have stopped slaughtering hundreds of ordinary Afghan citizens. The Syrian army of occupation has pulled back from Lebanon, and no one is being killed in and around Beirut. Refugees are not fleeing Cuba in their thousands. All is quiet in Africa, particularly in the Sahara, the Maghreb and the Horn of Africa. Sweetness and light radiate from South-East Asia. International terrorism has been brought under control worldwide. In brief, the international scene is a happy one. Were it not for Israel, there would be no threats to international peace—or at least the Security Council does not know of them.

The resolution which has just been adopted is highly reminiscent of resolution 467 (1980) adopted two weeks ago.

As will be recalled, that resolution was the product of a debate which came in the wake of a despicable outrage perpetrated by PLO terrorists who took hostage babes in arms at Kibbutz Misgav Am. That criminal act resulted in the deaths of an infant and a civilian, as well as the wounding of four toddlers, not to mention the death of an Israel Defence Forces soldier and the injury of 11 other soldiers in the action to free the little hostages. Nonetheless, the Council's resolution in question made no reference to that atrocity and confined itself mainly to placing blame on Israel, regardless of the wider context and of the implications for Israel's security. An act of hypocrisy and of selective conscience of precisely the same kind is being played out in the Council today.

The resolution which has just been adopted makes no reference to the background to the events mentioned in it. The Council's vision is eclectic, to put it mildly: it sees what it wants to see. It ignores what it is told to ignore.

The Government of Israel, like any Government, has a primary duty and responsibility for the preservation of law and order and the maintenance of security. It has taken a number of steps in order to prevent the recurrence of outrages of the kind which occurred in Hebron last Friday night. These steps included the deportation of the mayors of Hebron and Halhul and the Qadi of Hebron.

Over the last few months, these three individuals have, on the instructions of the PLO and the Arab rejectionist States, been actively and systematically engaged in inciting the local Arab population to acts of violence and subversion against Israel and Israelis alike. In so doing, they have abused their public offices, and even channelled PLO funds for these purposes. I could cite at length inflammatory statements made at open meetings by the two mayors and from the pulpit by the Qadi of Hebron, despite repeated warnings that they were far exceeding the norms of freedom of expression guaranteed and protected by the authorities. However, since this Council is not a court of law—even though it frequently chooses to act as though it were one—I shall perhaps limit myself to three of four instances of what Israel has had to deal with and had chosen not to act upon until the murders in Hebron last Friday night.

At the beginning of February of this year, the Mayor of Halhul spoke at a meeting at the Municipal Building and declared that there had been enough of words. He said that

the time has come to act, and one must not recoil from the use of any means.

He concluded by expressing the hope that the *Jihad*—the Holy War—would go on forever.

On 23 March 1980, the Qadi of Hebron raised a call for violence until the Palestinian flag flew not only in Hebron, but also in Jaffa, Haifa and Acre—in other words, in Israel.

The Mayor of Hebron has a long record of subversive activities. The disturbances in the Tomb of Patriarchs—the Cave of Machpelah—in October 1976 were fanned by an inflammatory broadsheet which Mr. Kawasmeh issued himself and in which he incited the Moslem community to despoil the things held holy by the Jews in the Cave of Machpelah. Instead of trying to ensure public order in Hebron, Mr. Kawasmeh worked openly in the opposite direction. In the last few days he has again given unrestrained expression to his views. According to the PLO radio in Lebanon, Mr. Kawasmeh called yesterday on Palestinian refugees in Sidon to return to Jaffa and Haifa over the blood of innocent Israelis.

The deportations of these three individuals were based on the Defence (Emergency) Regulations of 1945 issued by the British Mandatory authorities, regulation 112 of which authorizes deportation on grounds of certain activities against security. These regulations were in force and were acted upon on several occasions in Judea and Samaria under the Jordanian occupation prior to 4 June 1967. I do not recall any Council meeting being called to discuss those deportations. These regulations have remained in force since that date, 4 June 1967, in accordance with the principles of article 43 of the Hague Regulations of 1907 and article 64 (1) of the Fourth Geneva Convention of 1949, and that without prejudice to Israel's well-known position of principle with regard to the non-applicability of the Fourth Geneva Convention in the present context.

One of the tragedies of the Palestinian Arabs has been that for almost 60 years they have been dominated by an extremist and fanatical leadership. Starting with the notorious Mufti of Jerusalem, Amin al-Husseini, that leadership has had no compunction about terrorizing and assassinating its political rivals. It was totally lacking in political realism and obstinately opposed to compromise. It led the Palestinian Arabs, whom it claimed to represent, from one disaster to another.

The direct heir to that political legacy is the terrorist PLO. That organization has also waged a steady campaign of intimidation and assassination against Palestinian Arabs in Judea, Samaria and the Gaza District willing to co-exist peacefully with Israel. Moreover, that organization has used Judea and Samaria as a launching pad for acts of hostility and terror against Israel. In recent months it has stepped up its campaign against the peace process and the current talks aimed at achieving full autonomy for the Palestinian Arabs in Judea, Samaria and the Gaza District. And prominent among those involved in this campaign were the mayors of Hebron and Halhul and the Qadi of Hebron, whom Israel decided to deport only after their words and activities had led to bloodshed. The deportations had as one of their major purposes the prevention of further outrages of the kind perpetrated in Hebron last Friday night and the unnecessary and unforgivable shedding of more blood.

Those both inside and beyond this Council who have rushed to the defence of the three individuals in question are in fact those who have taken the lead in trying to frustrate the inexorable process leading to peace in the Middle East.

I have on numerous occasions indicated in this Council and in other organs of the United Nations who those Arab enemies of peace are and also who their supporters in other parts of the globe are. The most extreme of them within the Arab world are those who call themselves the Steadfastness Front and who met in Tripoli in the middle of last month with the participation of Yassar Arafat. The declaration which that Front issued at the conclusion of their meeting and recently had distributed as an official document both of the General Assembly and the Security Council, as document

A/35/133-S/13912, was one expression of their implacable opposition to peace and their active campaign against Israel, no matter how brutal and inhuman the means. The murders in Hebron last Friday night were another expression of the same phenomenon. Their repeated resort to the United Nations, and particularly to the Security Council, which they are confident they can always manipulate for their bellicose purposes, adds a third dimension to their tactics.

Israel, for its part, will not take risks with its security. Similarly, it will not be deterred from continuing its efforts to achieve peace within the framework of the Camp David Agreement, which offers the only practical approach for the achievement of a stable, just and comprehensive peace in our area. Israel will not be deflected by acts of terror in the area or by transparent exercises in hypocrisy and selective conscience in this Council.

158. Report of the Secretary-General Under Security Council Resolution 468, May 13, 1980*

* 35 U.N. SCOR Supp. (Apr–June 1980) at 48, U.N. Doc. S/13938 (1980).

1. In its resolution 468 (1980) of 8 May 1980 concerning the expulsion of the Mayors of Hebron and Halhoul and of the Sharia Judge of Hebron, the Security Council called upon the Government of Israel, as the occupying Power, to rescind those illegal measures and to facilitate the immediate return of the expelled Palestinian leaders so that they could resume the functions for which they were elected and appointed. The Council further requested the Secretary-General to report upon the implementation of the resolution.

2. The text of the above resolution was immediately brought to the attention of the Government of Israel by the Secretary-General, who had also previously made representations to the Government of Israel in this regard.

3. On 9 May the Permanent Mission of Israel informed the Secretary-General that the Government of Israel was unable to allow the expelled Mayors of Hebron and Halhoul and the Sharia Judge of Hebron to return, for reasons indicated in the statement made by the representative of Israel before the Security Council [*2221st meeting*].

4. In this connexion, the Secretary-General has noted reports that the Mayors of Hebron and Halhoul and the Sharia Judge of Hebron were denied re-entry into the West Bank by the Israeli authorities on 11 May.

159. Security Council Resolution 469 Deploring the Israeli Failure to Implement Resolution 468, May 20, 1980*

* S.C. Res. 469, 35 U.N. SCOR (2223rd mtg.) at 9, U.N. Doc. S/INF/36 (1980).

The Security Council,

Having considered the report[37] submitted by the Secretary-General on 13 May 1980, under Security Council resolution 468 (1980),

Recalling the Geneva Convention relative to the Protection of Civilian Persons in Time of War, of 12 August 1949,[22] and in particular article 1, which reads "The High Contracting Parties undertake to respect and to ensure respect for the present Convention in all circumstances", and article 49, which reads "Individual or mass forcible transfers, as well as deportations of protected persons from occupied territory to the territory of the occupying Power or to that of any other country, occupied or not, are prohibited, regardless of their motive",

1. *Strongly deplores* the failure of the Government of Israel to implement resolution 468 (1980);

2. *Calls again upon* the Government of Israel, as the occupying Power, to rescind the illegal measures taken by the Israeli military occupation authorities in expelling the Mayors of Hebron and Halhoul and the Sharia Judge of Hebron, and to facilitate the immediate return of the expelled Palestinian leaders so that they can resume the functions for which they were elected and appointed;

3. *Commends* the Secretary-General for his efforts and requests him to continue his efforts in order to ensure the immediate implementation of the present resolution and to report to the Security Council on the result of his efforts at the earliest possible date.

Adopted at the 2223rd meeting by 14 votes to none, with 1 abstention (United States of America).

[22] United Nations, *Treaty Series*, vol. 75, p. 287.

[37] *Official Records of the Security Council, Thirty-fifth Year, Supplement for April, May and June 1980*, document S/13938.

160. Political Programme Approved by the Fourth General Conference of the Palestinian Liberation Movement Fateh, Damascus, May 22–31, 1980*

* 10 J. Palestine Stud. 189 (Autumn 1980).

I. At the Palestinian Level

In the light of the unity of the Palestinian people, and the unity of their territory and their political representation, and in affirmation of their independent national will for the continuation and victory of their revolution;

Inasmuch as armed popular revolution is the sole and inevitable road to the liberation of Palestine, and inasmuch as the road to liberation is the road to unity; and in confirmation of the principle that democracy governs relations in the Palestinian arena and that democratic dialogue is the proper way to develop these relations, the Conference affirms the following:

1. Ceaseless efforts to consolidate Palestinian national unity at all levels inside and outside the occupied territory under the leadership of our Movement and within the framework of the PLO, so as to ensure the continuing escalation of all forms of Palestinian struggle.

2. The importance of stepping up our Movement's participation—with its proper weight—in the PLO, so as to ensure that it plays an effective role and so as to develop its internal regulations and organs in such a way as to guarantee the independence of all its institutions.

3. The escalation of armed struggle inside the occupied territory and via all lines of confrontation with the Zionist enemy.

4. Increasing concern for the organization of our people wherever they may reside, and expansion of the framework of the activities of popular and professional organizations and federations; protection of our people in their places of temporary residence and defence of them against persecution, exploitation or absorption.

5. Support at all levels for the steadfastness of our people inside the occupied territory, and provision of the necessary material support to enable them to maintain their steadfastness, escalate their struggle and develop all their national institutions and, in particular, efforts to strengthen the links with the Palestinian masses in the territories occupied in 1948 to enable them to resist the plans to fragment their unity and suppress their Arab identity.

6. Stress on the necessity of independent Palestinian decision-making, and efforts to develop the ability of all organizations of the Palestinian revolution to abide by the independent Palestinian decision.

7. In conformity with the leading position occupied by our Movement in the PLO, with what the political programme outlines on this subject and with the legitimacy of the PLO in the Arab and international arenas, the resolutions of the PLO's Palestinian National Council currently in force are to be regarded as complementing the Movement's Political Programme, since they do not conflict with goals and principles of our Movement and its political programmes.

8. Consolidation of the role of the Palestinian woman in all the fields of struggle, and efforts to ensure that she participates effectively in all frameworks and at all levels.

II. At the Arab Level

A. At the Mass Level:

Inasmuch as Palestine is part of the Arab homeland, and the Palestinian people are part of the Arab nation and their struggle part of its struggle, and inasmuch as the Palestinian revolution is the vanguard of the Arab nation in the battle for the liberation of Palestine, [the Conference affirms that:]

1. The relationship with the Arab masses is a strategic relation that enjoins more extensive participation by these masses in the protection of the revolution and in the conduct of all forms of struggle against the imperialist Zionist base in Palestine and against all the enemies of our people and our nation, and in the liquidation of imperialist and colonialist interests in the region.

2. There must be closer cohesion with the Arab national liberation movements and the Arab nationalist and progressive forces for the joint battle for the liberation of Palestine, and the achievement of the objectives of the Arab nation in the liberation of its regions and the building of a unified progressive Arab society.

3. [There must be] consolidation of the militant cohesion with the Lebanese national movement and all other nationalist forces that are valiantly fighting in the same trench as the Palestinian revolution against the enemies of the Palestinian and Lebanese peoples and the Arab nation, and participation with them in the struggle to protect Lebanon's unity, Arab character and territorial integrity. This requires strenuous efforts [both] to eliminate all negative manifestations that threaten relations with the masses, and to consolidate our relations with them by all ways and means.

4. The cohesion of the Lebanese masses with, and heroic support for, the Palestinian revolution in confronting the war of liquidation and annihilation must be safeguarded, supported and developed so that it may become a model for relations with the masses throughout the Arab homeland on the basis of kinship ties; this requires further support with all our energies and resources.

5. The special importance of the Jordanian arena requires that special attention be devoted to its recovery as one of the principal bases of support in the struggle against the Zionist enemy; the energies of the masses must be harnessed for the achievement of this goal.

6. [It is necessary to] reinforce the common struggle with the Egyptian people, represented by their nationalist and progressive forces, to abort the Camp David conspiracy and its consequences, and to bring Egypt back into Arab ranks to assume its natural position in the Arab struggle.

B. At the level of Relations with Arab Regimes:

Inasmuch as the aim of relations with the Arab regimes is to develop their positive aspects, these relations must be governed by the following principles:

1. The principles, goals and methods of the Movement.

2. These relations must not conflict with the strategic relations with the masses.

3. The position of each regime with regard to the cause of Palestine and the armed revolution of its people and, in particular, recognition of and commitment to the PLO as the sole legitimate representative of the Palestinian people, and rejection of any attempt from any quarter to prejudice this.

4. No interference in our internal affairs, and confrontation of any attempts to impose tutelage on or to subjugate our people, or to persecute or exploit them; also confrontation of any attempt to settle [our people] in any land other than their homeland, Palestine.

5. Confrontation of any attempt to deny the revolution freedom of action within the ranks of our people, wherever they reside.

6. The revolution exercises its responsibilities at the pan-Arab level and via any Arab territory for the sake of [regaining] the occupied Palestinian Arab territories, and every effort must be made to mobilize the human and material resources of the Arab nation, in particular its oil wealth, as a weapon for the achievement of this goal.

7. Efforts to develop the Steadfastness and Confrontation Front so that it may become a primary instrument of action based on supporting the PLO, continuing the struggle against the Zionist enemy and confronting and thwarting all liquidationist solutions; efforts to harden Arab positions with a view to confronting and foiling the settlement in whatever form and under whatever name, and resolute resistance to any attempt to provide the Camp David agreements with a cover of legitimacy.

8. Efforts to create a broad Arab front, as stipulated by the resolutions of the Steadfastness and Confrontation Front, for the confrontation of all imperialist and Zionist conspiracies, and first and foremost, the Camp David conspiracy in all its forms.

III. At the International Level

Inasmuch as the cause of Palestine is the central cause of the Arab nation in its just struggle against the Zionist-imperialist enemy;

And inasmuch as the Middle East area is of international strategic importance, the cause of Palestine, in addition to its justice and the struggle of its people, has always had an important international dimension and [has always] been the focus of world conflict that has led to the emergence of two camps: that of the enemies, and that of the friends of the cause and the struggle of our people.

Our Movement is part of the international liberation movement in the common struggle against imperialism, Zionism, racism and their agents, and we establish our alliances with all international parties in conformity with our principles and with the Palestinian National Charter.

A. International Organizations:

[The Conference affirms the need for:]

1. Efforts through the PLO to secure the adoption of more comprehensive resolutions on the rights of the Palestinian Arab people in all interna-

tional forums and organizations—in particular the UN—so as to increase the isolation of the Zionist-American enemy in these organizations and in the international arena.

2. Efforts to embody the UN General Assembly resolution condemning Zionism as a form of racism and racial discrimination in measures and sanctions against the imperialist and settler Zionist base in Palestine, as stipulated by the UN Charter.

3. Intensification of efforts to maintain the UN positions rejecting the Camp David agreements, and to develop these positions to involve the rejection of all forms of settlement reached at the expense of our people and their cause.

B. Friendly Forces:

[The Conference affirms the importance of:]

1. Consolidating the strategic alliance with the socialist countries, headed by the USSR, since this alliance is essential for the serious and effective confrontation of American and Zionist conspiracies against the cause of Palestine and liberation causes in the world.

2. Consolidating our relations with the world liberation movements that are fighting in the same trench with us against American imperialism, Zionism, racism, Fascism and reaction; Fateh supports the struggle of all liberation movements and all freedom-fighters against injustice, coercion and tyranny.

3. Consolidating our Movement's external relations and intensifying its political activity on the basis of the Movement's principles and programmes, for the establishment of alliances with democratic and progressive political forces that support our just struggle and our legitimate rights.

4. Consolidating relations with the Islamic revolution in Iran which has swept away the most arrogant fortress of American imperialism in the region, and which supports us in our struggle for the liberation of Palestine.

5. Strengthening relations with the peoples and governments of the Islamic, African and the non-aligned countries, with a view to developing their positions towards greater support of the Palestinian cause and our struggle, and to winning greater recognition of the PLO as the sole legitimate representative of the Palestinian people.

C. The American Position:

The US heads the enemies of our people and our nation in that it pursues a policy hostile to our people, our revolution and the Arab nation, and to all Arab and international forces of liberation; it supports the Zionist enemy and its agents in the area, and establishes military pacts with the aim of subjecting the area to its military influence so that it may continue to plunder the wealth of our nation. It is, therefore, imperative to consolidate the international front opposed to US policy, to fight against it and abort it, and to strike at American interests in the area.

D. The Positions of Western Europe (EEC), Japan and Canada:

1. [The Conference affirms the need to] intensify political activity in these countries and benefit from the support of democratic and progressive polit-

ical forces in them to reduce and then halt support for the Zionist entity, and achieve its isolation through the recognition by these forces of the PLO as the sole legitimate representative of the Palestinian people, and [the need to] achieve maximum political and material support for our cause, our struggle and our national rights.

2. Many of the Western European countries and Canada still pursue a policy that does not recognize the national rights of our people, and they provide support at all levels to the Zionist enemy. They are following a policy in conformity with that of the US and of its schemes in the area, and Japan's policy is not dissimilar. Therefore, efforts must be intensified to resist and thwart any plan or initiative that conflicts with the national rights of our people.

In conclusion, the General Conference of our Movement stresses the need to safeguard and consolidate the political gains that have been achieved in the international political arena, and that have kept the cause of Palestine a living cause that enjoys such extensive international support that it is now the vanguard and standard-bearer of the world liberation movement.

161. Security Council Resolution 471 Reaffirming Resolution 465 and Expressing Concern for Israeli Settlements Policy in the Occupied Arab Territories, June 5, 1980*

---

* S.C. Res. 471, 35 U.N. SCOR (2226th mtg.) at 10, U.N. Doc. S/INF/36 (1980).

The Security Council,

Recalling once again the Geneva Convention relative to the Protection of Civilian Persons in Time of War, of 12 August 1949,[22] and in particular article 27, which reads,

> Protected persons are entitled, in all circumstances, to respect for their persons . . . They shall at all times be humanely treated, and shall be protected especially against all acts of violence or threats thereof . . . ,

Reaffirming the applicability of the Geneva Convention relative to the Protection of Civilian Persons in Time of War to the Arab territories occupied by Israel since 1967, including Jerusalem,

Recalling also its resolutions 468 (1980) and 469 (1980),

Reaffirming its resolution 465 (1980), by which the Security Council determined "that all measures taken by Israel to change the physical character, demographic composition, institutional structure or status of the Palestinian and other Arab territories occupied since 1967, including Jerusalem, or any part thereof have no legal validity and that Israel's policy and practices of settling parts of its population and new immigrants in those territories constitute a flagrant violation of the Geneva Convention relative to the Protection of Civilian Persons in Time of War and also constitute a serious obstruction to achieving a comprehensive, just and lasting peace in the Middle East" and strongly deplored the "continuation and persistence of Israel in pursuing those policies and practices",

Shocked by the assassination attempts against the Mayors of Nablus, Ramallah and Al Bireh,

Deeply concerned that the Jewish settlers in the occupied Arab territories are allowed to carry arms, thus enabling them to perpetrate crimes against the civilian Arab population,

1. *Condemns* the assassination attempts against the Mayors of Nablus, Ramallah and Al Bireh and calls for the immediate apprehension and prosecution of the perpetrators of these crimes;

2. *Expresses deep concern* that Israel, as the occupying Power, has failed to provide adequate protection to the civilian population in the occupied territories in conformity with the provisions of the Geneva Convention relative to the Protection of Civilian Persons in Time of War;

3. *Calls upon* the Government of Israel to provide the victims with adequate compensation for the damages suffered as a result of these crimes;

4. *Calls again upon* the Government of Israel to respect and to comply with the provisions of the Geneva Convention relative to the Protection of Civilian Persons in Time of War, as well as with the relevant resolutions of the Security Council;

5. *Calls once again upon* all States not to provide Israel with any assistance

---

[22] United Nations, *Treaty Series*, vol. 75, p. 287.

to be used specifically in connexion with settlements in the occupied territories;

6. *Reaffirms* the overriding necessity to end the prolonged occupation of Arab territories occupied by Israel since 1967, including Jerusalem;

7. *Requests* the Secretary-General to report on the implementation of the present resolution.

Adopted at the 2226th meeting by 14 votes to none, with 1 abstention (United States of America).

162. Declarations on the Middle East, Euro-Arab Dialogue, and Lebanon Issued by the Leaders of the European Community at the Venice Summit, June 12–13, 1980*

* 13 Bull. Eur. Comm. (No. 6) 10 (1980).

Middle East

1.1.6. '1. The Heads of State or Government and the Ministers of Foreign Affairs held a comprehensive exchange of views on all aspects of the present situation in the Middle East, including the state of negotiations resulting from the agreements signed between Egypt and Israel in March 1979. They agreed that growing tensions affecting this region constitute a serious danger and render a comprehensive solution to the Israel-Arab conflict more necessary and pressing than ever.

2. The nine Member States of the European Community consider that the traditional ties and common interests which link Europe to the Middle East oblige them to play a special role and now require them to work in a more concrete way towards peace.

3. In this regard, the nine countries of the Community base themselves on Security Council Resolutions 242 and 338 and the positions which they have expressed on several occasions, notably in their Declarations of 29 June 1977,[1] 19 September 1978,[2] 26 March[3] and 18 June 1979,[4] as well as in the speech made on their behalf on 25 September 1979 by the Irish Minister of Foreign Affairs at the thirty-fourth United Nations General Assembly.[5]

4. On the bases thus set out, the time has come to promote the recognition and implementation of the two principles universally accepted by the international community: the right to existence and to security of all the States in the region, including Israel, and justice for all the peoples, which implies the recognition of the legitimate rights of the Palestinian people.

5. All of the countries in the area are entitled to live in peace within secure, recognized and guaranteed borders. The necessary guarantees for a peace settlement should be provided by the UN by a decision of the Security Council and, if necessary, on the basis of other mutually agreed procedures. The Nine declare that they are prepared to participate within the framework of a comprehensive settlement in a system of concrete and binding international guarantees, including (guarantees) on the ground.

6. A just solution must finally be found to the Palestinian problem, which is not simply one of refugees. The Palestinian people, whe [*sic*] are conscious of existing as such, must be placed in a position, by an appropriate process defined within the framework of the comprehensive peace settlement, to exercise fully their right to self-determination.

7. The achievement of these objectives requires the involvement and support of all the parties concerned in the peace settlement which the Nine are endeavouring to promote in keeping with the principles formulated in the

---

[1] Bull. EC 6-1977, point 2.2.3.
[2] Bull. EC 9-1978, point 2.2.8.
[3] Bull. EC 3-1979, point 2.2.74.
[4] Bull. EC 6-1979, point 2.2.59.
[5] Bull. EC 9-1979, point 3.4.1.

declaration referred to above. These principles apply to all the parties concerned, and thus the Palestinian people, and to the PLO, which will have to be associated with the negotiations.

8. The Nine recognize the special importance of the role played by the question of Jerusalem for all the parties concerned. The Nine stress that they will not accept any unilateral initiative designed to change the status of Jerusalem and that any agreement on the city's status should guarantee freedom of access for everyone to the Holy Places.

9. The Nine stress the need for Israel to put an end to the territorial occupation which it has maintained since the conflict of 1967, as it has done for part of Sinai. They are deeply convinced that the Israeli settlements constitute a serious obstacle to the peace process in the Middle East. The Nine consider that these settlements, as well as modifications in population and property in the occupied Arab territories, are illegal under international law.

10. Concerned as they are to put an end to violence, the Nine consider that only the renunciation of force or the threatened use of force by all the parties can create a climate of confidence in the area, and constitute a basic element for a comprehensive settlement of the conflict in the Middle East.

11. The Nine have decided to make the necessary contacts with all the parties concerned. The objective of these contacts would be to ascertain the position of the various parties with respect to the principles set out in this declaration and in the light of the results of this consultation process to determine the form which such an initiative on their part could take.'

Euro-Arab Dialogue

1.1.7. 'The Nine noted the importance which they attach to the Euro-Arab Dialogue at all levels and the need to develop the advisability of holding a meeting of the two sides at political level. In this way, they intend to contribute towards the development of cooperation and mutual understanding between Europe and the Arab world.'

Lebanon

1.1.8. 'The Nine reiterate once again their total solidarity with Lebanon, a friendly country whose equilibrium is seriously jeopardized by the clashes in the region, and renews its urgent appeal to all the countries and parties concerned to put an end to all acts liable to affect Lebanon's independence, sovereignty and territorial integrity as well as the authority of its government. The Nine will support any action or initiative likely to guarantee the return of peace and stability in Lebanon, a factor which constitutes an essential element in the equilibrium of the region.

The Nine stress the importance of the role which should be played by the United Nations Interim Force in Lebanon (UNIFIL) in southern Lebanon.

The Nine recall the Declaration which they made in Luxembourg on 22 April[1] and stress that it is essential for all the parties concerned to allow the UNIFIL to implement to the full the mandate assigned to it, including that of taking control of the territory up to the internationally recognized boundaries.'

[1] Bull. EC 4-1980, point 2.2.61.

163. Position of the Government of Israel on the
Declaration on the Middle East Issued by the Leaders of
the European Community at the Venice Summit,
June 12–13, 1980*

---

* Embassy of Israel, Washington, D.C.

The heads of governments of the nine European countries who met in Venice on the 12th and the 13th of June issued a declaration on the Middle East. In view of the political activity which went on in Europe recently, this declaration does not come as a surprise. Nonetheless, the Government of Israel takes a grave view of the declaration on the following grounds.

1. The nine European countries concerned have not taken part in the peace process initiated by the Camp David accords. This process is founded on principles agreed after long negotiations and is the result of compromise. It represents a delicate balance of the claims of the parties and the obligations undertaken by them. In their declaration, the nine European countries not only decline to support the one peace-seeking effort which has so far been successful, but they actually endanger it by encouraging holders of extremist attitudes.

2. The Venice declaration is yet another stage in a declaratory policy purporting to show involvement in a process from which Europe has so far withheld its participation. Yet this time the heads of government of the nine have also added what it reveals is a readiness to adopt publicly views contradictory to the peace process in an effort to win Arab favour.

3. The declaration is couched in a-priori biased terms, ignoring the interests of Israel as well as the actual situation in the Middle East. It is one-sided in that its authors accept the Arab views in their entirety and in complete disregard of Israel's position. Here are examples of this one-sidedness:

(a) The question of Jerusalem. The declaration calls for free access to the Holy Places, while its authors, the Nine, are well aware that free access to all Holy Places in Jerusalem is in fact assured for, and enjoyed by, people of all religions and all nationalities since 1967, and that it is precisely Israel who has brought about and safeguards this freedom of access. This is in contrast with the situation which existed before 1967, when Jordan was in occupation of East Jerusalem, and did not allow free access to Jews, Christians and Moslems living in Israel.

(b) The association or involvement of the PLO, as the declaration demands, in the peace process (which is a process of making peace with Israel) is a contradiction in terms, for the PLO's principal demand is the dissolution of the State of Israel and its replacement by another state. Indeed, only a week before the Nine issued their declaration in Venice, Fatah, the PLO's main constituent and the one reputed to be its most moderate member, passed resolutions reaffirming the PLO's well-known tenets. How then do the Nine propose to resolve this contradiction? How, in their opinion, can a body whose aim and policy are to annihilate Israel be a party to a process of making peace with her?

(c) The Nine proclaim the principle of self-determination on behalf of the Palestinians without pausing to consider its application and relation to a territory. The Government of Israel is of the opinion that the self-determination of the Palestinians has already found expression in the state of which they form the demographic and cultural majority, which is Jordan. The fact that Jordan's newly appointed prime minister is again, as on several occasions before, a Palestinian, lends support to this view. Now if the self-determination claimed should mean a second state for Palestinians, then Israel must reject this interpretation, for it cannot operate except at the cost of the Jewish people's own self-determination in its homeland. May it be observed that indiscriminate application of this principle may well carry the risk of disruption to many existing states in Europe, Africa and elsewhere.

4. The declaration of the Nine in effect attempts to dictate a settlement of the conflict without leaving room for negotiations. Expressions such as "put an end to territorial occupation," and "occupied Arab territories" precondition the result which the authors of the declaration wish to see attained.

5. The Nine declare themselves ready to take part in a system of guarantees to be offered to the parties to the settlement they advocate. Israel has had bitter experience with what European states term "guarantees." A poignant example from relatively recent history is what happened on the eve of the Six-Day War to the Tripartite Guarantee concerning the Middle East and, of course, to the guarantees by the maritime countries concerning the freedom of navigation through the Straits of Tiran. No country can place its security in the hands of other countries, more especially in an era when those countries are inclined to eschew any involvement.

6. An example of prominent lop-sidedness in the statements the Nine have made in Venice is provided by their respective comments on the invasion of Afghanistan and on the Arab-Israel conflict. It is ironic that when referring to Afghanistan, the Nine consider the Soviet invasion merely to "threaten to jeopardize the climate of international relations;" whereas the situation resulting from the Camp David accords, which have after all achieved a breakthrough to peace and relaxation for a part of the conflict area—that, they define precisely as "serious danger."

7. The declaration of the Nine of the Middle East comes at a time when the European Community itself is undergoing a grave crisis, and the Middle East question has proved to be one of the few subjects on which the Community can display unity.

On June 14, 1980 The Guardian (London) listed a few of the subjects which somehow eluded Community success:

> . . . The Europeans were less united on the internal reforms necessary to reinforce their new found foreign-policy cohesion . . .
> . . . Europe's leaders were even less unanimous on what should be done to combat the rapid deterioration in the world economy.
> . . . Despite (the) common recognition of the danger of a synchronised world recession, the summiteers were short of answers to the problem.
> . . . There is no consensus within the Community for an increase in aid to the developing countries, unless it is aid paid for by OPEC . . .

Europe then seems to be united on one issue—the Middle East. In order to dilute these problems, will it be Israel who will have to pay the price?

8. Israel has always welcomed, and continues to welcome, constructive efforts by all who are ready to bring the parties to the negotiating table. She acknowledges gratefully the role the United States is playing in this matter, but she cannot consider in the same light the one-sided way in which the European countries have chosen to act.

164. Senate Resolution 473 on Palestinian Women as a Separate Issue at the U.N. Mid-Decade Conference for Women, June 26, 1980*

---

* S. Res. 473, 96th Cong., 2d Sess., 126 Cong. Rec. 16548 (1980).

Whereas a UN-Mid-Decade Conference for Woman has been scheduled for July 14-30, 1980, in Copenhagen to review and evaluate "the progress made and obstacles encountered in attaining the objectives of the United Nations Decade for Women"; and

Whereas a separate item was included in the agenda of that Conference on "The Effects of Israeli Occupation on Palestinian Women Inside and Outside the Occupied Territories" despite US opposition and despite the existence of the more general item of "Women as Refugees" on the agenda; and

Whereas a document drafted by the Arab states and the PLO and adopted as official documentation for the Conference, "The Social and Economic Conditions of Palestinian Women Inside and Outside the Occupied Territories", presents a biased account of the conditions of Palestinian women by arguing that the Arab-Israeli conflict is responsible for the problems faced by Palestinian women; and

Whereas the addition of this document and separate agenda item in the proceedings of the Mid-Decade Conference is an obvious attempt to inject a highly politicized discussion into an apolitical meeting; and

Whereas the spectre of an irrelevant, politically-motivated debate threatens to detract from the positive results that may emerge in achieving the objectives of the Decade: Now, therefore, be it

Resolved that it is the sense of the Senate that

(1) the inclusion of a separate agenda item on Palestinian women and the acceptance of a 66-page document relating to that item present an unfortunate intrusion of political issues into a conference devoted directly to questions of health, education and employment for women throughout the world and as such is deplored by the Senate; and

(2) the U.S. delegation to the Conference should be instructed to oppose any resolutions or amendments introduced at the Copenhagen Conference on issues which do not relate directly to the goals of the Conference, such as the separate issue of Palestinian women, and should actively work with other delegations to ensure that they voice similar opposition.

165. Security Council Resolution 476 Deploring Israeli Settlements Policy in the Occupied Territories and Jerusalem, June 30, 1980*

* S.C. Res. 476, 35 U.N. SCOR (2242nd mtg.) at 13, U.N. Doc. S/INF/36 (1980).

The Security Council,

Having considered the letter of 28 May 1980 from the representative of Pakistan, the current Chairman of the Organization of the Islamic Conference, contained in document S/13966,[25]

Reaffirming that the acquisition of territory by force is inadmissible,

Bearing in mind the specific status of Jerusalem and, in particular, the need to protect and preserve the unique spiritual and religious dimension of the Holy Places in the city,

Reaffirming its resolutions relevant to the character and status of the Holy City of Jerusalem, in particular resolution 252 (1968), 267 (1969), 271 (1969), 298 (1971) and 465 (1980),

Recalling the Geneva Convention relative to the Protection of Civilian Persons in Time of War, of 12 August 1949,[22]

Deploring the persistence of Israel in changing the physical character, demographic composition, institutional structure and the status of the Holy City of Jerusalem,

Gravely concerned about the legislative steps initiated in the Israeli Knesset with the aim of changing the character and status of the Holy City of Jerusalem,

1. *Reaffirms* the overriding necessity for ending the prolonged occupation of Arab territories occupied by Israel since 1967, including Jerusalem;

2. *Strongly deplores* the continued refusal of Israel, the occupying Power, to comply with the relevant resolutions of the Security Council and the General Assembly;

3. *Reconfirms* that all legislative and administrative measures and actions taken by Israel, the occupying Power, which purport to alter the character and status of the Holy City of Jerusalem have no legal validity and constitute a flagrant violation of the Geneva Convention relative to the Protection of Civilian Persons in Time of War and also constitute a serious obstruction to achieving a comprehensive, just and lasting peace in the Middle East;

4. *Reiterates* that all such measures which have altered the geographic, demographic and historical character and status of the Holy City of Jerusalem are null and void and must be rescinded in compliance with the relevant resolutions of the Security Council;

5. *Urgently calls* on Israel, the occupying Power, to abide by the present and previous Security Council resolutions and to desist forthwith from persisting in the policy and measures affecting the character and status of the Holy City of Jerusalem;

---

[22] *United Nations, Treaty Series,* vol. 75, p. 287.

[25] See *Official Records of the Security Council, Thirty-fifth Year, Supplement for April, May and June 1980.*

6. *Reaffirms* its determination, in the event of non-compliance by Israel with the present resolution, to examine practical ways and means in accordance with relevant provisions of the Charter of the United Nations to secure the full implementation of the present resolution.

Adopted at the 2242nd meeting by 14 votes to none, with 1 abstention (United States of America).

166. Letter from the Permanent Representative of Israel to the U.N. Secretary-General Concerning an Israeli-Sponsored Study of the Rights of Palestinians Under International Law, June 27, 1980*

---

* S/14045, U.N. Doc. A/35/316 (1980).

I have the honour to refer to my letters of 16 November 1978 and 20 December 1978 (A/33/376 and A/33/543), in which I registered my Government's strong objection to the release of a United Nations Secretariat publication entitled *The Origins and Evolution of the Palestine Problem, Part I: 1917-1947;*[1] and *Part II: 1947-1977*[2] (ST/SG/SER.F/1). In those letters I expressed regret that the United Nations had been drawn into the pattern, so characteristic of certain régimes, of rewriting history according to the transient interests of a political body.

Since submitting those letters to you, three other "studies" have been released in the same series. They are entitled: *The Right of Return of the Palestinian People* (ST/SG/SER.F/2);[3] *The Right of Self-Determination of the Palestinian People* (ST/SG/SER.F/3);[4] and *An International Law Analysis of the Major United Nations Resolutions Concerning the Palestine Question* (ST/SG/SER.F/4).[5]

As in the case of the first "study", all the others were prepared by or under the aegis of the "Special Unit on Palestinian Rights" within the Secretariat, "under the close guidance" of the "Special Committee on the Exercise of the Inalienable Rights of the Palestinian People". The first three "studies" were published anonymously; the fourth is said to express the views only of its authors, W. Thomas Mallison and Sally Mallison.

The three new pseudo-scientific publications are no less objectionable than the first one. Emblazoned with the emblem of the United Nations, and carrying the imprimatur of the Secretary-General, these later "studies" are designed not only to give further currency to a completely misleading version of the history of the Arab-Israel conflict, but also to propagate bogus theories with regard to a number of complex legal issues connected with the Arab-Israel conflict.

The partisan views expressed in all the "studies", like the recommendations of the Committee under whose "guidance" they have been prepared, accord fully with those held by the terrorist PLO, an organization which is committed to the destruction of Israel, a Member State of the United Nations.

By producing and disseminating these publications, the United Nations is serving the cause of international terror, not the cause of international peace. In the process, the United Nations has once again misused international funds, gravely compromised the integrity of the Secretariat and exposed the Organization to severe and more than justified criticism.

The Government of Israel does not intend to reply to the gross distortions, misrepresentations and other improprieties taken with history and law in these "studies".

That notwithstanding, it has requested learned counsel, in the person of

---

[1] United Nations publication, Sales No. E.78.I.19.
[2] United Nations publication, Sales No. E.78.I.20.
[3] United Nations publication, Sales No. E.78.I.21.
[4] United Nations publication, Sales No. E.78.I.22.
[5] United Nations publication, Sales No. E.79.I.19.

Professor Julius Stone, Member of the Institute of International Law; Distinguished Professor of International Law and Jurisprudence, University of California Hastings College of the Law; Professor of Law, University of New South Wales; Emeritus Challis Professor of International Law and Jurisprudence, University of Sydney; author of numerous authoritative works in the field of international law, to peruse these "studies" from the legal point of view. I now enclose a memorandum of law which he has written and which deals with some of the main propositions which the "studies" seek to establish.

As will be seen, this memorandum of law shows that all the "studies" in the series rest on flawed foundations and that their conclusions are untenable.

The opinions expressed in the memorandum are those of learned counsel, and do not necessarily reflect those of the Government of Israel.

I have the honour to request that this letter and its enclosure be circulated as an official document of the General Assembly, under items 26, 51, 53, 57, 92, 106 and 109 of the preliminary list, and of the Security Council.

(*Signed*) Yehuda Z. BLUM
Ambassador
Permanent Representative of
Israel to the United Nations

167. Israel, the United Nations, and International Law:

Memorandum of Law, June 1980*

---

* S/14045/Annex, U.N. Doc. A/35/316 (1980).

ANNEX

Israel, the United Nations and International Law Memorandum of Law
by *Julius Stone*

S.J.D. (Harvard), LL.D. (Leeds, honoris causa), D.C.L. (Oxford), O.B.E.

Member, Institute of International Law; Distinguished Professor of International
Law and Jurisprudence, University of California Hastings College of the Law;
Professor of Law, University of New South Wales; Emeritus Challis Professor of
International Law and Jurisprudence, University of Sydney; Barrister-at-Law,
etc.

June, 1980

CONTENTS

INTRODUCTION

1. It is a commonplace among international lawyers that each organ of
the United Nations is the interpreter of its own powers and procedures.
This applies to the General Assembly, even when regrettably the majorities
in that body are marshalled by means, such as the oil weapon, which do not
reflect the legal or moral merits of the issues before it. General Assembly
resolution 3376 (XXX) of 10 November 1975 established a "Committee on
the Exercise of the Inalienable Rights of the Palestinian People". In its resolution 32/40 B of 2 December 1977, the General Assembly set up a "Special
Unit on Palestinian Rights" in the Secretariat, which in 1978 and 1979 prepared and disseminated a series of tendentious studies "under the close
guidance" of that Committee. A list of those "studies" and their brief titles
as employed in this memorandum is as follows:

  (a) *The Origins and Evolution of the Palestine Problem* (ST/SG/SER.F/1)
     (herein *"Origins"*, published in two parts);
  (b) *The Right of Return of the Palestinian People* (ST/SG/SER.F/2) (herein
     "Return");
  (c) *The Right of Self-Determination of the Palestinian People* (ST/SG/SER.F/
     3) (herein *"Self-Determination"*);

(d) *An International Law Analysis of the Major United Nations Resolutions Concerning the Palestine Question* (ST/SG/SER.F/4) (herein *"Resolutions"*).

2. *Resolutions*, the latest of the "studies", rehearsing and overlapping much that appears in its predecessors, differs from them in that it discloses the identity of its authors, namely, W. T. Mallison, Professor of Law and Director, International Comparative Law Program, George Washington University, and Sally V. Mallison, Research Associate. Although that "study", like the others, was prepared and published "at the request of the Committee on the Exercise of the Inalienable Rights of the Palestinian People", the Secretariat found it necessary to distance itself from it by stating that "the views expressed are those of the authors", a caveat which does not appear in the three earlier anonymous "studies". The present examination of this entire series of explicitly partisan "studies", strangely emblazoned with the official emblem of the United Nations, indicates that the sponsoring Committee's caution in dissociating itself from *Resolutions* was well-advised and might well have been extended to all the anonymous "studies".

3. The structure of argument which the authors pursue to their conclusions is as follows. First, they seek to establish that the United Nations, and particularly the General Assembly, is "an international lawmaker". Second, they elaborate various implications of the Partition resolution, before its destuction by Arab rejection and armed aggression in 1947–8, and argue that that resolution remains now as "law" created by the General Assembly, still binding more than three decades later. Third, they seek to show that repeated recitals in General Assembly resolutions, from resolution 194 (III) to resolution 3236 (XXIX), establish in international law a "right of return" for the benefit of Palestinian Arab refugees. Fourth, the authors likewise seek to show that repeated references in General Assembly resolutions since 1970 constitute a legal determination of the right of self-determination of Palestinian Arabs and that the General Assembly is empowered to redraw the boundaries of Israel in order to satisfy that right.

4. The legal merit of this single-minded argument depends not only on its internal coherence but also on the soundness of the premises on which it is based. I shall examine it in both those aspects, beginning immediately with the fundamental premise from which all the conclusions flow: the status and force in international law of General Assembly resolutions.

5. While I originally set out to examine the consistency with international law of the assertions and assumptions of the "studies", I soon found it necessary to transcend this *ad hoc* design. I realized that the outcomes of the legal analysis were likely to have critical effects, not only on the Arab-Israel conflict, but on some basic doctrines of international law. Thus, this memorandum analyses legal aspects of many complex problems directly relating to the Middle East, and in so doing clarifies central issues of current international law. In addition to the legal status of General Assembly resolutions,

this memorandum will discuss the effect of coercion of the Assembly membership by, for example, the oil weapon, the legal status of the supposed right of self-determination of peoples, the content and limits of that right and its relation to the limits on the use of force set by international law, the application of the fundamental international law principle *ex injuria non oritur jus*, and other international law issues of similar gravity.

I. LEGAL EFFECTS OF GENERAL ASSEMBLY RESOLUTIONS

6. The basic general rule on the legal effect of General Assembly resolutions was stated by Judge Sir Hersch Lauterpacht in his opinion in the *South West Africa—Voting Procedure* case. He observed that save where otherwise provided for in the United Nations Charter (as for example with regard to the budget under Art. 17, or the admission of new members under Art. 4, para. 2), "decisions of the General Assembly . . . are not legally binding upon the Members of the United Nations". Apart from such Charter exceptions, "resolutions" of this body, even if framed as declarations or decisions, "refer to recommendations . . . whose legal effect although not altogether absent . . . appears to be no more than a moral obligation". The *binding* legal quality of such resolutions must be established by conformity with the recognized requirements for creation of customary law or treaty law.[1]

7. A generation later, in an equally considered pronouncement, another distinguished former judge of the International Court of Justice, Sir Gerald Fitzmaurice, was no less unequivocal in rejecting the "illusion" that a General Assembly resolution could have "legislative effect". He pointed out, *inter alia*, that a Philippines proposal to expressly permit such a legislative effect was overwhelmingly rejected at the San Francisco Conference; that the general structure of the Charter limits the General Assembly (as distinct from the Security Council) to merely recommendatory functions; that it was precisely this limitation which explains why United Nations Members are so often prepared to acquiesce in allowing so many resolutions to be adopted by abstaining or not casting a negative vote; and that such relevance as General Assembly resolutions might have to international law is, at most, that the content of a particular resolution may come to be considered for adoption by States in "a separate treaty or convention", binding by virtue of its adoption.[2]

8. These scholarly observations were confirmed the following year, at the 1492nd meeting of the General Assembly's Sixth (Legal) Committee, by a remarkable manifestation of concurrent views by Members of the United Nations. The Committee had before it a draft resolution on the role of the

---

[1] *I. C. J. Reports, 1955*, 155 ff. His further explanation that repeated flouting of such recommendtions may overstep the "line between impropriety and illegality" (p. 20), has reference to the special case of exercise of supervisory competence over the trusteeship system under the Charter. It is not of general application.

[2] Institute of International Law, *Livre du Centenaire* (1973) 268 ff. For the discussion of the San Francisco Conference, see 9 *UNCIO Documents* 70.

International Court of Justice. Its preamble referred to the possibility that in deciding disputes the Court might take into consideration declarations and resolutions of the General Assembly. A wide spectrum of States from all parts of the world rejected even this rather mild reference. The proposal was, some said, an attempt at "indirect amendment" of Article 38 of the Statute of the International Court, and a "subversion of the international structure of the United Nations". It was capable of meaning "that General Assembly resolutions could themselves develop international law". The proposal attributed to the General Assembly "powers which were not within its competence". It was an attempt to "issue directives regarding sources of law", departing from the view that resolutions and declarations of the General Assembly are "essentially recommendations and not legally binding". Declarations and resolutions of the General Assembly could not be considered a source of international law, "particularly in view of their increasing political content which was often at variance with international law".[3]

9. Therefore, before their massive reliance on General Assembly resolutions as creating legal obligations, the authors of the "studies" owe their readers a full, careful and candid consideration of the requirements involved in justifying this reliance under Article 38 of the Statute of the International Court of Justice. The authors' inability to establish the propriety of grounding the legal basis of their theses in recent General Assembly resolutions is especially manifest in the whole structure of the *Resolutions* "study". It opens with a section devoted to "The Juridical Competence of the Political Organs of the United Nations", obviously intended to maximize the legal effect of those General Assembly resolutions favourable to their theses.

10. Despite the contentiousness of the issue and the vast literature on it, *Resolutions* purports to dispose of the matter by two carefully selected quotations. One is from Professor Rosalyn Higgins' general statement[4] that votes and views of States in international organizations have "come to have legal significance", and that "collective acts of States repeated by and *acquiesced in by sufficient numbers [of States]* with sufficient frequency, *eventually* attain the status of law" (emphasis supplied). The other is Judge Tanaka's dissenting opinion in the *South West Africa* cases.[5] But Judge Tanaka there only pointed out that the traditional requirements for the creation of a new rule of customary law (practice, repetition, and *opinio juris sive necessitatis*) remain unchanged. However, they may mature at a quicker pace under modern techniques of communication and international organization.

11. From these carefully qualified generalities the "study" proceeds immediately (p. 5) to its own statement of its sponsors' desired law, namely, that "the State practice requirement for customary law-making [is to be

---

[3] *Official Records of the General Assembly, Twenty-ninth Session*, Sixth Committee, at 166 ff.
[4] *The Development of International Law Through the Political Organs of the United Nations* (1963) 2.
[5] Second Phase, *I. C. J. Reports, 1966*, 6 at 248.

found] in the collective acts of States (as in voting in favour of a particular General Assembly resolution) as well as in their individual acts". For this summary to represent correctly the opinions of the learned authorities whom they quote, the authors should then have proceeded, with the same care as Professor Higgins and Judge Tanaka, to consider additional requirements. These include the acquiescence of States, the demonstration of *opinio juris sive necessitatis*, the *sufficiency* of the number of States involved (judged by the nature of their interest, self-serving or adverse, in the subject-matter), as well as the sufficiency of the *number of instances* when these requirements are met. Thus, the quotations relied on by the authors proceeded by analogy with these requirements of customary law. By neglecting the relevant specifications for customary law, the authors distort the analogy into a vague notion of "consensus."

12. The Mallisons' wish for a simplistic rule translating General Assembly resolutions into international law, and their failure to establish this proposition, are understandable. What is difficult to understand is why, as international lawyers, they show so little awareness of the range and depth of the controversies among their colleagues, which forbid such simplification. Half a dozen hypotheses—each with its own consequential criteria and limits— are current in the literature and divide the authorities. They include the treatment of voting behaviour (1) as an extension of treaty-making; (2) as authoritative interpretation of existing treaties; (3) as expression of "general principles of law"; (4) as declaratory of the existence of rules of international law; (5) as a new source of international law supplementing the inadequacies of the sources laid down in Article 38 of the Statute of the International Court of Justice; and (6) as a means of creating informal expectations among States. According to the sixth hypothesis, expectations can mature into binding rules depending on whether the votes of States (a) represent the interests of all affected sides in controversial matters; (b) avoid extreme and intransigent positions; (c) are free of vague and indeterminate language; (d) are free of politically motivated double standards; (e) are not used to champion *ex parte* positions in political quarrels; and (f) proceed from an international organ which maintains on the particular matter impartial methods of deliberation and resolutions.

13. Hypotheses (1)–(5), as well as that which proceeds on the analogy of customary law, all remain inchoate, with applicable criteria surrounded by doubt and dispute. As to hypothesis (6), it will be apparent, as this examination proceeds, that much recent General Assembly action on the Middle East, especially since the deploying of the oil weapon in 1973, is a veritable paradigm of that kind of United Nations action which will *not* mature into law.[6]

---

[6] See generally for a recent and most valuable survey of the literature manifesting these doubts and disputes, Christoph Schreuer, "Recommendations and the Traditional Sources of International Law" (1977) 20 *German Yearbook of International Law* 103–118.

14. But the authors do not trouble to explore these vital questions. Instead, they fill the lacuna with a superficial summary of the subject matters on which the Security Council and General Assembly are authorized to adopt resolutions under Articles 12 to 14 and 33 to 38 of the Charter. It is surprising that in doing so, they make no reference to the point, relevant to their thesis, that only as to certain decisions of the Security Council can Article 25 of the Charter create legally binding obligations for Members. No legal force is attributed by the Charter to resolutions of the General Assembly.

15. Ignoring or side-stepping all of these issues, the authors invite the reader (p. 8) to accept the proposition that all assertions of law repeated in General Assembly resolutions become *ipso facto* international law by "consensus". Indeed, by a singular begging of the question, the only real guidance offered in *Resolutions* for selecting those General Assembly resolutions which qualify as customary law, is to say (pp. 3–4) that "this practice [i.e. of expressing consensus of legal issues through the General Assembly] is particularly evident in General Assembly resolutions concerning Palestine, Israel and the Middle East". Thus, after setting out to establish, as a basis for their claim that certain resolutions on the Palestinian Arabs are law, the limits within which General Assembly resolutions may be offered to establish the existence of new international law by direct action of the participating States, the authors then simply tender those very resolutions as examples of how such new customary law is created in the General Assembly. This failure of the authors to lay a firm legal foundation for their interpretation of General Assembly resolutions negates all the main submissions in the "study". Their submissions that a formidable series of legal obligations, arising outside traditional international law and the Charter, have been imposed on Israel by General Assembly resolutions, do not bear scrutiny and so must be rejected.

16. Professor Schreuer wisely observed in his survey of the state of international law in 1977:

> A recommendation's significance will not least depend on the moral authority of the adopting organ. Only the maintenance of high and impartial standards of decision-making in the international organ will endow its recommendations with persuasive force for all sectors of the international community. The application of politically motivated double standards or the use of general resolutions to champion positions in political quarrels are liable to undermine the credibility of the international organ even in areas of relative agreement.[7]

There are several reasons for suspecting that this rather self-evident prerequisite for attributing binding force to resolutions of the General Assembly has often not been fulfilled in recent years.

---

7 *Ibid.*, at 117.

17. One obvious reason is that some pronouncements of that body, even when they purport to "declare" or "interpret" law, smack of short-term power politics rather than of a deliberative legislative process. In a General Assembly of over 150 Members, operating on the basis of one State—one vote, major Powers like the Soviet Union, or alliances controlling a major resource like oil, together with large blocs of third world States, are in a position to convert that body into one more instrument of their own political warfare. In a General Assembly with the limited powers envisioned by the Charter this parliamentary situation would afford a tolerable (perhaps even desirable) arena for international politics. It becomes unacceptable and dangerous when the majority of groupings made up of temporary and shifting alliances attempts to attribute legally binding force to the resolutions it forces through this body. Such usurped power is at present being targeted against much of the western world, and even more particularly against Israel.

18. A second reason for denying General Assembly resolutions law-making effect is to be found in the duress or political pressures regularly brought to bear on States voting in the General Assembly. For example, the coercive oil embargo power wielded by a few States, diminutive in population but formidable in the importance of the resource they control, constantly inhibits Members who might wish to vote no, or even to abstain, on a range of matters notably but not exclusively affecting the Middle East. Under adequate duress, enough Members can be "obliged" to support, or at least abstain from opposing, such resolutions, so as to secure a majority for them. But to be "obliged" in this manner certainly does not satisfy the time-honoured requirement of *opinio juris sive necessitatis* in the international law-making process. In the jurisprudential commonplace, to be "obliged" to yield to an armed bandit is not to have a legal obligation to do so. No process of this kind, whether on issues affecting the Middle East or on other matters, can create international legal obligations.

19. General Assembly resolutions 34/65 B of 29 November 1979, purporting to declare the Camp David Accords and other agreements, including the Peace Treaty between Israel and Egypt to "have no validity" poses, at a new height of visibility, the threat to international legal order from automatic attribution of legal (or even moral) force to resolutions of the General Assembly. That extraordinary pronunciamento on the legal validity of agreements freely negotiated and arrived at between sovereign States blatantly expresses the policy of the Arab "rejectionist" States, and the Soviet determination to secure its super-Power role in the Middle East. But these political statements cannot be transformed into "law" by means of a vote in the General Assembly. The 38 States which voted against that resolution and the 32 which abstained included the United States, the nine members of the European Economic Community, and nearly 60 other Members. When this voting pattern is analysed more closely, it emerges that many of the abstentions would have been negative votes but for fear of the use of

the oil weapon against them. The majority includes more than a score of Members who are either oil producers or Arab or Moslem in affiliation, and no less than that number of Communist or Communist-aligned States.

20. That this is now a regular voting pattern in the General Assembly is clear from a comparison with the notorious resolution 3379 (XXX) of 1975, which solemnly pretended to "determine" that "Zionism" is a form of "racism". There too almost half the Members of the United Nations voted against or abstained, and the majority consisted of only 72 out of the 142 Members of the United Nations. The coercion by oil-producing States, in alliance with Communist States, was only too apparent in that vote. It is obviously not possible to prevent such resolutions from being adopted. But that is not the pertinent issue. That issue is whether, as the manipulators demand, there should be added to these extravagant expressions an attribution of binding force in international law.

21. It would indeed be extraordinary if a legal order which holds void treaties procured by the threat or use of force (see article 52 of the Vienna Convention on the Law of Treaties), would simultaneously attribute binding legal force to resolutions of the General Assembly for which States vote under extreme duress. No doubt the use of bargaining power, whether deriving from oil resources or from military force, cannot be prevented altogether from influencing the outcomes of negotiations between States. Yet, just as the Vienna Convention on the Law of Treaties sets limits to the lawful role of military power in inducing a party to accede to a demand, there must be corresponding limits to other means of coercion, including threats of economic strangulation by deprivation of essential oil supplies.[8]

22. There are a number of specific provisions of the Charter governing the employment of extreme economic duress. First, Article 53 expressly lays down that "no enforcement action shall be taken under regional arrangements, or by regional agencies without the authorization of the Security Council". Yet in fact this is what the 1973 Arab States' oil embargo against the United States, the Netherlands, Japan and other States amounted to. Such unilateral measures would not be in conformity with the Charter even if the political demands of the Arab States against Israel had conformed (which they did not) to the relevant Security Council resolutions. Second, the extreme coercion of the concerted oil measures probably constituted a threat or use of force, forbidden by Article 2, paragraph 4, of the United Nations Charter. There is a great difference between this degree of economic coercion based on monopoly power over oil supplies, and mere legal embargoes by one State against another when the fact of monopolistic control is absent. If this is so, the Vienna Convention on the Law of Treaties renders void any consensual obligation which States are thereby induced to accept. Third, many United Nations Members have taken the view in connexion with the Definition of Aggression that it includes "economic aggres-

---

[8] See on the history and scope of article 52, Stone, *Of Law and Nations* (1974), 231–251.

sion", and that its victims may lawfully take appropriate measures of self-defence. Fourth, a conspiratorial design of this kind by a group of Members to cripple the economies of other Members for collateral political ends obviously flouts the "Purposes" and "Principles" of Articles 1 and 2 of the Charter, as well as the Declaration on Principles of International Law Concerning Friendly Relations and Co-operation Among States in Accordance with the Charter of the United Nations, adopted by the General Assembly in resolution 2625 (XXV). Fifth, as a number of States urged in the Special Committee on the Definition of Aggression, the "sovereignty" of States protected by Article 2 of the Charter, as well as by the Definition of Aggression, may embrace economic attributes in addition to "territorial integrity" and "political independence". Hence, the extreme coerciveness and dubious legality of the Arab oil boycott under Article 53 of the Charter would seem to constitute "a threat or use of force in violation of the principles of the Charter".

23. If the exercise of modes and degrees of duress against individual States or regional groups are thus unlawful, it would be strange to think that they could remain lawful when exercised against the collectivity of Member States of the United Nations in the General Assembly. And it would become correspondingly grotesque to argue, as do all these "studies", that once assertions in resolutions of that body are sufficiently repeated they are transformed into international law, regardless of any duress by way of oil or other pressures which induced many Members to vote or abstain so as to allow them to be adopted. The grotesqueness arises not merely from ignoring the unlawful pressure by which the mere appearance of *consensus* is produced, and which, in principle, should of itself taint the resolution *qua* resolution. The grotesqueness is raised to breath-taking proportions by the claim that such resolutions are transmuted into precepts of international law binding on all States.

24. A third reason for rejecting claims that General Assembly resolutions as such create binding law is the rather indiscriminate fashion current today in the General Assembly of endorsing assertions made in the name of "international law", merely because they seem "progressive" in the sense of constricting the legal rights of States not belonging to the so-called Non-Aligned Group. Such positions are sometimes taken by publicists of some sincerity; yet they often represent a naive view not only of international law, but also of both morality and international politics. These publicists can be found to take stern restrictive views of the range of lawful resort to force by States, while insisting, with no sense of the incongruity, that States are also free to initiate or support "wars of liberation" of their own choice, provided that they can control by any means sufficient protective votes in the General Assembly. Such doctrines are a veritable forcing-bed for the double standards which Dr. Schreuer, as seen, correctly stigmatizes as fatal to any attribution of law-making to the General Assembly.

25. This "softening" of the doctrine which has been a mainstay of state-

craft since before the Peace of Westphalia (1648), is due in part to changing power-constellations, cultural styles and ideological commitments, and sometimes to post-colonial guilt feelings. But it is also due in part to the skill, imagination and persistence with which Soviet, Arab and other diplomats and publicists have co-ordinated, disguised and pressed the accumulation of their demands against the existing legal order. It is not the present thesis that in this new situation the give and take in the conflict of claims and the power that backs them may not yield new principles for a viable legal order. Yet to qualify as international law *any* assertion for which a majority can be marshalled in the General Assembly is to undermine both the United Nations and the international legal order as hitherto understood. The effect may be to block or vaporize that law, so as to foreclose any chance of adjusting it to changing conditions, as well as to invite political and military disasters.

26. Professor Gaetano Arangio-Ruiz's work, *The Normative Role of the General Assembly of the United Nations and the Declaration of Principles and Friendly Relations*,[9] is perhaps the most comprehensive and up-to-date examination of this matter. That learned author and experienced diplomat has diligently assembled, scrupulously commented upon, patiently organized and critically analysed the practice and growing literature which seeks to establish, explain or support pretensions to law-making authority by the General Assembly. It is a work which commands attention from all who value juristic and intellectual integrity above fashion and ideology. Professor Arangio-Ruiz ranges over numerous theories which purport to attribute law-making authority to the General Assembly. These include the supposed legitimation by the Charter or other contractual rule; a supposedly authorizing rule of customary law, the supposed "will" of the "Organised International Community", and the supposed binding force of particular resolutions seen as the practice of States maturing into custom or as "treaty" obligations based on "consensus".

27. On every such ground he is led to conclude that the General Assembly lacks authority either to "enact" or "declare" or "determine" or "interpret" international law in a way legally binding on any State, whether or not a Member of the United Nations and regardless of how that State voted on the particular resolution. His demonstration is relevant both for attempts at abstract "declaration" of law made by the General Assembly and for usurpation of the power to "determine" matters on which States are at variance, despite the lack of authority from the Charter to so "determine". He calls upon international lawyers to resist and reject what he calls the "soft-law method" associated with loose attribution of independent law-making power to the General Assembly. In response to arguments like those made in these "studies", that sufficiently frequent repetition of a statement in the

---

[9] 137 *Académie de Droit International, Recueil des Cours* (1972), 419.

General Assembly can in itself transmogrify that statement into a rule of customary law, Professor Arangio-Ruiz offers a fitting answer:

> It would be too easy if the "shouting out" of rules through General Assembly resolutions were to be law-making simply as a matter of "times" shouted and size of the choir. By all means, we would urge that one let the General Assembly shout as often and as loud as it is able and willing to shout. However, for the shouted rule to be customary law there still remains to consider the conduct and the attitudes of States with regard to the actual behaviour, positive or negative, contemplated as due by the rule (p. 476).

28. Among the more dramatic examples of the dangers to the international legal order from loose attempts to turn General Assembly resolutions into international law is that body's resolution 3236 (XXIX) of 22 November 1974 on the rights of the Palestinian people. Since the resolution is also a centre-piece of all four "studies" it is instructive to examine it in terms of the preceding general analysis.

29. The basic issues and principles for the settlement of the Middle East situation were set forth in Security Council resolution 242 (1967), reaffirmed in resolution 338 (1973), which required the parties to proceed forthwith to negotiations for a just and durable peace. During the period from 1967 to 1973, various cease-fires ordered by the Security Council and consented to by the parties were beyond any doubt in full legal force. Under those circumstances, the hostilities initiated by Egypt and Syria in 1969–1970 and 1973, and the Arab States' harbouring and support of terrorist operations against Israel under the auspices of the PLO and its military wings, should have incurred the censure of the United Nations. However, the geo-political drives of Soviet policy, the multiplication of United Nations Members aligned in voting blocs with Communist and Arab Members, the political use of the Soviet veto and the coercive use of the oil weapon, rendered the Security Council impotent through most of the Yom Kippur War of 1973.

30. Then, on 22 November 1974, the General Assembly adopted resolution 3236 (XXIX) which made explicit this travesty of the applicable principles of international and Charter law. No one can second-guess the voting fate of that resolution had not the damoclean sword of an oil boycott hung over the proceedings. Even under such coercion, one third of the Members of the General Assembly either voted against or abstained. Resolutions adopted in such circumstances are not likely to reflect or promote international law, much less justice or morality.

31. In resolution 3236 (XXIX), the General Assembly purported to reaffirm "the inalienable rights of the Palestinian people in Palestine". It also recognized the PLO as the appropriate claimant in respect of such rights. In so doing, the General Assembly endorsed by implication prior PLO actions, including terrorist activities deliberately aimed at men, women and

children, as well as the citizens, airports and aircraft of numerous States not involved in the Middle East dispute. By the same token, and by a later express provision, it also offered dispensation for the continuance of such activities.

32. Second, the resolution violated various legal principles and rights guaranteed under international law and under other authoritative long-standing United Nations resolutions. By its endorsement of the PLO's aspirations, which (under art. 6 of the Palestinian National Covenant) call for the destruction of the State of Israel, the measure violated the sovereign equality of Israel, guaranteed by Article 2, paragraph 1, of the Charter. It also violated Israel's right to be free from the threat or use of force under Article 2, paragraph 4, and to be free from armed attack under Article 51.

33. Third, the resolution contradicted the assurance embodied in Security Council resolution 242 (1967) of Israel's right "to live in peace within secure and recognized boundaries free from threats or acts of force".

34. Fourth, by reaffirming what it called "the inalienable rights of the Palestinian people in Palestine", with no geographical limitation placed on those last two words, the resolution contradicted the General Assembly's 1947 Partition resolution. Although Arab aggression prevented that resolution from ever coming into legal operation, the General Assembly was certainly committed to recognizing the entitlement of the Jewish people, and later of Israel, to *some part* of Palestine. Historic and geographic "Palestine" includes not only Judea and Samaria and Gaza, but also the whole of pre-1967 Israel and the Kingdom of Jordan. This notwithstanding, the representative of Jordan in the debate on the 1974 resolution made clear his country's view that Israel *was* included in the "Palestine" claimed for the Palestinians, whereas Jordan was not!

35. Fifth, while the General Assembly in 1947 had requested the Security Council to treat the use of force by Arab States as "a threat to the peace, breach of the peace or act of aggression", the General Assembly in 1974 placed itself in the role of a virtual accomplice by encouraging the resumption of the very kind of aggression which it formerly singled out for peremptory condemnation. This lamentable *volte-face* is underscored by the express approval in paragraph 5 of the resolution of the use by the PLO of "all means" to achieve its ends, and its appeal to all States and international organizations to *assist with such means!*[10]

36. The representative of the United States spoke for many Members when he referred to the dangers to the authority of the United Nations posed by such one-sided resolutions. He cited the handling of the global economic crisis and the Middle East conflict as examples of what he viewed as arbitrary disrespect for the Charter. He warned that if the United

---

[10] Resolution 3236 (XXIX), para. 6. The succeeding words—"in accordance with the Purposes and Principles of the Charter"—are ambivalent as to whether any limits are to be read into that extraordinary appeal.

Nations continued to proceed on the basis of arithmetical majorities, a "sterile form of international activity" would result and the United Nations would no longer be regarded as a responsible forum of world opinion.[11] Yet this resolution typifies the resolutions of the recent period on which these "studies" base their untenable conclusions.

II. GENERAL ASSEMBLY RESOLUTION 181 (II) OF 29 NOVEMBER 1947

37. Two distinct and basic legal questions are wholly overlooked in the Mallisons' analysis of the Partition resolution. One: What would have been its effects on sovereign title in the territories concerned had the Arab States not rejected it? Two: What residual binding effect (if any) survived the destruction of the resolution by Arab aggression? Both these questions are certainly part of what the authors call (p. v) "the context of international law" in which they claim to be examining the United Nations resolutions concerned. Legal relations of States cannot be frozen at a point in time over a quarter of a century ago, even at the behest of these authors.

38. The first issue is the potential legal effect of the Partition resolution *had it come into legal operation*. On this issue the authors involve themselves a somewhat tortuous struggle. On the one hand, they do not dissociate themselves from Arab claims that the resolution was invalid *ab initio*, violating (in their view) the Mandate for Palestine, as interpreted by Arab protagonists (pp. 22–23).[12] Acceptance of these claims would obviously tend to justify the Arab States' forcible rejection of the resolution. On the other hand, after failure of that Arab aggression to destroy Israel, the authors, writing over three decades later, wish for rather obvious reasons to attach great value to certain provisions of the 1947 resolution which would, on their interpretation, be legally embarrassing to Israel (pp. 24–25). In this schizophrenic posture, their analysis suggests that the General Assembly was in 1947 both a legitimate United Nations successor to the League of Nations Mandates System, and a usurping authority acting *ultra vires*. The tension of simultaneous validity and invalidity which they suggest for the 1947 resolution infects and cripples the whole of their account of the role of the General Assembly at that time.

39. If we address ourselves directly to the potential effects on sovereign title had the Partition resolution not been aborted by Arab aggression, the answer is not complicated. On 2 April 1947, the United Kingdom, as the Mandatory Power, gave formal notice to the United Nations and authorized the General Assembly to attempt a settlement on the question.[13] Since the Charter refers to the Mandate System, the United Kingdom's request was

[11] Press Release US-UN 191 (74), 6 December 1974.

[12] See, e.g. H. Cattan, *Palestine and International Law* (London, 2nd ed., 1964), on which the authors rely heavily.

[13] See *Official Records of the General Assembly, First Special Session*, Plenary Meeting (A/286), 183.

properly a "question or . . . matter within the scope" of the Charter, for purposes of General Assembly discussion under Article 10.

40. It is no less certain, however, that the powers of the General Assembly acting on a matter within Article 10 are limited to the non-binding mode of "recommendations" (paras. 6–36, *supra*). Moreover, the language of the 1947 resolution was scarcely such as to convey titles *instanter*. Nor was it clear that the General Assembly had any territorial title in Palestine to convey. Elihu Lauterpacht correctly concludes that the Partition resolution had no legislative character as is necessary to vest territorial rights in either Jews or Arabs. Any binding force would have had to arise from the principle *pacta sunt servanda*, that is, from the agreement of the *parties* concerned to the proposed plan. Such agreement was frustrated *ab initio* by the Arab rejection,[14] a rejection underscored by the armed invasion of Palestine by the forces of Egypt, Lebanon, Transjordan, Syria, Iraq and Saudi Arabia launched hard on the heels of the British withdrawal on 14 May 1948, and aimed at destroying Israel.

41. Israel thus does not derive its legal existence from the Partition plan.[15] Rather, its independence rests (as does that of most other States in the world) on its own assertion of independence, on the vindication of that independence against assault by other States, and on the establishment of an orderly government within the territory under its control. At most, as Israel's Declaration of Independence expressed it, the General Assembly resolution was a "recognition" of the "natural and historical right" of the Jewish people in Palestine. The immediate recognition of Israel by the United States and other states, and its admission in 1949 into the United Nations, were in no way predicated on its creation by the Partition resolution.

42. Israel's Declaration of Independence of 14 May 1948, made under the immediate shadow of armed attack from the Arab States, predicated independence on the following grounds: (1) *Eretz Israel* (the Land of Israel, the Hebrew name for "Palestine") was the birthplace of the Jewish people where "their spiritual, religious and national identity was shaped", where they first attained statehood, created cultural values of national and universal significance, and gave the Bible to the world; (2) Jews in exile had never

---

[14] E. Lauterpacht, *Jerusalem and the Holy Places* (London, 1968), 39.

[15] Certainly, in so far as all the parties concerned allowed it to become operative, it would become binding on them and on all concerned. It was on that assumption that Moshe Shertok, speaking for the Jewish Agency, distinguished at the time between the Partition resolution and other resolutions of the General Assembly, and stated on 27 April 1948 that the Partition resolution would (that is, if it became operative) have *a* (emphasis supplied) binding force. *Official Records of the General Assembly, Second Special Session*, vol. II, at 108. Mr. Shertok was dealing with the particular problem which arose in 1948, namely, whether the General Assembly could revoke the 1947 resolution and impose a United Nations trusteeship on Palestine. The Mallisons quote a part of that section of his statement (*Resolutions*, pp. 25–26), without due reference to the context in which it was made, and to the assumption underlying it, namely that the 1947 resolution was to become operative.

ceased to pray and hope for their return to political freedom in the Land of Israel; (3) efforts to return to *Eretz Israel* had continued throughout successive generations, and in recent decades had become a mass movement, bringing a revival of the Land of the Hebrew language, and progress for all inhabitants; (4) the historic connexions between the Jewish people and *Eretz Israel* and the right of the Jewish people to rebuild its National Home there were internationally recognized in the League of Nations Mandate; and (5) the contribution of the Jewish people to the victory of the freedom-loving nations over the nazi tyranny had gained for them the right to be reckoned among the peoples who founded the United Nations. These elements are summed up in a concluding affirmation that "it is the natural right of the Jewish people to be master of their own fate, like all other nations, in their own sovereign state".

43. All these elements of Israel's entitlement to sovereignty were independent of the United Nations. They refer to facts existing before the United Nations was established. However, the Declaration did also refer to the General Assembly's Partition resolution. It recited that on 29 November 1947 the General Assembly had adopted a resolution *"calling for"* the establishment of a Jewish state in "Eretz-Israel", and that "this *recognition* by the United Nations of the right of the Jewish people to establish their state is *irrevocable"* (emphasis supplied).[16]

44. I have emphasized certain of the words used in the official translation of the Declaration because the Mallisons' version in *Resolutions* (p. 26) alters them in ways tending to support the otherwise untenable assertion that "Israel has placed heavy reliance upon the Partition resolution as providing legal authority" and that it "is the pre-eminent juridical basis for the State of Israel". The authors interpret (without adducing any support) the expression "calling for" in the Declaration of Independence as though it was *authorizing*. They also take liberties with the phrase that the United Nations' "recognition" is "irrevocable". In context, this means that the preceding five elements of Jewish peoplehood and entitlement to national independence, as elucidated earlier in the Declaration, justify "this recognition" by the United Nations. The authors substitute for the word "recognition" the word "resolution", thus rewriting Israel's Declaration of Independence as if it read, This *resolution* by the United Nations . . . is *irrevocable"*. This distortion is obviously essential to their argument that Israel remained and still remains bound by the 1947 resolution despite its rejection by the Arab States and other authorities concerned. It is, however, pure fabrication.

45. Returning to the question: What *would have been* the legal binding effect of the Partition resolution had its coming into operation not been aborted by the Arab States? The answer is that the "Plan of Partition with Economic Union" set out in the annex to that resolution, would, *if accepted*,

---

[16] Official translation in 1 *Laws of the State of Israel* (5708–1948) 4. Reproduced in J. N. Moore (editor), *The Arab-Israel Conflict*, III, Documents, (Princeton, 1974) 349.

have been binding on Israel and on the Arab States, including the new Palestinian Arab State once it was established, on the basis of the rule *pacta sunt servanda*. The effect of the *agreement* would have been to allocate sovereign titles, *inter alia*, to Israel, the proposed new Arab State, and the proposed *corpus separatum* comprising Jerusalem and its environs. Israel stood ready to enter into this agreement. On the other hand, as even the authors have to admit (pp. 25–27), the Arab States rejected it, and used armed aggression to destroy the Plan.[17] There was in fact no such agreement, no such effect in vesting and delimiting titles, and no such entities as the proposed Arab State and *corpus separatum* ever came into being, in fact or in law.

46. The chronology of events is essential in assessing whether the Partition resolution could affect sovereign titles in Mandated Palestine. The resolution recommended to the Mandatory Power the adoption and implementation of the revised majority plan of the United Nations Special Committee on Palestine (UNSCOP); it requested the Security Council to "take measures" to implement the Plan; it called upon the inhabitants of Palestine to take steps necessary to put the Plan into effect; and it appealed to all Governments and peoples to refrain from any action which might hamper or delay the Plan's coming into effect. The Plan envisaged the termination of the Mandate and the withdrawal of British forces no later than 1 August 1948. It provided that the Arab and Jewish States and the international rgime in the City of Jerusalem should come into existence not later than 1 October 1948. The Plan also described their future boundaries and included chapters on the Holy Places, religious buildings and sites, religious and minority rights and citizenship, international conventions and financial obligations.

47. The Jewish Agency for Palestine reluctantly accepted this resolution, in the belief that it contained the elements upon which the parties could together construct a peaceful future.[18] The Jewish Agency did so on the understanding that, despite the negative attitudes of the Arab States in the General Assembly, they would accept the appeal of that body not to oppose its implementation by violence. This understanding was implicit in the principle of reciprocity in international relations founded on mutual consent. The Arab States, however, rejected the resolution as infringing Arab rights, and *ultra vires* of the General Assembly. They proceeded in May 1948 to attempt to seize the whole of Palestine by armed force. Consequently, all basis for bringing the plan into legal operation was finally destroyed by the Arab States in May, months before the termination of the Mandate.[19]

---

[17] In fact, the Arab States were on this account subject, under the resolution, to Security Council action against them as aggressors. The Mallisons, as already observed, blow hot and cold as to whether, at its moment of proposed implementation, the resolution was or was not "valid", let alone binding on the States concerned (*Resolutions*, pp. 23–25).

[18] Cf. *Israel and the United Nations* in the Carnegie Endowment Series of *National Studies on International Organization* (New York, 1956), 67.

[19] As early as 20 February 1948, the Security Council received a report from the Pales-

48. The authors of *Resolutions* pay virtually no regard to these dates and events, despite their crucial importance for vesting titles in international law. After their opening vacillation as to whether or not the resolution was "invalid" *ab initio*, they confuse matters further by vigorously asserting that the resolution is certainly of continuing validity today (pp. 25–27), over 30 years later.

49. The miracle to be wrought by the Arab States, and by the Mallisons in their wake, is almost as impressive as the revival of something dead. It is no less than the resuscitation of a resolution which they had guaranteed would be still-born and which they had buried by their own aggression over three decades ago.[20] Since, as shown, none of the resolution's potential legal effects ever came into being in the first place, they cannot have any "continuing validity" today.

50. The opposite view pressed by the authors of *Resolutions* is grossly repugnant to elementary considerations of justice and equity and good faith common to most legal systems, including international law. There are additional grounds, rooted in basic notions of justice and equity, on which the Arab States and the Palestinian Arabs should not, in any case, be permitted after so lawless a resort to violence against the resolution, to claim legal entitlements under it. Several of "the general principles of law" mentioned in Article 38, paragraph 1, of the Statute of the International Court of Justice preclude it. These Arab claimants do not come with clean hands seeking equity; their case is mired by the illegal bid to destroy by aggression the very resolution from which they now seek equity. They may also be thought by their representations concerning those documents to have led others to act to their own detriment, and thus are now debarred by their conduct from espousing, in pursuit of present expendiencies, positions they formerly denounced. Their position also resembles that of a party to a transaction who has unlawfully repudiated the transaction, and then comes to court years later claiming that selected provisions of it should be meticulously enforced against the wronged party. Similarly, it resembles that of a party who has by unlawful violence wilfully destroyed the subject-matter which is "the fundamental basis" on which consent was to rest, and now clamours to have the original terms enforced against the other party.

51. The authors of *Resolutions* seek to salvage some continuing binding effect for the Partition resolution by suggesting (p. 27) that the gist of some later General Assembly resolutions, especially those concerning Palestinian

---

tine Commission that "powerful Arab interests, both inside and outside Palestine, are defying the resolution of the General Assembly [181 (II) of 29 November 1947] and are engaged in a deliberate effort to alter by force the settlement envisaged therein" (S/676, 16 February 1948). *Official Records of the Security Council, Third Year, Special Supplement* No. 2 at 11.

[20] For the quite explicit objectives of the attack see the official statements of Arab Governments and their representatives, assembled in the letter dated 12 December 1978 of the Permanent Representative of Israel to the United Nations (A/33/488-S/12966).

peoplehood, somehow retroactively instilled new life into the still-born resolution of 1947. They argue that these later resolutions now "constitute a
world-wide consensus of support". I have already submitted that these authors have not adequately examined the limits within which votes in international bodies can be the equivalent of statements of rules of international
law. This deficiency also undermines this final basis of their claim that the
provisions of the abortive 1947 Partition resolution constitute binding
norms of international law of 1979. General Assembly resolutions having
no law-making authority on their own, certainly cannot revive a resolution
which never had any legal effect to begin with.

III. The Right of Return

52. An examination of the General Assembly resolutions on the right of
return or compensation of Palestinian refugees shows that the heavy reliance on them displayed by the authors of *Resolutions* (pp. 31–37) is mis-
placed. The authors themselves observe (pp. 31–32) that paragraph 11 of
General Assembly resolution 194 (III), which they properly recognize as the
starting point and basis of their argument, did not even purport to be in
mandatory terms. It was simply part of the terms of reference of the Palestine Conciliation Commission. A recital in resolution 273 (III), on the admission of Israel into the United Nations, "recalled" that resolution 194 (III)
provided an option for refugees to return to their homes or to receive compensation, but it immediately "noted" the declaractions and explanations
made by Israel with respect to implementation of that resolution. Since Israel's declarations and explanations did not unqualifiedly accept the resolution, it can in no way be regarded as creating a legal obligation. As Elihu
Lauterpacht observes the General Assembly "could not by its resolution give
the Jews and Arabs in Palestine rights which they did not otherwise possess;
nor, correspondingly, could it take away such rights as they did possess".[21]

53. It is clear that the next resolution, General Assembly resolution 513
(VI), was designed to facilitate the resettlement of the refugees in order to
end their virtual confinement in concentration camps on Arab territory. Resettlement was the effective solution for the far larger and more complex
refugee problems in Europe after the Second World War. With regard to
the Arab refugees, it is a melancholy fact that this more humane and effective course has been followed to so small an extent, for so long, that some
observers have concluded that, for the Arab States concerned, the refugee
problem was more useful than its *solution*. Resolutions 2452 (XXIII), 2535
(XXIV), 2963 (XXVII), 3089 (XXVIII) and 3236 (XXIX), concerned with
refugees fleeing in the aftermath of the Arab aggression of both 1947–1948
and 1967, aim at supporting the activities of the Commissioner-General of
the United Nations Relief and Works Agency for Palestine Refugees in the
Near East (UNRWA). Although they contain various calls upon Israel and

---

[21] E. Lauterpacht, *supra*, note 14, at 27 ff.

expressions of regret in the matter of repatriation and compensation, the peremptory assertions vital for the "studies" only finally mature in resolution 3236 (XXIX) of 22 November 1974. In the era of the oil weapon which then ensued, General Assembly resolutions indeed began regularly to insert the adjective "inalienable" before the words "right to return".

54. Even if those resolutions are taken as declaratory of international law, the question still arises why the authors of these "studies" have ignored the fact that Israel has absorbed and rehabilitated even larger numbers of Jewish refugees uprooted from Arab lands since 1948. In their doggedly meticulous analysis of General Assembly resolutions, the authors nowhere refer to Jewish refugees, nor do they even seek to explain why the general judicial principles on this matter which they so eloquently invoke (pp. 28–30), running from Magna Carta (1215) to the International Covenant on Civil and Political Rights (1966), should apply only to Arab refugees and not to Jewish refugees.

55. The members of each of these groups suffered similar wrongs. The duty of providing homes for the 700,000 Jewish refugees involved was assumed by Israel in its fundamental Law of Return of 1950, as a first responsibility of the new State. This great burden of rehabilitation assumed by Israel should, both in law and justice, be brought into account in assessing contributions to be made by the Arab States and Israel to what Security Council resolution 242 (1967) called a "just" solution to the refugee problem. The point is even more pertinent because the misfortunes of both peoples arose from unsuccessful ventures in aggressive use of armed force in defiance of the United Nations Charter and resolutions by Arab States, and not by Israel.

56. In this connexion, the authors of *Resolutions* exhibit a curious astigmatism. Most remarkable is their failure to look carefully at relevant Security Council resolutions, especially resolutions 242 (1967) and 338 (1973). After all, the title of their "study" is *Major United Nations Resolutions*, not *Major General Assembly Resolutions*. In their tangled doctrine about "the right of return" of Palestinian refugees, they pay no regard whatsoever to the fact that the Security Council in 1967 did not feel that it could invoke any such hard-and-fast rule of international law as the authors assert. Nor do the authors deign to notice the fact that the formula of resolution 242 calling for "a just settlement of the refugee question", does not suffer from their own one-sidedness in ignoring Jewish refugees from Arab lands, while insisting on redress to Arab refugees from Palestine. They fail to notice that, as late as 1973, the Security Council reaffirmed in resolution 338 (1973) all the provisions of resolution 242 (1967), and called for urgent negotiation on their basis. This means that even in 1973 the resolutions of the Security Council, also a principal organ of the United Nations, did not conform to the reconstructed version of international law offered in *Resolutions*.

IV. Self-Determination and the Arab-Israel Conflict

57. Is self-determination, whatever its specific content, the subject-matter of a precept of international law itself, or is it only a consideration of policy or of justice, to be weighed as one among other facts and values in the interpretation and application of legal rules? The authors of the *Self-Determination* "study" ask (p. 1) whether the doctrine is "a principle" or "a right". To this rather abstruse question, they give an even more abstruse answer. Conceding that the complexities of the issue are not within their ambit, they nevertheless announce that they will proceed "on the axiom" that "the right of self-determination exists as a crucial element in contemporary international life and is recognized as such by the political world community". Note that this supposed axiom studiously avoids any juridical reference, and might be better suited to a textbook on the sociology of the international community. A careful lawyer knows that a notion of "right" may or may not refer to a "*legal* right". I propose to analyse the evidence and process by which the authors of *Self-Determination* and of *Resolutions* seek to demonstrate the transmogrification of this sociological observation into a precept of international law currently in force.

58. The demonstration proceeds (pp. 2–13) by culling the views of publicists who have asserted that "self-determination has developed into an international legal right". Some of these are experts whose distinction is certainly not in the field of international law;[22] but as a token of objectivity the "study" also mentions (though scarcely exhaustively) one or two publicists who hold the opposing view. The anonymous writers have perforce to admit (p. 12) that, even today, there is a "variety of opinions on the issue of the juridical position in international law of the right of self-determination". Yet this in no way inhibits them from assuming that the right of self-determination *is* "an established principle of international law", because this is "the consistent stand of the General Assembly". Moreover, this stand "reflects the will of the international community". This is nothing more than a reassertion of their opening axiom, of no legal significance unless the General Assembly "stand", as reflected in its resolutions, can be said to have a legislative character. But, as has been shown, although *Resolutions* opens with a laborious effort to demonstrate that the "stand" of the General Assembly on a matter becomes international law, its efforts were unsuccessful. Hence, proceeding from faith (or prejudice) rather than any juristic demonstration, the anonymous authors of *Self-Determination* perform the extraordinary feat of elevating the self-determination principle to the level of *jus cogens*.[23]

---

[22] For instance, here and elsewhere the references in the "studies" to W. E. Hocking, *The Spirit of World Politics* (1932), 354, 372–74.

[23] At 12–13. Their main authority on *jus cogens* is a somewhat complicated *ipse dixit* of M. Gros Espiel in his study prepared for the Subcommittee on the Prevention of Discrimination and the Protection of Minorities, entitled *Implementation of United Nations Resolutions Relating to the Right of Peoples under Colonial and Alien Domination to Self-Determination* (E/CN.4/Sub.2/405), especially at 33–35. Contra, see study for the same Subcommittee by

59. In both the "studies" on *Self-Determination* and *Resolutions*, therefore, the standing in law of the right of self-determination in general is asserted in conclusional terms, but nowhere is any demonstration proferred. Within this hazardous frame the authors produce a collage of documents critical of the League of Nations Mandate and of Zionism, the national liberation movement of the Jewish people. With similar selectivity, they rehearse (pp. 22–28) the history of the British administration in Palestine and the first phase of the United Nations involvement up to the abortion of the Partition resolution by what the authors delicately call the "sending" by "the Arab States" of "forces" into Palestine (p. 31). Nowhere in this presentation do they give any reason why self-determination, as the legal right they claim it to be, does not spread its blessings over the Jewish people as well as the Palestinian Arab people. Equally irrelevant for them is the unlawful occupation and annexation by Jordan of the West Bank and its failure, from 1948 to 1967, to accord the slightest degree of autonomy to the Palestinian Arabs living there.

60. Up to 1970, General Assembly resolutions dealt only with the claims of Arab refugees to return to their homes and "their repatriation, resettlement and economic and social rehabilitation and payment of adequate compensation for the property of those choosing not to return".[24] It is only with General Assembly resolution 2672 C (XXV) of 8 December 1970 that "the General Assembly moved towards acknowledging the correlation between the right of self-determination and other inalienable rights" (*Resolutions*, p. 44). From this resolution and from a phrase in resolution 2649 (XXV) of 30 November 1979, the authors of *Resolutions* make so bold as to argue that all earlier resolutions on the self-determination of peoples in general, have later and retroactively become "specifically applicable to the Palestinian people" (*id.*). They are thus accepting as an historical fact that, so far as the

---

A. Critescu entitled *The Historical and Current Development of the Right to Self-Determination on the Basis of the Charter of the United Nations and Other Instruments Adopted by United Nations Organs, with Particular Reference to the Promotion and Protection of Human Rights and Fundamental Freedoms* (E/CN.4/Sub.2/404), para. 154, who squarely states: "No United Nations instrument confers such a peremptory character on the right of peoples to self-determination." The anonymous authors also cite a dictum of Professor Georg Schwarzenberger to the effect that since international law has always been a system of nation-States, it has always in that sense been based on the self-determination of these nations. See G. Schwarzenberger, *International Law and Order* (1971), 27–28. How much Professor Schwarzenberger's position is here misunderstood is indicated by the fact that in his important *Frontiers of International Law* (London, 1962) neither the notion of *jus cogens* nor the self-determination principle receive any discussion even under the head of "fundamental rights and freedoms". *Loc. cit.*, 308 ff. And see his essay "International *Jus Cogens*", 43 *Texas Law Review* 455 (1965). It is to be recalled that no treaty and no serious scholar has yet given *jus cogens* any function other than the negative one of making void an inconsistent treaty.

[24] Count Folke Bernadotte, Progress Report of 16 September 1948, 3 UN *Official Records of the General Assembly, Supplement No. 11*, 1–19, at 18, United Nations Document A/648.

General Assembly is concerned, *no* rights of the Palestinian Arabs under the Charter were recognized until 1970.

61. Even resolution 2672 C (XXV) of 8 December 1970, claimed as an epoch-making recognition of Palestinian self-determination, was hesitant at that late stage. No less than 72 States out of a total of the 139 Members of the United Nations at the time either opposed it or abstained in the vote, and only 47 States voted for it. This scarcely signals a whole-hearted flash of recognition, even a belated one, by the international community of an age-old self-evident truth!

62. Moreover, unprecedented coercion was exercised in the General Assembly by the Arab States' oil boycott in support of the Syrian-Egyptian attack on Israel in 1973 in order to induce a majority to vote for resolutions asserting the existence of the fact of a separate Palestinian Arab national identity. Even under such threats and duress, in 1973, the pertinent resolution 3089 D (XXVIII) marshalled only 87 affirmative votes (with 39 States voting against or abstaining). It is noteworthy that when, a year later, resolution 3236 (XXIX) attempted to strengthen the self-determination claim by "reaffirmation", there were increases in both the number of Members who opposed, and the number who abstained.[25]

63. The "study" on *Self-Determination* concludes (pp. 33–37) with a section entitled "The Affirmation by the United Nations of the Right of Self-Dtermination [*sic*] of the Palestinian People". While the *Resolutions* "study" blurs the precise time of full recognition by the General Assembly of the claim of the Palestinian Arabs, *Self-Determination* is crystal clear and accurate on the point. The anonymous authors of *Self-Determination* point out that the General Assembly's repeated assertions of Palestinian qualification as a nation do not begin until resolution 2672 (XXV) of 8 December 1970. They even stress (p. 33), with perspicacity, but without mentioning the oil weapon, that it was with the Arab war of aggression of October 1973 that the cause of self-determination for the Palestinian people "began a rapid advance". They also stress the close relation between the affirmations by Arab Heads of State at the Rabat Summit in 1974 of the right of self-determination for the Palestinian Arabs and the status of the PLO, and the General Assembly's adoption of the PLO resolution 3236 (XXIX) of 22 November 1974. All this leads inexorably to the admission that the General Assembly's action was taken under pressure of the Arab States, including those now flexing their muscles through OAPEC.

[25] See the voting figures in *Resolutions*, pp. 57 ff. In this connexion, it is recalled that the United Nations Conference on the Law of Treaties adopted its well-known Declaration on the Prohibition of Military, Political or *Economic* Coercion in the Conclusion of Treaties, solemnly condemning the threat or use of pressure "*in any form*", by any State in order to coerce and another State "*to perform any act*", in violation of the "principles of the sovereign equality of States and freedom of consent" (emphasis supplied). United Nations Conference on the Law of Treaties, *Official Records*, Documents of the Conference, at 285 (A/CONF.39/26).

64. The authors of *Self-Determination* admirably summarize (p. 37) the main point as to *national* claims of the Palestinian Arabs in this striking way:

Thus it will be seen that the right of self-determination of the Palestinian people, denied for three decades during the Mandate, ignored for two decades in the United Nations, have over almost the last decade received consistent recognition and strong assertion by a preponderant majority of Member States of the United Nations . . .

It is ironic that this eloquence, applied to the Palestinian Arabs, admits, indeed insists, that the proper date for the application of the self-determination principle is placed about 1970, and certainly not half a century before, in 1917. The implications of this admission are examined below (paras. 66–82).

65. It is also curious that in a 10-page section on "The National Rights of the People of Palestine" (*Resolutions*, pp. 39–48), the authors continue avoiding reference to the most important and influential of recent resolutions on the Middle East, Security Council resolutions 242 (1967) and 338 (1973). As international lawyers, the authors must be aware of the importance of resolution 242 as the only authoritative and unanimously accepted formulation by the Security Council of the issues between Israel and the Arab States. They ignore its implications for the self-determination issue in that Security Council resolution 242 (1967) significantly excludes all reference to any *national* claims of Palestinian Arabs against Israel. This was simply not an issue in the Middle East conflict in 1967, nor was it in 1973 when resolution 338 (1973) reaffirmed resolution 242 (1967).

66. A basic assumption underlying this whole series of "studies" is that the peoples whose competing claims of self-determination are to be reconciled are the Jewish people on the one hand, and the Palestinian Arab people on the other. A corollary to this assumption is that the relevant date for applying the self-determination principle in the Middle East is 1947, the date of the Partition resolution. Alternatively, it may be 1974, when the General Assembly first pronounced, in resolution 3236 (XXIX), that "the Palestinian people is entitled to self-determination in accordance with the Charter of the United Nations".

67. Such assumptions fly in the face of the history of the struggle over Palestine by ignoring the critical importance of the decades before 1947. The main conclusion of *Self-Determination* (p. 37) is that no such right of *Palestinian Arabs* as a separate people was recognized "during three decades" of the League Mandate, or "the first two decades" of the United Nations. This admission confirms what is in any case clear from the post-First World War settlement: the rival claimants to the former Ottoman territories concerned were limited to the Jewish and Arab national movements, and given the historical context, properly so.

68. For centuries preceding 1917, the name "Palestine" never referred to

a defined political, demographic, cultural or territorial entity. In the immediately preceding centuries, the area formed part of the Ottoman Empire,
and for much of that time its provincial capital was in Damascus. In 1917,
its larger part, north of a line from Jaffa to the River Jordan, was part of
the Vilayet of Beirut and the whole of it was considered part of *Sham* (a
broad area comprising what is today Syria and beyond). The Arabs living
there were not regarded by themselves or by others as "Palestinians", nor
did they in any major respect differ from their brethren in Syria and Lebanon. This "Syrian" rather than "Palestinian" identification of Arabs living
in Palestine underlay the request of the Syrian General Congress on 2 July
1919, "that there should be no separation of the southern part of Syria
known as Palestine, nor of the littoral Western Zone which includes Lebanon, from the Syrian country".[26]

69. Indeed, the main argument made by Arabs in the post-First World
War negotiations was not that "Palestinians" would resent the loss of *Palestinian* identity by the establishment of the Jewish National Home, but that
the inhabitants would *resent the severance of their connexion with their fellow Syrians*. In the light of these facts, the notion that the Arabs living in Palestine
regarded themselves in 1917 as a *Palestinian people* in the sense required by
President Wilson's self-determination principle (for brevity "the liberation
principle") is thus a figment of an unhistorical imagination. To respect these
historical facts is not to impugn the liberation principle; it is merely to point
out that the principle must be applied at the appropriate time to group life
as they truly exist.

70. Even some PLO leaders have disavowed a distinct Palestinian identity.
On 31 March 1977, for example, the head of the PLO Military Operations
Department, Zuhair Muhsin, told the Netherlands newspaper *Trouw* that:

> There are no differences between Jordanians, Palestinians, Syrians and
> Lebanese . . . We are one people. Only for political reasons do we care-
> fully underline our Palestinian identity. For it is of national interest for
> the Arabs to encourage the existence of the Palestinians against Zion-
> ism. Yes, the existence of a separate Palestinian identity is there only
> for tactical reasons. The establishment of a Palestinian state is a new
> expedient to continue the fight against Zionism and for Arab unity.

71. Thus, the fact relevant to a correct application of the self-determination doctrine in the present case go back to 1917. For whether this doctrine
is already part of international law *stricto sensu*, or (as many international
lawyers think) a precept of politics or policy or justice, to be considered

---

[26] Cf. *Foreign Relations of the United States*, Paris Peace Conference, 1919, vol. 12, 781
(Report of the King-Crane Commission). This historical fact continues to reverberate today in Arab circles. President Assad of Syria in 1974 stated that "Palestine is a basic part
of Southern Syria" (*New York Times*, 9 March 1974). On 17 November 1978, Yasser Arafat
commented that Palestine is southern Syria and Syria is northern Palestine (*Voice of Palestine*, 18 November 1978).

where appropriate, it is clear that its applications must be predicated on facts. One such fact is *when* in time the claimant group lacking a territorial home first constituted a people or nation, with the requisite common endowment of distinctive language, ethnic origin, history, tradition and the like.

72. The point in time at which it can be confidently said that a distinctively Palestinian Arab claim for self-determination emerged on the Middle East scene was around the adoption of the Palestinian National Charter in 1964 (revised as a "Covenant" in 1968).[27] The Covenant itself testifies with striking clarity that the belatedness of this self-recognition as Palestinian Arabs undermined the demands for territorial sovereignty. It was, after all, nearly half a century after the non-Turkish territories of the Ottoman Empire had already been allocated between the Jewish and Arab liberation claimants (the latter including the Palestinian Arabs, but not as a distinctive part). The Covenant sought to side-step these historical facts by two devices. It claimed that the Palestinian Arabs were part of "the Arab nation" to which the post-First World War allocation was made, and which by 1964 had come to control a dozen new independent States in the Middle East (arts. 14–15). But it also insisted that Palestinians were a separate people entitled to the whole of Palestine as an indivisible territorial unit for its homeland (arts. 1–5).

73. This design still left the problem of how, conceding the emergence of a distinctive Palestinian people only *in the 1960s*, such subsequent events could affect the prior correct application of the "self-determination" or "liberation" principle *in 1919*. To meet that problem the Covenant adopted the ingenious fiction of declaring Palestinian nationhood retrospectively to have existed in 1917. To this end it provided that only Jews who had "normally resided" in Palestine before the "Zionist invasion" (presumably around 1917) could qualify for membership in the Palestinian state, and, by clear implication, that all others would be expelled (arts. 6, 20–23).

74. In order to examine the assumptions on which the "studies" on *Self-Determination* and *Resolutions* proceed, the year 1917 must be utilized for testing the application of the self-determination principle to the Jewish and Arab peoples. At that time none of the present Arab States in the former provinces of the Ottoman Empire in the Middle East had come into existence, so "the Arab Nation", on whose behalf wide-ranging claims were made, was certainly an eligible claimant under that principle. By the same token, however, the Jewish people was also a proper claimant under it. Indeed, historically the Jewish claims began earlier than did the Arab claims. The Emir Feisal, in his well-known letter of March 1919 to Felix Frankfurter, recognized the concurrence of the Jewish and Arab liberation movements. He thanked Chaim Weizmann and other Zionist leaders for being "a great helper of our [the Arab] cause", and expressed the hope that "the Arabs may soon be in a position to make the Jews some return for their

[27] For English translation, see Moore, *op cit.* note 16, at 698, 705.

kindness". And as a signal reminder that, among Arabs too in 1919, there was no distinguisable [sic] Palestinian Arab nationhood, he added: "There is room in *Syria* for us both" (emphasis added).[28]

75. This historical context was clearly set out in the Agreement of Understanding and Co-operation of 3 January 1919 signed by the Emir Feisal, representing Arab national aspirations at the Paris Peace Conference, and Dr. Weizmann, representing the Zionist movement. Its preamble envisaged the closest possible collaboration in the development of "the Arab State and Palestine" as the surest means of "the consummation of their national aspirations". It is obvious from article 1 of that Agreement, providing for the exchange of "Arab and Jewish accredited agents" between "the Arab State" and "Palestine" that what was envisaged was the allocation of "Palestine" for self-determination of the Jewish nation, and of the rest of the region for that of "the Arab nation".[29] The Ottoman Empire was so vast that a dozen independent Arab States came later to be established on it alone. In fact, the Arab claim for territory in which to exercise their right of self-determination extends beyond these dozen Middle East States. Several other States in Asia and North Africa also realize the Arab nation's claim to self-determination. Together these make up the Arab League, which comprises over 20 members today.

76. Thus, no liberty is being taken with history when it is recalled that representatives of the Jewish and Arab national movements presented themselves simultaneously after the First World War as claimants for liberation. Each people, Jewish and Arab, shared within itself cultural and religious traditions and experiences deeply rooted in the Middle East region. The Jewish people claimed one part, Palestine, with which it had nearly four millenia of unbroken connexion, as its historic home. The Arabs claimed virtually the whole of the territories detached after the First World War from the Ottoman Empire. These were the two claimant peoples, the Jews and the Arabs, between whom the Principal Allied and Associated Powers made the territorial allocations which began the modern history of Palestine.

77. The myth propagated in the Palestinian National Covenant that the "Palestinian people" was unjustly displaced by "Jewish invasion" of Palestine is widely disseminated, and in unquestioningly and dogmatically espoused in the United Nations "studies" under consideration. It is therefore necessary to recall not only the Kingdom of David and the Succession of Jewish politics in Palestine down to the Roman conquest and Dispersion, but also the continuous Jewish presence in Palestine even after that conquest. In 1914 the Jews in Palestine were a closely-knit population of almost 100,000.

78. The connexion of the Jews with Palestine is eloquently stressed by the

---

[28] *Ib.*, 43.
[29] *Ib.*, 40. The significance of this document receives little attention in the "studies". Cf. *Origins*, Part I, p. 82, n. 7.

Report of the Royal Commission (headed by the late Lord Peel) in 1937. The zeal with which the "studies" cite passages from that Report fails to include the following:

> While the Jews had thus been dispersed over the world, they had never forgotten Palestine. If Christians have become familiar through the Bible with the physiognomy of the country and its place-names and events that happened more than two thousand years ago, the link which binds the Jews to Palestine and its past history is to them far closer and more intimate. Judaism and its ritual are rooted in those memories. Among countless illustrations it is enough to cite the fact that Jews, wherever they may be, still pray for rain at the season it is needed in Palestine. And the same devotion to the Land of Israel, *Eretz Israel*, the same sense of exile from it, permeates Jewish secular thought. Some of the finest Hebrew poetry written in the Diaspora has been inspired, like the Psalms of the Captivity, by the longing to return to Zion. Nor has the link been merely spiritual or intellectual. Always or almost always since the fall of the Jewish State, some Jews have been living in Palestine. Under Arab rule there were substantial Jewish communities in the chief towns.[30]

79. In terms of modern ideas concerning the liberation of peoples, it is critical to identify the two peoples whose competing claims were adjusted when the future of the former Ottoman territories in the Middle East was being negotiated. For it is fatal to any judgement of justice to misidentify the claimants among whom a territorial distribution is to be made. The facile assertion that Israel came into existence on the basis of an injustice to a *Palestinian nation* proceeds on a gross error of this very kind. In historical fact the Arab claimants after the First World War embraced Arabs of the whole Middle East area, including Arabs in Palestine, who were then in no sense a distinctive national group. The consequence is that now in 1980, to recognize a "Palestinian nation", and to endow it retroactively with an 80-year history as a rival claimant for Palestine, is to play impermissible games with both history and justice.

80. Arab national aspirations were certainly realized in the territorial distribution between Arabs and Jews after the First World War. Arab claims to sovereignty also received extensive fulfilment in the settlements following the Second World War, not only in the Middle East but in other parts of Asia and in Africa as well. Altogether this historical process included the following features:

(a) Despite all the extraneous Great Power manoeuvrings, Jewish and Arab claims in the vast area of the former Ottoman Empire came to the

---

[30] *Report of the Palestine Royal Commission*, Great Britain, Parliamentary Papers, Cmd. 5479 (1937), 8–9. Contrast *Origins*, Part I, pp. 55–57.

forum of liberation *together*, and not (as is usually implied) by way of Jewish encroachment on an already vested and exclusive Arab domain.

(b) The territorial allocation made to the Arabs after the First World War was more than 60 times greater in area, and hundreds of times richer in resources, than the "Palestine" designated in 1917 for the Jewish National Home. Indeed, the area of the territories *ultimately* made available to satisfy the claims of the Arab nation to self-determination is *500* times greater than the area of Israel.

(c) By successive steps after 1917, further encroachments were made upon this already tiny allocation to Jewish claims. As early as 1922, a major part of it (namely 35,468 out of 46,339 square miles, over three quarters) was cut away to establish what was to become the independent Hashemite Kingdom of Transjordan.

81. The liberation principle was thus applied to the rival claims of the Jewish people and the "Arab Nation" in the period following the First World War. Moreover, the principle was applied correctly to the facts of peoplehood then existing, by allocating the overwhelming share of territory and resources of the whole of the Middle East to the Arab nation (including the Palestinian Arabs). This share was ample enough to form in later decades the territorial basis for a dozen independent Arab States. The principle was also applied by allocating to the Jewish people, as part of the same settlement, a minute fraction of the area, embracing both Cisjordan and Transjordan. That tiny fraction was then reduced by four fifths in 1922, leaving the share allotted to the Jewish people under the liberation principle as 10,871 square miles, poor in resources, about one two hundredth of the entire territory distributed. This distribution in no way impaired any right of self-determination of any other nation. As has been seen, neither at the time of distribution, nor until decades later, did any distinct grouping of Palestinian Arabs come to be recognized *as a separate nation* either by themselves, or by other Arabs.

82. This presentation of the historical context belies the attempt in the Palestinian National Covenant, now emulated by the named and anonymous authors of the "studies", to present the Palestinian issue as a struggle which began in 1917 between the Jews of the world on the one hand, and *"Palestinian Arab Nation"* on the other, in which the Jews seized the major share. The underlying error here is the failure to recognize that the liberation principle has to be applied at particular points in time to the facts as they exist at the particular time. The self-determination claim on behalf of Palestinian Arabs was first pressed in United Nations resolutions at the end of the 1960s. If indeed they were wronged by not having been given an appropriate share of the vast territorial allocation made in 1919 to the "Arab Nation", of which they were then and now remain a part, such wrongs must be laid at the door of the dozen sovereign Arab States which arose from the lion's share of the distribution of the territory of the former Ottoman Empire.

83. The detaching in 1922 of four fifths of the territory within which the Jewish National Home was to be established in order to create first the Emirate of Transjordan and subsequently the present Kingdom of Jordan is of double significance in the context of applying the principle of self-determination. On the one hand, as already indicated, it drastically reduced the already tiny allocation for the exercise of the Jewish people's right to self-determination. But, conversely, in addition to satisfying the claims of Hashemite leadership, it provided a reserve of land for Arabs across the River Jordan *in Palestine*. Both Cisjordan and Transjordan made up historic Palestine. Hence the erroneous premise of these "studies" as to the identity of the claimants to self-determination in 1917 immediately gives rise to another dramatic error. That is their assumption that the Palestinian Arabs as a people do not *already* have a homeland and a base for statehood, and that these prerogatives must be wrested from the State of Israel. The fact is that after the First World War Transjordan arose as an encroachment on the small area properly allocated to the Jewish Nation, and subsequently the Jewish National Home provisions of the Mandate were made non-applicable there.[31] Yet these "studies" do not, as far as can be observed, refer to any duty on the part of the Kingdom of Jordan to accommodate the claims of the Palestinian Arabs.

84. The relevant consideration for the application of the self-determination principle in 1980, however, is that the origins and present position of the Arab Kingdom of Jordan in Palestine give the lie to the very claim that the Palestinian people lacks a homeland. Not only did the Kingdom of Jordan arise in Palestine over Jewish protests at the expense of territory allocated for the Jewish nation; it also inexorably became, by the same course of history, a Palestinian Arab State.

85. Therefore, in terms of any meaningful application of the self-determination principle, Jordan was certainly a Palestinian Arab State before 1948. Whether the King and his Palestinian subjects chose to conduct their affairs as a unitary or a federated State, the Palestinian Arabs already had a homeland in the State of Jordan. This reality may be concealed from time to time by the difficult relations between the King and his Palestinian subjects. Yet for much of the period 1948 to 1967, and perhaps until the bloody hostilities with the PLO in 1970, the Palestinian Arabs in the Kingdom of Jordan regarded Jordan as their State. Indeed it seems that in 1970 most Palestinian Arabs sided with the King and his Government against the PLO. That underlying reality continues to this day.

86. The assumption of these "studies" that the existence of Israel deprives the Palestinian Arabs of a national home is thus erroneous. It is understandable that the rejectionist Arab States and the PLO should refuse to entertain

---

[31] It is to be noted that *Origins*, although containing several maps, significantly omits one crucial map, namely the map of Palestine to which the Mandate for Palestine applied; and this, until 1946, included the area now called Jordan, covering almost four fifths of the territory of Mandated Palestine.

any mention of these errors. Only by propagating them can they twist the liberation claims of Palestinian Arabs into a demand against Israel, and move towards their avowed goal of destroying that State.[32] But it is strange that the authors of these "studies" ostensibly engaged in the exposition of international law, should indulge these unjustified positions so unquestioningly.

V. Appeasement of Self-Determination Claims by Redrawing the Boundaries of Sovereign States

87. With apparent pain, the authors of the *Resolutions* study conclude (p. 27) that the Partition resolution was not necessarily void *ab initio* merely because it recognized the "national rights" of the Jewish people as well as those of the Arabs of Palestine:

> The self-determination issue may have been resolved in an unusual manner, but it is not possible to conclude as a matter of law that the particular method of self-determination in two States was invalid *per se*.

Given these writers' premises this does indeed have the air of a major concession. They head the title of their relevant section (p. 39) "The National Rights of the People of Palestine", which implies that there is only one "people of Palestine" entitled to self-determination. It is clear from all they have written, and from all the output of the "Committee on the Exercise of the Inalienable Rights of the Palestinian People" that if there is only one people of Palestine, the Arabs are *the one*. This logical inference conforms openly to the claims of article 6 of the Palestinian National Covenant (1968) that all Jews who had not normally resided in Palestine *before 1917* should be barred from citizenship in the projected Palestinian Arab state and presumably expelled. There is consequently an air of magnanimity in the admission that the Jewish people, as well as the Arabs in Palestine, might be entitled to self-determination. Yet as these authors expatiate on this apparent concession it becomes clear that there is little substance to it.

88. Proceeding throughout as if any resolution of the General Assembly is law (despite their failure, as noted, to provide any foundation for this), the authors review the assertions of Palestinian national identity in General Assembly resolutions since 1970. They then attempt (pp. 46, ff.) to delineate the precise geographical area, presumably within Palestine, "to which Palestinian self-determination applies". Next they struggle to show how two States in Palestine may be warranted by the self-determination principle, despite the fact that the self-determination these authors are vindicating is only that of "the people of Palestine".

---

[32] Thus it was stated in the political programme approved by the Fourth Congress of Al-Fatah (the largest single component within the PLO, headed by Yasser Arafat) held in Damascus at the end of May 1980, that its purpose is "to liberate Palestine completely and to liquidate the Zionist entity politically, economically, militarily, culturally and ideologically" (published by *"al-Liwa"* of Beirut on 2 June 1980).

89. Their solution is regrettably of little comfort either to international law as hitherto understood, or to the State of Israel. What they seriously assert is that the General Assembly now has a new power deriving its legal authority from resolution 2625 (XXV), commonly known as the "Declaration on Principles of International Law Concerning Friendly Relations and Co-operation Among States in Accordance with the Charter of the United Nations" (herein "Declaration on Principles"). Whenever any group hitherto connected with a State asserts a right to self-determination against it, the General Assembly is now purportedly empowered to redraw the frontiers of that State in accordance with the same body's view of the extent to which the Government of the target State "represents" the whole of the people in its territory.

90. In a remarkable *tour de force*, the authors infer this extraordinary power of the General Assembly from the following proviso in the Declaration on Principles:

> Nothing in the foregoing paragraphs shall be construed as authorizing or encouraging any action which would dismember or impair, totally or in part, the territorial integrity or political unity of sovereign and independent States conducting themselves in compliance with the principle of equal rights and self-determination of peoples as described above and thus possessed of a government representing the whole people belonging to the territory without distinction as to race, creed or colour.
>
> *Every State shall refrain from any action aimed at the partial or total disruption of the national unity and territorial integrity of any other State or country* (emphasis supplied).

I do not propose to canvass the question of whether that passage supports any proposition that the General Assembly can by resolution usurp the drastic power of cutting up and even dismantling Member States of the United Nations. Any such assumption transcends the bounds of credulity of both international lawyers and national political leaders.

91. The threat posed to the territorial integrity and political unity and independence of all States by a General Assembly with such omnipotence scarcely needs elaboration. The self-determination principle is now increasingly invoked not merely against Western ex-colonial Powers, but also within and between the populations of new States which have attained independence since the Second World War. Consequently, those States too would become subject to these asserted powers of the General Assembly to make and unmake States by redefining their boundaries.

92. The authors do display some awareness of the dangers to which all States would be exposed by their extraordinary proposal. They try to minimize these dangers by arguing that the case of Israel is *sui generis*. The boundaries of Israel, they contend (p. 47), are merely *de facto* because they exist "at a particular time as a result of military conquest and of illegal an-

nexation". But this egregiously false assertion of both fact and law, lifted almost literally from the first report of the "Committee on the Exercise of the Inalienable Rights of the Palestinian People",[33] ignores the considered opinions to the contrary of many reputable international lawyers, as well as the necessary contrary implications of repeated actions by the General Assembly and the Security Council.

93. If the case of Israel cannot be so cavalierly singled out, then no less a threat is posed to all other States in the international community. Any State with neighbours entertaining predatory designs against it, which are able to find, promote or manipulate any specious "self-determination" claims, will be vulnerable to similar machinations. The sinister game in which the Committee sponsoring these pseudo-scientific "researches" into international law is engaged, is a deep and wide-ranging threat to the whole international legal order and to the United Nations itself.

94. In a pamphlet issued late in 1979, following the *Resolutions* study, the "Committee on the Exercise of the Inalienable Rights of the Palestinian People" made this threat even more explicit. It asks, somewhat disingenuously: "If a series of General Assembly resolutions on the right of self-determination in general has the effect of creating a principle of international law, then do not a series of resolutions on the specific right of self-determination of a particular people create obligations on the part of the international community?"[34] The Committee here frankly reveals its intent to invest General Assembly majorities with binding power to disrupt, dismember, and even destroy the life of sovereign independent States, Members of the United Nations, under the pretext of satisfying self-determination claims of one dissident group or another.

95. The fact that the States which are the intended victims of this draconian power would be picked off one by one in no way alleviates the threat to them all.

96. The *Resolutions* "study" finally and grudgingly admits (p. 47) that Israel's pre-1967 boundaries "may have received some international assent". This is the undeniable implication of Security Council resolution 242 (1967) which clearly contemplates withdrawal of Israel's armed forces only from "territories occupied in the recent conflict", and also affirms the principle of "the sovereignty, territorial integrity and political independence of every State in the area". These provisions of resolution 242 (1967) are set out as bases for the negotiations to be promoted between the States concerned, and they are in full accord with principles of international law. Any other approach, especially one suggesting that the General Assembly has any power under international law to determine the boundaries of Israel, is not merely naive, but is demonstrably unfounded and dangerous.

[33] A/31/35, para. 33.
[34] *The International Status of the Palestinian People (1979)* 27.

VI. The Use of Force and Alleged Liberation Struggles

97. Among the more outrageous assertions in these "studies" is the proposal that any asserted legal right of self-determination gives rise under international law to the legal licence for any people claiming self-determination, and for third States supporting it, to use armed force against a sovereign State in its vindication.

98. At the same time when this supposed legal liberty to use force in liberation struggles was being asserted in the General Assembly against the State of Israel in 1974, the Special Committee on the Question of Defining Aggression was concluding its seven years of labour. No question was more hotly debated than the question whether the use of force in liberation struggles was lawful, notwithstanding the prohibitions of the Charter. That Special Committee was composed of 35 Member States, and it was never suggested that they were not a fair representation of the entire membership of the United Nations. For scholars genuinely concerned about the extent to which the voting behaviour of States in the General Assembly manifests either the *opinio juris sive necessitatis* necessary for the formation of a rule of customary law, or the kind of assent which can be treated as equivalent to consent to be bound by a treaty, these debates are an indispensable and decisive body of research material. The significance of these materials is enhanced by the fact that the General Assembly accepted and endorsed the outcome of the Committee's work.

99. Yet among the material which they invoke against Israel, there is no sign that the authors of the "studies" have evinced the slightest interest in these proceedings which touch so closely their ostensible intellectual concerns. Had they studied the records of the Special Committee and those of the Sixth Committee, or even only resolution 3314 (XXIX), they would certainly have been more guarded before leaping to their simplistic conclusions. They would have found that the practice of States is in stark contrast to the thesis pressed by these researchers, namely, that the "consensus" of States as manifested in repeated General Assembly resolutions makes the contents of those resolutions binding international law. State practice demolishes a point crucial to these "studies", which is that international law today permits the use of armed force in liberation struggles and by third States supporting them.

100. In the seven years during which the General Assembly and the Special Committee debated the question of the use of armed force by peoples struggling for independence and by third States supporting them, various arguments advanced to legitimize the use of force in liberation struggles were considered and rejected. Those arguments asserted, *inter alia*, that Article 51 of the Charter accords "a right of self-defence of peoples and nations against colonial domination", and that the use of force is authorized by an accumulation of recent General Assembly pronouncements, including resolution 1514 (XV) on the Granting of Independence to Colonial Coun-

tries, resolution 2131 (XX) on the Inadmissibility of Intervention in the Domestic Affairs of States and the Protection of their Independence, resolution 2625 (XXV) (the "Declaration on Principles" already mentioned), resolution 2734 (XXV) on the Strengthening of International Security and, finally, resolution 3314 (XXIX) itself on the Definition of Aggression.

101. The crucial provisions of the Definition of Aggression for our purposes are article 3 (g) and article 7. Article 3 (g) of the Definition stigmatizes as an act of aggression:

> The sending by or on behalf of a State of armed bands, groups, irregulars or mercenaries, which carry out acts of armed force against another State of such gravity as to amount to the acts listed above. [i.e. acts constituting "aggression"], or its substantial involvement therein.

In apparent contradiction is article 7:

> Nothing in this Definition, and in particular article 3, could in any way prejudice the right to self-determination, freedom and independence, as derived from the Charter, of peoples forcibly deprived of that right and referred to in the Declaration on Principles of International Law Concerning Friendly Relations and Co-operation Among States in accordance with the Charter of the United Nations, particularly peoples under colonial and racist régimes or other forms of alien domination; nor the right of these peoples to struggle to that end and to seek and receive support, in accordance with the principles of the Charter and in conformity with the above-mentioned Declaration.

102. The full antithesis between the drafts of the self-determination saving clause finally embodied in article 7 and the indirect aggression armed bands provision (art. 3 (g)) emerged late in the course of the deliberations. There were three main earlier drafts of that saving clause. The Soviet draft did not only propose to save the "struggle" for self-determination; it unambiguously went on to make licit "the use of armed force in accordance with the Charter", *including* its use in order to exercise the inherent right of self-determination.[35] The 13-Power (non-aligned) draft, on the other hand, protected the provisions of the Charter as to "the right of peoples to self-determination, sovereignty and territorial integrity", but was not express in stating whether armed force could be used in seeking this right.[36] The six-Power (Western) draft, on the other hand, carefully provided that a non-recognized "political entity" could be considered a victim of aggression only if (a) it was delimited by international boundaries of internationally agreed lines of demarcation, and (b) the "political entity" concerned is not "subject to the authority" of the State alleged to be committing aggression against

---

[35] A/AC.134/L.12, reproduced in the 1971 Report of the Special Committee on the Question of Defining Aggression, *Official Records of the General Assembly, Twenty-sixth Session, Supplement No. 19* (A/8419), 23.

[36] A/AC.134/L.16, *ib.*, 24.

it.[37] This, of course, includes the most characteristic class of self-determination struggles. Some Members resisted even that limited concession towards non-State political entities, and thought that victims of aggression should be limited by definition to States.

103. It was in the context of the failure of the 13-Power draft to free the use of armed bands and other modes of indirect aggression from the stigma of aggression that the provision which ultimately became article 7 of the Definition first appeared. In its original form (as art. 5) the bid to legitimize the *use of force* by non-State groups and by States assisting them was (as in the above Soviet draft) quite explicit. There was nothing in the proposed definition to prevent peoples "from using force and seeking or receiving support and assistance" in exercise of "their inherent right to self-determination in accordance with the principles of the Charter".[38] If those words had survived to the final text of article 7, they would have compensated the proponents of "wars of liberation" for the failure of their bid to free the sending, etc. of armed bands from the stigma of aggression. *But the quoted words did not survive.*

104. In the version of article 7 ultimately adopted, the range of conduct saved from inculpation was narrowed in several significant respects. The reference to "peoples under military occupation" disappeared (a matter especially relevant to the problem of the Middle East). Not "foreign domination" as such, but only "forcible deprivation" of the Charter right of self-determination could justify the right to "struggle". *Above all, article 7 was stripped of any express reference to a right to use force* in the "struggle", and of any right of third States to use force to assist. What remains is the radically reduced formula of "the right of these peoples to struggle to that end".[39] In other words, the States which rejected the view that international law permitted the use of armed bands by non-State political entities, or of force by States assisting them under the banner of "self-determination" or "liberation", won the day, while those States which tried to claim that international law had legalized such uses of force were simply outnumbered and failed.

105. The Definition of Aggression, therefore, was established against the background of those very General Assembly resolutions which the researchers of the "Committee on the Exercise of the Inalienable Rights of the Palestinian People" assert have established rules of international law legalizing the use of force in self-determination struggles. The attitudes of the States participating in the Special Committee, whose work was subsequently en-

---

[37] A/AC.134/L.17, *ib.*, 26. The texts of this and the other earlier drafts are reprinted in *Official Records of the General Assembly, Twenty-eighth Session, Supplement No, 19* (A/9019), 7–12, from Annex 1 to the 1967 Committee's 1970 Report, *Official Records of the General Assembly, Twenty-fifth Session, Supplement No. 19* (A/5019), 55–60.

[38] See the Committee's 1973 Report, *Official Records of the General Assembly, Twenty-eighth Session, Supplement No. 19* (A/9019), 16, 17.

[39] Grammatically, it is not clear what "to that end" refers to—presumably "the right of self-determination, etc."

dorsed by the General Assembly, clearly show that this claim is wrong. In three critical respects, the text finally adopted *absolutely denies* any such claim. First, the Definition deliberately omits mention of any right to use force in self-determination struggles. Second, no right to receive assistance by way of force from third States is expressed or implied. Third, all reference to "peoples under military occupation" was removed. On all these counts spurious claims such as those asserted in the "studies" were decisively rejected by a preponderance of States clearly not limited to Western States.

VII. Israel's Rights under International Law Arising from Lawful Self-Defence Against Arab Aggression

106. Any legal import of any of the United Nations resolutions discussed so far cannot operate in a vacuum. Its effects must be determined by reference to the context of the rights and duties of the States concerned under general international law, including the provisions of the Charter and any pertinent binding determinations of the Security Council.

107. Although some may wish it otherwise, it is an axiom of international law, even under the Charter, that States live within an international legal order in which force is *not* the monopoly of the organized community, but rather is under the control of individual nations. In the absence of predominant community force there has been a constant accumulation of force (notably military potential) in the control of individual States. The most that can be done in support of legal order and community is to marshal, on occasion, some private forces against others for public ends. Unfortunately, the fact is that such forces are from time to time marshalled *against* the international legal order. It is for these reasons that international law has always given legal effect *ex post facto* to the outcomes of its collision with the overwhelming power of individual States. By allowing the military victor through an imposed treaty of peace to incorporate his terms into the body of international law, international law at least preserved the rest of its rules and ensured its own continued existence.

108. In international law until recently, these legal positions held for the relations between States, whether the victor was himself an aggressor or whether the victor was an innocent victim of aggression, responding by way of legitimate self-defence. The recent modification of this position, especially under the Covenant of the League of Nations and Charter of the United Nations, arises from the application of the principle *ex injuria non oritur jus*. Whether applied to treaties procured through duress, or the acquisition of territory, this modification seeks to strip of legal effect, not the use of force as such, but the *unlawful* use of force.

109. From its inception, Israel has maintained an unusually strong record of compliance with international law despite ceaseless provocations by its neighbours. It was armed aggression by Arab States (denounced as such in the Security Council) which aborted the Partition Plan accepted by the Jewish people in 1947. From that point onward, to President Sadat's journey to

Jerusalem in 1977 in response to Prime Minister Begin's invitation, Egypt as well as other Arab States persisited in maintaining a state of belligerency against Israel. For three decades they flouted their basic obligations as Members of the United Nations to refrain from the threat or use of force and armed attack against Israel's independence and territorial integrity. They did so not merely by wars and threats of wars; the also gave shelter to and promoted attacks by armed bands against Israel from Syria, Egyptian-controlled Gaza, Jordan and Lebanon. Those terrorist attacks massacred and maimed hundreds of innocent men, women and children. From Jordan first and subsequently from Lebanon, the PLO and its associated terror organizations have operated for years since 1967 aided and abetted by their Arab hosts and other Arab States. This situation was re-endorsed by the Members of the Arab League at their Tunis Conference as recently as 22 November 1979.

110. Israel's repeated requests, directly or to the United Nations, that these unlawful attacks be stopped have been left unanswered. Its own military actions in southern Lebanon were accordingly designed to abate them. Its actions conform to international law, as set out, for example, in such an authoritative work as Oppenheim's *International Law* edited by Sir Hersch Lauterpacht. That work states that on failure of the host State to prevent or, on notice, to abate these attacks, "a case of necessity arises and the threatened State is justified in invading the neighbouring country and disarming the intending raiders".[40] This rule of international law makes clear that this is a case of necessity, of self-defence, authorizing a State to enter another and destroy or remove the weaponry and bases being used against it. Majorities in the United Nations organs which, from time to time, have purported to condemn such responses by Israel, have no competence to alter such fundamental precepts of international law. This is especially so when the actual conduct of States observed in the international community bears no relation to the norms of conduct proscribed in those resolutions. No State has yet abandoned its inherent right of self-defence, preserved in Article 51 of the Charter.

111. After cease-fires were accepted by the Arab States concerned in the 1967 and 1973 wars, the illegality of continued hostilities by them became (if possible) even more heinous. Their continued hostilities flouted not only the Charter, but the very cease-fire agreements for which they had supplicated and which they had solemnly accepted. Here again, the fact that Soviet and other pro-Arab interests in the United Nations were able to marshal majorities to shield those illegalities from censure in no way sanctioned them or impugned the legality of Israel's responses.

112. All the States concerned (including Israel) are Members of the United Nations, bound by the Charter. Refusal by a Member to acknowledge the *statehood* and *Membership* of a State duly admitted is incompatible

[40] Oppenheim-Lauterpacht, *International Law*, vol. 1, para. 130.

with the Charter, and in particular with Article 2, paragraph 1, enshrining the principle of the sovereign equality of all Members. This is surely *a fortiori* so when the refusal, as in the case of several Arab States denying Israel's right to exist, carries with it the claim to be at liberty to destroy that State by force, despite Article 2, paragraph 4, of the Charter. However one interprets that difficult text, the openly articulated claims of Arab States since 1948 to destroy Israel or, as their jargon has it today, "to liquidate the Zionist entity", violate Charter prohibitions against the threat or use of force, and the positive duties implied in Article 2, paragraph 1, and elsewhere concerning the assurance to Israel of the benefits of membership, and the peaceful settlement of disputes.[41]

113. The basic precept of international law concerning the rights of a State which has been the victim of aggression, and which is lawfully administering territory of the attacking State, is also clear. The precept *ex injuria non oritur jus* holds that a lawful occupant such as Israel is entitled to remain in control of the territory involved pending conclusion of a treaty of peace. Security Council resolutions 242 (1967) and 338 (1973), adopted after the respective wars of those years, expressed this requirement for settlement by negotiations between the parties, the latter resolution using those very words. Through the decade 1967–1977, the Arab States and the Arab League compounded the illegality of their continued hostilities by proclaiming at their Khartoum Summit in September 1967, the notorious three "No's": no recognition of, no peace and no negotiation with Israel.[42] This effectively blocked the regular processes for post-war pacification and settlement.

114. In the meanwhile, oil pressure upon countries throughout the globe, and the propaganda machines of the Arab-Soviet blocs, set out to blur and if possible expunge all record of these gross illegalities. Though the general law (as well as resolutions 242 and 338) required the Arab States to negotiate with Israel among other things the extent of Israel's withdrawal from territories, those States demanded withdrawal from *all* the territories *before negotiation*. There is no historical instance in which aggressor States have been granted that kind of prerogative after the defect of their aggression.

115. Israel's territorial rights after 1967 are best seen by contrasting them with Jordan's lack of rights in Jerusalem and Judea and Samaria (the West Bank) after the Arab invasion of Palestine in 1948. The presence of Jordan in Jerusalem and elsewhere in Cisjordan from 1948 to 1967 was only by virtue of its illegal entry and occupation in 1948. Under the international law principle *ex injuria non oritur jus* Jordan acquired no legal title. Egypt itself denied Jordanian sovereignty and never tried to claim Gaza as Egyptian territory.

---

[41] Cf. Q. Wright, "Legal Impacts of the Middle East Situation" (1968) 33 *Law and Contemporary Problems* 5, 17.

[42] Moore, *op. cit.* in note 16, at 788.

116. By contrast, Israel's presence in all those areas pending the conclusion of negotiations for the establishment of secure and recognized boundaries is entirely lawful, since Israel entered those areas legally in exercise of its inherent right of self-defence. International law forbids acquisition of territory *by unlawful force*, but not where, as in this case, the entry into the territory was lawful. In particular, it does not forbid it when force is used to stop an aggressor, for the effect of such prohibition would be to guarantee to all potential aggressors that, even if their aggression failed, all territory lost in the attempt would be automatically returned to them. Such a rule would, of course, be utterly absurd.

117. International law, therefore, supports on three counts Israel's claim that it is under no obligation to hand the territories back automatically to Jordan or any other State. First, those lands never legally belonged to Jordan. Second, even if they had, Israel's present control is lawful, and it is entitled to negotiate the extent and the terms of its withdrawal. Third, international law would not in such circumstances require the automatic handing back of territory even to an aggressor who was the former lawful sovereign, which Jordan certainly was not. It requires the extent and conditions of the handing back to be negotiated between the parties.

118. As many have shown, all attempts to amend the draft of Security Council resolution 242 of 1967 so as explicitly to call for Israel to withdraw to the 1967 frontiers, failed.[43] That resolution did not call for withdrawal from *all* territories occupied in the 1967 War, but only withdrawal to lines to be negotiated, which were then to become "secure and recognised boundaries". Indeed, any other provision would have been at odds with the plain fact that, immediately after the War, at the 1,360th meeting of the Security Council on 14 June 1967, the Soviet resolution seeking to brand Israel as the aggressor was rejected by 11 votes to four. Also, the General Assembly at its 1,548th meeting of 4 July 1967, long before the entry of the oil weapon into that voting arena, also repeatedly refused to endorse such a proposition.[44]

119. Because the operative parts of resolution 242 are so explicit, Arab arguments began to focus on the preamble which refers to "the inadmissibility of the acquisition of territory by war", in the hope of weakening through that delphic phrase the clear international legal basis of Israel's territorial standing in the territories. They have had to argue that this phrase must be taken literally in its widest sense. Having stretched it in this way, they extract from it a meaning which other States have not been willing to

[43] Stone, *No Peace-No War in the Middle East* (1969), 34–35. Also A. Lall, *The United Nations and the Middle East Crisis* (1967), *passim.*

[44] See *Official Records of the Security Council, Twenty-second Year*, 1360th meeting at 18. In the General Assembly the majorities rejecting (including abstentions in each case) were of the order of 88 against 32, 98 against 22, 81 against 36, and 80 against 36. *Official Records of the General Assembly, Fifth Emergency Special Session*, 1548th plenary meeting, 14–16. And see Stone, *The Middle East under Cease-Fire* (1967), Sections II–IX, at 2–40.

accept. That meaning indeed yields such absurd results that while they press it against Israel, they implicitly deny its application to themselves.

120. The international lawyer, faced with this recital in the preamble to resolution 242 juxtaposed with its operative provisions, will recognize no less than three logically possible interpretations. He must ask which of them makes sense in its immediate context, bearing in mind the existing principles of international law, and what many call the "world order" policies underlying those principles.

121. The Arab States' interpretation is one logical possibility, and it does yield their desired result, that Israel must automatically and fully withdraw from all the territories, *however perfectly lawful its presence there*. A second interpretation is that the recital merely recalls, with the eloquent flourish common in preambles, the established *ex injuria* principle of international law as this applies to unlawful war. In this reading, "acquisition . . . by war" would refer to the initiation of war *for the purpose of* acquiring territory; such initiation, being unlawful, would bring the *ex injuria* principle into play. Israel's action being in self-defence, this principle would in no way affect its rights under international law as set out above. Third, no less plausibly, the recital could be a restatement of the rather commonplace technical principle of international law that mere occupation of territory does not itself vest in the occupant sovereign title over it. Transfer of title requires some further act, such as formal annexation or cession by a treaty of peace or other accepted instrument. That third meaning would fit particularly well the operative provisions calling for negotiations on such matters as "secure and recognised boundaries", the fixing of "demilitarised zones", and the like, and again would not affect Israel's rights as set out herein.

122. As indicated, the first interpretation, favoured by the Arab States, would be at odds with the operative provisions of resolution 242. Moreover, it would conflict with existing international law. It could scarcely be regarded as an amendment of the law, offered by the Security Council *de lege ferenda* for the future. For, in that eventuality, the recital would mean that an occupant must withdraw even before peace terms are agreed, even if he entered lawfully in self-defence against an aggressor. A rule presented *de lege ferenda* must by definition be a rule the consequences of which would be regarded as desirable for all members of the community generally. But it is apparent that this *proposed* rule would be disastrous and undesirable. It would assure every prospective aggressor that, if he fails, he will be entitled to the restoration of every inch of any territory he may have lost. This proposed rule would yield this result even if the defeated aggressor still openly reserves the liberty to renew his aggressive design, and even if the territories concerned had been seized unlawfully by the claimants, who have consistently used them since as a base for aggressive activity against the present occupant. In short, that interpretation would unconditionally underwrite the risks of loss from any contemplated aggression. Such a rule would turn *ex injuria* principle on its head: rather than discourage aggressors, it would

positively encourage them. To put forward such a rule *de lege ferenda* is to sanction a new and cynical legal maxim which might run: "If you cannot stop the aggressor, help him!" The interpretation yielding such a result cannot, therefore, be accepted when two others, each more consonant with both international law and common sense are, as shown above, readily available.

123. In this connexion, it must be added regarding both Egypt in Gaza and Jordan in Judea and Samaria, that even if their entry had not been unlawful or in defiance of the Security Council's cease-fire and truce resolutions of April and May 1948, the proposed rule would bar any right of theirs to remain in those territories. For in those circumstances their continued presence would fall within the meaning they seek to give to "the inadmissibility of the acquisition of territory by war". The consequence is that even were the rule now newly adopted with retrospective effect, it could not improve *their* present legal position vis-à-vis Israel except by an entirely unprincipled discriminatory application of the new rule in favour of—or rather against—one side only.[45]

124. Finally, it should be noted that this kind of Arab activity, designed to "amend" international law for *ad hoc* use against Israel, has become persistent since 1967 in all organs and contexts of international activity. The work of the 1967 Special Committee on the Question of Defining Aggression has already been discussed at length in another context (paras. 97–105). But of relevance here is the fact that its work was also characterized by efforts on the part of the Arab States to include a provision that territorial acquisition *even by lawful force* would be invalid. Those efforts failed abjectly.[46]

125. The only operative provision concerning acquisition of territory by force (art. 5, para. 3) strictly limits any invalidity by imposing no less than three requirements: (1) It is not acquisition by mere threat or use of force, but only acquisition by "aggression", which is invalid, so entry in the course of self-defence as in the case of Israel in 1967 would not be proscribed. (2) The acts of force there enumerated (in arts. 2 and 3) are stated to be aggression only *if first committed* by the occupant, thus doubly excluding acts in self-defence from the taint. (3) Even such acts, to be tainted, must be "in contravention of the Charter", thus triply excluding acts of self-defence.

126. Through all the meetings of the Special Committee and of the Sixth Committee of the General Assembly between 1967 and 1974, a version of the rule concerning acquisition of territory by force based on the principle *ex injuria non oritur jus* maintained itself against all Arab efforts to mutate it into a tool for condemning Israel. The attempt to twist this principle of

---

[45] Cf. A. Lall, *op. cit.*, in note 43, citing Abba Eban in the Security Council, *Official Records of the Security Council, Twenty-second Year*, 1375th meeting (13 November 1967), para. 49.

[46] See the analysis of the drafting in Stone, *Conflict Through Consensus* (1977) 55–56. The Thirteen-Power draft ("Third World" draft) (A/AC.134/L.16 and Add.1 and 2), para. 8, had proposed a text harmonious with the Arab position. It was not followed.

international law for *ad hoc* use against one particular State thus wholly failed. This must be attributed not simply to the legal skills and learning of most State representatives but also to a keen awareness by many of them of the dangers to their own security likely to ensue from a change in international law of which the operative implications are, as shown, quite absurd.[47]

Julius Stone

10 June 1980   Sydney, New South Wales

APPENDIX

Political Bias in Legal Argument: The Mallison Study

1. The foregoing memorandum establishes the international law context, including the prevailing rules as to the territorial entitlements of States, in situations emerging from the lawful and unlawful use of force. In the same context it examines the assumptions of the Mallisons in their *Resolutions* "study" concerning the legal effects of the General Assembly resolutions. A conscientious inquiry in the context of international law is also what those authors *claim* to pursue in their "study". It is thus dismaying to find that major questions and principles which have been shown to be part of the essential international legal context of the matters they discuss receive virtually no consideration or even mention from these authors. Moreover, where, as with the question of the legal value to be attributed to General Assembly resolutions, they do consider this context, their consideration is slim, if not perfunctory, and ignores most of the authorities. In the end they patently beg the question. In this, the Mallison "study" is no different than the three anonymous "studies" which preceded it. The following exposition highlights some of their more egregious errors in fact and law. It is meant to be illustrative, and is by no means exhaustive.

2. The authors presumably are not aware of some of their inadequacies. But other inadequacies are highlighted by them in their introduction. One of these is their declaration (p. v) that "consistent with the consulting arrangements with the United Nations, no direct use has been made of the formal negotiation history of the resolutions or of the informal unrecorded consultation which led to the adoption of particular wording".[1] Consultation

---

[47] After the above failure of their main efforts, the Arab States then sought the inclusion in paragraph 20 of the Special Committee's Report of an enigmatic Note 4: "With reference to the third paragraph of article 5 . . . this paragraph should not be construed so as to prejudice the established principle of international law relating to the inadmissibility of territorial acquisition resulting from the threat or use of force." *Official Records of the General Assembly, Twenty-Ninth Session, Supplement No. 19* (A/9619 and Corr.1). Since, as indicated, international law is precisely what article 5 affirmed, the purport of the note seems to be to keep alive the precise words of the relevant recital of resolution 242, in the hope presumably that its *superficial* ambiguity could continue to be exploited by the Arab side in the Middle East conflict. See Stone, *op. cit.*, note 46, at 63–64.

[1] A curiosity within a curiosity. That remark presumably refers to *travaux préparatoires* available other than in official United Nations records. Sed quaere? It is positively startling later to find the authors deliberately invoking the negotiating history of the Palestine Mandate to make a point which they believe favourable to Arab claims (p. 26).

of the *travaux préparatoires* is an essential part of international techniques of interpretation. The reader is entitled to wonder why either any United Nations officials of the "Committee on the Exercise of the Inalienable Rights of the Palestinian People", or these authors, should wish to renounce it. This is especially so since such preparatory materials are sometimes critical to the issues on which the authors engage. As Lord Caradon himself testified, for example, the legislative history is essential background for understanding the effect of the references to withdrawal of Israel's armed forces in Security Council resolution 242.[2] They are equally essential to ascertaining the meaning of references to acquisition of territory by force in contravention of the Charter in the General Assembly's Definition of Aggression.

3. The Mallisons' renunciation of the *travaux* was not necessarily inspired by a sense that foreshortened inquiries would yield better results for their particular theses [*sic*]. However, no such neutral explanation is plausible for another statement in their introduction, namely:

> The terms "Jew" and "Jewish" are used to refer to adherents of a particular monotheistic religion of universal moral values. The terms "Zionism" and "Zionist" refer to a particular national movement, with its political programme of first "a national home" and then a national state located in Palestine.

The authors innocently declare that *this is a "basic distinction" which it is necessary to make "because this is a juridical study"* (p. v). But it is no more "basic" from a juridical point of view than an analogous distinction between "Irishmen as adherents to a particular form of Christian Catholicism", and some other term for those "who are adherents to a political programme of securing (formerly) the independence of Ireland, or now of Northern Ireland". The authors are certainly aware that the designations "Zionism" and "Zionist" have been falsely and arbitrarily translated into "racist" by one of the most lamentable resolutions of the General Assembly (3379 (XXX)). It is just such resolutions which they are attempting to extricate from the morass of international politics to the more sheltered level of international law. No reputable international lawyer has accepted that meretricious pronouncement as other than an adventure in expedient pejoration. The authors should, as international lawyers, have avoided demeaning their brief in this way, especially since it is difficult to find any important legal argument of theirs which would not be equally strong (or equally weak) without this so-called "basic distinction".[3]

4. On the other hand, there is another distinction which would indeed

---

[2] See Stone, *No Peace-No War in the Middle East* (1969), pp. 33–35.

[3] The only real use the authors seek to make of this supposedly "basic juridical distinction" is for ventilating some criticisms of the early Jewish liberation movement, or of Israel by isolated Jewish individuals and a few extreme Jewish religious sects. See *Resolutions*, pp. 9–14, *passim*. Whatever else is to be said about this, it is in no sense "juridically basic" to the Mallisons' terms of reference.

have been "basic", not only for the Mallisons' juridical "study" but also for their exposition of what they claim (pp. 9–17) to be "the background of the Partition Resolution". That is the distinction in time, demonstrated earlier, between what they in 1979 identify as "the Palestinian Nation", on the one hand, and the "Arab Nation" of 1917, on the other. That distinction is no invention of the present writer, for as seen the "Palestinian National Covenant" insists precisely on it. The Mallisons may or may not agree with my conclusion that the burden of redress due to the Palestinian Arabs, like the redress due to Jews displaced by this distribution, should be shared equitably between the Arab States of the Middle East and Israel. *But it is difficult to see how they could fail to address themselves at all* to a distinction so relevant and central, and at the same time so damaging by its omission to both the structure of their argument and its main conclusions.

5. A further observation is called for particularly in the light of the Mallisons' dogged efforts (sometimes even to the point of misquoting important documents) to show that the General Assembly's Partition Resolution is "the pre-eminent juridical basis for the State of Israel", and that Israel is bound by that resolution even though the Arab States rejected it and, by blatant acts of armed aggression, wholly aborted its operation. The Mallisons have, as shown, an exalted if somewhat undiscriminating view of the legal effects of General Assembly resolutions. They are particularly enthusiastic about the Partition Resolution. But there is one central provision of that resolution, reference to which they asiduously avoid. That is the General Assembly's request that: "The Security Council determine as a threat to the peace, breach of the peace or act of aggression, in accordance with Article 39 of the Charter, any attempt to alter by force the settlement envisaged by this resolution." By this omission, they are able to ignore the consequences of the Arab side's rejection of the resolution, and their armed aggression against it and against Israel, which prevented it ever coming into legal operation. Such consideration, had it been given, would, as demonstrated in the memorandum have proved fatal for the main legal conclusions to which the Mallisons seek to lead their readers.

6. Perhaps these unfortunate lapses in purportedly objective "studies" are explained in part by the need of the "Committee on the Exercise of the Inalienable Rights of the Palestinian People" to find lawyers whose known opinions on the issues would produce the conclusions desired by the Committee. One dramatic instance of reliance on very questionable sources appears in *Origins*, Part I, pp. 35 ff., in relation to the "validity" of the Palestine Mandate. The Committee there can apparently only marshall two writers to support the desired conclusion. One is Mr. Henry Cattan, a former member of the Arab Higher Committee in Palestine. The other is our familiar Professor W. T. Mallison, who has written introductions to works by H. Cattan. The reader can assess for himself the scholarly and dispassionate objectivity of such manoeuvring.

168. Excerpt from the Resolutions Adopted by the
Conference of Foreign Ministers of Islamic Countries at an
Extraordinary Session to Discuss the Present Situation in
Occupied Palestine, Amman, July 11–12, 1980*

---

* 10 J. Palestine Stud. 199 (Winter 1981).

After study and discussion of recent developments in occupied Palestine, and having heard the various opinions, proposals and working papers that were submitted, the Conference adopted the following resolutions:

1. The Conference affirmed the inalienable national rights of the Palestinian people in their homeland, Palestine, and in particular their right to self-determination without outside interference and to establish their independent state on the soil of their homeland, and the right of the Palestinian people to continue their legitimate struggle to liberate their homeland and recover their rights in conformity with the relevant UN resolutions, under the leadership of the PLO, their sole legitimate representative both inside and outside the occupied homeland.

2. The Conference reaffirmed previous resolutions, and in particular the resolutions of the Eleventh Conference in Islamabad, on the Palestine question and Jerusalem. The Conference also affirmed that a just peace in the Middle East can only be established on the basis of the full and unconditional withdrawal of the Israeli enemy from all the Palestinian and Arab occupied territories, and first and foremost Jerusalem, the capital of Palestine, and of the Palestinian people being enabled to exercise their inalienable national rights in conformity with the relevant UN resolutions, and in particular resolutions 3236 and 3237.

3. The Conference condemned the official and organized racist, expansionist and terrorist policies being pursued by the enemy authorities in occupied Palestine, regarding these as a defiance of the will of the Islamic world and a flagrant violation of international law. In this context, the Conference affirmed that any state which supports Israeli aggression against the Palestinian people and the Islamic holy places in Palestine is the enemy of Islam and the Muslims.

4. The Conference affirmed the commitment of all Islamic states to sever all kinds of relations with any state that supports the Israeli enemy's decision to annex Jerusalem and to regard it as the capital of its entity, or that participates in the implementation of that decision, or transfers its embassy there.

The Conference called on those states that have established their diplomatic missions in Jerusalem to transfer them, and in the event of their not responding, the next Conference of Foreign Ministers will study what measures and moves should be adopted against them, including the severing of diplomatic relations.

5. The Conference decided to form a committee of legal experts to study what measures should be taken vis-à-vis the crimes that the Israeli enemy is committing as a war criminal in occupied Palestine.

6. The Conference affirmed the commitment of member states to supply the necessary support and to increase it, to assist the Palestinian people to hold out and endure in their homeland, and called on the Islamic peoples to participate in this support.

7. The Conference condemned the Israeli enemy for its continuing ag-

gression against Lebanon, especially in the South, and affirmed its support for the unity of the territory and people of Lebanon and for its independence and sovereignty, and for its efforts to restore its legitimate authority over all Lebanese territory.

8. The Conference called on the UN General Assembly, when it meets in its next session, as regards Palestine, to study ways and means—including the imposition of sanctions under Chapter VII of the UN Charter—of securing the implementation of the General Assembly resolutions on Palestine, and in particular resolution 3236, as being the basis of the solution of the Palestine question, and to take the necessary measures, in view of the fact that the Security Council has proved unable to secure the implementation of these resolutions.

9. The Conference called on the European Community to terminate its bilateral and collective economic agreements with Israel, in implementation of its undertakings that these agreements should not be applicable to the Palestinian and Arab occupied territories, and so as to induce Israel to withdraw from these territories.

10. The Conference condemned the US policy of supporting the Israeli occupation authorities in their settlement policies and aggressive practices, and the US position, in international forums, of support for Israel against Palestinian rights in a manner which is not in conformity with the UN Charter, the General Assembly resolutions and the Declaration of Human Rights.

169. **Speech Before the U.N. General Assembly by the President of the European Council Concerning the Stand Taken by the European Community on the Palestine Issue, July 24, 1980***

---

* 13 Bull. Eur. Comm. (No. 7/8) 85 (1980).

'The nine member countries of the European Community, on whose behalf I have the honour to address you today, have watched with distress the developments taking place in this tormented region. They deeply regret the hardening of positions on both sides, whereas only dialogue and a spirit of understanding can clear the way to peace.

They have frequently made known their views before this Assembly through a joint spokesman or the heads of the individual delegations.

They consider today that it is more important than ever that Europe should make itself heard and work in a more concrete way for a return to peace. That is the aim of the declaration issued on 13 June[2] by the nine countries of the European Community after the European Council meeting at Venice.

Quite clearly—and I should like to stress this point—the statement by the nine member countries of the European Community is fundamentally rooted in their concern to promote and encourage a comprehensive solution to the Israel-Arab conflict. In this connection the Nine are determined to encourage all positive initiatives whatever their sources.

But they consider that the close traditional ties and common interests binding Europe to the Middle East compel them to enter the search for a peaceful solution.

Too much passion, suffering and hate has accumulated in a land which had seemed promised a future of concord and fraternity between its peoples. It is time for an end to the language of violence and for all the parties to start talking to one another as equals. And it is time to move from rhetoric to the negotiation of terms and arrangements for restoring peace.

It is in this context that the declaration issued at Venice is to be regarded. There must be an end to ambiguities and a coming to terms with the realities which we have been only too inclined to fudge hitherto. Those realities are the State of Israel and the Palestinian people. The solution to the Middle Eastern problem lies in reconciling these two essential realities and enabling them to coexist.

In the view of the nine member countries of the European Community, two fundamental principles rule the search for a comprehensive peace settlement:

· the right to existence and security of all States in the region, including Israel;
· justice for all the peoples, which implies recognition of the legitimate rights of the Palestinian people.

Everything follows logically from this basic requirement. Firstly, as set out in the Venice declaration, "all the countries in the area are entitled to live in peace within secure, recognized and guaranteed borders. The necessary guarantees for a peace settlement should be provided by the UN by a deci-

[2] Bull. EC 6-1980, point 1.1.6.

sion of the Security Council and, if necessary, on the basis of other mutually agreed procedures. The Nine declare that they are prepared to participate within the framework of a comprehensive settlement in a system of concrete and binding international guarantees, including (guarantees) on the ground".

Secondly, "a just solution must finally be found to the Palestinian problem, which is not simply one of refugees. The Palestinian people, who are conscious of existing as such, must be placed in a position, by an appropriate process defined within the framework of the comprehensive peace settlement, to exercise fully their right to self-determination".

The negotiations which are to lead to a comprehensive peace settlement will be based on the recognition and implementation of Israel's right to existence and security and the right of the Palestinian people to self-determination. Within the framework of the settlement Israel will have to put an end to the territorial occupation which it has maintained since the conflict of 1967. Under such a settlement it will also be possible to define frontiers for the State of Israel which will be internationally recognized and guaranteed.

The Nine are convinced that no comprehensive and lasting peace settlement is possible in the Middle East if the occupation of territories by force continues.

They are also convinced that the Israeli settlements constitute a serious obstacle to the peace process. Likewise recognizing the special significance of the question of Jerusalem for all the parties concerned, they will not accept any initiative designed to change that city's status, and stress that any agreement on its status should guarantee freedom of access to the Holy Places for everyone.

The Nine consider the renunciation of violence a precondition for constructive negotiations. It is necessary to create a climate of trust, which is vital if a just and equitable solution is to be found to the conflict in the Middle East.

Those are the bases and principles upon which the member countries of the European Community will endeavour to seek a peace settlement. These principles apply to all the parties concerned, and that includes the Palestinian people and the PLO, which will have to be involved in the negotiations.

The Nine have decided to establish the necessary contacts with those parties to find out how they stand and to determine, in the light of the outcome of the consultations, what form an initiative on their part might take.

The day before yesterday the foreign ministers of the European Community approved the detailed arrangements for the round of contacts which I am to have the privilege—and also the grave responsibility—of conducting personally in my capacity as current President of the Council. I will be setting off shortly, and the Nine are aware that the contacts with all the parties concerned will be imbued with the feelings of friendship and cooperation which characterize the traditional links between Europe and the Middle East.

I have just indicated the standpoint and concerns of the nine member countries of the European Community on the conflict in the Middle East. It is on that basis that those countries will be participating in this session. Unfortunately they do not feel that the draft resolution which has been distributed contributes to the search for a comprehensive, just and lasting solution which they advocate.

As you are aware, the Nine have always supported Security Council resolution 242, and continue to do so vigorously. They recognize that the resolution has shortcomings, particularly with regard to the Palestinian people, and they have made their attitude on that point known several times. Nevertheless, despite that failing, the basic principles set out in resolution 242 remain fundamentally relevant to any settlement of the conflict. It would therefore be essential for any resolution adopted during this session to refer explicitly to resolution 242 and not to contradict it, as would be the case if Israel were simply exhorted and invited to negotiate without being offered the necessary guarantees for its existence.

The Nine will determine their votes in this session in accordance with the general criteria I have just indicated. But I should like to express the hope that the results of this session will ultimately contribute to pacification rather than confrontation.

The Nine are convinced that only through negotiation can peace be restored to a region which has suffered all too greatly from bloody strife.

In conclusion, I should like to emphasize the will of Europe, as an independent, unanimous and committed political force, to work in a concrete way for a return to peace, and to do this we must create a climate of trust, in other words abandon all extremist positions. I shall be calling upon all those I meet to show understanding and engage in dialogue, in the conviction that this will pave the way towards peace.'

170. House of Representatives Resolution 748 on

Palestinian Women as a Separate Issue at the U.N.

Mid-Decade Conference for Women, July 29, 1980*

---

* H.R. Res. 748, 96th Cong., 2d Sess., 126 Cong. Rec. 20048 (1980).

Whereas the World Conference of the United Nations Decade for Women: Equality, Development and Peace, is currently meeting in Copenhagen, Denmark;

Whereas the principal aims of the Conference are to review and evaluate the progress made and obstacles faced by women in member states of the United Nations in improving their access to health, educational opportunities, and employment;

Whereas the agenda of the Conference also includes items on women refugees, the effect of apartheid on women, and the situation of Palestinian women in the occupied territories;

Whereas a document drafted by the Economic Commission for West Asia on the subject of Palestinian women for discussion in relation to agenda items on the same subject threatens to detract from the positive results that could emerge in achieving the principal aims of the Conference and of the United Nations Decade for Women; and

Whereas United Nations foreign policy interests are best served by the positive results of constructive resolutions that could emerge from the Conference including a reaffirmation of the World Plan of Action for the Integration of Women in societies throughout the world: Now, therefore, be it

Resolved, That it is the sense of the House of Representatives that—

(1) the United States delegation to the Copenhagen Conference on the United Nations Decade for Women should support appropriate resolutions on the principal agenda items relating to health, education, and employment;

(2) the United States delegation should oppose any resolutions or amendments introduced at the Copenhagen Conference on issues which do not directly relate to the goals of the Conference, such as the separate issue of Palestinian women, and should work actively with other delegations to ensure that they voice similar opposition; and

(3) the United States delegation should report to the Congress on the results of the Conference.

171. General Assembly Resolution ES-7/2 on the Question of Palestine, July 29, 1980*

---

* G.A. Res. ES-7/2, ES-7 U.N. GAOR Supp. (No. 1) at 3, U.N. Doc. A/ES-7/14.

The General Assembly,

Having considered the question of Palestine at an emergency special session,

Convinced that the failure to solve this question poses a grave threat to international peace and security,

Noting with regret and concern that the Security Council, at its 2220th meeting on 30 April 1980, failed to take a decision, as a result of the negative vote of the United States of America, on the recommendations of the Committee on the Exercise of the Inalienable Rights of the Palestinian People endorsed by the General Assembly in its resolutions 31/20 of 24 November 1976, 32/40 A of 2 December 1977, 33/28 A of 7 December 1978 and 34/65 A of 29 November 1979,

Having considered the letter dated 1 July 1980 from the Permanent Representative of Senegal to the United Nations, Chairman of the Committee on the Exercise of the Inalienable Rights of the Palestinian People,[4]

Having heard the statement by the Observer of the Palestine Liberation Organization, the representative of the Palestinian people,[5]

1. *Recalls and reaffirms* its resolutions 3236 (XXIX) and 3237 (XXIX) of 22 November 1974 and all other relevant United Nations resolutions pertinent to the question of Palestine;

2. *Reaffirms,* in particular, that a comprehensive, just and lasting peace in the Middle East cannot be established, in accordance with the Charter of the United Nations and the relevant United Nations resolutions, without the withdrawal of Israel from all the occupied Palestinian and other Arab territories, including Jerusalem, and without the achievement of a just solution of the problem of Palestine on the basis of the attainment of the inalienable rights of the Palestinian people in Palestine;

3. *Reaffirms* the inalienable right of the Palestinians to return to their homes and property in Palestine, from which they have been displaced and uprooted, and calls for their return;

4. *Reaffirms also* the inalienable rights in Palestine of the Palestinian people, including:

(*a*) The right to self-determination without external interference, and to national independence and sovereignty;

(*b*) The right to establish its own independent sovereign State;

5. *Reaffirms* the right of the Palestine Liberation Organization, the representative of the Palestinian people, to participate on an equal footing in all efforts, deliberations and conferences on the question of Palestine and the situation in the Middle East within the framework of the United Nations;

6. *Reaffirms* the fundamental principle of the inadmissibility of the acquisition of territory by force;

[4] *Ibid.* [*Official Records of the General Assembly, Seventh Emergency Special Session, Annexes*], agenda item 5, document A/ES-7/1, annex.

[5] *Ibid., Seventh Emergency Special Session, Plenary Meetings,* 1st meeting, paras. 171-217.

7. *Calls upon* Israel to withdraw completely and unconditionally from all the Palestinian and other Arab territories occupied since June 1967, including Jerusalem, with all property and services intact, and urges that such withdrawal from all the occupied territories should start before 15 November 1980;

8. *Demands* that Israel should fully comply with provisions of resolution 465 (1980) adopted unanimously by the Security Council on 1 March 1980;

9. *Further demands* that Israel should fully comply with all United Nations resolutions relevant to the historic character of the Holy City of Jerusalem, in particular Security Council resolution 476 (1980) of 30 June 1980;

10. *Expresses its opposition* to all policies and plans aimed at the resettlement of the Palestinians outside their homeland;

11. *Requests and authorizes* the Secretary-General, in consultation, as appropriate, with the Committee on the Exercise of the Inalienable Rights of the Palestinian People, to take the necessary measures towards the implementation of the recommendations contained in paragraphs 59 to 72 of the report of the Committee to the General Assembly at its thirty-first session[6] as a basis for the solution of the question of Palestine;

12. *Requests* the Secretary-General to report to the General Assembly at its thirty-fifth session on the implementation of the present resolution;

13. *Requests* the Security Council, in the event of non-compliance by Israel with the present resolution, to convene in order to consider the situation and the adoption of effective measures under Chapter VII of the Charter;

14. *Decides* to adjourn the seventh emergency special session temporarily and to authorize the President of the latest regular session of the General Assembly to resume its meetings upon request from Member States.

11th plenary meeting
29 July 1980

[6] *Ibid., Thirty-first Session, Supplement No. 35* (A/31/35).

172. Security Council Resolution 478 Censuring Israeli "Basic Law" on Jerusalem, August 20, 1980*

---

* S.C. Res. 478, 35 U.N. SCOR (2245th mtg.) at 14, U.N. Doc. S/INF/36 (1980).

The Security Council,

Recalling its resolution 476 (1980),

Reaffirming again that the acquisition of territory by force is inadmissible,

Deeply concerned over the enactment of a "basic law" in the Israeli Knesset proclaiming a change in the character and status of the Holy City of Jerusalem, with its implications for peace and security,

Noting that Israel has not complied with resolution 476 (1980),

Reaffirming its determination to examine practical ways and means, in accordance with the relevant provisions of the Charter of the United Nations, to secure the full implementation of its resolution 476 (1980), in the event of non-compliance by Israel,

1. *Censures* in the strongest terms the enactment by Israel of the "basic law" on Jerusalem and the refusal to comply with relevant Security Council resolutions;

2. *Affirms* that the enactment of the "basic law" by Israel constitutes a violation of international law and does not affect the continued application of the Geneva Convention relative to the Protection of Civilian Persons in Time of War, of 12 August 1949,[22] in the Palestinian and other Arab territories occupied since June 1967, including Jerusalem;

3. *Determines* that all legislative and administrative measures and actions taken by Israel, the occupying Power, which have altered or purport to alter the character and status of the Holy City of Jerusalem, and in particular the recent "basic law" on Jerusalem, are null and void and must be rescinded forthwith;

4. *Affirms also* that this action constitutes a serious obstruction to achieving a comprehensive, just and lasting peace in the Middle East;

5. *Decides* not to recognize the "basic law" and such other actions by Israel that, as a result of this law, seek to alter the character and status of Jerusalem and calls upon:

(*a*) All Member States to accept this decision;

(*b*) Those States that have established diplomatic missions at Jerusalem to withdraw such missions from the Holy City;

6. *Requests* the Secretary-General to report to the Security Council on the implementation of the present resolution before 15 November 1980;

7. *Decides* to remain seized of this serious situation.

Adopted at the 2245th meeting by 14 votes to none, with 1 abstention (United States of America).

[22] United Nations, *Treaty Series*, vol. 75, p. 287.

173. Secretary of State Muskie's Statement Before the
U.N. Security Council on Jerusalem and the Peace
Negotiations, August 20, 1980*

* 80 U.S. Dep't State Bull. No. 2043, at 78 (October 1980).

I come here today out of my deep respect for the United Nations and all it has represented for 35 years. It is a force for peace and reason in the world. It is a forum where nations may air their differences and seek out the common ground. We should all be grateful that this institution has worked so well, on so many issues, in its relatively short span of time.

Therefore, I also come here today with a feeling of sorrow, for I believe that in its work on the Middle East over the past 5 months the United Nations has been the focus of attempts not to advance the cause of peace but to restrain it, contrary to the ideals and purposes of this institution.

The succession of resolutions before this Council and the emergency special session of the General Assembly has neither aided the Camp David process nor offered a single alternative with the slightest chance of success. Eight times in these 5 months resolutions on the Middle East have come before us. For our part, the United States has joined the debate and the voting. We have done that because we respect this institution, and we honor those who have labored hard for a positive approach.

But eight times, those resolutions have failed the critical tests of reason, of balance, of accounting for the concerns of both sides, of genuinely serving the objective of peace. The resolution before us today is illustrative of a preoccupation which has produced this series of unbalanced and unrealistic resolutions on Middle East issues. It fails to serve the goal of all faiths that look to Jerusalem as holy.

We must share a common vision of this ancient city's future—an undivided Jerusalem, with free access to the holy places for people of all faiths. But how can that vision be realized? Certainly it cannot be realized by unilateral actions nor by narrow resolutions in this forum. Rather the question of Jerusalem must be addressed in the context of negotiations for a comprehensive, just, and lasting Middle East peace.

That is the position of my government. But it is more. The status of Jerusalem cannot simply be declared; it must be agreed to by the parties. That is a practical reality. It will remain so despite this resolution or 100 more like it. We have encouraged all parties to refrain from unilateral actions which seek to change the character or status of Jerusalem. In line with this position we will not vote against the resolution as presently written.

So there can be no mistake, let me note that we will continue firmly and forcefully to resist any attempt to impose sanctions against Israel under Chapter VII [of the U.N. Charter]. That step is contained in a draft resolution to be presented here but not to be voted upon. We are unalterably opposed to it. We will vote against any such resolution.

But if we do not vote against the version before us today, neither can we find cause to support it. For the resolution is still fundamentally flawed. It fails even to reaffirm Resolution 242 as the basis for a comprehensive peace. Israel, for example, is to be censured—yet there is no censure, indeed no mention at all, of violence against Israel or of efforts that undermine Israel's legitimate security needs. Further, the resolution before us calls upon those states that have established diplomatic missions in Jerusalem to withdraw them from the holy city. In our judgment this provision is not binding. It is without force. And we reject it as a disruptive attempt to dictate to other nations. It does nothing to promote a resolution of the difficult problems facing Israel and its neighbors. It does nothing to advance the cause of peace. On these specific grounds, we abstain on the resolution.

And on broader grounds, we ask that the United Nations return to first principles in addressing the Middle East. Let us resist useless pronouncements and resume the practical search for results—on Jerusalem and on all other issues.

There are few problems in the world today as much in need of resolution—and of patient, constructive effort to achieve it. Four cruel wars in 30 years—and the peril and suffering that remain—underscore the urgency of this task. And it is underscored again by recent fighting in Lebanon, renewing that violent cycle. For all those 30 years there was no peace. Plans were tried and abandoned. Partial solutions came apart. Modest, stablizing steps were the very most to be achieved; and they were all too fragile.

Then in November 1977, President Sadat of Egypt took the courageous step of going to Jerusalem in an inspired act of statesmanship to break the deadlock. With equal statesmanship the Israeli Government responded. At Camp David the next September, for 13 days, President Sadat, Prime Minister Begin, and President Carter joined to create a framework for peace in the Middle East. Thus was born the first real chance to bring the goals of Resolution 242 into being. Then, following President Carter's trip to the Middle East in February 1979, peace between Israel and Egypt—the first real peace—was achieved.

Even so, it was only a beginning. Camp David was designed not just for a limited settlement between Israel and one of its neighbors but as a framework for a truly comprehensive and final peace among all parties to the conflict. A year ago last May, the second stage of the Camp David process began—negotiations between Egypt and Israel, with the United States as full partner, to provide full autonomy for the inhabitants of the West Bank and Gaza. This is to be a transitional arrangement of 5 years. Not later than the third year after the start of that period, negotiations to settle the final status of the territories would begin.

This may be an imperfect process. But let me remind you of this. It is also the first time the twin issues of Palestinian rights and Israeli security—issues at the core of the Arab-Israeli conflict—have been at the top of the agenda together. It is the first time there has been real hope—not a mirage or a wish—that a comprehensive settlement could be attained.

My government has stated many times in the past, and I will restate it again today: We are absolutely and firmly commited to the success of the process begun at Camp David and its ultimate goal of a just and lasting peace throughout the region. There is no issue on which President Carter has spent more time and effort than this great cause. And that will continue to be the case until the job is done.

This is difficult and painstaking work. It is precisely the kind of effort that inspired the creation of the United Nations. It is precisely the work to which the United Nations should now rededicate itself. We desire to work closely with the Islamic states in order that their legitimate goals set out in Resolution 242 may be attained in peace and honor.

It is vital that a political climate be preserved within which the hard work of peace can succeed. That is why we have urged all the parties not to take unilateral steps that could prejudice the outcome of the negotiations. That is why we have counseled patience and sought wider support for our efforts. And it is why events here in the last several months have been so profoundly disturbing. We do not expect everyone to support the Camp David process. We do, however, seek an end to efforts that work in the contrary direction—not just to undermine the Camp David process but to disrupt the search for peace itself.

Let me, therefore, repeat our belief that this constant recourse to debates and resolutions that are not germane to the peace process—and even harmful to it—should stop. Elsewhere in Southwest Asia and in Southeast Asia warfare is a present reality. The aggressor nations make no effort to find peace. Yet this Council is continuously drawn to the Middle East, where authentic work for peace is under way.

The United States will not be deterred from this historic enterprise. Indeed, I would like to reiterate our firm determination to finish what has so well begun. At Camp David, as a result of statesmanship and courage, the two parties with the help of the United States designed a framework for comprehensive peace. They agreed to start with a treaty of peace between Egypt and Israel. This was a goal which many thought to be utterly unattainable but which was achieved through negotiation and on the basis of Resolution 242.

As a further step toward a comprehensive peace, the parties agreed to launch serious negotiations aimed at providing autonomy for the Palestinian inhabitants of the West Bank and Gaza for a transitional period. The final objective is clear: resolution of the Palestinian problem in all its aspects and, ultimately, peace treaties between Israel and all of its other neighbors—Jordan, Syria, and Lebanon.

We intend to persevere in this effort regardless of all distractions, diversions, and difficulties.

174. Address by Ambassador Sol M. Linowitz Before the National Press Club, September 18, 1980*

---

* 80 U.S. Dep't State Bull. No. 2045, at 53 (December 1980). *See also* Ambassador Linowitz's Press Conference, 80 U.S. Dep't State Bull. No. 2045, at 48 (December 1980).

Just 2 years ago yesterday an event took place which was as dramatic as it was historic. After 13 days of arduous and intensive negotiations, President Anwar Sadat of Egypt and Prime Minister Menahem Begin of Israel, having met with President Carter at Camp David, announced to the world that they had reached agreement on the so-called Camp David framework for Middle East peace. In a moving ceremony at the White House, the Camp David accords were signed, and a new chapter in the history of the Middle East was opened.

Today I want to talk with you about where that process stands 2 years later. I want to report to you on my recent discussions with Prime Minister Begin and President Sadat and to affirm to you that the Camp David peace process has managed to survive its premature obituaries and is once again moving forward.

Before discussing with you details of my recent trip and our current negotiating efforts, I would like to focus on some of the most significant elements of the present situation—elements that give us reason for hope that the way to comprehensive peace in the Middle East will yet be found.

Elements of the Present Situation

First, there is today a growing global awareness of the stakes involved in peace in the Middle East. It is trite, but undeniably true, that the greatest impetus for peace is the constant danger of war. And the stark fact is that another Middle East war would invite global disaster.

Our own unrelenting efforts for peace between Israel and its neighbors proceed from an unshakable commitment to the security of Israel and a recognition that Israel's long-term security is best assured by the achievement of a stable peace throughout the region. Moreover, our work for peace in the Middle East is an essential element of our strategy for maintaining and defending our vital interests in Southwest Asia and the Persian Gulf.

Clearly, the strategic importance of this region has never been greater. It is equally manifest that the threats to peace in the region have multiplied as a result of the Soviet invasion of Afghanistan. And the danger that the spark of local conflict could ignite a major conflagration has never been more serious. So today the world understands, perhaps better than ever before, the vital significance of finding the way to peace in the Middle East.

The United States, Israel, the Arab states, our allies outside the Middle East—all have a strategic interest in a just and lasting peace in the Middle East. And each of us can find in peace the possibilities of bountiful new progress—in our relations with one another, in our economies, in our efforts toward the resolution of disputes in other areas.

Second, there is reason for hope and satisfaction in what has already been accomplished in the search for the Middle East peace. For over 30 years, the Arab-Israel conflict provided fertile ground for the congenital nay-say-ers and the traditional prophets of doom. Except for such historic moments as the visit of President Sadat to Jerusalem or the signing of the Camp David accords, the problems always loomed larger than the possibilities. Yet the most important fact is that since Camp David there has been very significant progress.

We have only to think back to the situation in 1947—or 1967—or even 1977 and compare it with the situation now.

- Then there was a formal state of war and, on occasion, its terrible reality. Now we have a peace treaty between Egypt and Israel.
- Then there was a gulf of hostility and distrust and suspicion. Now there is real and evident determination in both Egypt and Israel to find a larger peace.
- Then the mechanism for achieving a peaceful settlement did not exist. Now it does in the Camp David process.

The treaty between Egypt and Israel marks a peace without victor or vanquished, entered into by two nations determined to reject a legacy of hostility and warfare. The terms of the Peace Treaty have been scrupulously followed. Israel has given up on schedule not only most of the Sinai—won and defended at such cost in blood—but also the Alma oil fields from which it had derived the majority of its energy needs. Egypt, for its part, has proceeded to normalize its relations with Israel in the face of the strong, even fierce, reaction of its Arab neighbors and former allies.

Embassies have been opened, ambassadors exchanged. In civil aviation, in agriculture, in tourism, in other areas—Egypt and Israel have signed agreements that will enable their relations to move forward in defiance of their history of antagonism. Today the flag of Israel flies in Egypt and the flag of Egypt flies in Israel.

As important as these achievements are, they are not, in my judgment, the most important result of this new era of peace between two old enemies. More significant are changes of attitudes—on both sides. Everytime I sit down with President Sadat and Prime Minister Begin and with my colleagues in these negotiations, I am reminded that these shifts in perception are deep and genuine and permanent. Neither Egypt nor Israel is willing to return to the situation as it was before President Sadat's electrifying initiative in the fall of 1977. Both have set their feet on the road to peace and cooperation. Both understand that there can be no turning back. And both are determined that they will not turn back.

The third reason for hope in these negotiations is the fact that we have launched and are pursuing a practical process for future progress. In saying this I do not in any respect underestimate the immense difficulties before us. By the same token, however, none of us can overlook the opportunities.

Significant as it was, the treaty between Israel and Egypt was not the most far-reaching accomplishment of Camp David. Recognizing the potential vulnerability of their own treaty if left to stand alone, Egypt and Israel committed themselves to work as partners to achieve a comprehensive peace. And they decided that the next logical step toward that broader peace would be an agreement assuring Israel's security and well-being while providing full autonomy for the people of the West Bank and Gaza during a transition period.

These are the negotiations in which we are now engaged—negotiations which for the first time place on the same agenda the security of Israel and the legitimate rights of the Palestinians. The agreed objective of these negotiations is to provide for the free election of a self-governing authority by the Palestinian inhabitants of the West Bank and Gaza and for transitional arrangements not to exceed 5 years in duration.

No one at Camp David in September 1978 believed that this process would be easy. The Camp David accords call on the negotiating parties to translate the words "full autonomy" from a verbal concept to a practical reality. Never before had there been an attempt to define "full autonomy" in similar circumstances. So it is small wonder that progress has been slow—sometimes agonizingly slow.

But the fact is that there has been progress in the past 2 years—considerable progress. The parties have already agreed upon a very substantial number of powers and responsibilities to be transferred to the self-governing authority. They have also made very significant progress in agreeing on the modalities—the mechanisms—for the free election in which the members of the self-governing authority will be chosen. And both parties remain determined to reach their common goal.

Recent Egyptian-Israeli Agreement

Clear and gratifying proof of that lies in the agreement reached 2 weeks ago between President Sadat and Prime Minister Begin—an agreement few anticipated. After my meetings with them earlier this month, Prime Minister Begin and President Sadat authorized me to announce a joint statement of agreement on their behalf. The agreement is short in length but its importance should not be underestimated.

It contains four major points and I would like to focus on them separately.

First, it states: "Both parties are agreed that they are and remain firmly committed to the Camp David accords and process and are convinced that they offer the only viable path toward comprehensive peace in the Middle East. Both are determined to see the process through to a successful conclusion regardless of temporary difficulties that may arise along the way."

All of us involved in the negotiations recognize that we have in the past—and surely will again in the future—encounter temporary difficulties. By the same token, we recognize that frustrations and disappointments are to be expected in these as in any other negotiations. I can assure you that as the

President's Personal Representative since last December, I have often felt firsthand that disappointment and frustration.

In recent weeks our frustrations have been intensified by a myriad of external disturbances and disruptions—matters that have diverted attention from the issues actually under negotiation. Such developments as violence on the West Bank, the seemingly endless stream of U.N. resolutions, and the various statements and actions touching on the status of Jerusalem—all have buffeted the negotiating process at the very time the parties have been trying to focus on the most difficult and complex issues. For example, the deeply sensitive issue of Jerusalem suddenly was pushed from the wings onto center stage, bringing with it predictable storm clouds and thunderclaps.

The leaders who met at Camp David knew that the problem of Jerusalem would need time for solution, and they agreed not to try to solve it in the current negotiations. They understood that Jerusalem touches the very souls of hundreds of millions of people—Jews, Muslims, and Christians alike. This is the reason for our belief that the city should remain forever undivided, with free access to the Holy Places for believers of all faiths. Its final status, however, can only be resolved at the right moment, in an atmosphere of deep trust, cooperation, and understanding among all the parties. And that moment has not yet come.

Until it does, there are other important issues to be dealt with. Recognizing this, President Sadat and Prime Minister Begin have once again committed themselves to the Camp David accords and process as the only—let me repeat only—available path toward comprehensive peace in the Middle East.

Some will say—and indeed some already have—that this is merely a reaffirmation of commitment to an inadequate process. They point out—correctly—that the Camp David accords do not settle the Jerusalem problem; they do not answer Palestinian questions about the final status of the West Bank and Gaza; they do not guarantee permanent Israeli security. Some outside the present negotiations, seduced by the illusion of easy answers and quick solutions, contend that the pace of the negotiations evidences their ineffectiveness and ultimate failure.

But these arguments miss the central point. The genius of the negotiators at Camp David was that they understood that past efforts to achieve peace in the Middle East had failed precisely because they had grasped for too much too soon. They recognized that the issues in this region are so complex, the emotions so deep, the contending forces so many, the stakes so great that the problems defy shortcut solutions. The wisdom of Camp David was to recognize this fact, to understand that bitterness dies hard while trust grows slowly. The key to Camp David was its recognition that the best hope for enduring peace lay in a phased process—one in which agreements attainable at one stage become building blocks for future progress on more difficult issues.

So by abandoning the quest for comprehensive "breakthroughs," Camp David itself become a breakthrough. By deciding to pursue peace in relatively modest steps, the parties at Camp David took a giant step.

What was sensible then remains sensible today. Our goal remains not dramatic breakthroughs but steady incremental progress.

With full awareness of this, President Sadat and Prime Minister Begin have now reaffirmed their belief in the soundness of this approach. They have recommitted their countries to see this process through to success.

The second point in the recent agreement between President Sadat and Prime Minister Begin was their joint recognition that "for the negotiations to succeed, they must rest on a firm foundation of mutual trust and friendship." Not only did they concur in the statement of principle; they affirmed their intention to act in order to strengthen that foundation during the coming weeks.

The most profoundly disturbing aspect of the period between May and August of this year was the growing rift between Israel and Egypt. Exchanges between them had become increasingly sharp; tensions were exacerbated; and each side began to see in the other's actions and inactions cause to doubt the other's good faith. This deteriorating situation invited the critics and opponents of the Camp David process to intensify their rhetoric and essential negativism.

Prime Minister Begin and President Sadat both recognized the dangers in this situation. Both are aware that their mutual trust and respect and friendship—today as at Camp David—remain the cornerstones for progress. They know that in any negotiation the opposing parties must develop and maintain mutual trust and respect if they are to be able to work together constructively in an effort to bridge their differences and that this is especially true in negotiations such as those in which we are now involved, where the issues are so complex and arouse such strong emotions. Both Prime Minister Begin and President Sadat know that to fulfill their continued commitment to the Camp David process, each must be sensitive to the concerns of the other and responsive to the opportunities to reassure the other. And this awareness is already reflected in their very recent actions.

Third, President Sadat and Prime Minister Begin agreed to resume the autonomy negotiations at a mutually agreed date. Prior to this agreement, there had been some who doubted whether Egypt or Israel were truly committed to meaningful progress in the coming weeks. Others doubted whether such resumed negotiations could be productive prior to the U.S. elections. The present undertaking to go back to the negotiating table next month indicates the seriousness of the commitment by all parties.

Given the difficulty of the issues with which we are now grappling, there is a natural temptation to seek to avoid coming to grips with the formidable problems. Consider the questions the parties are trying to resolve.

· How can Israel be assured that its security interests will be fully preserved and protected under the new autonomy arrangement?

- How can the water resources of the region best be fairly and equitably shared?
- How should we deal with the public lands in the West Bank and Gaza areas during the 5-year transitional period?
- What powers should be exercised by the self-governing authority during the transitional period, recognizing that the final status of the territories will later have to be determined by agreement among Israel, Egypt, Jordan, and the Palestinians?
- And should the Arab inhabitants of East Jerusalem participate in the election of the self-governing authority?

At the direction of President Carter, I made clear in my talks with both Prime Minister Begin and President Sadat that the United States is prepared to work intensively and actively with them during the weeks ahead to help them resolve the key issues that still separate the parties. In other words, they are assured that the United States stands ready to play its role as a full partner.

In that spirit of full partnership, I gave both Prime Minister Begin and President Sadat a document we had prepared in an effort to help the parties bridge the differences between them. In accepting our document and agreeing to study it, both parties reaffirmed their continuing commitment to serious exchanges on the outstanding issues. And both welcomed the active and substantive participation by the United States.

Finally, in their joint statement, Prime Minister Begin and President Sadat agreed that a summit meeting with President Carter could contribute significantly to the peace process. Accordingly, they agreed to consult about when and where such a summit might be held later this year, and preparations will soon begin to lay the groundwork for the summit.

This recent agreement gives me as a negotiator new reason for hope and even optimism that the way to a broader Middle East peace will one day be found. Indeed, I remain today—2 years after Camp David—convinced that despite the frustrations, anxieties, and disappointments, the prospect of achieving a just, lasting, and comprehensive peace between Arabs and Israelis is still better than at any time in the past 30 years.

As a negotiator I cannot allow myself the temptations of impatience or discouragement. Pessimism at this important time does not serve our nation's interests or the interests of peace. It does not serve the interests of those—both Arab and Israeli—who have the most at stake. It holds in cheap regard the historic accomplishments of the leaders of Egypt and Israel. It ignores the overriding fact that seemingly intractable obstacles have been overcome before. And it overlooks the fact that what was considered merely a dream but 2 years ago is today a reality.

Because we care about Israel's security, because we care about a more promising future for the Palestinians, because we care about continued progress for Egypt and Israel and the entire region, and because we understand our strategic interests as well as our moral obligations, we must continue to be resolute in our efforts to fulfill the promise of Camp David.

In the Chinese language, the word crisis is written by combining two symbols—the symbol for the word "danger" and the symbol for the word "opportunity."

In the Middle East, the danger is great and we know it. But the opportunity is also great—and that we also know. At this extraordinary moment in history, we are determined that this opportunity not be lost.

175. Resolutions Adopted by the Emergency Session of the Conference of Foreign Ministers of Islamic Countries (excerpt), Fez, Morocco, September 18–20, 1980*

* 10 J. Palestine Stud. 146 (Winter 1981).

The Conference of Foreign Ministers of Islamic Countries, meeting in emergency session in Fez from September 18-20, 1980 at the recommendation of the Jerusalem Committee, studied the grave situation through which the cause of Jerusalem and Palestine is passing as a result of the Israeli Knesset's decision to annex Jerusalem and claim it the unified and eternal capital of the Zionist entity. The Conference regarded this decision as a flagrant defiance of the sentiments of Muslims, and an act of aggression against the Islamic countries. It is also an affirmation of Israel's refusal to abide by the recent Security Council resolution 478 regarding as null and void all Israel's legislative and administrative measures and actions involving a change in the identity and status of Jerusalem, and calling for their immediate rescindment.

The Islamic countries, from their commitment to confrontation of this challenge and to the liberation of Jerusalem and their insistence on Arab Islamic sovereignty over the Holy City; in affirmation of their support for the people of Palestine and their determination to confront this Israeli aggression with all their energies and resources; and from their resolution to continue to provide support to the heroic struggle of the people of Palestine until Jerusalem is liberated and the Palestinian people recover their inalienable rights, including their right to return, to self-determination and to establish their independent state on the soil of their land; and in the light of the spirit of Islamic solidarity, the Conference adopted the following resolutions:

1. To adopt the recommendations and resolutions of the Jerusalem Committee at its emergency session in Casablanca, and to affirm the obligation of all the Islamic countries to implement them.

2. To affirm the commitment of all the Islamic countries to use all their political, financial, oil and military resources to confront the Israeli decision to annex Jerusalem, and to endorse the enforcement of a political and economic boycott on countries that recognize the Israeli decision, facilitate its implementation, or establish embassies in Jerusalem.

3. The Conference calls on all countries in the world to refuse dealings of any kind with the Israeli authorities that the latter could construe as constituting recognition of the *fait accompli* in Jerusalem and all the other occupied Palestinian and Arab territories. Failure in this respect would result in these countries being boycotted.

4. To welcome Security Council resolution 478 of August 20, 1980 and to call on the Council to take the necessary measures for the enforcement of such military and economic sanctions against Israel as are provided for by the UN Charter.

5. The Conference expresses its full satisfaction at the response of those countries that have transferred their embassies from Jerusalem, thereby recognizing the invalidity and illegality of the Israeli decision. It notes that the response of all countries to the call of the Islamic countries to transfer their embassies from Jerusalem is an affirmation of the international com-

munity's unanimous rejection of Israel's move to annex Jerusalem and make it the capital of its entity.

6. The Conference observes with satisfaction the refusal of the Federal Government of Switzerland to sign an agreement with Israel in Jerusalem and calls on all countries to follow this example.

7. To affirm the support of the Islamic countries for the PLO by all available means, and to provide the support necessary for the confrontation of the aggressive war that Israel is waging against the Palestinian people in occupied Palestine and South Lebanon with the aim of liquidating and annihilating them.

The Conference condemns the Israeli aggressions against South Lebanon and calls on member states to assist the Lebanese state to halt these aggressions.

8. To provide material and political support to the Palestinian Arab people inside and outside the occupied homeland and to reinforce their capability to confront the schemes of the self-government conspiracy and to resist the occupation and its racist measures.

9. To call on the member states of the Islamic Conference that have previously recognized Israel to withdraw their recognition and to sever all political and economic relations with it.

10. To continue to resist the course and the accords of Camp David and to close the doors leading to them until they are foiled.

11. The Conference condemns the US policy of support for the Israeli occupation authorities' settlement measures and their aggressions against Islamic holy places in the occupied Palestinian and Arab territories, and US support for Israel against Palestinian rights in international forums. This conflicts with the UN Charter, the resolutions of the General Assembly and the Universal Declaration of Human Rights, and the Conference regards this as a defiance of the Islamic world.

12. [Not] to accept any political settlement of the Palestine question and the Arab-Israeli conflict that is reached under the umbrella of the [present] imbalance of forces resulting from the signing of the Camp David accords. . . . Also, to regard Security Council resolution 242 as incompatible with Arab and Islamic rights, and not constituting a sound basis for the solution of the Middle East crisis, and in particular the Palestine question. Furthermore, to insist on the implementation of the UN resolutions on the Palestine question, in particular resolution No. 1[1] adopted by the seventh emergency special session of the General Assembly, and to reject any initiatives that conflict with these resolutions.

13. To initiate political activity at the UN and with the major countries, headed by the European Community, with a view to winning greater support for the Palestinian cause and to strengthening the cordon of isolation around Israel.

[1] In fact, the resolution referred to is No. 2—*Ed.*

14. To take action to induce the General Assembly to adopt a resolution requesting a judgement from the International Court of Justice on Israeli practices and measures that violate the inalienable national rights of the Palestinian people, and on the aggressive activities of the Israeli authorities against the Palestinian people in Palestine and the occupied Arab territories, on condition that the measures relative to the submission of this request for a judgement do not impair the inalienable national rights of the Palestinian people, and that this step be taken with the approval of the PLO, the sole legitimate representative of the Palestinian people.

15. To call on the UN General Assembly not to accept the credentials of the Israeli delegation to the UN because it represents a government that has violated international legality in making Jerusalem its capital.

16. To call on the great powers and the international organizations to shoulder their responsibilities and confront Israeli defiance by imposing sanctions against Israel, in implementation of the UN Charter.

17. To call on the countries of the world to take action to prevent Jewish immigration to the occupied Palestinian and Arab territories, in view of the Zionist policy of settlement in those territories and Israel's persistent refusal to recognize the right of the Palestinian people to return to their homeland and exercise their right to self-determination, to sovereignty and to establish their independent state on the soil of their homeland.

18. To step up contacts with the Vatican and Christian circles with the object of expounding the Islamic view of the new Israeli decision and asking them to support the inalienable rights of the Palestinian people, and to recognize the PLO.

19. To launch a wide-scale information campaign condemning the Israeli decision and to take action to secure the implementation of the information plan for the confrontation of Israeli defiance.

20. To call on member states to cut off their loans and contributions to the International Monetary Fund and the World Bank unless these institutions accept the PLO as a member with observer status.

21. To establish an Islamic Boycott of Israel Office in implementation of the relevant resolutions of the Islamic Conference, to operate in coordination with the Arab League Secretariat General's main Boycott of Israel Office.

22. To cover the capital and endowments of the Jerusalem Fund.

23. The Islamic countries declare their commitment to a holy war with all the wide human dimensions therein, including steadfastness and confrontation of the Zionist enemy on all fronts, military, political, economic, information and cultural.

24. To call on the Jerusalem Committee to draw up a comprehensive plan for the mobilization of all the resources of the Islamic countries for the confrontation of the Israeli aggression, and to refer the Syrian-Palestinian working paper on economic and military issues to the Committee and submit this plan to the next Islamic summit conference which is to be held in Saudi Arabia.

176. Written Question to the EEC Foreign Ministers on
Recognition of Jerusalem as "the Sole and Indivisible
Capital of Israel," September 22, 1980—Answer,
January 20, 1981*

---

* 24 O.J. Eur. Comm. (No. C 49) 4 (1981).

WRITTEN QUESTION NO 1177/80
by Mr Glinne
to the Foreign Ministers of the nine Member States of the
European Community meeting in political cooperation
(22 September 1980)

Subject: Recognition of Jerusalem as 'the sole and indivisible capital of Israel'

The Israeli Parliament has just proclaimed Jerusalem the 'sole and indi-visible capital of Israel' in defiance of United Nations resolutions on this issue.

Do the Nine recognize Jerusalem in this capacity? Do they have a common position on this issue? What is this position?

ANSWER
(20 January 1981)

At the European Council held in Venice on 13 June 1980, the Nine stated their recognition of the special importance of the role played by the question of Jerusalem for all the parties concerned. They stressed that they would not accept any unilateral initiative designed to change the status of Jerusalem and that any agreement on the city's status should guarantee freedom of access for everyone to the Holy Places.

The Nine, therefore, keenly regret the Israeli decision referred to by the Honourable Member.

177. Text of the Treaty of Friendship between the Soviet Union and the Syrian Arab Republic, Signed in Moscow by Soviet President Brezhnev and Syrian President Hafez Al-Assad, October 8, 1980*

* 10 J. Palestine Stud. 148 (Winter 1981).

The Union of Soviet Socialist Republics and the Syrian Arab Republic,

Inspired by the wish to develop and strengthen the relations of friendship and all-round co-operation that have taken shape between them, in the interests of the peoples of both states, of the cause of peace and security all over the world and of the consolidation of international *détente*, and the development of peaceful co-operation among states,

Determined to administer a firm rebuff to the policy of aggression pursued by imperialism and its accomplices, to continue the struggle against colonialism, neo-colonialism and racialism in all their forms and manifestations, including Zionism, and to come out in favour of national independence and social progress,

Attaching great significance to the continuation of co-operation between the two countries in establishing a just and lasting peace in the Middle East,

Reaffirming their allegiance to the goals and principles of the United Nations Charter including the principles of respect for sovereignty, national independence, territorial integrity and non-interference in internal affairs,

Have decided to conclude the present Treaty and have agreed on the following:

ARTICLE 1

The high contracting parties proclaim their resolve to develop steadily and strengthen friendship and co-operation between both states and peoples in the political, economic, military, scientific, technological, cultural and other spheres on the basis of the principles of equality, mutual advantage, respect for sovereignty, national independence and territorial integrity and non-interference in one another's internal affairs.

ARTICLE 2

The high contracting parties will promote in every way the strengthening of universal peace and the security of the peoples, the relaxation of international tensions and its implementation in concrete forms of co-operation among states, and the settlement of disputed questions by peaceful means, removing any manifestations of the policy of hegemonism and aggression from the practice of international relations.

The two sides will co-operate intensively with each other in solving the tasks of ending the arms race and achieving general and complete disarmament, including nuclear disarmament under effective international control.

ARTICLE 3

The high contracting parties, guided by their belief in the equality of all peoples and states, regardless of race and religious beliefs, condemn colonialism, racialism, and Zionism as one of the forms and manifestations of racialism, and reaffirm their determination to wage a tireless struggle against them. The two sides will co-operate with other states in supporting the just aspirations of the peoples in their struggle against imperialism, for the ultimate and complete elimination of colonialism and racial domination, and for freedom and social progress.

ARTICLE 4

The Union of Soviet Socialist Republics will respect the policy of non-alignment pursued by the Syrian Arab Republic, which constitutes a major factor contributing to the preservation and consolidation of international peace and security and to a lessening of international tensions.

The Syrian Arab Republic will respect the peaceful foreign policy pursued by the Union of Soviet Socialist Republics, aimed at strengthening friendship and co-operation with all countries and peoples.

ARTICLE 5

The high contracting parties will develop and broaden the practice of the mutual exchange of opinions and regular consultations on questions concerning bilateral relations and international problems of interest to both sides, and above all on the problems of the Middle East. Consultation and exchanges of views shall be held at different levels, above all through meetings of the leading state figures of both sides.

ARTICLE 6

In cases of the emergence of situations jeopardizing peace or the security of one of the parties, or posing a threat to peace, or violating peace and security throughout the world, the high contracting parties shall enter without delay into contact with each other with a view to co-ordinating their positions and co-operating in order to remove the threat that has arisen and to restore peace.

ARTICLE 7

The high contracting parties will carry out close and comprehensive co-operation in assuring conditions for the preservation and development of the social and economic achievements of their peoples and for respecting the sovereignty of each of the two parties over their natural resources.

ARTICLE 8

The high contracting parties will contribute to the steady consolidation and broadening of mutually beneficial economic and also scientific and technical co-operation and the exchange of experience between them in the fields of industry, agriculture, irrigation and water resources and the utilization of oil and other natural resources, in the fields of communications, transport and other economic sectors as well as in the training of national personnel. The two sides undertake to extend trade and maritime navigation between them on the basis of the principles of equality, mutual benefit and most-favoured-nation treatment.

ARTICLE 9

The high contracting parties will continue to develop their co-operation and exchange of experience in the fields of science, art, literature, education, health, information, cinematography, tourism, sports and other fields.

The two sides undertake to contribute to the expansion of contacts and co-operation between the organs of state power and mass organizations, including the trade union and other public organizations, enterprises, and cultural and scientific establishments in order that the peoples of both countries may become increasingly familiar with each other's life, work, experience and achievements.

ARTICLE 10

The high contracting parties will continue to develop co-operation in the military field on the basis of appropriate agreements concluded between them in the interests of strengthening their defence capacity.

ARTICLE 11

Each of the high contracting parties states that it will not enter into alliances, or participate in any groupings of states, or in actions or activities directed against the other high contracting party.

ARTICLE 12

Each of the high contracting parties states that its obligations under present international agreements do not contradict the provisions of this treaty, and undertakes not to conclude any international agreements which are incompatible with it.

ARTICLE 13

Any differences that may arise between the high contracting parties in the interpretation or application of any provision of this treaty shall be resolved on a bilateral basis, in a spirit of friendship, mutual understanding and respect.

ARTICLE 14

This treaty shall be effective for 20 years as from the day it comes into force.

If neither of the high contracting parties states, six months prior to the expiry of the above-mentioned period, its desire to terminate the Treaty, it will remain effective for the following five years until one of the high contracting parties gives notification in writing, six months prior to the expiry of the current five-year period, of its intention to terminate it.

ARTICLE 15

This Treaty is subject to ratification and shall enter into force on the day of the exchange of the ratification instruments, which shall be done in Damascus.

Done in Moscow on October 8, 1980, in duplicate, each copy in the Russian and Arabic languages, with both texts being equally authentic.

178. General Assembly Resolution 35/75 on

the Living Conditions of the Palestinian People,

December 5, 1980*

* G.A. Res. 75, 35 U.N. GAOR Supp. (No. 48) at 135, U.N. Doc. A/35/48 (1980).

The General Assembly,

Recalling the Vancouver Declaration on Human Settlements, 1976,[134] and the relevant recommendations for national action[135] adopted by Habitat: United Nations Conference on Human Settlements,

Recalling also resolution 3, entitled "Living conditions of the Palestinians in the occupied territories", contained in the recommendations for international co-operation adopted by Habitat: United Nations Conference on Human Settlements[136] and Economic and Social Council resolutions 2026 (LXI) of 4 August 1976 and 2100 (LXIII) of 3 August 1977,

Recalling further its resolutions 31/110 of 16 December 1976, 32/171 of 19 December 1977, 33/110 of 18 December 1978 and 34/113 of 14 December 1979,

1. *Takes note with satisfaction* of the report of the Secretary-General on the living conditions of the Palestinian people in the occupied Arab territories;[137]

2. *Deplores* the refusal of the Government of Israel to allow the Group of Experts on the Social and Economic Impact of the Israeli Occupation on the Living Conditions of the Palestinian People in the Occupied Arab Territories[138] to visit the Palestinian and other Arab territories occupied by Israel;

3. *Condemns* Israeli policy resulting in the deterioration of the living conditions of the Palestinian people in the occupied territories;

4. *Calls upon* all States to co-operate with United Nations agencies, organizations and organs and local Palestinian authorities to alleviate the tragic living conditions of the Palestinian people caused by the Israeli occupation;

5. *Requests* the Secretary-General to submit a comprehensive and analytical report to the General Assembly at its thirty-sixth session, through the Economic and Social Council, on the progress made in the implementation of the present resolution.

83rd plenary meeting
5 December 1980

[134] See *Report of Habitat: United Nations Conference on Human Settlements, Vancouver, 31 May-11 June 1976* (United Nations publication, Sales No. E.76.IV.7 and corrigendum) chap. I.

[135] *Ibid.*, chap. II.

[136] *Ibid.*, chap. III.

[137] A/35/533 and Corr.1.

[138] For the report of the Group of Experts, see A/35/533 and Corr.1, annex I.

179. General Assembly Resolution 35/111 on Assistance to
the Palestinian People, December 5, 1980*

* G.A. Res. 111, 35 U.N. GAOR Supp. (No. 48) at 165, U.N. Doc. A/35/ 48 (1980). *See also* subsequent resolution, G.A. Res. 70, 36 U.N. GAOR Supp. (No. 51) at 101, U.N. Doc. A/36/51 (1981).

The General Assembly,

Recalling its resolutions 33/147 of 20 December 1978 and 34/133 of 14 December 1979,

Recalling also its resolutions 3236 (XXIX) and 3237 (XXIX) of 22 November 1974,

Recalling further Economic and Social Council resolutions 1978 (LIX) of 31 July 1975, 2026 (LXI) of 4 August 1976 and 2100 (LXIII) of 3 August 1977,

Taking note with satisfaction of the report of the Secretary-General on assistance to the Palestinian people,[241]

Also taking note of the report of the Governing Council of the United Nations Development Programme on its twenty-seventh session,[242]

1. *Notes with satisfaction* the action taken by the Administrator and the Governing Council of the United Nations Development Programme in response to General Assembly resolution 34/133;

2. *Urges* the relevant agencies, organizations, organs and programmes of the United Nations system to take the necessary steps for the full implementation of Economic and Social Council resolutions 2026 (LXI) and 2100 (LXIII);

3. *Requests* that assistance to the Palestinian people in the West Bank and Gaza should be rendered through United Nations agencies and organs in co-operation and consultation with the local Palestinian economic, social, educational and municipal organizations in these occupied territories;

4. *Requests* that assistance to the Palestinian people in the Arab host countries should be rendered through United Nations agencies, in consultation with the parties concerned and in accordance with the relevant resolutions of the Economic and Social Council;

5. *Requests* the Secretary-General to report to the General Assembly at its thirty-sixth session, through the Economic and Social Council, on the progress made in the implementation of the present resolution.

84th plenary meeting
5 December 1980

---

[241] A/35/227 and Add.1.

[242] *Official Records of the Economic and Social Council, 1980, Supplement No. 12* (E/1980/42/Rev.1).

180. General Assembly Resolution 35/122 on the Report of the Special Committee to Investigate Israeli Practices Affecting the Human Rights of the Population of the Occupied Territories, December 11, 1980*

* G.A. Res. 122, 35 U.N. GAOR Supp. (No. 48) at 89, U.N. Doc. A/35/48 (1980).

A

The General Assembly,

Recalling its resolutions 3092 A (XXVIII) of 7 December 1973, 3240 B (XXIX) of 29 November 1974, 3525 B (XXX) of 15 December 1975, 31/106 B of 16 December 1976, 32/91 A of 13 December 1977, 33/113 A of 18 December 1978 and 34/90 B of 12 December 1979,

Considering that the promotion of respect for the obligations arising from the Charter of the United Nations and other instruments and rules of international law is among the basic purposes and principles of the United Nations,

Bearing in mind the provisions of the Geneva Convention relative to the Protection of Civilian Persons in Time of War, of 12 August 1949,[18]

Noting that Israel and those Arab States whose territories have been occupied by Israel since June 1967 are parties to that Convention,

Taking into account that States parties to that Convention undertake, in accordance with article 1 thereof, not only to respect but also to ensure respect for the Convention in all circumstances,

1. *Reaffirms* that the Geneva Convention relative to the Protection of Civilian Persons in Time of War, of 12 August 1949, is applicable to Palestinian and other Arab territories occupied by Israel since 1967, including Jerusalem;

2. *Strongly deplores* the failure of Israel to acknowledge the applicability of that Convention to the territories it has occupied since 1967;

3. *Call again upon* Israel to acknowledge and to comply with the provisions of that Convention in Palestinian and other Arab territories it has occupied since 1967, including Jerusalem;

4. *Urges once more* all States parties to that Convention to exert all efforts in order to ensure respect for and compliance with its provisions in Palestinian and other Arab territories occupied by Israel since 1967, including Jerusalem.

92nd plenary meeting
11 December 1980

B

The General Assembly,

Recalling its resolutions 32/5 of 28 October 1977, 33/113 B of 18 December 1978 and 34/90 C of 12 December 1979,

Expressing grave anxiety and concern at the present serious situation in the occupied Arab territories as a result of the continued Israeli occupation and the measures and actions taken by the Government of Israel, as the occupying Power, and designed to change the legal status, geographical nature and demographic composition of those territories,

[18] United Nations, *Treaty Series*, vol. 75, No. 973, p. 287.

Considering that the Geneva Convention relative to the Protection of Civilian Persons in Time of War, of 12 August 1949,[18] is applicable to all the Arab territories occupied since 5 June 1967,

1. *Determines* that all such measures and actions taken by Israel in the Palestinian and other Arab territories occupied since 1967 have no legal validity and constitute a serious obstruction of efforts aimed at achieving a just and lasting peace in the Middle East;

2. *Strongly deplores* the persistence of Israel in carrying out such measures, in particular the establishment of settlements in the Palestinian and other occupied Arab territories;

3. *Calls again upon* Israel to comply strictly with its international obligations in accordance with the principles of international law and the provisions of the Geneva Convention relative to the Protection of Civilian Persons in Time of War, of 12 August 1949;

4. *Calls once more upon* the Government of Israel, as the occupying Power, to desist forthwith from taking any action which would result in changing the legal status, geographical nature or demographic composition of the Arab territories occupied since 1967, including Jerusalem;

5. *Urges* all States parties to the Geneva Convention relative to the Protection of Civilian Persons in Time of War to respect and to exert all efforts in order to ensure respect for and compliance with its provisions in all the Arab territories occupied by Israel since 1967, including Jerusalem.

92nd plenary meeting
11 December 1980

C

The General Assembly,

Guided by the purposes and principles of the Charter of the United Nations as well as the principles and provisions of the Universal Declaration of Human Rights,[19]

Bearing in mind the provisions of the Geneva Convention relative to the Protection of Civilian Persons in Time of War, of 12 August 1949,[18] as well as of other relevant conventions and regulations,

Recalling all its resolutions on the subject, in particular resolutions 32/91 B and C of 13 December 1977, 33/113 C of 18 December 1978 and 34/90 A of 12 December 1979, as well as those adopted by the Security Council, the Commission on Human Rights and other United Nations organs concerned and by the specialized agencies,

Having considered the report of the Special Committee to Investigate Israeli Practices Affecting the Human Rights of the Population of the Occupied Territories[20] which contains, *inter alia*, public statements made by leaders of the Government of Israel,

[19] Resolution 217 A (III).
[20] See A/35/425.

1. *Commends* the Special Committee to Investigate Israeli Practices Affecting the Human Rights of the Population of the Occupied Territories for its efforts in performing the task assigned to it by the General Assembly and for its thoroughness and impartiality;

2. *Deplores* the continued refusal by Israel to allow the Special Committee access to the occupied territories;

3. *Calls again upon* Israel to allow the Special Committee access to the occupied territories;

4. *Deplores* the continued and persistent violation by Israel of the Geneva Convention relative to the Protection of Civilian Persons in Time of War, of 12 August 1949, and other applicable international instruments, and condemns in particular those violations which that Convention designates as "grave breaches" thereof;

5. *Condemns* the following Israeli policies and practices:

(*a*) Annexation of parts of the occupied territories, including Jerusalem;

(*b*) Establishment of new Israeli settlements and expansion of the existing settlements on private and public Arab lands, and transfer of an alien population thereto;

(*c*) Evacuation, deportation, expulsion, displacement and transfer of Arab inhabitants of the occupied territories and denial of their right to return;

(*d*) Confiscation and expropriation of private and public Arab property in the occupied territories and all other transactions for the acquisition of land involving the Israeli authorities, institutions or nationals on the one hand and the inhabitants or institutions of the occupied territories on the other;

(*e*) Destruction and demolition of Arab houses;

(*f*) Mass arrests, administrative detention and ill-treatment of the Arab population;

(*g*) Ill-treatment and torture of persons under detention;

(*h*) Pillaging of archaeological and cultural property;

(*i*) Interference with religious freedoms and practices as well as family rights and customs;

(*j*) Illegal exploitation of the natural wealth, resources and population of the occupied territories;

6. *Reaffirms* that all measures taken by Israel to change the physical character, demographic composition, institutional structure or status of the occupied territories, or any part thereof, including Jerusalem, are null and void, and that Israel's policy of settling parts of its population and new immigrants in the occupied territories constitutes a flagrant violation of the Geneva Convention relative to the Protection of Civilian Persons in Time of War and of relevant United Nations resolutions;

7. *Demands* that Israel desist forthwith from the policies and practices referred to in paragraphs 5 and 6 above;

8. *Reiterates its call* upon all States, in particular those States parties to the Geneva Convention relative to the Protection of Civilian Persons in Time of War, in accordance with article 1 of that Convention, and upon interna-

tional organizations and the specialized agencies not to recognize any changes carried out by Israel in the occupied territories and to avoid actions, including those in the field of aid, which might be used by Israel in its pursuit of the policies of annexation and colonization or any of the other policies and practices referred to in the present resolution;

9. *Requests* the Special Committee, pending the early termination of the Israeli occupation, to continue to investigate Israeli policies and practices in the Arab territories occupied by Israel since 1967, to consult, as appropriate, with the International Committee of the Red Cross in order to ensure the safeguarding of the welfare and human rights of the population of the occupied territories and to report to the Secretary-General as soon as possible and whenever the need arises thereafter;

10. *Requests* the Special Committee to continue to investigate the treatment of civilians in detention in the Arab territories occupied by Israel since 1967;

11. *Requests* the Secretary-General:

(*a*) To provide all necessary facilities to the Special Committee, including those required for its visits to the occupied territories, with a view to investigating the Israeli policies and practices referred to in the present resolution;

(*b*) To continue to make available additional staff as may be necessary to assist the Special Committee in the performance of its tasks;

(*c*) To ensure the widest circulation of the reports of the Special Committee, and of information regarding its activities and findings, by all means available through the Department of Public Information of the Secretariat and, where necessary, to reprint those reports of the Special Committee which are no longer available;

(*d*) To report to the General Assembly at its thirty-sixth session on the tasks entrusted to him in the present paragraph;

12. *Decides* to include in the provisional agenda of its thirty-sixth session the item entitled "Report of the Special Committee to Investigate Israeli Practices Affecting the Human Rights of the Population of the Occupied Territories".

92nd plenary meeting
11 December 1980

D

The General Assembly,

Recalling Security Council resolutions 468 (1980) of 8 May 1980 and 469 (1980) of 20 May 1980,

Deeply concerned at the expulsion by the Israeli military occupation authorities of the Mayors of Hebron and Halhul and of the Sharia Judge of Hebron,

Gravely concerned at the imprisonment by the Israeli military occupation authorities of the Mayors of Hebron and Halhul,

Recalling the Geneva Convention relative to the Protection of Civilian Persons in Time of War of 12 August 1949,[18] in particular article 1 and the first paragraph of article 49, which read as follows:

Article 1

The High Contracting Parties undertake to respect and to ensure respect for the present Convention in all circumstances.

Article 49

Individual or mass forcible transfers, as well as deportations of protected persons from occupied territory to the territory of the occupying Power or to that of any other country, occupied or not, are prohibited, regardless of their motive. . . . ,

Reaffirming the applicability of the Geneva Convention relative to the Protection of Civilian Persons in Time of War to Palestinian and other Arab territories occupied by Israel since 1967, including Jerusalem,

1. *Calls upon* the Government of Israel, as the occupying Power, to rescind the illegal measures taken by the Israeli military occupation authorities in expelling and imprisoning the Mayors of Hebron and Halhul and in expelling the Sharia Judge of Hebron and to facilitate the immediate return of the expelled Palestinian leaders so that they can resume the functions for which they were elected and appointed;

2. *Requests* the Secretary-General to report to the General Assembly as soon as possible on the implementation of the present resolution.

92nd plenary meeting
11 December 1980

E

The General Assembly,

Gravely concerned at reports indicating the intention of the Israeli authorities to enact legislation embodying changes in the character and status of the occupied Syrian Arab Golan Heights,

Deeply concerned that the Arab territories occupied since 1967 have been under continued illegal Israeli occupation,

Recalling its previous resolutions, in particular resolutions 3414 (XXX) of 5 December 1975, 31/61 of 9 December 1976, 32/20 of 25 November 1977, 33/28 and 33/29 of 7 December 1978 and 34/70 of 6 December 1979, in which it, *inter alia*, called upon Israel to put an end to its illegal occupation of the Arab territories and to withdraw from all those territories,

Reaffirming that the acquisition of territory by force is inadmissible under the Charter of the United Nations and that all territories thus occupied by Israel must be returned,

Recalling the Geneva Convention relative to the Protection of Civilian Persons in Time of War of 1949,[18]

1. *Condemns* the persistence of Israel in changing the physical character, demographic composition, institutional structure and legal status of the Syrian Arab Golan Heights;

2. *Strongly condemns* the refusal by Israel, the occupying Power, to comply with relevant resolutions of the General Assembly and the Security Council;

3. *Determines* that all legislative and administrative measures and actions which might be taken by Israel, the occupying Power, that purport to alter the character and legal status of the Syrian Arab Golan Heights are null and void, constitute a flagrant violation of international law and the Geneva Convention relative to the Protection of Civilian Persons in Time of War and have no legal effect;

4. *Calls upon* Member States not to recognize such legislative and administrative measures and actions;

5. *Calls upon* Israel, the occupying Power, to desist from enacting such legislation.

92nd plenary meeting
11 December 1980

F

The General Assembly,

Bearing in mind the Geneva Convention relative to the Protection of Civilian Persons in Time of War, of 12 August 1949,[18]

Recalling Security Council resolutions 468 (1980) of 8 May 1980 and 469 (1980) of 20 May 1980,

Deeply shocked by the most recent atrocities committed by Israel, the occupying Power, against educational institutions in the occupied Palestinian territories,

Taking cognizance of the recent repeated expulsion by Israel, the occupying Power, of the Mayors of Hebron and Halhul,

Condemning the rejection of Israel to accept and carry out the above-mentioned decisions of the Security Council,

1. *Reaffirms* the applicability of the Geneva Convention relative to the Protection of Civilian Persons in Time of War, of 12 August 1949, to the Palestinian and other Arab territories occupied by Israel, including Jerusalem;

2. *Condemns* Israeli policies and practices against Palestinian students and faculty in schools, universities and other educational institutions in the occupied Palestinian territories, especially the policy of opening fire on defenceless students, causing many casualties;

3. *Condemns* the systematic Israeli campaign of repression against universities in the occupied Palestinian territories, restricting and impeding academic activities of Palestinian universities by subjecting selection of courses, textbooks and educational programmes, admission of students and appoint-

ment of faculty members to the control and supervision of the military occupation authorities, in clear contravention of the Geneva Convention relative to the Protection of Civilian Persons in Time of War;

4. *Demands* that Israel, the occupying Power, comply with the provisions of the fourth Geneva Convention relative to the Protection of Civilian Persons in Time of War and rescind all actions and measures against all educational institutions and ensure the freedom of these institutions;

5. *Requests* the Security Council to convene urgently in order to take the necessary measures, in accordance with the provisions of the Charter of the United Nations, to ensure that the Government of Israel, the occupying Power, rescinds the illegal measures taken against the Palestinian mayors and the Sharia Judge Tamimi, and to facilitate their immediate return so that they can resume the functions for which they were elected.

92nd plenary meeting
11 December 1980

181. General Assembly Resolution 35/169 on the Question of Palestine, December 15, 1980*

* G.A. Res. 169, 35 U.N. GAOR Supp. (No. 48) at 26, U.N. Doc. A/35/48 (1980).

A

The General Assembly,

Recalling and reaffirming its resolutions 181 (II) of 29 November 1947, 194 (III) of 11 December 1948, 3236 (XXIX) of 22 November 1974, 3375 (XXX) and 3376 (XXX) of 10 November 1975, 31/20 of 24 November 1976, 32/40 A and B of 2 December 1977, 33/28 A to C of 7 December 1978, 34/ 65 A to D of 29 November and 12 December 1979 and ES-7/2 of 29 July 1980,

Having considered the report of the Committee on the Exercise of the Inalienable Rights of the Palestinian People,[38]

Having heard the statement of the Palestine Liberation Organization, the representative of the Palestinian people,[39]

1. *Expresses its grave concern* that no just solution to the problem of Palestine has been achieved and that this problem therefore continues to aggravate the Middle East conflict, of which it is the core, and to endanger international peace and security, and that Security Council resolution 242 (1967) of 22 November 1967 does not provide for the future and for the inalienable rights of the Palestinian people, the attainment of which is a *conditio sine qua non* for a just solution of the question of Palestine;

2. *Reaffirms* that a just and lasting peace in the Middle East cannot be established without the achievement, *inter alia*, of a just solution of the problem of Palestine on the basis of the attainment of the inalienable rights of the Palestinian people, including the right of return and the right to self-determination, national independence and sovereignty in Palestine, in accordance with the Charter of the United Nations and the principles of international law;

3. *Stresses* the basic principle that the future of the Palestinian people cannot be discussed in their absence and, therefore, calls once more for the invitation of the Palestine Liberation Organization, the representative of the Palestinian people, to participate, on the basis of General Assembly resolution, 3237 (XXIX) of 22 November 1974, in all efforts, deliberations and conferences on the Middle East which are held under the auspices of the United Nations, on an equal footing with other parties;

4. *Endorses* the recommendations of the Committee on the Exercise of the Inalienable Rights of the Palestinian People contained in paragraphs 45 to 48 of its report and draws the attention of the Security Council to the need for urgent action thereon;

5. *Reaffirms* the inalienable right of the Palestinians to return to their homes and property in Palestine, from which they have been displaced and uprooted, and calls for their return;

6. *Reaffirms also* the inalienable rights in Palestine of the Palestinian people, including:

---

[38] *Ibid.,* [*Official Records of the General Assembly*], *Thirty-fifth Session, Supplement No. 35* (A/35/35).

[39] *Ibid., Thirty-fifth Session, Plenary Meetings,* 75th meeting, paras. 85-141.

(*a*) The right to self-determination without external interference, and to national independence and sovereignty;

(*b*) The right to establish its own independent sovereign State;

7. *Strongly reaffirms* its repeated endorsement of the recommendations of the Committee on the Exercise of the Inalienable Rights of the Palestinian People, as contained in paragraphs 59 to 72 of its report on its thirty-first session, and as reproduced in the annex to the present resolution;

8. *Demands* the complete and unconditional withdrawal by Israel from all the Palestinian and other Arab territories occupied since June 1967, including Jerusalem, in conformity with the fundamental principle of the inadmissibility of the acquisition of territory by force;

9. *Demands* that Israel should fully comply with the provisions, in particular, of Security Council resolution 465 (1980) adopted unanimously on 1 March 1980;

10. *Further demands* that Israel should fully comply with all the resolutions of the United Nations relevant to the historic character of the Holy City of Jerusalem, in particular Security Council resolutions 476 (1980) of 30 June 1980 and 478 (1980) of 20 August 1980, and rejects the declaration of Israel that Jerusalem is its capital;

11. *Expresses its opposition* to all policies and plans aimed at the resettlement of the Palestinians outside their homeland;

12. *Condemns* Israel for its non-compliance with the provisions of General Assembly resolution ES-7/2 and Security Council resolutions 465 (1980) and 478 (1980) and other relevant resolutions of the United Nations;

13. *Requests* the Security Council to convene in order to consider the situation and the adoption of effective measures under Chapter VII of the Charter;

14. *Decides* to include in the provisional agenda of its thirty-sixth session the item entitled "Question of Palestine".

95th plenary meeting
15 December 1980

Annex
Recommendations of the Committee on the Exercise of the Inalienable Rights of the Palestinian People, endorsed by the General Assembly at its thirty-first session[40]

I. BASIC CONSIDERATIONS AND GUIDELINES

59. The question of Palestine is at the heart of the Middle East problem, and, consequently, the Committee stressed its belief that no solution in the Middle East can be envisaged which does not fully take into account the legitimate aspirations of the Palestinian people.

60. The legitimate and inalienable rights of the Palestinian people to re-

---

[40] The recommendations endorsed by the General Assembly in its resolution 31/20 were originally issued as part two of *Official Records of the General Assembly, Thirty-first Session, Supplement No. 35* (A/31/35).

turn to their homes and property and to achieve self-determination, national independence and sovereignty are endorsed by the Committee in the conviction that the full implementation of these rights will contribute decisively to a comprehensive and final settlement of the Middle East crisis.

61. The participation of the Palestine Liberation Organization, the representative of the Palestinian people, on an equal footing with other parties, on the basis of General Assembly resolutions 3236 (XXIX) and 3375 (XXX) is indispensable in all efforts, deliberations and conferences on the Middle East which are held under the auspices of the United Nations.

62. The Committee recalls the fundamental principle of the inadmissibility of the acquisition of territory by force and stresses the consequent obligation for complete and speedy evacuation of any territory so occupied.

63. The Committee considers that it is the duty and the responsibility of all concerned to enable the Palestinians to exercise their inalienable rights.

64. The Committee recommends an expanded and more influential role by the United Nations and its organs in promoting a just solution to the question of Palestine and in the implementation of such a solution. The Security Council, in particular, should take appropriate action to facilitate the exercise by the Palestinians of their right to return to their homes, lands and property. The Committee, furthermore, urges the Security Council to promote action towards a just solution, taking into account all the powers conferred on it by the Charter of the United Nations.

65. It is with this perspective in view and on the basis of the numerous resolutions of the United Nations, after due consideration of all the facts, proposals and suggestions advanced in the course of its deliberations, that the Committee submits its recommendations on the modalities for the implementation of the exercise of the inalienable rights of the Palestinian people.

II. RIGHT OF RETURN

66. The natural and inalienable right of Palestinians to return to their homes is recognized by resolution 194 (III), which the General Assembly has reaffirmed almost every year since its adoption. This right was also unanimously recognized by the Security Council in its resolution 237 (1967); the time for the urgent implementation of these resolutions is long overdue.

67. Without prejudice to the right of all Palestinians to return to their homes, lands and property, the Committee considers that the programme of implementation of the exercise of this right may be carried out in two phases.

Phase one

68. The first phase involves the return to their homes of the Palestinians displaced as a result of the war of June 1967. The Committee recommends that:

(*a*) The Security Council should request the immediate implementation of its resolution 237 (1967) and that such implementation should not be related to any other condition;

(*b*) The resources of the International Committee of the Red Cross and/ or of the United Nations Relief and Works Agency for Palestine Refugees in the Near East, suitably financed and mandated, may be employed to assist in the solution of any logistical problems involved in the resettlement of those returning to their homes. These agencies could also assist, in co-operation with the host countries and the Palestine Liberation Organization, in the identification of the displaced Palestinians.

Phase two

69. The second phase deals with the return to their homes of the Palestinians displaced between 1948 and 1967. The Committee recommends that:

(*a*) While the first phase is being implemented, the United Nations in cooperation with the States directly involved, and the Palestine Liberation Organization as the interim representative of the Palestinian entity, should proceed to make the necessary arrangements to enable Palestinians displaced between 1948 and 1967 to exercise their right to return to their homes and property, in accordance with the relevant United Nations resolutions, particularly General Assembly resolution 194 (III);

(*b*) Palestinians not choosing to return to their homes should be paid just and equitable compensation as provided for in resolution 194 (III).

III. RIGHT TO SELF-DETERMINATION, NATIONAL INDEPENDENCE AND SOVEREIGNTY

70. The Palestinian people has the inherent right to self-determination, national independence and sovereignty in Palestine. The Committee considers that the evacuation of the territories occupied by force and in violation of the principles of the Charter and relevant resolutions of the United Nations is a *conditio sine qua non* for the exercise by the Palestinian people of its inalienable rights in Palestine. The Committee considers, furthermore, that upon the return of the Palestinians to their homes and property and with the establishment of an independent Palestinian entity, the Palestinian people will be able to exercise its rights to self-determination and to decide its form of government without external interference.

71. The Committee also feels that the United Nations has a historical duty and responsibility to render all assistance necessary to promote the economic development and prosperity of the Palestinian entity.

72. To these ends, the Committee recommends that:

(*a*) A time-table should be established by the Security Council for the complete withdrawal by Israeli occupation forces from those areas occupied in 1967; such withdrawal should be completed no later than 1 June 1977;

(*b*) The Security Council may need to provide temporary peacekeeping forces in order to facilitate the process of withdrawal;

(*c*) Israel should be requested by the Security Council to desist from the establishment of new settlements and to withdraw during this period from settlements established since 1967 in the occupied territories; Arab property and all essential services in these areas should be maintained intact;

(*d*) Israel should also be requested to abide scrupulously by the provisions of the Geneva Convention relative to the Protection of Civilian Persons in Time of War, of 12 August 1949,[41] and to declare, pending its speedy withdrawal from these territories, its recognition of the applicability of that Convention;

(*e*) The evacuated territories, with all property and services intact, should be taken over by the United Nations, which, with the co-operation of the League of Arab States, will subsequently hand over these evacuated areas to the Palestine Liberation Organization as the representative of the Palestinian people;

(*f*) The United Nations should, if necessary, assist in establishing communications between Gaza and the West Bank;

(*g*) As soon as the independent Palestinian entity has been established, the United Nations, in co-operation with the States directly involved and the Palestinian entity, should, taking into account General Assembly resolution 3375 (XXX), make further arrangements for the full implementation of the inalienable rights of the Palestinian people, the resolution of outstanding problems and the establishment of a just and lasting peace in the region, in accordance with all relevant United Nations resolutions;

(*h*) The United Nations should provide the economic and technical assistance necessary for the consolidation of the Palestinian entity.

B

The General Assembly,

Recalling and reaffirming its resolutions 34/65 A to D of 29 November and 12 December 1979,

Taking note of paragraphs 31 and 47 of the report of the Committee on the Exercise of the Inalienable Rights of the Palestinian People,[42]

1. *Reaffirms* its rejection of those provisions of the accords which ignore, infringe, violate or deny the inalienable rights of the Palestinian people, including the right of return, the right of self-determination and the right to national independence and sovereignty in Palestine, in accordance with the Charter of the United Nations and the principles of international law, and which envisage and condone continued Israeli occupation of the Palestinian territories occupied by Israel since 1967;

2. *Expresses its strong opposition* to all partial agreements and separate treaties which constitute a flagrant violation of the rights of the Palestinian people, the principles of the Charter and the resolutions adopted in the various international forums on the Palestinian issue, as well as the principles of international law, and declares that all agreements and separate treaties have no validity in so far as they purport to determine the future of the

---

[41] United Nations, *Treaty Series*, vol. 75, No. 973, p. 287.
[42] *Official Records of the General Assembly, Thirty-fifth Session, Supplement No. 35* (A/35/35).

Palestinian people and of the Palestinian territories occupied by Israel since 1967;

3. *Declares* that no State has the right to undertake any actions, measures or negotiations that could affect the future of the Palestinian people, its inalienable rights and the occupied Palestinian territories without the participation of the Palestine Liberation Organization on an equal footing, in accordance with the relevant United Nations resolutions, and rejects all such actions, measures and negotiations.

95th plenary meeting
15 December 1980

C

The General Assembly,

Recalling its resolutions 3376 (XXX) of 10 November 1975, 31/20 of 24 November 1976, 32/40 A and B of 2 December 1977, 33/28 A to C of 7 December 1978, 34/65 A to D of 29 November and 12 December 1979 and ES-7/3 of 29 July 1980,

Having considered the report of the Committee on the Exercise of the Inalienable Rights of the Palestinian People,[42]

1. *Expresses its appreciation* to the Committee on the Exercise of the Inalienable Rights of the Palestinian People for its efforts in performing the tasks assigned to it by the General Assembly;

2. *Requests* the Committee to keep the situation relating to the question of Palestine under review and to report and make suggestions to the General Assembly or the Security Council, as appropriate;

3. *Authorizes* the Committee to continue to exert all efforts to promote the implementation of its recommendations, to send delegations or representatives to international conferences where such representation would be considered by it to be appropriate, and to report thereon to the General Assembly at its thirty-sixth session and thereafter;

4. *Requests* the United Nations Conciliation Commission for Palestine, established under General Assembly resolution 194 (III) of 11 December 1948, as well as other United Nations bodies associated with the question of Palestine, to co-operate fully with the Committee on the Exercise of the Inalienable Rights of the Palestinian People and to make available to the Committee, at its request, the relevant information and documentation which they have at their disposal;

5. *Decides* to circulate the report of the Committee to all the competent bodies of the United Nations and urges them to take the necessary action, as appropriate, in accordance with the Committee's programme of implementation;

6. *Requests* the Secretary-General to continue to provide the Committee with all the necessary facilities for the performance of its tasks.

95th plenary meeting
15 December 1980

D

The General Assembly,

Having considered the report of the Committee on the Exercise of the Inalienable Rights of the Palestinian People,[42]

Noting, in particular, the information contained in paragraphs 20 to 29 and 38 to 44 of that report,

Recalling its resolutions 32/40 B of 2 December 1977, 33/28 C of 7 December 1978 and 34/65 D of 12 December 1979,

1. *Notes with appreciation* the action taken by the Secretary-General in compliance with General Assembly resolution 34/65 D;

2. *Requests* the Secretary-General to ensure that the Special Unit on Palestinian Rights of the Secretariat, in consultation with the Committee on the Exercise of the Inalienable Rights of the Palestinian People and under its guidance, continues to discharge the tasks detailed in paragraph 1 of General Assembly resolution 32/40 B and paragraph 2 (*b*) of resolution 34/65 D;

3. *Also requests* the Secretary-General to keep under constant review the question of the strengthening of the Special Unit on Palestinian Rights and to provide it with the resources necessary to discharge the responsibilities assigned to it by the General Assembly as well as the redesignation of the Special Unit as requested in paragraph 1 of resolution 34/65 D;

4. *Further requests* the Secretary-General to ensure the continued co-operation of the Department of Public Information and other units of the Secretariat in enabling the Special Unit of Palestinian Rights to perform its tasks;

5. *Invites* all Governments and organizations to lend their co-operation to the Committee on the Exercise of the Inalienable Rights of the Palestinian People and the Special Unit on Palestinian Rights in the performance of their tasks;

6. *Notes with appreciation* the action taken by Member States to observe annually on 29 November the International Day of Solidarity with the Palestinian People and the issuance by them of special postage stamps for the occasion.

95th plenary meeting
15 December 1980

E

The General Assembly,

Recalling and reaffirming its resolutions 2253 (ES-V) of 4 July 1967 and 2254 (ES-V) of 14 July 1967,

Recalling the resolutions of the Security Council relevant to the character and status of the Holy City of Jerusalem, in particular resolutions 252 (1968) of 21 May 1968, 267 (1969) of 3 July 1969, 271 (1969) of 15 September 1969, 298 (1971) of 25 September 1971, 465 (1980) of 1 March 1980, 476 (1980) of 30 June 1980 and 478 (1980) of 20 August 1980,

Reaffirming that the acquisition of territory by force is inadmissible,

Bearing in mind the specific status of Jerusalem and, in particular, the need for protection and preservation of the unique spiritual and religious dimension of the Holy Places in the city,

Expressing its satisfaction at the decision taken by the States which have responded to Security Council resolution 478 (1980) and withdrawn their diplomatic representatives from the Holy City of Jerusalem,

Recalling the Geneva Convention relative to the Protection of Civilian Persons in Time of War, of 12 August 1949,[43]

Deploring the persistence of Israel in changing the physical character, demographic composition, institutional structure and the status of the Holy City of Jerusalem,

Deeply concerned over the enactment of a "basic law" in the Israeli Knesset proclaiming a change in the character and status of the Holy City of Jerusalem, with its implications for peace and security,

1. *Censures* in the strongest terms the enactment by Israel of the "Basic Law" on Jerusalem;

2. *Affirms* that the enactment of the "Basic Law" by Israel constitutes a violation of international law and does not affect the continued application of the Geneva Convention relative to the Protection of Civilian Persons in Time of War, of 12 August 1949, in the Palestinian and other Arab territories occupied since June 1967, including Jerusalem;

3. *Determines* that all legislative and administrative measures and actions taken by Israel, the occupying Power, which have altered or purport to alter the character and status of the Holy City of Jerusalem, and, in particular, the recent "Basic Law" on Jerusalem and the proclamation of Jerusalem as the capital of Israel, are null and void and must be rescinded forthwith;

4. *Affirms also* that this action constitutes a serious obstruction to achieving a comprehensive, just and lasting peace in the Middle East;

5. *Decides* not to recognize that "Basic Law" and such other actions by Israel that, as a result of this law, seek to alter the character and status of Jerusalem and calls upon all States, specialized agencies and other international organizations to comply with the present resolution and other relevant resolutions and urges them not to conduct any business which is not in conformity with the provisions of the present resolution and the other relevant resolutions.

95th plenary meeting
15 December 1980

43 United Nations, *Treaty Series*, vol. 75, No. 973, p. 287.

182. General Assembly Resolution 35/207 on the Situation in the Middle East, December 16, 1980*

* G.A. Res. 207, 35 U.N. GAOR Supp. (No. 48) at 39, U.N. Doc. A/35/48 (1980).

The General Assembly,

Having discussed the item entitled "The situation in the Middle East",

Taking into account the support extended to the just causes of the Palestinian people and the other Arab countries in their struggle against Israeli aggression and occupation in order to achieve a comprehensive, just and lasting peace in the Middle East and the full exercise by the Palestinian people of its inalienable national rights, as affirmed by previous resolutions of the General Assembly relating to the question of Palestine and the situation in the Middle East,

Deeply concerned that the Arab and Palestinian territories occupied since June 1967, including Jerusalem, still remain under illegal Israeli occupation, that the relevant resolutions of the United Nations have not been implemented and that the Palestinian people is still denied the restoration of its land and the exercise of its inalienable national rights in conformity with international law, as reaffirmed by resolutions of the United Nations,

Reaffirming that the acquisition of territory by force is inadmissible under the Charter of the United Nations and the principles of international law and that Israel must withdraw from all the occupied Palestinian and other Arab territories, including Jerusalem,

Reaffirming further the necessity of establishing a comprehensive, just and lasting peace in the region, based on full respect for the Charter and the principles of international law,

1. *Condemns* Israel's continued occupation of Palestinian and other Arab territories, in violation of the Charter of the United Nations, the principles of international law and the relevant resolutions of the United Nations, and renews its call for the immediate, unconditional and total withdrawal of Israel from all these occupied territories;

2. *Reaffirms* its conviction that the question of Palestine is at the core of the conflict in the Middle East and that no comprehensive, just and lasting peace in the region will be achieved without the full exercise by the Palestinian people of its inalienable national rights;

3. *Reaffirms further* that a just and comprehensive settlement of the situation in the Middle East cannot be achieved without the participation on an equal footing of the parties to the conflict, including the Palestine Liberation Organization as the representative of the Palestinian people;

4. *Declares once more* that peace in the Middle East is indivisible and that a just and lasting settlement of the Middle East problem must be based on a comprehensive solution, under the auspices of the United Nations, which ensures complete and unconditional withdrawal from all the Palestinian and other Arab territories occupied since June 1967, including Jerusalem, and enables the Palestinian people to exercise its inalienable rights, including the right of return, and the right to self-determination, national independence and the establishment of its independent State in Palestine under the leadership of the Palestine Liberation Organization, in accordance with resolu-

tions of the United Nations relating to the question of Palestine, in particular General Assembly resolutions ES-7/2 of 29 July 1980 and 35/169 A of 15 December 1980;

5. *Rejects* all partial agreements and separate treaties which violate the recognized rights of the Palestinian people and contradict the principles of just and comprehensive solutions to the Middle East problem to ensure the establishment of a just peace in the area;

6. *Further reaffirms* its strong rejection of Israel's decision to annex Jerusalem, declare it as its "capital" and alter its physical character, demographic composition, institutional structure and status, considers all these measures and their consequences null and void, requests that they should be rescinded immediately and calls upon all Member States, specialized agencies and other international organizations to abide by the present resolution and all other relevant resolutions, including General Assembly resolution 35/169 E of 15 December 1980;

7. *Strongly condemns* Israel's aggression against Lebanon and the Palestinian people as well as its practices in the occupied Palestinian and other Arab territories, particularly the Syrian Golan Heights, including annexation, the establishment of settlements, assassination attempts and other terrorist, aggressive and repressive measures which are in violation of the Charter and the principles of international law;

8. *Calls* for strict respect for the territorial integrity, sovereignty and political independence of Lebanon within its internationally recognized boundaries;

9. *Requests* the Secretary-General to report to the Security Council periodically on the development of the situation and to submit to the General Assembly at its thirty-sixth session a report covering the developments in the Middle East in all their aspects.

98th plenary meeting
16 December 1980

183. Security Council Resolution 484 Expressing Concern for Israeli Expulsion of Mayors from Hebron and Halhoul and Calling for Their Return, December 19, 1980*

* S.C. Res. 484, 35 U.N. SCOR (2260th mtg.) at 16, U.N. Doc. S/INF/36 (1980).

The Security Council,

   Recalling its resolutions 468 (1980) and 469 (1980),

   Taking note of General Assembly resolution 35/122 F of 11 December 1980,

   Expressing its grave concern at the expulsion by Israel of the Mayor of Hebron and the Mayor of Halhoul,

   1. *Reaffirms* the applicability of the Geneva Convention relative to the Protection of Civilian Persons in Time of War, of 12 August 1949, to all the Arab territories occupied by Israel in 1967;

   2. *Calls upon* Israel, the occupying Power, to adhere to the provisions of the Convention;

   3. *Declares it imperative* that the Mayor of Hebron and the Mayor of Halhoul be enabled to return to their homes and resume their responsibilities;

   4. *Requests* the Secretary-General to report on the implementation of the present resolution as soon as possible.

Adopted unanimously at the 2260th meeting.

184. Excerpt from the Final Resolutions of the Third Islamic Summit on Palestine and Jerusalem, Taif, January 25–28, 1981*

* 10 J. Palestine Stud. 182 (Spring 1981).

The Conference endorsed the following political resolutions:

1. *Jerusalem: Basic Programme of Action for the Confrontation of the Zionist Enemy:*

Commitment to liberate Arab Jerusalem so that it may be the capital of the Palestinian state, and to call on all countries in the world to respect the UN resolutions by refusing to treat the Zionist occupation authorities in such a manner as to enable them to claim that this treatment amounts to implicit recognition or acceptance of the *fait accompli* they have imposed by declaring Jerusalem to be the undivided capital of the Zionist entity.

It was decided to make use of all the Islamic countries' economic capabilities and natural resources with a view to weakening the Zionist economy, and to halt the financial, economic and political support received by Israel; also, to make every effort to change international political positions in favour of the Palestinian people and in support of the PLO.

2. *The Question of Palestine and the Middle East:*

The Conference resolves to regard the cause of Palestine as the essence of the Middle East problem, the first cause of the Islamic nation, and affirms its commitment to liberate all the occupied Palestinian and Arab territories and not to accept any situation liable to prejudice Arab sovereignty over Jerusalem, nor to permit any Arab or Islamic party to reach any unilateral solution of the Palestine question or the question of the occupied Arab territories.

The Conference affirmed that there can only be a just peace in the Middle East if it is based on the full and unconditional withdrawal of the Zionist entity from all the occupied Palestinian and Arab territories and the recovery of the inalienable rights of the Palestinian people, including the right to return, to self-determination and to establish their independent state in the land of Palestine under the leadership of the PLO.

The Conference resolves to continue to resist the Camp David agreement, and to regard Security Council resolution 242 as incompatible with Palestinian and Arab rights and as not constituting a sound basis for the solution of the Middle East crisis and the Palestine question.

The Conference resolves that the Islamic countries are committed to using all their military, political and economic capabilities and their natural resources, including oil, as an effective means of supporting the inalienable national rights of the Palestinian people and the Arab nation and for the confrontation of the countries that provide the Zionist entity with military, economic and political support.

The Conference calls on the countries of the European Community to implement their undertakings as regards the invalidity of their bilateral and collective economic agreements with Israel in the occupied Palestinian Arab territories.

3. *The Situation in Afghanistan:*

The Conference expressed its extreme concern at continued Soviet armed intervention in Afghanistan and renewed the demand for the withdrawal of all foreign forces from the territory of Afghanistan.

It also expressed extreme concern at the situation of the Afghan refugees and urged that they be provided with aid, and that a situation favourable to their return to their homes be ensured.

The Conference called for redoubled efforts to ensure that Afghanistan remains an independent non-aligned Islamic country, and affirms the Islamic Conference Organization's commitment to continue efforts to solve this issue, and recommended that the Ministerial Committee, composed of the Secretary-General of the Islamic Conference Organization and the foreign ministers of Guinea, Iran, Pakistan and Tunisia, cooperate with the Secretary-General of the UN and his special representative in their efforts to reach a just solution of the situation in Afghanistan.

4. *Islamic Solidarity:*

The Conference stressed the importance of the Islamic member states coexisting on a basis of justice, equality and mutual respect, and of their commitment to non-interference in internal affairs.

The Conference urged coordination of efforts and solidarity with a view to achieving the independence of all peoples and protecting their full sovereignty and legitimate interests. . . .

It urged the member states to increase their cooperation in the economic, commercial and technical fields in the interests of Islamic solidarity.

The Conference called on the member states to refrain from joining the military pacts now existing within the framework of the conflict between the great powers, and not to permit the establishment of foreign military bases in their territory.

The Conference declared its total commitment to the principles of non-interference—direct or indirect—in internal affairs and of refraining from inciting discord and promoting disunity, which are incompatible with the ordinances of Islam on which the Islamic Conference Organization is based. It also resolved to make every effort to eliminate such differences of view or tenets as may arise between members, by stressing the fundamental spiritual, moral and social values that unite all Muslims and by eliminating all that is incompatible with the essence of Islam.

5. *Jihad:*

The Kings, Emirs and Presidents of the Islamic countries agreed to declare *jihad* to rescue Jerusalem, support the Palestinian people and ensure withdrawal from the occupied Arab territories. The Islamic countries made it clear in their resolution that the word *jihad* is used in its Islamic sense, which is not susceptible to interpretation or misunderstanding, and that the practical measures for its implementation will be taken in conformity with this and in constant consultation between the Islamic countries.

6. *The Conflict Between Iran and Iraq:*

The Conference expressed profound concern at the continued fighting between Iran and Iraq and, in the light of the resolution adopted by the Extraordinary Conference of Foreign Ministers held in New York on September 26, 1980, on the formation of a good offices committee, the Conference resolved to call on Iran and Iraq to accept Islamic mediation and to facilitate the task of the good offices committee. It was decided to expand the membership of this committee to include the Secretary-General, Senegal, Gambia, Pakistan, Bangladesh, Turkey, Guinea and the PLO.

The Conference called on the two conflicting states to impose an immediate cease-fire, and announced that the member states had approved the formation of an Islamic force to enforce the cease-fire, if necessary, and at the recommendation of the good offices committee.

185. Excerpt from the Resolutions Adopted by the Fourth
Congress of the PFLP, April 1981*

* 10 J. Palestine Stud. 189 (Summer 1981).

International Level

1. The congress emphasized that the Palestinian Revolution is part of the revolutionary anti-imperialist front, and stressed the necessity of enhancing the solidarity with the socialist community, led by the Soviet Union, the world national liberation movements, and the working class and democratic forces in the capitalist countries, who are confronting international imperialism and its allies.

2. The congress salutes and expressed its gratitude to the Soviet Union and its great communist party, and to the other socialist countries, for their principled support of all the struggling peoples of the world, based on the principle of proletarian internationalism, and in particular their active support of and solidarity on all levels with the Palestinian Revolution. In addition, the congress highly evaluated the economic, political, social and military achievements which have enhanced and strengthened the international socialist community and their confrontation with international imperialism and its aggressive policies. While the congress noted its strong satisfaction with the growth and development of relations between the PFLP and the Soviet Union and all the socialist countries, it emphasized our sincere desire to achieve increased development of this relation, based on our resolute belief in the strategic alliance between the Palestinian Revolution and the socialist community, led by the Soviet Union - the loyal friend of the struggling people.

3. The congress saluted the struggle and victories of the world national liberation movements; these victories constitute a primary part of the struggle of the forces of the international revolutionary process against imperialism. The congress noted the development taking place in the class structure of the world national liberation movements and the deepening of their social content and goals. It reaffirmed that the solidarity and linkage of the struggle of this movement with that of the struggle of the other forces of the world revolutionary process, in particular the support of the Soviet Union, constitutes another primary factor in its ability to achieve victory.

4. The congress saluted the working class and democratic forces in the capitalist countries in their struggle against capitalist exploitation and local monopolies, and their solidarity with the national liberation movements, in particular their support of the struggle of the Palestinian people for their inalienable rights.

5. The congress militantly saluted the peoples who have achieved victory over the reactionary and backward forces, and succeeded in directing their countries on the road to the national democratic development opposing imperialism and its allies. We salute the peoples of Ethiopia, Nicaragua, Grenada and Afghanistan, and appreciate the international support and aid given by the Soviet Union to the Afghani people to assist them in confronting the attacks of imperialism, reaction and renegade forces.

6. The congress saluted and expressed its militant solidarity with all the

world national liberation movements, especially the struggle in El Salvador under the leadership of Farabundo Marti Front for National Liberation, in South Africa under the leadership of the African National Congress and in Namibia under the leadership of SWAPO.

7. The congress saluted and appreciated the steadfastness of socialist Cuba, in its forefront position in confronting US imperialism. We salute its achievements on the road to constructing a socialist society. We salute the revolutionary example it represents in its rich experience, its revolutionary leadership and the ability to build a communist party through struggle and determination.

8. The congress warmly saluted the victory of the great Vietnamese people and the reunification of their country. We reaffirm our complete support of their struggle to reconstruct and develop their country and of their confrontation with the aggressions of the renegade Chinese leadership.

9. The congress completely condemned the policies of imperialism, led by the US, of military build-up and increasing international tension, threatening the world with the return of the cold war atmosphere. These policies are manifested in imperialism's delay in the negotiations for nuclear arms limitations and the ratification of SALT II; the placing of medium-range nuclear missiles in Western Europe; the increase of its fleets in the Indian Ocean, the Arabian Sea, the Arab Gulf, the Red Sea, the Mediterranean Sea, and the Caribbean; the building of aggressive military bases in Diego Garcia, Egypt, Kenya, Somalia, Oman and Saudi Arabia. By adopting these policies, world imperialism, under the leadership of the US, is completely responsible for threatening world peace, security and stability.

Arab Level

1. The 4th national congress of the PFLP, which was held in Lebanon under the protection of the patriotic Lebanese masses, sincerely declares its appreciation of the great Lebanese masses and the Lebanese Patriotic [National] Movement (LPM). The congress reaffirmed the militant solidarity between the Lebanese masses under the leadership of the LPM, and the Palestinian masses, under the leadership of their armed revolution, in their confrontation against the imperialist-Zionist-reactionary conspiracy which aims at liquidating the Palestinian Revolution and the LPM in order to impose the isolationist-Zionist project in Lebanon. The congress reaffirmed the leading role of the LPM in the confrontation of this conspiracy, to protect the unity and Arab identity of Lebanon, and to guarantee its democratic development. The congress highly esteemed the militant consolidation between the LPM and the Palestinian Revolution. This is a concrete example of Arab solidarity: Arab mass solidarity forged in the struggle against the enemy, as opposed to reactionary Arab solidarity whose aim is to halt the Arab mass movement.

2. The congress reaffirmed the necessity to deepen Palestinian, Syrian

and patriotic Lebanese solidarity, to confront the imperialist-Zionist-reactionary conspiracy aimed at striking Syrian's steadfastness, liquidating the Palestinian Revolution and imposing the isolationist-Zionist project in Lebanon.

3. The congress saluted Syria for its confrontation position against the Camp David conspiracy, and reaffirmed our support for Syria against the moves of external and internal reactionary forces that are attempting to undermine its steadfastness.

4. The congress saluted the Egyptian Arab masses, under the leadership of the patriotic and progressive forces, and reaffirmed solidarity with and complete support of their struggle to overturn Sadat's treacherous policies, to foil the Camp David conspiracy, to protect Egypt's sovereignty, and to return Egypt to its natural position as the vanguard of our Arab nation's struggle against Zionism.

5. The congress warmly saluted our masses in Jordan, and reaffirmed Jordanian-Palestinian mass solidarity in the struggle to establish a democratic patriotic regime in Jordan, which will end the exploitation of the masses and pave the road for social democracy and development. This would broaden the mobilization of the masses in the struggle against the Zionist enemy.

6. The congress sent comradely salutes to the toiling masses in Democratic Yemen and their vanguard, the Yemeni Socialist Party, in their confrontation of the reactionary plots to liquidate their progressive regime, and their successful struggle to protect and deepen their social democratic and national achievements.

7. The congress saluted the struggling masses of the Arab Peninsula and Gulf, under the leadership of the patriotic and progressive forces, and reaffirmed our complete solidarity with and support of their struggle against the reactionary regimes in the region. We absolutely condemn the imperialist military bases and the increase of imperialist military presence in the area in general. The congress called upon democratic and progressive Arab forces to struggle to eliminate these bases and all forms of imperialist military presence in the region, and welcomed the proposal of comrade Ali Nassar Mohammed and the initiative of comrade Brezhnev, which call for peace and security in the region, and guarantee the freedom and sovereignty of its peoples, rather than threatening it with military invasion. On this occasion the congress militantly saluted the struggle of our comrades in the Peoples Front for the Liberation of Oman, the National Democratic Front in North Yemen, the Popular Front and the Liberation Front in Bahrain, the struggling forces in the Arab Peninsula and those forces opposing the Saudi regime.

8. The congress saluted the Libyan Jamahiriya and reaffirmed our solidarity with it in confronting reactionary forces and the attempts of the Egyptian regime to invade its territory. The congress welcomed the unconditional aid offered to the people of Chad in their just struggle against the

reactionary and colonialist forces; this is a blow to the parties of Camp David in that region.

9. The congress saluted the brotherly Arab people in Algeria, their party and government, and highly commended their commitment to the patriotic line against Camp David and the imperialist activities.

10. The congress saluted the POLISARIO Front and its fighters, and supports its struggle to liberate the people of the Western Sahara from the exploitation of the Moroccan regime, and to achieve their right to self-determination on their land.

11. The congress emphasized the position of the PFLP as an integral part of the Arab national liberation movement, and its commitment and participation in the struggles of this movement to achieve the objectives of the Arab nation: liberation, democracy, socialism and unity.

12. The congress saluted the Steadfastness and Confrontation Front call for developing this front and its programmes and implementing its resolutions on the basis of struggle.

13. The congress emphasized the importance of the role played by the Arab Peoples' Conference, and the necessity to develop its potential and content in order to radicalize and strengthen it.

14. The congress condemned the Iraqi war against the revolution of the Iranian masses, which comes as part of the retreating policies of the Iraqi regime, especially after the Iranian masses had succeeded in overthrowing the puppet Shah regime, placing Iran in the anti-imperialist camp, confronting imperialism and supporting the struggle of the Palestinian people.

15. The congress saluted the struggle of the masses in Iraq against the retreating policies of the regime in Iraq; welcomed the establishment of the national democratic front in Iraq, supports its programme and admires its role and that of all the democratic and progressive forces fighting for a democratic patriotic Iraq.

16. The congress condemned the oil policy of the Arab reactionary regimes, which is completely dependent on the imperialist plans, and the greed and exploitation of the monopolies The congress also condemned the policies of Arab reaction, that draws benefits from the oil revenues while most of the money pours back into the pockets of imperialism and its monopolies in the form of investments, stocks and deals. The congress views these policies as aiding the world capitalist system, serving imperialism and its objectives, and supporting the aggressive militaristic capabilities of the Zionist enemy. At the same time, these policies lead to the development of the comprador class in the Arab countries, whose interests are strongly tied to world imperialism and accordingly [members of this class] are obedient tools to execute its plans.

Palestinian Level

1. The congress saluted the heroic steadfastness of our people in the occupied homeland and our militants in Zionist prisons. The PFLP renews its

pledge to be faithful to their struggle and sacrifices, their goals and national aspirations, and to continue to uphold the militant and effective armed struggle until the achievement of the full national aims of our Palestinian struggle are achieved.

2. The congress saluted the militants of the Palestinian Resistance and the LPM, who are steadfast in South Lebanon, defending the Lebanese masses, the Palestinian Revolution and the honour and integrity of the Arab nation.

3. The congress reaffirmed that the PLO is the sole legitimate representative of the Palestinian Arab people wherever they are. We will protect the PLO's achievements and struggle against all attempts to undermine its representation of the Palestinian Arab people. We call for enhancement of Palestinian national unity within the framework of the PLO, based upon the political and organizational programme adopted at the 14th session of the PNC.

4. The congress reaffirmed the necessity of placing all efforts, with the cooperation of all patriotic Palestinian forces, to activate the Palestine National Front in the occupied land, increase its effectiveness and develop its potentials on the basis that it is the primary and actual arm of the PLO in occupied Palestine.

5. The congress noted the necessity to increase the efforts to crystallize the role of the democratic and progressive forces in the Palestinian arena as a step towards forming the unified Palestinian communist party.

6. The congress saluted the democratic, progressive, anti-Zionist Jewish forces, who oppose the ideology, practice and material entity of Zionism, and who support the struggle of the Palestinian people to achieve their national goals under the leadership of the PLO. The congress strongly condemned any contacts with any Zionist forces or elements, and any attempt to cover up such contacts, and demands that those that make such contacts be exposed, judged and disciplined.

7. The congress reaffirmed the PFLP's firm confrontation, by all possible means, of the policy of capitulationist political settlement, under any form or name, such as the so-called European initiative or the Jordanian option, etc.

8. The congress considers it our just right to struggle within and from the Arab lands and those bordering Palestine, against the imperialist-Zionist enemy. We reject any interventions, obstacles or terrorism against the Palestinian people wherever they are. We will protect their national militant identity from annihilation and oppression. We consider the struggle of our people as part of the struggle of the Arab masses and their revolutionary movement.

186. Senate Concurrent Resolution 39 on Anwar El-Sadat—Expressions of Gratitude and Sympathy, October 6, 1981*

* S. Con. Res. 39, 95 Stat. 1774 (1981).

Whereas, the Congress of the United States has learned with profound sorrow and deep regret of the tragic death of President Anwar el-Sadat of the Arab Republic of Egypt; and

Whereas, President Sadat has been a true friend of the United States and a true partner in the search for peace in the Middle East; and

Whereas, President Sadat has earned the affection and respect of the people of the United States for his historic leadership and statesmanship in the cause of international peace; and

Whereas, the Congress has confidence that Egypt's leaders and institutions will carry on the responsibilities of government with full competence and dedication, including moving forward in the search for an enduring peace settlement in the Middle East and in promoting the economic well being of all Egyptians; and

Whereas, the leaders of Egypt have today reaffirmed their intent to follow the policies of President Sadat: Now, therefore, be it

Resolved by the Senate (the House of Representatives concurring), That:

(1) The United States expresses its deep sympathies to the family of President Sadat and the people of Egypt for their tragic loss; and

(2) the United States reaffirms its friendship with and full support for the Government and people of Egypt.

Agreed to October 6, 1981.

187. Written Question to the European Council on Follow-up to the Declaration of Venice, October 14, 1981—Answer, November 27, 1981*

* 24 O.J. Eur. Comm. (No. C 338) 18 (1981).

WRITTEN QUESTION No 1127/81
by Mr Israel
to the Foreign Ministers of the ten Member States of the European
Community, meeting in political cooperation
(*14 October 1981*)

Subject: Follow-up to the Declaration of Venice

Do the Foreign Ministers not agree that, one year and three months after it was made, the Declaration of Venice has remained a dead letter? Is this state of affairs not the result of a contradiction inherent in the said declaration? The call which the 'Nine' made in paragraph 4 for 'recognition . . . of the right to existence and to security of all the States in the region, including Israel . . .' and in paragraph 7 for application on the 'universally accepted' principles defined in paragraph 4 'to all the parties concerned, and thus to the Palestinian people, and to the PLO . . .' is hard to reconcile with their recommendation, also contained in paragraph 7, that 'the PLO will have to be associated with the negotiations'.

At all events is it not clear from an objective reading of the Declaration of Venice that the PLO will have to participate in the negotiations even if it rejects, as it seems to do at present, the principles enshrined in paragraph 4 and in particular, of course, the right to existence and security of the State of Israel?

This being the case, how can the Foreign Ministers claim that the two principles defined as being those on which any settlement of the conflict between Israel and certain Arab States must be based are universally accepted when the PLO appears to be exempted by the 'Nine' from the obligation to recognize one of these principles?

ANSWER
(*27 November 1981*)

Paragraph 7 of the Venice Declaration states that the principles set out in Paragraph 4 'must be respected . . . by the PLO, which will have to be associated with negotiations'. The PLO are in no way exempted by the Ten from the need to adhere to the first principle; and it is evident from public statements over the past months that the Ten are continuing to urge the PLO to accept the right of Israel to exist. It would be unrealistic to expect any progress toward negotiations between all parties without the PLO making clear such acceptance.

188. General Assembly Resolution 36/73 on the Living Conditions of the Palestinian People, December 4, 1981*

* G.A. Res. 73, 36 U.N. GAOR Supp. (No. 51) at 103, U.N. Doc. A/36/51 (1981).

The General Assembly,

Recalling the Vancouver Declaration on Human Settlements, 1976,[24] and the relevant recommendations for national action[25] adopted by Habitat: United Nations Conference on Human Settlements,

Recalling also resolution 3, entitled "Living conditions of the Palestinians in occupied territories", contained in the recommendations for international co-operation adopted by Habitat: United Nations Conference on Human Settlements,[26] and Economic and Social Council resolutions 2026 (LXI) of 4 August 1976 and 2100 (LXIII) of 3 August 1977,

Recalling further its resolutions 3236 (XXIX) and 3237 (XXIX) of 22 November 1974, 31/110 of 16 December 1976, 32/171 of 19 December 1977, 33/110 of 18 December 1978, 34/113 of 14 December 1979 and 35/75 of 5 December 1980,

1. *Takes note* of the report of the Secretary-General on the living conditions of the Palestinian people;[27]

2. *Denounces* Israel for refusing to allow the Group of Experts on the Social and Economic Impact of the Israeli Occupation on the Living Conditions of the Palestinian People in the Occupied Arab Territories[28] to visit the Palestinian territories occupied by Israel;

3. *Condemns* Israel for the deteriorating living conditions of the Palestinian people in the occupied Palestinian territories;

4. *Affirms* that the elimination of the Israeli occupation is a prerequisite for the social and economic development of the Palestinian people in the occupied Palestinian territories;

5. *Recognizes* the need for a comprehensive report on the deterioration of the social and economic conditions of the Palestinian people in the occupied Palestinian territories;

6. *Requests* the Secretary-General to prepare a comprehensive and analytical report on the deteriorating living conditions of the Palestinian people in the occupied Palestinian territories and to submit it to the General Assembly at its thirty-seventh session, through the Economic and Social Council;

7. *Also requests* the Secretary-General, in preparing the above-mentioned report, to consult and co-operate with the Palestine Liberation Organization, the representative of the Palestinian people.

84th plenary meeting
4 December 1981

[24] *Report of Habitat: United Nations Conference on Human Settlements, Vancouver, 31 May-11 June 1976* (United Nations publication, Sales No. E.76.IV.7 and corrigendum), chap. I.
[25] *Ibid.*, chap. II.
[26] *Ibid.*, chap. III.
[27] A/36/260 and Add. 1-3.
[28] For the report of the Group of Experts, see A/35/533 and Corr. 1, annex I.

189. General Assembly Resolution 36/120 on the Question
of Palestine, December 10, 1981*

* G.A. Res. 120, 36 U.N. GAOR Supp. (No. 51) at 26, U.N. Doc. A/36/51
(1981).

A

The General Assembly,

Recalling its resolutions 3376 (XXX) of 10 November 1975, 31/20 of 24 November 1976, 32/40 A and B of 2 December 1977, 33/28 A to C of 7 December 1978, 34/65 A and B of 29 November 1979, 34/65 C and D of 12 December 1979, ES-7/2 of 29 July 1980 and 35/169 A to E of 15 December 1980,

Having considered the report of the Committee on the Exercise of the Inalienable Rights of the Palestinian People,[51]

1. *Expresses its appreciation* to the Committee on the Exercise of the Inalienable Rights of the Palestinian People for its efforts in performing the tasks assigned to it by the General Assembly;

2. *Requests* the Committee to keep the situation relating to the question of Palestine under review and to report and make suggestions to the General Assembly or the Security Council, as appropriate;

3. *Authorizes* the Committee to continue to exert all efforts to promote the implementation of its recommendations, to send delegations of representatives to international conferences where such representation would be considered by it to be appropriate, and to report thereon to the General Assembly at its thirty-seventh session and thereafter;

4. *Requests* the United Nations Conciliation Commission for Palestine, established under General Assembly resolution 194 (III) of 11 December 1948, as well as other United Nations bodies associated with the question of Palestine, to co-operate fully with the Committee and to make available to it, at its request, the relevant information and documentation which they have at their disposal;

5. *Decides* to circulate the report of the Committee to all the competent bodies of the United Nations and urges them to take the necessary action, as appropriate, in accordance with the Committee's programme of implementation;

6. *Requests* the Secretary-General to continue to provide the Committee with all the necessary facilities for the performance of its tasks.

93rd plenary meeting
10 December 1981

B

The General Assembly,

Having considered the report of the Committee on the Exercise of the Inalienable Rights of the Palestinian People,[51]

Taking note, in particular, of the information contained in paragraphs 39 to 48 of that report,

Recalling its resolutions 32/40 B of 2 December 1977, 33/28 C of 7 Decem-

[51] *Official Records of the General Assembly, Thirty-sixth Session, Supplement No. 35* (A/36/35).

ber 1978, 34/65 D of 12 December 1979 and 35/169 D of 15 December 1980,

1. *Takes note with appreciation* of the action taken by the Secretary-General in compliance with General Assembly resolution 35/169 D;

2. *Requests* the Secretary-General to ensure that the Special Unit on Palestinian Rights of the Secretariat continues to discharge the tasks detailed in paragraph 1 of General Assembly resolution 32/40 B and paragraph 2 (*b*) of Assembly resolution 34/65 D, in consultation with the Committee on the Exercise of the Inalienable Rights of the Palestinian People and under its guidance;

3. *Requests* the Secretary-General to provide the Special Unit on Palestinian Rights with the necessary additional resources to accomplish its tasks and to expand its work programme, *inter alia* through:

(*a*) The organization annually of a seminar in North America in addition to the regional seminars;

(*b*) More widespread dissemination of its publications in all the official languages;

(*c*) The translation of those publications into languages other than the official languages of the United Nations;

4. *Also requests* the Secretary-General to take necessary action on the re-designation of the Special Unit on Palestinian Rights, as requested in paragraph 1 of resolution 34/65 D, in keeping with the political importance of its work and its expanded work programme;

5. *Further requests* the Secretary-General to ensure the continued co-operation of the Department of Public Information and other units of the Secretariat in enabling the Special Unit on Palestinian Rights to perform its tasks, *inter alia* through the production, in consultation with the Committee, of a film on Palestinian rights and through the provision of copies of the photographic exhibit on Palestinian rights installed at United Nations Headquarters and of other visual material for use by the Special Unit and United Nations information centres;

6. *Invites* all Governments and organizations to lend their co-operation to the Committee and the Special Unit on Palestinian Rights in the performance of their tasks;

7. *Takes note with appreciation* of the action taken by Member States to observe annually on 29 November the International Day of Solidarity with the Palestinian People and the issuance by them of special postage stamps for the occasion.

93rd plenary meeting
10 December 1981

C

The General Assembly,

Having considered the report of the Committee on the Exercise of the Inalienable Rights of the Palestinian People,[51]

Recalling its relevant resolutions, particularly resolutions 31/20 of 24 November 1976 and ES-7/2 of 29 July 1980,

Gravely concerned that no just solution to the problem of Palestine has been achieved and that this problem therefore continues to aggravate the Middle East conflict, of which it is the core, and to endanger international peace and security,

Convinced that wider international recognition of the facts underlying the question of Palestine will lead to a just solution of the problem,

Recognizing that a lasting peace in the Middle East requires a just solution of the problem of Palestine through the attainment and exercise by the Palestinian people of its inalienable rights,

Emphasizing the need for a comprehensive effort to seek effective ways and means to enable the Palestinian people to attain and to exercise those rights,

1. *Decides* to convene, under the auspices of the United Nations, an International Conference on the Question of Palestine not later than 1984, on the basis of General Assembly resolution ES-7/2;

2. *Authorizes* the Committee on the Exercise of the Inalienable Rights of the Palestinian People to act as the Preparatory Committee for the Conference and to take all the necessary steps for its organization, to hold sessions particularly for this purpose and to make recommendations regarding, *inter alia*, the site, scheduling of and participation in the Conference, and the provisional agenda of the Conference;

3. *Invites* all appropriate United Nations bodies, the specialized agencies and other intergovernmental and nongovernmental organizations to co-operate with the Committee in the implementation of the present resolution;

4. *Requests* the Secretary-General to appoint a Secretary-General of the Conference and to provide all the necessary assistance to the Committee in the organization of the Conference.

93rd plenary meeting
10 December 1981

D

The General Assembly,

Having considered the report of the Committee on the Exercise of the Inalienable Rights of the Palestinian People[51] and the recommendations contained therein,[52]

Having heard the statement of the Palestine Liberation Organization, the representative of the Palestinian people,[53]

Expressing its extreme concern that no just solution to the problem of Palestine has been achieved and that this problem therefore continues to aggra-

[52] *Ibid.*, sect. V.
[53] *Ibid.*, *Thirty-sixth Session, Plenary Meetings*, 80th meeting, paras. 79-134.

vate the Middle East conflict, of which it is the core, and to endanger international peace and security,

Reaffirming that a just and comprehensive lasting peace in the Middle East
requires a just solution to the problem of Palestine through the attainment
by the Palestinian people of its inalienable rights,

Resolutely emphasizing the inadmissibility of the acquisition of territory by
force,

Recognizing the need to work for a comprehensive, just and lasting peace
in the Middle East,

Recalling and reaffirming its previous relevant resolutions, particularly resolutions 181(II) of 29 November 1947, 194 (III) of 11 December 1948, 3236
(XXIX) of 22 November 1974 and ES-7/2 of 29 July 1980,

1. *Reaffirms* the inalienable right of the Palestinians to return to their
homes and property in Palestine, from which they have been displaced and
uprooted, and calls for their early return;

2. *Reaffirms also* the inalienable rights in Palestine of the Palestinian people, including:

(*a*) The right to self-determination without external interference, and to
national independence and sovereignty;

(*b*) The right to establish its own independent sovereign State;

3. *Reaffirms*, in particular, that a comprehensive, just and lasting peace in
the Middle East cannot be established without the withdrawal of Israel from
all the occupied Palestinian and other Arab territories, including Jerusalem,
and without the achievement of a just solution of the problem of Palestine
on the basis of the attainment by the Palestinian people of its inalienable
rights in Palestine, in accordance with the Charter of the United Nations
and the relevant resolutions of the United Nations;

4. *Expresses its opposition* to all policies and plans aimed at the resettlement
of the Palestinians outside their homeland;

5. *Demands* that Israel should withdraw completely and unconditionally
from all the Palestinian and other Arab territories occupied since June
1967, including Jerusalem, with all property and services intact;

6. *Further demands* that Israel should fully comply with all the resolutions
of the United Nations relevant to the historic character of the Holy City of
Jerusalem, in particular Security Council resolutions 476 (1980) of 30 June
1980 and 478 (1980) of 20 August 1980, and rejects the enactment of a
"Basic Law" by the Israel Knesset proclaiming Jerusalem the capital of Israel;

Demands that Israel should fully comply with the provisions, in particular,
of Security Council resolution 465 (1980) adopted unanimously on 1 March
1980;

8. *Reaffirms* the basic principle that the future of the Palestinian people
can only be considered with its participation and calls for the participation
of the Palestine Liberation Organization, the representative of the Palestinian people, in all efforts, deliberations and conferences on the question of

Palestine and on the situation in the Middle East to be held under the auspices of the United Nations, on an equal footing and on the basis of the relevant resolutions of the United Nations;

9. *Endorses* the recommendations of the Committee on the Exercise of the Inalienable Rights of the Palestinian People contained in paragraphs 49 to 53 of its report[51] and draws the attention of the Security Council to the fact that action on the Committee's recommendations, as endorsed by the General Assembly in its resolution 31/20 of 24 November 1976,[54] is long overdue;

10. *Requests* the Security Council to convene in order to consider the situation and the adoption of effective measures to implement the recommendations of the Committee as endorsed by the General Assembly in its resolution 31/20;

11. *Decides* to include in the provisional agenda of its thirty-seventh session the item entitled "Question of Palestine".

93rd plenary meeting
10 December 1981

E

The General Assembly,

Recalling and reaffirming its resolutions 2253 (ES-V) of 4 July 1967, 2254 (ES-V) of 14 July 1967, 35/169 E of 15 December 1980 and 36/15 of 28 October 1981,

Recalling the resolutions of the Security Council relevant to the character and status of the Holy City of Jerusalem, in particular resolutions 252 (1968) of 21 May 1968, 267 (1969) of 3 July 1969, 271 (1969) of 15 September 1969, 298 (1971) of 25 September 1971, 465 (1980) of 1 March 1980, 476 (1980) of 30 June 1980 and 478 (1980) of 20 August 1980,

Reaffirming that the acquisition of territory by force is inadmissible,

Bearing in mind the specific status of Jerusalem and, in particular, the need for protection and preservation of the unique spiritual and religious dimension of the Holy Places in the city,

Recalling the Geneva Convention relative to the Protection of Civilian Persons in Time of War, of 12 August 1949,[55]

Deploring the persistence of Israel in changing the physical character, the demographic composition, the institutional structure and the status of the Holy City of Jerusalem,

1. *Determines once again* that all legislative and administrative measures and actions taken by Israel, the occupying Power, which have altered or purport to alter the character and status of the Holy City of Jerusalem, and, in particular, the so-called "Basic Law" on Jerusalem and the proclamation of Je-

---

[54] For the text of the recommendations, see resolution 35/169 A, annex.
[55] United Nations, *Treaty Series*, vol. 75, No. 973, p. 287.

rusalem as the capital of Israel, are null and void and must be rescinded forthwith;

2. *Affirms* that such actions constitute a serious obstruction to achieving a comprehensive, just and lasting peace in the Middle East, and a threat to international peace and security;

3. *Reaffirms* its resolution not to recognize that "Basic Law" and such other actions by Israel that, as a result of this law, seek to alter the character and status of Jerusalem and calls upon all States, specialized agencies and other international organizations to comply with the present resolution and other relevant resolutions and urges them not to conduct any business which is not in conformity with the provisions of the present resolution and the other relevant resolutions;

4. *Demands* that Israel should fully comply with all the resolutions of the United Nations relevant to the historic character of the Holy City of Jerusalem, in particular Security Council resolutions 476 (1980) and 478 (1980);

5. *Requests* the Secretary-General to report on the implementation of those resolutions within six months.

93rd plenary meeting
10 December 1981

F

The General Assembly,

Recalling and reaffirming its resolutions 34/65 A and B of 29 November 1979, 34/65 C and D of 12 December 1979 and 35/169 B of 15 December 1980,

Taking note of paragraphs 26, 27 and 52 of the report of the Committee on the Exercise of the Inalienable Rights of the Palestinian People,[51]

1. *Strongly reaffirms* its rejection of those provisions of the accords which ignore, infringe, violate or deny the inalienable rights of the Palestinian people, including the right of return, the right of self-determination and the right to national independence and sovereignty in Palestine, in accordance with the Charter of the United Nations and the principles of international law, and which envisage and condone continued Israeli occupation of the Palestinian territories occupied by Israel since 1967, including Jerusalem;

2. *Expresses its strong opposition* to all partial agreements and separate treaties which constitute a flagrant violation of the rights of the Palestinian people, the principles of the Charter and the resolutions adopted in the various international forums on the Palestinian issue, as well as the principles of international law, and declares that all agreements and separate treaties have no validity in so far as they purport to determine the future of the Palestinian people and of the Palestinian territories occupied by Israel since 1967, including Jerusalem;

3. *Declares* that no State has the right to undertake any actions, measures

or negotiations that could affect the future of the Palestinian people, its inalienable rights and the occupied Palestinian territories without the participation of the Palestine Liberation Organization on an equal footing, in accordance with the relevant resolutions of the United Nations, rejects all such actions, measures and negotiations, and considers all such actions, measures and negotiations as a flagrant violation of the inalienable rights of the Palestinian people;

4. *Decides* that all actions, measures and negotiations to implement or execute such accords and agreements, or any part thereof, are null and void in so far as they purport to determine the future of the Palestinian people and of the Palestinian territories occupied by Israel since 1967, including Jerusalem.

93rd plenary meeting
10 December 1981

190. Israel: Law on the Golan Heights,

December 14, 1981*

* Text provided by the Embassy of Israel, Washington, D.C., *reprinted in* 21 Int'l Legal Materials 163 (1982).

Golan Heights Law—5742/1981

1. The law, jurisdiction and administration of the State shall apply to the Golan Heights, as described in the appendix.

2. This law shall become valid on the day of its passage in the Knesset.

3. The Minister of the Interior shall be charged with the implementation of this law, and he is entitled, in consultation with the Minister of Justice, to enact regulations for its implementation and to formulate in regulations transitional provisions and provisions concerning the continued application of regulations, orders, administrative orders, rights and duties which were in force on the Golan Heights prior to the application of this law.

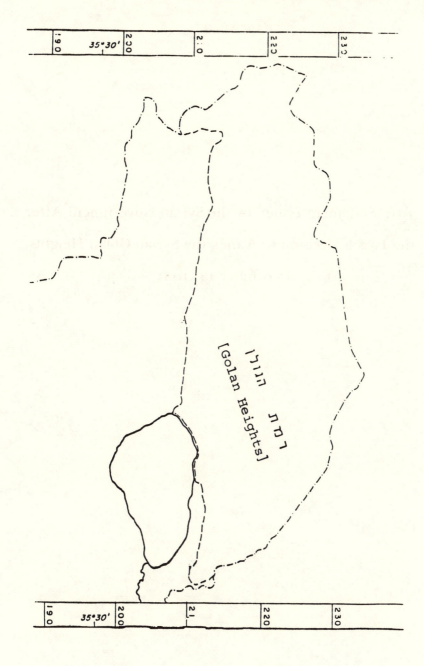

הגולן
[Golan Heights]

191. Statement Issued by the Syrian Government After the Israeli Decision to Annex the Syrian Golan Heights, December 14, 1981*

* 11 J. Palestine Stud. 199 (Spring 1982).

Within the framework of the Zionist enemy's aggressive and expansionist policy—the operations of Judaization, the building of settlements and the expulsion and persecution of the Arab population—the government of the Zionist enemy has taken a decision to enforce Israeli law in the occupied Syrian Arab territories.

In drawing the attention of Arab public opinion and of the international community to the gravity of this move, and to its repercussions on the security and peace of the region and the world, the government of the Syrian Arab Republic wishes to make clear the following:

1. That Syria reserves the right to take the appropriate measures as regards this major and flagrant violation of the Charter of the UN and its resolutions, including resolution 338.

2. That this Israeli decision means the annexation of the occupied Syrian territories, a declaration of war on Syria and the annulment of the cease-fire.

3. That this Israeli decision is an affirmation of the aggressive and expansionist policy of the aggressive Zionist entity, and reveals what kind of peace that entity wants.

In expressing its profound concern at this new aggressive move, the government of the Syrian Arab Republic affirms that it will confront this situation in the light of its national and pan-Arab responsibilities. It calls on world public opinion to support it in confronting this dangerous development which will have repercussions, not only on the region, but also on the international situation as a whole.

As a first step, the government of the Syrian Arab Republic has called for an urgent meeting of the Security Council to deal with this grave situation which threatens security and peace in the region and in the world, and to adopt a resolution rescinding these Israeli measures and imposing sanctions against the Zionist enemy, in implementation of the Charter and the resolutions of the UN.

In this connection, the Syrian government affirms that it will spare no effort to defend its territory and its national interests. It calls the attention of Arab public opinion to what Israel is preparing against the Arab nation and its national interests, and calls on the Arab governments and masses to apprehend the gravity of the present situation and the measures required to confront these dangerous developments.

192. Excerpts from the Statement Issued by the Jordanian Government After the Israeli Decision to Annex the Syrian Golan Heights, December 15, 1981*

* 11 J. Palestine Stud. 200 (Spring 1982).

Israel has taken a new step in its aggressive and expansionist policy aimed at Judaizing and annexing the occupied Arab territories by deciding . . . to enforce Israeli law in the occupied Golan Heights.

This measure which, in effect, means the annexation to Israel of that section of Arab territory, is one more in the series of steps taken by Israel in its expansion at the expense of Arab territory and rights. These measures include the usurpation of precious parts of Palestine in 1948, the occupation of other Arab territories in 1967, the Judaization and annexation of Arab Jerusalem, and the establishment of settlements. Further moves have been to initiate the project for the construction of a canal linking the Mediterranean and Dead seas, the bombing of the Iraqi nuclear installations, the violation of Arab airspace, and Israel's continuous aggressions against Lebanon and the Palestinian resistance. To this list must be added Israel's inhuman treatment of the Palestinian Arab people living under its occupation, who are heroically and unceasingly resisting Israel's schemes aimed at pushing through the self-government conspiracy, perpetuating the occupation and annexing Arab territory.

This decision lies within the framework of the aggressive and expansionist policy pursued by successive Israeli governments. It is also the natural result of the deteriorating Arab situation in which, in the absence of a correct perspective on matters, the real danger has been ignored and efforts have been dissipated in disagreements over side issues. . . .

The government of the Hashemite Kingdon [sic] of Jordan, in condemning Israel's decision to annex the occupied Arab Golan Heights, calls on the international community in general and those states that are influential in matters related to world peace in particular, to face up to their responsibility for preventing Israel's further implementation of its schemes. These infringe all the resolutions unanimously adopted by the international community with regard to the bases for the establishment of a just, permanent and comprehensive peace in the area.

The international community is called on to deal with the grave consequences of the Israeli concept of peace in the region, which is based on the usurpation of Arab territory and rights. For such a move presents a constant threat to the security, peace and stability of the countries and people of the region and, consequently, to the security and stability of the world.

193. Statement by the EEC Foreign Ministers on the Extension of Israeli Law to the Golan Heights, December 15, 1981*

---

* 14 Bull. Eur. Comm. (No. 12) 69 (1981).

2.2.63. The Ministers also issued the following statement concerning the Golan Heights:

'The Foreign Ministers of the Member States of the European Community strongly deplore the decision of the Government and Knesset of Israel to extend Israeli law, jurisdiction and administration to occupied Syrian territory in the Golan Heights. Such an extension, which is tantamount to annexation, is contrary to international law, and therefore invalid in our eyes. This step prejudices the possibility of the implementation of Security Council Resolution 242 and is bound to complicate further the search for a comprehensive peace settlement in the Middle East to which we remain committed.'

194. General Assembly Resolution 36/146 on the U.N.
Relief and Works Agency for Palestine Refugees in the
Near East, December 16, 1981*

---

* G.A. Res. 146, 36 U.N. GAOR Supp. (No. 51) at 85, U.N. Doc. A/36/51
(1981).

A

PALESTINE REFUGEES IN THE GAZA STRIP

The General Assembly,

Recalling Security Council resolution 237 (1967) of 14 June 1967,

Recalling also its resolutions 2792 C (XXVI) of 6 December 1971, 2963 C (XXVII) of 13 December 1972, 3089 C (XXVIII) of 7 December 1973, 3331 D (XXIX) of 17 December 1974, 3419 C (XXX) of 8 December 1975, 31/15 E of 23 November 1976, 32/90 C of 13 December 1977, 33/112 E of 18 December 1978, 34/52 F of 23 November 1979 and 35/13 F of 3 November 1980,

Having considered the report of the Commissioner-General of the United Nations Relief and Works Agency for Palestine Refugees in the Near East, covering the period from 1 July 1980 to 30 June 1981,[9] and the report of the Secretary-General of 30 September 1981,[10]

Recalling the provisions of paragraph 11 of its resolution 194 (III) of 11 December 1948 and considering that measures to resettle Palestine refugees in the Gaza Strip away from the homes and property from which they were displaced constitute a violation of their inalienable right of return,

Alarmed by the reports received from the Commissioner-General of the United Nations Relief and Works Agency for Palestine Refugees in the Near East that the Israeli occupying authorities persist in their policy of demolishing, on punitive grounds, shelters occupied by refugee families,[11]

1. *Demands* that Israel desist from the removal and resettlement of Palestine refugees in the Gaza Strip and from the destruction of their shelters;

2. *Requests* the Secretary-General, after consulting with the Commissioner-General of the United Nations Relief and Works Agency for Palestine Refugees in the Near East, to report to the General Assembly before the opening of its thirty-seventh session on Israel's compliance with paragraph 1 above.

100th plenary meeting
16 December 1981

B

POPULATION AND REFUGEES DISPLACED SINCE 1967

The General Assembly,

Recalling Security Council resolution 237 (1967) of 14 June 1967,

Recalling also its resolutions 2252 (ES-V) of 4 July 1967, 2452 A (XXIII) of 19 December 1968, 2535 B (XXIV) of 10 December 1969, 2672 D (XXV)

---

[9] *Official Records of the General Assembly, Thirty-sixth Session, Supplement No. 13* (A/36/13 and Corr. 1).

[10] A/36/559.

[11] *Ibid.*, para. 5.

of 8 December 1970, 2792 E (XXVI) of 6 December 1971, 2963 C and D (XXVII) of 13 December 1972, 3089 C (XXVIII) of 7 December 1973, 3331 D (XXIX) of 17 December 1974, 3419 C (XXX) of 8 December 1975, 31/15 D of 23 November 1976, 32/90 E of 13 December 1977, 33/112 F of 18 December 1978, 34/52 E of 23 November 1979, ES-7/2 of 29 July 1980 and 35/13 E of 3 November 1980,

Having considered the report of the Commissioner-General of the United Nations Relief and Works Agency for Palestine Refugees in the Near East, covering the period from 1 July 1980 to 30 June 1981,[9] and the report of the Secretary-General of 30 September 1981,[12]

1. *Reaffirms* the inalienable right of all displaced inhabitants to return to their homes or former places of residence in the territories occupied by Israel since 1967 and declares once more that any attempt to restrict, or to attach conditions to, the free exercise of the right of return by any displaced person is inconsistent with that inalienable right and inadmissible;

2. *Considers* any and all agreements embodying any restriction on or condition for the return of the displaced inhabitants as null and void;

3. *Deplores* the continued refusal of the Israeli authorities to take steps for the return of the displaced inhabitants;

4. *Calls once more upon* Israel:

(a) To take immediate steps for the return of all displaced inhabitants;

(a) To desist from all measures that obstruct the return of the displaced inhabitants, including measures affecting the physical and demographic structure of the occupied territories;

5. *Requests* the Secretary-General, after consulting with the Commissioner-General of the United Nations Relief and Works Agency for Palestine Refugees in the Near East, to report to the General Assembly by the opening of its thirty-seventh session on Israel's compliance with paragraph 4 above.

100th plenary meeting
16 December 1981

C

REVENUES DERIVED FROM PALESTINE REFUGEE PROPERTIES

The General Assembly,

Recalling its resolutions 35/13 A to F of 3 November 1980 and all its previous resolutions on the question, including resolution 194 (III) of 11 December 1948,

Taking note of the report of the United Nations Conciliation Commission for Palestine, covering the period from 1 October 1980 to 30 September 1981,[13]

Recalling that the Universal Declaration of Human Rights[14] and the prin-

---

[12] A/36/558.
[13] A/36/529.
[14] Resolution 217 A (III).

ciples of international law uphold the principle that no one shall be arbitrarily deprived of private property,

Considering that the Palestinian Arab refugees are entitled to their property and to the income derived from their property, in conformity with the
principles of justice and equity,

Recalling, in particular, its resolution 394 (V) of 14 December 1950, in
which it directed the United Nations Conciliation Commission for Palestine,
in consultation with the parties concerned, to prescribe measures for the
protection of the rights, property and interests of the Palestinian Arab refugees,

Taking note of the completion of the programme of identification and
evaluation of Arab property, as announced by the United Nations Conciliation Commission for Palestine in its twenty-second progress report,[15] of 11
May 1964, and of the fact that the Land Office has a schedule of Arab owners and file of documents defining the location, area and other particulars
of Arab property,

1. *Requests* the Secretary-General to take all appropriate steps, in consultation with the United Nations Conciliation Commission for Palestine, for
the protection and administration of Arab property, assets and property
rights in Israel, and to establish a fund for the receipt of income derived
therefrom, on behalf of their rightful owners;

2. *Calls upon* the Governments concerned to render all facilities and assistance to the Secretary-General on the implementation of the present resolution;

3. *Requests* the Secretary-General to report to the General Assembly at its
thirty-seventh session on the implementation of the present resolution.

100th plenary meeting
16 December 1981

D

ASSISTANCE TO PERSONS DISPLACED AS A RESULT OF THE JUNE 1967
HOSTILITIES

The General Assembly,

Recalling its resolution 35/13 C of 3 November 1980 and all previous resolutions on the question,

Taking note of the report of the Commissioner-General of the United
Nations Relief and Works Agency for Palestine Refugees in the Near East,
covering the period from 1 July 1980 to 30 June 1981,[9]

Concerned about the continued human suffering resulting from the June
1967 hostilities in the Middle East,

---

[15] *Official Records of the General Assembly, Nineteenth Session, Annex No. 11*, document
A/5700.

1. *Reaffirms* its resolution 35/13 and all previous resolutions on the question;

2. *Endorses*, bearing in mind the objectives of those resolutions, the efforts of the Commissioner-General of the United Nations Relief and Works Agency for Palestine Refugees in the Near East to continue to provide humanitarian assistance as far as practicable, on an emergency basis and as a temporary measure, to other persons in the area who are at present displaced and in serious need of continued assistance as a result of the June 1967 hostilities;

3. *Strongly appeals* to all Governments and to organizations and individuals to contribute generously for the above purposes to the United Nations Relief and Works Agency for Palestine Refugees in the Near East and to the other intergovernmental and non-governmental organizations concerned.

100th plenary meeting
16 December 1981

E

WORKING GROUP ON THE FINANCING OF THE UNITED NATIONS RELIEF AND
WORKS AGENCY FOR PALESTINE REFUGEES IN THE NEAR EAST

The General Assembly,

Recalling its resolutions 2656 (XXV) of 7 December 1970, 2728 (XXV) of 15 December 1970, 2791 (XXVI) of 6 December 1971, 2964 (XXVII) of 13 December 1972, 3090 (XXVIII) of 7 December 1973, 3330 (XXIX) of 17 December 1974, 3419 D (XXX) of 8 December 1975, 31/15 C of 23 November 1976, 32/90 D of 13 December 1977, 33/112 D of 18 December 1978, 34/52 D of 23 November 1979 and 35/13 D of 3 November 1980,

Having considered the report of the Working Group on the Financing of the United Nations Relief and Works Agency for Palestine Refugees in the Near East,[16]

Taking into account the report of the Commissioner-General of the United Nations Relief and Works Agency for Palestine Refugees in the Near East, covering the period from 1 July 1980 to 30 June 1981,[9]

Gravely concerned at the critical financial situation of the United Nations Relief and Works Agency for Palestine Refugees in the Near East, which has already reduced the essential minimum services being provided to the Palestine refugees and which threatens even greater reductions in the future,

Emphasizing the urgent need for extraordinary efforts in order to maintain, at least at their present minimum level, the activities of the United Nations Relief and Works Agency for Palestine Refugees in the Near East,

1. *Commends* the Working Group on the Financing of the United Nations

[16] A/36/615.

Relief and Works Agency for Palestine Refugees in the Near East for its efforts to assist in ensuring the Agency's financial security;

2. *Takes note with approval* of the report of the Working Group;

3. *Requests* the Working Group to continue its efforts, in co-operation with the Secretary-General and the Commissioner-General of the United Nations Relief and Works Agency for Palestine Refugees in the Near East, for the financing of the Agency for a further period of one year;

4. *Requests* the Secretary-General to provide the necessary services and assistance to the Working Group for the conduct of its work.

100th plenary meeting
16 December 1981

F

ASSISTANCE TO PALESTINE REFUGEES

The General Assembly,

Recalling its resolution 35/13 A of 3 November 1980 and all previous resolutions on the question, including resolution 194 (III) of 11 December 1948,

Taking note of the report of the Commissioner-General of the United Nations Relief and Works Agency for Palestine Refugees in the Near East, covering the period from 1 July 1980 to 30 June 1981,[9]

1. *Notes with regret* that repatriation or compensation of the refugees as provided for in paragraph 11 of General Assembly resolution 194 (III) has not been effected, that no substantial progress has been made in the programme endorsed by the Assembly in paragraph 2 of its resolution 513 (VI) of 26 January 1952 for the reintegration of refugees either by repatriation or resettlement and that, therefore, the situation of the refugees continues to be a matter of serious concern;

2. *Expresses its thanks* to the Commissioner-General and to all the staff of the United Nations Relief and Works Agency for Palestine Refugees in the Near East, recognizing that the Agency is doing all it can within the limits of available resources, and also expresses its thanks to the specialized agencies and private organizations for their valuable work in assisting the refugees;

3. *Reiterates its request* that the headquarters of the United Nations Relief and Works Agency for Palestine Refugees in the Near East should be relocated within the area of its operations as soon as practicable;

4. *Notes with regret* that the United Nations Conciliation Commission for Palestine has been unable to find a means of achieving progress in the implementation of paragraph 11 of General Assembly resolution 194 (III)[17] and requests the Commission to exert continued efforts towards the imple-

---

[17] For the report of the United Nations Conciliation Commission for Palestine covering the period from 1 October 1980 to 30 September 1981, see A/36/529.

mentation of that paragraph and to report to the Assembly as appropriate, but not later than 1 October 1982;

5. *Directs attention* to the continuing seriousness of the financial position of the United Nations Relief and Works Agency for Palestine Refugees in the Near East, as outlined in the report of the Commissioner-General;

6. *Notes with concern* that, despite the commendable and successful efforts of the Commissioner-General to collect additional contributions, this increased level of income to the United Nations Relief and Works Agency for Palestine Refugees in the Near East is still insufficient to cover essential budget requirements in the present year and that, at currently foreseen levels of giving, deficits will recur each year;

7. *Calls upon* all Governments as a matter of urgency to make the most generous efforts possible to meet the anticipated needs of the United Nations Relief and Works Agency for Palestine Refugees in the Near East, particularly in the light of the budgetary deficit projected in the report of the Commissioner-General, and therefore urges non-contributing Governments to contribute regularly and contributing Governments to consider increasing their regular contributions.

100th plenary meeting
16 December 1981

G

UNIVERSITY OF JERUSALEM FOR PALESTINE REFUGEES

The General Assembly,

Recalling its resolution 35/13 B of 3 November 1980,

Having examined with appreciation the report of the Secretary-General concerning the establishment of the university of Jerusalem in pursuance of paragraphs 5 and 6 of resolution 35/13 B,[18]

Having also examined with appreciation the report of the Commissioner-General of the United Nations Relief and Works Agency for Palestine Refugees in the Near East, covering the period from 1 July 1980 to 30 June 1981,[9]

1. *Commends* the constructive efforts made by the Commissioner-General of the United Nations Relief and Works Agency for Palestine Refugees in the Near East, the Council of the United Nations University and the United Nations Educational, Scientific and Cultural Organization in exploring ways and means of establishing at Jerusalem a university of arts and sciences to cater to the needs of Palestine refugees in the area, under the aegis of the United Nations;

2. *Further commends* the close co-operation of the competent educational authorities in the host countries as well as those of the Palestine Liberation Organization;

[18] A/36/593.

3. *Recognizes* the urgent necessity of establishing the proposed university;

4. *Calls upon* Israel as the occupying Power to desist from obstructing the implementation of the resolution of the General Assembly and to remove the obstacles which it has put in the way of establishing the university at Jerusalem;

5. *Requests* the Secretary-General to take all necessary measures, including a functional feasibility study, for establishing the university at Jerusalem;

6. *Further requests* the Secretary-General to report to the General Assembly at its thirty-seventh session on the progress made in the implementation of the present resolution.

100th plenary meeting
16 December 1981

H

OFFERS BY MEMBER STATES OF GRANTS AND SCHOLARSHIPS FOR HIGHER EDUCATION, INCLUDING VOCATIONAL TRAINING, FOR THE PALESTINE REFUGEES

The General Assembly,

Recalling its resolution 212 (III) of 19 November 1948 on assistance to Palestine refugees,

Recalling also its resolution 35/13 B of 3 November 1980,

Cognizant of the fact that the Palestine refugees have, for the last three decades, lost their lands and means of livelihood,

Having examined with appreciation the report of the Secretary-General on offers of grants and scholarships for higher education for Palestine refugees and the scope of the implementation of resolution 35/13 B,[19]

Having also examined with appreciation the report of the Commissioner-General of the United Nations Relief and Works Agency for Palestine Refugees in the Near East, covering the period from 1 July 1980 to 30 June 1981,[9] dealing with this subject,

Noting that fewer than one per thousand of the Palestine refugee students have the chance to continue higher education, including vocational training,

Noting also that over the past several years the number of scholarships offered by the United Nations Relief and Works Agency for Palestine Refugees in the Near East has dwindled to half of what it was because of the Agency's recurring budgetary difficulties,

1. *Urges* all States to respond to the appeal contained in General Assembly resolution 32/90 F of 13 December 1977 in a manner commensurate with the needs of the Palestine refugees for higher education and vocational training;

2. *Strongly appeals* to all States, specialized agencies and non-governmental organizations to augment the special allocations for grants and scholarships to Palestine refugees in addition to their contributions to the regular budget

---

[19] A/36/385 and Add. 1 and 2.

of the United Nations Relief and Works Agency for Palestine Refugees in the Near East;

3. *Expresses its appreciation* to all Governments, specialized agencies and non-governmental organizations that responded favourably to General Assembly resolution 33/112 C of 18 December 1978;

4. *Invites* the relevant United Nations agencies to continue to expand the inclusion within their respective spheres of competence of assistance for higher education for the Palestine refugee students;

5. *Appeals* to all States, specialized agencies and the United Nations University to contribute generously to the Palestinian universities in the territories occupied by Israel since 1967;

6. *Also appeals* to all States, specialized agencies and other international bodies to contribute towards the establishment of vocational training centres for Palestine refugees;

7. *Requests* the United Nations Relief and Works Agency for Palestine Refugees in the Near East to act as recipient and trustee for such special allocations and scholarships and to award them to qualified Palestine refugee candidates;

8. *Requests* the Secretary-General to report to the General Assembly at its thirty-seventh session on the implementation of the present resolution.

100th plenary meeting
16 December 1981

195. General Assembly Resolution 36/147 on the Report

of the Special Committee to Investigate Israeli Practices

Affecting the Human Rights of the Population of the

Occupied Territories, December 16, 1981*

* G.A. Res. 147, 36 U.N. GAOR Supp. (No. 51) at 88, U.N. Doc. A/36/51
(1981). *See also* subsequent resolution, G.A. Res. 88, 37 U.N. GAOR Supp.
(No. 51) at 92, U.N. Doc. A/37/51 (1982).

A

The General Assembly,

Recalling its resolutions 3092 A (XXVIII) of 7 December 1973, 3240 B (XXIX) of 29 November 1974, 3525 B (XXX) of 15 December 1975, 31/106 B of 16 December 1976, 32/91 A of 13 December 1977, 33/113 A of 18 December 1978, 34/90 B of 12 December 1979 and 35/122 A of 11 December 1980,

Recalling also Security Council resolution 465 (1980) of 1 March 1980 in which, *inter alia*, the Council affirmed that the Geneva Convention relative to the Protection of Civilian Persons in Time of War, of 12 August 1949,[20] is applicable to the Arab territories occupied by Israel since 1967, including Jerusalem,

Considering that the promotion of respect for the obligations arising from the Charter of the United Nations and other instruments and rules of international law is among the basic purposes and principles of the United Nations,

Bearing in mind the provisions of the Geneva Convention,

Noting that Israel and those Arab States whose territories have been occupied by Israel since June 1967 are parties to that Convention,

Taking into account that States parties to that Convention undertake, in accordance with article 1 thereof, not only to respect but also to ensure respect for the Convention in all circumstances,

1. *Reaffirms* that the Geneva Convention relative to the Protection of Civilian Persons in Time of War, of 12 August 1949, is applicable to Palestinian and other Arab territories occupied by Israel since 1967, including Jerusalem;

2. *Condemns* the failure of Israel as the occupying Power to acknowledge the applicability of the Geneva Convention to the territories it has occupied since 1967, including Jerusalem;

3. *Demands* that Israel acknowledge and comply with the provisions of the Geneva Convention in Palestinian and other Arab territories it has occupied since 1967, including Jerusalem;

4. *Urgently calls upon* all States parties to the Geneva Convention to exert all efforts in order to ensure respect for and compliance with its provisions in Palestinian and other Arab territories occupied by Israel since 1967, including Jerusalem.

100th plenary meeting
16 December 1981

B

The General Assembly,

Recalling its resolutions 32/5 of 28 October 1977, 33/133 B of 18 December 1978, 34/90 C of 12 December 1979 and 35/122 B of 11 December 1980,

[20] United Nations, *Treaty Series*, vol. 75, No. 973, p. 287.

Recalling also Security Council resolution 465 (1980) of 1 March 1980,

Expressing grave anxiety and concern at the present serious situation in the occupied Palestinian and other Arab territories, including Jerusalem, as a result of the continued Israeli occupation and the measures and actions taken by the Government of Israel, as the occupying Power, designed to change the legal status, geographical nature and demographic composition of those territories,

Considering that the Geneva Convention relative to the Protection of Civilian Persons in Time of War, of 12 August 1949,[20] is applicable to all Arab territories occupied since 5 June 1967, including Jerusalem,

1. *Determines* that all such measures and actions taken by Israel in the Palestinian and other Arab territories occupied since 1967, including Jerusalem, are in violation of the relevant provisions of the Geneva Convention relative to the Protection of Civilian Persons in Time of War, of 12 August 1949, and constitute a serious obstruction of efforts to achieve a just and lasting peace in the Middle East, and therefore have no legal validity;

2. *Strongly deplores* the persistence of Israel in carrying out such measures, in particular the establishment of settlements in the Palestinian and other occupied Arab territories, including Jerusalem;

3. *Demands* that Israel comply strictly with its international obligations in accordance with the principles of international law and the provisions of the Geneva Convention;

4. *Demands once more* that the Government of Israel, the occupying Power, desist forthwith from taking any action which would result in changing the legal status, geographical nature or demographic composition of the Palestinian and other Arab territories occupied since 1967, including Jerusalem;

5. *Urgently calls upon* all States parties to the Geneva Convention to respect and to exert all efforts in order to ensure respect for and compliance with its provisions in all Arab territories occupied by Israel since 1967, including Jerusalem.

100th plenary meeting
16 December 1981

C

The General Assembly,

Guided by the purposes and principles of the Charter of the United Nations and by the principles and provisions of the Universal Declaration of Human Rights,[21]

Bearing in mind the provisions of the Geneva Convention relative to the Protection of Civilian Persons in Time of War, of 12 August 1949,[20] as well as of other relevant conventions and regulations,

Recalling all its resolutions on the subject, in particular resolutions 32/91 B and C of 12 December 1977, 33/113 C of 18 December 1978, 34/90 A of 12 December 1979 and 35/122 C of 11 December 1980, and also those

[21] Resolution 217 A (III).

adopted by the Security Council, the Commission on Human Rights and other United Nations organs concerned and by the specialized agencies,

Having considered the report of the Special Committee to Investigate Israeli Practices Affecting the Human Rights of the Population of the Occupied Territories,[22] which contains, *inter alia*, public statements made by the leaders of the Government of Israel,

1. *Commends* the Special Committee to Investigate Israeli Practices Affecting the Human Rights of the Population of the Occupied Territories for its efforts in performing the tasks assigned to it by the General Assembly and for its thoroughness and impartiality;

2. *Deplores* the continued refusal by Israel to allow the Special Committee access to the occupied territories;

3. *Demands* that Israel allow the Special Committee access to the occupied territories;

4. *Reaffirms* the fact that occupation itself constitutes a grave violation of the human rights of the civilian population of the occupied Arab territories;

5. *Condemns* the continued and persistent violation by Israel of the Geneva Convention relative to the Protection of Civilian Persons in Time of War, of 12 August 1949, and other applicable international instruments, and condemns in particular those violations which the Convention designates as "grave breaches" thereof;

6. *Declares* that Israel's grave breaches of the Geneva Convention are war crimes and an affront to humanity;

7. *Strongly condemns* the following Israeli policies and practices:

(*a*) Annexation of parts of the occupied territories, including Jerusalem;

(*b*) Establishment of new Israeli settlements and expansion of the existing settlements on private and public Arab lands, and transfer of an alien population thereto;

(*c*) Evacuation, deportation, expulsion, displacement and transfer of Arab inhabitants of the occupied territories and denial of their right to return;

(*d*) Confiscation and expropriation of private and public Arab property in the occupied territories and all other transactions for the acquisition of land involving the Israeli authorities, institutions or nationals on the one hand and the inhabitants or institutions of the occupied territories on the other;

(*e*) Excavations and transformations of the landscape and the historical, cultural and religious sites, especially in Jerusalem;

(*f*) Destruction and demolition of Arab houses;

(*g*) Mass arrests, administrative detention and ill-treatment of the Arab population;

(*h*) Ill-treatment and torture of persons under detention;

(*i*) Pillaging of archaeological and cultural property;

(*j*) Interference with religious freedoms and practices as well as family rights and customs;

[22] See A/36/579.

(*k*) Interference with the system of education and with the social and economic development of the population in the occupied Palestinian and other Arab territories;

(*l*) Interference with the freedom of movement of individuals within the occupied Palestinian and other Arab territories;

(*m*) Illegal exploitation of the natural wealth, resources and population of the occupied territories;

8. *Reaffirms* that all measures taken by Israel to change the physical character, demographic composition, institutional structure or status of the occupied territories, or any part thereof, including Jerusalem, are null and void, and that Israel's policy of settling parts of its population and new immigrants in the occupied territories constitutes a flagrant violation of the Geneva Convention and of the relevant resolutions of the United Nations;

9. *Demands* that Israel desist forthwith from the policies and practices referred to in paragraphs 7 and 8 above;

10. *Urges* the international organizations and the specialized agencies, in particular the International Labour Organisation, to examine the conditions of the Arab workers in the occupied Palestinian and other Arab territories, including Jerusalem;

11. *Reiterates* its call upon all States, in particular those States parties to the Geneva Convention, in accordance with article 1 of the Convention, and upon international organizations and the specialized agencies not to recognize any changes carried out by Israel in the occupied territories and to avoid actions, including those in the field of aid, which might be used by Israel in its pursuit of the policies of annexation and colonization or any of the other policies and practices referred to in the present resolution;

12. *Requests* the Special Committee, pending the early termination of the Israeli occupation, to continue to investigate Israeli policies and practices in the Arab territories occupied by Israel since 1967, to consult, as appropriate, with the International Committee of the Red Cross in order to ensure the safeguarding of the welfare and human rights of the population of the occupied territories and to report to the Secretary-General as soon as possible and whenever the need arises thereafter;

13. *Requests* the Special Committee to continue to investigate the treatment of civilians in detention in the Arab territories occupied by Israel since 1967;

14. *Requests* the Secretary-General:

(*a*) To provide all necessary facilities to the Special Committee, including those required for its visits to the occupied territories, with a view to investigating the Israeli policies and practices referred to in the present resolution;

(*b*) To continue to make available additional staff as may be necessary to assist the Special Committee in the performance of its tasks;

(*c*) To ensure the widest circulation of the reports of the Special Committee and of information regarding its activities and findings, by all means available through the Department of Public Information of the Secretariat, and, where necessary, to reprint those reports of the Special Committee that are no longer available;

(*d*) To report to the General Assembly at its thirty-seventh session on the tasks entrusted to him in the present paragraph;

15. *Requests* the Security Council to ensure Israel's respect for and compliance with all the provisions of the Geneva Convention relative to the Protection of Civilian Persons in Time of War, of 12 August 1949, in Palestinian and other Arab territories occupied since 1967, including Jerusalem, and to initiate measures to halt Israeli policies and practices in those territories;

16. *Decides* to include in the provisional agenda of its thirty-seventh session the item entitled "Report of the Special Committee to Investigate Israeli Practices Affecting the Human Rights of the Population of the Occupied Territories".

100th plenary meeting
16 December 1981

D

The General Assembly,

Recalling Security Council resolutions 468 (1980) of 8 May 1980, 469 (1980) of 20 May 1980 and 484 (1980) of 19 December 1980,

Deeply concerned at the expulsion by the Israeli military occupation authorities of the Mayors of Hebron and Halhul and of the Sharia Judge of Hebron,

Recalling the Geneva Convention relative to the Protection of Civilian Persons in Time of War, of 12 August 1949,[20] in particular article 1 and the first paragraph of article 49, which read as follows:

"Article 1
"The High Contracting Parties undertake to respect and to ensure respect for the present Convention in all circumstances."

"Article 49
"Individual or mass forcible transfers, as well as deportations of protected persons from occupied territory to the territory of the occupying Power or to that of any other country, occupied or not, are prohibited, regardless of their motive . . .",

Reaffirming the applicability of the Geneva Convention to the Palestinian and other Arab territories occupied by Israel since 1967, including Jerusalem,

1. *Demands* that the Government of Israel, the occupying Power, rescind the illegal measures taken by the Israeli military occupation authorities in expelling and imprisoning the Mayors of Hebron and Halhul and in expelling the Sharia Judge of Hebron and that it facilitate the immediate return of the expelled Palestinian leaders so that they can resume the functions for which they were elected and appointed;

2. *Requests* the Secretary-General to report to the General Assembly as soon as possible on the implementation of the present resolution.

100th plenary meeting
16 December 1981

E

The General Assembly,

Deeply concerned that the Arab territories occupied since 1967 have been under continued illegal Israeli military occupation,

Recalling its previous resolutions, in particular resolutions 3414 (XXX) of 5 December 1975, 31/61 of 9 December 1976, 32/20 of 25 November 1977, 33/28 and 33/29 of 7 December 1978, 34/70 of 6 December 1979 and 35/122 E of 11 December 1980, in which it, *inter alia,* called upon Israel to put an end to its illegal occupation of the Arab territories and to withdraw from all those territories,

Gravely concerned at reports indicating measures being taken by the Israeli authorities to enact legislation embodying changes in the character and status of the occupied Syrian Arab Golan Heights,

Reaffirming that the acquisition of territory by force is inadmissible under the Charter of the United Nations and that all territories thus occupied by Israel must be returned,

Recalling the Geneva Convention relative to the Protection of Civilian Persons in Time of War, of 12 August 1949,[20]

1. *Condemns* the persistence of Israel in changing the physical character, demographic composition, institutional structure and legal status of the occupied Syrian Arab Golan Heights;

2. *Strongly condemns* the refusal by Israel, the occupying Power, to comply with the relevant resolutions of the General Assembly and the Security Council;

3. *Determines* that all legislative and administrative measures and actions taken or to be taken by Israel, the occupying Power, that purport to alter the character and legal status of the Syrian Arab Golan Heights are null and void and constitute a flagrant violation of international law and of the Geneva Convention relative to the Protection of Civilian Persons in Time of War, of 12 August 1949, and have no legal effect;

4. *Strongly condemns* Israel for its attempts and measures to impose forcibly Israeli citizenship and Israeli identity cards on the Syrian citizens in the occupied Syrian Arab Golan Heights and calls upon it to desist from its repressive measures against the population of the Syrian Arab Golan Heights;

5. *Calls upon* Member States not to recognize any of the legislative or administrative measures and actions referred to above;

6. *Calls upon* Israel, the occupying Power, to desist forthwith from enacting such legislative or administrative measures;

7. *Requests* the Secretary-General to submit to the General Assembly at its

thirty-seventh session a report on the implementation of the present resolution.

100th plenary meeting
16 December 1981

F

The General Assembly,

Bearing in mind the Geneva Convention relative to the Protection of Civilian Persons in Time of War, of 12 August 1949,[20]

Deeply shocked by the most recent atrocities committed by Israel, the occupying Power, against educational institutions in the occupied Palestinian territories,

1. *Reaffirms* the applicability of the Geneva Convention relative to the Protection of Civilian Persons in Time of War, of 12 August 1949, to the Palestinian and other Arab territories occupied by Israel since 1967, including Jerusalem;

2. *Condemns* Israeli policies and practices against Palestinian students and faculty in schools, universities and other educational institutions in the occupied Palestinian territories, especially the policy of opening fire on defenceless students, causing many casualties;

3. *Condemns* the systematic Israeli campaign of repression against the closing of universities in the occupied Palestinian territories, restricting and impeding academic activities of Palestinian universities by subjecting the selection of courses, textbooks and educational programmes, the admission of students and the appointment of faculty members to the control and supervision of the military occupation authorities, in clear contravention of the Geneva Convention;

4. *Demands* that Israel, the occupying Power, comply with the provisions of the Geneva Convention and rescind all actions and measures against all educational institutions and ensure the freedom of these institutions, and that it rescind immediately orders for the closure of the universities of Bir Zeit, Bethlehem and Al-Najah and facilitate the resumption of education in the above-mentioned institutions;

5. *Requests* the Secretary-General to submit to the General Assembly, before the end of 1981, a report on the implementation of the present resolution.

100th plenary meeting
16 December 1981

G

The General Assembly,

Recalling Security Council resolution 471 (1980) of 5 June 1980, in which the Council condemned the assassination attempts against the Mayors of

Nablus, Ramallah and Al Bireh and called for the immediate apprehension and prosecution of the perpetrators of these crimes,

Recalling once again the Geneva Convention relative to the Protection of Civilian Persons in Time of War, of 12 August 1949,[20] in particular article 27, which states, *inter alia*:

> Protected persons are entitled, in all circumstances, to respect for their persons. . . . They shall at all times be humanely treated, and shall be protected especially against all acts of violence or threats thereof . . . ,

Reaffirming the applicability of the Geneva Convention to the Arab territories occupied by Israel since 1967, including Jerusalem,

1. *Expresses deep concern* that Israel, the occupying Power, has failed so far to apprehend and prosecute the perpetrators of the assassination attempts;

2. *Demands* that Israel, the occupying Power, inform the Secretary-General of the results of the investigations relevant to the assassination attempts;

3. *Requests* the Secretary-General to submit to the General Assembly, not later than 31 December 1981, a report on the implementation of the present resolution.

100th plenary meeting
16 December 1981

196. Security Council Resolution 497 Deploring Annexation of the Golan Heights, December 17, 1981*

* S.C. Res. 497, 36 U.N. SCOR (2319th mtg.) at 6, U.N. Doc. S/INF/37 (1981).

The Security Council,

Having considered the letter of 14 December 1981 from the Permanent Representative of the Syrian Arab Republic contained in document S/14791,[26]

Reaffirming that the acquisition of territory by force is inadmissible, in accordance with the Charter of the United Nations, the principles of international law and relevant Security Council resolutions,

1. *Decides* that the Israeli decision to impose its laws, jurisdiction and administration in the occupied Syrian Golan Heights is null and void and without international legal effect;

2. *Demands* that Israel, the occupying Power, should rescind forthwith its decision;

3. *Determines* that all the provisions of the Geneva Convention relative to the Protection of Civilian Persons in Time of War, of 12 August 1949,[33] continue to apply to the Syrian territory occupied by Israel since June 1967;

4. *Requests* the Secretary-General to report to the Security Council on the implementation of the present resolution within two weeks and decides that, in the event of non-compliance by Israel, the Council would meet urgently, and not later than 5 January 1982, to consider taking appropriate measures in accordance with the Charter of the United Nations.

Adopted unanimously at the 2319th meeting.

[26] *Official Records of the Security Council, Thirty-sixth Year*, 2292nd meeting.
[33] United Nations, *Treaty Series*, vol. 75, p. 287.

197. General Assembly Resolution 36/226 on the Situation in the Middle East, December 17, 1981*

A

The General Assembly,

Having discussed the item entitled "The situation in the Middle East",

Taking note of the report of the Secretary-General of 11 November 1981,[106]

Welcoming the world-wide support extended to the just cause of the Palestinian people and the other Arab countries in their struggle against Israeli aggression and occupation in order to achieve a comprehensive, just and lasting peace in the Middle East and the full exercise by the Palestinian people of its inalienable national rights, as affirmed by previous resolutions of the General Assembly relating to the question of Palestine and the situation in the Middle East,

Gravely concerned that the Arab and Palestinian territories occupied since 1967, including Jerusalem, still remain under Israeli occupation, that the relevant resolutions of the United Nations have not been implemented and that the Palestinian people is still denied the restoration of its land and the exercise of its inalienable national rights in conformity with international law, as reaffirmed by resolutions of the United Nations,

Reaffirming the applicability of the Geneva Convention relative to the Protection of Civilian Persons in Time of War, of 12 August 1949,[107] to all the occupied Palestinian and other Arab territories, including Jerusalem,

Reiterating all relevant United Nations resolutions which emphasize that the acquisition of territory by force is inadmissible under the Charter of the United Nations and the principles of international law and that Israel must withdraw unconditionally from all the occupied Palestinian and other Arab territories, including Jerusalem,

Reaffirming further the imperative necessity of establishing a comprehensive, just and lasting peace in the region, based on full respect for the Charter and the principles of international law,

Gravely concerned also at recent Israeli actions involving the escalation and expansion of the conflict in the region, which further violate the principles of international law and endanger international peace and security,

1. *Condemns* Israel's continued occupation of the Palestinian and other Arab territories, including Jerusalem, in violation of the Charter of the United Nations, the principles of international law and the relevant resolutions of the United Nations, and demands the immediate, unconditional and total withdrawal of Israel from all these occupied territories;

2. *Reaffirms* its conviction that the question of Palestine is the core of the conflict in the Middle East and that no comprehensive, just and lasting

---

[106] A/36/655-S/14746. For the printed text, see *Official Records of the Security Council, Thirty-sixth Year, Supplement for October, November and December 1981.*

[107] United Nations, *Treaty Series,* vol. 75, No. 973, p. 287.

peace in the region will be achieved without the full exercise by the Palestinian people of its inalienable national rights;

3. *Reaffirms further* that a just and comprehensive settlement of the situation in the Middle East cannot be achieved without the participation on an equal footing of all the parties to the conflict, including the Palestine Liberation Organization as the representative of the Palestinian people;

4. *Declares once more* that peace in the Middle East is indivisible and must be based on a comprehensive, just and lasting solution of the Middle East problem, under the auspices of the United Nations, which ensures the complete and unconditional withdrawal of Israel from the Palestinian and other Arab territories occupied since 1967, including Jerusalem, and which enables the Palestinian people, under the leadership of the Palestine Liberation Organization, to exercise its inalienable rights, including the right to return and the right to self-determination, national independence and the establishment of its independent sovereign State in Palestine, in accordance with the resolutions of the United Nations relevant to the question of Palestine, in particular General Assembly resolutions ES-7/2 of 29 July 1980 and 36/120 A to F of 10 December 1981;

5. *Rejects* all partial agreements and separate treaties in so far as they violate the recognized rights of the Palestinian people and contradict the principles of just and comprehensive solutions to the Middle East problem to ensure the establishment of a just peace in the area;

6. *Deplores* Israel's failure to comply with Security Council resolutions 476 (1980) of 30 June 1980 and 478 (1980) of 20 August 1980 and General Assembly resolution 35/207 of 16 December 1980, determines that Israel's decision to annex Jerusalem and to declare it its "capital", as well as the measures to alter its physical character, demographic composition, institutional structure and status, are null and void and demands that they be rescinded immediately, and calls upon all Member States, the specialized agencies and all other international organizations to abide by the present resolution and all other relevant resolutions, including Assembly resolution 36/120 E;

7. *Condemns* Israel's aggression and practices against the Palestinian people in the occupied Palestinian territories and outside these territories, particularly in the Palestinian refugee camps in Lebanon, including the expropriation and annexation of territory, the establishment of settlements, assassination attempts and other terrorist, aggressive and repressive measures, which are in violation of the Charter and the principles of international law and the pertinent international conventions;

8. *Strongly condemns* Israeli annexationist policies and practices in the occupied Syrian Golan Heights, the establishment of settlements, the confiscation of lands, the diversion of water resources, the intensification of repressive measures against the Syrian citizens therein and the forcible imposition of Israeli citizenship on Syrian nationals, and declares all these measures null and void as they constitute violations of the Geneva Conven-

tion relative to the Protection of Civilian Persons in Time of War, of 12 August 1949;

9. *Strongly condemns* the Israeli aggression against Lebanon and the continuous bombardment and destruction of its cities and villages, and all acts that constitute a violation of its sovereignty, independence and territorial integrity and the security of its people and prevent the full implementation of Security Council resolution 425 (1978) of 19 March 1978, including the full deployment of the United Nations Interim Force in Lebanon up to the internationally recognized borders;

10. *Calls* for strict respect of the territorial integrity, sovereignty and political independence of Lebanon and supports the efforts of the Government of Lebanon, with regional and international endorsement, to restore the exclusive authority of the Lebanese State over all of its territory up to the internationally recognized boundaries;

11. *Deplores* Israeli violations of the airspace of various Arab countries and demands their immediate cessation;

12. *Considers* that the agreements on strategic co-operation between the United States of America and Israel signed on 30 November 1981 would encourage Israel to pursue its aggressive and expansionist policies and practices in the Palestinian and other Arab territories occupied since 1967, including Jerusalem, would have adverse effects on efforts for the establishment of a comprehensive, just and lasting peace in the Middle East and would threaten the security of the region;

13. *Calls upon* all States to put an end to the flow to Israel of any military, economic and financial resources that would encourage it to pursue its aggressive policies against the Arab countries and the Palestinian people;

14. *Requests* the Secretary-General to report to the Security Council periodically on the development of the situation and to submit to the General Assembly at its thirty-seventh session a comprehensive report covering the developments in the Middle East in all their aspects.

103rd plenary meeting
17 December 1981

B

The General Assembly,

Gravely alarmed by Israel's decision of 14 December 1981 to apply Israeli law to the occupied Syrian Arab Golan Heights,

Reaffirming that acquisition of territory by force is inadmissible under the Charter of the United Nations, the principles of international law and relevant United Nations resolutions,

Reaffirming once more the applicability of the Geneva Convention relative to the Protection of Civilian Persons in Time of War, of 12 August 1949,[107] to the occupied Syrian territory,

Recalling its resolutions 35/122 A to F of 11 December 1980,

1. *Declares* that Israel's decision to apply Israeli law to the occupied Syrian Arab Golan Heights is null and void and has no legal validity whatsoever;

2. *Determines* that the provisions of the Geneva Convention relative to the Protection of Civilian Persons in Time of War, of 12 August 1949, continue to apply to the Syrian territory occupied by Israel since 1967;

3. *Strongly deplores* the persistence of the Israeli policy of annexation, which escalates tension in the region;

4. *Demands* that Israel, the occupying Power, rescind forthwith its decision and all administrative and other measures relating to it, which constitute a flagrant violation of all relevant principles of international law;

5. *Calls upon* all States, specialized agencies and other international institutions not to recognize that decision;

6. *Requests* the Security Council, in the event of Israel's failure to implement the present resolution, to invoke Chapter VII of the Charter of the United Nations;

7. *Requests* the Secretary-General to report to the General Assembly and the Security Council on the implementation of the present resolution not later than 21 December 1981.

103rd plenary meeting
17 December 1981

198. Excerpt from the Statement Issued by the PLO
Central Council at the End of Its Meetings in Damascus,
December 29, 1981*

* 11 J. Palestine Stud. 202 (Spring 1982).

The Council reviewed the outcome of the Arab summit conference in Fez, endorsing the stand of the Palestinian delegation to the Foreign Ministers' conference and the summit.

The Council affirmed its adherence to the resolutions of the National Council and the interim political programme of the PLO. It stressed that the position towards any initiative or solution must stem from the resolutions of the Palestinian National Council and the political programme.

The Council condemned the decision taken by the Zionist enemy's Knesset to annex the Golan and stressed that, coming as it has after the decision to annex Jerusalem, this decision is an embodiment of the Zionist enemy's expansionist policy and its designs on the Arab world as a whole.

The Council stressed the importance of pursuing a decisive Arab policy in confrontation of American and Zionist schemes aimed at dominating the Arab region and its resources, destroying the achievements of Palestinian and Arab national struggle, and liquidating the Arab-Israeli conflict in favour of American imperialism and Zionism.

The Council reviewed the situation in Lebanon in the light of Israel's mobilization and threats against the Lebanese and Palestinian peoples, the Palestinian revolution, the Lebanese nationalist movement and Syria. The Council stressed the importance of reinforcing and consolidating Palestinian-Syrian cohesion and strengthening the strategic relations between them and the Lebanese national movement and forces and the Lebanese people, with a view to repelling Israeli aggression in defence of Lebanon's Arab character, the unity of its territory and people and its national independence, and to thwarting all the partitionist plans devised by the enemies of Lebanon and the Arab nation.

The Council stressed the importance of reinforcing the National Front for Steadfastness and Confrontation and confronting all the dangers and provocations to which the parties to this Front are being subjected. The Council also stressed the importance of strengthening joint Arab action and Arab solidarity on the basis of confronting American and Zionist policy in the region and the plans resulting from that policy. The Council condemned the strategic alliance between the US and Israel as being directed against all the countries of the Arab nation, and aimed at imposing American-Israeli hegemony on the whole Arab nation.

The Council expressed its concern at and condemned Europe's intention to participate in the multinational force in Sinai as constituting European involvement in the Camp David accords and a violation of Egyptian national sovereignty.

The Council expressed profound satisfaction at the development of Palestinian relations with the friendly USSR and the other socialist countries, which constitutes an important guarantee in support of the struggle of our people against Zionist occupation and Zionist-American plans.

The Council also reviewed the situation in the occupied homeland in the light of the heroic uprising of our steadfast people against the occupation, the self-government conspiracy and the enemy plan to impose civil govern-ment with the aim of entrenching the occupation of the whole of the land of Palestine.

The Council stressed the importance and necessity of supporting the steadfastness of our people in the occupied homeland and of consolidating national unity in their ranks, and called for directing all efforts to resisting occupation and liquidationist projects.

The Council expressed great pride in the valiant popular uprising in the West Bank and the Gaza Strip, which continued for nearly two months, in all the cities, villages and camps in the occupied homeland. Through this heroic resistance our people have affirmed their firm resolve to foil the civil government plan, and their adherence to their inalienable national rights.

199. Excerpts from the Syrian-Soviet Joint Communiqué
Issued at the End of Talks between Syrian Foreign
Minister Abd Al-Halim Khaddam and Soviet Foreign
Minister Gromyko, Moscow, January 16, 1982*

---

* 11 J. Palestine Stud. 205 (Spring 1982).

The talks between Comrade Abd al-Halim Khaddam and Mr. Andrei Gromyko, Member of the Politburo of the Central Committee of the Soviet Communist Party and Foreign Minister of the USSR, covered the grave and tense situation prevailing in the Middle East, especially since the Israeli decision to annex the occupied Syrian territories in the Golan. This move is a flagrant violation of the Charter and the resolutions of the United Nations and a serious threat to security and peace in the region and throughout the world. The two sides agreed that it is necessary to counteract the dangerous developments in that area.

The two parties reviewed the other issues related to the situation in the Middle East and Israel's aggressions against the Arab countries. They condemned the American-Israeli plans aimed at imposing US hegemony in the Middle East and encouraging Israeli expansion against the Arabs. All this constitutes an aggression against the whole Arab nation, including the Palestinian Arab people, and a threat to international security and peace. They view the agreement on strategic cooperation between the US and Israel as a dangerous move, the consequences of which go beyond the framework of the Middle East.

The two sides affirmed their rejection of the policy of separate deals, and their continuing condemnation of the Camp David accords and the Egyptian-Israeli treaty, and the negotiations the parties to Camp David are conducting on so-called self-administration for the Palestinians. They affirm that a just peace must rest on the basis of full withdrawal from all the Arab territories occupied in 1967 and on recognition of the inalienable national rights of the Palestinian Arab people, including their right to self-determination and to establish their independent state, as well as the right of the Palestinians to return to their homes in conformity with the resolutions of the UN.

The two sides examined the international situation and American imperialism's attempts to complicate it through interference in the internal affairs of other states. They condemn the attempts of the US and its Nato allies to interfere in the internal affairs of the Polish People's Republic, which are contrary to the Charter of the UN and the recognized norms of international law.

The two parties expressed their satisfaction with the continuing development of Syrian-Soviet relations which have been raised to a new and higher level as a result of the Treaty of Friendship and Cooperation between the Syrian Arab Republic and the USSR in all fields, including the military field.
. . .

Great importance was accorded to the current political consultations between Syria and the USSR on Middle East issues and other current international issues of common interest.

The two parties are resolved to continue to promote this beneficial process in conformity with the Treaty of Friendship and Cooperation between the Syrian Arab Republic and the USSR. . . .

200. General Assembly Resolution ES-9/1 on the Situation

in the Occupied Arab Territories, February 5, 1982*

---

* G.A. Res. ES-9/1, ES-9 U.N. GAOR Supp. (No. 1) at 3, U.N. Doc. A/ES-9/7.

The General Assembly,

Having considered the item entitled "The situation in the occupied Arab territories" at its ninth emergency special session, in accordance with Security Council resolution 500 (1982) of 28 January 1982,

Noting with regret and concern that the Security Council, at its 2329th meeting, on 20 January 1982, failed to take appropriate measures against Israel, as requested by the Council in resolution 497 (1981) of 17 December 1981, as a result of the negative vote of a permanent member of the Council,

Recalling Security Council resolution 497 (1981),

Recalling its resolution 35/122 E of 11 December 1980,

Reaffirming its resolution 36/226 B of 17 December 1981,

Having considered the reports of the Secretary-General of 21 December 1981[3] and 31 December 1981,[4]

Recalling its resolution 3314 (XXIX) of 14 December 1974, in which it defined an act of aggression as, *inter alia*, "the invasion or attack by the armed forces of a State of the territory of another State, or any military occupation, however temporary, resulting from such invasion or attack, or any annexation by the use of force of the territory of another State or part thereof", and provided that "no consideration of whatever nature, whether political, economic, military or otherwise, may serve as justification for aggression",

Stressing once again that the acquisition of territory by force is inadmissible under the Charter of the United Nations, the principles of international law and relevant United Nations resolutions,

Reaffirming once more the applicability of the Geneva Convention relative to the Protection of Civilian Persons in Time of War, of 12 August 1949,[5] to the occupied Syrian territory,

Noting that Israel's record and actions establish conclusively that it is not a peace-loving Member State and that it has not carried out its obligations under the Charter,

Noting further that Israel has refused, in violation of Article 25 of the Charter, to accept and carry out the numerous relevant decisions of the Security Council, the latest being resolution 497 (1981),

1. *Strongly condemns* Israel for its failure to comply with Security Council resolution 497 (1981) and General Assembly resolution 36/226 B;

2. *Declares* that Israel's decision of 14 December 1981 to impose its laws, jurisdiction and administration on the occupied Syrian Golan Heights constitutes an act of aggression under the provisions of Article 39 of the Charter of the United Nations and General Assembly resolution 3314 (XXIX);

---

[3] A/36/846 and Corr. 1-S/14805 and Corr. 1. For the printed text, see *Official Records of the Security Council, Thirty-sixth Year, Supplement for October, November and December 1981*, document S/14805.

[4] *Official Records of the Security Council, Thirty-sixth Year, Supplement for October, November and December 1981*, document S/14821.

[5] United Nations, *Treaty Series*, vol. 75, No. 973, p. 287.

3. *Declares once more* that Israel's decision to impose its laws, jurisdiction and administration on the occupied Syrian Golan Heights is null and void and has no legal validity and/or effect whatsoever;

4. *Determines* that all actions taken by Israel to give effect to its decision relating to the occupied Syrian Golan Heights are illegal and invalid and shall not be recognized;

5. *Reaffirms* its determination that all the provisions of the Hague Conventions of 1907[6] and the Geneva Convention relative to the Protection of Civilian Persons in Time of War, of 12 August 1949, continue to apply to the Syrian territory occupied by Israel since 1967, and calls upon all parties thereto to respect and ensure respect of their obligations under these instruments in all circumstances;

6. *Determines* that the continued occupation of the Syrian Golan Heights since 1967 and its effective annexation by Israel on 14 December 1981, following Israel's decision to impose its laws, jurisdiction and administration on that territory, constitute a continuing threat to international peace and security;

7. *Strongly deplores* the negative vote by a permanent member of the Security Council which prevented the Council from adopting against Israel, under Chapter VII of the Charter, the "appropriate measures" referred to in resolution 497 (1981) unanimously adopted by the Council;

8. *Further deplores* any political, economic, military and technological support to Israel that encourages Israel to commit acts of aggression and to consolidate and perpetuate its occupation and annexation of occupied Arab territories;

9. *Firmly emphasizes* its demands that Israel, the occupying Power, rescind forthwith its decision of 14 December 1981 to impose its laws, jurisdiction and administration on the Syrian Golan Heights, which has resulted in the effective annexation of that territory;

10. *Reaffirms* the overriding necessity of the total and unconditional withdrawal by Israel from all the Palestinian and other Arab territories occupied since 1967, including Jerusalem, which is a primary requirement for the establishment of a comprehensive and just peace in the Middle East;

11. *Declares* that Israel's record and actions confirm that it is not a peace-loving Member State and that it has carried out neither its obligations under the Charter nor its commitment under General Assembly resolution 273 (III) of 11 May 1949;

12. *Calls upon* all Member States to apply the following measures:

(a) To refrain from supplying Israel with any weapons and related equipment and to suspend any military assistance which Israel receives from them;

[6] Carnegie Endowment for International Peace, *The Hague Conventions and Declarations of 1899 and 1907* (New York, Oxford University Press, 1915).

(*b*) To refrain from acquiring any weapons or military equipment from Israel;

(*c*) To suspend economic, financial and technological assistance to and co-operation with Israel;

(*d*) To sever diplomatic, trade and cultural relations with Israel;

13. *Also calls upon* all Member States to cease forthwith, individually and collectively, all dealings with Israel in order totally to isolate it in all fields;

14. *Urges* non-member States to act in accordance with the provisions of the present resolution;

15. *Calls upon* all specialized agencies of the United Nations system and international institutions to conform their relations with Israel to the terms of the present resolution;

16. *Requests* the Secretary-General to follow up the implementation of the present resolution and to report thereon at intervals of two months to Member States as well as to the Security Council and to submit a comprehensive report to the General Assembly at its thirty-seventh session under the item entitled, "The situation in the Middle East".

12th plenary meeting
5 February 1982

201. General Assembly Resolution ES-7/4 on the Question of Palestine, April 28, 1982*

* G.A. Res. ES-7/4, ES-7 U.N. GAOR Supp. (No. 1) at 4, U.N. Doc. A/ES-7/14/Add. 1 (1982).

The General Assembly,

Having considered the question of Palestine at its resumed seventh emergency special session,

Noting with regret and concern that the Security Council, at its 2348th meeting, on 2 April 1982, and at its 2357th meeting, on 20 April 1982, failed to take a decision as a result of the negative votes of the United States of America,

Having heard the statement by the Head of the Political Department of the Palestine Liberation Organization, the representative of the Palestinian people,[4]

Convinced that the worsening situation in the Middle East and the failure to find a solution to this question pose a grave threat to international peace and security,

Deploring the repressive measures taken by the Israeli authorities in the illegally occupied Palestinian Arab territories, including Jerusalem,

Recalling the relevant United Nations resolutions pertaining to the status and unique character of the Holy City of Jerusalem, in particular Security Council resolutions 465 (1980) of 1 March 1980, 476 (1980) of 30 June 1980 and 478 (1980) of 20 August 1980,

Affirming once more that the Geneva Convention relative to the Protection of Civilian Persons in Time of War, of 12 August 1949,[5] is applicable to all territories occupied by Israel since 1967, including Jerusalem,

Noting with regret that, owing to the negative vote of one of its permanent members, the Security Council has, so far, failed to take a decision on the recommendations of the Committee on the Exercise of the Inalienable Rights of the Palestinian People endorsed by the General Assembly in its resolutions 31/20 of 24 November 1976, 32/40 A of 2 December 1977, 33/28 A of 7 December 1978, 34/65 A of 29 November 1979, 35/169 A of 15 December 1980 and 36/120 D of 10 December 1981,

1. *Reaffirms* its resolutions ES-7/2 of 29 July 1980 and 3236 (XXIX) and 3237 (XXIX) of 22 November 1974 and all other relevant United Nations resolutions pertinent to the question of Palestine;

2. *Reaffirms* the fundamental principle of the inadmissibility of the acquisition of territory by force;

3. *Reaffirms* that all the provisions of the Hague Convention of 1907[6] and the Geneva Convention relative to the Protection of Civilian Persons in Time of War, of 12 August 1949, apply to all territories occupied by Israel since 1967, including Jerusalem, and calls upon all parties to these instruments to respect and ensure respect of their obligations in all circumstances;

---

[4] A/ES-7/PV.12, p. 16.

[5] United Nations, *Treaty Series*, vol. 75, No. 973, p. 287.

[6] Carnegie Endowment for International Peace, *The Hague Conventions and Declarations of 1899 and 1907* (New York, Oxford University Press, 1915).

4. *Demands* that Israel should comply with the provisions of Security Council resolution 465 (1980);

5. *Further demands* that Israel should comply with all United Nations resolutions relevant to the status and unique character of the Holy City of Jerusalem, in particular with Security Council resolutions 476 (1980) and 478 (1980);

6. *Expresses its rejection* of all policies and plans aiming at the resettlement of the Palestinians outside their homeland;

7. *Condemns* Israel, the occupying Power, for its:

(*a*) Failure to fulfil its obligations under the provisions of the Geneva Convention relative to the Protection of Civilian Persons in Time of War;

(*b*) Disbanding of the elected municipal council of El-Bireh;

(*c*) Dismissal of the elected mayors of Ramallah and Nablus;

(*d*) Violation of the sanctity of the Holy Places, particularly of Al-Haram Al-Shareef, in Jerusalem;

(*e*) Shooting and killing and wounding of worshippers in the precincts of Al-Haram Al-Shareef by members of the Israeli army on 11 April 1982;

(*f*) Repressive measures, including shooting at the unarmed civilian population in the occupied Palestinian territory and in the occupied Syrian Golan Heights, resulting in death and injury;

(*g*) Attacks against and interference with the functions of various civic and religious institutions in the occupied Palestinian territory, including Jerusalem, in particular educational institutions;

8. *Condemns* all policies which frustrate the exercise of the inalienable rights of the Palestinian people, in particular providing Israel with military, economic and political assistance and the misuse of the veto by a permanent member of the Security Council, thus enabling Israel to continue its aggression, occupation and unwillingness to carry out its obligations under the Charter and the relevant resolutions of the United Nations;

9. *Urges* all Governments which have not yet done so:

(*a*) To recognize the inalienable rights of the Palestinian people;

(*b*) To renounce the policy of providing Israel with military, economic and political assistance, thus discouraging Israel from continuing its aggression, occupation and disregard of its obligations under the Charter and the relevant resolutions of the United Nations;

(*c*) To act accordingly in all the organs of the United Nations;

10. *Condemns* the policies which encourage the flow of human resources to Israel, enabling it to implement and to proceed with its colonization and settlement policies in the occupied Arab territories;

11. *Declares once again* that Israel's record and actions confirm that it is not a peace-loving Member State and that it has carried out neither its obligations under the Charter nor its commitment under General Assembly resolution 273 (III) of 11 May 1949;

12. *Calls again upon* Israel, the occupying Power, to observe and apply scrupulously the provisions of the Geneva Convention relative to the Pro-

tection of Civilian Persons in Time of War and the principles of international law governing military occupation in all the occupied Palestinian and other Arab territories, including Jerusalem;

13. *Demands* that Israel, the occupying Power, should permit entry into the occupied territories of the Special Committee to Investigate Israeli Practices Affecting the Human Rights of the Population of the Occupied Territories and of the Commission established by Security Council resolution 446 (1979), in order to facilitate the fulfilment of the mandates entrusted to them by the General Assembly and by the Council, respectively;

14. *Urges* the Security Council to recognize the inalienable rights of the Palestinian people as defined in General Assembly resolution ES-7/2 and to endorse the recommendations of the Committee on the Exercise of the Inalienable Rights of the Palestinian People, as endorsed by the Assembly in its resolution 31/20 and in subsequent resolutions;

15. *Calls upon* the Secretary-General, in concurrence with the Security Council and in consultation as appropriate with the Committee on the Exercise of the Inalienable Rights of the Palestinian people, to initiate contacts with all parties to the Arab-Israeli conflict in the Middle East, including the Palestine Liberation Organization, the representative of the Palestinian people, with a view to finding concrete ways and means to achieve a comprehensive, just and lasting solution, conductive to peace, in conformity with the principles of the Charter and relevant resolutions and based on the implementation of the recommendations of the Committee as endorsed by the General Assembly at its thirty-first session;

16. *Requests* the Secretary-General to follow up the implementation of the present resolution and to report thereon at appropriate intervals to Member States as well as to the Security Council and to submit a comprehensive report to the General Assembly at its thirty-seventh session under the item entitled, "Question of Palestine";

17. *Decides* to adjourn the seventh emergency special session temporarily and to authorize the President of the latest regular session of the General Assembly to resume its meetings upon request from Member States.

20th plenary meeting
28 April 1982

C. Natural Resources in the Occupied Territories

202. General Assembly Resolution 34/136 on Permanent Sovereignty Over National Resources in the Occupied Arab Territories, December 14, 1979*

* G.A. Res. 136, 34 U.N. GAOR Supp. (No. 46) at 125, U.N. Doc. A/34/46 (1979). *See also* subsequent resolutions, G.A. Res. 110, 35 U.N. GAOR Supp. (No. 48) at 164, U.N. Doc. A/35/48 (1980) and G.A. Res. 173, 36 U.N. GAOR Supp. (No. 51) at 109, U.N. Doc. A/36/51 (1981).

The General Assembly,

Bearing in mind the relevant principles of international law and the provisions of the international conventions and regulations, in particular Convention IV of The Hague of 1907[113] and the fourth Geneva Convention of 12 August 1949,[114] concerning the obligations and responsibilities of the occupying Power,

Recalling its previous resolutions on permanent sovereignty over natural resources, particularly the provisions supporting resolutely the efforts of the developing countries and the peoples of territories under colonial and racial domination and foreign occupation in their struggle to regain effective control over their natural and all other resources, wealth and economic activities,

Bearing in mind the pertinent provisions of its resolutions 3201 (S-VI) and 3202 (S-VI) of 1 May 1974, containing the Declaration and the Programme of Action on the Establishment of a New International Economic Order, and 3281 (XXIX) of 12 December 1974, containing the Charter of Economic Rights and Duties of States,

Recalling further its resolutions 3175 (XXVIII) of 17 December 1973, 3336 (XXIX) of 17 December 1974, 3516 (XXX) of 15 December 1975, 31/186 of 21 December 1976 and 32/161 of 19 December 1977 on permanent sovereignty over national resources in the occupied Arab territories,

1. *Emphasizes* the right of the Arab States and peoples whose territories are under Israeli occupation to full and effective permanent sovereignty and control over their natural and all other resources, wealth and economic activities;

2. *Reaffirms* that all measures undertaken by Israel to exploit the human, natural and all other resources, wealth and economic activities in the occupied Arab territories are illegal and calls upon Israel immediately to desist forthwith from all such measures;

3. *Further reaffirms* the right of the Arab States and peoples subjected to Israeli aggression and occupation to the restitution of, and full compensation for the exploitation, depletion and loss of and damages to, their natural, human and all other resources, wealth and economic activities, and calls upon Israel to meet their just claims;

4. *Calls upon* all States to support and assist the Arab States and peoples in the exercise of their above-mentioned rights;

5. *Calls upon* all States, international organizations, specialized agencies, investment corporations and all other institutions not to recognize, or cooperate with or assist in any manner in, any measures undertaken by Israel to exploit the resources of the occupied territories or to effect any changes

[113] Carnegie Endowment for International Peace, *The Hague Conventions and Declarations of 1899 and 1907* (New York, Oxford University Press, 1915), p. 100.

[114] United Nations, *Treaty Series*, vol. 75, No. 973, p. 287.

in the demographic composition, geographic character or institutional structure of those territories;

6. *Requests* the Secretary-General to prepare and submit to the General Assembly at its thirty-fifth session a report which takes into consideration the provisions of paragraph 2 of resolution 32/161.

104th plenary meeting
14 December 1979

203. General Assembly Resolution 36/15 on Recent

Developments in Connection with Excavations

in Eastern Jerusalem, October 28, 1981*

---

* G.A. Res. 15, 36 U.N. GAOR Supp. (No. 51) at 82, U.N. Doc. A/36/51 (1981).

The General Assembly,

Reaffirming that the Geneva Convention relative to the Protection of Civilian Persons in Time of War, of 12 August 1949,[3] is applicable to Palestinian and other Arab territories occupied by Israel since 1967, including Jerusalem,

Recalling its resolutions 2253 (ES-V) of 4 July 1967, 2254 (ES-V) of 14 July 1967, 3092 (XXVIII) of 7 December 1973, 3240 B (XXIX) of 29 November 1974, 3525 B (XXX) of 15 December 1975, 31/106 B of 16 December 1976, 32/91 A of 13 December 1977, 33/113 A of 18 December 1978, 34/90 B of 12 December 1979 and 35/122 of 11 December 1980,

Recalling Security Council resolutions 252 (1968) of 21 May 1968, 267 (1969) of 3 July 1969, 271 (1969) of 15 September 1969, 465 (1980) of 1 March 1980, 476 (1980) of 30 June 1980 and 478 (1980) of 20 August 1980,

Bearing in mind the need to protect and preserve the unique spiritual and religious character and dimensions of the Holy City of Jerusalem,

Expressing its very grave concern that Israel, as the occupying Power, persists in excavating and transforming the historical, cultural and religious sites of Jerusalem,

Noting with alarm that the excavations and transformations in progress seriously endanger the historical, cultural and religious sites of Jerusalem as well as its over-all configuration and that these sites have never been as endangered as they are today,

Noting with satisfaction and approval the decision of the World Heritage Committee of the United Nations Educational, Scientific and Cultural Organization to include the Old City of Jerusalem and its walls on the World Heritage List,

Noting with appreciation the recommendation of the Executive Board of the United Nations Educational, Scientific and Cultural Organization during its one hundred and thirteenth session that the World Heritage Committee should speed up the procedure for including the Old City of Jerusalem and its walls in the List of World Heritage in Danger,

1. *Determines* that the excavations and transformations of the landscape and of the historical, cultural and religious sites of Jerusalem constitute a flagrant violation of the principles of international law and the relevant provisions of the Geneva Convention relative to the Protection of Civilian Persons in Time of War, of 12 August 1949;

2. *Decides* that such violations by Israel constitute a serious obstruction to achieving a comprehensive and just peace in the Middle East as well as a threat to international peace and security;

3. *Demands* that Israel desist forthwith from all excavations and transformations of the historical, cultural and religious sites of Jerusalem, particularly beneath and around the Moslem Holy Sanctuary of Al-Haram Al-Sha-

---

[3] United Nations, *Treaty Series*, vol. 75, No. 973, p. 287.

rif (Al Masjid Al Aqsa and the Sacred Dome of the Rock), the structures of which are in danger of collapse;

4. *Requests* the Security Council to consider this situation in case Israel fails to comply immediately with the present resolution;

5. *Requests* the Secretary-General to report to the General Assembly and the Security Council, not later than 23 November 1981, on the implementation of the present resolution.

42nd plenary meeting
28 October 1981

204. General Assembly Resolution 36/150 on Israel's
Decision to Build a Canal Linking the Mediterranean Sea
to the Dead Sea, December 16, 1981*

* G.A. Res. 150, 36 U.N. GAOR Supp. (No. 51) at 95, U.N. Doc. A/36/51 (1981).

The General Assembly,

Recalling the Geneva Convention relative to the Protection of Civilian Persons in Time of War, of 12 August 1949,[43]

Reaffirming the applicability of the Geneva Convention to all Arab territories occupied by Israel since 1967, including Jerusalem,

Taking into account that the Israeli project to build a canal linking the Mediterranean Sea and the Dead Sea is in violation of the rules of international law, in particular those relating to the fundamental rights and duties of States,

Also taking into account that this project, if completed, will cause direct and irreparable damage to the rights and the legitimate vital interests of Jordan and of the Palestinian people,

Expressing concern that the proposed canal, to be constructed partly through the Palestinian territories occupied since 1967, will violate the principles of international law,

1. *Demands* that Israel cease forthwith the implementation of its project of a canal linking the Mediterranean Sea and the Dead Sea;

2. *Requests* the Security Council to consider initiating measures to halt the execution of this project;

3. *Requests* the Secretary-General to prepare and submit to the General Assembly and the Security Council, by 30 June 1982, a study on the Israeli canal and its effects on Jordan and the Palestinian territories occupied since 1967;

4. *Calls upon* all States not to assist, either directly or indirectly, in the preparation for and the execution of this project and to urge the compliance of national and international corporations to this effect;

5. *Decides* to include in the provisional agenda of its thirty-seventh session the item entitled, "Israel's decision to build a canal linking the Mediterranean Sea to the Dead Sea".

100th plenary meeting
16 December 1981

---

[43] United Nations, *Treaty Series*, vol. 75, No. 973, p. 287.

*D. The Threat of Nuclear Instability and
the Israeli Air Strike on Iraq's Osirak Reactor*

205. General Assembly Resolution 33/64 on the Establishment of a Nuclear-Weapon-Free Zone in the Region of the Middle East, December 14, 1978*

* G.A. Res. 64, 33 U.N. GAOR Supp. (No. 45) at 43, U.N. Doc. A/33/45 (1978). *See also* subsequent resolutions, G.A. Res. 77, 34 U.N. GAOR Supp. (No. 46) at 49, U.N. Doc. A/34/46 (1979) and G.A. Res. 147, 35 U.N. GAOR Supp. (No. 48) at 65, U.N. Doc. A/35/48 (1980).

The General Assembly,

Recalling its resolution 3263 (XXIX) of 9 December 1974, in which it overwhelmingly commended the idea of the establishment of a nuclear-weapon-free zone in the region of the Middle East,

Recalling also its resolution 3474 (XXX) of 11 December 1975, in which it recognized that the establishment of a nuclear-weapon-free zone in the Middle East enjoyed wide support in the region,

Bearing in mind its resolution 31/71 of 10 December 1976, in which it expressed the conviction that progress towards the establishment of a nuclear-weapon-free zone in the Middle East would greatly enhance the cause of peace in the region and in the world,

Considering its resolution 32/82 of 12 December 1977, in which it expressed the conviction that the development of nuclear capability would further complicate the situation and immensely damage the efforts to create an atmosphere of confidence in the Middle East,

Guided by its relevant recommendations in the Final Document of the Tenth Special Session of the General Assembly, dealing with the establishment of a nuclear-weapon-free zone in the Middle East,[20]

Recognizing that the establishment of a nuclear-weapon-free zone in the Middle East would greatly enhance international peace and security,

1. *Urges* all parties directly concerned seriously to consider taking the practical and urgent steps required for the implementation of the proposal to establish a nuclear-weapon-free zone in the Middle East in accordance with the relevant resolutions of the General Assembly and, as a means of promoting this objective, invites the countries concerned to adhere to the Treaty on the Non-Proliferation of Nuclear Weapons;[21]

2. *Invites* these countries, pending the establishment of such a zone in the Middle East and during the process of its establishment, to declare solemnly that they will refrain on a reciprocal basis from producing, acquiring or in any other way possessing nuclear weapons and nuclear explosive devices;

3. *Calls upon* these countries to refrain, on a reciprocal basis, from permitting the stationing of nuclear weapons on their territory by any third party, and to agree to place all their nuclear activities under International Atomic Energy Agency safeguards;

4. *Further invites* these countries, pending the establishment of a nuclear-weapon-free zone in the Middle East and during the process of its establishment, to declare, consistent with paragraph 63 (*d*) of the Final Document of the Tenth Special Session, their support for establishing such a zone in the region and to deposit these declarations with the Security Council;

5. *Reaffirms again* its recommendation to the nuclear-weapon States to refrain from any action contrary to the spirit and purpose of the present resolution and the objective of establishing in the region of the Middle East a

[20] *Ibid.*, [Resolution S-10/2], para. 63 (*d*).
[21] Resolution 2373 (XXII), annex.

nuclear-weapon-free zone under an effective system of safeguards, and to extend their co-operation to the States of the region in their efforts to promote these objectives;

6. *Renews its invitation* to the Secretary-General to continue to explore the possibilities of making progress towards the establishment of a nuclear-weapon-free zone in the Middle East;

7. *Decides* to include in the provisional agenda of its thirty-fourth session the item entitled "Establishment of a nuclear-weapon-free zone in the region of the Middle East".

84th plenary meeting
14 December 1978

206.   General Assembly Resolution 33/71 on the Review of the Implementation of the Recommendations and Decisions Adopted by the General Assembly at Its Tenth Special Session: A) Military and Nuclear Collaboration with Israel, December 14, 1978*

---

* G.A. Res. 71, 33 U.N. GAOR Supp. (No. 45) at 47, U.N. Doc. A/33/45 (1978).

A

MILITARY AND NUCLEAR COLLABORATION WITH ISRAEL

The General Assembly,

Gravely concerned over the continued and rapid Israeli military build-up,

Alarmed by the increasing evidence regarding Israeli attempts to acquire nuclear weapons,

Expressing its alarm over the use by Israel of cluster bombs against refugee camps and civilian targets in southern Lebanon,

Recalling its resolutions 3263 (XXIX) of 9 December 1974, 3474 (XXX) of 11 December 1975, 31/71 of 10 December 1976 and 32/82 of 12 December 1977 on the establishment of a nuclear-weapon-free zone in the region of the Middle East,

Recognizing that the continued escalation of Israeli armament constitutes a threat to international peace and security and underlies Israel's persistent defiance of General Assembly resolutions and its policy of expansion, occupation and denial of the inalienable rights of the Palestinian people,

Further recalling its repeated condemnations of the intensification of military collaboration between Israel and South Africa and its resolution 32/105 F of 14 December 1977, entitled "Military and nuclear collaboration with South Africa",

1. *Calls upon* all States to co-operate fully in effective international action, in accordance with Chapter VII of the Charter of the United Nations, to avert this grave menace to international peace and security;

2. *Requests* the Security Council, in particular, to call upon all States, under Chapter VII of the Charter and irrespective of any existing contracts:

(*a*) To refrain from any supply of arms, ammunition, military equipment or vehicles, or spare parts therefor, to Israel, without any exception;

(*b*) To ensure that such supplies do not reach Israel through other parties;

(*c*) To end all transfer of nuclear equipment or fissionable material or technology to Israel;

3. *Further requests* the Security Council to establish machinery for supervising the implementation of the measures referred to in paragraph 2 above;

4. *Invites* all Governments and organizations to take all appropriate action to promote the purposes of the present resolution.

84th plenary meeting
14 December 1978

207. General Assembly Resolution 34/89 on Israeli Nuclear Armament, December 11, 1979*

* G.A. Res. 89, 34 U.N. GAOR Supp. (No. 46) at 65, U.N. Doc. A/34/46 (1979). *See also* subsequent resolution, G.A. Res. 157, 35 U.N. GAOR Supp. (No. 48) at 79, U.N. Doc. A/35/48 (1980).

The General Assembly,

Alarmed by the increasing information and evidence regarding Israel's activities aiming at the acquisition and development of nuclear weapons,

Recalling its resolution 33/71 A of 14 December 1978 on military and nuclear collaboration with Israel,

Recalling its repeated condemnation of the military and nuclear collaboration between Israel and South Africa,

Reaffirming its resolutions 3263 (XXIX) of 9 December 1974, 3474 (XXX) of 11 December 1975, 31/71 of 10 December 1976, 32/82 of 12 December 1977 and 33/64 of 14 December 1978 on the establishment of a nuclear-weapon-free zone in the region of the Middle East,

Convinced that the development of nuclear capability by Israel would further aggravate the already dangerous situation in the region and further threaten international peace and security,

1. *Appeals* to all States to put an end to any co-operation with Israel which may assist it in acquiring and developing nuclear weapons and also to dissuade corporations, institutions and individuals within their jurisdiction from any co-operation that may result in providing Israel with nuclear weapons;

2. *Calls upon* all States to take all necessary measures to prevent the transfer to Israel of fissionable material and nuclear technology which could be used for nuclear arms;

3. *Calls upon* Israel to submit all its nuclear facilities to inspection by the International Atomic Energy Agency;

4. *Strongly condemns* any attempt by Israel to manufacture, acquire, store or test nuclear weapons or introduce them into the Middle East;

5. *Requests* the Security Council to adopt appropriate measures to ensure the implementation of the relevant resolutions concerning Israeli nuclear armament;

6. *Requests* the Secretary-General, with the assistance of qualified experts,[92] to prepare a study on Israeli nuclear armament and to report to the General Assembly at its thirty-sixth session;

7. *Further requests* the Secretary-General to submit a progress report on the work of the group of experts to the General Assembly at its thirty-fifth session;

8. *Decides* to include in the provisional agenda of its thirty-fifth session the item entitled "Israeli nuclear armament".

97th plenary meeting
11 December 1979

---

[92] Subsequently referred to as the Group of Experts to Prepare a Study on Israeli Nuclear Armament.

208. Statement by the International Atomic Energy Agency Director-General on the Application of Safeguards to the Tamuz (Osirak) Reactor Facility, June 12, 1981*

---

* U.N. Press Release, IAEA/989 of June 12, 1981, *reprinted in* 20 Int'l Legal Materials 965 (1981).

Statement by Director-General

The IAEA Director-General, Sigvard Eklund, made the following statement on the application of safeguards to the Tamuz reactor facility at the Board's meeting today in Vienna:

"I have received the following report from the Department of Safeguards.

"The task of the Agency in the implementation of safeguards is to verify that no safeguarded nuclear material is diverted from peaceful purposes. In a research reactor of the Osiris type this means, in the first place, to ensure that fuel elements supplied from abroad are checked on arrival and that, from that moment on, continuity of knowledge is maintained on their location and integrity. The primary measures used for this purpose are item counting, identification, and containment and surveillance. The design of the facility and of the fuel elements is such that provide assurance that the diversion of fuel elements would be detected with very high probability.

"The second possibility of diversion in a facility of the Osiris type is based on the undeclared production of plutonium. As the fuel elements consist of highly enriched uranium, only very small quantities of plutonium can be produced in them. Larger quantities perhaps up to the order of one significant quantity per year could only be produced if the core of the (Tamuz I) reactor were surrounded by a blanket of fertile elements made of natural or depleted uranium. The size and location of this blanket would be such that ordinary visual inspection would reveal its presence. The production of plutonium in fertile elements located underneath the reactor is practically impossible since the core is placed on a thick concrete slab which in turn is lined with a heavy steel plate. These provide shielding to permit maintenance work on control elements drives located in a vault below the reactor to be carried out. The existence or otherwise of undeclared underground installations has no influence on the detection capability of the IAEA's inspectorate at reactors of the Osiris type. In such a transparent pool reactor, the absence of fuel elements or the presence of undelcared [*sic*] fertile elements for plutonium production would be easily detected.

"In conclusion, in a reactor of this type, diversion of fuel elements or of undeclared plutonium produced at low rate cannot be technically excluded, but would be detected with very high probability.

"It should, of course, be borne in mind that it is not the task of the Agency to search facilities or installations which do not contain safeguarded material.

"May I end by saying that the presence of a large number of technicians from the country which has delivered the reactor could also be expected to provide some assurance."

209. Iraq's Statement Before the Security Council Concerning Israel's Attack on the Osirak Reactor, June 12, 1981*

---

* 36 U.N. SCOR (2280th mtg.) at 16, U.N. Doc. S/PV.2280 (1981).

Mr. HAMMADI (Iraq): Mr. President , allow me first to express to you, and through you to the members of the Security Council, my gratitude for convening this meeting and for giving me the opportunity to address the Council on the question of the flagrant act of aggression committed by Israel against Iraq.

On Sunday, 7 June 1981, at 1837 hours Baghdad local time, Israeli warplanes raided the nuclear installations situated near Baghdad, causing many civilian casualties and much material damage. The Zionist aggressors announced on the following day their responsibility for the attack, brazenly claiming the total destruction of the installations.

It is worth recalling that this was not the first attack of its kind carried out by the Zionist aggressor. We believe that Zionist warplanes carried out two raids aimed at the same installations on 27 September 1980.

In order to put the Israeli act of aggression in its proper perspective, it is necessary to deal with the motives and objectives of Zionist policies, and particularly those in the nuclear field.

It is no longer a secret that the founders of the Zionist entity had contemplated from the very beginning the possession of nuclear weapons as a means to guarantee the continued exile of the Palestinians, and continued expansion over Arab territories in order to realize the Zionist dream of "Greater Israel".

The Israeli nuclear programme goes back as far as 1949. The most important experiments conducted by the Weizman Institute in the early 1950s concerned the development of techniques of uranium extraction from phosphates in the Negev Desert, as well as those relating to the production of heavy water. In 1952 the Ben Gurion Government established the Atomic Energy Commission within the framework of the Ministry of Defence, with a separate budget and special laboratories. The existence of that Commission was kept secret until 1954. In 1953 a nuclear co-operation agreement was concluded with France which marked a turning point in the Israeli nuclear programme. The fact remains, however, that the United States was the first country to provide Israel with a nuclear reactor under an agreement concluded in 1955—namely, the reactor at Nahal Sorek, which had a five-megawatt capacity. The United States contributed $350,000 towards the cost of that reactor and provided Israel with a vast library of books, studies and reports, as well as six kilograms of enriched uranium-235. Furthermore, 56 Israelis were trained in American nuclear establishments. Subsequently, Israel obtained another American reactor with an eight-megawatt capacity; it was installed at the Technion Institute. In 1957 the decision was taken to construct the highly secret reactor at Dimona, and in 1958 a reactor at Rishon Lizion with a five-megawatt capacity was constructed in co-operation with the United States.

The decade of the 1950s also witnessed the provision to Israel of nuclear material and technology by the Central Intelligence Agency (CIA) and the beginning of co-operation in the nuclear field with the Federal Republic of

Germany. In 1964 the Dimona reactor became operational with a 24-mega-watt capacity and a possible production of 5 to 7 kilograms of plutonium annually. That quantity is sufficient for the production of a nuclear bomb with 1.2 times the force of the Hiroshima type.

It is to be noted that the Dimona reactor was obtained from France, and the truth about it was not disclosed until the CIA revealed in 1960 that what the Americans were told was a textile factory was in fact a nuclear reactor. *The New York Times* stated on 20 December 1960 that the Dimona reactor was "particularly well-suited for producing fissionable plutonium used in nuclear bombs". The same newspaper reported in its issue of 18 July 1970 that American experts who had visited the reactor had complained in 1969 that there was no guarantee that work relating to armament was not being undertaken in Dimona, in view of the restrictive procedures imposed by Israel on inspection.

It is well known that Israel has had a nuclear capability for a number of years. As far back as 1969, the Buffalo *Evening News* carried on its front page on 9 May a *Reuters* report published in the West German magazine *Der Spiegel* stating that Israel has become the world's sixth nuclear Power and had six Hiroshima-type bombs of 20 kilotons, produced at Dimona.

On 5 December 1974, *The New York Times* quoted Israeli President Ephraim Katzir as saying that Israel "possesses the potential to produce atomic weapons" and will do so "if we need it".

At the Conference on a Non-Nuclear Future, held at Salzburg in May 1977, Paul Levanthal, a former staff nuclear-weapons expert for the Senate Government Operation Committee of the United States, revealed that 200 tons of natural uranium, enough to build 42 nuclear weapons, which had been placed on a ship that had disappeared nine years before, had ended up in Israel. The uranium had been loaded onto a cargo ship named *The Scheersburg A* which had sailed out of Antwerp bound for Genoa, where it never arrived. The cargo of *The Scheersburg A* was reported to be capable of keeping a Dimona-type reactor operating and producing plutonium for 20 years.

Shortly after the Salzburg revelation, Norway's former chief prosecutor stated that Israeli agent Dan Aerbel had admitted taking part in the opera-tion to divert the uranium-laden ship. Aerbel had been seized in 1974 by the Norwegians with four other members of Israel's Mossad, the Israeli se-cret service, for the killing of a Moroccan national who was mistaken for a Palestinian by the Israeli agents at a small town in Norway.

According to one article published in *The Times* of London on 14 August 1980, the American Central Intelligence Agency (CIA) had mistakenly re-leased the text of a five-page secret document in 1974 which stated categor-ically that Israel was engaged in a nuclear-weapons programme. Part of the uranium was described as having been obtained by "clandestine means" which, although this not spelled out, was understood to refer to various raids in Europe by squads of underground Mossad agents. The report—all but two paragraphs of which would have remained classified, had a bureaucratic slip not led to its publication—stated in a key section:

We believe that Israel already has produced nuclear weapons. Our judgement is based on Israeli acquisition of large quantities of uranium, partly by clandestine means, the ambiguous nature of Israeli efforts in the field of uranium enrichment, and Israel's large investment in a costly missile system destined to accommodate nuclear warheads.

The Times went on to say that recent foreign reports had suggested that South Africa was not Israel's main partner in a secret nuclear-weapons development programme. The article also referred to a mysterious blast detected off the coast of South Africa in September 1979 by an American spy satellite. It also referred to the manuscript of a book written by two Israeli journalists entitled *None Will Survive Us: The Story of the Israeli A-Bomb*, which contained information to the effect that the said blast was the result of a joint nuclear test by Israel and South Africa. The blast of September 1979 was followed by another in December of the same year, and the second event was recorded by another United States satellite.

The Middle East Magazine, in its issue published in London in April 1981 which contained an investigative report on the Israel-South Africa nuclear link, states that:

. . . once again the White House said that the flash was "probably not" a nuclear blast and suggested it was a "micro-meteor hit", although scientists say this is likely to occur only once in 10 years. Even the CIA is not prepared to accept this a second time and has pointed out that, as in the previous incident, South African warships were positioned secretly at sea just below the flash point.

The magazine further quotes Marvin Cetron, the Pentagon's private weapons analyst, as saying:

Were I in the White House, I would try and give as many different possible alternatives as could be technically feasible, hoping to take off the high probability of its being a nuclear explosion. Obviously, it is a cover-up.

Nor was that the first attempted White House cover-up of its kind. In the mid-1960s the United States Government discovered that more than 200 pounds of highly enriched weapons-grade uranium, enough for at least four atomic bombs, was missing from the Nuclear Materials and Equipment Corporation (NUMEC) plant in Apollo, Pennsylvania. In his well-documented book *The Zionist Connection*, Dr. Alfred Lilienthal states that:

The most serious nuclear safeguards case the United States ever faced broke into the open in late February 1978 when the Nuclear Regulatory Commission (NRC) released a 550-page report in response to a

House Committee inquiry over previous testimony given by NRC Executive Director Lee V. Gossick. In revealing that Gossick had "testified incorrectly", the report confirmed that the CIA had evidence that Israel had the atomic bomb by 1968 and that bomb material in fact had been diverted from the Apollo plant. Equally important to the report was that CIA third-ranking official Carl Duckett had informed a closed meeting of the NRC in 1976 that President Johnson had been told eight years earlier that Israel had atomic weapons. The President had told CIA Director Richard Helms: "Don't tell anyone else, not even Dean Rusk or Robert McNamara"—then the Secretaries of State and Defence respectively.

The story was broken by *The Washington Post* in its issue of 2 March 1978.

The same Carl Duckett, who is currently a consultant to the United States Senate, repeated in an interview broadcast by ABC Television on 27 April 1981 that there was a clear consensus in the CIA that indeed NUMEC material had been diverted and had been used by the Israelis in fabricating weapons. He also confirmed that President Johnson had ordered Director Helms not to tell anybody else. Duckett further stated:

The key impression to me was that indeed it was taken very seriously by the President, and obviously he was very concerned that we protect that information.

That was stated on the ABC News Close-up broadcast over the ABC Television Network on Monday, 27 April 1981.

Iraq has embarked upon a vast and ambitious programme of development. In doing so my Government recognized at an early stage the importance of science and technology, including the peaceful application of nuclear energy, for the achievement of social and economic development. Working towards that goal, we have made efforts to expand our nuclear-research facilities and to widen the scope of the peaceful uses of atomic energy. We have also recognized that the development of alternative sources of energy is becoming increasingly vital and that the peaceful use of atomic energy will be one of the most important alternatives for some time to come.

Despite the basic imbalances and discrimination which are to be found in the Treaty on the Non-Proliferation of Nuclear Weapons, Iraq was one of its first adherents. We signed the Treaty on 1 July 1968 and ratified it on 29 October 1969. In 1972 my country concluded an agreement with the International Atomic Energy Agency for the application of safeguards to all our nuclear activities, as required by the Non-Proliferation Treaty. On numerous occasions my Government has expressed its conviction that full and faithful implementation of the Non-Proliferation Treaty would make a major contribution to its twin objectives—namely, horizontal and vertical non-proliferation and the promotion of nuclear energy for peaceful purposes.

We attach special importance to international co-operation in the field of the peaceful uses of atomic energy. Besides being a member of the International Atomic Energy Agency, Iraq has concluded bilateral co-operation agreements with a number of countries. With a view to strengthening and promoting co-operation in scientific and technical research, the Iraqi Atomic Energy Commission has, together with other organizations, sponsored several conferences and seminars, with the participation of scientists from other countries.

It can no longer be denied that it is the sovereign right of every country to seek knowledge and to pursue the application of science and technology, including nuclear technology for peaceful purposes, in the interests of economic and social development. We firmly believe that the widening gap between the developed and the developing countries cannot be narrowed without the full utilization of science and technology, including the peaceful application of nuclear energy.

Article IV of the Non-Proliferation Treaty provides as follows:

1. Nothing in this Treaty shall be interpreted as affecting the inalienable right of all the Parties to the Treaty to develop research, production and use of nuclear energy for peaceful purposes without discrimination and in conformity with articles I and II of this Treaty.

2. All the Parties to the Treaty undertake to facilitate, and have the right to participate in, the fullest possible exchange of equipment, materials and scientific and technological information for the peaceful uses of nuclear energy. Parties to the Treaty in a position to do so shall also co-operate in contributing alone or together with other States or international organizations to the further development of the applications of nuclear energy for peaceful purposes, especially in the territories of non-nuclear weapons States Party to the Treaty, with due consideration for the needs of the developing areas of the world. (*General Assembly resolution 2373 (XXII)*)

Moreover, at the Havana Summit Conference in 1979, the non-aligned countries reaffirmed the inalienable right of every country to undisturbed and independent development of the peaceful uses of atomic energy. A similar position was adopted by the Extraordinary Meeting of Foreign Ministers of Islamic Countries held in Fez, Morocco, in September 1980. In addition, repeated resolutions of the General Assembly have reaffirmed that right, subject to appropriate safeguards.

Israel prepared the ground for its act of aggression by a vast propaganda campaign alleging that Iraq was engaged in a programme of nuclear-weapons production. The countries which had concluded co-operation agreements with Iraq were denounced and vilified. The severity of the campaign prompted Mr. Jean François-Poncet, the then Foreign Minister of France, to question the reasons for such a campaign. He recalled that Iraq was, after all, the thirty-fifth country to buy a nuclear research reactor. There were 34 other countries which had imported 78 atomic reactors for such purposes, working with enriched uranium. Most of the reactors were of American construction. The countries included South Africa, South Korea, Thailand, Philippines, Zaire, and so on. The French Government also issued a statement on 29 July 1980 which expressed astonishment at the fabricated accusations being levelled against it for its co-operation with Iraq. The statement pointed out Iraq's right, together with that of all other States, to utilize nuclear energy for peaceful purposes and found no basis upon which Iraq could be prevented from exercising that right. In conclusion, the statement reaffirmed that the co-operation of the French Government with Iraq was carried out with perfectly legitimate objectives and was covered by all the necessary safeguards.

The Zionist campaign did not stop at that. There were acts of terrorism, sabotage, international piracy and physical liquidation carried out by Zionist undercover agents in order to obstruct Iraq's peaceful nuclear programme.

The motives behind the Zionist campaign and aggression against Iraq are, first, the desire to cover up Israel's possession of nuclear weapons and secondly and more importantly, the determination not to allow the Arab Nation to acquire the scientific or technical knowledge necessary for their development and progress. The Zionists believe that they can thus impose their *diktat* on the Arab Nation. The more the Arabs advance in their scientific knowledge, the weaker the Zionist chances of maintaining their occupation of Arab territories and their denial of the inalienable rights of the Palestinian people.

It is evident that the Israel nuclear programme has been geared to military purposes from its very inception and that all sorts of illegal means have been employed for its enhancement, in total violation of internationally accepted standards. Despite the repeated calls upon Israel to accede to the Non-Proliferation Treaty (NPT), it has bluntly refused to do so. Iraq, in contrast, by accepting the terms of the Non-Proliferation Treaty, has fully subscribed to those standards in its nuclear programme. In that context, I should like to quote the following from the statement made by the Director-General of the International Atomic Energy Agency (IAEA) at the opening meeting of that Agency's Board of Governors on 9 June 1981:

> Iraq has been a party to the Non-Proliferation Treaty since it came into force in 1970. In accordance with that Treaty, Iraq accepts Agency safeguards on all its nuclear activities. These safeguards have been satisfactorily applied to date, including during the recent period of armed conflict with Iran. The last safeguard inspection at the Iraqi nuclear centre took place in January of this year and all nuclear material there was satisfactorily accounted for. This material included the fuel so far delivered for the Tammuz reactors.

Iraq, being mindful of the danger posed to international peace and security by the Israeli armament programmes, has taken the initiative since the convening of the special session of the General Assembly on disarmament in 1978, in bringing to the attention of the world the dangers of those Israeli programmes. The General Assembly, at its thirty-third session, adopted a resolution sponsored by 36 States Members of the Organization entitled "Military and Nuclear Collaboration with Israel". The second paragraph of that resolution requested the Security Council in particular to call upon all States under Chapter VII of the Charter and irrespective of any existing contracts:

(a) to refrain from any supply of arms, ammunition, military equipment or vehicles, or spare parts therefor, to Israel, without any exception;
(b) to ensure that such supplies do not reach Israel through other parties;
(c) to end all transfer of nuclear equipment or fissionable material or technology to Israel. (*General Assembly resolution 33/71 A, para. 2*)

The resolution further requested the Security Council to establish machinery for the supervision and implementation of the measures referred to in the paragraph just quoted.

During the thirty-fourth session of the General Assembly, Iraq, supported by 25 other States Members of the Organization, inscribed an item on the agenda entitled "Israeli nuclear armament". The Assembly adopted resolution 34/89, in which it called upon Israel to submit all its nuclear facilities to inspection by the International Atomic Energy Agency. It also strongly condemned any attempt on the part of Israel to manufacture, acquire, store, test or introduce nuclear weapons into the Middle East. It further requested the Security Council to adopt appropriate measures to ensure the implementation of the relevant resolutions concerning Israeli nuclear armament.

Furthermore, Iraq has actively supported the initiatives taken in the General Assembly concerning the establishment of nuclear-weapon-free zones, particularly in the Middle East and in the Indian Ocean.

The attack carried out by Israel against Iraq is clearly an act of aggression in accordance with the provisions of the Charter as expounded on in the definition of aggression in resolution 3314 (XXIX) of the twenty-ninth session of the General Assembly. The Israeli allegation that it acted in legitimate self-defence is totally unfounded, in fact and in law.

The Israeli act of aggression is a severe blow to the internationally accepted system for the use of atomic energy for peaceful purposes. The Director-General of the International Atomic Energy Agency, in his statement to the Board of Governors, which I referred to earlier, said:

This attack on the Iraqi nuclear reactor is a serious development with far-reaching implications. The Agency's safeguards system is a basic element of the Non-Proliferation Treaty. During my long time here, I do not think we have been faced with a more serious question than the implications of this development. The Agency has inspected the Iraqi reactors and has not found evidence of any activity not in accordance with the Non-Proliferation Treaty. A non-NPT country has evidently not felt assured by our findings and about our ability to continue to discharge our safeguarding responsibilities effectively. . . . From a point of principle, one can only conclude that it is the Agency's safeguards régime which has also been attacked. Where would this lead us in the future? This is a matter of grave concern which should be pondered well.

Iraq had already warned the Security Council in a letter distributed in document S/14073 and dated 29 July 1980 that the Zionist campaign against Iraq was a prelude to an air strike against the Iraqi nuclear reactor, as Israel had in its possession American-manufactured aeroplanes with a range that enabled it to strike within Iraqi territory. This Zionist act of aggression against Iraq constitutes a qualitative change in the aggressor's policy in the area. It is a clear indication of the determination of the Zionists, after the failure of Camp David, to escalate their provocations with acts of armed aggression prior to launching a full-scale war in order to subjugate the Arab countries and to impose full Zionist domination over the whole Middle East.

In conclusion, I should like once again to emphasize that the Israeli attack against my country is a clear-cut act of premeditated aggression. The whole world has recognized that fact. The elaborate preparations that preceded the commission of that act were fully described by the Prime Minister of Israel and other Israeli leaders in their press conference held in Tel Aviv on 10 June. What is worse is that Mr. Begin stated categorically at that press conference that, if Iraq tried to rebuild the reactor, Israel would do all it can to destroy it again.

Faced with this grave situation, the Security Council cannot, in our opinion, limit itself to a mere condemnation of this act of Israeli aggression. The Council should reaffirm the right of all States to develop nuclear programmes for peaceful purposes. Mandatory sanctions in accordance with the provisions of Chapter VII of the Charter should be imposed upon Israel to remove the grave menace to international peace and security posed by its actions. Israeli lawlessness should be brought to an end. The Security Council must decide that all States—and especially the United States of America—shall, under Chapter VII of the Charter, refrain from providing Israel with any military material or technical co-operation or assistance which might encourage it to pursue its policy of expansion and aggression. Something more than condemnation should take place if we really want to have a world of law rather than a world of blind force. In addition, the Security Council should, in the interest of peace and stability in the Middle East, demand that all Israeli nuclear installations be opened to inspection, and subject to the safeguards system of the IAEA.

There should be very little doubt, especially among the members of the Council, that Israel's real target on Sunday, 7 June 1981, was not merely our peaceful nuclear installations. The Zionists and their friends were actually aiming at Iraq's crucial role in rallying the Arab nations against the Camp David conspiracy, in making a real contribution towards strengthening the world of Islam and the Non-aligned Movement, and in being the vanguard of the fight against colonialism, racism including Zionism, and all other forms of domination. They want to undermine the new Iraq and all that it stands for. That target is indestructible.

2 10. Israel's Statement Before the Security Council Concerning Its Actions Regarding the Osirak Reactor, June 12, 1981*

---

* 36 U.N. SCOR (2280th mtg.) at 37, U.N. Doc. S/PV.2280 (1981).

Mr. BLUM (Israel): Mr. President, at the outset, let me take this opportunity of conveying to you our felicitations on your assumption of the presidency of the Council for the month of June. You, Sir, represent a country with which mine has the friendliest and most cordial of relations. Since Mexico's election to the Council last year, you personally have exhibited great qualities of diplomacy and statesmanship. That was particularly the case when you acted as President of the Council in April of last year, a month in which a series of difficult debates took place. We have every confidence that, as President of the Council for a second time, you will handle its business with the same wisdom and expertise.

I should like to take this opportunity also to express my compliments to the Permanent Representative of Japan, Ambassador Nisibori, who conducted the Council's business last month in an exemplary fashion, with all his well-known skill and grace.

On Sunday, 7 June 1981, the Israel Air Force carried out an operation against the Iraqi atomic reactor called "Osiraq". That reactor was in its final stages of construction near Baghdad. The pilots' mission was to destroy it. They executed their mission successfully.

In destroying Osiraq, Israel performed an elementary act of self-preservation, both morally and legally. In so doing, Israel was exercising its inherent right of self-defence as understood in general international law and as preserved in Article 51 of the United Nations Charter.

A threat of nuclear obliteration was being developed against Israel by Iraq, one of Israel's most implacable enemies. Israel tried to have that threat halted by diplomatic means. Our efforts bore no fruit. Ultimately we were left with no choice. We were obliged to remove that mortal danger. We did it cleanly and effectively. The Middle East has become a safer place. We trust that the international community has also been given pause to make the world a safer place.

Those facts and the potentials for a safer world are widely recognized. Several States in the Middle East and beyond are sleeping more easily today in the knowledge that Saddam Hussein's nuclear arms potential has been smashed.

But all this will not preclude a hypocritical parade here in the Security Council. Nothing will prevent numerous Members of the United Nations from the usual ganging-up on Israel for reasons of spite and expediency. Nothing will stop them from hurling abuse at us, even though they know in their heart of hearts that it is Israel that has relieved them of an awesome menace. Their cant and crocodile tears will do this Organization no credit. The sham and charade will not add to the stature of this Council, and pontification will not further the cause of peace.

Israel has long believed in a different, more constructive approach. We advocate the establishment of a nuclear-weapon-free zone in the Middle East, grounded in a multilateral treaty, reached through direct negotiations by all the States concerned. This is the moment for the Security Council to lend its support to Israel's proposal. I shall return to our proposal at greater length towards the end of my statement.

Ever since the establishment of the State of Israel over 33 years ago, Iraq has been conspiring to destroy it. Iraq joined several other Arab States which attacked Israel the day after it became independent in 1948. But while other Arab States—Egypt, Lebanon, Jordan and Syria—signed armistice agreements with Israel in 1949, Iraq adamantly refused to do so. Instead, it fomented and supported the unrelenting Arab belligerency and terrorism against Israel. It also took part in the Arab wars against Israel in 1967 and 1973. And it has doggedly rejected any international measure or instrument which might imply even the most indirect recognition of Israel and its right to exist.

On 22 October 1973, when this Council called for a cease-fire in the Yom Kippur War, the Baghdad Government announced:

> Iraq does not consider itself a party to any resolution, procedure or measure in armistice or cease-fire agreements or negotiations of peace with Israel, now or in the near future.

In June 1977, the then President of Iraq, Ahmad Hasan Al-Bakr, asserted that:

> Efforts . . . must be consolidated . . . to support the liquidation of the racist Zionist entity so as to build a democratic society.

More recently, the Iraqi ambassador in New Delhi had the following to say at a press conference reported by the Middle East News Agency on 24 October 1978:

> Iraq does not accept the existence of a Zionist State in Palestine . . . the only solution is war.

And only last year, during the seventh emergency special session of the General Assembly, the representative of Iraq found it necessary to restate his Government's opposition to the very existence of my country.

In sum, Iraq declares itself to have been in a state of war with Israel since 1948. Hence, it has rejected all United Nations efforts to seek a peaceful settlement of the Arab-Israel dispute. It has publicly rejected Security Council resolutions 242 (1967) and 338 (1973).

Iraq has missed no opportunity to make it clear that it will not abide by international law in respect to Israel and that it reserves its freedom of action with regard to Israel. This perverse doctrine found expression in the so-called "National Charter" of Iraq, proclaimed by its President, Saddam Hussein, in February of last year and circulated as document A/35/110-S/13816 at the request of the Permanent Representative of Iraq.

The principles allegedly underlying that Charter were said to include, *inter alia*, the non-use of force and the peaceful settlement of disputes. Yet they were specifically excluded with regard to my country on the grounds that it is a "deformed entity [which] is not considered a State" (*A/35/110-S/ 13816, annex, p. 1*). That same Charter committed Iraq in no uncertain terms to all-out warfare against Israel and enjoined other Arab States to participate in that war, using "all means and techniques" (*ibid., p. 2*).

In a letter to the Secretary-General of 11 March 1980, circulated both as a document of the General Assembly and of this Council (A/35/131-S/ 13838), I drew attention to the fact that this undisguised denial by one Member State of the right of another Member State to exist is in flagrant violation of the purposes and principles of the United Nations Charter. I observed that it was a matter for surprise that a document so violently opposed to everything that the United Nations stands for should be circulated at all as a document of this Council, whose primary responsibility is the maintenance of international peace and security. The United Nations, and this Council in particular, were unmoved.

Not by accident has Iraq taken a lead among those Arab States which reject out of hand any solution of the Arab-Israel dispute by peaceful means. To translate its words into deeds, Iraq has used its petro-dollars to develop a sophisticated technological and military infrastructure. It sees itself as the leader and linchpin of the so-called Eastern Front which the Arab rejectionist States established in Baghdad in 1978 against Israel. Despite its involvement in a war of aggression against Iran, Iraq has continued to indicate its willingness to send men and material to take part in any military hostilities that the rejectionist Arab States may initiate against Israel.

Over and beyond the development of its conventional forces, Iraq has in recent years entered the nuclear armaments field methodically and purposefully, while at the same time piously appending its signature to international instruments specifically prohibiting it from doing so.

As far back as 8 September 1975, Saddam Hussein was quoted in the Lebanese weekly *al-Usbu al-Arabi* as saying that the acquisition of nuclear technology by his country was the first Arab attempt towards nuclear armament. By way of comment on reports that Iraq would be the first Arab country to acquire an atomic bomb, the Iraqi oil minister at the time was reported on 30 November 1976 in the Kuwaiti paper *al-Qabas* to have declared a week earlier that all Arab States should participate in a project to produce an atomic bomb. And according to the *International Herald Tribune* of 27 June 1980, Na'im Haddad, a senior member of Iraq's Revolutionary Command Council, stated at a meeting of the Arab League in 1977 that "the Arabs must get an atom bomb".

In brief, this Council is now confronted with an absurd situation. Iraq claims to be at war with Israel. Indeed it prepares for atomic war. And yet it complains to the Security Council when Israel, in self-defence, acts to avert nuclear disaster.

I would like to remind the representative of Iraq that a State cannot invoke in its favour benefits deriving from certain provisions of international law without being prepared at the same time also to abide by the duties flowing from international law. Arab States, including Iraq, seek to impose on Israel duties stemming from the international law of peace while simultaneously claiming for themselves the privileges of the international law of war.

In recent years, Iraq has been the most active Arab State in the nuclear field. Its goal has been the acquisition of a military nuclear option. Permit me to elaborate.

In 1974, Iraq attempted to acquire a 500-megawatt nuclear power reactor of the graphite-gas type which had been developed in the 1950s primarily for the production of large quantities of plutonium for military use. Although that request was turned down, it was nevertheless agreed to supply Iraq with a 70-megawatt nuclear reactor of the Osiris type, which is considered one of the most advanced reactors of its kind in the world.

Iraq demanded that its supplier provide it with weapons-grade nuclear fuel—that is, uranium enriched to a level of 93 per cent. When it comes to research, this type of fuel is generally confined to use in nuclear facilities with an extremely low capacity—from 1 to 10 megawatts.

Iraq's supplier undertook to provide it with about 80 kilograms of this weapons-grade uranium. In 1979, the supplier tried to persuade Iraq to accept a far lower grade of uranium, but the Iraqis insisted on the previous deal. To fulfil it, the supplier had to draw from stockpiles in its own military nuclear arsenal.

During 1980 the supplier dispatched to Iraq the first shipment of the enriched uranium concerned, containing 12 kilograms. This shipment enabled Iraq to put into operation a smaller nuclear reactor provided by the same supplier. Israel learned from unimpeachable sources that following the delivery, expected soon, of two additional shipments of weapons-grade uranium weighing about 24 kilograms, Osiraq would be completed, and put into operation within the next few weeks—and not later than the beginning of September 1981. Thirty-six kilograms of weapons-grade uranium in Iraq's possession would enable it to make a nuclear bomb.

This, of course, is by no means the end of the story. Iraq has also purchased complementary fuel-cycle technology: namely, four research laboratories for the study of the chemical processes of fuel preparation and its recycling, as well as the reprocessing of irradiated fuel. From the nuclear weapons point of view, the most significant is a radio-chemistry laboratory, known as the "hot cell", used for the separation of irradiated fuel and the extraction of plutonium. This project is scheduled for completion in 1981.

Together with the construction of these facilities, Iraq has been energetically investigating the possibility of acquiring nuclear power reactors which operate on natural uranium and heavy water. Such reactors produce large quantities of plutonium which, as is well known, is used in the manufacture of nuclear weapons.

In order to build up the reserves of uranium needed to attain self-sufficiency, Iraq has operated in four parallel directions: (a) it has bought weapons-grade enriched uranium on the international black market; (b) it has acquired uranium through bilateral deals; (c) it has obtained enrichment facilities; and (d) it has begun an intensive search for uranium on its own territory.

Iraq already possesses aircraft capable of delivering nuclear warheads. In addition, it is involved in the development of a new surface-to-surface missile with an effective range of up to 3,000 kilometres, also capable of delivering a nuclear warhead. Unlike Israel, Iraq, for well-known reasons, has not embarked on its large-scale nuclear programme for reasons of pure research, despite its protestations to the contrary. And again unlike Israel, Iraq has certainly not embarked upon its nuclear programme because it faces an energy crisis. Iraq is blessed with abundant supplies of natural oil and, when not engaged in foreign adventures against one of its neighbours, it is normally one of the largest oil suppliers in OPEC.

No amount of bluster can hide one simple, basic fact: Iraq's nuclear programme has, beyond a shadow of doubt, just one aim—to acquire nuclear weapons and delivery systems for them.

Academic and public figures who follow these matters have had no illusions about Iraq's nuclear objectives in the military field. For example, on 5 August 1980, the Paris newspaper *France-Soir*, published an article on Iraq's nuclear programme containing a warning by the eminent French atomic scientist Francis Perrin, who had served as head of the French Nuclear Energy Commission from 1951 to 1971. Referring to Osiraq, Perrin explained that it is fuelled by highly enriched uranium which can be used to produce an atomic weapon.

Similarly, on 27 March 1981, Senator Alan Cranston told the United States Senate:

> This massive Iraqi nuclear development program is under way despite the fact that Iraq has no parallel program for developing commercial nuclear power.

Senator Cranston went on to say that he had been informed authoritatively that Iraq was pursuing a nuclear-weapons capability option:

> Iraq, though at the present time Party to the Nuclear Non-Proliferation Treaty, is embarked on a full-scale program that appears designed to develop the capability to extract plutonium suitable for weapons purposes.

Senator Cranston explained that Iraq had vigorously embarked on an approach of the Manhattan Project type, which could provide it with nuclear explosives of the Hiroshima size. Senator Cranston's concerns were heightened by the fact that Iraq is governed by what he terms "a radical, militarily aggressive régime which routinely employs terrorism to advance its aims".

The combination of an Osiris reactor, and about 80 kilograms of weapons-grade nuclear fuel, together with laboratories for the production of plutonium would have enabled Iraq to acquire a nuclear-weapons capability by the mid-1980s. To produce nuclear weapons, Iraq could have opted for one of two paths: (a) the production of three to four nuclear explosive devices on the enriched uranium path, by using the fuel supplied for operating Osiraq, or (b) the use of plutonium produced by Osiraq and the reprocessing laboratory for the production of one plutonium bomb a year.

Further cause for anxiety was given by the delivery of weapons-grade nuclear material without proper provision for the return of the fuel rods after use.

Any lingering doubts about Iraq's intentions to acquire nuclear weapons to be used against Israel were removed just two days ago by the Iraqi Minister of Information. According to yesterday's *New York Times*, Latif Jassem wrote in the State-run newspaper *al-Jumhuriya* on 10 June 1981 that the Israel attack on Osiraq last Sunday showed that Israel knew that its "real and decisive danger" came from Iraq.

In plain terms, Iraq was creating a mortal danger to the people and State of Israel. It had embarked on ramified programmes to acquire nuclear weapons. It had acquired the necessary facilities and fuel. Osiraq was about to go critical, in a matter of weeks.

Over the last few years Israel has followed Iraq's nuclear development programme with growing concern. We have repeatedly expressed our demand both publicly and through diplomatic channels that nuclear assistance to Iraq be terminated. On various occasions, Israel representatives drew the attention of the United Nations General Assembly and of its First Committee to the frantic efforts being made by Iraq and its supporters to establish a nuclear axis aimed against Israel. The Government of Israel has repeatedly urged the European countries involved to stop assisting Iraq's systematic drive to attain a military nuclear capability, stressing the grave implications of such aid to Iraq for all concerned. We also urged other friendly Governments to use their influence in that direction. All these public and diplomatic efforts by Israel went unheeded while, at the same time, the pace of Iraq's nuclear development increased.

I should add that Israel was not alone in its apprehensions. Several neighbours of Iraq and other States in the Middle East also expressed their deep concern to Iraq's suppliers over Iraq's nuclear ambitions—but to no avail.

Precious time was lost, and Israel was left facing the stark prospect that within a very short period of time Osiraq would become critical, or, in the jargon of nuclear scientists, was about to go "hot". Israel was left with an agonizing dilemma. Once Osiraq had become hot, any attack on it would have blanketed the city of Baghdad with massive radioactive fallout. The effect of that would have been lethal and tens of thousands, and possibly hundreds of thousands, would have been grievously harmed.

On the other hand, Israel could not possibly stand idly by while an irresponsible, ruthless and bellicose régime, such as that of Iraq, acquired nuclear weapons, thus creating a constant nightmare for Israel. Saddam Hussein's régime has amply demonstrated its total disregard for innocent human life both at home and in its war with Iran. Given the nature and record of that unscrupulous régime, the vast dangers for Israel inherent in the creation of an Iraqi military nuclear potential are self-evident.

The Government of Israel, like any other Government, has the elementary duty to protect the lives of its citizens. In destroying Osiraq last Sunday, Israel was exercising its inherent and natural right of self-defence, as understood in general international law and well within the meaning of Article 51 of the United Nations Charter.

Commenting on the meaning of Article 51 of the Charter, Sir Humphrey Waldock, now President of the International Court of Justice, stated in a lecture delivered at the Hague Academy of International Law in 1952 that

> . . . it would be a travesty of the purposes of the Charter to compel a defending State to allow its assailant to deliver the first and perhaps fatal blow . . . To read Article 51 otherwise is to protect the aggressor's right to the first strike.

In similar vein, Professor Morton Kaplan and Nicholas de B. Katzenbach wrote in their book, *The Political Foundations of International Law*:

> Must a State wait until it is too late before it may defend itself? Must it permit another the advantages of military build-up, surprise attack, and total offence, against which there may be no defence? It would be unreasonable to expect any State to permit this—particularly when given the possibility that a surprise nuclear blow might bring about total destruction or at least total subjugation, unless the attack were forestalled.

And Professor Derek Bowett of Cambridge University, in his authoritative work on *Self-Defence in International Law*, observed:

> No State can be expected to await an initial attack which, in the present state of armaments, may well destroy the State's capacity for further resistance and so jeopardize its very existence.

So much for the legalities of the case. Still, we have been accused of acting unlawfully. Presumably it is lawful for a sovereign State to create an instrument capable of destroying several hundred thousand Israelis; it is unlawful to halt that fatal process before it reaches completion.

The decision taken by my Government in the exercise of its right of self-defence, after the usual international procedures and avenues had proved futile, was one of the most agonizing we have ever had to take. We sought to act in a manner which would minimize the danger to all concerned, including a large segment of Iraq's population. We waited until the eleventh hour after the diplomatic clock had run out, hoping against hope that Iraq's nuclear arms project would be brought to a halt. Our Air Force was only called in when, as I have said, we learned on the basis of completely reliable information that there was less than a month to go before Osiraq might have become critical. Our Air Force's operation was consciously launched on a Sunday, and timed for late in the day, on the assumption that the workers on the site, including foreign experts employed at the reactor, would have left. That assumption proved correct, and the loss in human life, which we sincerely regret, was minimal.

I should add that those same considerations worked in the opposite direction as regards Iraq's other nuclear facilities and constrained Israel from taking action against the smaller Western-supplied research reactor, as well as a small Soviet research reactor. Both of those facilities are operational and, if attacked, could release substantial amounts of radiation.

In this connexion, I wish to deny in the most categorical terms the false allegation made here by the Foreign Minister of Iraq—who had the courtesy to leave the Chamber when I started my statement—that Iraq's nuclear installations were attacked by Israel on any date prior to 7 June 1981.

With regard to the statement of the Foreign Minister of Baghdad as a whole, let me just observe that he added yet another tale to the *Tales of a 1,001 Nights* which, if I am not mistaken, were also written, like his statement, in Baghdad.

Iraq has unashamedly used the United Nations as an instrument to divert international attention from its nuclear weapons programme. By way of a smokescreen, it launched an attack on Israel, which came to be known as the "Iraqi initiative", at the tenth special session of the General Assembly in 1978 devoted to disarmament. Despite its manipulation of that special session and of the First Committee of the General Assembly ever since, in its unremitting campaign against Israel, nothing can or could camouflage its own nuclear weapons programme.

By contrast, Israel has long been committed to the concept that the most effective way to prevent the spread of nuclear weapons to the Middle East would be the creation of a nuclear-weapon-free zone in the region, modelled on the Tlatelolco Treaty which is based on an initiative of the Latin American countries and on direct negotiations among them.

Israel has repeatedly given expression to this idea. Since 1974 Israel has proposed it annually in the General Assembly and in other international forums. At the thirty-fifth session of the General Assembly in 1980 Israel submitted a draft resolution on this subject in document A/C.1/35/L.8, which spelled out in precise terms our proposal for the establishment of a nuclear-weapon-free zone in the Middle East. To our great regret this proposal was rejected out of hand by a number of Arab States, first and foremost by Iraq, whose representative even challenged Israel's right to sit in the First Committee. The Iraqi position could only mean that Iraq rejects any possibility of creating a nuclear-weapon-free zone in the Middle East.

Israel's proposal stands. With full awareness of the many political differences among the States of the Middle East, and without prejudice to any political or legal claim, it behoves all the States of the region, for the sake of their common future, to take concrete steps towards the establishment of a nuclear-weapon-free zone in the Middle East.

It is for that reason that, in a letter to the Secretary-General of 9 June 1981, in document A/36/315, Israel further elaborated its proposal and formally and urgently requested all States of the Middle East and States adjacent to the region to consent in the course of the current year to the holding of a preparatory conference to discuss the modalities of such a conference of States of the Middle East with a view to negotiating a multilateral treaty establishing a nuclear-weapon-free zone in the Middle East.

The Security Council now has a clear-cut choice before it. Either it can resign itself to the perpetuation of the well-established pattern of one-sided denunciations of my country which can only serve as a cover and encouragement for those who entertain destructive designs against it; alternatively, the Council can address itself seriously to the perils and challenges that confront us all.

It is in keeping with this latter approach that I invite the Council to consider carefully Israel's proposal regarding the establishment of a nuclear-weapon-free zone in the Middle East. We believe that the advancement of our proposal will constitute a significant contribution to the future well-being and security of all the States of the Middle East.

Beyond that, the time has come for serious stock-taking, for we are concerned here with a matter of grave import, crucial to the future of the Middle East and, I dare say, to the entire world.

Certain lessons must be drawn.

Israel has always held the conviction that no international conflict can be solved by the use of force. By the same token it must also be clear that the selfish pursuit of narrow interests, economic and other, can only exacerbate international tensions.

For its part, Israel will not allow itself to be the victim of such a cynical approach. We are an ancient people. We are imbued with an indomitable will to live. That will has been forged in a crucible of 3,000 years of suffering. We have survived the most terrible of tests. We have re-established our national independence. We are firmly rooted in our own land. We have the means and the determination to defend ourselves and we are resolved to do so.

For 30 years and more the world has watched with equanimity the unrestrained and unending aggression of Iraq and others against my country. Iraq and its supporters, both in the Arab world and beyond, have been encouraged by the apathy and appeasement of the international community and by their own ability to manipulate this world Organization for their bellicose ends and lawless policies.

The time has surely come for the United Nations in general, and this Council in particular, to persuade Iraq and its supporters that international conflicts cannot be solved by plotting the demise of a sovereign State. The only way to solve any conflict is to negotiate its peaceful resolution, for peace and peace alone will ensure the rights of all the States involved and guarantee their well-being and security.

211. Resolution by the International Atomic Energy
Agency on the Military Attack on Iraqi Nuclear Research
Center and Its Implications for the Agency,
June 15, 1981*

---

* 36 U.N. SCOR Supp. (Apr–June 1981) at 64, U.N. Doc. S/14532 (1981).

The Board of Governors,

"(*a*) *Recalling* that according to article II of the Statute the Agency shall seek to accelerate and enlarge the contribution of atomic energy to peace, health and prosperity throughout the world,

(*b*) *Recalling further* that, according to Article 2.4 of the Charter of the United Nations, all Members shall refrain in their international relations from the threat or use of force against the territorial integrity or political independence of any State, or in any other manner inconsistent with the purposes of the United Nations,

(*c*) *Recognizing* the inalienable right of all member States of the Agency to develop nuclear energy for peaceful purposes to further their scientific, technological and economic development,

(*d*) Mindful of the fact that Iraq fully subscribes to the Agency's safe-guards system and is a party to the Treaty on the Non-Proliferation of Nuclear Weapons,

(*e*) *Noting* the statement of the Director-General to the effect that Iraq has fulfilled its obligations under Agency safeguards, pursuant to the Non-Proliferation Treaty to the satisfaction of the Agency,

(*f*) *Informed* that, on 1 June 1981, Israel carried out a military attack on the Iraqi nuclear research centre, damaging the nuclear facilities and causing loss of human life,

(*g*) *Conscious* that this military action, besides affecting the security and peace of the region, has shown clear disregard for the Agency's safeguards régime and the Non-Proliferation Treaty and could do great harm to the development of nuclear energy for peaceful purposes,

(*h*) *Gravely concerned* by the far-reaching implications of such a military attack on the peaceful nuclear facilities in a member State,

1. *Strongly condemns* Israel for this premeditated and unjustified attack on the Iraqi nuclear research centre, which is covered by Agency safeguards;

2. *Recommends* to the General Conference at its forthcoming regular session to consider all the implications of this attack, including suspending the exercise by Israel of the privileges and rights of membership;

3. *Reminds* the member States of the Agency of the United Nations General Assembly resolution 35/157, calling for an end to all transfer of fissionable material and nuclear technology to Israel;

4. *Recommends* that the General Conference suspend provision of any assistance to Israel under the Agency's technical assistance programme;

5. *Urges* the Agency's member States to provide emergency assistance to Iraq to deal with the aftermath of this attack;

6. *Reaffirms* its confidence in the effectiveness of the Agency's safeguards system as a reliable means of verifying peaceful use of a nuclear facility;

7. *Requests* the Director-General to transmit the present resolution to the United Nations Security Council.["]

The resolution was adopted by 29 votes to 2, with 3 abstentions.

I have also been requested by the Board of Governors to transmit to the Security Council summary records of the proceedings of the Board relevant to this agenda item. These will be express mailed as soon as possible.[3]

(*Signed*) Sigvard EKLUND
Director-General of the
International Atomic Energy Agency

[3] The Acting Director-General of the Agency transmitted to the President of the Security Council copies of the summary records—563rd-567th meetings, held between 9 and 12 June 1981—by a letter of 15 June 1981 (S/14532/Add.1 of 31 July 1981); they may be consulted in the Dag Hammarskjöld Library.

212. Iraq's Statement on Behalf of the Islamic Group Before the Security Council Concerning Israel's Attack on the Osirak Reactor, June 16, 1981*

* 36 U.N. SCOR (2285th mtg.) at 61, U.N. Doc. S/PV.2285 (1981).

Mr. HAMMADI (Iraq): I should like to inform the Council that, on the request of the Government of Iraq, the representatives of the Islamic Group met this afternoon and debated the subject-matter of this series of Council meetings—namely, the aggression of Israel against Iraq's nuclear installations—and that at the end of the debate the following resolution was adopted unanimously:

The Islamic Group,

Having met at United Nations Headquarters on 16 June 1981 at the request of the Republic of Iraq to consider the act of aggression committed by Israel against the Republic of Iraq,

Having heard the statement of His Excellency Sheikh Jabber Al-Ahmad Al-Sabah, the Deputy Prime Minister and Minister for Foreign Affairs of Kuwait, on behalf of the Council of the League of Arab States,

Recalling the position of the member countries of the Organization of the Islamic Conference on strengthening the security of non-nuclear-weapon States against the use or threat of use of nuclear weapons (resolution No. 28/12-P), as well as the establishment of nuclear-weapon-free zones in Africa, in the Middle East and in South Asia (resolution No. 29/12-P),

Considering the grave situation arising from the premeditated attack on the Iraqi nuclear installations, devoted exclusively to peaceful purposes,

Recalling the various resolutions adopted by the Islamic Conference in connexion with Israel's acts of aggression against the Palestinian people and the Arab countries,

Affirming that aggression entails international responsibility, with the payment of prompt and adequate compensation for the damages suffered,

1. Strongly condemns the premeditated and unprovoked aggression by Israel as an act of State terrorism and a blatant violation of the sovereignty of a non-aligned country and a member of the Organization of the Islamic Conference;

2. Requests that the international community take the measures envisaged in the Charter to prevent Israel from pursuing such acts in future;

3. Demands that Israel pay prompt and adequate compensation for the damages suffered by Iraq;

4. Reaffirms the inalienable right of all States to apply and develop their programmes for the peaceful uses of nuclear energy for economic and social development in conformity with their priorities, interests and needs;

5. Affirms its solidarity with and support of Iraq in its endeavours to exercise that inalienable right and to resist Israeli aggression;

6. Reaffirms the resolutions of the General Assembly relating to Is-

rael nuclear armament and demands that the international community make Israel comply with the said resolutions;

7. Pledges to work together during the forthcoming session of the General Assembly to achieve the application by the United Nations of the measures envisaged in the Charter to prevent Israel from committing such acts of aggression and to comply with the norms of international law, the principles of the Charter and the provisions of the relevant resolutions of the United Nations.

213. Security Council Resolution 487 Condemning Israel's Air Strike on Iraq's Osirak Reactor, June 19, 1981*

* S.C. Res. 487, 36 U.N. SCOR (2288th mtg.) at 10, U.N. Doc. S/INF/37 (1981).

The Security Council,

Having considered the agenda contained in document S/Agenda/2280,

Having noted the contents of the letter dated 8 June 1981 from the Minister of Foreign Affairs of Iraq,[54]

Having heard the statements made on the subject a its 2280th through 2288th meetings,

Taking note of the statement made by the Director-General of the International Atomic Energy Agency to the Agency's Board of Governors on the subject on 9 June 1981 and his statement to the Security Council at its 2288th meeting on 19 June 1981,

Taking note also of the resolution adopted by the Board of Governors of the Agency on 12 June 1981 on the "military attack on Iraqi nuclear research centre and its implications for the Agency",[55]

Fully aware of the fact that Iraq has been a party to the Treaty on the Non-Proliferation of Nuclear Weapons[56] since it came into force in 1970, that in accordance with that Treaty Iraq has accepted Agency safeguards on all its nuclear activities, and that the Agency has testified that these safeguards have been satisfactorily applied to date,

Noting furthermore that Israel has not adhered to the Treaty on the Non-Proliferation of Nuclear Weapons,

Deeply concerned about the danger of international peace and security created by the premeditated Israeli air attack on Iraqi nuclear installations on 7 June 1981, which could at any time explode the situation in the area, with grave consequences for the vital interests of all States,

Considering that, under the terms of Article 2, paragraph 4, of the Charter of the United Nations, "all members shall refrain in their international relations from the threat or use of force against the territorial integrity or political independence of any State, or in any other manner inconsistent with the purposes of the United Nations",

1. *Strongly condemns* the military attack by Israel in clear violation of the Charter of the United Nations and the norms of international conduct;

2. *Calls upon* Israel to refrain in the future from any such acts or threats thereof;

3. *Further considers* that the said attack constitutes a serious threat to the entire safeguards régime of the International Atomic Energy Agency, which is the foundation of the Treaty on the Non-Proliferation of Nuclear Weapons;

4. *Fully recognizes* the inalienable sovereign right of Iraq and all other States, especially the developing countries, to establish programmes of technological and nuclear development to develop their economy and industry

---

[54] *Official Records of the Security Council, Thirty-sixth Year, Supplement for April, May and June 1981*, document S/14509.

[55] *Ibid.*, document S/14532.

[56] General Assembly resolution 2373 (XXII) of 12 June 1968.

for peaceful purposes in accordance with their present and future needs and consistent with the internationally accepted objectives of preventing nuclear-weapons proliferation;

5. *Calls upon* Israel urgently to place its nuclear facilities under the safeguards of the International Atomic Energy Agency;

6. *Considers* that Iraq is entitled to appropriate redress for the destruction it has suffered, responsibility for which has been acknowledged by Israel;

7. *Requests* the Secretary-General to keep the Security Council regularly informed of the implementation of the present resolution.

Adopted unanimously at the 2288th meeting.

214. Israel's Statement Before the Security Council Concerning Its Actions Regarding the Osirak Reactor, June 19, 1981*

* 36 U.N. SCOR (2288th mtg.) at 18, U.N. Doc. S/PV.2288 (1981).

Mr. BLUM (Israel): This has been a lengthy debate. It has been deliberately protracted in a conscious effort to confound and confuse the issues. In the course of it, we have heard many statements which, regretably any change, are simply not worthy of serious consideration.

How, for example, are we to regard the profound concern for human life expressed in such high-minded terms by Viet Nam in the light of the atrocities that that country has perpetrated and is perpetrating in South-East Asia? How, for example, are we supposed to react to protestations by the Soviet Union concerning aggression and violation of national sovereignty when the Soviet occupation of the whole of Afghanistan is still going on, and, indeed, naked Soviet aggression against the Afghan people is still being perpetrated. And when Hungary and Czechoslovakia entered the fray, they in fact only served to remind us that Afghanistan is not the first victim of Soviet aggression.

On the other hand, there have been those who have taken part in this debate with great sincerity. Besides them, there are no doubt many outside this chamber for whom the subject of this debate has also raised far-reaching questions.

My country has approached the matter before the Council with the utmost seriousness and has raised questions of great import, to which we have not received any substantive answers.

We have been told that Iraq's nuclear programme was designed for peaceful purposes. Yet solid and decisive evidence points emphatically in the opposite direction.

Iraq's nuclear activities have troubled many Governments and experts around the world. We indicated some of the questions arising in this regard but the representative of Iraq did not answer the questions we raised. He chose not to answer them simply because Iraq has not acted in good faith.

Because of their extreme importance, permit me to repeat and enlarge upon those questions which I should like to address to the Foreign Minister of Iraq.

1. Why did Iraq first try in 1974 to acquire a 500-megawatt nuclear reactor of a kind designed primarily to produce large quantities of plutonium for military use? Moreover, why is it now trying to buy an up-scaled, Cirene type plutogenic reactor, whose military use is clear, but whose commercial use is not proven?

2. Why did Iraq insist on receiving a 70-megawatt reactor which has no usable application as an energy source, which does not correspond to any peaceful energy plan and which, incidentally, is far too large for Iraq's most ambitious scientific needs?

3. Why did Iraq insist on receiving weapons-grade nuclear fuel, rather than the less proliferant alternative of "Caramel" fuel which it was offered?

4. What is Iraq's demonstrable need for nuclear energy, given its abundant oil reserves?

5. If Iraq has a need of this kind for either the short or the long term,

why has it not developed a commercial nuclear energy programme? Why has it not made any transactions which would be relevant to such a programme?

6. Why, if it is genuinely interested in nuclear research, did it rush to buy plutonium separation technology and equipment that cannot be justified on scientific or economic grounds?

7. Why has Iraq been making frantic efforts to acquire natural uranium, wherever and however it can, in at least four continents, some of which uranium is not under International Atomic Energy Agency (IAEA) safeguards? Why has Iraq taken the highly unusual step of stockpiling uranium, before it has built power reactors?

I think that all these questions are fairly intelligible to the layman and must make everyone think. They are certainly intelligible to the expert, who will confirm that they point in one direction only—namely, a weapons-oriented nuclear programme.

Let me, just for the sake of illustration, elaborate on one of these questions: Iraq's insistence on receiving weapons-grade nuclear fuel and its adamant refusal to accept a less proliferant variety when offered. The International Nuclear Fuel Cycle Evaluation (INFCE), an international body, convened under the auspices of the IAEA, to deal, *inter alia*, with the non-proliferation aspects of the nuclear fuel cycle, was greatly concerned with the already wide distribution of enriched uranium and the production of fissile material in nuclear reactors of the 1 to 5 megawatt size, not to speak of a 70-megawatt facility like Osiraq. Consequently, the INFCE has set up study groups under the auspices of the IAEA, to make recommendations on the subject. The report of Working Group Eight, entitled "Advanced fuel cycle and reactor concepts", document INFCE/PC/2/8 of January 1980, is most illuminating.

In Section 4.2., headed "Measures to increase proliferation resistance", the report states:

> The trade in and widespread use of highly enriched uranium and the production of fissile materials constitute proliferation risks with which INFCE is concerned.

It recommended that proliferation resistance can be increased by:

> Enrichment reduction preferably to 20% or less which is internationally required to be a fully adequate isotopic barrier to weapons usability of $U235$.

In another section of the same report, dealing with French reactors of the Osiris type—which would include Osiraq—the authors state:

> The Osiris core was converted from the highly enriched uranium to the low enriched UO_2 Caramel fuel, with startup of the reactor in June

1979. The general success of the work developed on Caramel fuel . . . permits Osiris to be completely loaded with Caramel assemblies.

In layman's terms, had Iraq so wished, it could have successfully operated Osiraq on Caramel-type fuel, thereby at least eliminating the option of diverting weapons-grade nuclear fuel. But it refused to do so, and insisted on receiving weapons-grade enriched uranium.

But to come back to my list of questions as a whole: if Iraq's representatives could not address themselves to them, other people have done so. They include three eminent French nuclear scientists, who have made a serious examination of these and other disturbing questions related to Iraq's nuclear development programme.

The French scientists are: George Amsel, Director of Research at the *Centre National de la Recherche Scientifique*, Unit for Solid Physics at the *Ecole Normale Supérieure*; Jean-Pierre Pharabaud, Engineer at the *Centre National de la Recherche Scientifique*, Laboratory of High Energy Physics at the *Ecole Polytechnique*; and Raymond Sehe, Chief of Research at the *Centre National de la Recherche Scientifique*, Laboratory of Particle Physics at the *Collège de France*.

The analysis and conclusions of these three prominent scientists are to be found in a comprehensive memorandum entitled *Osirak et la prolifération des armes atomiques*, which they presented to the French Government and public in May of this year.

It is of great interest and relevance to compare their scientific findings and conclusions with the version presented to this Council. It was alleged here that two "hypotheses"—namely the diversion of enriched uranium and the production of plutonium, for the manufacture of a nuclear weapon— are both groundless.

Let us look at what the French scientists say about each of these hypotheses—or, to be more accurate, about these possibilities. Chapter II of their memorandum is entitled *"Possibilités de prolifération"*. Pargraph 5 thereof is headed *Les possibilités d'obtention d'explosifs nucléaires liées à Osirak*.

Concerning the uranium path, they indicate that two options exist: (a) the use of fresh enriched uranium; and (b) the use of slightly irradiated enriched uranium.

Even assuming that the diversion of the enriched uranium were to be detected and that the supplier would immediately halt further deliveries of enriched uranium, the authors of the memorandum conclude that Iraq already possesses sufficient weapons-grade material to produce two nuclear bombs.

As regards the production of plutonium, the French scientists observe in their memorandum that by introducing a blanket of natural uranium around the reactor core of Osiraq, plutonium can be produced. After the chemical separation of the plutonium, the yield per annum would be sufficient for one nuclear bomb. This separation can be carried out in the facility based on the hot-cell installation supplied to Iraq by Italy. This method does not involve any diversion of the enriched uranium fuel. In addition, pluto-nium production can be accomplished even if the supplier imposes the use of the less enriched "Caramel" type of fuel in the nuclear reactor.

Given the nuclear facilities and materials and the complementary tech-nology that Iraq had at its disposal, to try to dismiss in this Council either of these paths leading to the manufacture of a nuclear weapon as "ground-less hypotheses", or even to make light of them, is irresponsible. Such an attitude flies in the face of incontrovertible scientific data, readily available to informed observers.

Indeed, it also flies in the face of statements by French officials. As re-ported in *The New York Times* of 18 June 1981, Dr. Michel Pecqueur, the Head of the French Atomic Energy Agency, while trying to defend the agreements between his country and Iraq, conceded that:

> ... in theory the reactor could be used to produce a "significant quan-tity" of plutonium, which means enough for a bomb, by irradiating a large amount of natural or depleted uranium. The plutonium could then be extracted in a "hot-cell" laboratory supplied by Italy, although this reprocessing is technically difficult. (*The New York Times, 18 June 1981, p. A18*)

Then there are the admissions made by the Chief Nuclear Attaché at the French Embassy in Washington who, according to *The New York Times* of 17 June 1981, agreed that Osiraq had what he termed "high neutron flux" which "meant that it could have produced a considerable amount of pluto-nium". The French official concerned took issue with the estimate of the annual production of 10 kilograms of plutonium, and suggested that "5 ki-lograms was a better figure". In other words, the only point at issue is whether Osiraq could have produced enough plutonium for one bomb in a period of 12 months or in something between 12 and 24 months. And does anyone here seriously believe that there is an essential difference if it were to take Iraq one year or a few months longer to produce a nuclear bomb?

In another article in *The New York Times* of 18 June, two professors of nuclear science and engineering at Columbia University explain how Osiraq provides the neutron bombardment for converting natural uranium into plutonium. In the same article, the Chief Nuclear Attaché at the French Embassy in Washington is quoted as saying that:

> ... the basic design of the French export model, known as Osiris, shows a cavity in the reactor that can hold material for neutron bombardment.

In the course of this debate great play has been made of the fact that Iraq is a signatory to the nuclear Non-Proliferation Treaty (NPT) and that its nuclear reactors have been inspected periodically by the International Atomic Energy Agency (IAEA). Let me again draw the attention of mem-bers of the Council to the French scientists' memorandum. Chapter III is entitled *"Les sauvegardes"*. It is an extensive analysis of the NPT safeguards systems and takes up about one third of the whole paper. Among the more significant points made are:

First, the country being inspected has to approve in advance the name of the individual inspector whom the IAEA wishes to designate. The country being inspected can reject the inspector whom the Agency has nominated.

Parenthetically, let me mention in this regard that, according to information submitted yesterday, since 1976 only Soviet and Hungarian inspectors have inspected Osiraq.

To come back to the scientists' memorandum: the second point they make is that the frequency of routine inspections is a function of the size of the reactor. For Osiraq, this means no more than three or four inspections a year.

Thirdly, for routine inspections, advance notice is given.

Fourthly, in principle, the possibility exists of unscheduled inspections, that is to say, surprise visits; but in practice advance notice of three or four days is given, even for such unscheduled inspections.

Fifthly, the inspectors must have access to everything relating to fissible material. However, they are not policemen; they can only inspect what has been declared. Thus, any hot-cells and chemical-separation facilities constructed in secret elsewhere will escape all inspection.

Sixthly, the inspectors within the facility are always accompanied by representatives of the State concerned.

Seventhly, the effectiveness of the safeguard measures depends on the cooperation of the country concerned. In this connexion the authors of the memorandum observe that for the IAEA and France, Iraq's good faith has been taken for granted and its assurances at face value, without any guarantees.

Eightly [*sic*], experience shows that inspections can be blocked for a certain period without causing any reaction. On this point the authors of the memorandum rightly recall:

(*spoke* [*sic*] *in French*)
That is what happened on 7 November 1980 at the beginning of the Iran-Iraq war, when Iraq informed the IAEA that the inspectors from the Agency could not at that time get to Baghdad to monitor the two reactors . . . A well-informed French source at that time stated: We are in a completely new situation which has not been foreseen in any international treaty.

(*continued in English*)
In brief, there are several serious loopholes in the NPT safeguards system that can easily be exploited by a country, such as Iraq, if it is determined to obtain a nuclear weapon.

The flaws in the safeguards system are now coming into the open. No less an authority than the former Director of Safeguards Operations at the IAEA in Vienna, Mr. Slobodan Nakicenovic, attested to the inadequacies of the NPT safeguards on Austrian Radio on 17 June. Incidentally, Mr. Naki-cenovic was appointed Director of Division of Safeguards and Inspections of the IAEA in September 1964. He was initially responsible for the development of instruments used in the Agency's inspection work. As Director of the Division, he was charged with the task of implementing all the safeguards agreements to which the Agency was a party.

These serious weaknesses in the safeguards system were incisively analysed in a leading article in the *Washington Post* of 16 June 1981 entitled "Nuclear Safeguards or Sham", in which the NPT safeguards system was shown to be hollow. Having asked why the IAEA had done nothing about several suspicious features of the Iraqi nuclear programme, the article observed that the NPT

> is written in such a way that a violation does not technically occur until nuclear material—uranium or plutonium—is diverted from its approved use. But this may occur within a few days of its insertion into a nuclear bomb. Since IAEA inspectors come around only a few times a year, the international safeguards system amounts to only an elaborate accounting procedure that relies on the good intentions of the parties being safeguarded.

In these circumstances, it is surely not unreasonable to raise serious doubts about the efficacy of the NPT safeguards system. There is certainly room for grave reservations when the country supposedly bound by these safeguards makes no secret of its ambitions to obliterate another country.

In this connexion, let me refer to a report in today's *New York Times* based on information from officials and diplomats at the IAEA in Vienna. One of them has lifted the veil from Iraq's nuclear programme. He is quoted as saying:

> If you ask whether Iraq had it in mind to make nuclear weapons one day, then I'd say a lot of people at the agency thought it probably did. A lot of things it was doing made sense only on that assumption. (*The New York Times, 19 June 1981, p. A1*)

Could it be that this was the reason why Israel was muzzled last week in Vienna and denied the possibility of presenting its case to the Board of Governors of the IAEA before it proceeded to condemn my country?

There is no question that Iraq regards itself as being in a state of war with Israel. Its leaders admit this openly and have called time and again for the liquidation of my country. Such a flagrant violation of Article 2, paragraph 4 of the United Nations Charter is apparently perfectly in order. As far as we have been able to ascertain, the Security Council, or for that matter the United Nations as a whole, has never called Iraq to account for this, over the last 30 or so years. It is apparently perfectly in order to use the threat of force against Israel, to train and send in terrorists to commit mindless acts of murder, and to join in Arab wars of aggression against Israel in 1948, in 1967 and in 1973, and then to retreat to safety, using other Arab countries as a buffer between its heroic army and Israel.

In the light of Iraqi declarations and deeds, and Iraq's refusal even to sign an armistice agreement with Israel, Israel had full legal justification to exercise its inherent right of self-defence to abort the Iraqi nuclear threat to Israel.

We have been reminded here of the Caroline affair. But that incident, as is well known—and the representatives of the United Kingdom and the United States will bear me out in this—occurred almost a century and a half ago. It occurred precisely 108 years before Hiroshima. To try and apply it to a nuclear situation in the post-Hiroshima era makes clear the absurdity of the position of those who base themselves upon it. To assert the applicability of the Caroline principles to a State confronted with the threat of nuclear destruction would be an emasculation of that State's inherent and natural right of self-defence.

In this connexion [sic], I cited in my statement of 12 June Sir Humphrey Waldock, who observed a few short years after Hiroshima that:

> it would be a travesty of the purposes of the Charter to compel a defending State to allow its assailant to deliver the first and perhaps fatal blow. . . . To read Article 51 otherwise is to protect the aggressor's right to the first strike.

Yet some of those who have taken part in this debate obviously consider themselves greater authorities in international law than Sir Humphrey Waldock, who happens to be the President of the International Court of Justice.

No doubt they would also dismiss the views of another eminent international lawyer, Stephen Schwebel, who was only recently elected to the International Court of Justice, and who in a lecture at the Hague Academy of International Law some 10 years ago, observed:

> Perhaps the most compelling argument against reading Article 51 to debar anticipatory self-defence whatever the circumstances is that, in an age of missiles and nuclear weapons, it is an interpretation that does not comport with reality.

Serious people do not haughtily brush aside the views of the President of the International Court of Justice and of its judges. Nor are they cavalier about the views of such a pre-eminent authority on international law as Professor Myres McDougal of Yale Law School, who, writing in the *American Journal of International Law* in 1963, stated:

> Under the hard conditions of the contemporary technology of destruction, which makes possible the complete obliteration of States with still incredible speed from still incredible distances, the principle of effectiveness requiring that agreements be interpreted in accordance with the major purposes and demands projected by the parties could

scarcely be served by requiring States confronted with necessity for defence to assume the posture of "sitting ducks".

Any such interpretation could only make a mockery, both in its acceptability to States and in its potential application, of the Charter's major purpose of minimizing unauthorized coercion and violence across State lines.

Indeed, the concept of a State's right to self-defence has not changed throughout recorded history. Its scope has, however, broadened with the advance of man's ability to wreak havoc on his enemies. Consequently the concept took on new and far wider application with the advent of the nuclear era. Anyone who thinks otherwise has simply not faced up to the horrific realities of the world we live in today and that is particularly true for small States whose vulnerability is vast and whose capacity to survive a nuclear strike is very limited.

We have been told in the course of this debate that one cannot isolate the subject before the Council from the root cause of the Arab-Israel conflict. Israel agrees, and this debate has, if nothing else, been an object lesson of what the root cause of the Arab-Israeli conflict really is—that is, the absolute refusal of most Arab States to recognize Israel and its right to exist.

Take, for example, the new Syrian Ambassador whose maiden speech we had the pleasure of hearing on Tuesday of this week. It goes without saying that Syria deeply laments the smashing of Saddam Hussein's nuclear capability. With his bosom friend and ally the representative of Iraq sitting at his side, the representative of Syria made his country's attitude towards Israel patently clear by describing my country as a "cancer in the region" suffering from "congenital deformities". He is obviously a soul-mate of the representative of another Arab State with which his country has fraternal relations, namely the distinguished representative of the Palestinian Arab State of Jordan, who has in the past delicately alluded to bubonic plague and venereal disease in referring to my country. Those epithets are more than mere pejoratives. They demonstrate the inability of most Arab States to reconcile themselves to Israel's existence and to its right to exist like any other sovereign State[.]

This, and only this, is the root cause of the Arab-Israel conflict. And there will be no solution to the conflict until the rejectionist Arab States come to terms with Israel and negotiate peace with us.

But that does not mean that the Middle East is doomed to live under the threat of nuclear war until a comprehensive peace is achieved. Israel has always supported the principle of non-proliferation. In 1968 Israel voted in favour of General Assembly resolution 2373 (XXII), on the NPT. Since then Israel has studied carefully various aspects of the NPT as they relate to conditions prevailing in the Middle East—conditions which, regrettably, preclude its implementation in the region.

The NPT envisages conditions of peace. However, as I have just pointed out, most Arab States not only deny Isarel's [*sic*] right to exist but are also bent on destroying my country and hence reject any peace negotiations with us.

Amost half the States in the new Arab League—the new Arab League, with its headquarters in Tunis—are not bound by the NPT régime. And some Arab States which are parties to the NPT have entered reservations specifically dissociating themselves from any obligation towards Israel in the context of the Treaty.

Moreover, other Arab States, also parties to the NPT, are not only suspected of searching for a nuclear-weapons option but are known to have been involved in unsafeguarded transfer of nuclear material. Libya, for instance, was reported in 1979 to be involved in an unsafeguarded international uranium deal between Niger and Pakistan—that is, two States not party to the NPT. Libya has also purchased several hundred tons of uranium from Niger, apparently without involving the IAEA.

Beyond the Middle East, Pakistan is considered to have all its known nuclear facilities under safeguards. But, as is also well known, it has in parallel embarked on the reprocessing and uranium-enrichment courses through the acquisition of unsafeguarded equipment by exploiting loopholes in the export guidelines of the London Club member States.

In the light of the foregoing it is clear that the NPT is no effective guarantee against the proliferation of nuclear weapons in the Middle East.

In such circumstances, Israel of the view that the most effective and constructive step which could be taken would be to establish a nuclear-weapon-free zone in the Middle East, based on the Tlatelolco model, freely arrived at by negotiations among all the States concerned and anchored in a binding multilateral treaty to which they would all be signatories. It is for this reason that Israel has resubmitted its proposal for a nuclear-weapon-free zone in the Middle East. The details of that proposal are set out in my letter of 15 June to you, Mr. President, which has been circulated as document S/14534. While obviously it would not solve the Arab-Israel conflict as a whole, we believe that our proposal, if advanced, would constitute a significant contribution to the future well-being and security of all the States of the Middle East.

It is for this reason also that Israel has submitted its proposal independent of other efforts being made to reach a comprehensive solution to the conflict. Hence Israel's proposal is an unlinked deal, standing on its own, separate and independent from anything else which may delay its fulfilment. Hence, too, we have submitted our proposal without prejudice to any political or legal claim which any of the States concerned may have on any other.

This is a moment of truth for all of us. We have been confronted with one of the most momentous questions facing mankind today.

Yet another biased, anti-Israel resolution by this Council will not bring peace any closer. But much may be achieved for the common good and security of all the States in the Middle East if they and the States adjacent to the region indicate their consent without delay to the holding of a preparatory conference to discuss the modalities of a conference where a treaty establishing a nuclear-weapon-free zone in the Middle East would be negotiated. Israel therefore reiterates its call to all the States concerned to give serious and urgent consideration to our proposal.

215. U.N. Ambassador Kirkpatrick's Statement on the Israeli Raid Before the Security Council, June 19, 1981*

* 81 U.S. Dep't State Bull. No. 2053, at 84 (August 1981). For Congressional reaction, see calls for greater international safeguards in S. Res. 179, 97th Cong., 1st Sess., 127 Cong. Rec. S7858 (1981) and H.R. Res. 177, 97th Cong., 1st Sess., 127 Cong. Rec. H4513 (1981).

I wish to thank the Ambassador from Mexico, who has acquitted himself with such distinction in carrying out the difficult responsibilities, showing so keen a sense of the importance which the international community attaches to these deliberations. May I also congratulate the distinguished Ambassador from Japan, who last month earned the esteem of the entire Council by managing our affairs with singular deftness.

The issue before the Security Council in the past week—Israel's attack upon the Iraqi nuclear reactor—raises profound and troubling questions that will be with us long after the conclusion of these meetings. The Middle East, as one prominent American observed last week, "provides combustible matter for international conflagration akin to the Balkans prior to World War I," a circumstance made all the more dangerous today by the possibility that nuclear weapons could be employed in a future conflict.

The area that stretches from Southwest Asia across the Fertile Crescent and Persian Gulf to the Atlantic Ocean, is, as we all know, torn not only by tension and division but also by deeply rooted, tenacious hostilities that erupt repeatedly into violence. In the past 2 years alone, one country in the area, Afghanistan, has been brutally invaded and occupied but not pacified. Afghan freedom fighters continue their determined struggle for their country's independence. Iraq and Iran are locked in a bitter war. And with shocking violence, Libya, whose principal exports to the world are oil and terror, invaded and now occupies Chad. Lebanon has its territory and its sovereignty violated almost routinely by neighboring nations. Other governments in the area have, during the same brief period, been the object of violent attacks and terrorism. Now comes Israel's destruction of the Iraqi nuclear facility. Each of these acts of violence undermines the stability and well-being of the area. Each gravely jeopardizes the peace and security of the entire area. The danger of war and anarchy in this vital strategic region threatens global peace and presents this Council with a grave challenge.

My government's commitment to a just and enduring peace in the Middle East is well-known. We have given our full support to efforts by the Secretary General to resolve the war between Iran and Iraq. Our abhorrence of the Soviet Union's invasion and continued occupation of Afghanistan—against the will of the entire Afghan people—requires no elaboration on this occasion. For weeks, our special representative Philip Habib has been in the area conducting talks which we still hope may help to end the hostilities in Lebanon and head off a conflict between Israel and Syria. Not least, we have been engaged in intensive efforts to assist in the implementation of the Egyptian-Israeli treaty, efforts that have already strengthened the forces for peace in the Middle East and will, we believe, lead ultimately to a comprehensive peace settlement of the Arab-Israeli conflict in accordance with Resolutions 242 and 338 of the Security Council.

As in the past, U.S. policies in the Middle East aim above all at making the independence and freedom of people in the area more secure and their daily lives less dangerous. We seek the security of all the nations and peoples of the region.

· The security of all nations to know that a neighbor is not seeking technology for purposes of destruction.

· The security of all people to know they can live their lives in the absence of fear of attack and do not daily see their existence threatened or questioned.

· The security of all people displaced by war, violence, and terrorism.

The instability that has become the hallmark and history of the Middle East may serve the interests of some on this Council; it does not serve our interests; it does not serve the interests of our friends, be they Israeli or Arab.

We believe, to the contrary, that the peace and security of all the nations in the region are bound up with the peace and security of the area.

It is precisely because of my government's deep involvement in efforts to promote peace in the Middle East that we were shocked by the Israeli air strike on the Iraqi nuclear facility and promptly condemned this action, which we believe both reflected and exacerbated deeper antagonisms in the region which, if not ameliorated, will continue to lead to outbreaks of violence.

However, although my government has condemned Israel's act, we know it is necessary to take into account the context of this action as well as its consequences. The truth demands nothing less. As my President, Ronald Reagan, asserted in his press conference:

"... I do think that one has to recognize that Israel had reason for concern in view of the past history of Iraq, which has never signed a cease-fire or recognized Israel as a nation, has never joined in any peace effort for that .... it does not even recognize the existence of Israel as a country.["]

With respect to Israel's attack on the Iraqi nuclear reactor, President Reagan said: "... Israel might have sincerely believed it was a defensive move."

The strength of U.S. ties and commitment to Israel is well known to the members of this Council. Israel is an important and valued ally. The warmth of the human relationship between our peoples is widely understood. Nothing has happened that in any way alters the strength of our commitment or the warmth of our feelings. We in the Reagan Administration are proud to call Israel a friend and ally.

Nonetheless we believe the means Israel chose to quiet its fears about the purposes of Iraq's nuclear program have hurt and not helped the peace and security of the area. In my government's view, diplomatic means available to Israel had not been exhausted, and the Israeli action has damaged the regional confidence that is essential for the peace process to go forward. All of us with an interest in peace, freedom, and national independence have a high stake in that process. Israel's stake is highest of all.

My government is committed to working with the Security Council to remove the obstacles to peace. We made clear from the outset that the United States will support reasonable actions by this body which might be likely to contribute to the pacification of the region. We also made clear that my government would approve no decision that harmed Israel's basic interests, was unfairly punitive, or created new obstacles to a just and lasting peace.

The United States has long been deeply concerned about the dangers of nuclear proliferation. We believe that all nations should adhere to the Non-proliferation Treaty. It is well known that we support the International Atomic Energy Agency (IAEA) and will cooperate in any reasonable effort to strengthen it.

We desire to emphasize, however, that security from nuclear attack and annihilation will depend ultimately less on treaties signed than on the construction of stable regional order. Yes, Israel should be condemned; yes, the IAEA should be strengthened and respected by all nations. And yes, too, Israel's neighbors should recognize its right to exist and enter into negotiations with it to resolve their differences.

The challenge before this Council was to exercise at least the same degree of restraint and wisdom that we demand of the parties directly involved in Middle East tensions. Inflammatory charges, such as the Soviet statement that the United States somehow encouraged the raid or that we knew of the raid beforehand, are false and malicious. One can speculate about whose interest is served by such innuendo. Certainly the spirit of truth, restraint, or peace is not served by such innuendo. Certainly the process of peace is not forwarded.

Throughout the negotiations of the last days, my government had sought only to move us closer to the day when genuine peace between Israel and its Arab neighbors will become a reality. We have searched for a reasonable outcome of the negotiations in the Security Council, one which would protect the vital interests of all parties, and damage the vital interests of none, which would ameliorate rather than exacerbate the dangerous passions and division of the area. In that search we were aided by the cooperative spirit, restrained positions, and good faith of the Iraqi Foreign Minister Sa'dun Hammadi. We sincerely believe the results will move that turbulent area a bit closer to the time when all the states in the region have the opportunity to turn their energies and resources from war to peace, from armaments to development, from anxiety and fear to confidence and well-being.

216. General Assembly Resolution 36/27 on Armed Israeli Aggression Against the Iraqi Nuclear Installations and Its Grave Consequences for the Established International System Concerning the Peaceful Uses of Nuclear Energy, the Non-Proliferation of Nuclear Weapons, and International Peace and Security, November 13, 1981*

* G.A. Res. 27, 36 U.N. GAOR Supp. (No. 51) at 17, U.N. Doc. A/36/51 (1981).

The General Assembly,

Having considered the item entitled "Armed Israeli aggression against the Iraqi nuclear installations and its grave consequences for the established international system concerning the peaceful uses of nuclear energy, the non-proliferation of nuclear weapons and international peace and security",

Expressing its deep alarm over the unprecedented Israeli act of aggression against the Iraqi nuclear installations on 7 June 1981, which created a grave threat to international peace and security,

Recalling its resolutions 33/71 A of 14 December 1978 concerning military and nuclear collaboration with Israel and 34/89 of 11 December 1979 on Israeli nuclear armament,

Further recalling Security Council resolution 487 (1981) of 19 June 1981 and noting with concern Israel's refusal to comply with that resolution,

Taking note of the resolution adopted on 12 June 1981 by the Board of Governors of the International Atomic Energy Agency[23] and of resolution GC(XXV)/RES/381 adopted on 26 September 1981 by the General Conference of the Agency, in which the Conference, *inter alia*, considered that the Israeli act of aggression constituted an attack against the Agency and its safeguards régime and decided to suspend the provision of any assistance to Israel,

Fully aware of the fact that Iraq, being a party to the Treaty on the Non-Proliferation of Nuclear Weapons,[24] has subscribed to the International Atomic Energy Agency safeguards régime, and that the Agency has testified that these safeguards have been satisfactorily applied,

Noting with concern that Israel has refused to adhere to the Treaty on the Non-Proliferation of Nuclear Weapons and, in spite of repeated calls, including that of the Security Council, to place its nuclear facilities under International Atomic Energy Agency safeguards,

Alarmed by the increasing information and evidence regarding Israel's activities aiming at the acquisition and development of nuclear weapons,

Gravely concerned over the misuse by Israel, in committing its acts of aggression against Arab countries, of aircraft and weapons supplied by the United States of America,

Condemning the Israeli threats to repeat such attacks on nuclear installations if and when it deems it necessary,

Affirming the inalienable sovereign right of all States to develop technological and nuclear programmes for peaceful purposes, in accordance with the internationally accepted objectives of preventing the proliferation of nuclear weapons,

1. *Strongly condemns* Israel for its premeditated and unprecedented act of aggression in violation of the Charter of the United Nations and the norms

[23] See GC (XXV)/643.
[24] Resolution 2373 (XXII), annex.

of international conduct, which constitutes a new and dangerous escalation in the threat to international peace and security;

2. *Issues a solemn warning* to Israel to cease its threats and the commission of such armed attacks against nuclear facilities;

3. *Reiterates its call* to all States to cease forthwith any provision to Israel of arms and related material of all types which enable it to commit acts of aggression against other States;

4. *Requests* the Security Council to investigate Israel's nuclear activities and the collaboration of other States and parties in those activities;

5. *Reiterates its request* to the Security Council to institute effective enforcement action to prevent Israel from further endangering international peace and security through its acts of aggression and continued policies of expansion, occupation and annexation;

6. *Demands* that Israel, in view of its international responsibility for its act of aggression, pay prompt and adequate compensation for the material damage and loss of life suffered as a result of that act;

7. *Requests* the Secretary-General to keep Member States and the Security Council informed of progress towards the implementation of the present resolution and to submit a report to the General Assembly at its thirty-seventh session;

8. *Decides* to include in the provisional agenda of its thirty-seventh session the item entitled "Armed Israeli aggression against the Iraqi nuclear installations an its grave consequences for the established international system concerning the peaceful uses of nuclear energy, the non-proliferation of nuclear weapons and international peace and security".

56th plenary meeting
13 November 1981

217. General Assembly Resolution 36/87 on the Establishment of a Nuclear-Weapon-Free Zone in the Region of the Middle East, December 9, 1981*

* G.A. Res. 87, 36 U.N. GAOR Supp. (No. 51) at 57, U.N. Doc. A/36/51 (1981).

A

The General Assembly,

Recalling its resolutions 3263 (XXIX) of 9 December 1974, 3474 (XXX) of 11 December 1975, 31/71 of 10 December 1976, 32/82 of 12 December 1977, 33/64 of 14 December 1978, 34/77 of 11 December 1979 and 35/147 of 12 December 1980 on the establishment of a nuclear-weapon-free zone in the region of the Middle East,

1. *Requests* the Secretary-General to transmit General Assembly resolution 35/147 to the Assembly at its second special session devoted to disarmament, to be held from 7 June to 9 July 1982;

2. *Decides* to include in the provisional agenda of its thirty-seventh session the item entitled "Establishment of a nuclear-weapon-free zone in the region of the Middle East".

91st plenary meeting
9 December 1981

B

The General Assembly,

Recalling its resolutions concerning the establishment of a nuclear-weapon-free zone in the region of the Middle East,

Recalling also the recommendations for the establishment of such a zone in the Middle East consistent with paragraphs 60 to 63, in particular paragraph 63 (*d*), of the Final Document of the Tenth Special Session of the General Assembly,[21] the first special session devoted to disarmament,

Recalling further Security Council resolution 487 (1981) of 19 June 1981,

Taking into consideration the resolution adopted on 12 June 1981 by the Board of Governors of the International Atomic Energy Agency[22] and resolution GC(XXV)/RES/381 adopted on 26 September 1981 by the General Conference of the Agency,

Recalling further the report of the Secretary-General concerning Israeli nuclear armament,[23]

Realizing that adherence to the Treaty on the Non-Proliferation of Nuclear Weapons[24] by all parties of the region will be conducive to a speedy establishment of a nuclear-weapon-free zone,

Deeply concerned that the future of the Treaty on the Non-Proliferation of Nuclear Weapons in the region has been gravely endangered by the attack carried out by Israel, which is not a party to the Treaty, on the nuclear installations of Iraq, which is a party to that Treaty,

1. *Considers* that the Israeli military attack on the Iraqi nuclear installations

[21] Resolutions S-10/2.
[22] See GC(XXV)/643.
[23] A/36/431.
[24] Resolution 2373 (XXII), annex.

adversely affects the prospects of the establishment of a nuclear-weapon-free zone in the region of the Middle East;

2. *Declares* that it is imperative, in this respect, that Israel place forthwith all its nuclear facilities under International Atomic Energy Agency safeguards;

3. *Requests* the Secretary-General to transmit the present resolution to the General Assembly at its second special session devoted to disarmament.

91st plenary meeting
9 December 1981

218. General Assembly Resolution 36/98 on Israeli
Nuclear Armament, December 9, 1981*

---

* G.A. Res. 98, 36 U.N. GAOR Supp. (No. 51) at 75, U.N. Doc. A/36/51 (1981).

The General Assembly,

Recalling its relevant resolutions on the establishment of a nuclear-weapon-free zone in the region of the Middle East,

Recalling also its resolutions 33/71 A of 14 December 1978 on military and nuclear collaboration with Israel and 34/89 of 11 December 1979 and 35/157 of 12 December 1980 on Israeli nuclear armament,

Alarmed by the increasing evidence regarding Israel's attempts to acquire nuclear weapons,

Noting with concern that Israel has persistently refused to adhere to the Treaty on the Non-Proliferation of Nuclear Weapons[82] despite repeated calls by the General Assembly and the Security Council to place its nuclear facilities under International Atomic Energy Agency safeguards,

Recalling Security Council resolution 487 (1981) of 19 June 1981,

Recalling the resolution adopted on 12 June 1981 by the Board of Governors of the International Atomic Energy Agency[83] and resolution GC (XXV)/RES/381 adopted on 26 September 1981 by the General Conference of the Agency, in which the Conference, *inter alia*, considered the Israeli act of aggression as an attack against the Agency and its safeguards régime and decided to suspend the provision of any assistance to Israel,

Recalling its repeated condemnation of the nuclear collaboration between Israel and South Africa,

Taking note of the report of the Secretary-General[84] transmitting the study of the Group of Experts to Prepare a Study on Israeli Nuclear Armament,

1. *Expresses its appreciation* to the Secretary-General for his report on Israeli nuclear armament;

2. *Expresses its deep alarm* at the fact that the report has established that Israel has the technical capability to manufacture nuclear weapons and possesses the means of delivery of such weapons;

3. *Also expresses its deep concern* that Israel has undermined the credibility of the International Atomic Energy Agency safeguards, in particular by the bombing of the Iraqi nuclear facilities which were under Agency safeguards;

4. *Reaffirms* that Israel's attack on the Iraqi nuclear facilities and Israel's capability constitute a serious destabilizing factor in an already tense situation in the Middle East, and a grave danger to international peace and security;

5. *Requests* the Security Council to prohibit all forms of co-operation with Israel in the nuclear field;

6. *Calls upon* all States and other parties and institutions to terminate forthwith all nuclear collaboration with Israel;

---

[82] Resolution 2373 (XXII), annex.

[83] See GC(XXV)/643.

[84] A/36/431. The study was subsequently issued with the title *Study on Israeli Nuclear Armament* (United Nations publication, Sales No. E.82.IX.2).

7. *Requests* the Security Council to institute effective enforcement action against Israel so as to prevent it from endangering international peace and security by its nuclear-weapon capability;

8. *Demands* that Israel should renounce, without delay, any possession of nuclear weapons and place all its nuclear activities under international safeguards;

9. *Requests* the Secretary-General to give maximum publicity to the report on Israeli nuclear armament and to distribute it to Member States, the specialized agencies and the International Atomic Energy Agency and non-governmental organizations, so that the international community and public opinion may be fully aware of the danger inherent in Israel's nuclear capability;

10. *Also requests* the Secretary-General to follow closely Israeli military nuclear activity and to report thereon as appropriate;

11. *Further requests* the Secretary-General to transmit the report on Israeli nuclear armament to the General Assembly at its second special session devoted to disarmament;

12. *Decides* to include in the provisional agenda of its thirty-seventh session the item entitled "Israeli nuclear armament".

91st plenary meeting
9 December 1981

E. Continuing Terrorism and Response

219. Agreement Concerning the Application of the European Convention on the Suppression of Terrorism Among the Member States of the European Communities, December 4, 1979*

* 12 Bull. Eur. Comm. (No. 12) 90 (1979).

'The Member States of the European Activities,

Concerned to strengthen judicial cooperation among these States in the fight against acts of violence;

While awaiting the ratification without reservations of the European Convention on the Suppression of Terrorism signed at Strasbourg on 27 January 1977, described below as "the European Convention", by all the Member States of the European Communities, described below as "the Member States",

Have agreed as follows:

ARTICLE 1

This Agreement shall apply in relations between two Member States of which one at least is not a party to the European Convention or is a party to that Convention, but with a reservation.

ARTICLE 2

1. In the relations between two Member States which are parties to the European Convention, but of which one at least has made a reservation to that Convention, the application of the said Convention shall be subject to the provisions of this Agreement.

2. In the relations between two Member States of which one at least is not a party to the European Convention, Articles 1 to 8 and 13 of that Convention shall apply subject to the provisions of this Agreement.

ARTICLE 3

1. Each Member State which has made the reservation permitted under Article 13 of the European Convention shall declare whether, for the application of this Agreement, it intends to make use of this reservation.

2. Each Member State which has signed the European Convention but has not ratified, accepted or approved it, shall declare whether, for the application of this Agreement, it intends to make the reservation permitted under Article 13 of that Convention.

3. Each Member State which has not signed the European Convention may declare that it reserves the right to refuse extradition for an offence listed in Article 1 of that Convention which it considers to be a political offence, an offence connected with a political offence or an offence inspired by political motives, on condition that it undertakes to submit the case without exception whatsoever and without undue delay, to its competent authorities for the purpose of prosecution. Those authorities shall take their decision in the same manner as in the case of any offence of a serious nature under the law of that State.

4. For the application of this Agreement, only the reservations provided for in paragraph 3 of this Article and in Article 13 of the European Convention are permitted. Any other reservation is without effect as between the Member States.

5. A Member State which has made a reservation may only claim the application of this Agreement by another State to the extent that the Agreement itself applies to the former State.

ARTICLE 4

1. The declarations provided for under Article 3 may be made by a Member State at the time of signature or when depositing its instrument of ratification, acceptance or approval.

2. Each Member State may at any time, wholly or partially, withdraw a reservation which it has made in pursuance of paragraphs 1, 2 or 3 of Article 3 by means of a declaration addressed to the Department of Foreign Affairs of Ireland. The declaration shall have effect on the day it is received.

3. The Department of Foreign Affairs of Ireland shall communicate the declarations to the other Member States.

ARTICLE 5

Any dispute between Member States concerning the interpretation or application of this Agreement which has not been settled by negotiation shall, at the request of any party to the dispute, be referred to arbitration in accordance with the procedure laid down in Article 10 of the European Convention.

ARTICLE 6

1. This Agreement shall be open for signature by the Member States of the European Communities. It shall be subject to ratification, acceptance or approval. Instruments of ratification, acceptance or approval shall be deposited with the Department of Foreign Affairs of Ireland.

The Agreement shall enter into force three months after the deposit of the instruments of ratification, acceptance or approval by all States which are members of the European Communities on the day on which this Agreement is opened for signature.

ARTICLE 7

1. Each Member State may, at the time of signature or when depositing its instrument of ratification, acceptance or approval, specify the territory or territories to which this Agreement shall apply.

2. Each Member State may, when depositing its instrument of ratification, acceptance or approval or at any later date, by declaration addressed to the Department of Foreign Affairs of Ireland extend this Agreement to any other territory specified in the declaration and for whose international relations it is responsible or on whose behalf it is authorized to give undertakings.

3. Any declaration made in pursuance of the preceding paragraph may, as regards any territory specified in that declaration, be denounced by means of a notification addressed to the Department of Foreign Affairs of

Ireland. The denunciation shall have effect immediately or at such later date as may be specified in the notification.

4. The Department of Foreign Affairs of Ireland shall communicate these declarations and notifications to the other Member States.

ARTICLE 8

This Agreement shall cease to have effect on the date when all the Member States become parties without reservation to the European Convention.

Done at Dublin, this 4th day of December 1979 in German, English, Danish, French, Irish, Italian and Dutch, all texts being equally authoritative, in a single copy, which shall remain deposited in the archives of the Department of Foreign Affairs of Ireland, which shall transmit certified copies to each of the Member States.'

220. General Assembly Resolution 34/145 on Measures to Prevent International Terrorism Which Endangers or Takes Innocent Human Lives or Jeopardizes Fundamental Freedoms and Study of the Underlying Causes of Those Forms of Terrorism and Acts of Violence Which Lie in Misery, Frustration, Grievance and Despair and Which Cause Some People to Sacrifice Human Lives, Including Their Own, in an Attempt to Effect Radical Change, December 17, 1979*

* G.A. Res. 145, 34 U.N. GAOR Supp. (No. 46) at 244, U.N. Doc. A/34/46 (1979). *See also* subsequent resolution, G.A. Res. 109, 36 U.N. GAOR Supp. (No. 51) at 241, U.N. Doc. A/36/51 (1981).

The General Assembly,

Recalling its resolutions 3034 (XXVII) of 18 December 1972, 31/102 of 15 December 1976 and 32/147 of 16 December 1977,

Recalling also the Declaration on Principles of International Law concerning Friendly Relations and Co-operation among States in accordance with the Charter of the United Nations,[13] the Declaration on the Strengthening of International Security,[14] the Definition of Aggression[15] and the Protocols Additional to the Geneva Conventions of 1949,[16]

Deeply concerned about continuing acts of international terrorism which take a toll of innocent human lives,

Convinced of the importance of international co-operation for dealing with acts of international terrorism,

Reaffirming the inalienable right to self-determination and independence of all peoples under colonial and racist régimes and other forms of alien domination, and upholding the legitimacy of their struggle, in particular the struggle of national liberation movements, in accordance with the purposes and principles of the Charter and the relevant resolutions of the organs of the United Nations,

Having examined the report of the *Ad Hoc* Committee on International Terrorism,[17]

1. *Welcomes* the results achieved by the *Ad Hoc* Committee on International Terrorism during its last session, held from 19 March to 6 April 1979;

2. *Adopts* the recommendations submitted to the General Assembly relating to practical measures of co-operation for the speedy elimination of the problem of international terrorism;

3. *Unequivocally condemns* all acts of international terrorism which endanger or take human lives or jeopardize fundamental freedoms;

4. *Condemns* the continuation of repressive and terrorist acts by colonial, racist and alien régimes in denying peoples their legitimate right to self-determination and independence and other human rights and fundamental freedoms;

5. *Takes note* of the study of the underlying causes of international terrorism contained in the report of the *Ad Hoc* Committee;

6. *Urges* all States, unilaterally and in co-operation with other States, as well as relevant United Nations organs, to contribute to the progressive elimination of the causes underlying international terrorism;

7. *Calls upon* all States to fulfil their obligations under international law to refrain from organizing, instigating, assisting or participating in acts of civil

---

[13] Resolution 2625 (XXV), annex.
[14] Resolution 2734 (XXV).
[15] Resolution 3314 (XXIX), annex.
[16] A/32/144, annexes I and II.
[17] *Official Records of the General Assembly, Thirty-fourth Session, Supplement No. 37* (A/34/37).

strife or terrorist acts in another State, or acquiescing in organized activities within their territory directed towards the commission of such acts;

8. *Appeals* to States which have not yet done so to consider becoming parties to the existing international conventions relating to various aspects of the problem of international terrorism, specifically, the Convention on Offences and Certain Other Acts Committed on Board Aircraft, signed at Tokyo on 14 September 1963,[18] the Convention for the Suppression of Unlawful Seizure of Aircraft, signed at The Hague on 16 December 1970,[19] the Convention for the Suppression of Unlawful Acts against the Safety of Civil Aviation, signed at Montreal on 23 September 1971,[20] and the Convention on the Prevention and Punishment of Crimes against Internationally Protected Persons, including Diplomatic Agents, adopted at New York on 14 December 1973;[21]

9. *Invites* all States to take all appropriate measures at the national level with a view to the speedy and final elimination of the problem of international terrorism, such as the harmonization of domestic legislation with international conventions, the implementation of assumed international obligations and the prevention of the preparation and organization in their territory of acts directed against other States;

10. *Recommends* to the appropriate specialized agencies and regional organizations that they should consider measures to prevent and combat international terrorism within their respective spheres of responsibility and regions;

11. *Urges* all States to co-operate with one another more closely, especially through the exchange of relevant information concerning the prevention and combating of international terrorism, the conclusion of special treaties and/or the incorporation into appropriate bilateral treaties of special clauses, in particular regarding the extradition or prosecution of international terrorists;

12. *Invites* Governments to submit their observations and concrete proposals, in particular on the need for an additional international convention or conventions on international terrorism;

13. *Recognizes* that, in order to contribute to the elimination of the causes and the problem of international terrorism, both the General Assembly and the Security Council should pay special attention to all situations, including, *inter alia*, colonialism, racism and situations involving alien occupation, that may give rise to international terrorism and may endanger international peace and security, with a view to the application, where feasible and necessary, of the relevant provisions of the Charter of the United Nations, including Chapter VII thereof;

14. *Requests* the Secretary-General:

[18] United Nations, *Treaty Series*, vol. 704, No. 10106, p. 219.
[19] *Ibid.*, vol. 860, No. 12325, p. 106.
[20] *United States Treaties and Other International Agreements*, vol. 24, part one (1973), p. 568.
[21] Resolution 3166 (XXVIII) annex.

(*a*) To prepare a compilation on the basis of material provided by Member States of relevant provisions of national legislation dealing with the combating of international terrorism;

(*b*) To follow up, as appropriate, the implementation of the recommendations contained in the report of the *Ad Hoc* Committee and to submit a report to the General Assembly at its thirty-sixth session;

15. *Decides* to include the item in the provisional agenda of its thirty-sixth session.

105th plenary meeting
17 December 1979

221. International Convention Against the Taking of Hostages, December 17, 1979*

* G.A. Res. 146, 34 U.N. GAOR Supp. (No. 46) at 245, U.N. Doc. A/34/46 (1979).

The General Assembly,

Considering that the progressive development of international law and its codification contribute to the implementation of the purposes and principles set forth in Articles 1 and 2 of the Charter of the United Nations,

Mindful of the need to conclude, under the auspices of the United Nations, an international convention against the taking of hostages,

Recalling its resolution 31/103 of 15 December 1976, by which it established the *Ad Hoc* Committee on the Drafting of an International Convention against the Taking of Hostages and requested it to draft at the earliest possible date an international convention against the taking of hostages,

Further recalling its resolutions 32/148 of 16 December 1977 and 33/19 of 29 November 1978,

Having considered the draft Convention prepared by the *Ad Hoc* Committee in pursuance of the above-mentioned resolutions,[22]

Adopts and opens for signature and ratification or for accession the International Convention against the Taking of Hostages, the text of which is annexed to the present resolution.

105th plenary meeting
17 December 1979

ANNEX

INTERNATIONAL CONVENTION AGAINST THE TAKING OF HOSTAGES

The States Parties to this Convention,

Having in mind the purposes and principles of the Charter of the United Nations concerning the maintenance of international peace and security and the promotion of friendly relations and co-operation among States,

Recognizing, in particular, that everyone has the right to life, liberty and security of person, as set out in the Universal Declaration of Human Rights[23] and the International Covenant on Civil and Political Rights,[24]

Reaffirming the principle of equal rights and self-determination of peoples as enshrined in the Charter of the United Nations and the Declaration on Principles of International Law concerning Friendly Relations and Co-operation among States in accordance with the Charter of the United Nations,[25] as well as in other relevant resolutions of the General Assembly,

Considering that the taking of hostages is an offence of grave concern to the international community and that, in accordance with the provisions of this Convention, any person committing an act of hostage taking shall be either prosecuted or extradited,

---

[22] *Official Records of the General Assembly, Thirty-fourth Session, Supplement No. 39* (A/34/39), sect. IV.

[23] Resolution 217 A (III).

[24] Resolution 2200 A (XXI), annex.

[25] Resolution 2625 (XXV), annex.

Being convinced that it is urgently necessary to develop international co-operation between States in devising and adopting effective measures for the prevention, prosecution and punishment of all acts of taking of hostages as manifestations of international terrorism,

Have agreed as follows:

ARTICLE I

1. Any person who seizes or detains and threatens to kill, to injure or to continue to detain another person (hereinafter referred to as the "hostage") in order to compel a third party, namely, a State, an international intergovernmental organization, a natural or juridical person, or a group of persons, to do or abstain from doing any act as an explicit or implicit condition for the release of the hostage commits the offence of taking of hostages ("hostage-taking") within the meaning of this Convention.

2. Any person who:

(*a*) Attempts to commit an act of hostage-taking, or

(*b*) Participates as an accomplice of anyone who commits or attempts to commit an act of hostage-taking

likewise commits an offence for the purposes of this Convention.

ARTICLE 2

Each State Party shall make the offences set forth in article 1 punishable by appropriate penalties which take into account the grave nature of those offences.

ARTICLE 3

1. The State Party in the territory of which the hostage is held by the offender shall take all measures it considers appropriate to ease the situation of the hostage, in particular, to secure his release and, after his release, to facilitate, when relevant, his departure.

2. If any object which the offender has obtained as a result of the taking of hostages comes into the custody of a State Party, that State Party shall return it as soon as possible to the hostage or the third party referred to in article 1, as the case may be, or to the appropriate authorities thereof.

ARTICLE 4

States Parties shall co-operate in the prevention of the offences set forth in article 1, particularly by:

(*a*) Taking all practicable measures to prevent preparations in their respective territories for the commission of those offences within or outside their territories, including measures to prohibit in their territories illegal activities of persons, groups and organizations that encourage, instigate, organize or engage in the perpetration of acts of taking of hostages;

(*b*) Exchanging information and co-ordinating the taking of administrative and other measures as appropriate to prevent the commission of those offences.

ARTICLE 5

1. Each State Party shall take such measures as may be necessary to establish its jurisdiction over any of the offences set forth in article 1 which are committed:

(a) In its territory or on board a ship or aircraft registered in that State;

(b) By any of its nationals or, if that State considers it appropriate, by those stateless persons who have their habitual residence in its territory;

(c) In order to compel that State to do or abstain from doing any act; or

(d) With respect to a hostage who is a national of that State, if that State considers it appropriate.

2. Each State Party shall likewise take such measures as may be necessary to establish its jurisdiction over the offences set forth in article 1 in cases where the alleged offender is present in its territory and it does not extradite him to any of the States mentioned in paragraph 1 of this article.

3. This Convention does not exclude any criminal jurisdiction exercised in accordance with internal law.

ARTICLE 6

1. Upon being satisfied that the circumstances so warrant, any State Party in the territory of which the alleged offender is present shall, in accordance with its laws, take him into custody or take other measures to ensure his presence for such time as is necessary to enable any criminal or extradition proceedings to be instituted. That State Party shall immediately make a preliminary inquiry into the facts.

2. The custody or other measures referred to in paragraph 1 of this article shall be notified without delay directly or through the Secretary-General of the United Nations to:

(a) The State where the offence was committed;

(b) The State against which compulsion has been directed or attempted;

(c) The State of which the natural or juridical person against whom compulsion has been directed or attempted is a national;

(d) The State of which the hostage is a national or in the territory of which he has his habitual residence;

(e) The State of which the alleged offender is a national or, if he is a stateless person, in the territory of which he has his habitual residence;

(f) The international intergovernmental organization against which compulsion has been directed or attempted;

(g) All other States concerned.

3. Any person regarding whom the measures referred to in paragraph 1 of this article are being taken shall be entitled:

(a) To communicate without delay with the nearest appropriate representative of the State of which he is a national or which is otherwise entitled to establish such communication or, if he is a stateless person, the State in the territory of which he has his habitual residence;

(b) To be visited by a representative of that State.

4. The rights referred to in paragraph 3 of this article shall be exercised in conformity with the laws and regulations of the State in the territory of which the alleged offender is present, subject to the proviso, however, that the said laws and regulations must enable full effect to be given to the purposes for which the rights accorded under paragraph 3 of this article are intended.

5. The provisions of paragraphs 3 and 4 of this article shall be without prejudice to the right of any State Party having a claim to jurisdiction in accordance with paragraph 1 (*b*) of article 5 to invite the International Committee of the Red Cross to communicate with and visit the alleged offender.

6. Tbe State which makes the preliminary inquiry contemplated in paragraph 1 of this article shall promptly report its findings to the States or organization referred to in paragraph 2 of this article and indicate whether it intends to exercise jurisdiction.

ARTICLE 7

The State Party where the alleged offender is prosecuted shall, in accordance with its laws, communicate the final outcome of the proceedings to the Secretary-General of the United Nations, who shall transmit the information to the other States concerned and the international intergovernmental organizations concerned.

ARTICLE 8

1. The State Party in the territory of which the alleged offender is found shall, if it does not extradite him, be obliged, without exception whatsoever and whether or not the offence was committed in its territory, to submit the case to its competent authorities for the purpose of prosecution, through proceedings in accordance with the laws of that State. Those authorities shall take their decision in the same manner as in the case of any ordinary offence of a grave nature under the law of that State.

2. Any person regarding whom proceedings are being carried out in connexion with any of the offences set forth in article 1 shall be guaranteed fair treatment at all stages of the proceedings, including enjoyment of all the rights and guarantees provided by the law of the State in the territory of which he is present.

ARTICLE 9

1. A request for the extradition of an alleged offender, pursuant to this Convention, shall not be granted if the requested State Party has substantial grounds for believing:

(*a*) That the request for extradition for an offence set forth in article 1 has been made for the purpose of prosecuting or punishing a person on account of his race, religion, nationality, ethnic origin or political opinion; or

(*b*) That the person's position may be prejudiced:

(i) For any of the reasons mentioned in subparagraph (*a*) of this paragraph, or

(ii) For the reason that communication with him by the appropriate authorities of the State entitled to exercise rights of protection cannot be effected.

2. With respect to the offences as defined in this Convention, the provisions of all extradition treaties and arrangements applicable between States Parties are modified as between States Parties to the extent that they are incompatible with this Convention.

ARTICLE 10

1. The offences set forth in article 1 shall be deemed to be included as extraditable offences in any extradition treaty existing between States Parties. States Parties undertake to include such offences as extraditable offences in every extradition treaty to be concluded between them.

2. If a State Party which makes extradition conditional on the existence of a treaty receives a request for extradition from another State Party with which it has no extradition treaty, the requested State may at its option consider this Convention as the legal basis for extradition in respect of the offences set forth in article 1. Extradition shall be subject to the other conditions provided by the law of the requested State.

3. States Parties which do not make extradition conditional on the existence of a treaty shall recognize the offences set forth in article 1 as extraditable offences between themselves, subject to the conditions provided by the law of the requested State.

4. The offences set forth in article 1 shall be treated, for the purpose of extradition between States Parties, as if they had been committed not only in the place in which they occurred but also in the territories of the States required to establish their jurisdiction in accordance with paragraph 1 of article 5.

ARTICLE 11

1. States parties shall afford one another the greatest measure of assistance in connexion with criminal proceedings brought in respect of the offences set forth in article 1, including the supply of all evidence at their disposal necessary for the proceedings.

2. The provisions of paragraph 1 of this article shall not affect obligations concerning mutual judicial assistance embodied in any other treaty.

ARTICLE 12

In so far as the Geneva Conventions of 1949 for the protection of war victims[26] or the Protocols Additional to those Conventions are applicable to a particular act of hostage-taking, and in so far as States Parties to this Convention are bound under those conventions to prosecute or hand over the

[26] United Nations, *Treaty Series*, vol. 75, Nos. 970-973.

hostage-taker, the present Convention shall not apply to an act of hostage-taking committed in the course of armed conflicts as defined in the Geneva Conventions of 1949 and the Protocols thereto, including armed conflicts, mentioned in article 1, paragraph 4, of Additional Protocol I of 1977,[27] in which peoples are fighting against colonial domination and alien occupation and against racist régimes in the exercise of their right of self-determination, as enshrined in the Charter of the United Nations and the Declaration on Principles of International Law concerning Friendly Relations and Co-operation among States in accordance with the Charter of the United Nations.

ARTICLE 13

This Convention shall not apply where the offence is committed within a single State, the hostage and the alleged offender are nationals of that State and the alleged offender is found in the territory of that State.

ARTICLE 14

Nothing in this Convention shall be construed as justifying the violation of the territorial integrity or political independence of a State in contravention of the Charter of the United Nations.

ARTICLE 15

The provisions of this Convention shall not affect the application of the Treaties on Asylum, in force at the date of the adoption of this Convention, as between the States which are parties to those Treaties; but a State Party to this Convention may not invoke those Treaties with respect to another State Party to this Convention which is not a party to those Treaties.

ARTICLE 16

1. Any dispute between two or more States Parties concerning the interpretation or application of this Convention which is not settled by negotiation shall, at the request of one of them, be submitted to arbitration. If within six months from the date of the request for arbitration the parties are unable to agree on the organization of the arbitration, any one of those parties may refer the dispute to the International Court of Justice by request in conformity with the Statute of the Court.

2. Each State may at the time of signature or ratification of this Convention or accession thereto declare that it does not consider itself bound by paragraph 1 of this article. The other States Parties shall not be bound by paragraph 1 of this article with respect to any State party which has made such a reservation.

3. Any State Party which has made a reservation in accordance with paragraph 2 of this article may at any time withdraw that reservation by notification to the Secretary-General of the United Nations.

---

[27] A/32/144, annex I.

ARTICLE 17

1. This Convention is open for signature by all States until 31 December 1980 at United Nations Headquarters in New York.

2. This Convention is subject to ratification. The instruments of ratification shall be deposited with the Secretary-General of the United Nations.

3. This Convention is open for accession by any State. The instruments of accession shall be deposited with the Secretary-General of the United Nations.

ARTICLE 18

1. This Convention shall enter into force on the thirtieth day following the date of deposit of the twenty-second instrument of ratification or accession with the Secretary-General of the United Nations.

2. For each State ratifying or acceding to the Convention after the deposit of the twenty-second instrument of ratification or accession, the Convention shall enter into force on the thirtieth day after deposit by such State of its instrument of ratification or accession.

ARTICLE 19

1. Any State Party may denounce this Convention by written notification to the Secretary-General of the United Nations.

2. Denunciation shall take effect one year following the date on which notification is received by the Secretary-General of the United Nations.

ARTICLE 20

The original of this Convention, of which the Arabic, Chinese, English, French, Russian and Spanish texts are equally authentic, shall be deposited with the Secretary-General of the United Nations, who shall send certified copies thereof to all States.

IN WITNESS WHEREOF, the undersigned, being duly authorized thereto by their respective Governments, have signed this Convention, opened for signature at New York on. . . .[28]

[28] The Convention was opened for signature on 18 December 1979.

222. Ottawa Economic Summit Conference Statement on Terrorism, July 20, 1981*

* 17 Weekly Comp. Pres. Doc. 780 (July 27, 1981).

1. The Heads of State and Government, seriously concerned about the active support given to international terrorism through the supply of money and arms to terrorist groups, and about the sanctuary and training offered terrorists, as well as the continuation of acts of violence and terrorism such as aircraft hijacking, hostage-taking and attacks against diplomatic and consular personnel and premises, reaffirm their determination vigorously to combat such flagrant violations of international law. Emphasizing that all countries are threatened by acts of terrorism in disregard of fundamental human rights, they resolve to strengthen and broaden action within the international community to prevent and punish such acts.

2. The Heads of State and Government view with particular concern the recent hijacking incidents which threaten the safety of international civil aviation. They recall and reaffirm the principles set forth in the 1978 Bonn Declaration and note that there are several hijackings which have not been resolved by certain states in conformity with their obligations under international law. They call upon the governments concerned to discharge their obligations promptly and thereby contribute to the safety of international civil aviation.

3. The Heads of State and Government are convinced that, in the case of the hijacking of a Pakistan International Airlines aircaft in March, the conduct of the Babrak Karmal government of Afghanistan, both during the incident and subsequently in giving refuge to the hijackers, was and is in flagrant breach of its international obligations under the Hague Convention to which Afghanistan is a party, and constitutes a serious threat to air safety. Consequently the Heads of State and Government propose to suspend all flights to and from Afghanistan in implementation of the Bonn Declaration unless Afghanistan immediately takes steps to comply with its obligations. Furthermore, they call upon all states which share their concern for air safety to take appropriate action to persuade Afghanistan to honour its obligations.

4. Recalling the Venice Statement on the Taking of Diplomatic Hostages, the Heads of State and Government approve continued cooperation in the event of attacks on diplomatic and consular establishments or personnel of any of their governments. They undertake that in the event of such incidents, their governments will immediately consult on an appropriate response. Moreover, they resolve that any state which directly aids and abets the commission of terrorist acts condemned in the Venice Statement, should face a prompt international response. It was agreed to exchange information on terrorist threats and activities, and to explore cooperative measures for dealing with and countering acts of terrorism, for promoting more effective implementation of existing anti-terrorist conventions, and for securing wider adherence to them.

NOTE: As printed above, the statement follows the text issued at the summit conference and made available by the White House Press office. It was not issued as a White House press release.

223. Council of Europe: Recommendation No. R (82) 1 of the Committee of Ministers to Member States Concerning International Co-operation in the Prosecution and Punishment of Acts of Terrorism, January 15, 1982*

* Council of Europe Press Release I (82)2, January 25, 1982, *reprinted in* 21 Int'l Legal Materials 199 (1982).

The Committee of Ministers, under the terms of Article 15 (b) of the Statute of the Council of Europe,

Considering that the aim of the Council of Europe is to achieve greater unity among its members;

Concerned at the increased number of acts of terrorism committed in certain member States;

Considering the prevention and suppression of such acts to be indispensable to the maintenance of the democratic institutions of member States;

Having regard to Council of Europe initiatives[x] in the past aimed at the suppression of terrorism which represent important contributions to the fight against this threat to society;

Convinced that it is necessary to develop further and to strengthen international co-operation in this field;

Desirous of rendering existing procedures of international judicial co-operation simpler and more expeditious, of improving the exchange of information between the competent authorities of member States, particularly between those with a common border, and of facilitating the prosecution and punishment of acts of terrorism;

Having regard to existing co-operation and channels of communications between the police forces of member States;

Recalling the Declaration on Terrorism adopted by the Committee of Ministers on 23 November 1978;

Emphasising that any measure of international co-operation must be fully compatible with the protection of human rights and particularly with the principles contained in the Convention for the Protection of Human Rights and Fundamental Freedoms signed in Rome on 4 November 1950,

RECOMMENDS the Governments of member States to give effect, by the most appropriate means, to the following measures aimed at improving international co-operation in the prosecution and punishment of acts of terrorism directed against the life, physical integrity or liberty of persons, or against property where they create a collective danger for persons, includ-

---

[x] In particular:

— European Convention on Extradition (1957) with two Additional Protocols (1975 and 1978) [17 I.L.M. 813 (1978)]
— European Convention on Mutual Assistance in Criminal Matters (1959) and Additional Protocol (1978) [17 I.L.M. 801 (1978)]
— European Convention on the Suppression of Terrorism (1977) [15 I.L.M. 1272 (1976)]
— Resolution (74) 3 on international terrorism adopted by the Committee of Ministers at its 53rd Session (January 1974)
— Declaration on Terrorism adopted by the Committee of Ministers at its 63rd Session (November 1978)
— Communique of the Committee of Ministers at its 67th (October 1980), 68th (May 1981) and 69th (November 1981) Sessions
— Assembly Recommendation Nos. 684 (1972), 703 (1973), 852 (1979), 916 (1981)
— Conference on the "Defence of democracy against terrorism in Europe—Tasks and problems" (November 1980)

ing, in accordance with domestic law, attempts of or threats of or participation as an accomplice in these acts (referred to as "acts of terrorism" in the present recommendation).

I. *Channels of communication for mutual judicial assistance in criminal matters*

1. Direct communication between the authorities concerned in the requesting and requested State, of requests for judicial assistance and the replies thereto should be encouraged in all cases where it is permitted by the law of these States or by any treaty to which these States are Party, if it is likely to render mutual judicial assistance more expeditious.

2. Where direct transmission is permitted, cases involving acts of terrorism should be treated with urgency according to the procedure provided by Article 15 (2) of the European Convention on Mutual Assistance in Criminal Matters or by other treaties in force between member States or by the law of these States, so that letters rogatory may be addressed by the authority concerned in the requesting State, it being understood that the requested State may require a copy to be sent to its Ministry of Justice or other competent ministry.

3. Where requests for assistance and the replies thereto may be communicated directly between the authorities concerned in the requesting and the requested State, their transmission should be effected as rapidly as possible, either through Interpol National Central Bureau, insofar as this is not contrary to Interpol's Constitution, or by other existing ways of transmission.

4. Where communication is effected between Ministries of Justice or other competent ministries, the authority concerned in the requesting State should be allowed directly to provide the authority concerned in the requested State with an advance copy of the request. The authority concerned in the requested State should be advised that the sole purpose of transmitting the copy is to enable it to prepare for the execution of the request.

II. *Exchange of information*

5. Exchanges of information between member States should be improved and reinforced. To that end, the competent authorities should, insofar as this is not contrary to domestic law, be enabled to furnish, of their own accord, information in their possession on such matters as:

i. measures concerning the prosecution of the alleged offender (e.g. arrest, indictment)
ii. the outcome of any judicial or administrative proceedings (e.g. conviction, decision on extradition)
iii. the enforcement of any sentence (including pardon, conditional release)
iv. other relevant information relating to the whereabouts of the person concerned (e.g. expulsion, escape, execution of an extradition decision)

to the authorities of any member State concerned, as for instance, the State where the act of terrorism was committed, the State which has jurisdiction over the offence, the State of which the offender is a national, the State where the offender has his habitual residence, or any other State likely to have an interest in the particular element of information.

6. The exchange of this information should be effected with all necessary expediency either through Interpol National Central Bureaux, insofar as this is not contrary to Interpol's Constitution, or by other existing ways of transmission.

III. *Prosecution and trial of offences of an international character*

7. Where one or several acts of terrorism have been committed in the territory of two or several member States and there is a link between those acts or their authors, the member States concerned should examine the possibility of having the prosecution and the trial conducted in only one State. To that end, the States concerned should agree on the competent State, in accordance with existing international treaties and their internal law. The same should apply, if possible, where one or several acts of terrorism of an international character have been committed in the territory of a single State by several persons acting in unison who have been apprehended in various States. In negotiating such agreements on the competent State, the States concerned should, with a view to ensuring that prosecution and trial take place in the State best suited for conducting the proceedings, take into account the number of offences committed in each State, the seriousness of the offences, the availability of evidence, the personal circumstances of the alleged offender, in particular his nationality and residence, and the prospects of rehabilitation.

F. U.S.-Israel Relations

224. Statement by Foreign Minister, Yitzhak Shamir, to the Knesset on the Issue of U.S. Arms Sale to Jordan and Saudi Arabia, June 25, 1980*

* Embassy of Israel, Washington, D.C.

A Strong Israel—Precondition for Peace
in the Middle East

Every responsible element in the world understands that a suitable balance of forces in the region between Israel and the Arab states is an essential precondition to every hope and move for peace in the Middle East.

It is easy to prove and explain the basic truth that the Arab states will one day be ready to establish peace only with a strong Israel that cannot be overcome by force of arms. That general rule applies also to the first peace treaty signed with an Arab state, with Egypt.

The American administration has always recognized the justice of the demand for a suitable arms balance in our region. The discussion always concerned not the principle, but rather the means of its application. This principle is in danger of being seriously undermined by the arms transactions to which reference has been made here by those who have submitted motions on the subject. The Government of Israel has lost no opportunity to apprise the U.S. administration and its agencies of the gravity of the danger.

U.S. Weapons to the Rejectionist Front

The supply of substantial quantities of advanced weapons to Jordan and Saudi Arabia, members of the Eastern Front and the rejectionist front, jeopardizes the security of Israel and the peace of the region and militates against the peace process in which we are currently engaged.

The weaponry to be supplied to Jordan and Saudi Arabia is liable to turn these states into regional powers, equipped with the most up-to-date, sophisticated and powerful means of warfare. These weapons are likely, in the main, to be used against us in coordination with the armed forces of Iraq and Syria, both of whom are equipped with vast quantities of excellent Soviet weapons.

Excess Arming of Jordan and Saudi Arabia Can
Ignite War Against Israel

Although these states are in conflict among themselves, they are liable, under the influence of the tremendous military power at their disposal, to unite around the one aim which can bring them together—the destruction of Israel. While weaponry is only a means of attaining political objectives, sometimes it is the means which determines the policy itself and influences the determination of the goals. The fact is that the very existence of military power on so tremendous a scale in the hands of states which advocate continual warfare against Israel, is liable to encourage and push them in the direction of war. The United States itself must appreciate the extent of the danger and the extent of the responsibility which it takes upon itself in supplying this weaponry.

The forces that the rejectionist states and the Eastern Front can bring to bear against us are very great. One need only note that already today there are at the disposal of these states 8,000 of the most modern tanks, most of which are equipped with highly sophisticated and efficient night-vision equipment.

We are particularly concerned at the recent apparent tendency on the part of the United States Government to supply unlimited quantities of sophisticated modern weaponry to Jordan and Saudi Arabia, which will provide them with a considerable offensive capability. It will be recalled that in 1967 it was Jordanian tanks supplied by the United States and Great Britain which crossed the River Jordan. We understand the concern of the United States Government for the security of the Saudi regime, but the Iranian experience has proved, in the most convincing fashion, that the best tanks and planes will not be able to ensure the regimes in Saudi Arabia or elsewhere, or the regular supply of oil, just as they were unable to ensure them in Iran.

If any use will ever be made of those weapons, it will only be against Israel.

Arms Sales to Arab States Undermine Peace Efforts

We are aware of and appreciate the serious efforts being made by the United States for peace in the region. Precisely because of that, it is difficult for us to come to terms with a method in which one hand brings peace nearer, while at the same time the other hand, by supplying large quantities of top-grade weapons to our neighbors in the East and in the South, increases the danger of war. The flow of these quantities of superior lethal weaponry to all the countries surrounding us imposes upon the State of Israel the most heavy economic burden, for we are obliged to act—above and beyond our economic ability—in order to redress, to some extent, the balance of forces. Likewise, the supply of weapons to Egypt, with all our appreciation for the participation of Egypt in the peace process, necessitates caution, a gradual approach and a careful stocktaking of the balance of considerations, declarations and developments which, above all, must stand the test of time.

In the future, as in the past, the Government of Israel will be diligent in its maintenance of the arms balance—and this with a double aim: to maintain the security of Israel, and to allow for progress in the peace process. The United States must realize that peace is not possible without the security of Israel—security that will be clearly visible to the eyes of our neighbors.

Israel—Only Democratic and Stable Country in Middle East

We would remind the U.S. Government and all Western Governments, particularly those of Great Britain and France, that the State of Israel is the only democratic country in this region, and only here—in Israel—is there a stable regime without the possibility of surprise coups which, overnight, can put massive and superior equipment into the hands of dangerous and hostile elements.

It would be a mistake to think that, in the Middle East, it is possible to act on behalf of global interests while neglecting the security of Israel. The undermining of Israel's security, through the irresponsible flooding of the region with Eastern and Western arms, impairs the chances of peace; any such impairment could in turn lead to war and jeopardize the peace of the world.

We shall appeal to all friendly elements anxious for the peace of Israel, and peace generally, to halt this dangerous flow of lethal weapons to the Middle East.

225. Agreement Settling Claims on Behalf of the U.S.
Ship *Liberty*, December 15 and 17, 1980*

---

* T.A.I.S. No. 9957 (slip agreement).

ISRAEL

Claims: U.S. Ship "Liberty"

Agreement effected by exchange of notes
Dated at Washington December 15 and 17, 1980;
Entered into force December 17, 1980.

The Israeli Ambassador to the Secretary of State

AO/315   15 December 1980

The Ambassador of Israel presents his compliments to the Secretary of State and has the honour to refer to the Embassy's note of 22 February 1978[1] and to consequent exchange of notes concerning physical damage to the U.S. ship "Liberty" on 8 June 1967.

Without prejudice to the legal position of the Government of Israel and to the question of liability for the tragic event the Government of Israel has the honour to propose as full and final settlement of the U.S. claim that Israel pay the United States Government the sum of $6,000,000 (six million dollars) to be paid in three annual payments of $2,000,000 each, commencing 15 January 1981.

The Ambassador of Israel avails himself of this opportunity to renew to the Secretary of State the assurances of his highest consideration.

The Honorable
Edmund S. Muskie
The Secretary of State
The Department of State
Washington, D.C.

The Secretary of State to the Israeli Ambassador

December 17, 1980

Excellency:

I have the honor to acknowledge the receipt of your note No. AO/315 of December 15, 1980 relating to the U.S. ship "Liberty," which reads as follows:

The Ambassador of Israel presents his compliments to the Secretary of State and has the honour to refer to the Embassy's note of 22 February 1978 and to consequent exchange of notes concerning physical damage to the U.S. ship "Liberty" on 8 June 1967.

Without prejudice to the legal position of the Government of Israel and to the question of liability for the tragic event the Government of Israel has the honour to propose as full and final settlement of the U.S. claim that Israel pay the United States Government the sum of

[1] Not printed.

$6,000,000 (six million dollars) to be paid in three annual payments of $2,000,000 each, commencing 15 January 1981.

The Ambassador of Israel avails himself of this opportunity to renew to the Secretary of State the assurances of his highest consideration.

I have the honor to inform you that the Government of the United States agrees with your proposed settlement and that your note and my reply thereto constitute the agreement of our two Governments concerning this matter.

Accept, Excellency, the renewed assurances of my highest consideration.

For the Secretary of State:
[David D. Newsom]

His Excellency
  Ephraim Evron,
    Ambassador of Israel.

226. Communiqué on American-Israeli Strategic Cooperation Issued by the Arab Foreign Ministers After Their Emergency Meeting in New York, October 3, 1981*

* 11 J. Palestine Stud. 194 (Winter 1982).

1. The agreements that have been concluded or that it is intended shall be concluded between the US and Israel are a qualititive [*sic*] development in American bias towards Israel and a legal commitment by the US to continue to support Israel in her expansionist and aggressive policy.

These agreements will not only assist Israel to continue her occupation of the Arab territories and of the city of Jerusalem and her usurpation of the national rights of the Palestinian people; they will also help Israel to escalate her aggressive policy by enabling her to rely on American military, political and economic support.

The Arab community believes that these agreements increase the military and political imbalance in the area, place the US in a state of hostility to the Arab nation and close the door to the search for a just peace in the Middle East, transforming this area into a focus of international conflict and inflicting the most grievous harm on the vital interests of the Arab nation and on international security and peace.

The Arab community believes that this strategic alliance with Israel will lead to a series of grave consequences for which the US must bear the full responsibility.

The Arab community believes that by impeding the achievement of a just solution that safeguards Arab rights, the US will bring about a situation for which the Arab states cannot be held responsible since, to protect their rights, they will be obliged to use all their resources to defend these rights.

2. Having reviewed recent developments in Lebanon, and Israel's continuing acts of aggression and occupation of Lebanese territory, which are leading to an explosion in Lebanon's security situation, internally and externally, and preventing Lebanon from reaching a final solution of the crisis, the Arab community draws the attention of the international community to the dangers of aggressive actions and urges the taking of measures that will deter Israel and ensure the full implementation of Security Council resolution 425 and the subsequent resolutions.

The Arab community supports Lebanon's unity, the sovereignty of her people, her security and her territorial integrity within the framework of her recognized international frontiers.

3. The Arab community condemns Irsael's terrorist measures both inside and outside the occupied territories. It also condemns the covert war that Israel is currently waging in Lebanon against the Lebanese and Palestinian peoples.

227. Memorandum of Understanding between the Government of the United States and the Government of Israel on Strategic Cooperation, November 30, 1981*

* 82 U.S. Dep't State Bull. No. 2058, at 45 (January 1982).

This Memorandum of Understanding reaffirms the common bonds of friendship between the United States and Israel and builds on the mutual security relationship that exists between the two nations. The Parties recognize the need to enhance strategic cooperation to deter all threats from the Soviet Union to the region. Noting the longstanding and fruitful cooperation for mutual security that has developed between the two countries, the Parties have decided to establish a framework for continued consultation and cooperation to enhance their national security by deterring such threats to the whole region.

The Parties have reached the following agreements in order to achieve the above aims.

ARTICLE I

United States-Israeli strategic cooperation, as set forth in this Memorandum, is designed against the threat to peace and security of the region caused by the Soviet Union or Soviet-controlled forces from outside the region introduced into the region. It has the following broad purposes:

A. To enable the Parties to act cooperatively and in a timely manner to deal with the above mentioned threat;

B. To provide each other with military assistance for operations of their forces in the area that may be required to cope with this threat;

C. The strategic cooperation between the Parties is not directed at any State or group of States within the region. It is intended solely for defensive purposes against the above mentioned threat.

ARTICLE II

1. The fields in which strategic cooperation will be carried out to prevent the above mentioned threat from endangering the security of the region include:

A. Military cooperation between the Parties, as may be agreed by the Parties;

B. Joint military exercises, including naval and air exercises in the eastern Mediterranean Sea, as agreed upon by the Parties;

C. Cooperation for the establishment and maintenance of joint readiness activities, as agreed upon by the Parties;

D. Other areas within the basic scope and purpose of this agreement, as may be jointly agreed.

2. Details of activities within these fields of cooperation shall be worked out by the Parties in accordance with the provisions of Article III below. The cooperation will include, as appropriate, planning, preparations, and exercises.

ARTICLE III

1. The Secretary of Defense and the Minister of Defense shall establish a Coordinating Council to further the purposes of this Memorandum:

A. To coordinate and provide guidance to Joint Working Groups;

B. To monitor the implementation of cooperation in the fields agreed upon by the Parties within the scope of this agreement;

C. To hold periodic meetings, in Israel and the United States, for the purposes of discussing and resolving outstanding issues and to further the objectives set forth in this Memorandum. Special meetings can be held at the request of either Party. The Secretary of Defense and Minister of Defense will chair these meetings whenever possible.

2. Joint Working Groups will address the following issues:

A. Military cooperation between the Parties, including joint U.S.-Israeli exercises in the eastern Mediterranean Sea;

B. Cooperation for the establishment of joint readiness activities including access to maintenance facilities and other infrastructure, consistent with the basic purposes of this agreement;

C. Cooperation in research and development, building on past cooperation in this area;

D. Cooperation in defense trade;

E. Other fields within the basic scope and purpose of this agreement, such as questions of prepositioning, as agreed by the Coordinating Council.

3. The future agenda for the work of the Joint Working Groups, their composition, and procedures for reporting to the Coordinating Council shall be agreed upon by the Parties.

ARTICLE IV

This Memorandum shall enter into force upon exchange of notification that required procedures have been completed by each Party. If either Party considers it necessary to terminate this Memorandum of Understanding, it may do so by notifying the other Party six months in advance of the effective date of termination.

ARTICLE V

Nothing in the Memorandum shall be considered as derogating from previous agreements and understandings between the Parties.

ARTICLE VI

The Parties share the understanding that nothing in this Memorandum is intended to or shall in any way prejudice the rights and obligations which devolve or may devolve upon either Government under the Charter of the United Nations or under international law. The Parties reaffirm their faith in the purposes and principles of the Charter of the United Nations and their aspiration to live in peace with all countries in the region.

For the Government of the United States:
CASPAR W. WEINBERGER
Secretary of Defense

For the Government of Israel:
ARIEL SHARON
Minister of Defense